Handbook of Research on Applications of AI, Digital Twin, and Internet of Things for Sustainable Development

Brojo Kishore Mishra
GIET University, India

A volume in the Advances in Computational Intelligence and Robotics (ACIR) Book Series

Published in the United States of America by
  IGI Global
  Engineering Science Reference (an imprint of IGI Global)
  701 E. Chocolate Avenue
  Hershey PA, USA 17033
  Tel: 717-533-8845
  Fax: 717-533-8661
  E-mail: cust@igi-global.com
  Web site: http://www.igi-global.com

Library of Congress Cataloging-in-Publication Data

Names: Mishra, Brojo Kishore, 1979- editor.
Title: Handbook of research on applications of AI, digital twin, and
  internet of things for sustainable development / Brojo Mishra, editor.
Description: Hershey, PA : Engineering Science Reference, [2023] | Includes
  bibliographical references and index. | Summary: "The increasing
  interest in Artificial Intelligence (AI), Digital Twin (DT) and Internet
  of Things (IoT) is progressively playing a wider impact on many
  different sectors, and and this book offers several applications and
  challenges in various vital roles such as Product design and lifecycle,
  Smart Cities, Agriculture, Environment automation, Healthcare, Farming,
  Wearable, Climate, Sensors, Transportation, Electrical generation,
  E-governance renewable energy, and eco-system for sustainable growth"--
  Provided by publisher.
Identifiers: LCCN 2022034124 (print) | LCCN 2022034125 (ebook) | ISBN
  9781668468210 (h/c) | ISBN 9781668468234 (eISBN)
Subjects: LCSH: Sustainable engineering--Data processing. | Sustainable
  development--Data processing. | Artificial intelligence. | Digital twins
  (Computer simulation) | Internet of things.
Classification: LCC TA170 .H363 2023 (print) | LCC TA170 (ebook) | DDC
  338.9/270285--dc23/eng/20220908
LC record available at https://lccn.loc.gov/2022034124
LC ebook record available at https://lccn.loc.gov/2022034125

This book is published in the IGI Global book series Advances in Computational Intelligence and Robotics (ACIR) (ISSN: 2327-0411; eISSN: 2327-042X)

British Cataloguing in Publication Data
A Cataloguing in Publication record for this book is available from the British Library.

All work contributed to this book is new, previously-unpublished material. The views expressed in this book are those of the authors, but not necessarily of the publisher.

For electronic access to this publication, please contact: eresources@igi-global.com.

Advances in Computational Intelligence and Robotics (ACIR) Book Series

Ivan Giannoccaro
University of Salento, Italy

ISSN:2327-0411
EISSN:2327-042X

MISSION

While intelligence is traditionally a term applied to humans and human cognition, technology has progressed in such a way to allow for the development of intelligent systems able to simulate many human traits. With this new era of simulated and artificial intelligence, much research is needed in order to continue to advance the field and also to evaluate the ethical and societal concerns of the existence of artificial life and machine learning.

The **Advances in Computational Intelligence and Robotics (ACIR) Book Series** encourages scholarly discourse on all topics pertaining to evolutionary computing, artificial life, computational intelligence, machine learning, and robotics. ACIR presents the latest research being conducted on diverse topics in intelligence technologies with the goal of advancing knowledge and applications in this rapidly evolving field.

COVERAGE

- Intelligent Control
- Synthetic Emotions
- Artificial Intelligence
- Machine Learning
- Artificial Life
- Cyborgs
- Fuzzy Systems
- Neural Networks
- Computational Intelligence
- Cognitive Informatics

IGI Global is currently accepting manuscripts for publication within this series. To submit a proposal for a volume in this series, please contact our Acquisition Editors at Acquisitions@igi-global.com or visit: http://www.igi-global.com/publish/.

Titles in this Series

For a list of additional titles in this series, please visit: www.igi-global.com/book-series

Applied AI and Multimedia Technologies for Smart Manufacturing and CPS Applications
Emmanuel Oyekanlu (Drexel University USA)
Engineering Science Reference • © 2023 • 300pp • H/C (ISBN: 9781799878520) • US $270.00

Constraint Decision-Making Systems in Engineering
Santosh Kumar Das (Sarala Birla University, Ranchi, India) and Nilanjan Dey (Techno International New Town, Kolkata, ndia)
Engineering Science Reference • © 2023 • 312pp • H/C (ISBN: 9781668473436) • US $270.00

Handbook of Research on Artificial Intelligence Applications in Literary Works and Social Media
Pantea Keikhosrokiani (School of Computer Sciences, Universiti Sains Malaysia, Malaysia) and Moussa Pourya Asl (School of Humanities, Universiti Sains Malaysia, Malaysia)
Engineering Science Reference • © 2023 • 376pp • H/C (ISBN: 9781668462423) • US $325.00

Convergence of Deep Learning and Internet of Things Computing and Technology
T. Kavitha (New Horizon College of Engineering (Autonomous), India & Visvesvaraya Technological University, India) G. Senbagavalli (AMC Engineering College, Visvesvaraya Technological University, India) Deepika Koundal (University of Petroleum and Energy Studies, Dehradun, India) Yanhui Guo (University of Illinois, USA) and Deepak Jain (Chongqing University of Posts and Telecommunications, China)
Engineering Science Reference • © 2023 • 349pp • H/C (ISBN: 9781668462751) • US $270.00

Multi-Disciplinary Applications of Fog Computing Responsiveness in Real-Time
Debi Prasanna Acharjya (Vellore Institute of Technology, India) and P. Ahmed Kauser (Vellore Institute of Technology, India)
Engineering Science Reference • © 2023 • 300pp • H/C (ISBN: 9781668444665) • US $270.00

Deep Learning Research Applications for Natural Language Processing
L. Ashok Kumar (PSG College of Technology, India) Dhanaraj Karthika Renuka (PSG College of Technology, India) and S. Geetha (Vellore Institute of Technology, India)
Engineering Science Reference • © 2023 • 290pp • H/C (ISBN: 9781668460016) • US $270.00

Controlling Epidemics With Mathematical and Machine Learning Models
Abraham Varghese (University of Technology and Applied Sciences, Muscat, Oman) Eduardo M. Lacap, Jr. (University of Technology and Applied Sciences, Muscat, Oman) Ibrahim Sajath (University of Technology and Applied Sciences, Muscat, Oman) M. Kamal Kumar (University of Technology and Applied Sciences, Muscat, Oman) and Shajidmon Kolamban (University of Technology and Applied Sciences, Muscat, Oman)
Engineering Science Reference • © 2023 • 269pp • H/C (ISBN: 9781799883432) • US $270.00

701 East Chocolate Avenue, Hershey, PA 17033, USA
Tel: 717-533-8845 x100 • Fax: 717-533-8661
E-Mail: cust@igi-global.com • www.igi-global.com

Editorial Advisory Board

List of Contributors

Table of Contents

Detailed Table of Contents

Iris-Panagiota Efthymiou, LABHEM, University of Pireaus, Greece
Theocharis Efthymiou Egleton, London School of Economics, UK

Artificial intelligence (AI) enables 'smart' solutions and brings multiple benefits, including the more efficient provision of energy and water, combined with better waste management and reductions in pollution, noise, and traffic congestion. Achieving the goal of universal AI implementation in smart cities is not a simple task. There are substantive challenges and both political and practical actions to slow progress. Practical issues often enter around the fundamental lack of infrastructure surrounding a potential AI revolution with a realignment of educational goals that is seemingly inevitable, something also necessary for the long-term politically and ethically sustainable application of artificial intelligence in social and civil settings. This chapter aims to address the associated regulatory and practical issues, both through de jure and de facto means.

K. Hemant Kumar Reddy, VIT AP University, India
Rajat Subhra Goswami, National Institute of Technology Arunachal Pradesh, India
Diptendu Sinha Roy, National Institute of Technology, Meghalaya, India

The rapid development of information and communication technology (ICT)-based solutions in the field of smart city applications becomes essential to cope with the ever-increasing urbanization requirements globally. These ever-increasing demands pose a great challenge to city infrastructure, particularly smart cities, and thus a sustainable approach is needed for the future smart cities. The ever-increasing service demand of the smart city archetype is prone to monitoring and managing such constrained smart city infrastructures in an effective way and to maintain the QoS (smart applications like transportation, healthcare, road traffic, and other utility services). In this work, the authors envisioned improving the QoS of smart transportation while employing a context-aware computing approach that helps to alleviate fog node data transfer, and a distributed smart transport service (DSTS) model is proposed that manages intelligent vehicles and road traffic of the traditional vehicles in an effective way to improve the QoS of the smart city.

Chapter 3

The chapter examines ML methods that appear to be applied in implementing systems with intelligent behaviour. It depends on two workshops on learning in system of intelligent manufacturing, an intensive survey of the literature, and various commitments. Symbolic, sub-symbolic, and hybrid approaches, as well as their applications in manufacturing, are also discussed, as are hybrid solutions that attempt to combine the advantages of several methodologies. The advantages, inadequacies, and impediments of different creation methods are illustrated to decide suitable strategies for explicit circumstances.

Chapter 4

A urologist confirms high risks of kidney stones just because of diabetic mellitus; however, other factors also exist, but a major cause is type 2 diabetes. Renal cyst and diabetes clinical features show 58% of affected subjects as the same. Research findings prove the high risk of renal cancer among diabetes patients. All these patients underwent abdominal MRI or CT scan to extract kidney high-definition 3D images. The dataset was gathered from two hospitals: the first is the SRMS IMS, and the second is the Bareilly MRI & CT Scan Centre, both located in the city of Bareilly in the state of Uttar Pradesh of India. Research has been analyzed to note the classification among four classes using seven transfer learning methods. Results have been compared with seven transfer learning methods. The methods are EfficientNetB0, Xception, VGG16, ResNet50, MobileNet, InceptionV3, DenseNet121. Out of these deep learning-based algorithms, EfficientNetB0 shows the best accuracy of 96.02%.

Chapter 5

In the modern era, the quantity of data, specifically the text data, has increased rapidly. Recently, fake news has gained a lot of attention worldwide. Generally, fake news is propagated through different social media. The effects of fake news may be economic, political, organizational, or personal. To save the life of community from fake news propagation, identification of fake news at an initial point is crucial. The fake news propagators target innocent people for spreading the fake news and they become a part of fake news propagation unknowingly. To prevent this kind of activity, fake news detection and its blueprint of propagation becomes crucial to community and government. This chapter makes an analysis related to the prediction of fake news through the help of supervised ML algorithms. The ML algorithms are adopted for the categorization of fake news as true or false with the help of NLP textual analysis and feature extraction. However, during the testing phase, the XGB algorithm gives the best result over other ML algorithms with an accuracy of 99%.

Chapter 6

Innovation and adoption of smart things are very fast in today's era. Everyone wants a smart device to solve any problem because it is effortless, affordable, and less time-consuming. Using artificial intelligence (AI), we have solved many more problems with great success. Some areas where AI is already used are healthcare, smart city, smart grid, agriculture, astronomy, gaming, finance, tourism, social media, robotics, automotive industries, entertainment, e-commerce, education, etc. As the number of users of AI and the number of smart devices increases, the risk of the data and information we are sharing with these devices are also becoming high. For the safety and privacy of users as well as the company, AI systems, their data, and their communications must be protected. Consequently, this chapter aims to provide an overview of how safety and security can be achieved in AI systems. Learners will get knowledge about AI systems and some security mechanisms that can be helpful to their further studies.

Chapter 7

The ethical issues of how the computer evolved to the artificial intelligence and machine learning era are explored in this chapter. To develop these intelligent systems, what are the basic principles, policies, and rules? How are these systems helpful to humankind as well as to society? How are businesses and other relevant organizations adapting AI and ML? AI and ML are booming technology. They have major applications in healthcare, computer vision, traffic networks, manufacturing, business trade markets, and so on.

Chapter 8

India is one of the world's largest food producers, creating the sustainability of its agricultural system of global significance. More than 67% of the Indian population still depend on agriculture or its allied sectors for their livelihood. There lies a requirement for the discussion on balancing or enriching the agriculture production in order to bring in food security for the growing population. Agriculture in recent years is facing great downfall due to uncertain monsoons, decline of soil fertility, population pressure, lack of support services, and so on. To overcome these, there is a need for communication such as dissemination of right information on right time to the farmers, which would help them towards advancing their knowledge on agriculture. The growth of active internet users over the past few years shall make this task easier. The chapter shall make an in-depth analysis on the need for the development of an agricultural social network and shall also present a prototype of the proposed system.

Chapter 9

Divya R., B.S. Abdur Rahman Crescent Institute of Science and Technology, India
Karthikeyan Ramalingam, B.S. Abdur Rahman Crescent Institute of Science and Technology, India
Sneha Unnikrishnan, B.S. Abdur Rahman Crescent Institute of Science and Technology, India

The world population will increase by two billion in the year 2050 as per the United Nations Food and Agriculture Organization. To meet the needs of people, more efficient farming practices must be identified and implemented, which can increase the yield of crops in the field. A study shows that one in five deaths globally, equivalent to 11 million deaths, are because of poor diet and unavailability of food for the underprivileged. Automation in the agricultural field will not just ease the process but also increase the yield, helping many households to afford at least two meals a day. Implementation of artificial intelligence in agriculture can ease the process. Some countries like the United States, Singapore, etc. use AI in agriculture; they have reported a good impact on the yield of crops. The main objective of this work is to analyze the applications to implement artificial intelligence technology in farming, the advantages and disadvantages of artificial intelligence in agriculture, and the opportunity in India to implement these technologies in farming.

Chapter 10

Ghalia Nasserddine, Jinan University of Lebanon, Lebanon
Mohamed Nassereddine, University of Wollongong in Dubai, UAE
Amal Adel El Arid, Rafik Hariri University, Lebanon

Recently, with the birth of globalization, the world has witnessed a huge growth in its energy consumption. From an agricultural society, the world has transformed itself into an industrial and knowledge society. This transformation leads to a surge in energy consumption which led to an increase in carbon emission. For this reason, renewable energy systems with zero carbon emission has become a vital need for economic comfort and environmental security. However, the main disadvantage of renewable energy is its intermittency and prediction. Solar and wind generation are usually unpredictable, which leads to several problems if the network heavily relies on renewable energy as the primary source of electricity. This chapter describes the integration of the internet of things (IoT) with renewable energy systems to cover these problems. The authors will start with an introduction to renewable energy systems and their limitations. Then, they focus on the advantage of using IoT to enhance renewable systems.

Chapter 11

Mitali Chugh, University of Petroleum and Energy Studies, India
Neeraj Chugh, University of Petroleum and Energy Studies, India

In the agricultural domain, the advent of IoT has paved the path for innovative research. Being promising yet at a budding stage, IoT must be extensively experimented upon to be applied widely in different agricultural applications. The rising demand for food has enhanced the necessity of industrialized progression and thorough production techniques in agricultural science. At the vanguard of the innovative farming age, an evolving internet of things (IoT) puts forward many innovative solutions. The agricultural parameters, such as environmental factors, soil conditions, etc., are traced in smart or precision agriculture to upsurge crop harvests, reduce costs, and sustain inputs for the process. Flourishing IoT technologies present several novel solutions and enhance growth prospects in the agricultural sector. To address the IoT's potential usage in the current scenario, this chapter looks at design principles, architectures, numerous challenges, and developments associated with smart agriculture. Also, a review of different perspectives on applications of IoT is conducted.

Chapter 12

Swatantra Kumar Jaiswal, National Institute of Technology, Raipur, India
Suraj Kumar Mukti, National Institute of Technology, Raipur, India
Kali Charan Rath, GIET University, India

Electrical and electronic equipment that has reached the end of its useful life produces e-waste for the society. It generates various problems for society sustainability. The time has come to take the remedial action for its preventive or recycle it for various usages. This chapter incorporates a correlation research of e-waste from distinct international locations and sufficiently illuminates the variables adding to the development of e-squander and its management structures. Accordingly, it gives reality to lower e-object usage at the customer facet and manipulates the estimate at the maker facet. Furthermore, it would be treasured by the leaders who are related to drafting India's future e-squander approach.

Chapter 13

Prabhakar Yadlapalli, Koneru Lakshmaiah Education Foundation, India
Leela Rajani Myla, Koneru Lakshmaiah Education Foundation, India
Naga Venkata Sai Deekshitha Sandaka, Koneru Lakshmaiah Education Foundation, India
S. Gopal Krishna Patro, Koneru Lakshmaiah Education Foundation, India

Systems for course arranging help city sightseers and suburbanites in settling on the best course between two irregular focuses. Nonetheless, while prompting multi-modular courses, present day organizer calculations frequently don't consider client inclinations or the aggregate insight. Multimodal courses can be suggested in light of the assessments of purchasers with comparative preferences as per a method called cooperative separating (CF). In this chapter, the authors present a component—a portable recommender system for redid, multimodal courses—that consolidates CF with information-based ideas to improve the nature of course proposals. They give a full clarification of the crossover strategy and show the way things are integrated into a functioning model. The consequences of a client concentrated on show that the model, which joins CF, information-based, and well-known course suggestions, outflanks cutting-edge course organizers.

Chapter 14

B. K. Tripathy, Vellore Institute of Technology, India
Apoorv Singh, Vellore Institute of Technology, India

There is a strong consensus that quantum computers are likely to solve previously intractable problems, especially in data science and AI. Nowadays, processing power of machine learning algorithms is limited by that of conventional computers. Quantum computing (QC) is one of the digital trends with the quickest rate of growth, and it seems to provide an answer to large data problems. It is a combination of the fields of computer science, information theory, and quantum physics. Quantum computers use the ability of subatomic particles to exist in more than one state at once to solve complex problems. In spite of its recent origin, quantum computing is already being used in the field of data analytics. QC can process huge datasets at much quicker rates and can provide data to AI models. By comparing schemas to swiftly assess and comprehend the link between two counterparts, QC can also aid in the integration of data. The ability to perform more sophisticated analysis and build machine learning models is a benefit of employing quantum computers.

Chapter 15

Ashish Anandrao Patil, KLE Institute of Technology, India
Manu T. M., KLE Institute of Technology, India
Basavaraj S. Anami, KLE Institute of Technology, India

Various enforced rules on human beings due to pandemic have made them spend more time indoors. Hence, improving indoor air quality (IAQ) is significant so that people can work efficiently under good indoor ambience. There are various plants in nature that absorb harmful ingredients from indoor environments based on their biological properties. This chapter presents an internet of things (IoT)-based biological plant recommendation system to improve indoor air quality. This system monitors a particular indoor environment and measures the concentration of various gases at the front-end. In the back-end subsystem, the data received from the front-end subsystem is assessed and a suitable plant/s from the cloud database is recommended. This is a very handy and cost-effective system and can be easily implemented in any indoor environment.

Chapter 16

K. S. Sastry Musti, Namibia University of Science and Technology, Nambia
Geetam Singh Tomar, Rajkiya Engineering College, Sonbhadra, India

The development of smart energy systems using the principles of Industry 4.0 to energize smart cities is of significant interest. On the other hand, digital twin systems are gaining popularity as they are expected to provide greater insights into the design, development, and maintenance processes of complex systems. This chapter first presents various salient operational requirements in energizing the smart cities through renewable energies, virtual power plants, and demand side management technologies. The tenets of digital twins and Industry 4.0 are the key drivers in the developmental process of cyber physical energy systems. The chapter illustrates the process of replicating the twins—physical and virtual systems—to function in synchronization for effective management. The digital transformation process of developing cyber physical systems from the conceptual living labs to the fully functional digital twins is presented.

Chapter 17

Hanène Babay, Faculty of Monastir, Tunisia
Nozha Erragcha, Higher Business School of Tunisia, Tunisia

Several reasons seem to justify the development trend of smart cities. Indeed, humanity is facing several challenges such as an increasing environmental impact, enormous difficulties in living in congested cities, and ever-increasing running costs. These challenges threaten the quality of life, especially in times of crisis, which has drawn attention to the relevance of using ICTs for governance purposes and has proliferated the awareness of stakeholders (authorities, citizens, civil society, etc.) to act in favor of the implementation of the mechanisms necessary for a new way of governing. This chapter presents the concept of smart cities and identifies the issues related to their development as well as the technologies that can intervene in the conversion of cities into smart and sustainable cities.

Chapter 18

    Tumburu Chandhana, Vellore Institute of Technology, India
    Anuhya Balija, Vellore Institute of Technology, India
    Siva R R Kumaran, Vellore Institute of Technology, India
    Brijendra Singh, Vellore Institute of Technology, India

Digital twin technology is starting to receive interest in the industry and, more recently, in academics. The digital twin is best described as the seamless integration of data between a physical and virtual system in either direction. The internet of things (IoT), cloud computing, edge computing, digital twins, and artificial intelligence all bring challenges, applications, and enabling technologies. Despite the fact that the idea of the "digital twin" has been well established over the past few years, there are still many different interpretations that result from varied professional viewpoints. The digital twin is primarily introduced in this chapter, along with its advantages and practical applications in different sectors. The authors have presented a detailed review of the artificial intelligence-driven digital twin, sensor-driven digital twin, cloud-driven digital twin, and edge computing-driven digital twin. It looks at the architectures, enabling technologies, potential obstacles, and challenges of current research on digital twins.

Chapter 19

    Megha Gupta, MSCW, University of Delhi, India
    Nida Khan, J.C. Bose University of Science and Technology, YMCA, India

The digital twin is a burgeoning technology that has just recently gained popularity. The term "digital twin" refers to a virtual twin that is put on site with sensors that collect real-time data. Hard real-time embedded operating systems are required for operating systems that enable digital twins, which use real-time data. Digital twin indicates a virtual replica that takes into account both device dynamics and individual component parts. The digital twin's primary dynamic is represented by each and every component or gadget. Regardless of the gadget's physical, internal, or functional aspects, the physical device handles them all. The use of digital twins has grown around the globe. Different technologies, such as IoT, AI, ML, data mining, cloud computing, and others, benefit from this technique. This chapter presented the detailed view of this rapidly expanding field of study along with several digital twins application fields, emerging concerns, and future prospects. Also, this chapter discussed the relation between digital twin and latest technologies such as IoT, AI, etc.

Chapter 20

Kunal Dhibar, Bengal College of Engineering and Technology, India
Prasenjit Maji, Bengal College of Engineering and Technology, India
Shiv Prasad, Bengal College of Engineering and Technology, India
Moumita Pal, JIS College of Engineering, India

Numerous industries have embraced cutting-edge computer technology as digitalization has progressed, including big data, artificial intelligence (AI), cloud computing, digital twins, and edge computing. In order to analyze the state of the application of digital twins in conjunction with AI, this chapter looks at the research findings of recently published literature. It then evaluates the applications and futures of AI in digital twins. High-fidelity computer simulations are used in modern engineering practice for the design and research of complex engineering systems. In the field of mechanical and aeronautical engineering, computational simulations have long been used to support conceptual design, prototyping, manufacturing, production, test-data correlation, and safety evaluation. In the last 10 years, there has been a change in how computational simulations are used to give assistance across the whole product life cycle.

Chapter 21

Abhishek Kumar Sinha, GIET University, India
S Gopal Krishna Patro, Koneru Lakshmaiah Education Foundation, India
Amrutashree Hota, GIET University, India

The recommendation system works on an idea of suggesting or recommending items, products, books, movies, etc. by analyzing and using some filtering to find the user's interest. To maximize the growth of business and profit gain, users need to be recommended with products belonging to their area of interest. To fulfill this requirement, the recommendation system has been implemented. In this study, the discussion is over recommendation system and how different concepts come to work out individually as well as together for recommendation. In this analysis, the focus is on recommending the method of e-commerce. In that scenario, "cold start problem" comes into consideration. Cold start problems are also studied, and a purposed idea has also been highlighted to reduce cold start problem to some extent. 'LCW Aspect' is going to execute and analyze user's culture, weather, local scarcity, and focused on solving recommendation problems for new emerging users.

Chapter 22

Neha Shekhawat, Banasthali Vidyapith, India
Seema Verma, Banasthali Vidyapith, India
Ankit Vijayvargiya, Swami Keshvanand Institute of Technology, Management, and
Gramothan, India
Manisha Agarwal, Banasthali Vidyapith, India
Manisha Jailia, Banasthali Vidyapith, India

Weeds are the major source of concern for farmers, who anticipate that weeds may lower crop productivity. Thus, it is essential and vital to detect weeds. Traditional weed classification methods such as hand cultivation with hoes have many hindrances such as labour cost and time consumption. Currently, weed reduction farmers are using herbicides, but they have a negative impact on farmer health as well as on the environment. So, farmers want to lower the use of herbicides. Precise spraying is one of the methods in present-day agriculture to lower the usage of herbicides and to destroy the weeds with the assistance of new technologies. Deep learning approaches are already being employed in a variety of agricultural and farming applications and gave better results. This chapter uses convolution neural networks to provide a short overview of some significant agricultural research endeavours. Different architectures of CNN for classification and detection were used. In the sector of agriculture, the authors have outlined the notion of CNNs.

Chapter 23

Akshay Mendon, Thakur College of Engineering and Technology, India
Bhavya Manoj Votavat, School of Computer Science and Engineering, VIT Bhopal
University, India
Vighnesh Hegde, Thakur College of Engineering and Technology, India
Megharani Patil, Thakur College of Engineering and Technology, India

The genesis of artificial intelligence (AI) has subsequently led to many machine learning algorithms being used for purposes like drug discovery. The strategies for developing drug targets and medication revelation have joined forces with AI and deep learning algorithms to improve the effectiveness, adequacy, and nature of created yields. Drug discovery is a very difficult endeavor as its success depends on data from several fields, yet it is very crucial and beneficial for us in the long run. In this chapter, the applications that have created novel techniques and produced significant yield in this field are reviewed.

Chapter 24

Meenu Vijarania, K.R. Mangalam University, India
Milind Udbhav, K.R. Mangalam University, India
Swati Gupta, K.R. Mangalam University, India
Robin Kumar, K.R. Mangalam University, India
Akshat Agarwal, Amity University, Gurgaon, India

Cost of living affects the maintenance if a certain standard of living, which includes housing, food, taxes, healthcare, etc. To overcome this issue, the project aims to analyze the amount of money needed to survive in different geographical areas and compare the cost of living in different areas. The analysis of the cheapest and most expensive places in the world is done for proper categorization. For getting proper data there is a need of extracting the latitude and longitude of all different locations. The comparison of expenses in different countries based on different parameters gives an idea about the living standards in different countries. Analyzing different parameters also helps to decide the lifestyle of people in different countries and whether their expenses will be high or low in the particular country. One major type of analysis, which is geospatial analysis, is also used here to study the entities using different topological or geographical properties. The project deals with real-life scenarios people face in day-to-day life when there is a need to decide the lifestyle of living.

Chapter 25

Shipra Shivkumar Yadav, IICC Nagpur, India

An agricultural digital twin is presented in this research using technologies from the sensing change and smart water management platform projects. Unlike the sensing change project, which created a soil probe, an internet of things is now being developed by the SWAMP project platform for managing water. The authors come to the conclusion that this system is capable of collecting data from the soil probe and displaying it in a dashboard, allowing for the deployment of additional soil probes, as well as other monitoring and controlling devices, to create a fully functional digital twin

Chapter 26

Fredrick Romanus Ishengoma, The University of Dodoma, Tanzania

As artificial intelligence (AI) gets more prevalent in our everyday lives, the issue of ethical concerns related to AI inevitably needs to be addressed. Currently ethical issues surrounding AI have been fragmented, and there is lack of studies that have provided a comprehensive taxonomy. While most existing research focuses on a single application domain (e.g., health or autonomous vehicles), AI ethics is currently a cross-disciplinary issue. This chapter presents a state-of-the-art argument and discussion on ethical dilemmas associated with AI advancement, thereby generating new research agendas within AI and ethics domain. Moreover, the taxonomy of AI ethical dilemmas is presented along with recommendations.

Chapter 27

Ali Yuce, Cappadocia University, Turkey

As information and communication technologies have had such a profound impact on every part of our lives, the globe has undergone significant transformation. This impact will not only increase productivity and efficiency, but will also have a substantial positive impact on all aspects of sustainable development. Recent developments in technologies that convey dynamic and real-time data, like the digital twin, have the great potential to revolutionize our concept of sustainability in smart manufacturing and monitoring natural resources. With the use of digital twin technology, one may decrease and potentially eliminate possible energy waste, maintenance expenses, and time waste by making quick predictions and taking prompt remedial action during the manufacturing process. This conceptual paper contends that digital twin can significantly boost an organization's productivity and profitability while enhancing destinations' values, including distinctive natural, cultural, and environmental resources, without endangering the lives of the next generation.

Preface

Artificial Intelligence (AI) is a branch of computer science by which we can create intelligent machines which can behave like a human, think like humans, and able to make decisions. The Internet of Things (IoT) is a system of interrelated computing devices, mechanical and digital machines, objects, animals or people that are provided with unique identifiers and the ability to transfer data over a network without requiring human-to-human or human-to-computer interaction. A Digital Twin (DT) is a virtual representation of an object or system that spans its lifecycle, is updated from real-time data, and uses simulation, machine learning and reasoning to help decision-making

The rapid growth and capability of artificial intelligence, digital twin, and the internet of things are unlocking incredible opportunities to overcome some of the greatest environmental and social impact challenges currently facing the global community, such as feeding a growing population, safety, affordable housing, and environmental sustainability. Sustainable development was defined by the UN in 1987 as development that meets the needs of the present without compromising the ability of future generations to meet their own needs.

This book *Handbook of Research on Applications of AI, Digital Twin, and Internet of Things for Sustainable Development* comprises a number of state-of-the-art contributions from both scientists and practitioners working in a large pool of fields where AI, DT, and IoT can open up new solutions for Sustainable Development Goals. The book is organized into 27 chapters. This book starts by presenting how AI, DT, and IoT can tackle the challenges of sustainable development in general and then focuses on the following axes:

Chapter 1: Rapid urbanization has created great stress internationally on the sustainability of cities. Artificial Intelligence (AI) has become one of the most powerful inventions in our lives, and its impact on urban settlements and activities is accelerating, ultimately influencing daily life. Cities are the primary drivers and hubs of most socioeconomic activity, environmental transformations, and political actions. It is essential to comprehend how the development of AI and city development are intertwined. Therefore, this chapter was conducted to identify the role of AI for sustainable smart cities. The descriptive analysis was used in this chapter. Data was collected through secondary sources. Sixty (60) secondary sources on AI and sustainable smart cities were read and fifty-three (53) of them were analyzed for the chapter. This chapter found that AI in the development of the smart city can play an important role in urban planning, management, and development with an advanced security system, disposal management, and traffic monitoring to make communities livable and secure, with access and control over their residences and other activities aimed at making life more comfortable and enjoyable. However there is a need to overcome the privacy issues to make AI usage reliable and secure to develop sustainable smart cities.

Chapter 2: Envisioned a Distributed Smart Transport Service model to improve the quality of Service of smart transportation while employing a context-aware computing approach that helps to alleviate effective data transfers among Fog nodes and vehicles in real-time. Use of intelligent approach at fog node level latency can be minimized and can manage intelligent vehicles and road traffic of the traditional vehicles in an effective manner, which further improves the QoS of the smart city

Chapter 3: Artificial intelligence and Machine Learning (ML) research algorithms that can learn on their own from data. Machine learning approaches have advanced significantly over the last decade, as evidenced by Deep Learning concepts used in electronic games and self-driving vehicle. As a result, scientists have begun to investigate machine learning for industrial applications, and numerous studies have identified machine learning as one of the vital empowering agents for transforming a conventional production system to Industry 4.0. Industrial applications, on the other hand are still rare and limited to a small group of worldwide firms. This study tackles these issues, with the goal of elucidating the true potential of machine learning algorithms in operation management, as well as their potential shortcomings. Continuous, consistent improvement is an important necessity for producing organizations, requiring flat and flexible organizations, and adaptable, learning data and material handling frameworks on the other. The chapter examines ML methods that appear to be applied in implementing systems with intelligent behavior.

Chapter 4 reviews that deep and machine learning has already sought assistance from various transfer learning algorithms such as VGG-19, ResNet-50, Inception V3, etc. to be reprocessed and achieved foreground for the classification of MRI and CT scan images. This model is constituted of four classes' cyst, stone, tumor, and healthy kidneys, and taken as input to mobile and web applications, further, inherently processed with the trained model to predict the desired output. Images can be trained and tested with other deep learning classifiers like V-net, MobileNet, Xception, NASNetMobile, DenseNet201, GLSM, etc. to compare the result.

Chapter 5 provides an analysis related to the prediction of fake news through the help of supervised ML algorithms. The ML algorithms are adopted for the categorization of the fake news as true or false with the help of NLP textual analysis and feature extraction. However, during the testing phase, the XG Boost algorithm gives the best result over the other machine learning algorithms with an accuracy of 99%. Researchers have looked into an algorithm that may more accurately discern between fake and real news. This new model will evaluate the fake news items based on the following criteria: spelling problems, jumbled sentences, punctuation errors, etc.

Chapter 6 discusses how safety and security can be achieved in AI systems. The authors gave a brief introduction about AI systems followed by some top security threats in AI systems and provided various solutions for that, also mentioned some important points for ensuring safety and discussed the important challenges in this area. Despite the fact that AI technology development is well underway, the growing security risks it poses require us to be more vigilant in order to safeguard its higher, quicker, and better development.

Chapter 7: The Ethical issues will describe the how the computer evolved to till to the Artificial intelligence and Machine learning era. Do develop these intelligent systems what the basic principles policies and rules should be followed. How these systems are helpful to the human kind and as well as to the society? How the business organization and other relevant organizations are adapting AI and ML. The AI and ML is very booming technology nowadays. It is having major applications in healthcare, computer vision, traffic network, manufacturing, business trade market and so on. These systems are evolved to help the human and expertise like man to develop and to create wonders in the world.

Chapter 8: Due to unpredictable monsoons, deteriorating soil fertility, growing population, a shortage of support programs, and other factors, agriculture has suffered greatly in recent years. The farmer would be able to advance their knowledge of agriculture by receiving the appropriate information at the appropriate moment, which would help them overcome these difficulties. This effort should be made simpler by the rise of online users over the previous few years. The chapter will analyze the need for the creation of an agricultural social network in great detail and will also demonstrate a working prototype of the idea.

Chapter 9 discusses the applications of Artificial Intelligence implemented in farming that can reduce the challenges farmers face in the field. The authors have reviewed the advantages, disadvantages of artificial intelligence in agriculture, and the opportunity in India to implement these technologies in agriculture.

Chapter 10 studies the integration of the Internet of Things (IoT) with renewable energy systems to cover electricity generation problems. The authors start with an introduction to renewable energy systems and their limitations. Then, they focus on the advantage of using IoT to enhance renewable systems. This chapter ends by conclusion that in the future, the Internet of Things will be a tool with incalculable and limitless potential, which has already had and will continue to have a significant impact on energy production.

Chapter 11: To address the IoT's potential usage in the current scenario, this chapter looks at design principles, architectures, numerous challenges, and developments associated with smart agriculture. Also, a review of different perspectives on applications of IoT is conducted.

Chapter 12 includes a correlation research of e-waste from different international locations and illuminates per users about the various variables that add to the development of e-waste. The reality to e-object usage is lower at the customer facet and the estimate is manipulated at the maker facet.

Chapter 13: Systems for course arranging help city sightseers and suburbanites in settling on the best course between two irregular focuses. Nonetheless, while prompting multi-modular courses, present day organizer calculations frequently don't consider client inclinations or the aggregate insight. Multimodal courses can be suggested in light of the assessments of purchasers with comparative preferences as per a method called cooperative separating (CF). In this part, we present a component — a portable recommender system for redid, multimodal courses — that consolidates CF with information-based ideas to improve the nature of course proposals. We give a full clarification of our crossover strategy and show the way things are integrated into a functioning model. The consequences of a client concentrate on show that our model, which joins CF, information based, and well-known course suggestions, outflanks cutting edge course organizers.

Chapter 14 gives an overview of Quantum computing and its role in Data Analytics Environment. Quantum computing (QC is one of the digital trends with the quickest rate of growth, and it seems to provide an answer to large data problems. It is a combination of the fields of computer science, information theory, and quantum physics. Quantum computers use the ability of subatomic particles to exist in more than one state at once to solve complex problems. In spite of its recent origin, quantum computing is already being used in the field of data analytics. QC can process huge datasets at much quicker rates and can provide data to AI models.

Chapter 15: Various enforced rules on human beings due to pandemic, have made them to spend more time indoor. Hence, improving indoor air quality (IAQ) is significant so that people can work efficiently under good indoor ambience. There are various plants in the nature which absorbs harmful ingredients from indoor environment based on their biological properties. Chapter 15 presents an Internet of things

(IoT) based biological plant recommendation system to improve indoor air quality. This system monitors a particular indoor environment and measures the concentration of various gases at the front-end. In the back-end subsystem, the data received from the front-end subsystem is assessed and a suitable plant/s from the cloud database is recommended. This is very handy and cost-effective system and can be easily implemented in to any indoor environment.

Chapter 16 presents the overall framework for developing energy system digital twins to supply futuristic smart cities. The framework considers various operational issues of legacy power systems and identifies an appropriate process for digitally transforming the legacy systems into modern cyber physical systems. The operational issues include the standard injection of renewable energies, virtual power transfer using power plants and demand side management technologies. The proposed framework uses the key tenets of digital twins and industry 4.0 in the digital transformation process. The chapter then takes up the process of replicating both the twins - physical and virtual systems to function in synchronization for effective management.

Chapter 17: Several reasons seem to justify the development trend of smart cities. Indeed, humanity is facing several challenges such as an increasing environmental impact, enormous difficulties in living in congested cities and ever-increasing running costs. These challenges threaten the quality of life especially in times of crisis, which has drawn attention to the relevance of using ICTs for governance purposes and has proliferated the awareness of stakeholders (authorities, citizens, civil society, etc.) to act in favor of the implementation of the mechanisms necessary for a new way of governing. This chapter presents the concept of smart cities, identifies the issues related to their development as well as the technologies that can intervene in the conversion of cities into smart and sustainable cities.

Chapter 18 gives an overview of digital twin enabling technologies, architectures, artificial intelligence based, sensor, cloud and edge computing based digital twin with its advantages, applications and challenges. It will also facilitate readers to identify the limitations and research gaps in implementation of digital twin technologies.

Chapter 19 introduces the notion of Digital Twins, a new and rapidly expanding field of study. The authors examine several Digital Twins application fields, emerging concerns and obstacles, and future prospects. Authors also discussed the relation between Digital twin and latest technologies such as IoT, AI, etc.

Chapter 20 generalizes that in order to analyze the state of the application of digital twins in conjunction with AI; this article looks at the research findings of recently published literature. In the field of mechanical and aeronautical engineering, computational simulations have long been used to support conceptual design, prototyping, manufacturing, production, test-data correlation, and safety evaluation.

Chapter 21: The Recommendation System works on an idea of suggesting or recommending items, products, books, movies etc. by analyzing and using some filtering to find the user's interest. To maximize the growth of business and profit-gain, users need to be recommended with products belonging to their area of interest. To fulfill this requirement, the recommendation system has been implemented. In this study, the discussion is over recommendation system and how different concepts come to workout individually as well as together for recommendation. In this analysis, the focus is on recommending method of e-commerce. In that scenario, "cold start problem" comes into consideration. Cold start problems are also studied and a purposed idea has also been highlighted to reduce cold start problem to some extent. In that purposed idea, 'LCW Aspect' is going to execute and analyze user's culture, weather, local scarcity and focused on solving recommendation problem for new emerging users.

Chapter 22 reviews the different models of deep learning for weed classification and weed detection. The author has reviewed the background of Convolution Neural Networks (CNNs), Different models of CNN for weed classification and CNN models for detection also; application of these deep learning models was also discussed.

Chapter 23 discusses and reviews the technologies that produce promising results in the deep learning incorporated algorithms that are used for lead and target discovery for drug development and discovery. Usage of virtual screening has also been highlighted for the development of lead synthesis pathways.

Chapter 24: Cost of living helps in maintaining a certain standard of living which includes housing, food, taxes, healthcare et. To overcome this issue the project aims to analyze the amount of money needed to survive in different geographical areas and compare the cost of living in different areas. The analysis of the cheapest and most expensive places in the world is done for proper categorization. For getting proper data there is a need of extracting the latitude and longitude of all different locations. The comparison of expenses in different countries based on different parameters gives an idea about the living standards in different countries. Analyzing different parameters also helps to decide the lifestyle of people in different countries and whether their expenses will be high or low in the particular country. One major type of analysis which is geospatial analysis is also used here to study the entities using different topological or geographical properties.

Chapter 25: An agricultural digital twin is presented in this research using technologies from the Sensing Change and Smart Water Management Platform projects. Unlike the Sensing Change project, which created a soil probe, An Internet of Things is now being developed by the SWAMP project. Platform for managing water in We come to the conclusion that our system is capable of collecting data from the soil probe and displaying it in a dashboard, allowing for the deployment of additional soil probes as well as other monitoring and controlling devices to create a fully functional digital twin.

Chapter 26 presents a comprehensive taxonomy of the ethical dilemmas in Artificial Intelligence (AI) and discusses how to deal with ethics in AI effectively. Based on the taxonomy, the author introduces open issues and specific areas where more research is needed when incorporating ethics in AI.

Chapter 27 stresses how the convergence of digital twins and other cutting-edge technologies can increase productivity and efficiency while lowering operating and manufacturing expenses. Furthermore, this chapter also examines the importance of digital twins in preserving unique environmental resources and cultural heritage assets for future generations.

Brojo Kishore Mishra
GIET University, India

Acknowledgment

The editor would like to acknowledge the help of all the people involved in this project and, more specifically, to the authors and reviewers that took part in the review process. Without their support, this book would not have become a reality.

First, the editor would like to thank each one of the authors for their contributions. Our sincere gratitude goes to the chapter's authors who contributed their time and expertise to this book.

Second, the editor wishes to acknowledge the valuable contributions of the reviewers and editorial advisory board members regarding the improvement of quality, coherence, and content presentation of chapters. Most of the authors also served as referees; we highly appreciate their double task.

Finally, the editor wishes to acknowledge the best supports received from the IGI Global publication house, GIET University team, past & present students, well wishers and my lovely family members.

Chapter 1
Artificial Intelligence for Sustainable Smart Cities

Iris-Panagiota Efthymiou
LABHEM, University of Pireaus, Greece

Theocharis Efthymiou Egleton
London School of Economics, UK

ABSTRACT

Artificial intelligence (AI) enables 'smart' solutions and brings multiple benefits, including the more efficient provision of energy and water, combined with better waste management and reductions in pollution, noise, and traffic congestion. Achieving the goal of universal AI implementation in smart cities is not a simple task. There are substantive challenges and both political and practical actions to slow progress. Practical issues often enter around the fundamental lack of infrastructure surrounding a potential AI revolution with a realignment of educational goals that is seemingly inevitable, something also necessary for the long-term politically and ethically sustainable application of artificial intelligence in social and civil settings. This chapter aims to address the associated regulatory and practical issues, both through de jure and de facto means.

INTRODUCTION

The increase in urban populations has resulted in economic, technological, and climate changes that have the potential to severely impact the standard of living in cities. In response, the concept of "smart city" has evolved, which refers to the use of innovative ICTs to mitigate negative consequences for cities and their residents. In this setting, AI is deployed alongside other technologies, growing fast and playing a crucial role in enabling intelligent citywide systems in different areas (Dominikovi et al., 2021). As technology has made enormous dives in enabling AI development, artificial intelligence has become a necessity for daily living and business operations (Raisch & Krakowski, 2021). AI in smart cities will play a significant role in making urbanization smarter to achieve sustainable growth by equipping cities with advanced features that allow people to live, walk, and shop in a safer and more comfortable envi-

DOI: 10.4018/978-1-6684-6821-0.ch001

ronment (Bisen, 2020). Globally, smart cities have made great development in their smart city projects and the adoption of breakthrough smart technologies to make their home cities more livable, energy efficient, and reduce carbon emission (Lai, 2022).

One of the United Nations (UN) "Sustainable Development Goals (SDGs)" for 2030 is to ensure that cities are resilient, inclusive, sustainable, and safe (Lim &Taeihagh, 2018). Following a decade of research, smart cities are moving into a new era. Digital solutions are among the most cost-effective and powerful additions to the toolkit for keeping a city great for many years, even though they are only one component of the entire toolkit for making a city great. Smart city development is not an end in itself, but a way to achieve a goal. The objective is to respond more quickly and dynamically to the preferences and needs of inhabitants (Bughin et al., 2018). Recent years have seen a rise in debate and research on the possible revolutionary effects of AI usage in "smart cities," including innovative discipline, decision-making, governance, and revolution prospects (Allam & Dhunny, 2019). Therefore, the objective of this chapter was to examine the role of AI in sustainable smart cities. To achieve the chapter objective, secondary data resources were reviewed, including journal articles, website content, reports, etc. This chapter includes a discussion of the application, advantages, and challenges of AI in sustainable smart cities. In addition, this chapter included prospects and suggestions for future research.

BACKGROUND

Artificial intelligence (AI): AI is a branch of computer science. It is the development of computer systems capable of doing activities that normally require human intellect (Muhammad, 2019). AI is a real revolutionary accomplishment of computer programming, destined to become an integral part of all software in the future years and decades ahead (Bughin et al., 2018).

Smart City: There is currently no widely accepted definition of the term "smart city." It relates to the application of digital technology and data to enhance communities by providing social, financial, and environmental benefits to residents (OpenLearn, 2019). It is an area where digital solutions are used to make traditional networks and operations more efficient for the benefit of its residents and businesses (European Commission, n.d.).

Sustainability: The word "sustainability" implies behavior that achieves a stable level within pre-determined criteria for the components considered for each dimension of sustainability, such as smart cities, in a manner that can be maintained over time (Kannegiesser & Günther, 2014).

The United Nations estimates that by 2050, 70% of the world's population will reside in cities and metropolitan regions, meaning that energy consumption and emissions will continue to rise every year. The demand for better urban transportation networks, eco-friendly water management facilities, and energy-efficient structures is greater than ever. This is where smart urban programs and projects come into play. Smart technology in cities enhances not only the quality of life of its residents but also public safety as a whole (Lai, 2022). Moreover, AI adds to the decision-making of smart cities because smart decision-making employs a systematic and structured approach to data collection and logical decision-making systems rather than relying on chance, instinct, or generalizations based on extensive knowledge (Berntzen, et al., 2018). According to the "Smart City Index 2020," Zurich, Helsinki, and Singapore are the world's smartest cities (Lai, 2022).

MAIN FOCUS OF THE CHAPTER

In recent times, the necessity to apply information and communication technology (ICT) to address key urban and societal concerns has been one of the most prevalent concepts in urban policy debates. This activity generated the concept of a "smart city" (Yigitcanlar & Cugurullo, 2020). The concept of smart cities dates back to 1994 when Amsterdam was the first city to attempt to construct and incorporate a virtual digital urban concept. Since then, particularly the internet emergence in the 2000s, companies such as Cisco (2005) and IBM (2008) have shown an interest in making investments in this new concept to demonstrate a desire for it (Allam & Jones, 2021). Since then, several significant technological, construction, and consultancy companies, together with city planners and policymakers, have jumped on the smart city bandwagon (Yigitcanlar & Inkinen, 2019). This has led to a plethora of "smart-city programmers" that are transforming current cities and constructing new ones throughout the globe (Karvonen et al., 2018). Essentially, the term "smart city" refers to an area where digital communications and technology are used to improve efficiency in several interrelated urban areas (such as security, electricity, and transportation), leading to economic growth, enhanced quality of life, and sustainable practices (Allam & Newman, 2018). Several urban problems can be ameliorated by AI, including traffic safety, poor air quality, waste management, and a reduced risk of disasters (Gupta et al., 2021).

Recent AI systems for improving the quality of life in urban centers include a tool for semi-automatic digitalization of sketch maps to help include indigenous communities by describing their rights to land; a framework for traffic control using wireless signals; strategies for effective waste management; air quality modeling; and urban health monitoring equipment (Kanschat et al., 2022). Still, there is an absence of methodically identified knowledge and a lack of multi-disciplinary perspectives that make it hard to agree on what AI can do to make cities more sustainable(Zheng et al., 2020). Smart cities are made with very complex, integrated technologies that include a large number of sensors and pieces of equipment that are connected to computerized systems. These systems include analytics, decision algorithms, monitoring, and the use of the Internet of Things (IoT) (Bokhari & Myeong, 2022).

The term "smart city" is complex, making its expression challenging. There have been a lot of attempts to study people or groups or to examine people's living conditions (Cardullo & Kitchin, 2019). Many scholars highlight the ecological impact of urbanization activities and the use of information and communication infrastructure, but few recognize the role played by individuals and organizations in raising people's living standards (Gaur et al., 2015). In addition, Israelites et al., (2021)point out that the existing research atmosphere is primarily concerned with technological issues, leaving behind the social influences, engagement capacities, and medium of instruction aspects of citizen-inclusive and multi-stakeholder development. As a result, the potential of AI is still inadequately understood. To address this gap, this chapter focuses on the role of AI in sustainable smart cities for human well-being.

Sustainable Smart Cities

Recently, about 55% of the world's people live in cities, which are growing quickly across the entire globe (Chen et al., 2022). In many countries, like the UK, Australia, and the Netherlands, the number is higher than 85%. This helps to make urban areas the main focus of sustainability strategy, not just because they are home to most of the world's people, but also because they are where most of the world's economic and social activities occur (Praharaj et al., 2018). By putting cities at the center of policy actions, the shift in focus from the country to the city has led to new and different ideas for building a sustainable future (Chu, 2016). Still, this isn't always the case in real life. Research results have demonstrated that, in reality, most smart cities are driven by economic goals and don't solve environmental or social issues (Cugurullo, 2016). In recent years, smart-city research has turned its attention to the "smart and sustainable city" to bring the social, environmental, and financial aspects of smart urbanism back into balance (Martin et al., 2018). A smart and environmentally friendly city is an urban area that works as a strong system of schemes with sustainability solutions, supported by unrestricted future technologies and policy, to make sure that all humans and non-humans have the futures they want (Yigitcanlar et al., 2019).

Applications of AI in Smart Cities

AI is rapidly becoming an integral part of our daily lives and our urban environments. Several countries across the world are conducting trials for AI-driven vehicles to prepare their cities and their citizens for the changes that autonomous driving will bring (Cugurullo et al., 2021). In the COVID-19 era, countries like Hong Kong used robot dogs to track social distancing (Schellin et al., 2020). A few years ago, Dubai started robot police to prevent minor crimes (Lakshmi &Bahli, 2020). Robotic doctors are being used in hospitals in Japan and other countries (Suwa et al., 2020). Smart home technologies and services are making many homes safer and more energy efficient. Home automation, also known as "domotics," is becoming increasingly important in the construction industry (Jaihar et al., 2020). Big companies and small businesses now have chatbots on their websites to answer customer questions (Brandtzaeg & Følstad, 2018). A large-scale artificial intelligence called "city brains" run the transportation, energy, and safety mechanisms of several cities in Malaysia and China (Cugurullo, 2020).

Air pollution and global warming's negative impacts on population health, and inequitable access to resources are all things that are due to the transportation industry (Pangbourne et al., 2018). "Smart" and "sustainable" cities can help to address the issues by using new technology to help people, businesses, and governments to live better while making sure that environmental and social systems will prevail (Gopalakrishnan et al., 2015). The negative effects of urban development on the environment, the economic system, and society can be lessened with sustainable transportation infrastructure and systems. Autonomous vehicles (AVs) have become a viable solution to transportation problems in the modern world. The widespread use of autonomous vehicles can help the environment by reducing energy use and emissions. It can also help the society and economy by increasing efficiency, road safety, traffic flow, and transportation accessibility among other things (Parkin et al., 2018). A lot of these benefits come from the fact that connected nature of AVs, which lets them communicate with other vehicles and important infrastructure to enhance traffic circulation and make cities more sustainable and smart (Petit &Shladover, 2014).

AI is also an important component of environmental studies in a variety of countries, including Australia, in which autonomous drones use to detect environmental hazards and endangered animals through machine learning (Aziz et al., 2017). Several smartphones today have an AI that can act as a virtual assistant (Kaplan & Haenlein, 2019). Overall, these examples are just the tip of the iceberg when it comes to AI. Analytics is where AI is used the most. AI starts by describing, prescriptive, and predictive analyses of data it collects and processes to make many decisions that affect our lives (El Morr& Ali-Hassan, 2019). In other words, AI-assisted urban Machine Learning (ML) is used a lot in cities all over the world today to address the uncertainty and complexity of urban life (Allam&Dhunny, 2019). Some of the more common applications of AI are described below (India Berry, 2021);

- Advanced Security Cameras & Monitoring Systems: Artificially intelligent cameras and sensors can monitor the environment to improve the security in the city's neighborhoods. These devices can identify individuals and faces, as well as observe their behavior in restricted locations.
- Traffic Management System: AI may also assist with traffic management. In urban areas, the vast majority of residents have their own automobiles, and there is a significant volume of commercial automobiles transporting both people and products. The public sector is also included in smart transportation, and according to AI, there are numerous chances to enhance public transit.
- Automated Flying Objects for Aerial View Tracking: Artificial Intelligence-enabled robots or autonomously flying objects with comparable capabilities can be used to display the internal city and residential areas, as well as other potentially hazardous locations. In-built cameras in drones give administrative and intelligence organizations real-time images of regions that humans cannot obtain quickly, enabling them to take prompt action. Drones with autonomous capabilities can track people, monitor traffic, and provide 2D aerial image mapping for better urbanization. It may be utilized for advanced surveillance and security by the law enforcement squads and security departments.
- Face Detection Cameras and Movement for Public Safety: Artificial intelligence in face recognition technologies may identify individuals based on their facial features. AI in surveillance cameras or drones may identify human faces and compare them to a trace to verify the identity of individuals entering cities, societies, and other restricted locations.

Benefits of AI for Smart City

Incorporating AI into smart cities provides various advantages for both the environment and humans. From an eco-friendly atmosphere to sustained development, AI in smart cities offers numerous advantages for everybody. Some of the benefits are described below (ThinkTank European Parliament, 2021);

- Positive Effect on the Environment: One of the greatest advantages of smart cities is that CO_2 emissions will decrease; this will be the primary driver for the creation of smart and sustainable cities.
- Water Management and Controlled Energy: Similarly, in smart cities, smart water management and power-producing grid are major contributors to the production of clean energy. Such a strategy also aids in obtaining clean drinking water for the preservation of the environment.
- More Convenient Transportation System: In smart cities, the movement of products and services must be safe and effective for people to prosper. To improve mobility, several cities are implementing smart technology to alleviate traffic jams and give customers real-time data.
- Advance Safety and Security in the Public: In such urban settings, citizen security is of the utmost importance. The advent of AI-powered "smart cities" has made it possible for governments to keep a closer eye on their residents, courtesy of CCTV cameras equipped with facial recognition software. In addition to providing enhanced security, AI-powered cameras may also act as smoke and motion sensors.

Challenges of AI for Smart Cities

Attaining AI in smart cities is not a simple process, since there are several challenges to achieving smart cities. A few of them are discussed below (Bisen, 2020);

- Costing and Infrastructure: Most of the gadgets, machines, buildings, and computers in smart cities use sensor systems to gather information, such as rush-hour statistics, a lot of data from AI surveillance systems or other security devices, crime rates, or air quality. For these sensors to work, they need a complicated and expensive infrastructure.
- Security and Privacy Issues: Another difficulty in building such metropolises is the privacy and security of the residents. As the Internet of Things (IoT) and sensor technologies become more widespread, it becomes more difficult to monitor individuals or observe their activities. Awareness, training, and disclosure on the aim of data collection are essential for the community to feel that they're contributing to the sustainability of their city.
- Risk of Socialization: Inclusive urbanization should be a priority in the development of such cities to address the growing susceptibility of slums and poor communities.

AI in Decision-Making Processes

AI has proven successful in various areas, including smart city decision-making (Kermany et al., 2018). Scientists have already proved the vital importance of machine learning in rational decision-making processes, making cities intelligent and promoting a good quality of life. Scholl and AlAwadhi (2016) emphasize how AI-enabled government empowers cities to cooperate to develop smart services that no one city can deliver alone. Effective governance in smart cities promotes data collection from monitors and other resources to enhance urban security management(Meijer &Thaens, 2018). For example, the South Korean government successfully employed artificial intelligence to battle the COVID-19 pandemic by promoting the preventive exchange of information, supporting residents in comprehending the situation, and implementing recently issued safety regulations (Park et al., 2020).

Smart cities have evolved into a crucial component of cities with enormous issues, such as verifying social presence, durability, public health and safety, prosperity, and making smart decisions. When cities confront such challenges, they use several smart city transformation strategies. This evolution includes several AI tactics that are often supported by urban politicians who construct governance systems, as well as other specialists from all over the globe (Giffinger & Kramar, 2021). Even though other ICT tools, such as databases and monitors, may aid in decision-making, machine learning stands out due to its three distinctive design qualities. However, the most significant aspect is automatic training and decision-making using advanced mathematical problem representations (Young et al., 2019).

SOLUTIONS AND RECOMMENDATIONS

Implementing AI in the appropriate areas of smart cities can have life-changing effects. AI has the potential to improve the effectiveness and efficiency of a variety of city services and infrastructure projects. Hence, AI can play a significant role in making advancement and management of smart cities more effective by facilitating the implementation of cutting-edge safety and livability features such as complicated security systems, traffic management, and waste disposal that give inhabitants greater control over their living environments. Moreover, AI companies need a vast quantity of training data for smart cities to train models like robots, AI video surveillance, and facial recognition systems to perform effectively and offer correct information, hence making smart cities actually smart for sustained development. This caused the issue of privacy. So, there is a need to overcome these kind of issues to make AI usage reliable and secure to develop sustainable smart cities. Smart cities must give priority to enhancing outcomes for residents and involving their active engagement in building their communities. Moreover, a smart city necessitates the use of computer technology for the connection and administration of its architectural, ecological, and economic infrastructure to provide its citizens with improved services while ensuring the efficient and effective use of existing resources.

FUTURE RESEARCH DIRECTIONS

A general limitation of the current study is that all the work was done through secondary sources in terms of AI and sustainable smart cities. It is suggested that future research may be conducted quantitatively. Local government may implement the findings of this chapter to plan for building smart cities such that the factor of social innovations should be involved in the decision-making process. This is because smart decision-making would share such collected data with entrepreneurs, businesses, and industries and would benefit society and all relevant stakeholders, including such social innovators. Future research may be conducted regarding other factors of smart cities, especially in the fields of health and education, for a better understanding of the importance of AI in these fields of life.

CONCLUSION

AI has become essential to our daily lives. With the increase of smart, internet-connected devices, data has become ubiquitous. Such information may be utilized to develop intelligent machines for smart cities. Today, most of the world's inhabitants exist in cities. Urban life is impacted positively by AI. AI is referred to as the fourth technological revolution owing to its enormous potential to transform all aspects of society. In smart cities, AI has transformed everything. Further, artificial intelligence can influence smart decision-making. The development of smart technology creates favorable conditions for governments and municipalities to build smart city systems for various purposes. The main aim is to increase the comfort of living in smart cities. The latest developments in artificial intelligence, robust hardware development, and the ability to process enormous datasets collected using millions of connected multisensory devices open up new opportunities for developing and improving smart city systems. This creates unique advantages for effective promotion and support of the transformation of urban areas. However, there are still several requirements to be addressed for the development and operation of such systems. Experts are increasingly considering the concept of smart sustainable cities that involve all the benefits of smart cities, as it focuses on a continuous transformative process. It must guarantee the sustainable growth of a city in the future and provide its residents with a variety of capabilities. To implement this approach, robust, secure, dependable, and extensible infrastructural technologies must be created to support ICT-based services and applications. The automation of many processes in smart city subsystems depends on the "reliability" and "security" of the AI-based solutions underlying them.

These two conditions are critical for smart sustainable city systems because the well-being and safety of people depend on them.

REFERENCES

Allam, Z., & Dhunny, Z. A. (2019). On big data, artificial intelligence and smart cities. *Cities (London, England)*, *89*, 80–91. doi:10.1016/j.cities.2019.01.032

Allam, Z., & Jones, D. S. (2021). Future (post-COVID) digital, smart and sustainable cities in the wake of 6G: Digital twins, immersive realities and new urban economies. *Land Use Policy*, *101*, 105201. doi:10.1016/j.landusepol.2020.105201

Allam, Z., & Newman, P. (2018). Redefining the smart city: Culture, metabolism and governance. *Smart Cities*, *1*(1), 4–25. doi:10.3390martcities1010002

Aziz, K., Haque, M. M., Rahman, A., Shamseldin, A. Y., & Shoaib, M. (2017). Flood estimation in ungauged catchments: Application of artificial intelligence based methods for Eastern Australia. *Stochastic Environmental Research and Risk Assessment*, *31*(6), 1499–1514. doi:10.100700477-016-1272-0

Berntzen, L., Johannessen, M. R., & El-Gazzar, R. (2018). Smart Cities, Big Data and Smart Decision-making-Understanding" Big Data" in Smart City Applications. *ICDS 2018, The Twelfth International Conference on Digital Society and eGovernments.*

Bisen, S. V. (2020). *HowAI Can be Used in Smart Cities: Applications Role & Challenge*. Retrieved May 14, 2020, https://medium.com/vsinghbisen/how-ai-can-be-used-in-smart-cities-applications-role-challenge-8641fb52a1dd

Bokhari, S. A. A., & Myeong, S. (2022). Use of artificial intelligence in smart cities for smart decision-making: A social innovation perspective. *Sustainability*, *14*(2), 620. doi:10.3390u14020620

Brandtzaeg, P. B., & Følstad, A. (2018). Chatbots: Changing user needs and motivations. *Interactions*, *25*(5), 38-43.

Bughin, J., Seong, J., Manyika, J., Chui, M., & Joshi, R. (2018). *Notes from the AI frontier: Modeling the global economic impact of AI*. McKinsey Global Institute.

Cardullo, P., & Kitchin, R. (2019). Smart urbanism and smart citizenship: The neoliberal logic of 'citizen-focused' smart cities in Europe. *Environment and Planning C: Politics and Space, 37*(5), 813-830.

Chen, G., Li, X., Liu, X., Chen, Y., Liang, X., Leng, J., Xu, X., Liao, W., Qiu, Y., Wu, Q., & Huang, K. (2020). Global projections of future urban land expansion under shared socioeconomic pathways. *Nature Communications*, *11*(1), 1–12. doi:10.103841467-020-14386-x PMID:31988288

Chu, E. K. (2016). The governance of climate change adaptation through urban policy experiments. *Environmental Policy and Governance*, *26*(6), 439–451. doi:10.1002/eet.1727

Cugurullo, F. (2016). Urban eco-modernisation and the policy context of new eco-city projects: Where Masdar City fails and why. *Urban Studies (Edinburgh, Scotland)*, *53*(11), 2417–2433. doi:10.1177/0042098015588727

Cugurullo, F. (2020). Urban artificial intelligence: From automation to autonomy in the smart city. *Frontiers in Sustainable Cities*, *2*, 38. doi:10.3389/frsc.2020.00038

Cugurullo, F., Acheampong, R. A., Gueriau, M., & Dusparic, I. (2021). The transition to autonomous cars, the redesign of cities and the future of urban sustainability. *Urban Geography*, *42*(6), 833–859. doi:10.1080/02723638.2020.1746096

Dominiković, I., Ćukušić, M., & Jadrić, M. (2021). The role of artificial intelligence in smart cities: systematic literature review. In *International conference on data and information in Online* (pp. 64-80). Springer. 10.1007/978-3-030-77417-2_5

El Morr, C., & Ali-Hassan, H. (2019). Descriptive, predictive, and prescriptive analytics. In *Analytics in Healthcare* (pp. 31–55). Springer. doi:10.1007/978-3-030-04506-7_3

European Commission. (n.d.). *Smart cities: Cities using technological solutions to improve the management and efficiency of the urban environment*. Retrieved from: https://ec.europa.eu/info/eu-regional-and-urban-development/topics/cities-and-urban-development/city-initiatives/smart-cities_en

Gaur, A., Scotney, B., Parr, G., & McClean, S. (2015). Smart city architecture and its applications based on IoT. *Procedia Computer Science*, *52*, 1089–1094. doi:10.1016/j.procs.2015.05.122

Giffinger, R., & Kramar, H. (2021). Benchmarking, profiling, and ranking of cities: The "European smart cities" approach. In *Performance Metrics for Sustainable Cities* (pp. 35–52). Routledge. doi:10.4324/9781003096566-4

Gopalakrishnan, K., Chitturi, M. V., & Prentkovskis, O. (2015). Smart and sustainable transport: Short review of the special issue. *Transport*, *30*(3), 243–246. doi:10.3846/16484142.2015.1099407

Gupta, S., & Degbelo, A. (2022). *An Empirical Analysis of AI Contributions to Sustainable Cities (SDG11)*. arXiv preprint arXiv:2202.02879.

Gupta, S., Langhans, S. D., Domisch, S., Fuso-Nerini, F., Felländer, A., Battaglini, M., Tegmark, M., & Vinuesa, R. (2021). Assessing whether artificial intelligence is an enabler or an inhibitor of sustainability at indicator level. *Transportation Engineering*, *4*, 100064. doi:10.1016/j.treng.2021.100064

India Berry. (2021). *10 ways AI can be used in Smart Cities*. Retrieved November 14, 2021, https://aimagazine.com/top10/10-ways-ai-can-be-used-smart-cities

Israilidis, J., Odusanya, K., & Mazhar, M. U. (2021). Exploring knowledge management perspectives in smart city research: A review and future research agenda. *International Journal of Information Management*, *56*, 101989. doi:10.1016/j.ijinfomgt.2019.07.015

Jaihar, J., Lingayat, N., Vijaybhai, P. S., Venkatesh, G., & Upla, K. P. (2020). Smart home automation using machine learning algorithms. In *2020 International Conference for Emerging Technology (INCET)* (pp. 1-4). IEEE. 10.1109/INCET49848.2020.9154007

Kannegiesser, M., & Günther, H. O. (2014). Sustainable development of global supply chains-part 1: Sustainability optimization framework. *Flexible Services and Manufacturing Journal*, *26*(1), 24–47. doi:10.100710696-013-9176-5

Kanschat, R., Gupta, S., & Degbelo, A. (2022). Wireless-Signal-Based Vehicle Counting and Classification in Different Road Environments. *IEEE Open Journal of Intelligent Transportation Systems*, *3*, 236–250. doi:10.1109/OJITS.2022.3160934

Kaplan, A., & Haenlein, M. (2019). Siri, Siri, in my hand: Who's the fairest in the land? On the interpretations, illustrations, and implications of artificial intelligence. *Business Horizons*, *62*(1), 15–25. doi:10.1016/j.bushor.2018.08.004

Karvonen, A., Cugurullo, F., & Caprotti, F. (2018). Introduction: Situating smart cities. In Inside smart cities (pp. 1-12). Routledge.

Kermany, D. S., Goldbaum, M., Cai, W., Valentim, C. C., Liang, H., Baxter, S. L., McKeown, A., Yang, G., Wu, X., Yan, F., Dong, J., Prasadha, M. K., Pei, J., Ting, M. Y. L., Zhu, J., Li, C., Hewett, S., Dong, J., Ziyar, I., ... Zhang, K. (2018). Identifying medical diagnoses and treatable diseases by image-based deep learning. *Cell*, *172*(5), 1122–1131. doi:10.1016/j.cell.2018.02.010 PMID:29474911

Lai, O. (2022). *Top 7 Smart Cities in the World*. Retrieved August 14, 2022, https://earth.org/top-7-smart-cities-in-the-world/

Lakshmi, V., & Bahli, B. (2020). Understanding the robotization landscape transformation: A centering resonance analysis. *Journal of Innovation & Knowledge*, *5*(1), 59–67. doi:10.1016/j.jik.2019.01.005

Lim, H. S. M., & Taeihagh, A. (2018). Autonomous vehicles for smart and sustainable cities: An in-depth exploration of privacy and cybersecurity implications. *Energies*, *11*(5), 1062. doi:10.3390/en11051062

Martin, C. J., Evans, J., & Karvonen, A. (2018). Smart and sustainable? Five tensions in the visions and practices of the smart-sustainable city in Europe and North America. *Technological Forecasting and Social Change*, *133*, 269–278. doi:10.1016/j.techfore.2018.01.005

Meijer, A., & Thaens, M. (2018). Quantified street: Smart governance of urban safety. *Information Polity*, *23*(1), 29–41. doi:10.3233/IP-170422

OpenLearn. (2019). *Smart Cities*. Retrieved September 4, 2019, https://www.open.edu/openlearn/science-maths-technology/smart-cities/content-section-overview?active-tab=description-tab

Pangbourne, K., Stead, D., Mladenović, M., & Milakis, D. (2018). The case of mobility as a service: A critical reflection on challenges for urban transport and mobility governance. In *Governance of the smart mobility transition*. Emerald Publishing Limited. doi:10.1108/978-1-78754-317-120181003

Park, Y. J., Choe, Y. J., Park, O., Park, S. Y., Kim, Y. M., Kim, J., Kweon, S., Woo, Y., Gwack, J., Kim, S. S., Lee, J., Hyun, J., Ryu, B., Jang, Y. S., Kim, H., Shin, S. H., Yi, S., Lee, S., Kim, H. K., ... Jeong, E. K. (2020). Contact tracing during coronavirus disease outbreak, South Korea, 2020. *Emerging Infectious Diseases*, *26*(10), 2465–2468. doi:10.3201/eid2610.201315 PMID:32673193

Parkin, J., Clark, B., Clayton, W., Ricci, M., & Parkhurst, G. (2018). Autonomous vehicle interactions in the urban street environment: A research agenda. *Proceedings of the Institution of Civil Engineers. Municipal Engineer*, *171*(1), 15–25. doi:10.1680/jmuen.16.00062

Petit, J., & Shladover, S. E. (2014). Potential cyberattacks on automated vehicles. *IEEE Transactions on Intelligent Transportation Systems*, *16*(2), 546–556.

Praharaj, S., Han, J. H., & Hawken, S. (2018). Urban innovation through policy integration: Critical perspectives from 100 smart cities mission in India. *City, Culture and Society, 12*, 35-43.

Raisch, S., & Krakowski, S. (2021). Artificial intelligence and management: The automation–augmentation paradox. *Academy of Management Review*, *46*(1), 192–210. doi:10.5465/amr.2018.0072

Schellin, H., Oberley, T., Patterson, K., Kim, B., Haring, K. S., Tossell, C. C., ... de Visser, E. J. (2020). Man's new best friend? Strengthening human-robot dog bonding by enhancing the doglikeness of Sony's Aibo. In *2020 Systems and Information Engineering Design Symposium (SIEDS)* (pp. 1-6). IEEE. 10.1109/SIEDS49339.2020.9106587

Scholl, H. J., & AlAwadhi, S. (2016). Creating Smart Governance: The key to radical ICT overhaul at the City of Munich. *Information Polity*, *21*(1), 21–42. doi:10.3233/IP-150369

Suwa, S., Tsujimura, M., Kodate, N., Donnelly, S., Kitinoja, H., Hallila, J., Toivonen, M., Ide, H., Bergman-Kärpijoki, C., Takahashi, E., Ishimaru, M., Shimamura, A., & Yu, W. (2020). Exploring perceptions toward home-care robots for older people in Finland, Ireland, and Japan: A comparative questionnaire study. *Archives of Gerontology and Geriatrics*, *91*, 104178. doi:10.1016/j.archger.2020.104178 PMID:32717586

ThinkTank European Parliament. (2021). *Artificial Intelligence in smart cities and urban mobility*. Retrieved July 23, 2021, https://www.europarl.europa.eu/thinktank/en/document/IPOL_BRI(2021)662937

Yigitcanlar, T., & Cugurullo, F. (2020). The sustainability of artificial intelligence: An urbanistic viewpoint from the lens of smart and sustainable cities. *Sustainability*, *12*(20), 8548. doi:10.3390u12208548

Yigitcanlar, T., Han, H., Kamruzzaman, M., Ioppolo, G., & Sabatini-Marques, J. (2019). The making of smart cities: Are Songdo, Masdar, Amsterdam, San Francisco and Brisbane the best we could build? *Land Use Policy*, *88*, 104187. doi:10.1016/j.landusepol.2019.104187

Yigitcanlar, T., & Inkinen, T. (2019). *Geographies of disruption*. Springer International Publishing. doi:10.1007/978-3-030-03207-4

Young, M. M., Bullock, J. B., & Lecy, J. D. (2019). Artificial discretion as a tool of governance: A framework for understanding the impact of artificial intelligence on public administration. *Perspectives on Public Management and Governance*, *2*(4), 301–313. doi:10.1093/ppmgov/gvz014

Zheng, C., Yuan, J., Zhu, L., Zhang, Y., & Shao, Q. (2020). From digital to sustainable: A scientometric review of smart city literature between 1990 and 2019. *Journal of Cleaner Production*, *258*, 120689. doi:10.1016/j.jclepro.2020.120689

Chapter 2
An Artificial Intelligence Approach to Enabled Smart Service Towards Futuristic Smart Cities

K. Hemant Kumar Reddy
VIT AP University, India

Rajat Subhra Goswami
National Institute of Technology Arunachal Pradesh, India

Diptendu Sinha Roy
National Institute of Technology, Meghalaya, India

ABSTRACT

The rapid development of information and communication technology (ICT)-based solutions in the field of smart city applications becomes essential to cope with the ever-increasing urbanization requirements globally. These ever-increasing demands pose a great challenge to city infrastructure, particularly smart cities, and thus a sustainable approach is needed for the future smart cities. The ever-increasing service demand of the smart city archetype is prone to monitoring and managing such constrained smart city infrastructures in an effective way and to maintain the QoS (smart applications like transportation, healthcare, road traffic, and other utility services). In this work, the authors envisioned improving the QoS of smart transportation while employing a context-aware computing approach that helps to alleviate fog node data transfer, and a distributed smart transport service (DSTS) model is proposed that manages intelligent vehicles and road traffic of the traditional vehicles in an effective way to improve the QoS of the smart city.

DOI: 10.4018/978-1-6684-6821-0.ch002

INTRODUCTION

Over the last decade or so, it has been observed that smart cities are metropolitan residences projected to offer a quality of life by offering the quality of service through essential and highly sophisticated cyber-physical systems (CPS). CPS is categorized as available pervasive services for improving lifestyle quality (Cicirelli, 2017), (Silva, 2018). Smart cities, and real-time smart services realization, can be achieved with new developments of cyber-physical systems which are more complex than the present form of IoT services. While incorporating concepts like cross-domain IoT applications and smart city, it can be viewed as an integration of a huge number of individual applications of the different domains to simplify and serve the complex services in a simpler and smarter way Intiza (2017), Soursos (2016). For example, when a person meets with an accident or a medical condition on road, then he has to give a call for an ambulance or known person for immediate help, which may not be feasible in critical cases, where a person is not in a situation to make a call to inform about his situation. In such cases, smart vehicle and smart city applications collaborate with each other to ensure that the proper medical facility should be made available, and information is sent to close relatives as well. This can be achieved only when different IoT applications of smart cities are seamlessly integrated to talk to one another and collaborate to achieve the diversified goal. This idea had motivated many researchers around the globe to work in this direction to come up with a robust design for a cross-domain IoT real-time applications system – a true all-inclusive smart IoT system in a real sense. For smart city big data analytics, cloud infrastructure is the best solution, where data is collected from different devices (intelligent vehicles, sensors, surveillance cameras, traffic lights, smart buildings, smart homes, & smart grids and meters) from different domains and from different layers. However, to achieve real-time services, a Fog/Edge layer has to be incorporated between the end devices and cloud layer to avoid the delay at the cloud layer Lilu (2019). In smart cities, a very large number of IoT devices obviously will generate enormous data, and thus both the storage and management of data in the fog layer need to be carefully considered. Ideally, these distributed environments required a huge amount of computation and storage capacity to handle and cloud servers are best suited for such scenarios, but today's smart city applications can't tolerate the delay of centralized cloud servers. In order to balance the two parameters like computation required and service delay, the Fog layer is introduced in between the cloud and access layer. Fog nodes are deployed to collect the data from devices that generate data like deployed sensors and moving autonomous vehicles on a real-time basis and process it on a real-time basis and send it back to vehicles for quick action. Periodically these collected data send to cloud servers for big data analytics. Network bandwidth and other network related parameters plays major role in sending collected data to upper layer and upper layer to cloud which are not considered in this work. To improve the network efficacy software defined networking can be an effective solution Hussain (2019), Hussain (2020) even in vehicular network SDN plays a major role improve the vehicular network efficacy (Renuka, 2021), whereas in this work, a standard network features considered. In this manuscript, both the pertinent concepts of context and context awareness are utilized to manage the collected data at the fog node level in an effective manner. Both context and context awareness has been excessively used by several researchers in Roy (2018), T. Gu (2005), Behera (2020), M. Baldauf(2006), and Renuka(2018). The concept learned from context generation and context processing is utilized as a context instance, and context instances are generated at fog nodes from raw data collected from either vehicles or roadside units. An application request can be processed in a Fog node if the required context instances and required resources like computation (CPU), Memory (Tcam), and Storage (disk) are available within. In a dynamic environment, the Fog node's resource status also keeps changing, and every time a Fog node may not satisfy every application's request.

The rest of this paper is organized as follows: Section 2 briefly presents the background study of related areas. Section 3 presents the proposed smart city model in detail, the experimental setup for simulating different scenarios resented in section 4. The experimental results are presented and analyzed in Section 5. Finally, the conclusions are presented in Section 6.

Literature Survey

This section deals with the state-of-the-art works which have been attempted in the field of smart city applications, and smart transportation systems. Most of these works have used machine learning and Deep learning-based approaches and have been categorized into two main types; works were focusing on traffic flow prediction and action prediction through multiple methods. Also, multiple researchers have also focused on autonomous vehicular systems' traffic flow prediction and traffic management and seamless service management of smart city applications. In Y. Lv (2014) proposed a deep learning (DL) approach-based model which utilized auto encoders as the main blocks for effective traffic flow prediction, and the results obtained were promising. In W. Huang(2014) proposed a DL model using a multi-task-based learning architecture for the evaluation of transportation network spatial and temporal patterns. whereas, Abdelhadi (2017) suggested a Long Short Term Memory- Recurrent Neural Network model for the prediction of Traffic Matrices (TM) for big networks. Where LSTMs are equipped to model temporal sequences and have better and more accurate long-range dependencies than conventional RNNs. The result of the proposed model effectively shows that the proposed LSTM-RNNs are better by several orders of magnitude than the traditional used linear methods. Lei (2015) proposed a novel framework for the selection of the informative features of a task from multiple heterogeneous feature groups. The proposed framework had two major functionalities, namely, features selection accompanying LASSO, which derives weight vector from ascertaining the pertinent feature groups, and multi-modal DNNs, which are required for conversion of multi-modal data into a unified representation. This method is prominent for the selection of the required feature groups and has better classification performance as compared with several methods.

The works whose focus was on the autonomous vehicular system are discussed here. Albin (2017) developed a system with a Deep Neural Network (DNN) for computer vision-based lane detection. The proposed system is safer and takes advantage of a centralized control algorithm for consolidation of the subsystems used to let the vehicle within the safer lane markings of the road. Xiong (2016) implemented autonomous driving without vehicles around through the combination of the Deep Reinforcement Learning model and safety-based control. The focus of this work was also on designing a proper collision avoidance algorithm utilizing the artificial vehicles around. Brody (2015) proposed an inexpensive, robust solution for autonomous driving with the combined usage of Deep Learning and Computer Vision. This work used the existing convolution neural networks (CNNs) while performing vehicle detection along with the lane for a real-time system. Tengchan (2019) proposed a framework that was novel for optimization of platoon operation while also taking into account the encountered delay. The delay analysis and stability analysis effectively conclude that control system parameters are better optimized to maximize derived wireless system reliability of the wireless V2V network and the stability of the vehicle's control system.

Provisioning of autonomous services using fog computing can be done on any object, which in turn increases system performance for the execution of services. Kai (2017) proposed a service management system platform, which consists of various components like service handler, service transporter, service manager, network sniffer, network router, and network utilization to support the migration of IoT services. Various parameters like hop count, throughput, latency, etc are considered to handle the migration service while ensuring communication costs to be kept at a minimum.

The disruption occurring due to migration can be handled by adaptive services which reschedule the services to neutralize the damage. Rzevski(2020) proposed a model named multi-agent technology (MAT) for handling migration in smart cities. This model detects variations in services using intelligent and fast decision-making technology and it consists of humans, physical resources, virtual software agents and a knowledge base. This model helps in the conversion of a normal city to a smart city with minimum disruptions. Chavhan (2021) proposed a context-based vehicle route service using Google maps. The model consists of the decision-management module (DMM) and an estimation-identification-finder module (EIAFM). DMM is used to find the probability of occurrence of a disruption event and EIAFM uses the usual speed of vehicles, and divergence of travel time to find the periphery of occurrence. The proposed system quickly tracks the vehicle density and improves the diverging vehicle density in various routes. The proposed system also reduces the average travel time of commuters.

Reddy (2020) proposed fog layer-based resource supervision in context-sensitive smart cities using a genetic algorithm approach to handle efficiency in energy consumption. Due to low latency, fog nodes can achieve service delay constraints. VM controller collects the information from the control units which in turn gets added to the service request queue to find the required context occurrence and the number of processing VMs. When the context occurrences are sufficiently available, the control from the VM controller is handed over to service requests. As the optimal VM scheduling for smart city tasks is an NP-complete problem that has to be solved by non-deterministic machine learning, the optimal VM allocation is attempted using a metaheuristic algorithm. The modified SCS () algorithm using GA along with optimization of VM management model will effectively reduce the number of migrations and energy utilization. Giuseppe (2020) proposed a smart city service system (SCSS) which consists of individuals, tools, parties, and pooled information, which is able to generate and cater value to providers, users, and other interested parties, through efficient services. A philosophical model using the scenario-based methodology is used for incorporating prevailing ontologies that allow for the swift development and alteration of the services by using the data which is collected from the citizens. The most valuable resource of a smart city which is, the illustration and utilization of knowledge, is achieved using the scenario-based model. One of the main drawbacks of the scenario-based method is it requires a long time for the reasoning process to complete which is a mismatch with the speed of the data that is generated.

This paper proposes a Distributed Smart Transport Service (DSTS) model, which improves the quality of service of smart transportation system of smart city. i) Smart Traffic Management (STM) Approach: it efficiently manage the road traffic of both traditional and intelligent vehicles with the help of employed context-aware computing and CNN based vehicle identification approach. ii) Smart Service Management (SSM) Approach: it efficiently uses the context aware computing concept toalleviate data transfers among Fog nodes and vehicles in real-time and a proposed servicing algorithms improve the service quality of smart city applications on cross vertical IoT platform. The DTS model through the use of IoT enabled fog-cloud system using an incremental federated learning approach for real-time identification and classification while eliminating the need for the expensive pre-processing techniques for IVS.

Distributed SmartTransport Service Model

Smart city distributed environment is formed by utilizing Fog nodes, autonomous vehicles, and roadside units. Fig. 1 depicts a scenario of an IoT-enabled smart city environment. It also depicts the scenario of how vehicles communicate with other vehicles and roadside units and nearby fog nodes. A large number of IoT devices obviously will generate enormous data, and thus both the storage and management of data in the distributed fog layer need to be carefully considered. In the scenario described in Fig. 1, Fog nodes are deployed to collect the data from moving autonomous vehicles on a real-time basis and process it on a real-time basis and send it back to vehicles for quick action. Periodically these collected data send to cloud servers for big data analytics.

The aforesaid smart service management model for the smart city has been envisioned and modeled as two different components. One that takes care of smart traffic management with help of deployed sensors, cameras, and fog nodes. The second component of the proposed model takes care of the complete, reliable, and real-time service management of smart cities. Figure 2 depicts the component-level diagram of the proposed DSTS model and the detailed architectural diagrams and working principles presented in the subsequent sections.

Figure 1. Live Traffic Management in Urban Areas

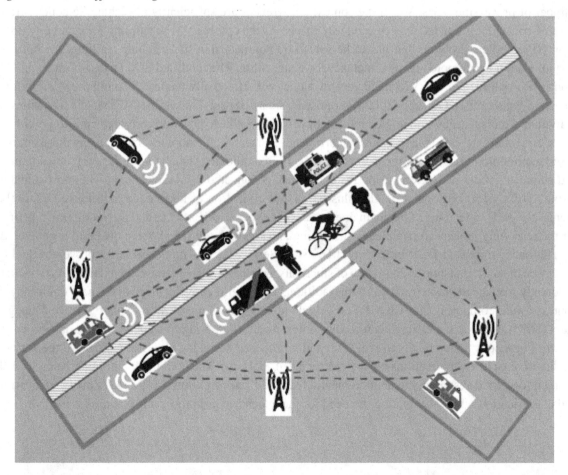

Figure 2. Abstract Level Component Diagram of DSTS model

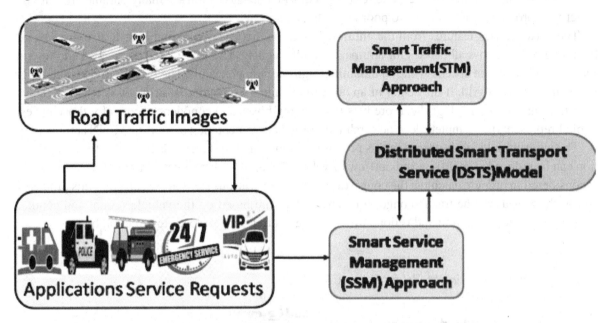

A. Smart Traffic Management (SAM)Approach

The two main objectives of this paper are as follows: first is proposing a robust model for a Fog-enabled smart city network architecture to provide complete and real-time service; and secondly, to provide service on a real-time basis by reduction of the overall service delay. To achieve the said objectives, a Fog enabled network architecture is modeled that receives traffic information from the deployed cameras and predicts the traffic conditions using a machine learning-based technique, which can extract the necessary traffic data from the surveillance footage and from past historical data from the season-wise. The extracted information is converted into a context form for sharing with other Fog nodes and based on this information, Fog nodes respond to the user's service request on a real-time basis.

In the case of the autonomous vehicle, vehicle devices generate an excessive amount of data, and at the same time, it requires real-time processing of this data. Also, it will result in increased computing requirements for both vehicles and deployed Fog nodes. These computation devices should be coupled with Artificial Intelligence algorithms like Machine learning and Deep learning for effective data processing. A prediction model is proposed to model the behavioral dynamics of pedestrians in real-time. Fig 3. depicts the traffic prediction model of a smart city, historical traffic data, real-time traffic data captured through CCTvs and deployed sensors, and environmental data like weather, temperature, pressure used for prediction. We have incorporated three different learning algorithms to predict the traffic flow, conjunction, and vehicle speed accurately. The deployed statistical approach is used to find or identify the traffic patterns during the day and night times, on different weekdays, and at different seasonal times. Statistical approaches are fastin nature and cheaper in implementation as compared to machine learning techniques but less accurate compared to machine learning techniques. In our model, we incorporated an auto-regressive integrated moving average model to identify the weekdays and seasonal traffic patterns. As it is a classical statistical data analysis approach that predicts the future based on the past regular interval time series data. However, due to today's drastic changes in traffic, many parameters can't be effectively processed and its leads to poor in prediction.

The network uses features from the entire image to predict each bounding box. It also predicts all bounding boxes across all classes for an image simultaneously. The YOLO design enables end-to-end training and real-time speeds while maintaining high average precision. The system divides the input image into an S ×S grid. If the center of an object falls into a grid cell, that grid cell is responsible for detecting that object. Each grid cell predicts B bounding boxes and conðdence scores for those boxes. Table 1 represents the complete designed architecture and implementation of modified CNN architecture.

The algorithm that is discussed in this proposed solution includes methods by which traffic congestion can be reduced. The inflow and outflow of vehicles in all four directions of a specific traffic signal is considered in order to calculate the congestion of the area. Various steps are involved in this proposed approach to measure the traffic congestion. These steps are based on the vehicles count and counter measure to avoid congestion and is done by assigning waiting time to specific direction traffic.

Figure 3. Traffic Prediction Model for Smart City

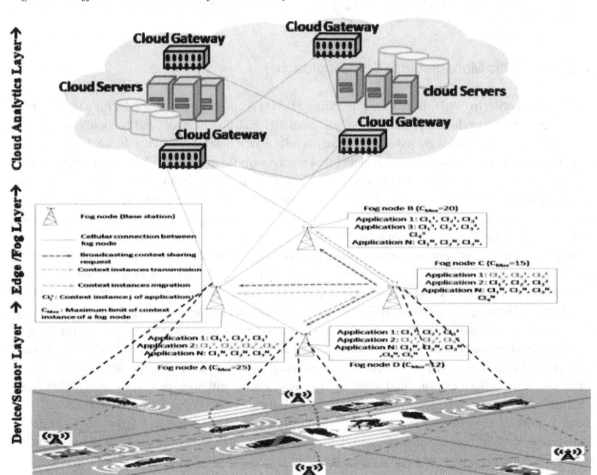

Table 1. Modified CNN Architecture

S NO.	PARAMETERS	VALUE
1	Input	Image of 416x416 size
2	Layer 1 (Convolutional)	32 filters of 3x3 size and output shape 256x256.
3	**Pooling**	2x2 filter with stride 2
4	Layer 2 (Convolutional)	32 filters of 1x1 size
5	Layer 3 (Convolutional)	64 filters of 3x3 size
	Residual Layer	Output size 128x128
6	**Pooling**	2x2 filter with stride 2.

Image Preprocessing

In this step, CCTV is used to capture high resolution images of the inflow and outflow of vehicles in all directions. These raw images are saved and pre-processed for edge detection.

Object Detection and Classification

In live traffic, the edges of the different vehicles present are detected and used to distinguish each distinct vehicle type. object detection is also used in this module to separate different vehicle shapes from the rest of the captured image. CNN technique is considered most suitable for this proposed solution after having analyzed various edge detectors Tahmid (2017), Canny (1986).

Time Allocation: The suggested division of time is based upon presumption. The contemporary allocation of time may depend on several different factors; for example, number of vehicles, and state of traffic at nearby intersections. Figure 4 depicts the workflow steps involved in the management of traffic.

There is an urgent need to incorporate new technologies and facilities to enhance traffic management networks, especially as the urban traffic jam problem continues to increase. Traffic issues are growing nowadays because of the rising number of vehicles and the limited resources that present infrastructures have. Based on the timer concept, the density of vehicle movement is considered and the results shows that the strict travel time saving strategy may be misguided, and perhaps better methods for managing the economic drag of traffic congestion lie in prioritizing the most important economic trips (possibly by assigning road pricing) or offering alternative means of travel to allow access to transportation despite obstruction due to traffic in Sweet (2013). The truth is that the town population and the number of cars on the road are increasing day by day. With a rising urban population and, thus an increase in the number of automobiles, the need for roadway, highway and road regulation is an important issue that needs to be addressed.

The biggest factors contributing to traffic issues today are the methods that are used to control the flow of traffic. The traffic control technology of today barely focuses on live traffic situations, resulting in unreliable traffic management structures.

Our approach was developed using PyCharm tools and aims to reduce heavy traffic congestion. The Image processing technique is also used in the implementation of this proposed solution. At first, a camera captures a picture of a street, and the other stages of the process are further explained:

A web camera is mounted in a traffic lane which takes photographs of the path where there is vehicle movement and traffic. Then, these images are stored effectively to learn the direction of the flow of traffic. Several forms of traffic control systems have been implemented to reduce the number of vehicles on the lane. A program where the total size of traffic is measured, using image processing methods, has been addressed. Another similar device proposed uses image processing techniques to monitor traffic lights and can be implemented in real time. At each point of the traffic light, a web camera is used to capture photos of the traffic lane that is chosen to be monitored. Then, these captured images are compared with an image matching method, using a reference image of the empty lane. Canny edge detection approach is employed to assess the image boundaries Krishna (2018). Traffic here is regulated according to the percentage of matches between the images. Many research papers are focused on methods of edge detection. There are also various other approaches that are proposed for traffic control networks. Manual monitoring applies to manpowered traffic control where Traffic police are assigned for traffic control in a given area. The monitoring of traffic signals by means of timers and electrical sensors is called automatic monitoring, but in scenarios, when there are no cars at all, time may be lost in giving a green signal in such approaches. With the assistance of image processing techniques, the proposed solution can overcome these limitations by regulating traffic lights. As the urban road flow crisis grows, there is a growing need to incorporate new technologies and infrastructure to enhance the state-of-the-art traffic management network. Traffic issues are growing today because of the rising number of cars and the scarce services that existing infrastructures have.

The recorded images are sequentially compared using picture matching. A picture of the road without traffic is used as a reference shot. Edge point detection is carried out using a Pre-edge detection operator for this purpose and can be managed based on the percentage of corresponding traffic signal durations. The received information in the form of contexts and current environment circumstance information is used to provide reliable and correct service to end-users and vehicles on the road on a real-time basis. The details of the service management approaches are discussed in the next section.

B. Smart Service Management (SSM)Approach

At present scenario of smart city, providing reliable and correct services to end users are prime important and challenging task due to increase in end-users and their demands. So, in this manuscript, we envision to incorporate smart service management approach in smart city transport system to provide secure and reliable services to end-users and vehicles. In order to address the aforesaid issues both the pertinent concepts of context and context awareness are utilized to manage the collected data at the fog node level in an effective manner. The concept of context and context awareness has been extensively used by several researchers in T. Gu(2005), Roy(2018). The concept learned from context generation and context processing is utilized as a context instance, and context instances are generated at fog nodes from raw data collected from either vehicles or roadside units. An application request can be processed in a Fog node if the required context instances and required resources like computation (CPU), Memory (Tcam), and Storage (disk) are available within. In a dynamic environment, the Fog node's resource status also keeps changing, and every time a Fog node may not satisfy every application's request.

To model the aforementioned scenario in an effective way, a three-layered architecture is proposed to handle the generated data as well as to provide the service to end user in real time basis.

Figure 4. Three Layered Enduser-Fog-Cloud (EFC) Architecture for Smart City

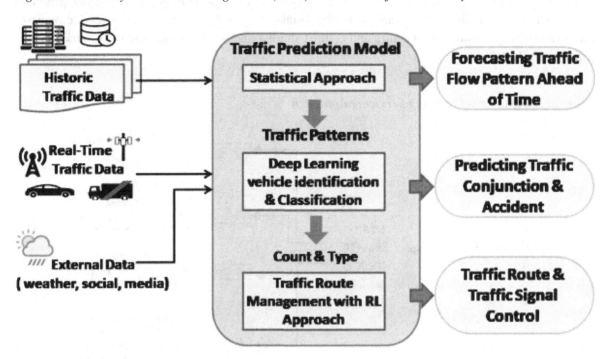

Fig. 4 depicts a three-layered End user-Fog-Cloud (EFC) architecture for sustainable smart city services, where Fog nodes act as a gateway between the device and cloud infrastructure. It has been experienced that the use of context-aware computing at the Fog node layer is very effective in managing the overall service time [9, 10]. In most of the metro cities, traffic-related services are not up to the mark due to traditional systems which are overburdened as a result of modern developments, and they are usually devoid of efficient ICT & IoT-based service applications. Even IoT (vertical applications) enabled smart city services are not fully effective in providing real-time complete services to customers. Fog-enabled architecture can be a solution and can offer a complete solution by incorporating context-aware computing at the fog layer to achieve real-time services T. Gu (2005), Behera (2020). Fig. 4 depicts the Fog environment scenario proposed, where deployed fog nodes collect environment information from environment sensors, vehicles, and other smart devices from users and process it for further processing. In the above figure 4, it can be clearly noticed that road blockage is due to colliding of vehicles and this information will be forwarded to the nearest fog nodes and the same information rippled to a point where vehicles can take a diversion to avoid the blockage. The same information will be sent to an authority for immediate action. To implement this distributed network scenario, a set of fogs are deployed within the sensing range of each other. Figure 4 depicts the fog network architecture for smart cities to enable smart services in real-time. An illustrative example of fog network architecture is presented with the help of 4 fog nodes, where all these fog nodes are deployed within the sensing range of each other and the different lines connecting these have a specific meaning presented in the right-side top corner of the figure. Each fog node is tagged with some specific applications that they can handle within it. A total of 14 applications have been used for service, out of which 6 to 8 applications were deployed in each fog node. For processing an application request that is requested from a user, the fog node required a certain number of numbers of context instances of such an application. As each Fog node is capable to handle a certain number of applications, when the received Fog node *Fi* is not able to complete the request within its deadline, then it finds a nearby suitable Fog node to hand over the service request. The details of Fog network architecture and context sharing and service migration is explained in our earlier work Roy (2018).

Figure 5. Multi-Channel Queuing Servicing Approach

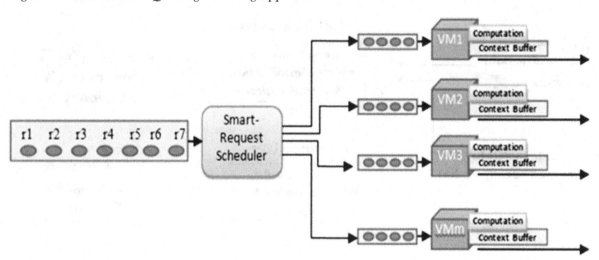

C. Combined Service Management Approach

As depicted in figure 2, the entire proposed DSTS model consist of two major components i. Smart Traffic Management (STM) Approach ii. Smart Service Management (SSM) Approach. Proposed SSM approach uses result of traffic prediction unit as well as vehicle class counter unit to find the traffic pattern of the season and to find the number of vehicles present on road respectively. The output of these units used for serve the service request of traffic type X. Xiong (2016). The presented servicing unit of Fog node receives the service requests from users and vehicles of different domain. These service requests are kept in a queue called service request queue (SRQ) which is a multi-channel queuing model, which takes service request from SRQ and scheduled in different available VMs based on the priority (DI: delay intolerable, DS: delay sensitive and DT: delay tolerable) these service requests are scheduled for servicing. The deployed smart request scheduler picks the high priority service requests to schedule immediately without any delay, whereas rest of the service requests are scheduled batch wise depending upon the availability of resources and context instance of required type. Each Fog node virtualized to multiple virtual machines to improve the performance, moreover a multi-channel servicing queuing approach incorporated to enhance the power of virtual machines. Fig. 5 depicts the multi-channel queuing servicing model of a Fog node, where a smart request scheduler sends the service requests to these virtual machines. Each virtual machine consists of computation and buffer space to store contexts of application types residing in virtual machines. In order to process any service request, a certain number of context instances are required. The detailed working principle of this model is presented in our earlier work Reddy(2020). Based on the availability and non-availability of both resources and context instances, the servicing approach is explained clearly in the following way;

Case-1: If the required computing resources and the context instances are available with the assigned virtual machine of a Fog node, then, the application will be processed immediately.

Case-2: if the required computing resources are available and the required context instances are unavailable in the assigned VM but available in other VM within the Fog node, then context instances are shared within VMs. If there is an unavailability of required context instances are in a Fog node, then a smart context sharing model (SCS) will be applied which we have discussed in our earlier paper [9].

Case-2.1 If required contexts buffer space is available then, a smart context sharing model (SCS) will be applied.

Case-2.2 If required contexts buffer space is not available then; Algorithm-2: context migration is carried out to create buffer space for incoming contexts before a smart context sharing model (SCS).

Case-3: If the required computing resources are not available and the required context instances are available in a Fog node, then the solution is dependent on the application's delay tolerant values.

Case-3.1: If the required resources will be available within the limit of delay tolerable value then the application will not be migrated i.e

Case-3.2: After forecasting, if it is found that the processing time of existing application exceeds the delay tolerance limit of requested application then the application will be migrated to a suitable Fog node using a combined forecast resource aware technique Algorithm 2 will be applied which we have discussed in our earlier paper Reddy(2020).

Case-4: If the required resources and contexts are un-available in a Fog node, then the application will be migrated to a suitable Fog node using a combined forecast resource aware technique then Algorithm 3 will be applied which we have discussed in our earlier paper Reddy(2020).

Table 2. Used notations and descriptions

Symbol	Discription
IFC	Traffic inflow/incoming vehicle count: total number of vehicles on incoming path
OFC	Traffic outflow/outgoing vehicle count: total number of vehicles on outgoing path
IFP	Traffic inflow vehicle path
OFP	Traffic outflow vehicle path
IFI	Road traffic inflow image for processing
OFI	Road traffic outflow image for processing
IFCThreashold	Max threshold incomming number of vehicles can allowed to pass through traffic point without conjuction
OFCThreashold	Max threshold outgoing number of vehicles can allowed to pass through traffic point without conjuction

SIMULATION DESIGN

This paper implemented with computer configuration is Pentium ® Dual Core CPU, E5700@3.00 GHz, RAM -2.00 GB, operating system for Ubuntu 14.04 (32-bit operating system, x64-based processor). To simulate the network, NS 3.26 (network simulator 3) and iFogsim simulator are used. Firstly, we declare the number of users and created fog devices by setting the parameters of FNs such as add node name, the rate per MIPS, bandwidth, a sensor with ifogsim, and power. The parameters setting for simulation are adopted as in Table 2. Figure 4 shows the simulation environment for smart city applications including predictive maintenance, and health monitoring systems. Here introduced a new group of stringent requirements like latency (low latency) requirement since resources of computing can be on-demand requested concurrently by several devices at multiple locations and it is implemented using spanning tree protocol. Next, the FN can be used for executing the task to another FN to the cloud system using a WRR algorithm. Based on the results from the scheduling algorithm, the task is scheduled to FN and then to the cloud system for allocating resources. Figure 5 shows the optimal FN selection

Table 3. Simulation parameters and values

Parameter	Value	Parameter	Value
Max. Cycles	100	Packet size	8
Local Link Transmission Delay	10	SP Tree Configuration	2
Switch	100_SW	Flit size	
Global Link Transmission Delay	100	Injection Queue Length	1000
Xbar Delay	3	Arbiter Iteration	2
Injection Delay	1	Local Queue Length	32
Internal Speedup	1	Local Link Channel	3
Global Queue Length	256	Global channels	2
Out Queue Length	32	Probability	0.5
Ring Injection Bubble	1	seed	10

The entire proposed model implemented in two different stages. In first stage, the real time streaming traffic video given as an input to the canny-detection algorithm, which identifies the number of vehicles. The output of first stage is given to input to the 2nd stage for traffic service management. Algorithm 1 presents the implemented workflow model of Intelligent Traffic Service Management Model. DSTS model showcase the components interaction and workflow of entire model. In order to measure the efficacy of the smart traffic service management, Kaggle traffic data set. Later on local road traffic videos ware captured processed using canny-detection algorithm and extracted the data set similar to Kaggle traffic set. The distributed fog network environment for the simulation was made with fog nodes. Initially the numbers of nodes were kept to be 50 and for every simulation 10 nodes were incremented till the nodes reached 100. This simulation network is similar with Roy(2018) presented by the authors earlier. In our simulation model it is assumed that fog nodes are deployed throughout the smart city within sensing range of each other. All these fog nodes are capable of processing and identifying number of vehicles and its type in real time basis. The real time traffic captured through the installed cameras and processed within the fog nodes. For our experimental purpose, we have processed traffic video separately and processed data feed as input to the simulation model for smart traffic service management. All these local trained models are integrated at cloud for formation of global training model. The model to be trained is pushed back to fog nodes for taking efficient decision at real time basis. This process is iterated throughout the simulation process. All these global trained models are used as service at Fog nodes and each fog node information can used the trained model for prediction and also train the model with its local data to further strengthen the model. All communications are in the form of context and fog node share its contexts with other fog nodes on demand basis. The concept of context sharing and context migration is discussed in our earlier work Roy(2018). These QoS violations are kept to minimum utilizing context sharing among Fog nodes. The results of the proposed DSTS model is compared with Greedy approach; while the parameter values of the aforesaid have been same for ready comparison. Despite the dynamic nature, performance of the simulation model is to be taken as mean value with associated standard deviation of multiple runs.

RESULT DISCUSSION

In this section, simulation-based experiments and results are described in order to evaluate the efficiency and effectiveness of the proposed model. Kaggle traffic detection Benchmarked is the dataset employed for these purposes. The said dataset consist of information of timestamp and number of vehicles on the traffic. based on the timestamp data smart traffic service management approach able to manage traffic effectively by adjusting the traffic signal waiting and diverting the traffic in another route with proper message. This is achieved with the help of collaboration of other fog nodes. The focus of this work is only on leveraging the truth predictions of the vehicles in the frame, but this work can be well adapted for other real-value ground truths simply by extension of the detection prediction matrix columns.

Figure 6. Predicted Traffic Signal waiting allocation time

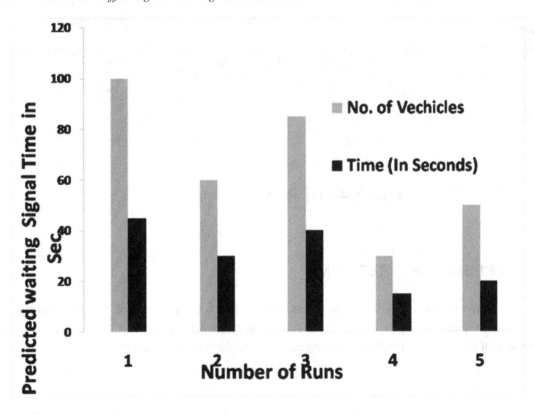

Fig. 6 depicts the predicted traffic signal waiting time based the other traffic parameter like incoming traffic load and traffic road width and it is observed that as the number of vehicles increases the waiting time predicted accordingly in the simulated environment the service time decreases.

Fig. 7 depicts the prediction accuracy of two different accuracy prediction approaches with respect to fixed input dataset. Prediction accuracy in case of decentralized model i.e. federated model, where traffic signal waiting time and point of diversion is much more the centralized model or single point and it is observed that as the global model get updates more and more with different data set of vehicles its prediction accuracy percentage is also increasing.

Figure 7. Prediction Accuracy Comparison

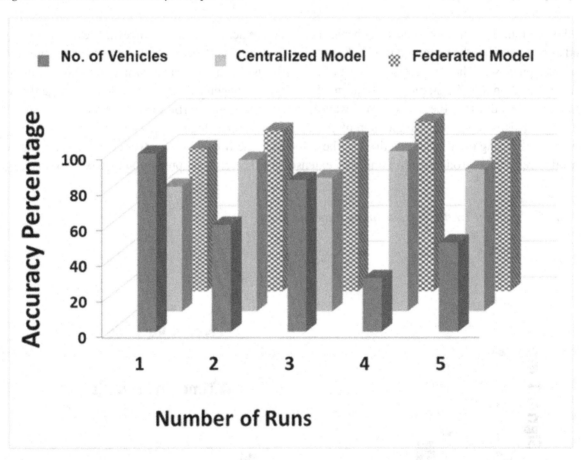

FUTURE RESEARCH DIRECTIONS

The proposed hybrid model work can be extended to enhance the efficacy of the proposed model in terms of incurred latency at processing and latency incurred at network level. Use of SDN can improve the efficacy of network and machine learning can be used for forecasting.

CONCLUSION

This paper presents a novel traffic management model for modern smart cities, that improves the QoS of smart traffic while employing a Canny-edge detection machine learning technique at the fog layer to manage the smart traffic services and an intelligent context-aware communication technique within the fog nodes that reduces the communication traffic. It utilizes a hybrid CNN model for real-time traffic load identification and classification of objects which is pertinent for effective distributed smart traffic service management system. The simulation-based results were found to be very encouraging to conclude that the proposed hybrid model of machine learning (canny-edge detection) and context-aware service enabled fog network model outperforms with RGB images showing accuracy more than 95%. The ITSM for smart city deals with the real time servicing with the help of incremental federated learning. The proposed approach shows better efficacy then the centralized approach and randomized approach.

REFERENCES

Ali, M. I., Patel, P., Datta, S. K., & Gyrard, A. (2017). Multi-layer cross domain reasoning over distributed autonomous IoT applications. *Open Journal of Internet Of Things*, *3*(1), 75–90.

Azzouni, A., & Pujolle, G. (2017). *A long short-term memory recurrent neural network framework for network traffic matrix prediction.* arXiv preprint arXiv:1705.05690.

Baldauf, M., Dustdar, S., & Rosenberg, F. (2007). A survey on context-aware systems. *International Journal of Ad Hoc and Ubiquitous Computing*, *2*(4), 263–277. doi:10.1504/IJAHUC.2007.014070

Behera, R. K., Reddy, K., & Roy, D. S. (2020). A novel context migration model for fog-enabled cross-vertical IoT applications. In *International Conference on Innovative Computing and Communications* (pp. 287-295). Springer. 10.1007/978-981-15-0324-5_25

Canny, J. (1986). A computational approach to edge detection. *IEEE Transactions on Pattern Analysis and Machine Intelligence*, (6), 679–698.

Canny, J. (1986). A computational approach to edge detection. *IEEE Transactions on Pattern Analysis and Machine Intelligence*, (6), 679–698.

Chavhan, S., Gupta, D., Nagaraju, C., Rammohan, A., Khanna, A., & Rodrigues, J. J. (2021). An efficient context-Aware vehicle incidents route service management for intelligent transport system. *IEEE Systems Journal*, *16*(1), 487–498.

Cicirelli, F., Guerrieri, A., Spezzano, G., & Vinci, A. (2017). An edge-based platform for dynamic smart city applications. *Future Generation Computer Systems*, *76*, 106–118. doi:10.1016/j.future.2017.05.034

D'Aniello, G., Gaeta, M., Orciuoli, F., Sansonetti, G., & Sorgente, F. (2020). Knowledge-based smart city service system. *Electronics (Basel)*, *9*(6), 965.

Falk, A., & Granqvist, D. (2017). *Combining Deep Learning with traditional algorithms in autonomous cars.* Academic Press.

Gu, T., Pung, H. K., & Zhang, D. Q. (2005). A service-oriented middleware for building context-aware services. *Journal of Network and Computer Applications, 28*(1), 1–18. doi:10.1016/j.jnca.2004.06.002

Huang, W., Song, G., Hong, H., & Xie, K. (2014). Deep architecture for traffic flow prediction: Deep belief networks with multitask learning. *IEEE Transactions on Intelligent Transportation Systems, 15*(5), 2191–2201. doi:10.1109/TITS.2014.2311123

Hussain, M. W., Reddy, K. H. K., Rodrigues, J. J., & Roy, D. S. (2020). An indirect controller-legacy switch forwarding scheme for link discovery in hybrid SDN. *IEEE Systems Journal, 15*(2), 3142–3149. doi:10.1109/JSYST.2020.3011902

Hussain, M. W., Reddy, K. H. K., & Roy, D. S. (2019). Resource aware execution of speculated tasks in Hadoop with SDN. *Int J Adv Sci Technol, 28*(13), 72–84.

Huval, B., Wang, T., Tandon, S., Kiske, J., Song, W., Pazhayampallil, J., . . . Ng, A. Y. (2015). *An empirical evaluation of deep learning on highway driving.* arXiv preprint arXiv:1504.01716.

Kientopf, K., Raza, S., Lansing, S., & Güneş, M. (2017, October). Service management platform to support service migrations for IoT smart city applications. In *2017 IEEE 28th Annual International Symposium on Personal, Indoor, and Mobile Radio Communications (PIMRC)* (pp. 1-5). IEEE.

Liu, Y., Yang, C., Jiang, L., Xie, S., & Zhang, Y. (2019). Intelligent edge computing for IoT-based energy management in smart cities. *IEEE Network, 33*(2), 111–117. doi:10.1109/MNET.2019.1800254

Lv, Y., Duan, Y., Kang, W., Li, Z., & Wang, F. Y. (2014). Traffic flow prediction with big data: A deep learning approach. *IEEE Transactions on Intelligent Transportation Systems, 16*(2), 865–873. doi:10.1109/TITS.2014.2345663

Reddy, K. H. K., Behera, R. K., Chakrabarty, A., & Roy, D. S. (2020). A service delay minimization scheme for qos-constrained, context-aware unified iot applications. *IEEE Internet of Things Journal, 7*(10), 10527–10534.

Renuka, K., Roy, D. S., & Reddy, K. H. K. (2021). An SDN empowered location aware routing for energy efficient next generation vehicular networks. *IET Intelligent Transport Systems, 15*(2), 308–319. doi:10.1049/itr2.12026

Renuka, K., Das, S. N., & Reddy, K. H. (2018). An Efficient Context Management Approach for IoT. *IUP Journal of Information Technology, 14*(2).

Ritwik, M. G., Krishna, D., Shreyas, T. R., & Phamila, Y. A. V. (2018, September). Road Congestion based Traffic Management System with Dynamic Time Quantum. In *2018 International Conference on Recent Trends in Advance Computing (ICRTAC)* (pp. 1-6). IEEE.

Roy, D. S., Behera, R. K., Reddy, K. H. K., & Buyya, R. (2018). A context-aware fog enabled scheme for real-time cross-vertical IoT applications. *IEEE Internet of Things Journal, 6*(2), 2400–2412.

Rzevski, G., Kozhevnikov, S., & Svitek, M. (2020, June). Smart city as an urban ecosystem. In *2020 Smart City Symposium Prague (SCSP)* (pp. 1-7). IEEE.

Silva, B. N., Khan, M., & Han, K. (2018). Towards sustainable smart cities: A review of trends, architectures, components, and open challenges in smart cities. *Sustainable Cities and Society*, *38*, 697–713. doi:10.1016/j.scs.2018.01.053

Soursos, S., Žarko, I. P., Zwickl, P., Gojmerac, I., Bianchi, G., & Carrozzo, G. (2016, June). Towards the cross-domain interoperability of IoT platforms. In *2016 European conference on networks and communications (EuCNC)* (pp. 398-402). IEEE. 10.1109/EuCNC.2016.7561070

Sweet, M. (2014). Traffic congestion's economic impacts: Evidence from US metropolitan regions. *Urban Studies (Edinburgh, Scotland)*, *51*(10), 2088–2110.

Tahmid, T., & Hossain, E. (2017, December). Density based smart traffic control system using canny edge detection algorithm for congregating traffic information. In *2017 3rd International Conference on Electrical Information and Communication Technology (EICT)* (pp. 1-5). IEEE.

Zeng, T., Semiari, O., Saad, W., & Bennis, M. (2019). Joint communication and control for wireless autonomous vehicular platoon systems. *IEEE Transactions on Communications*, *67*(11), 7907–7922.

Zhao, L., Hu, Q., & Wang, W. (2015). Heterogeneous feature selection with multi-modal deep neural networks and sparse group lasso. *IEEE Transactions on Multimedia*, *17*(11), 1936–1948.

Chapter 3
Applications of Machine Learning in Industrial Reliability Model

Suneel Kumar Rath
C.V. Raman Global University, India

Madhusmita Kumar Sahu
C.V. Raman Global University, India

Shom Prasad Das
Birla Global University, Bhubaneswar, India

ABSTRACT

The chapter examines ML methods that appear to be applied in implementing systems with intelligent behaviour. It depends on two workshops on learning in system of intelligent manufacturing, an intensive survey of the literature, and various commitments. Symbolic, sub-symbolic, and hybrid approaches, as well as their applications in manufacturing, are also discussed, as are hybrid solutions that attempt to combine the advantages of several methodologies. The advantages, inadequacies, and impediments of different creation methods are illustrated to decide suitable strategies for explicit circumstances.

INTRODUCTION

Machine learning will unharness the subsequent wave of virtual disruption. Businesses are predicted to be prepared. Companies that were among the first to put it in place have reaped the benefits. Future technology consists of robotics and self-using deep learning, natural language processing, machine learning, computer vision, and so on. The next generation of machine learning apps is built around digitization. Industries that have embraced digitization are typically at the forefront of machine learning. They are also expected to be a growth driver. Changes in marketplace share and revenue are probably to be elevated via way of means of using machine learning. Several adjustments to the original approach to industrial

DOI: 10.4018/978-1-6684-6821-0.ch003

automation are introduced by Industry 4.0. In this context, the Cyber-Physical System and Internet of Things technologies play a role in introducing intellectual automation and, thus implementing the notion of intelligent manufacturing, which is the main reason for smart products and best services (Kunst et al., 2019). Companies will encounter obstacles in a far more dynamic environment as a result of this unique approach. Many of these businesses are unprepared to deal with this new reality, in which a huge number of people do not always work together to boost productivity (Lee et al., 2014).

Predictive maintenance has several advantages, but it also has many drawbacks. On the one hand, productivity gains, system fault reduction (Chukwuekwe et al., n.d.), unexpected downtime minimization (Balogh et al., 2018), improved effectiveness in the utilization of human resources, financial(Schmidt & Wang, 2018), and optimization in maintenance intervention planning (Adhikari, 2018) are all benefits of Product data management. Machine Learning (ML) can be used for prognostics and failure prediction, such as estimating a machine's lifetime using a vast quantity of data to train an ML system (Balogh et al., 2018; Zhou & Tham, 2018), as well as diagnosing faults (Ansari et al., 2020; Bousdekis et al., 2019). Machine Learning (ML) research in areas directly related to design and manufacturing has not yet begun. It does, however, have a long history of success and failure, much like other disciplines of Artificial Intelligence (Lu, 1990) for a comprehensive assessment up to 1989. The adoption of a single ML approach or methodology into a current modeling and dynamic system for an explicit designing challenge has been the most typical feature of these R&D projects, with a few exceptions. Regardless, while learning is a universal process, machine learning in the context of engineering requires further investigation to completely appreciate the specifics. We hope to define and characterize "mutual human-machine learning" in future workplaces in this article. The key research difficulty is identifying how to characterize reciprocal learning when both human employees and intelligent computers of variable competence and intelligence participate in a shared endeavor. We investigate normal situations including humans and AI, just as human and machine skills in modern frameworks, to find an answer.

Figure 1. Relationship of human-machine collaboration.

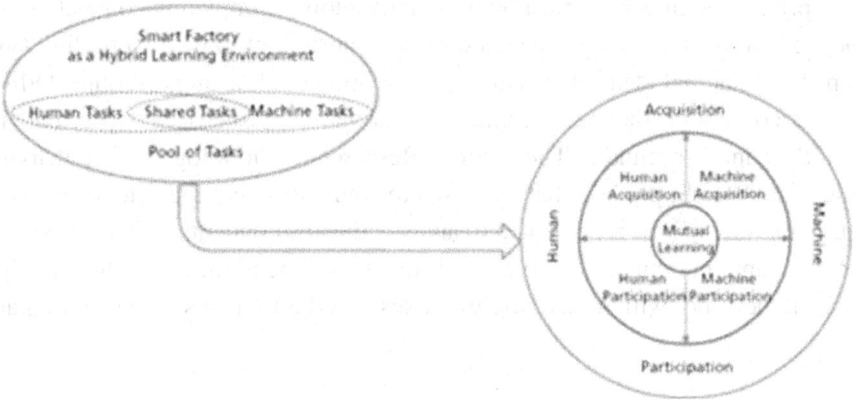

RESEARCH METHODOLOGY AND CONTRIBUTION

An efficient survey was conducted to achieve the study's two objectives, using the method described by Tranfield et al. (2003) in the year 2003, Who increased studies strategies from the clinical to the control sciences. Other authors have used this strategy to extract information from scientific literature with great success (Garengo et al. 2005). In the context of 4.0, this review focuses solely on ML applications in Production planning control. Zhong et al. (2016) supplied a bibliometric assessment of large records packages in several industries which include finance, healthcare, supply chain, and so on; however, its emphasis on assembling became limited. Wang et al. (2018) conducted a review on data-driven smart manufacturing and cited relevant sources. These sources, on the other hand, were not picked based on a comprehensive assessment of the literature. Due to the fact of the authors utilized a pre-described method to choose the papers to examine, Sharp et al. (2018) might be deemed as an observation much like this one. Despite this, they used Natural Language Processing (NLP) to analyze over 3000 distinct publications and give bits of knowledge into the scholarly literature of machine learning in 4.0. Although NLP can be beneficial for identifying major trends, it does now no longer permit writers to observe the info of the reviewed papers, where interesting research gaps and insights are likely to be discovered. A systematic review, on the other hand, enables the authors to adhere to a strict methodology while also conducting a thorough examination of each piece. Even though the PPC is closely tied to the supply chain domain, the latter isn't always covered inside the scope of this assessment because of its vastness, which will increase the chance of deviating from the PPC focus. As a result, the authors endorse that readers consult Hosseini et al. (2016) for a complete overview of quantitative techniques, technologies, terminology, and important supply chain flexibility factors. In reality, supply chain flexibility is a rising field of study that looks into a supply chain's ability to respond to disruptions also Hosseini et al. applied this topic in their research (2016), which used Bayesian networks to pick suppliers based on criteria for flexibility and also in this research they provided a function for assessing supplier resilience in identifying crucial supply network links using Bayesian networks.

Industry 4.0 aims to create digital twins, digital factories, or cyber-physical models that are computer representations of physical actions. Its purpose is to establish vertical and horizontal value chain integration by linking processes from the highest level to the low level, just as from providers to end clients. Also, another goal is to shorten the life cycle of product development by combining important design, manufacturing, operation, and maintenance operations into a digital thread. Several feedbacks from operation to product engineering must be built to develop a completely connected piece of equipment. The associated hardware, paying little heed to its arrangement in the assembling system, enables prescient upkeep. The principal idea is to accumulate a scope of online and disconnected signs from the hardware to take care of models that can recognize an anomaly or issue right off the bat. The following is a breakdown of the paper's reminder: The section "Research methodology and contribution" will talk about the precise writing audit process that was used to find and select the scientific article sample. A quick bibliometric analysis will be represented to analyze the key concepts utilized as string chains, and the main aim of this paper in comparison to related studies will be highlighted thoroughly. The section under "Analytical framework" will go over the four axes that the logical system encompasses.

DIFFERENT PARADIGMS FOR MACHINE LEARNING

Machine learning is a broad area with a generally normal set of aims and estimation methods that tight-spot it together. The general objective is to increase performance on a particular task, and the basic methods entail identifying and taking advantage of normality's in training data. Most of the assessments are exploratory, determined to show that the learning system brings about better execution on a different than set in at least one real space than without learning. Despite these parallels, AI analysts will quite often recognize prevalent execution on a different test set in at least one genuine area than without one of five significant ideal models. A subsequent structure, known as case-based or case-based learning, stores data as individual cases or encounters and uses adaptable matching calculations to recover and apply these guides to new circumstances. For example, the nearest neighbor approach chooses the stored case that is closest to the current condition (based on some distance metric) and uses it for prediction and classification. Case-based adapting typically stores preparing occurrences in memory; speculation happens during recovery, with the ordering system and comparability measure used to find relevant cases providing the majority of the power.

Genetic algorithms (GA), a third machine learning worldview, frequently express data using binary characteristics or Boolean, which are some of the time utilized as the actions and conditions of rules. The most famous mediator for this information is a go big or go home matching methodology to determine clashes, depending on the qualities related to rules. Production system architecture may allow rules to be applied in order, resulting in multi-step behavior in some instances. Mutation and Crossover, which are undifferentiated from genuine genetic mechanisms, are the best quality learning operators in GA that create new competitor rules from guardians with high qualities, where strength or "wellness" mirrors some proportion of execution. Decision trees, Condition-action rules, and other knowledge structures are used in a fourth model, which we can call rule enlistment. Utilizing an all-or-none match system, the exhibition component sorts examples down the decision tree branches or identifies the primary rule whose conditions fit the occasion. The activity sides of the standards or the tree leaves are utilized to store data about classes or expectations. In the standard rule-induction architecture, the different learning algorithms typically perform a greedy search across the space of decision trees, choosing attributes for inclusion into the information structure with the help of a statistical evaluation function. The last approach, known as analytic learning, encodes knowledge as logical principles and regularly utilizes a performance framework to solve multi-step problems via a finding procedure. One typical approach is to express information as Horn clauses (like in the Prolog programming language), then formulate questions as "theorems" and look for proofs. In this paradigm, learning components utilize past data to construct confirmations or "clarifications" of involvement, then, at that point, gather the pieces of evidence into more muddled guidelines that can deal with equivalent issues with less inquiry (utilizing nearby "search-control rules") or in a one-step (utilizing "macro-operators").

APPLICATIONS IN MANUFACTURING

A list of machine learning applications in manufacturing is described in the following parts, which are organized by topic. An overall introduction to every theme is trailed by a discussion of key research topics proposed by our contributors and distributed in significant distributions and gathering materials.

Design

Many research groups have separately solved a variety of design challenges using machine learning technologies. The discussion here begins with a confined issue setting that presupposes a particular design model and then moves on to a model development and optimization technique that is integrated. The latter two instances deal with specific production and system design challenges. A particular design retrieval system tries to reduce recurring design effort by filling in the plan and assembling subtleties of new, in some ways similar components using current part information: The algorithm predicts losing data on a new, partially specified part after viewing a set of representative, fully characterized parts. (Srinivasan & Moon, 1996) Treats design retrieval as a conceptual clustering problem, with pieces being displayed one at a time and identified as belonging to a particular existing group or forming another family based on the probability of predicting the proper attribute value. The algorithm's easy-to-understand hierarchical structure has proven to be a key feature. (Kopardekar & Anand, 1995) reports on tolerance allocation using ANN: in a tiny example, the method outperformed the exhaustive search. The method has the advantage of requiring no measurable presumptions and being able to tolerate dynamic mean shifts, making it suitable for use as part of a dynamic learning and quality control system. The central goal of the adaptive interactive modeling system (AIMS) framework (Lin & Lee, 1991; Lu et al., 1991) is to find a tradeoff between simulation method speed and accuracy in solving design problems: while a quick technique with lower precision is ideal in the early, exploratory phase of the plan, the last, calibrating stage ought to manage the cost of more assets for a more elevated level of exactness. The first phase, model creation, is to create models that meet the present modeling goals (such as speed of execution or readability of results) (Fig. 2).

Figure 2. The adaptive interactive modeling system comprises two phases: model formation and usage.

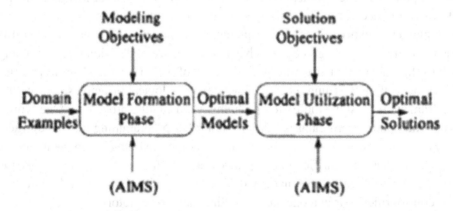

Several inductive learning techniques are utilized in the initial phases to build a large number of models, each with various modeling features (for example, one model recursively divides the qualities and returns steady execution esteems inside each class, while different utilizations a direct relapse of execution esteems).

Process Planning

The tremendous complexity of cycle arrangement expertise, as well as the deep relationships of knowledge from different resources, makes it one of the most successful areas for applying multiple learning approaches. Numerous applications employ ready-made tools and methodologies, as well as experiments that yield data that are useful outside of the technical community. This topic's experimentation is organized below by implementation area.

The Recognition and Processing of Machining Features

In (Chan & Case, 1994), the recognition of a preset set of artificial features is explained using a rule-based approach. Because new components may disclose unexpected feature interactions, the user should be able to adjust the recognition process in real time; this is accomplished here by adding new rules as needed. Identification capabilities are improved with the addition of new rules adapted to the specific situation, and the interaction arranging part is improved by factory-specific concerns. Albeit this moderate, intuitive change of acknowledgment limits can be viewed as a type of learning by instructing, more exploration is expected to see whether the new rule set additionally yields the right reactions to the old inquiries. Step-by-step learning, on the other hand, without the ability to generalize, may result in abysmal efficiency in both human and machine terms.

Machining Cells and Group Technologies

Due to some known limitations of standard, established different manual coding and categorization schemes, the establishment of part families and the accompanying group technology (GT) problem and machining cells necessitates unique solutions. Past endeavors with numerical programming or syntactic example acknowledgment were ineffectual, principally because they were hard proportional to new parts and adding machines, and particularly to evolving models. Since a connection between plan and assembling is being created in these, this subject of exploration is vital. Feature-based techniques are most commonly used. As a result, success in this field could narrow the distance between CAD (essentially, a composition activity) and CAM (mainly, decomposition), allowing the existing CAM cycle to be linked to the decomposition process' output (Subrahmanyan & Wozny, 1995).

Planning and Operation Selection

The overall issue setting in activity determination and arranging can be considered as the production of a plan from the necessary part detail (execution space) to the proper functional boundaries (choice space). Learning's role is to decide the backward of this planning productively and reliably by utilizing available handbooks and modeling tools (for example, simulation). (Kim & Lee, n.d.) Presents a case study in fiber optics production, in which a range of statistical and AI-based methodologies are merged in an integrated learning framework for material property forecasting. These methods are carefully evaluated, and the observed differences in predicting methods are demonstrated to be statistically significant.

Operation Sequence Planning

The use of AI approaches to automate process planning functions is an outstanding future trend in Computer-aided process planning (Eversheim & Schneewind, 1993). While flexibility demands and the accessibility of the organization's explicit qualities are referred to as driving drivers, the absence of successful business AI advances and the information procurement bottleneck are referred to as significant restricting issues. Overall, an integrated, hybrid strategy is recommended, just as it is in other domains. (Veloso, 1995) Describes the use of PRODIGY, planning, and learning system. An arranging area is characterized as a bunch of operators (nuclear tasks) with their effects on the world and the fundamental circumstances for their application, in everyday AI language. The underlying setup of the world and an objective assertion characterize an arranging challenge. The arranging issue is addressed by a progression of operators that, starting with the underlying state, change the world into one that meets the objective assertion. An arrangement of operators (an absolute request plan) is legitimate on the off chance that every one of their preconditions is met before they are executed, and it is right to assume each of their preconditions is met before they are executed.

GAPS DURING ML SOLUTION DEVELOPMENT

A Repository of Attacks That Have Been Carefully Curated

Attacks are deconstructed into shareable "strategies and methodology" in traditional software security, and the MITRE ATT&CK framework (FB, 2019; Sharif et al., 2017) organizes them all together. This creates a searchable database of attacks from both researchers and nation-state attackers. An explanation of the method, whose advanced persistent threat is known to employ it, detection ideas, and references to publications with the additional background, is included for each attack. The Technical Catalogue and Axes of Quality Evaluation are two of the most important sections of the guidelines. We suggest that a comparable organized chronicle of attacks be made, ideally by broadening the generally utilized Miter Framework. When adversarial ML specialists distribute another kind of attack, we urge them to enroll it in the Miter system so security investigators can see both customary and ill-disposed ML attacks in one spot.

Secure Coding for Adversarial Machine Learning

Secure coding practice allows engineers to eliminate exploitable vulnerabilities in their applications while also allowing other engineers to audit the source code in a traditional software context. Python, C, Java, and C++ (CMU, n.d.), for example, have clear-cut secure coding practices against common software vulnerabilities such as memory corruption. There is a lack of adversarial ML-specific security advice in the machine learning context. Although other toolkits include recommended practices (Tensor Flow (Tensorflow, n.d.), Pytorch, Keras, Tensor Flow(Github, n.d.a) is the main system that gives exhaustive rules around old-style programming threats just as admittance to devices for testing against adversarial attacks (McCallum & Nigam, 1998). Future adversarial ML research (Rath, Madhusmita, Sahu et al, 2022; Rath, Sahu, Das et al, 2022) should, in our opinion, focus on offering best practices for eliminating unclear program behavior and exploitable vulnerabilities. We recognize that providing clear suggestions is challenging due to the field's complexity (Hal, 1967).

Dynamic and Static Analysis of Machine Learning Systems

In classical programming security, static examination tools are utilized to reveal likely issues in the code without requiring implementation and to distinguish coding standard breaks. The source code is typically changed over into a theoretical language structure tree, as a result of which develops a control flow graph (CFG) (Carlini & Wagner, 2017). The control flow graph is searched for coding practices and checks that have been transformed into logic, and when they are found to be inconsistent with logic, they are raised as errors. When it comes to traditional software, for example, Python tools like Pyt (Github, n.d.b) discover security issues in traditional applications. We expect that static analysis tools will eventually connect with IDEs to provide scientific knowledge of the syntax and semantics of application code before it is committed to the code repository, preventing the introduction of security risks.

Machine Learning Systems Used in Auditing and Logging

To utilize a typical programming model, significant security occasions in the operating system, in the creation of process are logged in the host and relayed to Event Management (SIEM) and Security Information systems. This later enables security responders to perform anomaly detection (Twycross et al., 2010; Van der Aalst & de Medeiros, 2005) to determine whether a suspicious process (a sign of malware) has run on the machine. Paper not (Papernot, 2018) was the first to propose auditing in ML systems, along with arrangement outlines for instrumenting ML settings to collect telemetry. We advise ML system developers to identify the "high impact activities" in their systems also in the same way that they would in traditional software security. We advise carrying out the list of attacks deemed harmful to the company and ensuring that the telemetry events can be followed back to the attack. At last, these occasions should be exportable to customary event management and security information frameworks, so that the analysts may save records for future investigations.

ML System Detection and Monitoring

Because security analysts lack operational competence, ML environments are becoming incomprehensible. Some intriguing research has been done on the weakness of current ill-disposed location systems (Carlini & Wagner, 2017) and how to enhance them (Gilmer et al., 2018). Furthermore, we recommend that detection algorithms be built in a form that makes them easy to share among security specialists. In classical software security, for example, the logic of identification is written in a standard style and the most common of which is known as Sigma (Tranfield et al., 2003). By providing a means to self-doc, Sigma can translate one analyst's observations for many people into a protective mode of others. Where ATT&CK and MITRE provide a tremendous repository of understanding into adversarial approaches, Sigma may transform one expert's discoveries into protective activity for some by giving a way to the self-document substantial rationale for identifying an assailant's methods.

DATA, MACHINE LEARNING, AND ANALYTICS

In recent years, data has increased at an exponential rate. It gave rise to industries, technologies, and services based on analytics and machine learning. Manufacturing, healthcare, and retail are traditional businesses that are struggling and adopting the finest of ML and analytics at a breakneck pace. Simultaneously, relatively emerging businesses such as cloud-based customer service are primarily built on machine learning. Analytics and machine learning, on the other hand, are not limited to businesses, industries, or organizations. Policies of Government and world politics are both influenced by it on the border level. Before constructing a "smart city," for example, governments must conduct extensive data crunching and technology analyses based on data. Data analytics and insight production are gradually becoming required for government entities to make people-friendly policies and prevent crime. In the not-too-distant future, Big Data will govern all legislation, social welfare activities, and infrastructure construction. Machine learning analytics is becoming increasingly important as a result of numerous market and industry considerations. For example, the global economy's dynamics are constantly changing, knowledge workers' costs are rising, and clients are constantly pressuring businesses to cut costs. As a result, businesses are being forced to find new ways to address these problems. However, integrating machine learning analytics into the environment in which they are to be used is a difficult undertaking. It is opposed by existing forces.

Manufacturing Analytics based on Machine Learning

Manufacturing is known for its extensive reporting, quality frameworks, and risk detailed reporting. In the realm of technology, there has been growth, particularly in the areas of industrial organization and modern digitalization, as well as auxiliary production and technical logs containing granular information derived from sensors, telemetry, and other machine-generated data they use ML techniques, IoT, data science and cloud computing methodologies to help their clients. The various ways or procedures used to identify the optimal industrial model; in that situation, we can also apply ML techniques (Rath et al., n.d.; Rath et al., 2022a; Rath et al., 2022b). A quiet revolution is underway; transforming data can be transformed into a valuable tool for a variety of purposes, including productivity and profit. Among its applications are chemical, vehicle, meteorological, and a variety of other manufacturing applications. In comparison to other areas such as banking, customer service, and healthcare, the manufacturing industry has traditionally been hesitant to use Machine learning analytics and machine learning technologies. Extensive success across industries, on the other hand, has prompted industrial leaders to use it.

Banking and Finance Analytics Using Machine Learning

The financial markets are constantly changing, advancing, and preparing to adapt to new situations. This industry is continuously open to new technologies and systems that aid in the analysis of market behavior, mood, and financial professional attitudes. A new financial idea has recently emerged, combining the psychological characteristics valued by supporters of the quantitative procedures leaned toward by set-up neoclassical money specialists. Machine learning analytics is a great technique to combine behavioral and quantitative components of finance and assess, blend, and use them. Mobile banking apps that are both functional and clever, intelligent Chatbots, and search engines are just a few examples. Machine learning or AI implementations in finance and banking are triggered by the need to maintain and collect large amounts of customer data, maintain correct historical records, and comprehend the quantitative aspect of the financial or economic world.

Healthcare Analytics Using Machine Learning

The healthcare industry has an impact on all of us. Traditional healthcare institutions are evolving as a result of new and innovative technologies. In just a few years, it has gone from being a doctor-centric industry to one that is technology-enabled, with technologies like analytics playing a significant role in patient population health management. Machine learning analytics is a great technique to improve treatment results and results while keeping costs down. Deep learning, Machine learning together with AI, is revolutionizing healthcare and providing new meaning and directions. Deep learning strategies are utilized to help PCs how to dissect medical pictures by coordinating an imaging library with calculations and models that consequently discover and classify medical illnesses. Millions of people benefit from accurate imaging diagnosis that allows them to receive timely medication. As a result, millions of lives are saved.

Figure 3. Working with healthcare analytics.

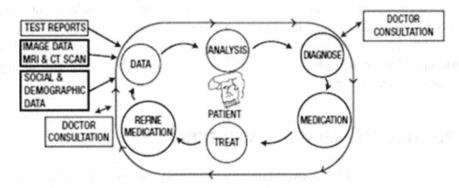

Marketing Analytics Using Machine Learning

Adaptation is the key to marketing success. Social technologies are being used by new-generation marketers to assess and analyze conceivably affecting customers. Web analytics tools enable businesses to track users across the internet and gain insight into their surfing habits. Intelligent machine learning technologies are a by-product of advancements in understanding and tracking technology. Machine learning analytics is beneficial to marketing in a variety of ways. The potential in areas like personalized messaging and product recommendations, for example, is enormous. Customers are transformed from casual site visitors to engaged customers of that site or business as a result of this. Machine learning-based analytics can help marketing companies acquire, analyze, and manage massive amounts of data from several sources (e.g., website visit flow, purchase behavior, responses to previous campaigns, and mobile app usage). ML analytics in marketing can help bridge the gap between analytics and information. ML-based analytics enable firms to turn data into a competitive advantage by extracting insights. Data science encompasses techniques such as predictive modeling, data mining, scenario-based "what if" research, simulation, and a new era of text analytics and smart statistics would be used to uncover important patterns and connections in data.

Machine Learning in the Retail Sector

The retail business is undergoing a positive transformation because of machine intelligence. It enables retailers to uncover crucial action areas buried beneath a sea of wasted data and also opportunities. It also gives them the ability to consume and analyses data that was previously thought to be beyond human ability to process (at least manually). The use of customer turnover data, allows retailers to foresee the future and make informed decisions. Mountains of data about products, price, sales, performance, consumer behavior, and logistic details are now available thanks to advances in data capture and storage technologies.

Machine Learning Analytics for Customers

Customer analytics give businesses the ability to foresee and anticipate what they will do for their consumers, as well as identify which customers are at risk, how to attract new customers, and which customers are loyal to their company. It also aids firms in customer segmentation so that the optimum business plan for client retention and acquisition may be implemented. It also determines whether or not high-value customers are in jeopardy and what propose to make to a particular client portion. At the point when a lot of information is free, it is basic to utilize AI-based examination to dissect purchaser information to settle on informed business choices. The achievement of AI-based examination, then again, is reliant upon having the right system, excellent information, thoroughly examined plans, and very much carried out arrangements.

STUDIES RELATED TO PREDICTIVE MAINTENANCE

In the literature, many different Predictive Maintenance techniques have been offered. Sensor data is typically acquired via IoT concept and assessed using ML and DL models in these studies (Lu, 1990), (Kunst et al., 2019). The received sensor data, such as temperature, vibration, and humidity, can be used to develop a model of the total system. The system may be alerted and, more crucially, maintained by recognizing irregularities in Big Data obtained from the model, permitting intercession at the primary stop of the machine previously it fails. With such scheduled maintenance interventions, unanticipated downtimes, personnel expenditures, and maintenance costs are avoided. Producing efficiency will improve as a result of this.

The data was collected using an IoT Structure regulating low-cost sensors and analyzed using an ML model in another work (Lee et al., 2014). With Azure IoT, data collection was simplified, and the information was stored in the cloud and delivered for ERP frameworks (Romeo et al., 2020), (Ali et al., 2019). Neural networks were supposed to be equipped for making exact and quick predictions. Neural organization geography is set up utilizing feed-forward layer rationale and a huge Electro Migration unwavering quality assessment was directed utilizing incorporated circuit bundles (O'Donovan et al., 2019). With such integrated circuit packages, the system's MTTF (mean time to failure) characteristics were computed, as well as the nature of failure estimations (Boyes et al., 2018). The analysis of Big Data generated by Distributed Control Systems and Industrial IoT with the advent of Industry 4.0 (Chukwuekwe et al., n.d.), (Wang & Wang, 2017) was the focus of a distinct application. In this scenario, the machine data was organized, and the failure estimates were generated using the FB100 function package from the machine learning library (Balogh et al., 2018). Big Data was generated using the help of IoT technology to manage equipment in another industrial activity, and data on operator failure alerts and failure interventions were collected (Adhikari, 2018), (Zhou & Tham, 2018). Maintenance 4.0, a new data analytics platform that integrates data mining, machine learning, and cloud technologies (Bousdekis et al., 2019), was used to assess the data. The system is dynamically monitored as a result of the analysis, and a prescient upkeep application was naturally enacted in the support expert's work plan (Ansari et al., 2020). Our study varies from the others, in that a subset of Big Data is developed using only the ERP system's previous failure warnings, with no consideration for IoT sensor technologies or additional equipment installation. This research looks at how a machine learning algorithm can detect errors before they happen.

THE SUGGESTIVE STRATEGY

In this study, the facility's downtime records from the previous three years were examined to forecast production line downtimes. Environmental and hardware concerns are the primary causes of unplanned downtime. Expert analyses have revealed certain commonalities in the places of the industrial packaging robots depicted in, such as working times, and seasonal considerations, An artificial intelligence framework is constructed based on expert knowledge to handle downtime and conversion data acquired from the system during working hours. Failure data in the training framework is used to impart expert knowledge to the artificial neural network. The data to be provided to the network is organized using a grouping approach. The system achieves a position where the failure predictions can provide scheduled maintenance through a procedure of weight refreshes including emphases using the preparation tests (Srinivasan & Moon, 1996). The investigation also includes a component reliability analysis of the system's hardware. The MTTF values for each component are calculated based on the current system downtimes. Theoretical and practical tests are carried out by feeding available data into the ANN and doing a reliability study.

FURTHER RESEARCH PERSPECTIVES

This cutting-edge study looked at several research publications that were picked using systematic literature review logic. An analytical framework consisting of four dimensions was used to analyze these studies. First, the elements of a technique were evaluated, allowing for a study of ML-PPC (Machine Learning in production planning and control system) activities, strategies, and tools. Second, the data sources that were used to create the ML-PPC model were identified and evaluated. Finally, a review of use cases revealed the different uses of data-driven models in Industry 4.0. The properties of 4.0 were discovered and analyzed as a result of their implementation. The findings from the activities led to the identification of eleven recurring tasks that were used to build an ML-PPC model. OUAs (Often Used Activities), CUAs (Commonly Used Activities), MUAs (Medium Use Activities) and SUAs (Sustained Use Activities) were the four groupings based on the percentage of time they were used (Seldom Use Activities). The OUAs and CUAs clusters' activities are thoroughly recorded in this literature, based on these clusters. Data pre-processing tasks constitute a big part of MUAs' activity, although they aren't well described by academics. The most commonly utilized families in the scientific literature were discovered after a thorough examination of the methodologies. The most effective methods were discovered to be Regression, Q-Learning, and Ensemble learning and clustering, and so on. Based on these findings, a temporary creation investigation of the best six most regularly utilized families has happened.

Findings indicated more interest in Ensemble learning, prompting more in-depth thinking about the approaches covered by each family. The most popular neural network approach was the multi-layer perceptron. However, specific deep learning approaches such as LSTM, Deep Neural Networks, and CNN are beginning to be used. When it comes to Ensemble learning, there are a couple of things to keep in mind. The most commonly utilized tools for constructing ML-PPC models in the research were MAT-LAB, R, Python, and Rapid Miner, based on the research the majority of authors, then again, neglected to refer to the apparatus they utilized, which is one of the review's flaws. It's also worth noting that these findings are based on a sample of scientific papers, implying that they are mostly applicable in a classroom setting. Other things to think about are the software's cost and scalability, labor market talent availability, interoperability with existing information systems, and so on. Artificial and management data are currently the most commonly used data sources. The previous recommends that enterprises are keen on esteeming the information held in data frameworks, while the last option proposes that acquiring each of the information needed to construct ML-PPC models is problematic. Data from IoT sources, such as Equipment and Product data, was used sparingly, indicating a keen interest in these data collection technologies. Finally, MLPPC models failed to integrate User data, most likely due to the difficulty of gathering it and the considerable amount of data privacy responsibility that it entails. In terms of 4.0 characteristics, the data suggest that much of the scientific literature in ML-PPC is devoted to achieving Self- the Organization of Resources, which is understandable given that one of the PPC's main goals is to manage resources to fulfill the business plan. At the subsequent level production process of self-guideline, self-learning and information revelation and age have all the earmarks of being dealt with all the more routinely. As found in the proposed cross-matrix, 76% of the potential study fields are either hardly handled or never studied. As a result, the ML-PPC remains a significant topic for the implementation of 4.0, with several research opportunities. The following three important points could be used to describe the primary future research perspectives:

Reinforce in ML-PPC the role of IoT: Here it allows for a better design of the data collection system as well as an update to the model to address the concept drift issue. To accomplish this, the Machine Learning approach and workflow ought to be changed from linear to circular, taking into account the need to retrain through new data regularly. This way of thinking would enable early identification of the retraining policy as well as the necessary factors, which could then be measured again at a low cost.

Improve the design, logistics, and integration of the PPC: Various use cases are said to assist the PPC. Recent literature, on the other hand, appears to disregard strategies, as well as product and process design applications in conjunction with the PPC.

Priorities are environmental considerations and human interaction to ensure the development of moral manufacturing in 4.0: understanding how humans interact with the best proposed ML-PPC models is critical to developing comprehensive methods that benefit society. To accomplish this, the impact of the MLPPC framework on employees' working conditions must be investigated in both the short and long term. If the system degrades them, a redesign is required.

Future work will be focused on the below points:

When ML-PPC models are implemented, the recommended to select an order, in the actions will be reviewed. Which should be completed, resulting in a strategy that will aid in the transition from a linear to a circular workflow?

Using sectorial information, the best applicable approaches and technologies will be linked to each activity: Connecting methodologies, tools, and the different activities is the key to developing a good utility that could be valuable to new practitioners in both research and industry.

A review of existing solutions of data availability and workarounds will be presented: because the availability of data has been identified as a major concern, a study of ways to address the class-imbalance problem, as well as the use of reliability learning in the context of PPC, will be carried out.

CONCLUSION

Machine-learning algorithms have proven to be extremely useful in a variety of real-world manufacturing applications. Commercial implementations of these techniques, as well as efficient linkages to commercial databases and user interfaces that are well-designed, are now available from dozens of companies all over the world. However, these algorithms are not without flaws. Using the methods described here, data sets with tens of thousands of training examples can be mined in a short period. Many critical data sets, on the other hand, are significantly larger. More research is required to develop effective AI or machine-learning approaches for such large data sets.

The goal of this systematic literature study was to look into the biggest problems within the framework of Industry 4.0, machine learning and reasoning are discussed. This industry's fundamentals and technology were investigated. We also discussed the difficulties of putting it into practice in the real world. This study looked for architectures or frameworks that leverage ontologies or machine learning models for reasoning. The study concentrated on cyber-physical system predictive maintenance, ignoring similar studies that used predictive maintenance in other contexts, such as software failure prediction.

REFERENCES

Adhikari. (2018). Machine Learning Based Data Driven Diagnostics & Prognostics Framework for Aircraft Predictive Maintenance. Academic Press.

Ali, M. I., Patel, P., & Breslin, J. G. (2019). Middleware for real-time event detection and predictive analytics in smart manufacturing. *2019 15th International Conference on Distributed Computing in Sensor Systems (DCOSS),* 370–376.

Ansari, F., Glawar, R., & Sihn, W. (2020). Prescriptive maintenance of cpps by integrating multimodal data with dynamic Bayesian networks. In *Machine learning for Cyber-Physical Systems* (pp. 1–8). Springer.

Balogh, Z., Gatial, E., Barbosa, J., Leitão, P., & Matejka, T. (2018). Reference architecture for a collaborative predictive platform for smart maintenance in manufacturing. *2018 IEEE 22nd International Conference on Intelligent Engineering Systems (INES),* 299–304.

Boetticher, Menzies, & Ostrand. (2007). *Promise repository of empirical software engineering data.* Available: http:// promisedata.org/repository

Bousdekis, A., Mentzas, G., Hribernik, K., Lewandowski, M., von Stietencron, M., & Thoben, K.-D. (2019). A unified architecture for proactive maintenance in manufacturing enterprises. In *Enterprise Interoperability VIII* (pp. 307–317). Springer.

Boyes, H., Hallaq, B., Cunningham, J., & Watson, T. (2018). The industrial internet of things (iiot): An analysis framework. *Computers in Industry, 101,* 1–12.

Bradley, P. (1997). The use of the area under the ROC curve in the evaluation of machine learning algorithms. *Pattern Recognition, 30*(7), 1145–1159.

Carlini, & Wagner. (2017). Adversarial examples are not easily detected: Bypassing ten detection methods. In *Proceedings of the 10th ACM Workshop on Artificial Intelligence and Security.* ACM.

Chan, A. K. W., & Case, K. (1994). Process planning by recognizing and learning machining features. *International Journal of Computer Integrated Manufacturing, 7*(2), 77–99.

Chukwuekwe, Glesnes, & Schjølberg. (n.d.). *Condition monitoring for predictive maintenance-towards systems prognosis within the industrial internet of things*. Academic Press.

CMU. (n.d.). https://wiki.sei.cmu.edu/confluence/display/seccode

Eversheim, W., & Schneewind, J. (1993). Computer-aided process planning - state of the art and future development. *Robotics and Computer-integrated Manufacturing, 10*(1/2), 65–70.

FB. (2019). https://about.fb.com/news/2019/01/designingsecurity- for-billions/

Garengo, P., Biazzo, S., & Bititci, U. S. (2005). Performance measurement systems in SMEs: A review for a research agenda. *International Journal of Management Reviews, 7*(1), 25–47.

Gilmer, Adams, Goodfellow, Andersen, & Dahl. (2018). *Motivating the rules of the game for adversarial example research*. arXiv preprint arXiv:1807.06732.

Github. (n.d.a). https://github.com/tensorflow/tensorflow/blob/master/SECURITY.md

Github. (n.d.b). Available: https://github.com/python-security/pyt

Hal. (1967, January). The WEKA data mining software: An update. *IEEE Transactions on Information Theory, IT-13*(1), 21–27.

Hosseini, S., & Barker, K. (2016). A Bayesian network model for resilience-based supplier selection. *International Journal of Production Economics, 180*, 68–87.

Kim, S. H., & Lee, C. M. (n.d.). *Advanced manufacturing systems through explicit and implicit learning*. Working Paper, KAIST Graduate School of Business, Seoul, South Korea.

Kopardekar, P., & Anand, S. (1995). Tolerance allocation using neural networks. *Int. J. of Advanced Manufacturing Techn., 10*.

Kunst, R., Avila, L., Binotto, A., Pignaton, E., Bampi, S., & Rochol, J. (2019). Improving devices communication in industry 4.0 wireless networks. *Engineering Applications of Artificial Intelligence, 83*, 1–12.

Lee, J., Kao, H.-A., & Yang, S. (2014). Service innovation and smart analytics for industry 4.0 and big data environment. *Journal of Theoretical and Applied Information Technology, 95*(1).

Lin, C. H., & Lee, C. S. G. (1991). Neural-network-based fuzzy logic control and decision system. *IEEE Transactions on Computers, 40*(Dec), 1320–1336.

Lu, S. C-VTcheng, D. KYerramareddy, S. (1991). Integration of simulation. learning and optimization to support engineering design. *CIRP Annals, 40*(1), 143–146.

Lu, S. Y. (1990). Machine learning approaches to knowledge synthesis and integration tasks for advanced engineering automation. *Computers in Industry, 15*, 105–120.

McCallum, & Nigam. (1998). A comparison of event models for naive Bayes text classification. *AAAI-98 Workshop on Learning for Text Categorization*.

O'Donovan, PGallagher, CLeahy, KO'Sullivan, D.T. (2019). A comparison of fog and cloud computing cyber-physical interfaces for industry 4.0 real-time embedded machine learning engineering applications. *Computers in Industry, 110*, 12–35.

Osakada, K., Yang, G. B., Nakamura, T., & Mori, K. (1990). Expert system for cold-forging process based on FEM simulation. *CIRP Annals, 39*(1), 249–252.

Papernot. (2018). *A marauder's map of security and privacy in machine learning.* arXiv preprint arXiv: 1811.01134.

Rath, Madhusmita, Sahu, Das, & Mohapatra. (2022). Hybrid Software Reliability Prediction Model Using Feature Selection and Support Vector Classifier. *2022 International Conference on Emerging Smart Computing and Informatics (ESCI)*, 1-4. doi: 10.1109/ESCI53509.2022.9758339

Rath, S. K., Sahu, M., & Das, S. P. (n.d.). Software Reliability Prediction: A Review. *International Journal of Engineering Research & Technology.*

Rath, S. K., Sahu, M., Das, S. P., & Bisoy, S. K. (2022). A Comparative Analysis of SVM and ELM Classification on Software Reliability Prediction Model. *Electronics (Basel), 11*(17), 2707.

Rath, S. K., Sahu, M., Das, S. P., & Pradhan, J. (2022a). Survey on Machine Learning Techniques for Software Reliability Accuracy Prediction. In *International Conference on Metaheuristics in Software Engineering and its Application* (pp. 43-55). Springer.

Rath, S. K., Sahu, M., Das, S. P., & Pradhan, J. (2022b). An Improved Software Reliability Prediction Model by Using Feature Selection and Extreme Learning Machine. In *International Conference on Metaheuristics in Software Engineering and its Application* (pp. 219-231). Springer.

Romeo, L., Loncarski, J., Paolanti, M., Bocchini, G., Mancini, A., & Frontoni, E. (2020). Machine learning-based design support system for the prediction of heterogeneous machine parameters in industry 4.0. *Expert Systems with Applications, 140*, 112869.

Schmidt, B., & Wang, L. (2018). Predictive maintenance of machine tool linear axes: A case from the manufacturing industry. *Proc. Manuf., 17*, 118–125.

Sharif, Bhagavatula, Bauer, & Reiter. (2017). *Adversarial generative nets: Neural network attacks on state-of-the-art face recognition.* arXiv preprint arXiv: 1801.00349.

Sharp, M., Ak, R., & Hedberg, T. (2018). A survey of the advancing use and development of machine learning in smart manufacturing. *Journal of Manufacturing Systems, 48*, 170–179.

Srinivasan, M., & Moon, Y. B. (1996). *A framework for a goal-driven approach to group technology applications using conceptual clustering.* Production Research.

Subrahmanyan, S., & Wozny, M. (1995). An overview of automatic feature recognition techniques for computer-aided process planning. *Computers in Industry, 26*, 1–21.

Tensorflow. (n.d.). https://bit.ly/2RDl3cm

Tian, Pei, Jana, & Ray. (2018). DeepTest: Automated testing of deep- neural-network-driven autonomous cars. *The 40th International Conference on Software Engineering (ICSE 2018)*, 303–314.

Tranfield, D., Denyer, D., & Smart, P. (2003). Towards a methodology for developing evidence-informed management knowledge utilizing systematic review. *British Journal of Management, 14*, 207–222.

Twycross, Aickelin, & Whitbrook. (2010). *Detecting anomalous process behavior using second generation artificial immune systems.* arXiv preprint arXiv: 1006.3654.

Van der Aalst, M., & de Medeiros, A. K. A. (2005). Process mining and security: Detecting anomalous process executions and checking process conformance. *Electronic Notes in Theoretical Computer Science, 121*, 3–21.

Veloso, M. (1995). Integrating planning and learning: The Prodigy architecture, 1. *Experimental and Theoretical AI, 7*, 81–120.

Wang, C., & Jiang, P. (2018). Manifold learning-based rescheduling decision mechanism for recessive disturbances in RFIDdriven job shops. *Journal of Intelligent Manufacturing, 29*(7), 1485–1500.

Wang, K., & Wang, Y. (2017). How AI affects the future predictive maintenance: a primer of deep learning. In *International Workshop of Advanced Manufacturing and Automation*. Springer.

Zhong, H. X., Jiang, S. L., Liu, M., & Lin, J. H. (2016). A prediction-based online soft scheduling algorithm for real-world steelmaking-continuous casting production. *Knowledge-Based Systems, 111*, 159–172.

Zhou, C., & Tham, C.-K. (2018). Graphel: A graph-based ensemble learning method for distributed diagnostics and prognostics in the industrial internet of things. In *2018 IEEE 24th International Conference on Parallel and Distributed Systems (ICPADS)*. IEEE.

Chapter 4
Classification of Kidney Diseases Using Transfer Learning

Sachin Kumar Saxena

https://orcid.org/0000-0002-6830-5930
Invertis University, India

Jitendra Nath Shrivastava
Invertis University, India

Gaurav Agarwal
Invertis University, India

Sanjay Kumar
SRMS IMS Hospital, India

ABSTRACT

A urologist confirms high risks of kidney stones just because of diabetic mellitus; however, other factors also exist, but a major cause is type 2 diabetes. Renal cyst and diabetes clinical features show 58% of affected subjects as the same. Research findings prove the high risk of renal cancer among diabetes patients. All these patients underwent abdominal MRI or CT scan to extract kidney high-definition 3D images. The dataset was gathered from two hospitals: the first is the SRMS IMS, and the second is the Bareilly MRI & CT Scan Centre, both located in the city of Bareilly in the state of Uttar Pradesh of India. Research has been analyzed to note the classification among four classes using seven transfer learning methods. Results have been compared with seven transfer learning methods. The methods are EfficientNetB0, Xception, VGG16, ResNet50, MobileNet, InceptionV3, DenseNet121. Out of these deep learning-based algorithms, EfficientNetB0 shows the best accuracy of 96.02%.

DOI: 10.4018/978-1-6684-6821-0.ch004

INTRODUCTION

There is a strong correlation between chronic kidney diseases and medical history showing that diabetic Mellitus causes diabetic symptoms. A high level of blood glucose level leads to CKD, cardiac issues, liver problems, nerve damage, etc. The asymptotic phase of renal disorder is crucial because the patient is not aware of the consequences and avoids taking precautionary steps to protect his kidney. In the later stage of CKD, symptoms are worse than vomiting, cardiac attack, retina damage, leg swelling, and congestive cardiac failure. The renal calculi, also called kidney stones, are hard particles stored at a single place or multi places, resulting in diminished functionality of the urinary system. Various kinds of kidney stones are existing in the human body, such as calcium depository, which is due to the excess amount of calcium in urine, the second type is uric acid stone, due to high level of acid existing in urine, third is struvite stone, which is due to infection in the urinary system, the fourth type is cysteine, which is due to family hierarchy disorder. Hypertension, older age, family history of kidney cancer, smoke, obesity, etc. are the main cause of kidney cancer, which is the worst case of kidney tumor. However, medical research does not claim any certain reason why kidney tumor particles are developed in the renal system.

In recent research, the association between kidney stones and diabetic Mellitus has come into the picture. Patients with type 2 diabetes are more prone to develop uric acid stones. There is a 33.9 percent risk factor of renal calculi or Nephrolithiasis inside the kidney of patients who are also suffering from type 2 diabetes (Daudon et al., 2006). A near about, 2.5 times is the risk factor to be developed kidney stones in the renal of type 2 diabetic patients. In addition, HbA1c ranges from 5.7 to 6.4 percent have a moderate chance of 34 percent, and HbA1c ranges above 6.4 percent have 92 percent to develop kidney stones (NICResearch, 2019). Based on the study of causes of renal calculi, an imbalance of insulin instances in the body, and high blood pressure levels are the major roots of Nephrolithiasis (Vieira, 2020). Kidney cancer or renal tumor is also one of the causes of kidney function deterioration. Tseng et al. (2015) extensively examined one million kidney cancer patients with diabetic and non-diabetic symptoms. They found a high number of cancer patients, who were also diagnosed with diabetic Mellitus. The ratio later hiked, when other parameters such as age, the high blood pressure were also added. The patients with type 2 diabetic Mellitus have much higher risk for kidney cancer as compared to other factors (Undzyte et al., 2020).

Figure 1. Cross section MRI image view

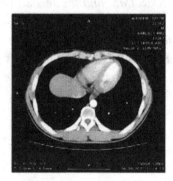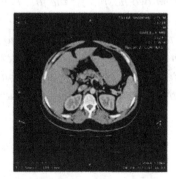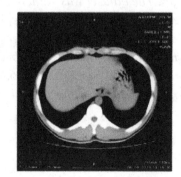

Figure 2. Patient abdominal raw CT scan image

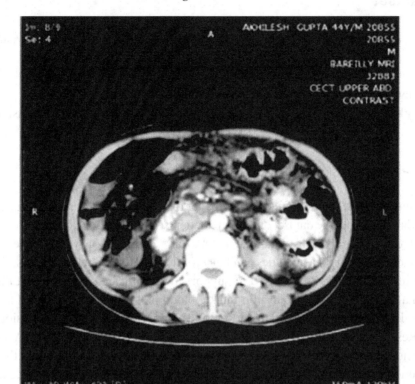

MOTIVATION

In the training stage, Kears API integrated with Python code to achieve the Deep Learning feature extractctions.

All the models have been trained on NVIDIA GeForce Experience recetly purchased by Shri Ram Murti Smarak College of Engineering and Technology, Bareilly, Uttar Pradesh, India. Further details are given in **Table 1 GPU hardware configuration** .

Table 1. GPU hardware configuration

Hardware Detail	Configuration
NVIDIA model number	3060
RAM	12 GB
SSD Graphic card	500 NVME
System Opearting system	Windows 10 Pro 64 Bits
Processor Model	Intel (R) Core (TM) i7-10700K
CPU prcessor	3.8 GHz
System RAM	32 GB

Code and Dataset

Code is accessble at author's GitHub repository: https://github.com/sachin365123/SevenDeepLearningAlgorithms

Dataset can retrieved from author private dataset repository: https://drive.google.com/drive/folders/1GltM4QEJiwuu6FUs4OAkfHtzBTchxVED?usp=sharing

RELATED WORK

Umair Muneer Butt et al. (2021), presented in their paper that resurging interest in the healthcare system is due to the availability of a large dataset of diabetic patients. The metabolic disorder leads to chronicle kidney disease, later, higher chances of cardiac attack. Early detection of type 2 diabetes can save the life of patients, and intelligent data analytics can be helpful to predict diabetic Mellitus. In this research paper, real-time IoT architecture is proposed to support the healthcare system. Renal diseases can be diagnosed when a few features such as insulin intake, blood pressure, and sugar level are measured at regular an interval, and further processed under multilayer perceptron, logistic regression, and random forest models. Researchers have performed their experimental studies on the PIMA Indian dataset, available to diagnose symptoms of diabetic Mellitus in the patient body. In addition, the authors have proposed a fin-tuned multilayer perceptron using a long short-term memory algorithm. Android mobile application with the Internet of Things implementation proposed to deploy to track real-time data, which is a novice concept in hypothetical healthcare architecture. As far as the accuracy of the proposed algorithm is concerned, it achieved 87.26 percent concerning state-of-art systems. However, the proposed algorithm has a comparison with artificial neural networks, J48, K nearest neighbor, FF-NN, and RB-Bayes algorithm. Placing sensors upon a patient's body is a challenging task, the authors proposed a virtual system to feed real-time data of patients and store it in Mongo DB, a database repository, further processed for machine learning algorithms.

Aishwarya Mujumdar et al. (2019), in their research work, authors have reviewed the parameters of the patient, for the purpose of predicting diabetic Mellitus. There are mainly several features like patient's service nature, the number of pregnancies available, glucose level, age, blood pressure, body mass index, skin thickness in millimeters, insulin intake, on which basis diabetes can be classified. various machine learning algorithms such as support vector classier, Random Forest, Decision Tree, Extra Tree, Ada Boost, Perceptron, Linear discrimination analysis, logistic regression, K nearest neighbor, Gaussian Naive, Bayes, Bagging algorithm, and gradient boost are implemented for predicting and identification of diabetic Mellitus. Accuracy ranges from 60 percent to 96 percent when machine algorithms are deployed at the PIMA Indian Dataset and diabetes dataset. Using pipeline, the accuracy of 97.2 percent is achieved for logistic regression, whereas the highest accuracy peaked at 98.8 percent for the Ada Boost classifier. Due to having large availability of datasets, big data analytics, at present, is useful to prevent diabetic Mellitus in the health care system. Data collection, data pre-processing, clustering, model building, and evaluation of trained dataset steps have been used in each model.

Rahulsingh G. Bisen et al. (2020) Designed a computer-aided diagnosis system to classify, detect, and segment liver tumors. Dynamic contrast-enhanced magnetic resonance imaging and computer tomography scan, ultrasound, and positron emission tomography scan images are used to classify tumors in livers. An automatic segmentation technique single block linear detection algorithm is introduced by the authors for texture features and extraction of region-of-interest.

Ravinder Kaur et al (2018) the intravenous urogram method is used for renal tracking. CT scans are also processed to segment the kidney images. The several other formats of medical images as X-rays, Ultrasounds, MRI, Nuclear medicine, and the OCT compared for various parameters cost involved, radiation, time involved spatial resolution.

S. R. Balaji et al. (2020) have obtained active counter segmentation to classify using a deep neural network method. Research has been performed upon MATLAB 2014 to classify cystine stones, calcium stones, uric acid stones, and struvite stones. A low pass Gaussian filter is used to find out the region of interest, and preprocessing of greyscale images leads to segmentation and feature selection.

Rati Goel et al. (2020) have achieved 90 percent accuracy, 78 percent precision, and 73 percent specificity while classifying kidney stones with the help of the morphological segmentation method. A graphical user interface has been designed for pre-processing, image enhancement, image filtering, morphological segmentation, and classification of kidney stones. The various parameters such as entropy, areas, correlation, contrast, and classification status are depicted on this MATLAB GUI.

The detail background history is given in **Table 2 Background study** below.

Problem Definition and Proposed Solution

Raw images contain patient name, id and other parameters; hence they are first preprocessed before primary outcome into low level feature of image, further undergone for various stages as given in figure 3. Less prior knowledge and predictive nature can result in to wrong classification; hence, once radiologist provides his correct opinion then high definition images are eventually stored at cloud storage, figure 4.

Four stages of chronic diseases are diagnosed in any patient namely end-stage kidney disease, acute kidney injury, chronic kidney disease, and no kidney disease, in previous research models, a deep belief network, softmax classifier, and Deep Learning model to produce prediction output with support of 25 features of any patient.

Figure 3. MRI Images representing Kidney with other organs

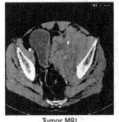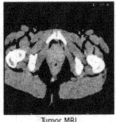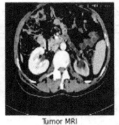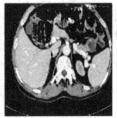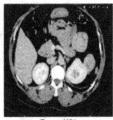

Table 2. Background study

S.No.	Author	Proposed Classification Models	Dataset Detail	Accuracy Rate	Outcome
1.	Sudharson S et al. (2019)	Singular Value Decomposition (SVD) for feature extraction and Support Vector Machine (SVM) as classifier	100 ultrasound images of kidney	90%	Proposed method for feature selection is better than other methods like GLCM, gradient, statistical and Gabor features
2.	Guozhen Chen et al. (2020)	Adaptive hybridized Deep Convolutional Neural Network (AHDCNN)	Image Dataset taken from NIH clinical centre	97.3%	IoMT model implemented for the prediction and diagnosis of Chronic Kidney Disease
3.	Pallavi Vaish et al. (2016)	Viola Jones algorithm, SVM classifier is used for texture feature extraction	Ultrasound Images	90.91%	Early detection of CKD using Smartphone Based Automatic Abnormality
4.	T. Mangayarkarasi (2017)	PNN-based classifciation method	Dr. Joe Antony-ULTRASOUNDSCAN CENTRE, Ernakulum, Cochin, Kerala, India	93.5%	Diagnostics of four classes: Normal, Cyst, Calculi and Tumor
5.	S.M.K. Chaitanya (2018)	Probabilistic principal component analysis (PPCA)	US Kidney Ultrasound and MRI Images	94%	Binary classification of kidney abnormality
6.	Renuka Marutirao Pujari (2014)	Proposed five steps for CKD detection	USG (ultrasonography), CAT (computed tomography) scan, and MRI (magnetic resonance imaging) collected from Satara hospital	--	detecting and diagnose of fibrosis conditions within kidney tissues followed by CKD stages
7.	Zarin Subah Shamma (2019)	Fuzzy Analytical Hierarchy Process (FAHP)	EEG and clinical data collected from Dhaka Medical college hospital using Mobile App	90.32%	Identify severity of CKD using Multicriteria decision making method
8.	Asif Ahmed Neloy (2019)	A generic architecture, and a classificatory model along with Naïve Bayes, Logistic Regression, KNeighbors Classifier, Decision Tree Classifier, Random Forest Classifier, Gradient Boosting Classifier, and MLP Classifier	5000 tabular sample data collected in Bangladesh using mobile APP and IBM Cloud	80-92%	Diagnostic of heart disease, stroke, Kidney Diseases, and Accident at hospital using PaaS cloud based method

System Design

Convolutional Neural Network

The convolutional neural network, a class of Deep Neural Networks, is of different kinds such as Conv1D layer, Conv2D layer, Conv3D layer, SeparableConv1D layer, SeparableConv2D layer, DepthwiseConv2D layer, Conv2DTranspose layer, Conv3DTranspose layer but most of the models are using Conv2D layer for feature extraction (Keras Team,).

EfficientNetB0

The Keras image classification model with ImageNet wights, softmax classifier activation function improves different surpasses for the image input. It also consists millions of FLOPs to train and test the pixels of input image (Tan & Le, 2019).

Xception

The Gradient Descent steps are having high relative accuracy with respect to ImageNet validation when ReLu activation function is used to train the images (Chollet, 2016).

VGG16

For large-scale image recognition, a very deep convolution neural network is compared for the results. The size of the initial Convolutional Neural Network is fixed at 224×224 RGB images (Simonyan & Zisserman, 2014).

ResNet50

The Input images of size 224×224 RGB images are undergoing Deep Residual Learning for image recognition, this model consists of 152 CNN layers, which is eight times denser than VGG and represents 3.57 percent of error (He et al., 2015).

MobileNet

There are several versions proposed by authors (Howard et al., 2017), such as MobilNet224, MobilNet192, MobilNet160, etc., out of which MobilNet 1.0 MobileNet-224 shows the highest accuracy with 83.3%.

InceptionV3

The Inception Architecture is the most widely used model for Computer Vision and Image Processing models. It costs 5 billion multiply-adds per inference, along with, it using less than 25 million parameters. The original model has been tested on ILSVRC 2012 classification (Szegedy et al., 2015).

DenseNet121

The Densely Connected Convolutional Networks consist of their feature maps that are used as inputs into all subsequent layers with convolution and pooling layers. The abdominal CT scan images are used to produce results (Huang et al., 2016).

Data Collection

The dataset was gathered from two hospitals, first, the Shri Ram Murti Smark Institute of Medical Sciences (SRMS IMS), and second is the Bareilly MRI & CT Scan Centre, both located in the city of Bareilly in the state of Uttar Pradesh of India. SRMS institute is established in 1990 and provides degree in medical education like MBBS (Bachelor of Medicine & Bachelor of Surgery) and Postgraduate (M.D./M.S.) in Pre, Para and Clinical Subjects. The SRMs hospital also possesses 950 bed multi super specialties to serve the patients. The performance analysis can obtain through two CT scans machines; with suitable facility of one single slice & other one dual source of 128 Slice CT. The SRMS hospital also comprises with two MRI machines; one is of 0.2 Tesla & other one is 3 Tesla large bore MRI, Dicom images are later undergone to various simulation models like Keras, Tensor Flow, and Python. Original private dataset can be retrieved from this Google drive link, raw Dicom images are having names like.

a.   DURGA_DATT_JOSHI_72Y_M_42215137,
b.   BAL_VINDER_KAUR_52Y_F_42200555,
c.   RAM_DEVI_65Y_F_42214353

Later, by using Python scripting language diacom images are renamed and converted to jpeg, finally cropped to remove extra parameters around the kidney feature.

Dataset can retrieved from author private dataset repository:

Figure 4. Testing image histogram for abdominal CT scan images

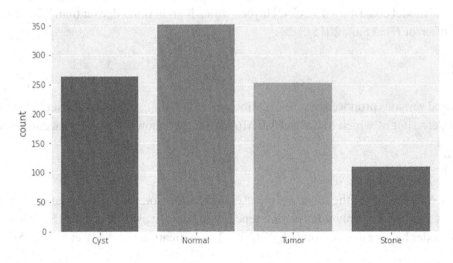

Figure 5. Testing image histogram for abdominal CT scan images

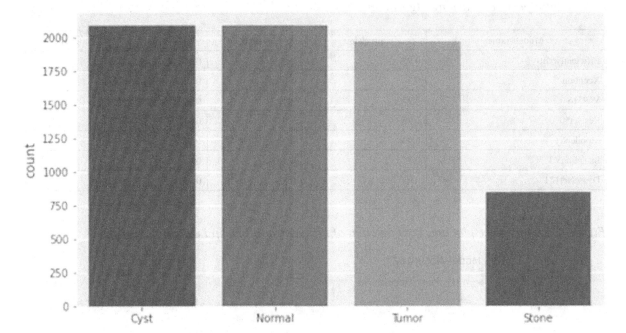

Result

This paper describes the classification among different MRI and CT scan images for four encoded classes: CYST, NORMAL, STONE, and TUMOR. **Table 3 Comprised estimated diabetics' classification precision, recall, f1-score and support for above mentioned supervised learning algorithms** shows precision, recall, f1-score and support for above mentioned seven supervised learning algorithms. Findings of deep learning algorithms with validation loss and validation accuracy for certain set of data conversion from grey level to binary color format for encoded classes: 'CYST': 0, 'NORMAL': 1, 'STONE': 2, 'TUMOR': 3. Figure 6 shows the EfficientNetB0 model loss and model accuracy and figure 7 representing the histogram diagram for EfficientNetB0 transfer model. Fiure 9 depicting output of the model while testing on random kidney images with various complexities. The precision value, recall, and f-score values of EfficientNetB0 is also highest among all transfer learning algorithms. While calculating the accuracy of the models on GPU, the EfficientNetB0 algorithm is taking run time of 4128 ms/step and validation loss is 30.26 percent, and validation accuracy is 96.02 percent. This research shows the classification amon different images consist of renal diseases. A deep learning system is used to analyse and classify the features of different kidney images.

Table 3. Comprised estimated diabetics' classification precision, recall, f1-score and support for above mentioned supervised learning algorithms

Model Name	precision	recall	f1-score	support
EfficientNetB0	0.96	0.96	0.96	979
Xception	0.92	0.89	0.90	979
VGG16	0.92	0.89	0.90	979
ResNet50	0.93	0.91	0.91	979
MobileNet	0.92	0.92	0.92	979
InceptionV3	0.85	0.82	0.83	979
DenseNet121	0.91	0.88	0.89	979

Figure 6. Performance plot and Loss function of EfficientNetB0 Deep Learning algorithm

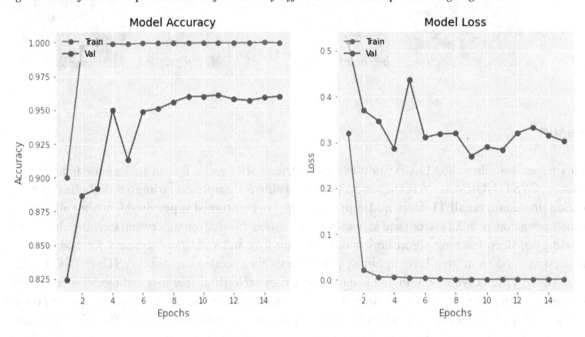

CONCLUSION

The proposed approach is based on deep neural networks and transfers learning. The efficient use of MRI and CT scan images is under consideration for the early prediction of different kidney diseases. The study of diabetic patient images and feature engineering is further helpful in the non-asymptomatic phase. This research shows the classification of kidney diseases with the help of MRI and CT images. Most of the patients were having diabetic history during their medical treatment. In future work, the authors are also planning to develop a Web-based portal for three parties, the doctor, the patient, and the medical insurance company. A systematic review of the correlation between renal diseases and diabetic Mellitus will be helpful to prevent chronic kidney diseases.

Figure 7. Histogram of different transfer learning algorithms

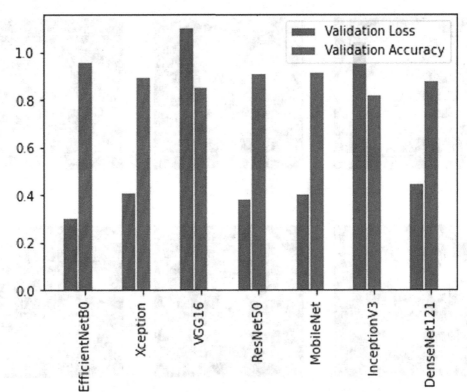

Figure 8. Heatmap of EfficientNetB0 model for training and testing MRI images

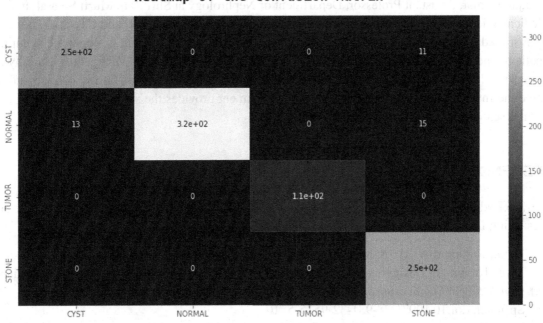

Figure 9. Testing of EfficientNetB0 model for random MRI images

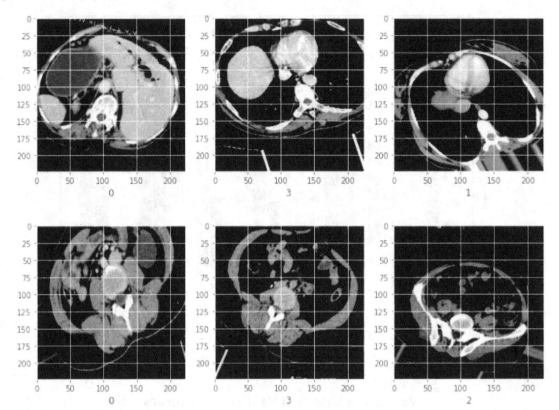

ACKNOWLEDGMENT

Dr. Sanjay Kumar, Assistant Professor, Department of Nephrology at Shri Ram Murti Smarak Institute of Medical Sciences, Bareilly assisted while reading the Dicom images of MRI and CT scan. The doctor also illustrated the length and breadth of chronic renal failures; from the point of nephrotic syndrome, the patient's nephritis symptoms, nephropathy, etc. Whole staff of Bareilly MRI center, Bareilly and radiologist to help me to understand the just of radiology reports of patients. Of my own accord, my institute the Invertis University, Bareilly, head of department provides the sum and substance of basic medical research.

REFERENCES

Balaji, S. RRadhakrishnan, MKarthikeyan, SSakthivel, R. (2020). Ultra Sound Imaging System of Kidney Stones Using Deep Neural Network. doi:10.1007/978-3-030-32150-5_117

Bisen, R. G., Rajurkar, A. M., & Manthalkar, R. R. (2020). Segmentation, Detection, and Classification of Liver Tumors for Designing a CAD System. In B. Iyer, P. Deshpande, S. Sharma, & U. Shiurkar (Eds.), *Computing in Engineering and Technology. Advances in Intelligent Systems and Computing* (Vol. 1025). Springer. doi:10.1007/978-981-32-9515-5_10

Butt, Letchmunan, Ali, Hassan, Baqir, & Sherazi. (2021). Machine Learning Based Diabetes Classification and Prediction for Healthcare Applications. *Journal of Healthcare Engineering*. doi:10.1155/2021/9930985

Chaitanya, S. M. K., & Rajesh Kumar, P. (2020). Oppositional Gravitational Search Algorithm and Artificial Neural Network-based Classification of Kidney Images. *Journal of Intelligent Systems*, *29*(1), 485–496. doi:10.1515/jisys-2017-0458

Chen, G., Ding, C., Li, Y., Hu, X., Li, X., Ren, L., Ding, X., Tian, P., & Xue, W. (2020). Prediction of Chronic Kidney Disease Using Adaptive Hybridized Deep Convolutional Neural Network on the Internet of Medical Things Platform. *IEEE Access: Practical Innovations, Open Solutions*, *8*, 100497–100508. doi:10.1109/ACCESS.2020.2995310

Chollet, F. (2016). *Xception: Deep learning with depthwise separable convolutions*. https://arxiv.org/abs/1610.02357

Daudon, M., Traxer, O., Conort, P., Lacour, B., & Jungers, P. (2006). Type 2 diabetes increases the risk for uric acid stones. *Journal of the American Society of Nephrology*, *17*(7), 2026–2033. doi:10.1681/ASN.2006030262 PMID:16775030

Goel, R., & Jain, A. (2020). Improved Detection of Kidney Stone in Ultrasound Images Using Segmentation Techniques. In M. Kolhe, S. Tiwari, M. Trivedi, & K. Mishra (Eds.), *Advances in Data and Information Sciences. Lecture Notes in Networks and Systems* (Vol. 94). Springer. doi:10.1007/978-981-15-0694-9_58

He, K., Zhang, X., Ren, S., & Sun, J. (2015). *Deep residual learning for image recognition*. https://arxiv.org/abs/1512.03385

Howard, A. G., Zhu, M., Chen, B., Kalenichenko, D., Wang, W., Weyand, T., Andreetto, M., & Adam, H. (2017). *MobileNets: Efficient Convolutional Neural Networks for Mobile Vision Applications*. https://arxiv.org/abs/1704.04861

Huang, G., Liu, Z., van der Maaten, L., & Weinberger, K. Q. (2016). *Densely connected convolutional networks*. https://arxiv.org/abs/1608.06993

Kaur, R., & Juneja, M. (2018). *Comparison of Different Renal Imaging Modalities: An Overview*. doi:10.1007/978-981-10-3373-5_4

Keras Team. (n.d.). *Conv2D layer*. Keras.Io. Retrieved April 19, 2022, from https://keras.io/api/layers/convolution_layers/convolution2d/

Mangayarkarasi, T., & Jamal, D. N. (2017). PNN-based analysis system to classify renal pathologies in Kidney Ultrasound Images. *2017 2nd International Conference on Computing and Communications Technologies (ICCCT)*, 123-126. 10.1109/ICCCT2.2017.7972258

Mujumdar & Vaidehi. (2019). Diabetes Prediction using Machine Learning Algorithms. *Procedia Computer Science, 165*, 292-299. doi:10.1016/j.procs.2020.01.047

Neloy, A. A., Alam, S., Bindu, R. A., & Moni, N. J. (2019). Machine Learning based Health Prediction System using IBM Cloud as PaaS. *2019 3rd International Conference on Trends in Electronics and Informatics (ICOEI)*, 444-450. 10.1109/ICOEI.2019.8862754

NICResearch. (2019, February 26). *Is there a connection between diabetes & kidney stones - NICResearch.* National Institute of Clinical Research. https://www.nicresearch.com/connection-diabetes-kidney-stones/

Pujari, R. M., & Hajare, V. D. (2014). Analysis of ultrasound images for identification of Chronic Kidney Disease stages. *2014 First International Conference on Networks & Soft Computing (ICNSC2014),* 380-383. 10.1109/CNSC.2014.6906704

Shamma, Z., Rumman, I., Saikot, A., Reza, S. M. S., Islam, M. M., Mahmud, M., & Kaiser, M. S. (2021). *Kidney Care: Artificial Intelligence-Based Mobile Application for Diagnosing Kidney Disease.* doi:10.1007/978-981-15-7561-7_7

Simonyan, K., & Zisserman, A. (2014). *Very deep convolutional networks for large-scale image recognition.* https://arxiv.org/abs/1409.1556

Subasi, A., Alickovic, E., & Kevric, J. (2017). Diagnosis of Chronic Kidney Disease by Using Random Forest. *CMBEBIH 2017. IFMBE Proceedings, 62.* 10.1007/978-981-10-4166-2_89

Sudharson, S., & Kokil, P. (2019). Abnormality classification in the kidney ultrasound images using singular value decomposition features. *2019 IEEE Conference on Information and Communication Technology,* 1-5. 10.1109/CICT48419.2019.9066200

Szegedy, C., Vanhoucke, V., Ioffe, S., Shlens, J., & Wojna, Z. (2015). *Rethinking the inception architecture for computer vision.* https://arxiv.org/abs/1512.00567

Tan, M., & Le, Q. V. (2019). *EfficientNet: Rethinking model scaling for convolutional Neural Networks.* https://arxiv.org/abs/1905.11946

Tseng, C.-H. (2015). Type 2 diabetes mellitus and kidney cancer risk: A retrospective cohort analysis of the National Health Insurance. *PLoS One, 10*(11), e0142480. doi:10.1371/journal.pone.0142480 PMID:26559055

Undzyte, G., Patasius, A., Linkeviciute-Ulinskiene, D., Zabuliene, L., Stukas, R., Dulskas, A., & Smailyte, G. (2020). Increased kidney cancer risk in diabetes mellitus patients: A population-based cohort study in Lithuania. The Aging Male. *The Official Journal of the International Society for the Study of the Aging Male, 23*(5), 1241–1245. doi:10.1080/13685538.2020.1755249 PMID:32342709

Vaish, P., Bharath, R., Rajalakshmi, P., & Desai, U. B. (2016). Smartphone based automatic abnormality detection of kidney in ultrasound images. *2016 IEEE 18th International Conference on e-Health Networking, Applications and Services (Healthcom),* 1-6. 10.1109/HealthCom.2016.7749492

Vasanthselvakumar, R. (2020). Automatic Detection and Classification of Chronic Kidney Diseases Using CNN Architecture. doi:10.1007/978-981-15-1097-7_62

Vieira, G. (2020, February 1). *Diabetes & kidney stones.* Diabetes Strong. https://diabetesstrong.com/diabetes-kidney-stones/

Wang, J., Zhu, H., Wang, S. H., & Zhang, Y.-D. (2021). A Review of Deep Learning on Medical Image Analysis. *Mobile Networks and Applications, 26*(1), 351–380. doi:10.100711036-020-01672-7

Chapter 5
A Comprehensive Approach to AI–Based Fake News Prediction in Digital Platforms by Applying Supervised Machine Learning Techniques

Sakya Sarkar

Asansol Institute of Engineering and Management-Polytechnic, India

Mauparna Nandan

Haldia Institute of Technology, India

ABSTRACT

In the modern era, the quantity of data, specifically the text data, has increased rapidly. Recently, fake news has gained a lot of attention worldwide. Generally, fake news is propagated through different social media. The effects of fake news may be economic, political, organizational, or personal. To save the life of community from fake news propagation, identification of fake news at an initial point is crucial. The fake news propagators target innocent people for spreading the fake news and they become a part of fake news propagation unknowingly. To prevent this kind of activity, fake news detection and its blueprint of propagation becomes crucial to community and government. This chapter makes an analysis related to the prediction of fake news through the help of supervised ML algorithms. The ML algorithms are adopted for the categorization of fake news as true or false with the help of NLP textual analysis and feature extraction. However, during the testing phase, the XGB algorithm gives the best result over other ML algorithms with an accuracy of 99%.

DOI: 10.4018/978-1-6684-6821-0.ch005

INTRODUCTION

In earlier times, generally, the individuals communicated with each other through verbal communication. But with the advent of new technologies, strategies to spread data among the common mass have arisen. But, wretchedly, the entire facts made available were not true. Counterfeit information was frequently disseminated as a type of rumor in order to mislead or hurt the opponent. A great deal of incorrect details was manufactured for misinformation goals, whether for political or commercial gain. Similarly, in today's Internet age, people are bombarded with a massive quantity of news related to numerous world events in the shape of pieces published in different forums, and frequently have no means of knowing whether the material offered is real or incorrect. As a result, an area of research known as fake news detection has emerged to assess the reliability of information and to detect fraudulent information. False or partially false news is referred to as fake news (Della Vedova et al., 2018). Generally, fake news is fabricated for political, financial, or ideological motives in attempt to deceive the receiver or to obtain fame (et al., 2018). The terminology "**fake news**" was relatively unknown and unpopular a few decades ago, but it has emerged as a huge giant in the digital era of social forum. Fake news, information bubbles, news manipulation, and a shortage of assurance in the social forum are the major drawbacks that are becoming increasingly ubiquitous in our culture. Fake news is normally promulgated in the form of articles in conventional media, but it has lately become increasingly common in social forum, allowing it to transmit at a very fast speed and on a massive scale (Shu et al., 2017). Furthermore, a typical approach employed to propagate fake news is to embrace captivating headlines, often known as clickbait (Bourgonje et al., 2017), in order to draw the attention of receivers. In today's digital age, when there are dozens of sharing sites regarding information through which false news or disinformation may spread, the combat is extremely hard against the pervasive problem of fake news. Because of the improvements in AI, which bring with them artificial bots that may be employed to produce and promulgate false news (Shao et al., 2017), it has become a bigger problem. The dilemma is serious because numerous persons think everything they study on the internet, and those who are unacquainted or modish to digital technologies and are susceptible to being duped. Scam is another issue that can arise as a consequence of spam or harmful emails and interactions. As a result, it is sufficiently compelling to identify the dilemma and take on the job of dipping crime, political turmoil, and sadness, as well as thwarting attempts to propagate counterfeit news. The primary motive of this article is to design a novel model for swiftly detecting false news on the basis of news headline without having to assess the whole substance of the news, based upon the inspection of the accessible problem. Due to the swift and widespread diffusion of varied information, such a methodology is specifically noteworthy in the case of prediction of news in the social forum. Furthermore, the researchers consider that analyzing the real-world data sets and employing the recommended models for classification based upon NLP and ML algorithms would allow swift identification of counterfeit news based on just on its title. There are many methods and areas of Artificial Intelligence (AI), Natural Language Processing (NLP), and Machine Learning (ML) that might aid us in battling this issue. Because of the numerous linguistic elements and styles, such as sarcasm, metaphors, etc., text, or natural language, is one form that might be challenging to understand. In addition, there are countless spoken languages, each with its own grammar, script, and syntax. A subfield of artificial intelligence, commonly known as "Natural Language Processing" includes methods that can use text, build models, and make predictions. The suggested approach is based upon machine learning and NLP approaches. Data set collected from Kaggle is utilized to verify the suggested model. This article demonstrates that it is possible to recognize counterfeit news on the basis of the title alone, without having the necessity to read the full article. This drastically cuts down the decision making time, especially when employing machine learning algorithms. For the mass circulation of information that hurts society, a solution like this is very crucial. Furthermore, the suggested technique applies to all the well-known supervised ML classifiers by converting natural language text into a matrix of token counts.

Background Study

Fake news is a broad topic that encompasses several scientific disciplines. Fake news detection based research is a relatively recent subject of study. Due to these factors, there isn't currently a universally recognized definition of false news. This phenomenon, which frequently goes by several names, is distinguished by a significant semantic capability. Over the phrase "fake news," several researchers and professionals prefer the term "disinformation." The most popular social networks in the world namely, Facebook, labels this information as false news, and Snopes is one of the first websites to offer fact-checking in the English language which prefers to replace it with debris news.

The way information is exchanged has altered as a consequence of social networking sites. A dataset made up of 15,500 Facebook posts was employed by Tacchini et al. These were divided into two categories with 99% accuracy, one based on crowd sourcing and the other on logistic regression (Balasundaram & Tanveer, 2012). Rubin et al. examined 360 news items by employing a SVM-based model and attained 90% accuracy, 84% recall, and an 87% F1Score (Rubin et al., 2016). Bilateral-weighted fuzzy support vector machine, a novel classifier, was suggested and its usefulness and efficacy were examined (Balasundaram & Tanveer, 2012).

In addition to discussing numerous supervised machine learning classification techniques, Osisanwo et al. also compared and clarified many attributes to assess the effectiveness of the various techniques. Data from the National Institute of Diabetes, Digestive and Kidney Diseases has been employed in research (Osisanwo et al., 2017). In order to achieve higher accuracy, Della Vedova et al. suggested an ML model that took into account social and news content aspects. They also applied this method in real-time by using Facebook Messenger chat bots, and achieved an accuracy rate of 81.7% (Gelfert, 2018).

Taking into account several media sources, the system analyses the reliability of the provided news piece. The study offers insight into how news articles are classified along with the many possible content kinds. The paper employs models that are inferior to the other models available, such as predictive modeling and linguistic features-based models (Parikh & Atrey, 2018). Fake news was foreseen using Naive Bayes classifier. This strategy was put into practice as a software system and evaluated against multiple data sets from Facebook and other sources, yielding an accuracy of 74%. Due to the lack of consideration for punctuation problems, the paper's accuracy was low (Granik & Mesyura, 2017). The several machine learning techniques examined percentage of the prediction. Different prediction models' accuracy was recorded, including Support Vector Machines, Gradient Boosting, and bounded Decision Trees. The models are assessed using probability thresholds, which aren't the most accurate (Gilda, 2017). Also found that Naive Bayes classifier was employed for fake news detection on various social forums. Facebook, Twitter, and other sites are the common data sources for news articles. Since the information on these sites is not entirely reliable, the accuracy gained is relatively poor (Jain & Kasbe, 2018). The rumor detection and countering false information in real time employs novelty-based functionality evaluated on data collected from Kaggle. The model has a 74.5% accuracy rate. Because clickbait (Yumeng, 2018) and dubious sources are not taken into account, accuracy is decreased (Perez-Rosas, 2018). Few techniques are used in Twitter to distinguish between spammers and non-spammers (Gupta & Kaushal,

2015). Naive Bayes classifier, Clustering, and Decision Tree are some of the models that are employed. The accuracy rate for identifying spammers is 70%, and the accuracy rate for identifying non-spammers is 71.2%. The utilized models only achieved a poor average accuracy in separating spammers from non-spammers. For the identification of bogus news using a variety of techniques, as language modeling was encouraged, the accuracy rate is restricted to 76%. If a predictive model is utilized in a variety of machine learning techniques to identify bogus news, accuracy can be enhanced (Perez-Rosas, 2018). The Naive Bayes classifier and Support Vector Machines are the machine learning models that have been offered and implemented. Since only these models were addressed, no specific accuracy was noted (Tapaswi, 2012). To determine the credibility of the provided Tweets, the Naive Bayes Classifier, Decision Trees, Support Vector Machines, and Neural Networks are the machine learning models that were implemented. The highest F1 score is 0.94 for both tweet and user features. By taking into account shaky news, greater accuracy might have been reached (Helmstetter & Paulheim, 2018). A method for automatically detecting fake news on Twitter involves learning to forecast accuracy ratings in two datasets that concentrate on the site's legitimacy. The accuracy rate for the models in use is 70.28%. The primary drawback is the structural distinction between CREDBANK and PHEME, which may interfere with model transfer (Buntain & Golbeck, 2017).

Generally websites and software committed to forums, social networks, microblogging, social bookmarking, and wikis are considered to be a part of social media. (Economic and Social Research Council, n.d.)(Gil, 2019). On the other hand, other academicians believe that fake news is an outcome of unintentional events, such as instructive distress or behaviors like those that occurred in the case of the Nepal Earthquake (Tandoc, 2017)(Radianti, 2016). In 2020, health-related false news was pervasive which have placed the world's health at danger. Earlier in February 2020, the WHO issued a warning stating that the COVID-19 epidemic has resulted in a significant "infodemic", or a burst of false and misleading information.

For the Fake News Prediction, NLP is mostly utilized to take into account one or more system or algorithm specialties. Speech interpretation and speech creation can be combined using an algorithmic system's Natural Language Processing (NLP) grade. It might also be used to track actions in different languages. (Granik & Mesyura, 2017) Proposed a new ideal system for extracting actions from English, Italian, and Dutch speeches by utilizing a variety of pipelines of different languages, such as Named Entity Recognition (NER), Parts of Speech (POS) Taggers, Chunking, and Semantic Role Labeling. This made NLP a good subject of the search (Granik & Mesyura, 2017) (Alkhodair et al., 2020). Sentiment analysis (Aphiwongsophon & Chongstitvatana, 2018) captures feelings about a certain topic. Extraction of a specific phrase for a subject, extraction of the sentiment, and coupling with connection analysis comprises sentiment analysis. Dual languages are used in the sentiment analysis. Analytical resources attempts to classify words on a scale of -5 to 5 by using a dictionary of meanings and a library of sentiment models for positive and negative terms. Research is being done to create parts of language taggers for languages like Sanskrit (Ranjan, 2003), Hindi (Diab, 2004), and Arabic using parts of speech taggers for languages like European languages. It may be effective to mark and classify words as adjectives, verbs, names, and so on. The majority of part-of-speech approaches work well in European languages but not in Asian or Arabic. The tree-bank approach is used especially in a portion of the Sanskrit word "speak." Arabic text is automatically exposed as basic sentences using a technique called the Vector Machine (SVM) (Rouse, 2018) that automatically recognizes symbols and components of speech (Dua & Du, 2016).

The two primary categories of data mining techniques are supervised and unsupervised. The supervised technique makes use of training data to anticipate concealed behaviors. Unsupervised data mining is an attempt to identify hidden data models using just pairs of input labels and categories as training data. Aggregate mines and a syndicate base are good examples of unsupervised data mining (Ray, 2017). Without the need to manually redesign software systems, machine learning (ML) methods enable them to provide results that are more accurate. Data scientists describe the changes or traits that the model must consider in order to make predictions. The algorithm divides the learnt levels into fresh data when training is complete (Dua & Du, 2016).

Traditional machine learning techniques have had good success in identifying bogus news. Using feature engineering, Reis et al. (2019) produced hand-crafted features like syntactic and semantic characteristics. The issue was then approached as a binary classification problem, with these features fed into well-known Machine Learning classifiers like K-Nearest Neighbor (KNN), Random Forest (RF), Naive Bayes, Support Vector Machine (SVM), and XGBOOST (XGB), with RF and XGB producing results that were quite favorable. TriFN, a novel framework proposed by Shu et al. (2019), offers a logical way to model tri-relationships among publishers, news items, and users at the same time. This framework performed noticeably better than both the standard Machine Learning models and previous state-of-the-art frameworks. The detection of fake news has undergone a considerable revolution since the introduction of deep learning in the field of text classification. In comparison to earlier methods that relied on manually created features, Karimi et al.'s (2018) proposed Multi-Source Multi-class Fake News Detection framework can automatically extract features using Convolution Neural Network (CNN) based models and combine these features from multiple sources using an attention mechanism. A deep diffusive network model was developed by Zhang et al. (2020) using the Gated Diffusive Unit (GDU), a novel type of diffusive unit model, to simultaneously learn the representations of news articles, creators, and subjects. Long Short-Term Memory (LSTM) network and doc2vec are used by Ruchansky et al. (2017) in their unique CSI(Capture-Score-Integrate) framework to capture the temporal spacing of user activity. Through the use of Graph Convolutional Networks and a geometric deep learning framework, Monti et al. (2019) have demonstrated that social network topology and propagation are significant features for the detection of bogus news. A Heuristic-driven Ensemble Framework is also implemented for COVID-19 Fake News Detection system (Das et al., 2021).

OBJECTIVES

- The main goal of this research is to develop a model that can distinguish between news that is fake and news that is true by using three distinct methods of NLP text vectorization to several ML classifiers
- The proposed model can easily identify false news based solely on the news title without reading the complete news article.
- The proposed model also identifies the fake news in the most optimized way.
- The classification method of XG Boost with TF-IDF and the Count Vectorizer feature extraction approach has achieved the maximum accuracy.

MAIN FOCUS OF THE CHAPTER

The people of the globe must acknowledge the significant involvement of technology with the aid of internet services for communication and information exchange in making modern living extremely acceptable. There is no denying that the internet has made life simpler and an effortless entrance to a wealth of knowledge possible.

This is a development in human history, but it also blurs the distinction between legitimate media and information that has been purposefully falsified. Today, anybody can create material that the internet can consume, regardless of how legitimate it is. Sadly, counterfeit news attracts a lot of attention online, particularly on social media. People are easily duped and don't hesitate to disseminate such inaccurate information to the remote reaches of the globe. Facebook, Twitter, Whatsapp and other social media platforms are listed as having a noteworthy impact on the distribution of fake news.

Many experts think that artificial intelligence and machine learning may be used to address the problem of fake news. This is because, recently, advances in technology and the availability of larger datasets have allowed artificial intelligence algorithms to perform better on many classification issues. A 60–85% accuracy range is achieved by using various models. It includes various algorithms such as Naive Bayes classifier, SVM, Decision Tree model, Linguistic features based and other classifiers. The parameters that are taken into account don't produce very accurate results. The objective of this study is to improve on the current outcomes in terms of false news detection accuracy with the help of efficient algorithms such as Multi Layer Perceptron, Ada Boost, XGBoost. Researchers have looked at an algorithm that can discern between fake and real news with an accuracy of 99.59%. By applying this new methodology, it will evaluate the fake news and real news with more accuracy.

The main goal of this research is to develop a model that can distinguish between news that is fake and news that is true by using three distinct methods of NLP text vectorization to several ML classifiers.

SOLUTIONS AND RECOMMENDATIONS

The key objective of the proposed model is to predict the counterfeit news by employing various supervised machine learning approaches. The proposed model is basically a classification task related to different types of news. The entire procedure is carried out in four stages as depicted in Fig. 1.

A. Data Collection and Pre-Processing

The problem of acquiring the right datasets in the right organization is one of the most toughest issues in machine learning to solve. It has nothing to do with complicated mathematics. Obtaining the proper information entails complying or identifying the data related to the conclusion that must be anticipated; for illustration, data that carries a flag about situations must be attended to. The datasets should correspond to the problem that is being tried to resolve. The efforts to put up an AI system must then return to the dataset collection stage if the proper information is not provided. Deep learning and machine learning more generally, require a good preparation set to function well. It takes some effort and some explicit understanding of where and how to amass relevant data in order to gather and grow the training set, which is a sizable assemblage of notorious information. Machine learning nets are prepared using the training set as their standard. Before they are released on information they haven't seen before, it is the thing that has to be remade. At this point, educated personnel's must discover the appropriate basic data and transform it into a numerical depiction that the machine learning algorithm can understand.In the fields of information science and critical thinking, test questions that demand a lot of time or skill might serve as a distinct advantage.

Figure 1. Control flow diagram

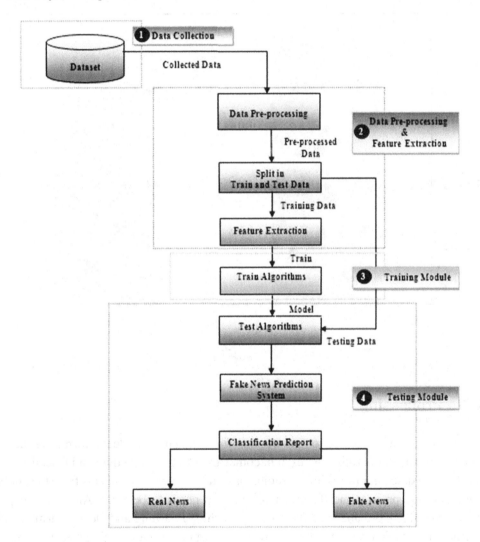

To make the AI model functional with the proper technique, choosing the appropriate dataset for machine learning is very crucial. There are a few guidelines that must be followed for machine learning on large data, even if choosing the proper quantity and quality of data is a difficult undertaking.

The dataset for the proposed work is sourced from kaggle.com. The dataset possesses two types of data - one having fake news and other having true news. The dataset measures 23481*4 and 21417*4 respectively. This indicates that there are 4 columns and 23481 rows corresponding to fake news and

4 columns and 21417 rows corresponding to true news. "Title," "Text," "Subject," and "Date" are the names of the columns. The statistics reveals that there are 21417 genuine news pieces and 23481 false news articles as depicted in Fig2. Now, it will be determined whether the algorithm can produce accurate results.

Figure 2. Count of fake and real news article

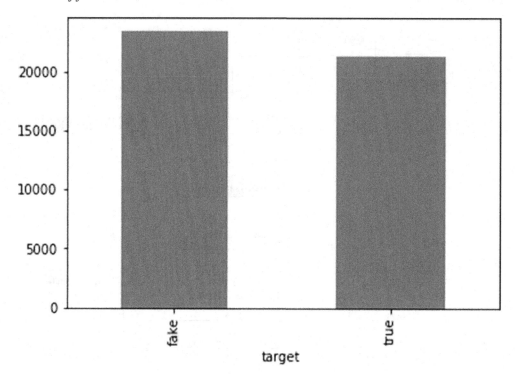

B. Data Pre-Processing

Data preprocessing is a method used to renovate unrefined data into an ideal informative index. If information is gathered from numerous sources, it becomes impossible to conduct an inspection to correctly format and clean the data. Preprocessing is crucial for achieving enhanced results from the applied model in a machine learning project, and the information setup needs to be legal. Another viewpoint holds that the dataset should be organized to allow many Machine Learning and Deep Learning calculations to be performed in a single informative index, with the best computation being selected. The data must undergo several adjustments before being represented using different assessing models. By deleting the data's existing useless information will assist in reducing the amount of the fake data.

A lot of manual and syntactic preparation was required since the data was in .csv format. In the initial phase, the dataset of fake news and the dataset of true news are concatenated. In the next phase, the entire dataset is shuffled to achieve robustness. After that, few fields are removed from the dataset like date and title. In the next phase, the dataset is converted into lowercase format. Finally, the punctuation and stop words are removed from the text using NLTK in Python. Removing the stop-words (referencing the NLTK stop-word list) helps in the lemmatizing procedure for the rest of the data. The subject wise number of articles is then generated from the dataset after the pre-processing phase as depicted in Fig.3.

The FreqDist statement tokenizer from the NLTK library is used to tokenize the text. This tokenizer gives the frequency of words the in dataset for both the fake news as depicted in Fig.4 and real news as depicted in Fig.5.

C. Feature Extraction

In Natural Language Processing, feature extraction techniques are often employed to examine textual similarities. In machine learning algorithms, the learning process is carried out by the production of output for the test data using a preset set of features from the training data. The algorithms cannot directly operate on the raw text. So, in order to turn text input into a matrix (or vector) of features, the system requires certain feature extraction algorithms. In the proposed model, various feature extraction techniques are implemented. The dataset has been used to execute the feature extraction approach in the proposed model. The various types of feature extraction techniques implemented for the proposed model are discussed in the section below.

Figure 3. Count of subject wise articles

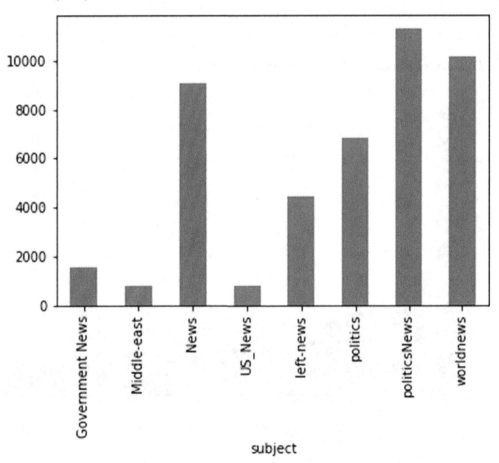

Figure 4. Frequently counted word for fake news

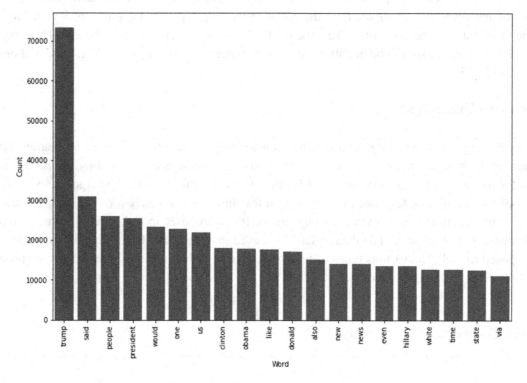

Figure 5. Frequently counted word for real news

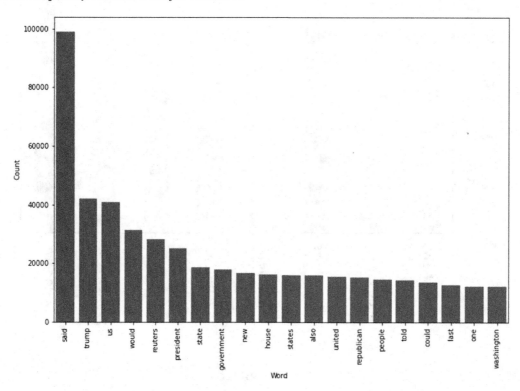

1. Bag of Words (BoW)

Bag of words is a text modeling technique used in natural language processing. In a technical aspect, it is defined as a technique employed for feature extraction from text data. This method is a non-complicated and implementable way to dig out characteristics from documents. A textual illustration of word recurrence in a document is called a "**Bag of Words**." It doesn't pay attention to grammatical conventions or word order; it only keeps track of word counts. It is referred to as a "bag" of words since any details on the arrangement or structure of the words inside the document are ignored. The model doesn't care where in the document recognized terms appear; it is simply interested in whether they do.

2. Word Cloud

A word cloud is a new visual representation of content information that is typically used to identify catchphrase labels (metadata) on websites or to envisage free-form material. Labels are frequently single words, and each tag's value is indicated by its size or color. This design is useful for discovering a phrase to determine its relative undeniable quality and for quickly identifying the most obvious terms. The phrases are hyperlinked to items relevant to the tag at the moment where they are used as site navigation aids. A word cloud has been formed for both fake news and real news as depicted in Fig. 6 and Fig. 7 respectively.

Figure 6. Word Cloud for fake news

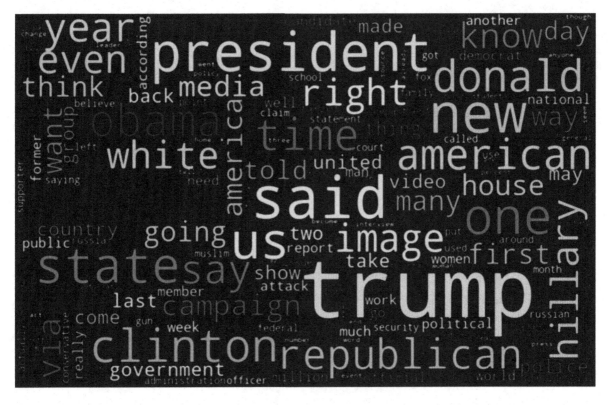

Figure 7. Word Cloud for Real news

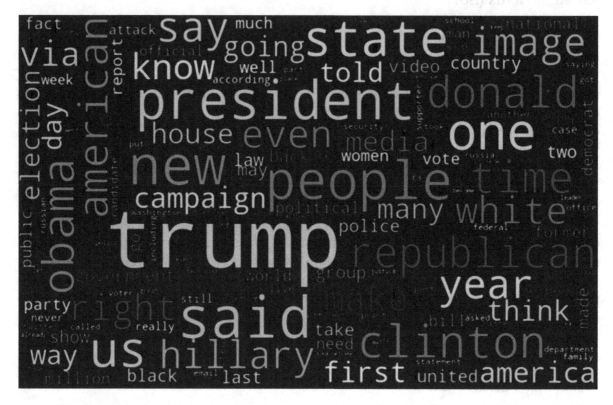

3. Count Vectorizer

A fantastic utility offered by the Python scikit-learn module is the CountVectorizer. It is used to convert a given text into a vector based on the number of times (count) each word appears across the full text. This is useful when there are numerous texts of this type and there occurs a need to turn each word in each text into a vector. Each unique word is represented by a column in the matrix that is created by the CountVectorizer and each sample of text from the document is represented by a row in the matrix. Each cell's value is just the number of words in that specific text sample.

4. TF-IDF Vectorizer

Term Frequency-Inverse Document Frequency is referred to as TF-IDF. It is made up of the following two sub-parts,

1. Term Frequency (TF)
2. Inverse Document Frequency (IDF)

Term Frequency (TF):

A term's TF indicates how frequently it appears in the whole manuscript. It is defined as the likelihood that a term will be found in the text. In relation to the overall number of words in the review r_j, it determines the frequency with which a word w_i appears in the review r_j.

TF(t) = Number of times term t appears in a document
Total number of terms in the document

Inverse Document Frequency (IDF):

A term's IDF value indicates how frequently or seldom it appears in the text. In other words, the words that are uncommon have a high IDF score. It accentuates those terms that onlyoccasionally appear throughout the entire manuscript. IDF is a log normalized value that is calculated by taking the logarithm of the overall term and dividing the total number of documents D in the corpus by the number of documents containing the term t.TF-IDF is the product of TF and IDF. It is formulated as:

Tfidf (t, d, D) = tf (t, d) * idf (d, D)

A word with a high frequency in a document and a low document frequency will have a high TF-IDF score. The IDF value for a term that appears in nearly all texts approaches 0, causing the tf-idf to likewise go closer to 0. When both IDF and TF values are high, or when a term is uncommon across the manuscript but common inside one section, the TF-IDF value is high.

D. Training and Testing the Model

To understand the problem that is being resolved, it is necessary to create an effective training set. Two informative collections are frequently used by machine learning algorithms: training data and testing data. A wider range of data should be randomly tested by each of the two. The larger of the two sets, the training set, is the major set that is being used. Putting a training set through a machine learning system teaches the network how to weigh various features, altering their coefficients according to how likely they can reduce errors in the results. Tensors containing those coefficients, also known as parameters, are collectively referred to as the model since they encapsulate a model of the data on which the model is being trained on. These are the most important lessons learned while developing a machine learning system. The test set comprises the second part. It is not used until the very end and serves as a seal of approval. The neural network can be put to test against this final arbitrary test after it has been set up and given the input. The results it generates should confirm that the internet accurately perceives images or at least remembers them to an extent of [x]. In the unlikely event where accurate predictions are not realized, the process requires tracing back to the training set and examining the errors that were made. If correct dataset is used, there won't be any issues and the system will run smoothly.

In the proposed methodology, the model is trained with 80% of the dataset values and the rest 20% of the dataset values have been employed for testing purpose. During this phase, multiple Supervised Machine Learning classifiers have been implemented for the training purpose. The training accuracy and their respective duration are depicted in Table 1 below:

The corresponding figure of Table 1 is depicted below in Fig. 8:

Table 1. Training accuracy and time

	LR	DT	RF	NB	ADB	XGB	SVM	MLP
Training Time(Sec.)	13.23	19.23	39.80	6.46	53.18	78.87	724	2078.16
Training Accuracy (%)	99.31	100	100	96	99.69	99.74	99.91	100

Figure 8. Training accuracy of different ML Classifiers

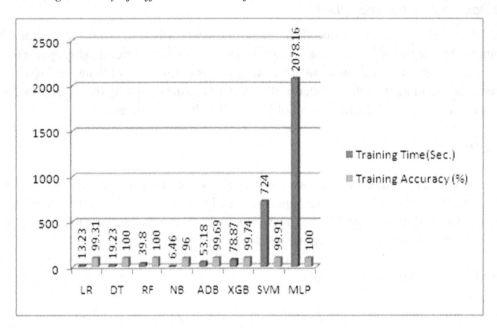

E. Machine Learning Classifiers

The proposed model imported multiple Machine Learning Classifier models using the Sklearn library. Sklearn is a Python library with several data processing features, such as model selection, clustering, and classification. Predicting the class of a set of data points is the process of classification. Targets, labels, and categories are other names for classes. Approximating a mapping function (f) from input variables (X) to discrete output variables is the problem of classification predictive modeling (y).The following machine learning classifiers have been used to classify the news as either fake or real.

Logistic Regression

LR is one of the ML algorithms that is most frequently employed in the Supervised Learning category. It is used to forecast the categorical reliant variable using a specified set of independent variables. Logistic Regression is used to predict the output for a dependent variable which is categorical in nature. The outcome must thereby, be a discrete or categorical value. It offers the probabilistic values that lie between 0 and 1 rather than the exact values between 0 and 1. It can be either True or False, 0 or 1, or

Yes or No. For the purpose of evaluating accuracy, the suggested system uses the LR algorithm. The result of the LR algorithm is depicted in the Table 2 below:

The corresponding confusion matrix of Table 2 is depicted below in Figure 9:

Table 2. Performance Evaluation of LR algorithm

Classifier	Performance Evaluation			
	Accuracy	Precision	Recall	F1 score
Logistic Regression	94.71	0.95	0.95	0.95

Figure 9. Confusion matrix for LR algorithm

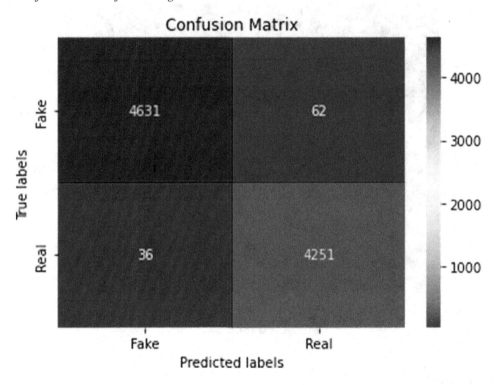

Decision Tree

Classification and regression problems can be resolved using the Supervised Machine Learning technique known as a Decision Tree. However, this approach is frequently preferred. It is a tree-structured classifier, where each leaf node represents the classification outcome and internal nodes represent the features of a dataset. The two nodes in a Decision Tree are the Decision Node and the Leaf Node. Decision nodes are used to make decisions and can have many branches, whereas Leaf nodes are the outcomes of decisions and do not have any branches. The features of the submitted dataset are utilized to run the test or develop the conclusions. The suggested system incorporates the Decision Tree method for accuracy evaluation. The result of the DT algorithm is depicted in the Table 3 below:

The corresponding confusion matrix of Table 3 is depicted below in Fig. 10:

Table 3. Performance Evaluation of DT algorithm

Classifier	Performance Evaluation			
	Accuracy	Precision	Recall	F1 score
Decision Tree	99.53	1.00	1.00	1.00

Figure 10. Confusion matrix for DT algorithm

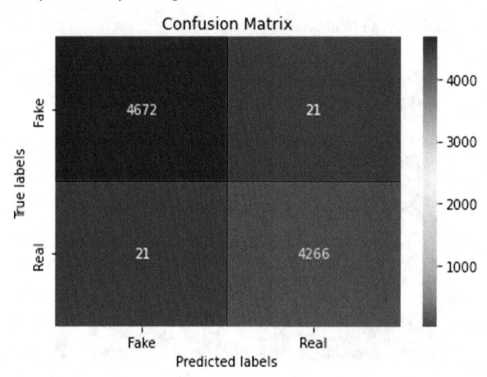

Random Forest

Random Forest is one of the favored algorithms for machine learning and a component of the supervised learning approach. It may be used to solve classification and regression-related ML problems. It is based on the concept of ensemble learning, a technique for combining several classifiers to solve complex problems and improve model performance. The Random Forest Classifier, as its name suggests, averages many decision trees applied to various subsets of the input dataset to improve the predictability of the dataset. The Random Forest takes predictions from each decision tree and predicts the outcome based on the votes of the majority of projections rather than relying just on one decision tree. The Random Forest algorithm is implemented in the proposed system for the evaluation of the accuracy. The result of the RF algorithm is depicted in the Table 4 below:

The corresponding confusion matrix of Table4 is depicted below in Figure 11:

Table 4. Performance Evaluation of RF algorithm

Classifier	Performance Evaluation			
	Accuracy	Precision	Recall	F1 score
Random Forest	99.11	0.99	0.99	0.99

Figure 11. Confusion matrix for RF algorithm

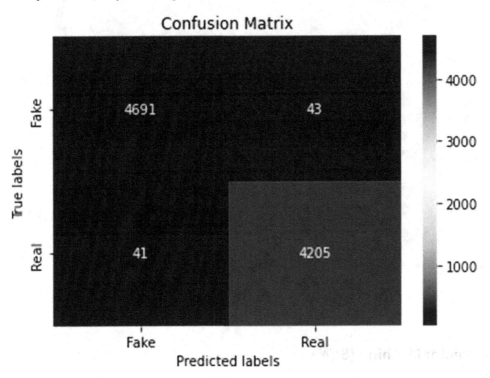

Naïve Bayes

Based on the Bayes theorem, the NB algorithm is a supervised learning technique for classification problems. It primarily uses a huge training set for text classification. One of the most simple and effective classification algorithms now in use is the Naive Bayes Classifier. It helps with the quick creation of predicatively accurate machine learning models. It provides predictions based on the likelihood that an object will occur since it is a probabilistic classifier. A few applications for Naive Bayes algorithms include spam filtration, sentiment analysis, and article categorization. The suggested system incorporates the Naive Bayes algorithm for accuracy evaluation. The result of the NB algorithm is depicted in the Table 5 below:

The corresponding confusion matrix of Table5 is depicted below in Figure 12:

Table 5. Performance Evaluation of NB algorithm

Classifier	Performance Evaluation			
	Accuracy	Precision	Recall	F1 score
Naïve Bayes	94.71	0.95	0.95	0.95

Figure 12. Confusion matrix for NB algorithm

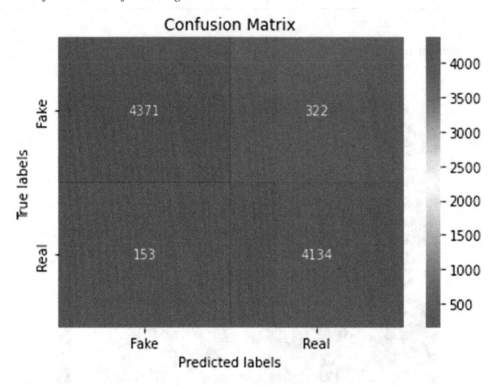

Support Vector Machine (SVM)

Classification and regression problems are resolved using Support Vector Machine, or SVM, one of the most used supervised learning techniques. It is mostly used, nevertheless, in Machine Learning Classification problems. In order to swiftly categorize new data points in the future, the SVM algorithm aims to define the best line or decision boundary that can split an-dimensional space into classes. The name of this best choice boundary is a hyperplane. The extreme vectors and points that help create the hyper plane are chosen via SVM. The SVM approach is based on support vectors, which are utilized to represent these extreme situations. The suggested system incorporates the SVM algorithm for the accuracy evaluation. The result of the SVM algorithm is depicted in the Table 6 below:

The corresponding confusion matrix of Table 6 is depicted below in Figure 13:

Table 6. Performance Evaluation of SVM algorithm

Classifier	Performance Evaluation			
	Accuracy	Precision	Recall	F1 score
Support Vector Machine	99	1.00	1.00	1.00

Figure 13. Confusion matrix for SVM algorithm

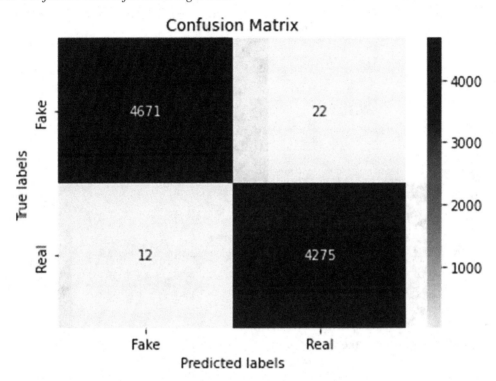

Multi Layer Perceptron

Multi-layer perception is referred to as MLP. It is composed of substantial, intricately interconnected layers that may transform any input dimension into the desired dimension. A multi-layer perception is a neural network that has many layers. The neurons are connected in such a fashion such that some of their outputs are also their inputs can create a neural network. One neuron (or node) per input is present in the input layer of a multi-layer perceptron, as is one node per output in the output layer, and any number of nodes may be present in the hidden layers of any number of multi-layer perceptrons. The accuracy of the proposed system is evaluated using the MLP algorithm. The result of the MLP algorithm is depicted in the Table 7 below:

The corresponding confusion matrix of Table 7 is depicted below in Figure 14:

Table 7. Performance Evaluation of MLP algorithm

Classifier	Performance Evaluation			
	Accuracy	Precision	Recall	F1 score
Ada Boost	99.54	1.00	1.00	1.00

Figure 14. Confusion matrix for MLP algorithm

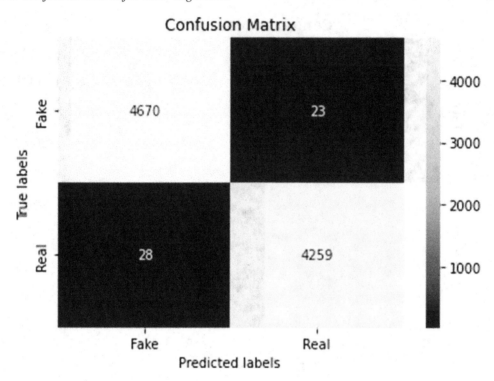

ADA Boost

An ensemble-based boosting classifier called Adaptive Boosting combines many classifiers to increase classifier precision. Iterative ensemble techniques are used. The main concept is to train the data sample in each cycle and set the classifier weights in order to ensure the accuracy of the unusual observational forecasts. The classifier must first be interactively trained using a range of weighted training cases. These criteria serve as the foundation for the algorithm. Secondly, it reduces training error with each iteration in an effort to provide a better match for these occurrences. In the suggested system, the Ada Boost method is used to evaluate accuracy. The result of the Ada Boost algorithm is depicted in the Table 8 below:

The corresponding confusion matrix of Table 8 is depicted below in Figure 15:

Table 8. Performance Evaluation of Ada Boost algorithm

Classifier	Performance Evaluation			
	Accuracy	Precision	Recall	F1 score
Multi Layer Perceptron	99.43	0.99	0.99	0.99

Figure 15. Confusion matrix for Ada Boost algorithm

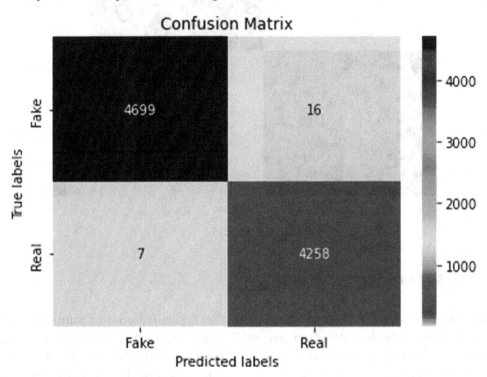

XG Boost

The foundation of XGB is a gradient boosting framework-based Dtree-based ensemble learning mechanism. It is generally used to solve prediction issues with unstructured data, such as text, photos, and other types of data. When dealing with small to medium-sized datasets, Dtree-based methods are thought to be best in class. The XG Boost algorithm is implemented in the proposed system for the evaluation of the accuracy. The result of the XG Boost algorithm is depicted in the Table 9 below:

The corresponding confusion matrix of Table 9 is depicted below in Figure 16:

Table 9. Performance Evaluation of XG Boost algorithm

Classifier	Performance Evaluation			
	Accuracy	Precision	Recall	F1 score
XG Boost	99.59	1.00	1.00	1.00

Figure 16. Confusion matrix for XG Boost algorithm

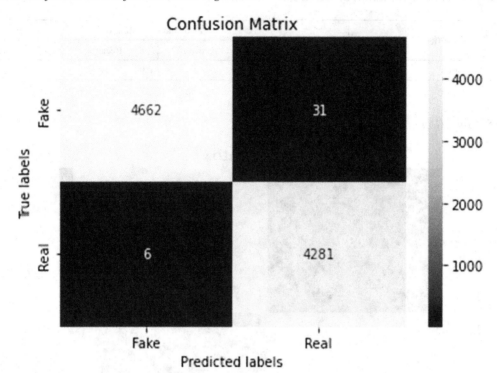

FUTURE RESEARCH DIRECTIONS

In machine learning challenges, having access to more data typically leads to a learning algorithm performing much better. Only about 45000 approx. articles make up the dataset that was discussed in this article. This is a somewhat small sample size, and a dataset containing more news articles from other sources would be very beneficial for the learning process because news from various sources will often include a wider vocabulary and more in-depth material.

In the future, different deep learning models like LSTM, Bi- LSTM, GRU and sentiment analysis using N-gram techniques will be implemented to categorize the news that might deliver higher accuracy may be taken into consideration, and more useful text like the publication of the news, URL domain, etc., could be extracted for the process. For greater accuracy, a dataset with more articles from a variety of sources that has more complex vocabulary and interesting content might be used.

CONCLUSION

The purpose of this study was to create a new model for swiftly identifying false news based solely on the news title without reading the complete news article. While full news text analysis was also done for comparison purposes to the proposed method. The news title and text were analyzed using NLP approaches before machine learning algorithms, including single classifiers and ensemble methods, were employed to make predictions. Four separate feature extraction techniques, including the count vectorizer, the TF-IDF vectorizer, the word cloud, and the bag of words, have been employed in the suggested system. Additionally, many categorization algorithms are employed. The classification method of XG Boost with TF-IDF and the count vectorizer feature extraction approach has the maximum accuracy, with a 99.59% accuracy rate. The performance of the other machine learning methods is rather good. The effectiveness of the algorithms is shown in Figure 17.

Figure 17. Accuracy level of different algorithm

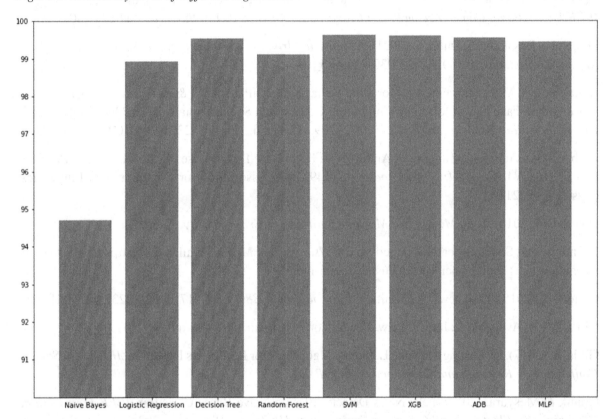

ACKNOWLEDGMENT

This research received no specific grant from any funding agency in the public, commercial, or not-for-profit sectors.

REFERENCES

Alkhodair, S. A., Ding, S. H. H., Fung, B. C. M., & Liu, J. (2020). Detecting breaking news rumors of emerging topics in social media. *Information Processing & Management*, *57*(2), 102018. doi:10.1016/j.ipm.2019.02.016

Aphiwongsophon, & Chongstitvatana. (2018). *Detecting Fake News with Machine Learning Method.* CP Journal.

Balasundaram & Tanveer. (2012). On proximal bilateral-weighted fuzzy support vector machine classifiers. *Int. J. Adv. Intell. Paradig.*. doi:10.1504/IJAIP.2012.052060

Bourgonje, P., Schneider, J. M., & Rehm, G. (2017). From clickbait to fake news detection: an approach based on detecting the stance of headlines to articles. *Proceedings of the 2017 EMNLP workshop: natural language processing meets journalism*, 84–89. 10.18653/v1/W17-4215

Buntain, C., & Golbeck, J. (2017). Automatically Identifying Fake News in Popular Twitter Threads. *IEEE International Conference on Smart Cloud (SmartCloud)*. 10.1109/SmartCloud.2017.40

Das, S. D., Basak, A., & Dutta, S. (2021). *A Heuristic-driven Ensemble Framework for COVID-19 Fake News Detection*. doi:10.1007/978-3-030-73696-5_16

Della Vedova, M. L., Tacchini, E., Moret, S., Ballarin, G., DiPierro, M., & de Alfaro, L. (2018). Automatic Online Fake News Detect ion Combining Content and Social Signals. *2018 22nd Conference of Open Innovations Association (FRUCT)*, 272–279. (Das et al., 2021)10.23919/FRUCT.2018.8468301

Diab. (2004). Automatic Tagging of Arabic Text: From Raw Text to Base Phrase Chunks. In *Proceedings of HLT-NAACL 2004: Short Papers* (pp. 149–152). Association for Computational Linguistics. (Das et al., 2021)

Dua & Du. (2016). *Data Mining and Machine Learning in Cybersecurity*. Auerbach Publications.

Economic and Social Research Council. (n.d.). *Using Social Media*. Available at: https://esrc.ukri.org/research/impact-toolkit/social-media/using-social-media

Gelfert, A. (2018). Fake news: A definition. *Informal Logic*, *38*(1), 84–117. doi:10.22329/il.v38i1.5068

GilP. (2019). Available at: https://www.lifewire.com/what-exactly-is-twitter-2483331

Gilda, S. (2017). Evaluating Machine Learning Algorithms for Fake News Detection. *IEEE 15th Student Conference on Research and Development (SCOReD)*.

Granik & Mesyura. (2017). Fake News Detection Using Naive Bayes Classifier. *IEEE First Ukraine Conference on Electrical and Computer Engineering (UKRCON)*.(Das et al., 2021)

Gupta, & Kaushal. (2015). Improving Spam Detection in Online Social Networks. *International Conference on Cognitive Computing and Information Processing(CCIP)*.

Helmstetter, & Paulheim. (2018). Weakly Supervised Learning for Fake News Detection on Twitter. *IEEE/ACM International Conference on Advances in Social Networks Analysis and Mining (ASONAM)*.

Jain & Kasbe. (2018). Fake News Detection. *IEEE International Students' Conference on Electrical, Electronics and Computer Sciences*.

Karimi, H., Roy, P., Saba-Sadiya, S., & Tang, J. (2018). Multi-source multi-class fake news detection. *Proceedings of the 27th International Conference on Computational Linguistics*, 1546-1557.

Monti, F., Frasca, F., Eynard, D., Mannion, D., & Bronstein, M. M. (2019). *Fake news detection on social media using geometric deep learning*. arXiv preprint arXiv:1902.06673.

Osisanwo, Akinsola, Awodele, Hinmikaiye, Olakanmi, & Akinjobi. (2017). Supervised Machine Learning Algorithms: Classification and Comparison. *Int. J. Comput. Trends Technol., 48*(3), 128–138. doi:10.14445/22312803/IJCTT-V48P126

Parikh, S. B., & Atrey, P. K. (2018). Media-Rich Fake News Detection: A Survey. *IEEE Conference on Multimedia Information Processing and Retrieval.*

Perez-Rosas. (2018). Automatic Detection of Fake News. Academic Press.

Radianti, J. (2016). An Overview of Public Concerns During the Recovery Period after a Major Earthquake: Nepal Twitter Analysis. In *HICSS '16 Proceedings of the 2016 49th Hawaii International Conference on System Sciences (HICSS)* (pp. 136-145). IEEE. 10.1109/HICSS.2016.25

Ranjan. (2003). Part of speech tagging and local word grouping techniques for natural language parsing in Hindi. In *Proceedings of the 1st International Conference on Natural Language Processing (ICON 2003)*. Semantic Scholar.

Ray, S. (2017). https://www.analyticsvidhya.com/blog/2017/09/common-machine-learning-algorithms/ (Das et al., 2021)

Reis, Correia, Murai, Veloso, & Benevenuto. (2019). Supervised learning for fake news detection. *IEEE Intelligent Systems, 34*(2), 76–81.

RouseM. (2018). https://searchenterpriseai.techtarget.com/definition/machine-learning

Rubin, V., Conroy, N., Chen, Y., & Cornwell, S. (2016). *Fake News or Truth?* Using Satirical Cues to Detect Potentially Misleading News. doi:10.18653/v1/W16-0802

Ruchansky, N., Seo, S., & Liu, Y. (2017). Csi: A hybrid deep model for fake news detection. *Proceedings of the 2017 ACM on Conference on Information and Knowledge Management*, 797-806. 10.1145/3132847.3132877

Shao, C., Ciampaglia, G. L, Varol, O., Flammini. A., & Menczer, K. (2017). *The spread of fake news by socialhots.* arXiv preprint arAiv: 1707.07592.

Shu, Wang, & Liu. (2019). Beyond news contents: The role of social context for fake news detection. *Proceedings of the Twelfth ACM International Conference on Web Search and Data Mining*, 312-320. 10.1145/3289600.3290994

Shu, K., Sliva, A., Wang, S., Tang, J., & Liu, H. (2017). Fake news detection on social media: A data mining perspective. *SIGKDD Explorations, 19*(1), 22–36. doi:10.1145/3137597.3137600

Tacchini, Ballarin, Della Vedova, Moret, & de Alfaro. (2017). *Some like it Hoax: Automated fake news detect ion in social networks.* Academic Press.

Tandoc. (2017). Defining fake news a typology of scholarly definitions. *Digital Journalism*, 1–17.

Tandoc, E.C., Lim, Z.W., & Ling, R. (2018). Defining "fake news" a typology of scholarly definitions. *Digital Journalism, 6*, 137–153.

Tapaswi. (2012). Treebank based deep grammar acquisition and Part-Of-Speech Tagging for Sanskrit m sentences. In Software Engineering (CONSEG), on Software Engineering (CONSEG) (pp. 1-4). IEEE. doi:10.1109/CONSEG.2012.6349476

Yi. (2003). Sentiment analyzer: Extracting sentiments about a given topic using natural language processing techniques. In *Data Mining, ICDM 2003. Third IEEE International Conference* (pp. 427-434). http://citeseerx.ist.psu.edu

Yumeng, Q. (2018). Predicting Future Rumours. *Chinese Journal of Electronics*.

Zhang, J., Dong, B., & Yu Philip, S. (2020). Fakedetector: Effective fake news detection with deep diffusive neural network. In *2020 IEEE 36th International Conference on Data Engineering (ICDE)* (pp. 1826-1829). IEEE. 10.1109/ICDE48307.2020.00180

Chapter 6
Safety and Security in AI Systems

Kshyamasagar Mahanta

https://orcid.org/0000-0002-5385-9463

Maharaja Sriram Chandra Bhanja Deo University, India

Hima Bindu Maringanti

Maharaja Sriram Chandra Bhanja Deo University, India

ABSTRACT

Innovation and adoption of smart things are very fast in today's era. Everyone wants a smart device to solve any problem because it is effortless, affordable, and less time-consuming. Using artificial intelligence (AI), we have solved many more problems with great success. Some areas where AI is already used are healthcare, smart city, smart grid, agriculture, astronomy, gaming, finance, tourism, social media, robotics, automotive industries, entertainment, e-commerce, education, etc. As the number of users of AI and the number of smart devices increases, the risk of the data and information we are sharing with these devices are also becoming high. For the safety and privacy of users as well as the company, AI systems, their data, and their communications must be protected. Consequently, this chapter aims to provide an overview of how safety and security can be achieved in AI systems. Learners will get knowledge about AI systems and some security mechanisms that can be helpful to their further studies.

1. INTRODUCTION

AI systems have the capacity to do calculations, reason, recognize patterns and links, Learn by experience, find solutions for problems, information management(store and retrieve), understand complicated concepts, speak effectively in natural language, classify circumstances, and adopt new things. According to Markets & Markets- a competitive intelligence and market research platform, the artificial intelligence (AI) business will be worth $190 billion by 2025. For us, today's fast breakthroughs in artificial intelligence (AI) and machine learning (ML) bring a variety of challenges and opportunities. Some areas where AI is already used are Healthcare, Smart City, Smart Grid, Agriculture, Astronomy, Gaming,

DOI: 10.4018/978-1-6684-6821-0.ch006

Finance, Tourism, Social media, Robotics, Automotive Industries, Entertainment, E-Commerce, Education, etc. As machine learning becomes more widely employed, the danger of system failures creating severe harm increases, particularly in areas where safety and security are crucial. Let's think about Self driving cars which are invented to save lives, reduce road accidents, giving a comfortable journey to people. But can you imagine if there will be any failure in the system then your life, as well as many others' life will be in danger who are traveling on the road. As all control is made automatically by its software, there is a chance that hackers will access the software and make some harmful activity. If AI control falls into the wrong hands, it might result in many devastating outcomes. It can be programmed to produce highly dangerous outcomes.

The history of robotics and artificial intelligence in many ways is also the history of humanity's attempts to control such technologies. From the Golem of Prague to the military robots of modernity, the debate continues as to what degree of independence such entities should have and how to make sure that they do not turn on us, their inventors. Careful analysis of proposals aimed at developing safe artificially intelligent systems leads to a surprising discovery that most such proposals have been analyzed for millennia in the context of theology (Yampolskiy & Spellchecker, 2016).

Robustness, assurance, and specification are the three categories into which problems in AI safety may be classified. A system must be robust to ensure that it continues to function within safe bounds even in new environments. It must also be assured that human operators can readily examine and comprehend it, and its specification is concerned with making sure that its behavior complies with the goals of the system designer. Safety considerations must precede the deployment of modern machine learning systems in high-stakes settings. Robustness, assurance, and specification are key areas of AI safety that can guide the development of reliably safe machine learning systems (Rudner & Toner, 2021).

In AI systems, in order to safeguard resources (such as apps and services) from unwanted access, security and privacy solutions must be properly developed. Building safe AI systems require a deep comprehension of the unique requirements of such systems. As every AI system is having unique design concept and unique functionality, the same security policy or safety measures cannot be applied everywhere. In this chapter, First, we introduced AI systems with some example, of how AI system works, and then we presented a brief idea about the safety and security of AI systems, which will help in designing and developing secure systems and the users will also be aware of it.

2. OVERVIEW OF AI SYSTEMS

The major technology behind AI are ML, Deep Learning (DL), and Natural Language Processing(NLP). Machine Learning is a subset of AI, where machines can learn by themselves to respond better or to take decisions by analyzing structured data sets. DL is a more advanced type of ML since it learns via representation, it uses Neural Network architecture which is also called Deep Neural Network (DNN) architecture. NLP is a linguistic method based on computer science. It enables computers to read and comprehend human language. NLP can be used by computers to interpret natural language into machine inputs.

Machine learning techniques are intended to extract relationships and patterns from data. A machine learning approach typically consists of an input-output statistical model (for instance, the connection between an audio file and a text transcription of it) and a learning algorithm that specifies how the model should evolve as it learns more about this input-output relationship. Training is the act of updating the model when new data becomes available, and recent developments in engineering and research have made it possible to effectively train extremely complicated models using massive quantities of data. A machine learning system may execute tasks like autonomous navigation once it has been effectively trained. It can also be used to create artificial data or make predictions about things like whether an image shows an object or a person (such as images, videos, speech, and text).

Data, rather than a predefined set of rules, is used by machine learning algorithms to discover relationships and patterns. As a result, these systems are only as good as the data that was used to train them. While current machine learning systems perform admirably in conditions comparable to those experienced during training, they frequently fail in settings that are significantly different. A deep neural network trained to categorize pictures of cats and dogs in black and white, for example, is likely to be successful in categorizing comparable images of cats and dogs in color. It will, however, be unable to accurately categorize a fish if it has never seen a picture of one during training.

Although machine learning methods do not employ explicit rules to express correlations and patterns, rules are used to update the model during training. These rules, sometimes known as "learning algorithms," represent how a machine learning system's human creator intends it to "learn" from data. For example, if the aim is to accurately categorize photos of cats and dogs, the learning algorithm should comprise a series of stages that gradually improve the model's ability to classify cats and dogs. This aim may be encoded in a learning algorithm in a variety of ways, and it is the human designer's responsibility to do so.

Deep neural networks are used by many current machine learning systems. Deep neural networks are statistical models that can represent a variety of complicated relationships and patterns and that perform particularly well with enormous volumes of data. Deep neural networks have practical applications in text, speech, image generation, sequential decision-making in autonomous systems, image classification, etc.

3. EXAMPLES OF AI SYSTEMS

Some common examples of AI applications are listed below:

- Virtual Assistant: NLP is used to train Virtual Assistants (some times called ChatBots) to mimic the conversational patterns of customer service agents . Advanced ChatBots no longer require precise input forms (for example, yes/no questions). They can provide extensive replies to complicated questions. In fact, if you rate the response negatively, the bot will discover the error and repair it for the next time, assuring optimum customer happiness.
- Voice Assistant: When our hands are busy, we frequently rely on voice assistants to do the task. You may ask the assistant to call someone while you're driving or you can ask for playing your favorite song. ' Siri', 'Alexa', 'OK google', and 'Cortana' are examples of voice assistants. Voice assistants use ML, NLP, and statistical analysis techniques to figure out what you want and attempt to get it for you.
- Social Media platform: AI is being used by social networking applications to monitor content, recommend connections, provide suggestions to targeted individuals, show advertisements of particular interest, etc. AI systems can discover and instantly remove or prohibit problematic content that breaches terms and conditions using keyword identification and image recognition.

- Text Editors: AI is used in word processors, messaging applications, and every other written media to recognize the wrong use of grammar and offer suggestions for any change. For teaching grammar to robots, Computer scientists and Linguists work together, the same way a student is taught in school. The algorithms are trained using high-quality linguistic data so that the editor can spot any grammatical or spelling errors.

- Maps and Navigation: AI has significantly enhanced peoples traveling experience. Without depending on paper maps or directions, you can now give your location to navigation applications like Waze, Google, or Apple Maps on your phone. The program has also been trained to recognize and do changes in traffic flow to offer the best path to avoid blockages and congestion. Using ML, the algorithms recall the boundaries of the structures they have learned, allowing for improved graphics on the map as well as recognition and comprehension of home and building numbers.

- Self Driving and Parking: To know the surrounding area of a vehicle, self-driving and parking automobiles employ the DL technique. A technology firm 'Nvidia', employs AI to offer automobiles "the ability to perceive, understand, and learn, allowing them to traverse a practically endless range of potential driving conditions". The company's AI-powered technology is already in Toyota, Mercedes-Benz, Audi, Volvo, and Tesla automobiles, and it is set to transform how humans drive—and enable vehicles to drive themselves.

- Transportation: UberEATS, ZOMATO, and SWIGGY have already started their food delivery facility in some cities using drones where no human intervention is needed. All these are possible only because of AI.

- Robotics: Roomba and iRobot have returned with a new, smarter robotic vacuum. The Roomba 980 model use AI techniques to scan a room, recognize barriers, and recall the most effective cleaning paths. The self-deploying Roomba can also assess how much vacuuming is required based on the size of the area, and it does not require human intervention to clean floors.

'Hanson Robotics' creates humanoid robots which use AI technology for business as well as consumer industries. 'Sophia' designed by Hanson, is an extremely advanced social-learning robot. Sophia can interact well with natural language and utilize facial expressions to portray human-like emotions. This robot has become an internet sensation in recent few years, seen on a variety of technical discussion forums. The robot has even received Saudi Arabian citizenship.

- Healthcare: Artificial intelligence is transforming healthcare, changing practically every area of the business starting from robotic surgeries to protecting vital information from attackers. Smart Virtual Assistants are minimizing unnecessary hospital visits and saving 20% of nurses' time for these processes; AI assistants are used for assisting doctors with a workflow which saves 17% of their schedules; pharmaceutical Industries are doing research on lifesaving medicines in a very short period of time and very low cost as it previously took.

- Finance: To make judgments, financial institutions depend on accuracy, real-time data, and the amount of data, all of which smart robots excel at. As the financial sector recognizes the efficiency and accuracy of AI, it is rapidly implementing automation, ChatBots, adaptive intelligence, algorithmic trading, and machine learning into financial operations. The computerized portfolio manager which is also called Robo-advisor is one of the most significant developments in finance sector. These automated advisers employ artificial intelligence and algorithms to monitor the financial market, collect related data and suggest the best portfolio or stock based on preferences.

Wealth management companies are adopting Robo-advisors because time and money can be saved for both the company and the customer and also it will deliver great returns.

4. TOP SECURITY THREATS IN AI SYSTEMS

Here some top security threats have been mentioned.

1. System Manipulation

One common threat to the AI system is designed to cause high-volume algorithms to predict results incorrectly. By providing falsified data as feedback to the system the attacker can able to accomplish this. Essentially, this type of attack is designed to present machines with a picture that does not exist in reality, forcing them to make decisions based on unverified data. The consequences of such an attack can be disastrous because the effects can be both long-lasting and far-reaching, making it a far more serious threat than many other security risks.

2. Data Poisoning

When hackers tamper with data used to train AI models, it becomes 'poisoned.' Because AI relies on that data to learn how to make accurate predictions, the algorithm's predictions will be wrong.

Threat actors are now tampering with data to use it in cyberattacks. They can do a lot, for example, by simply changing the data for a recommendation engine. They can then convince someone to download a malicious app or click on an infected link.

Data poisoning is so dangerous because it employs artificial intelligence against us. We are increasingly relying on AI predictions in many aspects of our personal and professional lives. It does everything from recommending a movie to predicting which customers will cancel their service.

Data poisoning attacks are difficult and time-consuming to detect. As a result, victims frequently discover that by the time they discover the problem, the damage has already been done.

3. Transfer Learning Attacks

Most ML systems rely on a previously trained machine learning model. The system's specifications are designed for achieving specific goals through specialized training algorithms. This is the window of opportunity for a transfer learning attack to be lethal to an AI/ML system. For example, if the selected model is well-known, an adversary can easily launch attacks that deceive a task-specific ML model. Security experts must check for suspicious activity or unexpected machine learning behaviors that can help in the identification of such attacks.

4. Online System Manipulation

The internet is very much crucial for the developing of AI/ML systems, and most of the machines are connected to the internet at the time of learning, which provides adversaries with a clear attack vertical. In such scenario, hackers can deceive ML systems by providing wrong inputs or gradually re-training them to give incorrect outputs. This type of attack can be prevented by streamlining and securing system operations and also by keeping records of data ownership.

5. Data Privacy

Data privacy is considered to be a fundamental requirement for consumer acceptance, which can be ensured through the data flow representation, authentication, and authorization of the performed activities such as data collection, retention, processing, and transmission. Data privacy risks are directly related to unauthorized collection, usage, access, storage, and sharing activities(Shahid et al., 2022). It is very difficult for professionals to safeguard the privacy and confidentiality of large amount of data. This is particularly accurate if the data is integrated into the machine learning model. In this scenario, attackers may conduct covert data extraction attacks, endangering the entire machine learning system. Attack verticals can also use smaller sub-symbolic function extraction attacks, which involve less work and resources. Organizations must create policies to stop function extraction attacks in addition to safeguarding ML systems against data extraction attacks to defend themselves.

5. ATTACKS AND SOLUTIONS

1. Data Collection-Related Attacks and Solutions

The primary factor accelerating AI development is data. It manifests itself in a variety of ways. Examples of data are image files and audio clips captured by any hardware devices (e.g., sensors), documents, and log files generated by computer systems or internet sources. The security threats associated with data collection are not similar to AI systems, but rather exist in all industries that require data collection. Data collection needs to meet the following security objectives: confidentiality, integrity, non-repudiation, authentication, privacy protection, and self-protection(Dear, 2021). There are two types of data collection methods: software-based data collection and hardware-based data collection. The software-based data collection method is used for representing the digital world and the hardware-based data collection method is used for representing the physical world, which is the key point for transforming physical data into digital forms.

Table 1. two types of data collection based methods

Data collection method	Security issues/Attacks	Solution
Software-based	• Data bias • Fake data • Data breach	• Detection and filtering • Detection and filtering • Encryption and Authentication
Hardware-based	Sensor spoofing attack	Filtering and enhancing Sensors

Data Collection Methods

a. Software-Based Data Collection

The majority of data in digital form is generated by Internet users' daily activities. Data collectors collect information using software program tools. For completing the data collection procedure, software-based data collection necessitates the collaboration of packet capture applications such as libraries for capturing packets, operating systems, device driver software, and network interface cards. Any problems in any part of the process will hamper the standard of data collection. Analyzing the data collection through online social networks as an example, we are going to discuss the security risks posed by software-based data collection methods and the corresponding countermeasures. Manipulation and falsification of data are two examples of security risks associated with data collection through social networks.

b. Hardware-Based Data Collection

Sensors, hardware probes, mobile terminals, cards used for data acquisition generation, inline taps, NIC(network interface cards), mobile terminals, and other hardware-related data collection devices are examples of this category. Each type of data collection method has different potential risks depending on the hardware's design principle. Sensors are the most widely used data collection tool because of their efficiency and flexibility.

1.1 Attacks

- *Data Bias*. Artificial intelligence is extremely sensitive to training data. Bias may be introduced by data source selection and data preparation. For example, a platform may be motivated by commercial interests (such as certain advertisements) or political maneuvers to "encourage" users to take action on social networks. Social platforms also prevent the collection of data by third parties and impose many restrictions on application programming interfaces (APIs). As a result, data collectors limit themselves to collecting limited data or data that differs from the data that the platform provides to regular users. We need to improve our data collection criteria and create tools to identify and reduce bias.
- *Fake Data*. Sometimes we use fake data to train our systems as there is a lack of actual data. The issue of fake data does not pose a significant challenge to the AI domain. To identify fake profiles in social networks on the internet, a convolutional neural network(CNN) or DNN model algorithm can be used.
- *Data Breach*. Unintentional information disclosure, and data leak is usually called as Data breach. It is an ongoing problem. Data breaches can occur not only in the data collection stage but also in the model training and inference stage.
- *Sensor Spoofing Attack*. For the training and subsequent inference of the model, the data generated from the real world must be digitized and collected using appropriate sensory elements. Sensors are ubiquitously integrated into smart portable devices, autonomous vehicles, and LIDAR (Light Detection and Ranging) systems, which are key components responsible for measuring and collecting data. Attackers can exploit the physical properties of sensors to create malicious patterns

that create sensors and interfere with data collection. For example, an attacker could block the magnetic field generated by the rotation mechanism, fooling the sensor into making a bad speed in a car. The magnetic field generated by the malicious actuator that detects the wrong speed is sent to the anti-lock braking sensor (ABS), resulting in a sensor spoofing attack.

1.2 Solutions

Data collection helps mitigate security risks by implementing data security strategies in hardware, software, and cybersecurity. There are numerous data collection security strategies. Furthermore, the protection strategies differ depending on the scenario. Some data collection protection measures based on data security strategies are mentioned below.

- *Detection and Filtering.* Sensor enhancement and baseband offset can help prevent sensor spoofing attacks. For microphones, you can suppress audio signals above 20 kHz by adding a low-pass filter and increasing the amplitude of the microphone, resulting in filtered-out human "inaudible" voice commands. To secure sensor networks, an iterative filtering technique with improved robustness and convergence can be used. We may also remove data collected by reliable or unreliable means.
- *Data Provenance and Authentication.* Sensor trust methods can be implemented to prevent data from untrusted or unauthorized devices from being captured. First, before aggregating data from sensor nodes, their identification should be validated using trustworthiness evaluations. And any strong encryption mechanism should be used to collect the data.
- *Standardized Management.* The small error made by humans can degrade the quality of data collected, necessitating training and management of the appropriate person. As a result, we must examine data collection security requirements like identity verification, confidentiality, integrity, etc., and create appropriate management procedures to ensure data collection. Furthermore, having the right incentive mechanisms in place can encourage data providers to share their data more honestly and accurately.

2. Scaling Attacks and Solutions

Typically, the size of the image data used to train the models is fixed. Because of the image pre-processing step, the image fed into the model is typically 220×220 or 32×32, which is smaller than the original. For example, during the data pre-processing phase, images must be scaled to match the model input size. Image scaling generates a new image with a lower or higher pixel resolution as compared to the original while retaining all features and scaling it proportionally. The attackers can modify the pixel-level information during the scaling process to generate a camouflage image, resulting in a significant change in visual interpretations before and after the scaling of the image.. Can you ever thought that, if you zoom out a teacup image, it can be transformed into a cat image. Such strange things can happen in the world of artificial intelligence research. carefully modifying the pixel values of any image can result in a completely different image when it is downscaled.

Attackers can use this image-scaling technique as a springboard for adversarial attacks on machine learning models, which are the artificial intelligence algorithms used in computer vision tasks like facial recognition and object detection. Adversarial machine learning is a subset of data manipulation techniques that alter the behavior of AI algorithms while remaining undetected by humans.

There are strong and weak strategies for implementing image scaling attacks. In a powerful strategy, the attacker can choose the source and target images. In the weak version, the enemy has no choice but to select the target, and the calculated attack image is useless and easy to detect.

2.1 Solutions

Robust scaling algorithms can be used to prevent such kinds of attacks. Area scaling, which is typically implemented in many scaling libraries, and Pillow's scaling algorithms are two secure scaling implementations that prevent image-scaling attacks. The relationship between down-sampling frequency and image scaling prevents Image Scaling Attacks, however, it reduces the quality of the input image.. Therefore integrating rescaling, filtering, and steganalysis into a scaling attack detection framework can be used for better results. The scaling detection method first downscales and then up-scales the input image to create a "copy" image, then compares the image's similarity on the color histogram before and after the input image as well as its "copy": Pixels injected by an attacker into the input image must be removed from the duplicate image for upscaling. Filter detection uses filters to filter images. Discrete Fourier Transform (DFT) is used to transform the samples suspected of attacking images into two-dimensional space, and steganalysis is used to detect perturbed pixels embedded by Image Scaling Attacks. Following that, to assess the similarity before and after, the Mean Squared Errors (MSE), Structural Similarity Index (SSIM), and Centered Spectrum Points (CSP) metrics are utilized, and the detection boundaries are generated independently for each detection method. Finally, to identify whether or not the entering image is an assault image, an ensemble technique can be used.

3. Data Poisoning Attacks and Solutions

AI systems are trained using large amounts of customized data. However, the quality of the data has a direct impact on the performance of the trained model. The training set can be poisoned by an attacker in order to manipulate the model's inference behavior. One example of a poisoning attack is: consider training a facial recognition-based security system that should admit Alice but reject Bob. If an attacker poisons the dataset by changing some of the images of "Alice" to ones of "Bob," the system would fail in its mission because it would learn to identify Bob as Alice. Therefore Bob would be incorrectly authenticated as Alice when the system was deployed(Comiter, 2019).

There are two types of poisoning attacks:

i)   availability attacks and ii) integrity attacks.

i)   Availability attacks are also known as denial-of-service attacks, with the goal of maximizing the overall loss of the model and causing model performance degradation as well as misclassification. For example, social media ChatBots have a large corpus that grows as a result of interactions with humans. When an attacker affects the ChatBot with statements that have no contextual relevance, the ChatBot will not engage in a normal logical conversation.

ii) The attacker compromises the target in an integrity attack by carefully crafting the poisoned data so that it does not influence the model categorization of the clean samples. The most prevalent sort of integrity assault is a backdoor attack. Backdoor attacks only classify entries based on explicit or implicit triggers, and back doors can still be detected in downstream transport activities. In order to identify malware, an attacker may mark a file with a certain location as harmless data and put it in the detector's training. After training and implementing the model, the attacker adds a specific path to the malware to evade detection, because every malware that executes a given path is linked with a benign class.

3.1 Solutions

Data poisoning attacks introduce contaminated data into the training set, causing learning algorithms to malfunction. Contaminated data differs from clean data in several ways, which means that it can be treated as an anomaly, so that anomaly detection techniques can be used to defend against data poisoning attacks. We have mentioned two methods i.e. Data sanitization and model robustness training, which can be used to protect against data poisoning attacks. Before training a classifier, data sanitization removes contaminated samples from a training data set, whereas robust learning focuses on increasing the robustness of a learning algorithm to reduce the influence of contaminated samples.

Data Sanitization:

One of the countermeasures to a poisoning attack is data sanitization. It is a method of pre-processing data that filters suspect samples before learning. 'Reject On Negative Impact' is one method of Data Sanitization. The data is regarded as poisoned and eliminated from the training set if it significantly harms the classifier. Although this method has shown remarkable performance in some situations, such as correctly recognizing attack emails, it is prohibitively expensive to test every data sample in the training set. influence has an effect In robust statistics, it is possible to determine how data points affect classifier prediction. The method can determine the impact of each data item without having to retrain the model.

Robustness Training:

In general, robust training is highly dependent on certain feature assumptions. By improving robust principal component regression and robust low-rank matrix approximation, these assumptions can be relaxed and strong defensive performance achieved. (Jagielski et al., 2018) proposed a principled approach to constructing a defense algorithm called TRIM, which provides high robustness and resilience against a large class of poisoning attacks. It offers great resilience and robustness against a broad range of poisoning threats. The TRIM technique employs a trimmed loss function to eliminate locations with high residuals while iteratively estimating the regression parameters. After a limited number of rounds, TRIM is able to identify the majority of poisoned spots and develop a reliable regression model. When compared to other approaches, TRIM performs much better and provides robustness considerably more effectively.

4. Adversarial Example Attacks and Solutions

Despite their high accuracy and performance, machine learning algorithms have been found to be vulnerable to subtle perturbations that can have catastrophic consequences in security-related environments. The threat becomes more grave when the applications operate in an adversarial environment. So, it has become an immediate necessity to devise robust learning techniques resilient to adversarial attacks(Chakraborty et al., 2018). How much knowledge the attacker has about the model, such as training data, feature sets, learning techniques, etc., determines the adversary's attack capabilities.

Adversarial Goals: An adversary makes an attempt to give a classification system an input x that leads to an incorrect output classification. The incorrectness of the model leads to the adversary's goal being inferred. The following broad categories can be used to classify adversarial goals according to their impact on the integrity of the classifier output:

(1) Confidence Reduction: The adversary tries to reduce the forecast confidence of the target model. For instance, a legitimate image of a "stop" sign at a traffic light can be predicted with less certainty because it is less likely to belong to a particular class.

(2) Misclassification: The adversary tries to change an input example's output categorization to a different class than the original class. For instance, any other class other than the class of a stop sign will be predicted for a real image of a "stop" sign.

(3) Targeted Misclassification: The adversary attempts to create inputs that cause the classification model's output to be a particular target class. For instance, the classification model will predict that any input image belongs to a class of photos with a "go" sign.

(4) Source/Target Misclassification: The adversary tries to cause a specific target class to be the result of classification for specific input. For instance, the classification model will predict that the input image of a "stop" sign is actually a "go" sign.

Attacks can be classified into three types based on the attacker's available knowledge:

i) white-box attack ii) black-box attack iii) grey-box attack

i) White-box attack: The attacker has complete knowledge of the target model, including the type of neural network model, parameters, and training algorithm, among other things. To generate adversarial examples, the adversary uses known knowledge to identify vulnerable feature spaces. Because white-box attacks require computing the gradient with respect to the input, and the gradient is discrete in the textual case, gradient-based white-box attack methods are difficult to apply to NLP.

ii) Black-box attacks: In contrast to white-box attacks, in Black-box attacks the adversary has no knowledge of the model but is permitted to analyze the model's vulnerability/weakness by querying the AI system with carefully devised inputs and observing the outputs. Black-box attacks are more practical, but they are more difficult to design.

iii) Grey-box attacks: Grey-box attacks are also called as semi-white box attacks. For the attacker to successfully attack the target model, they must gain partial knowledge of the model (aside from the model parameters). In actual practice, grey-box attacks are uncommon.

4.1 Solutions

While retaining the model's performance, the adversarial defensive technology should refrain from making too many changes to the original model structure (e.g., speed, memory usage, model classification accuracy). In addition to the NLP sector, methods for guarding against adversarial example attacks have also been thoroughly studied in the malware, speech recognition, and picture classification domains.

Defensive Distillation: Distillation is intended to move fine-grained knowledge from large-scale training models to small-scale models, allowing small-scale models to perform learning tasks more accurately and efficiently. To address the problem of missing information, a small model (distilled network) is provided to simulate a large, computationally intensive model (initial). Defensive distillation can defend against most adversarial example attacks and is simple to learn.

Gradient Regularization: Gradient regularization is the process of adding constraints to the objective function during training in order to avoid significant changes in the model output as the input changes. Small perturbations usually have no effect on the output. To defend against FGSM-based attacks, a model can be trained using a combination of regularization methods. It is worth noting that adversarial training can significantly reduce the curvature of loss functions and the decision boundary of the classifier. Furthermore, to defend against adversarial attacks, regularization methods and adversarial training can be combined, but the computational complexity is prohibitively high.

Feature Squeezing: In the field of image classification, there are two data compression methods: (i) Reduce color depth by encoding colors with lower values. (ii) Apply the spatial smoothing filter, which enables the mapping of multiple inputs into a single value. Feature squeezing is a model-enhancing technology that reduces the complexity of representation data by compressing the input features to withstand adversarial perturbations.

Detectors: A detector is a mechanism that determines whether or not an image detected is an adversarial sample. Typically, the detector's discrimination criteria for adversarial samples can be freely defined. The simplest approach is to label the adversarial and legitimate samples before training a classifier. Classifier training methods are classified into two types. One method is to train a classifier by labeling the adversarial examples and the original samples separately in the initial stage. Another method is to train a classifier by labeling the adversarial and clean samples only on the output values of a specific layer.

Network Verification: Network validation can be used to determine whether a sample violates certain DNN properties or if a sample within a specified range (distance from the original sample) changes its label value. An adversarial example is discriminated in the defense phase of adversarial example attacks if its input is detected to violate some DNN properties. As a result, network validation is based on the model's detection of new unknown attacks.

Adversarial Training: Adversarial training, as the name implies, involves adding adversarial examples generated by attack algorithms such as FGSM to the training set during the training phase. It is a brute force defense scheme as well as a regularization tool for dealing with the model's overfitting issue. Adversarial training necessitates a large number of adversarial examples in order to train networks against single-step attacks but is ineffective against iterative attacks.

Data Randomization: Data randomization refers to the use of randomization technology to mitigate adversarial effects. By randomly resizing the images and employing random padding technology to disrupt the structure of specific adversarial perturbations during the model's forward propagation phase, the adversarial effects can be mitigated. Specifically, it consists of two steps. I First, the input image is randomly resized. (ii) The resized image is then surrounded by zero random paddings. The padding's position is chosen at random. Data randomization works well in defending against both single-step and iterative attacks. The data random defense method is not only less computationally intensive and does not require additional training, but it is also compatible with other adversarial defense methods.

5. AI System Integration

AI technology is all around us. Despite our discussion of AI threats and countermeasures, the security issues appear to be more complex when AI is integrated into real-world applications. The security issues differ depending on the application scenario, and we should take a broad view of AI security. This section will look at several security risks that may arise during the integration process.

— AI confidentiality: AI confidentiality includes both data and model confidentiality. AI confidentiality is generally associated with model privacy, but it can also lead to security issues, such as model inversion and model extraction. The inverse analysis of a model to obtain private data based on the mapping relationship between inputs and outputs is referred to as model inversion. Model extraction is commonly defined as running a sufficient number of queries through an API and analyzing the output results (probabilities or labels) to infer model parameters or extract an approximate model that closely matches the target model. DP-differential privacy, homomorphic encryption, or model watermarking are frequently used to reduce privacy risks for both types of privacy issues.

— Code vulnerability protection: Utilizing data-driven techniques (such as AI/ML) for automated intelligent analysis performed directly on source code poses some challenges that must be overcome, such as properly representing source code to allow for further analysis in ML algorithms and localizing discovered vulnerabilities on source code. Modern AI system technologies are based on frameworks, such as deep learning (e.g., Caffe, Tensorflow, and Torch). All these frameworks depend on several external and basic libraries, which have greatly aided in the advancement of AI technologies. They do, however, have weaknesses and were not created to be faultless(Xiao et al., 2018). Although they are a necessary component for the implementation process of the model, code vulnerabilities are also a vital component of the security implementation of AI systems.

— A Google research team's new distributed ML method called federated learning(Brendan McMahan et al., 2017) has emerged as a significant new area of AI. Federated learning updates the global model by combining local models that have been trained on localized data that are stored by each client. Federated learning mostly reduces privacy concerns, but it lacks local data auditing and participant behavior management, which is likely to cause security problems. Attackers can easily access the communication channels, central server, and client-side of federated learning. The most frequent include user-side/server-side GAN attacks(Wang et al., 2019), privacy concerns in federated learning(Hardy et al., 2017), and poisoning attacks, which may be carried out by data poisoning or/and model poisoning(Bagdasaryan et al., 2018). Because of the restriction of access to data and control over clients, developing defenses against security attacks is extremely challenging than centralized training.

6. ENSURING SAFETY

AI is an incredibly efficient tool. And, like with any power tool, AI safety must be prioritized. Artificial Intelligence (AI) has come a long way, from Siri to self-driving automobiles. AI now includes anything from simple search engines to self-driving cars. To reap the commercial benefits of an AI system, we must first put AI safety policies in place. It implies that enterprises must develop best practices to guide the safe and ethical administration of AI systems. Alignment with business standards and objectives, computational responsibility, compliance with current business standards, data integrity assurance, and privacy and personal information protection are all part of this. For AI models to be used in safety- and security-critical areas such as (partly) autonomous driving in the years to come, a standardized methodology and concrete test criteria will be required in order to assess and evaluate the robustness of these models with respect to random as well as targeted perturbations. For ensuring an adequate level of safety and security, such criteria must be developed, and checking compliance with them must be made compulsory(Berghoff et al., 2021).

These are three helpful practices for adopting AI safety.

a)   Develop Guidelines
b)   Manage Data Integrity
c)   Validate and Verify

a) Develop Guidelines

Any physical or digital tool or even AI has the potential to be used unethically. Organizations must verify that AI systems are used appropriately. Companies might impose guidelines for the use of AI technologies. These principles include laws and regulations that can assist build trust among artificial intelligence creators, users, and beneficiaries. These principles should regulate both the ethical management of an AI system's operations and the behavior of its users. Organizations must make a policy to ensure compliance. These principles should also prohibit the company from engaging in any business that is potentially harmful to society. Before any data analysis or business work begins, the business goal and needs of any AI system should be explicitly articulated. AI technologies improve a company's ability to learn and identify new sources of revenue and get significant data insights. As a result, these AI systems must be used ethically.

b) Manage Data Integrity

Businesses must first properly maintain the integrity of the data and models that drive AI systems in order to ensure the overall integrity of AI systems. Anomalies can be caused by a variety of circumstances, including incompleteness and hostile attacks. Organizations should have strategies and systems in place to guard against, detect, fix, and minimize risks caused by anomalies. These strategies must be fully incorporated into the AI platform. An AI system's careful, risk-averting activities can help it provide more value than finely tuned but fragile insights or confident but unreliable conclusions. Managing data integrity and risk mitigation approaches is critical not just in intelligent devices, but also in systems based on human-machine interaction.

c) Validate and Verify

Validating and verifying AI systems is a way of determining their dependability and predictability. Before they are implemented, all AI systems should be verified, validated, and tested, both stochastically and logically. Techniques for confirming that a system can fulfill its tasks satisfactorily are included in the verification. As AI systems work in largely unknown settings and act on ambiguous information, new verification procedures must be implemented. Another important technique for determining predictability and hence confirming that an AI system does not exhibit undesired behaviors is validity. Organizations must know what is good or bad in a specific setting in order to characterize those unwanted behaviors.

7. FUTURE SCOPE AND CHALLENGES

There are various scopes and challenges related to this field. Some of them are mentioned below.

— Develop a protection mechanism that may be used for many types of sensor devices. Because new data gathering devices and tools are always being updated, there is plenty of space for advancement in data security during the data collection process. Sensor security vulnerabilities are mostly caused by the design of the hardware and malicious signal injection conducted on the hardware by attackers. On the hardware side, researchers must tweak and test the sensor's physical qualities and logical connections. On the software side, researchers must devise appropriate ways to detect and reject malicious data during the sensor's data gathering phase, such as cleaning the data and other pre-processing processes. Second, the generalization of sensor malicious signal identification technology is inadequate. It is critical to developing a defense mechanism that can be applied to various types of sensor devices, making it impossible for attackers to circumvent the defense mechanism.

— Improving the interpretability of AI models. The interpretability of models mounted in current AI research is lacking. Nonetheless, we struggle to precisely assess and explain what security issues arise in AI and under what conditions. As a result, attackers may always locate the AI attack surface, but we are unable to identify potential security vulnerabilities before they are exposed and exploited by attackers. We must urgently improve the mathematical validation of AI models and the interpretability of AI.

— Increase the security and privacy protections for AI technologies. Security and privacy are strongly linked, and AI systems face not just the aforementioned security concerns, but also privacy risks, such as model inversion and model extraction(Zhang et al., 2020). Current AI security and privacy concerns are handled separately. Future research on the integration of both privacy and security domains must be increased to assure data and model privacy while maintaining AI system security.

8. CONCLUSION

AI has been widely applied in a variety of industries, enabling a new era of the industrial revolution and propelling human society into the age of intelligence. But the development of AI technology is still in its early stages. Security threats arise throughout the AI system's lifespan. Even though multiple countermeasures have been proposed, there are still a number of issues that must be solved. This article discusses security risks in AI systems and offers remedies. Finally, a summary is provided to provide a sense of the future scope and challenges for AI security issues. Despite the fact that AI technology development is well underway, the growing security risks it poses require us to be more vigilant in order to safeguard its higher, quicker, and better development.

REFERENCES

Bagdasaryan, E., Veit, A., Hua, Y., Estrin, D., & Shmatikov, V. (2018). *How To Backdoor Federated Learning*. https://arxiv.org/abs/1807.00459

Berghoff, C., Bielik, P., Neu, M., Tsankov, P., & von Twickel, A. (2021). Robustness Testing of AI Systems: A Case Study for Traffic Sign Recognition. *IFIP Advances in Information and Communication Technology, 627,* 256–267. doi:10.1007/978-3-030-79150-6_21

Brendan McMahan, H., Moore, E., Ramage, D., Hampson, S., & Agüera y Arcas, B. (2017). Communication-efficient learning of deep networks from decentralized data. *Proceedings of the 20th International Conference on Artificial Intelligence and Statistics, AISTATS 2017,* 54.

Chakraborty, A., Alam, M., Dey, V., Chattopadhyay, A., & Mukhopadhyay, D. (2018). Adversarial Attacks and Defences. *Survey.* https://arxiv.org/abs/1810.00069

Comiter, M. (2019). *Attacking artificial intelligence: AI's security vulnerability and what policymakers can do about it.* Belfer Center for Science and International Affairs, Harvard Kennedy School.

Dear, K. (2021). Artificial intelligence, security, and society. *The World Information War: Western Resilience, Campaigning, and Cognitive Effects, 55*(1), 231–256. doi:10.4324/9781003046905-17

Hardy, S., Henecka, W., Ivey-Law, H., Nock, R., Patrini, G., Smith, G., & Thorne, B. (2017). *Private federated learning on vertically partitioned data via entity resolution and additively homomorphic encryption.* https://arxiv.org/abs/1711.10677

Jagielski, M., Oprea, A., Biggio, B., Liu, C., Nita-rotaru, C., & Li, B. (2018). Manipulating Machine Learning. *Poisoning Attacks and Countermeasures for Regression Learning., 3,* 19–35. Advance online publication. doi:10.1109/SP.2018.00057

Rudner, T. G. J., & Toner, H. (2021, Mar.). Key Concepts in AI Safety: An Overview. *CSET.*

Shahid, J., Ahmad, R., Kiani, A. K., Ahmad, T., Saeed, S., & Almuhaideb, A. M. (2022). Data Protection and Privacy of the Internet of Healthcare Things (IoHTs). *Applied Sciences (Switzerland), 12*(4), 1927. Advance online publication. doi:10.3390/app12041927

Wang, Z., Song, M., Zhang, Z., Song, Y., Wang, Q., & Qi, H. (2019). Beyond Inferring Class Representatives: User-Level Privacy Leakage from Federated Learning. *Proceedings - IEEE INFOCOM,* 2512–2520. doi:10.1109/INFOCOM.2019.8737416

Xiao, Q., Li, K., Zhang, D., & Xu, W. (2018). Security risks in deep learning implementations. *Proceedings - 2018 IEEE Symposium on Security and Privacy Workshops,* 123–128. 10.1109/SPW.2018.00027

Yampolskiy, R. V., & Spellchecker, M. S. (2016). *Artificial Intelligence Safety and Cybersecurity: a Timeline of AI Failures.* https://arxiv.org/abs/1610.07997

Zhang, J., Li, C., Ye, J., & Qu, G. (2020). Privacy threats and protection in machine learning. *Proceedings of the ACM Great Lakes Symposium on VLSI, GLSVLSI, September,* 531–536. 10.1145/3386263.3407599

Chapter 7
Ethical Issues, Fairness, Accountability, and Transparency in AI/ML

K. Sunitha

CMRCET, Hyderabad, India

ABSTRACT

The ethical issues of how the computer evolved to the artificial intelligence and machine learning era are explored in this chapter. To develop these intelligent systems, what are the basic principles, policies, and rules? How are these systems helpful to humankind as well as to society? How are businesses and other relevant organizations adapting AI and ML? AI and ML are booming technology. They have major applications in healthcare, computer vision, traffic networks, manufacturing, business trade markets, and so on.

INTRODUCTION

In this chapter, we are trying to explain how artificial intelligence and machine learning came into existence in the world. Is AI necessary for mankind? If this is the case, how important is AI in human life, and how much of it is required? Along with that, we are discussing how computers are evolving, starting from small abacuses to AI as robotics. Mainly, we are dealing with: what are the ethical issues of AI? How these are effective for AI development Are you eager to learn about AI? What is AI? How is it useful? How has the invention of AI made human life easier and more effective? What ethical issues are effective and useful for constructing AI robotics? So, let's start our journey towards the world of AI (Tutorials Point, n.d.).

Many changes have occurred since man began his civilization from monkey to man. As humans discovered their wants and needs in life, they began inventing things to make it easier and more meaningful. According to his knowledge, he invented many things, such as the motor bike for transportation, the electric light for lighting, the house for living, and numerous cookware pots for cooking. He began learning about things in the education and science sectors to broaden his knowledge. As science made

DOI: 10.4018/978-1-6684-6821-0.ch007

tremendous changes to human life, it found many branches like physics, chemistry, biology, mechanics, electronics, electrical engineering, and computers. But here, we are not discussing all the branches of science. So, here we are talking about only one demanding, curious branch of science: is Computers (Tutorials Point, n.d.).

Because of the history of computers, our journey began. Man made all the research and inventions with his knowledge to make man's life easier in an effective manner. So, in the history of computers, the first machine invented to calculate or for counting was the abacus. The abacus is a combination of rods and grooves, and it is used to do some mathematical calculations like addition, subtraction, division, and multiplication. An abacus is used to count the numbers by moving string balls to do mathematical operations (Tutorials Point, n.d.). An abacus looks like the image below.

Figure 1. Abacus, first calculating device

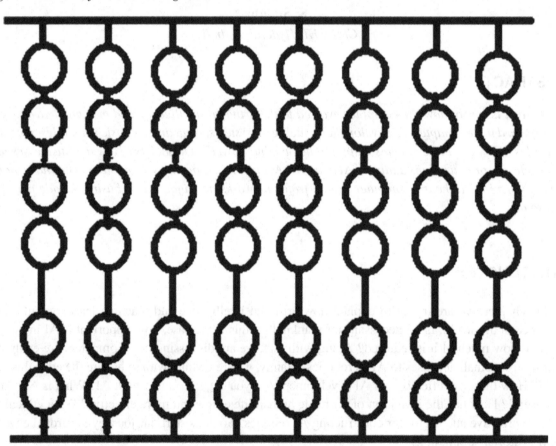

Humans improved the calculations by an abacus to some small calculating machine known as the calculator as inventions and requirements were noticed. This machine is used for some mathematical operations that need to be done quickly and easily to save time. The calculator looks like the one in the below figure.

Figure 2. The Calculator

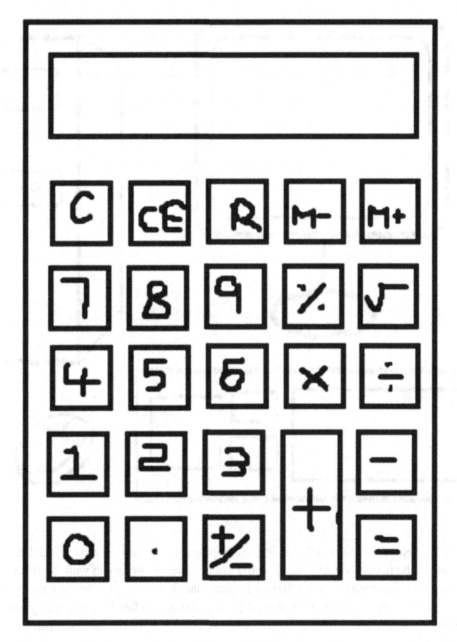

Along with calculations of numbers using combinations of alphabets and the concept of a typewriter, the scientists invented the first computer. This machine is used for both calculation and typing purposes. These machines were invented to make human work easier and faster to calculate. As inventions and research were done in science and technology, they moved to the computers, of which there are many types, like microcomputers, mainframe computers, and supercomputers. The man can complete many tasks more quickly. This computer is a piece of electronic equipment that accepts input from input devices such as keyboards. This data processes and displays the output on the monitor of the computer. The computer is faster than a human, so it replaces humans (Tutorials Point, n.d.).

Figure 3. The First Computer

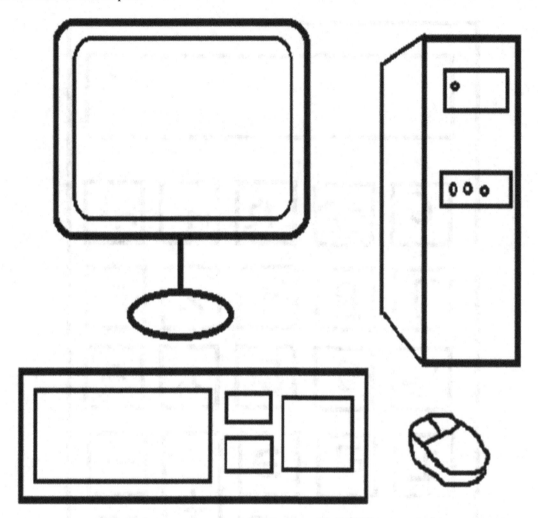

The man has invented these many things in the computer branch and then extended them towards the organization where he is working. His mind would not be quiet, so he began walking toward one of the many computers. As one computer is sufficient for one man, but many people are able to use it, then it is extended to many computers. The man started computerizing his fields. Then, many branches of his organization are computerized and need to share the data from one part of the organization with another part of the organization. To make it clear, the production department of the organization is used to share data from the stock department. As a result, only computers began to share data. Another example from the university: in the physics department, people began sharing data with other departments, including electrical. Then, within the university, a small network was started for sharing data and resources (Computer hardware, n.d.).

As the world's population grows, so do human requirements and needs. Many businesses and working environments are improved as a result of this. As a result, the need for computers is expanded from one organization to many. The computers were restricted to one organization, and then the organisation wanted to share the data, exchange the information, and share the resources. To achieve this, they implemented networking. This networking allows users to share data, send data, and exchange resources via information systems, among other things. Many technologies evolved as human needs increased and people began to use computers more. Many companies evolved in various sectors of science and technology, like the software industry, health care, manufacturing, pharmacy, banking, and so on. Computers have been used to study many aspects of human life and industry. Life became easier and faster with the introduction of computers and can compete with the outside world rigorously and effectively. The productivity of the industry also increased by making it more computerized or automated (Computer hardware, n.d.).

Figure 4. A Network Overview

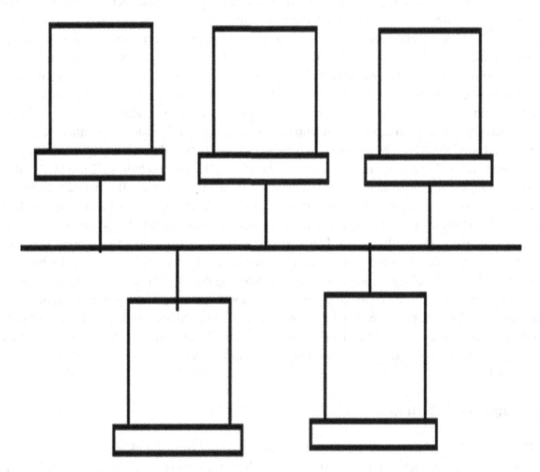

The AI is able to provide solutions to different kinds of problems that exist in the real world. By existing with the problem, only humans can think innovatively in terms of technologies to build new ones like AI, ML, robotics, deep learning, and block chain. To find a solution to the problem, a new innovative technology or combination of technologies is used. But in this chapter, we are discussing AI and ML (Kruse et al., 2013).

Nowadays, we can control the entire world with the tip of our fingers. Each and every work is based on human intervention. Machines, such as computers, can complete tasks on their own. To accomplish this, computers can work independently and make decisions on their own, just like humans, which expert systems can do. Expert systems can be invented for many applications to make human life easier and faster, increase productivity, and maintain competitiveness in the world with the invention of new technologies like artificial intelligence (AI) and machine learning (ML) (Kruse et al., 2013).

Artificial intelligence is one of the biggest technologies in computer science and information technology. AI is primarily concerned with using machine intelligence to increase productivity in an effective and efficient manner. This technology made the machine think like a man, act like a man, and take effective decisions without human intervention. The AI is being used to make better decisions and solve problems like a human. It means that a machine is able to think like a man and take decisions to solve problems without human intervention. This is done to increase productivity in various industries, like the software industry. These types of AI machines can also be invented to predict future problems that exist in the real world. With the invention of AI and ML, many problems in the health care industry can be properly predicted in order to provide better solutions and diagnose patients' diseases. In this AI and ML, a new technology called Computer Vision is used to receive objects and make precise decisions about the patient's diseases in order to cure and treat them correctly. In order to maintain competitiveness in the industry, the AI can be improved to increase productivity and efficiency by decreasing errors and repetition and giving intelligent automated solutions to real-world problems (Kruse et al., 2013).

Now we will see how these capabilities can be achieved with the help of ML. To add intelligence to the machine, we must implement machine learning algorithms in the machine so that it can think like a human. Machine learning is used to program the computers to find the optimal solution to a problem that exists in the real world (Mavridis, 2015). The optimum solution will increase the performance criterion by comparing it with the old technologies that are introduced in Computer Science and Technology. A model can be defined by using some parameters, and learning concepts are used to execute a computer program to get an optimal solution to the problem. The model defined may be predictive to make future predictions, descriptive to gain knowledge from massive amounts of data from around the world, or both.

Many applications are implemented and deployed to make human life easier and faster by utilizing AI and ML. There is so much useful technology in the world that we need to understand its benefits and drawbacks.

Advantages of AI and ML

- Easier and Faster: Nowadays, many tools are available to learn AI and ML, apply them, and use them. So it became very easy and faster to learn. In the real world, AI and ML are extremely demanding technologies. Every industry is being replaced by AI virtual assistants (Advantages and Disadvantages of Artificial Intelligence, n.d.).
- Saves time: AI and ML can be used to predict the results faster than humans. As a result, it saves more time than human labor by lowering labor costs effectively and efficiently through the use of cutting-edge technology (Advantages and Disadvantages of Artificial Intelligence, n.d.).
- Increases Productivity and Quality: As AI and ML replace human jobs. By implementing virtual assistants to operate any machine in large industries, we can increase productivity and improve the quality of our products (Advantages and Disadvantages of Artificial Intelligence, n.d.).

- Improves Efficiency and Accuracy Effectively: In the medical field, to diagnose a cancer patient, we need accurate results to predict. These accurate results can be achieved with the new subfield of AI and ML called computer vision. It captures the images of the patient with accurate data (Advantages and Disadvantages of Artificial Intelligence, n.d.).

- Faster Decision-Making: If the machines can think like a man and act like a man, then they can easily make decisions faster to solve any problem. With this faster problem-solving ability, work can progress very quickly.

- Future Prediction Becomes Simple: Using satellite technology, AI and ML can predict accurate weather forecasting results by predicting natural disasters. Then, it is possible to take better decisions effectively and efficiently to overcome it (Advantages and Disadvantages of Artificial Intelligence, n.d.).

- Optimum Solution to Increase Performance: In the financial sector, mostly in banking and the stock market, they are dealing with numbers only. With specific and correct data, they can be used and predicted for optimum trading by AI and ML machines, and the performance of the stock market is increasing day by day in the market.

- Data can be saved and secured in an organization so that hackers and fraudsters cannot access the data. AI and block chain technology together will provide better solutions for global security. Even AI and ML can decide which model is better for generating good revenue or profit from the market. They can apply different permutations and combinations to predict the solutions rigorously in order to achieve success (Advantages and Disadvantages of Artificial Intelligence, n.d.).

- Less Error Rate: Humans can make mistakes, but virtual assistants powered by AI and machine learning cannot. In the sense that a man can make mistakes but not a machine. By doing so, it reaches greater accuracy with a greater degree of precision. Nowadays, robots with high-quality supervision abilities in industries can achieve estimated results quickly and effectively by applying different techniques. As a result, work performance is improved with a very low error rate (Advantages and Disadvantages of Artificial Intelligence, n.d.).

- Humans can only work for a limited number of hours before becoming exhausted and tired. Virtual assistants, on the other hand, can be available around the clock to complete any task efficiently and effectively with the same accuracy without exhaustion or tiredness.

- Knowledge gathering is faster and deeper: Machines can easily gather knowledge in greater depths than humans. As a result, they can easily analyze and draw conclusions that effectively solve any problem (Advantages and Disadvantages of Artificial Intelligence, n.d.).

- The Best Techniques Can Be Learned: The human can store the data within his limitations, but AI and ML models can store huge amounts of data and can apply many techniques and combinations of techniques to solve any problem in the world. And in any field, it can apply its techniques and its expertise to find solutions. Any field like education, healthcare, manufacturing, construction, banking, and so on. Able to face any challenges in any field to solve the problem (Advantages and Disadvantages of Artificial Intelligence, n.d.).

Disadvantages of AI and ML

- Replace human jobs: Nowadays, everywhere we look, we are looking into automation, i.e., computerization, because of AI and ML around the globe. As AI and ML technology evolves, it is like adding a supplement to existing jobs. Most of the researchers found that most of the greatest things happened when humans and machines worked in combination. Together, they can create wonders by using technology and combinations of technologies (Advantages and Disadvantages of Artificial Intelligence, n.d.).

- Implementation Cost and Time are Very High: The cost of AI and ML models is based on the different kinds of portfolios. As per the premises, AI and ML tools are affordable nowadays. In some offices, most people are using machines powered by AI and ML. The price of each depends on the time it takes to develop and the complexities involved in the development. These tools are very expensive because there is a lot of code, mathematics, statistics, probability, science, and technology involved. As a result, these are effective AI and ML tools. Many companies are able to afford to enhance their processes, business transformation, and enterprise to maintain their competitiveness in the market by using AI and ML automation tools (Advantages and Disadvantages of Artificial Intelligence, n.d.).

- Leads to Unemployment: This aspect affects the globe in two ways: directly and indirectly. by the new technological inventions in computer science and technology, by directly replacing the workers that they were previously performing in the organization. As technology demands more AI and ML models, there is a need to develop these to fulfill the market's requirements. From a production standpoint, many labor requirements arise to implement or develop. This is for increasing machine productivity, which requires a large number of people to complete. This leads indirectly to unemployment from the productivity side (Advantages and Disadvantages of Artificial Intelligence, n.d.).

- More time to deploy software: the time taken to deploy AI and ML models depends on their complexity to implement. This refers to how long it takes to develop that model. Most complex models will take more time to deploy, while easier ones will take less time. The AI and ML model takes more time in data collection and preparation, and then analysts can analyze the data to build the AI algorithm to deploy. In today's competitive world of business, it is necessary to collect clean and clear data to develop a good modern machine learning model with good deep learning. Historically, developing and deploying AI and ML process models takes longer than good deep learning (Advantages and Disadvantages of Artificial Intelligence, n.d.).

- Increase in Human Laziness: It is the one assumption or belief of some researchers that the introduction of AI and ML makes people lazy and impatient. However, AI and ML experts and developers are optimistic about the future of this rapidly evolving technologies.AI and machine learning reduce the need for humans by eliminating many job opportunities. According to some experts, AI and ML machines are causing humans to become physically inactive, with less activity and less work, and even less intelligent towards their work (Advantages and Disadvantages of Artificial Intelligence, n.d.).

- Not adhering to and comprehending any ethics: Over the last ten years, experts in AI and ML technology have been developing safeguards for protecting against potential hazards. This means not following any ethics and principles during the development of AI and ML models, like not using the correct ethical patterns. These expert systems exist to supplement rather than replace human intelligence (Advantages and Disadvantages of Artificial Intelligence, n.d.). When AI and ML systems make decisions, society still bears many responsibilities because disastrous consequences may occur around the world, including loss of state or capital, human health, or even human life. This type of prediction becomes extremely difficult for humans; how can it be accomplished with these expert systems? When AI-based decisions must be made in a process involving lawyers, regulators, and citizens of society, the consequences must be considered.

- Lack of Creativity: The AI and ML systems can create but cannot be creative. It is like human replication to replace human work and intelligence. It is having the ability to read human emotions and understand those emotions. not having the creativity to create the required skill based on societal standards. AI and ML systems can never replicate or replace human consciousness, emotions, or creativity.

- The experience for improvement is not there: AI and ML are implemented with cutting-edge technology, but they are designed to aid in more personalized consumer knowledge and cannot replicate human experiences. Each and every consumer has his or her own knowledge and experience about things, and according to their knowledge, the AI systems are not developed to get or learn new instant experiences. So instantly, AI systems are not able to improve their experience. AI and ML work best if they are balanced with consumer knowledge and serve to improve the experience of great inventions like manufactured goods (Advantages and Disadvantages of Artificial Intelligence, n.d.).

- Unable to Control: According to the AI Institute study, humans cannot protect or prevent AI and ML from developing their own preferences. The scientists and researchers were shaping the technologies in accordance with human values and needs, but instead they are not allowing technologies to shape humans. Some aspects of AI and ML systems are extreme in comparison with humans and cannot be controlled. like the storage of data, but faster than humans (Advantages and Disadvantages of Artificial Intelligence, n.d.).

- Machine degradability: AI and ML machines cannot think like humans, and they cannot create anything. These machines do not have feelings. The machines are created, developed, implemented, and programmed by humans. For it is programmed to do only that work and is restricted beyond that, unable to take any decisions. Machines cannot be programmed to respond and question in the same way that human's do. If these systems are intended to perform work in their respective fields, such as agriculture, health care, politics, law, or socioeconomics, then only that work will be performed. The agriculture machine cannot do wonders in the healthcare domain, and so on. Even though the machine can perform tasks faster than a human, store massive amount of data, solve complex operations, and perform tasks accurately, effectively, and efficiently, it is still a machine. The equal importance of a human is not given (Advantages and Disadvantages of Artificial Intelligence, n.d.).

ETHICAL STANDARDS

The AI is like a fantasy world turned into reality. Like a fantasy world character, how they act in a novel story or in a comic world becomes reality, so does human imagination, which is created by AI and ML. Once upon a time, a man imagined that any machine could perform any human task; how would life be then?

AI and ML are being developed in such a way that they will change our daily lives in domains like the service industry, transportation, health care, education, politics, public safety and security, and entertainment. These systems were never introduced in such a way that they built trust or reliance, were appreciable, and respected human and civil rights. These AI and ML models need to follow some fundamental human principles and ethical values and protect the well-being of the people, the community, and the globe (Artificial Intelligence (AI) Ethics, 2020).

There is agreement amongst the research community that trust in AI and ML can only be achieved through fairness, transparency, accountability, regulation, and so on. Other issues would have an impact on how much trust we have in the AI and ML models we use. It means how much a human is able to control the AI and ML models and his role, or by giving the intelligent systems more autonomy (Artificial Intelligence (AI) Ethics, 2020).

The main and final goal of AI and ML machines is to create or develop a machine that itself follows an ideal ethical principle or set of principles to help society, individuals, and organizations in the real world. It is simple to explain theoretically, but applying ethical principles to AI and ML agents is difficult and challenging. Without any unbiased ethical standards or principles, how is it possible to implement or train machines ethically? How can we implement certain intelligent machines to understand ethical principles in the same way humans do? First, we need to train or program in such a way that the robots can understand what harm is. What are the consequences of that harm, and how can it be remedied? Each and every situation in human life is not planned and comes in unexpected ways, and solutions are also not planned early. On the spot, only the man had to solve the problem without harming anything or anyone by keeping ethical standards or principles under control. Likewise, only machines can be trained to solve any problem without harming anything, like society, humans, or a nation. For this, we need to train the machines according to ethical standards that apply universally or globally. To deploy such ethical standards in a machine, it is necessary to decrease the information irregularities between AI and ML programmers and the creators of ethical standards. While applying to invent these ethical standards for AI, ML, and intelligent systems, researchers and practitioners would try to better understand the existing principles so that they would be able to apply those ethical standards or principles for research activities and help train developers to develop ethical AI and ML models (Artificial Intelligence (AI) Ethics, 2020).

AI and machine learning (ML) are new and challenging technologies that are gaining traction in society. To improve our lives in business, industry, organization, politics, health care, education, and so on. These AI and ML systems are improving tremendously in every aspect of the real world. And it is improving at rocket speed by crossing the human limit and expectations as well. So AI and ML are virtually replacing the whole of human society and business very sensibly (Artificial Intelligence (AI) Ethics, 2020).

This uncontrollable AI and ML in society has raised some ethical, social, and political issues that require immediate action and the attention of the various stakeholders, namely the government, education, industrial, organizational, political, and policymaker roles, all of which are on the verge of being phased out. This AI and ML invention as automation and technology is nicely swallowing the aforementioned jobs and unexpectedly affecting and going out of human control. So it is necessary to follow this problem or to overcome it, but first we need to know: are these sensible issues or ethical issues? Now, we are going to discuss in detail the ethical issues of AI and ML in the present and future technology implementations that need to be understood (Artificial Intelligence (AI) Ethics, 2020).

Fairness

When combined with sensitive data, AI and ML provide a more in-depth look into our personal and professional lives. As humans, we are naturally vulnerable to biases, also called unfairness. The human is responsible for developing AI and ML models; there is the possibility for human unfairness or bias to be embedded in the intelligent systems that the human builds. It is a major responsibility of the development team and researchers to reduce the algorithmic bias or unfairness through research and data collection, which is representative of a huge population in the world (Barocas et al., 2022).

In real time, the research team must explore and recognize from where the bias of data becomes noticeable, from where it is initiated, and how it can be diminished. That should bring to notice both intentional and unintentional biases. The designing and development process without intentional biases can be reviewed by the schedule team to avoid unintentional biases. The unintentional biases must include stereotyping and confirmation bias. To raise awareness of user-defined biases or issues, introduce a feedback method or open a conversation with users to raise consciousness of user-defined biases or issues (Barocas et al., 2022).

To solve this unfairness or bias, we need to pose some questions to the research team. They are, but how can we identify and address the unintentional biases that we introduce when designing and developing AI and ML models? How do we introduce some methods and techniques that replicate that change in the ongoing data collection? How can we collect the best feedback from the users to correct unintentional biases in design or decision-making algorithms (Barocas et al., 2022)?

AI and machine learning algorithms are influencing every aspect of human life. These algorithms create movie proposals; recommend products to purchase, and so on. They are highly used in banking sector scenarios such as loans and in employment hiring decisions. Machines and humans make different decisions; machines do not become exhausted, bored, tired, or uninterested as easily as humans do. The machines can take decisions like humans without any vulnerability or unbalanced or unjustified appeal to the globe. While taking decisions, machines cannot be impartial to anyone; they will just do their work according to the algorithms fed into their implementation (Barocas et al., 2022).

The decision-making process can sometimes differ based on group fairness, individual fairness, or anti-discrimination and counterfactual fairness. A human can distinguish between these, but a machine has difficulty with them. These decision-making categories are again based on some AI and ML algorithms; we are specifically mentioning any one of them (Barocas et al., 2022).

Fairness and equality issues arise in the banking and finance sectors, criminal and illegal justice, public or social science programs, health care, employment, marketing, product advertising, product promotion, and so on.

Awakening of AI and ML

Many new technologies, such as AI and machine learning (ML), will be invented, developed, and created in digital marketing. So we need to be aware of them to improve our world. Organizations and many research centre institutions and metrics, according to those skills, are lagging and need to upgrade by awakening the technologies. The business cannot deal with these rapid changes and adapt to new technologies in the world; we must reinvent the skills required to develop, recreate, and accelerate technologies. By replacing some of the human labor, the visualization of AI and ML motivated the human potential for inventing new things through creativity and innovation. When humans and machines collaborate to achieve greater things while keeping humans in the loop, humans can do a lot more. Instead of looking for ways to replace humans and human work and degrade skills, AI and ML systems can add a lot of value and remain indispensable. There is a lot more mission to learn new technologies to increase the economic aspect of the organization with revolutionary changes in the workplace and in the organization as well.

The awakening describes the productivity explosion due to the ability to restructure the organizational process, methods, and workforce skills. This technology alone will not improve productivity. By means of these investments, organizations are able to restructure their business processes and practices to see continuous progress in productivity and performance. The awakening will give us advanced technologies to improve organizational and community levels in the real world.

There is a need to learn new incredible technologies as people become more aware of them. Training centers for humans and machines are required to create learning centers or education centers. Learning increases humans' and machines' ability to generate new discoveries, fostering the belief that society can use technology without harm. By striking into the worker's creativity, leadership, and training abilities.

Cyber Security and Ethical Hacking

This is a very deep-learning technology in the real world. Here we are discussing a few points about this topic. The AI and ML systems are used in cyber security and ethical hacking to rapidly and easily study huge amounts of data and millions of actions and to recognise many unusual types of threats, from malware zero-day vulnerabilities to dangerous actions that might lead to a phishing attack or the download of malicious code. And it is to prevent malicious behaviour from occurring, which reduces security risk and prevents data theft from hackers on the internet (Sani et al., 2019).

As technology advances on a national and global scale, humans can operate or work from the comfort of their own homes; however, internet access is required. The various activities and services are being offered through the internet only, like online banking, online trading, mostly working with social media, and so on. To do so, many users' public and personal data is available globally on the internet. Many technologies are now designed in such a way that they can directly attack the user's data, which is known as threatening, cyber attack, or cyber hacking (Sani et al., 2019).

The cyber security with AI and ML ensures that the organization and its people can use the internet freely. By utilizing AI and ML in approaches to risk management, training actions, assurance, technological services, and telecommunication systems, as well as all communicated and/or stored information or data in the cyber environment, cyber security issues many policies, tools, best practices, guidelines, and security safeguards.

All of the problems that exist on the internet are solved by the organization's implementation of cyber security with ethical hacking in AI and ML. The organization works towards the appropriate standards and the combination of solutions needs to be determined in order to generate the exact solutions to the problems. According to the research on this topic, policymakers recommend the following application of AI and ML to cyber security and ethical hacking:

Enhancing collaboration between policymakers and the technical team will provide the key for organizational-level representatives to do the best investigation, prevention, and mitigation of potential malicious uses of AI and ML in cyber security.

Certain policies, ethics, and standards underpin encouraging the sharing of cyber security-related information and data. Sometimes it is necessary to share the data of private and public sectors, like the legal and political realms, and any governance framework that would enable legal certainty when exchanging the data or information.

Focusing on the reliability of AI and ML, rather than its trustworthiness, in standards and some certification methods like improving the AI and ML systems' robustness, developing AI and ML applications in the organization, testing the data through those systems, and parallel monitoring and controlling the behavior with the original systems

Implementing and testing the security requirements for AI and ML systems in public policies Obedience to ethical and safety principles that are set by the organization is the basic requirement of AI and ML applications in certain critical sectors.

Evaluating how the use of AI and ML systems in cyber security and ethical hacking research and operations would be affected by the current and future regulatory environment

Suggesting suitable testing before an AAAI and ML system is developed in order to evaluate the related security risks Such testing can be done to avoid attacks' ease and damaging opportunities' cost (Sani et al., 2019).

The Big Tech Monopoly

The technology giants are the main active drivers behind the characterization of the global markets by the growth in digital services. A technological monopoly occurs when a single organization controls all technological methods and techniques required to create a certain invention or has limited privileges over the technology used to develop it. Technological monopolies occur when the product or service that the organization provides has legal protection in the form of a patent or copyright. The big organizations like Google, Apple, Amazon, and Microsoft organize their innovation activities toward the technology monopoly. They continuously monopolize knowledge while outsourcing the new innovations to other organizations and research institutions (Jacobs & Wallach, 2021; Steed & Caliskan, 2021).

The big tech monopoly is increasingly a natural monopoly. The natural monopoly phased by us is that we only experienced being completely blocked in homes during the COVID-19 pandemic. Because of the virus attack, no one can go outside to buy or conduct any transactions for our daily lives. In this kind of situation, if robots are implemented, they can move around and do transactions like humans. They can take decisions and involve themselves in many problem-solving mechanisms. The robots are like virtual assistants that can communicate, think, take decisions, and so on, leading to transformational change in the world over the last 3 years.

This type of technical monopoly happens, and they are so scale-driven that, once they get to that scale, it's very, very difficult to maintain competitiveness in the global market. In the organization, there are many different types of monopolies, such as private monopolies, which are firm monopolies owned and operated by private individuals. This technical monopoly has many advantages, like economies of scale, which are related to lower average costs from the increased scale of the organization. There is a chance of making a lot of money with the technology used for research and development known as "dynamic efficiency." The monopoly power can encourage investment in order to obtain a patent of reward. The organizations that become technological monopolies are very efficient, successful, and innovative in the global market (Jacobs & Wallach, 2021; Steed & Caliskan, 2021).

Once the technological monopolies occur, there are many disadvantages, too, like higher prices for consumers for the products. The people's incentives will be lower to cut costs. and even less inventive in terms of innovation and investment in new technologies. The new technological monopolies can gain the political authority to defend their vested interests. There is less choice for customers in the market because of a lack of knowledge regarding the new technology launches.

Here we discussed how technological and intellectual monopolies are built and organized to maintain competitiveness in the global market. Only the big organizations are able to compete with and adjust to these monopolies earlier than the small-scale organizations. It is necessary to expand the knowledge of patent or copy rights for new inventions and research works. They establish scientific collaborations with universities and other research industries to share knowledge regarding intellectual property and big tech monopolies in the global market.

Human-Machine Team Up

The most promising prospects from AI and ML will come knocking on the door of mutual learning between humans and machines. While AI and ML will ensure that human capabilities are supplemented and that organizations are redesigning and restructuring, many organizations are still finding that the results fall short of their expectations. This is a little bit disturbing and frustrating, but not unexpected. Often, organizations are trying to develop AI and ML systems without having understandable knowledge of how the technology will interact with people (Jacobs & Wallach, 2021; Steed & Caliskan, 2021).

In the past few years, a number of studies and research projects have examined how organizations use digital capabilities to become more competitive, including a recent study on human-machine collaboration in a cross-organizational trend. Finding the perfect balance of machines and humans can be extremely difficult for research-based organizations. The technologies of AI and ML systems, as well as how humans and machines interact and collaborate, are changing dramatically. These interactive data interactions are expected to yield huge benefits in advancing productivity and reducing human tiredness and strain in many strange areas, such as organizations, the traffic industry network, and the healthcare industry, where the environment is very complex and dynamic. The machines can perform any number of tasks repetitively with high speed and high accuracy without getting tired. On the other hand, humans are able to adopt a high level of perception capabilities and display higher flexibility than machines.

By collaborating with machine and human abilities, there is some possibility of connecting the strengths of both humans and machines, increasing the number of applications and purposes of the industry. Human and machine collaboration in organizational gathering and disassembly in official environments will shift from a fixed hierarchical relationship to flexible collaboration on shared data and information in team structures (Steed & Caliskan, 2021).

Always, teams will require trust between the team members, in the same way trust is required between humans and the AI and ML intelligent agent machines. Here, they maintain the peer-to-peer relationship to work together. First, the human workers must trust the machines to carry out any collaborative work. Conversely, the machine should also trust the human team members. The machines can be used for constructive work rather than destructive or distracted work. They are cognitively and emotionally developed to take over any work done by humans.

Human and machine can collaborate by supporting one another with new technologies, research, and inventions rather than dominating one another. Even though he has limitations, the man is a creature of AI and ML machine intelligence agents. Similarly, when compared to humans, the machine has some limitations. That's why they should work together as a team to bring bigger, more innovative inventions to the globe.

Inequality and Wealth Gaps

Automation, such as robots or AI and ML systems, will automatically increase working capacity and make it faster and more accurate than humanly possible. The inequality is not only limited to, but also associated with increases in the organization's wealth production and capital income. As AI and ML systems replace human work and workers, they are unable to generate income, neither for themselves nor for humans or organizations. As technological changes occur around the globe, globalization of the market to maintain the competitiveness of the industry will increase the value of the minimum wage (Jacobs & Wallach, 2021).

Machines can easily replace jobs that were previously done manually. As a result, automation is easily replacing low-skilled and uneducated workers. By replacing the machine, the organization may generate income rather than the machine. AI and ML can help in healthcare for life-critical applications with the aid of radiology in the process of detecting tumors by catching them in the MRI scans before the doctors are able to recognize them (Jacobs & Wallach, 2021).

The rise in income inequality is caused by automation, which affects low-wage jobs more than higher-wage jobs, resulting in an excess of lower-wage workers and higher unemployment relative to market labor demand. The one myth is that wage or income growth among less educated labor productivity is slow. Automation machines can be programmed to take higher risks than humans, so inequality has declined.

Machine Autonomy is Under Threat

The AI and ML machines are autonomous to the extent that they can take individual decisions without any human intervention at the moment. And in critical situations, they also have the capability to intervene, suspend, or adapt. As far as the dangers of giving machines autonomy are concerned, AI and Ml systems have been given the ability to learn and express some autonomy. Otherwise, controlling these systems will become a very tedious process. It can be dangerous to predict how these AI and ML systems will operate with their independence in mobility and decision-making, and these systems are equipped to solve problems using solutions unknown to the human being operating them. The autonomous technologies in AI and ML will significantly increase productivity at the organizational level by improving the overall effectiveness and efficiency of the system. Even these systems can reduce costs and improve overall safety and security in their respective fields, like the mining industry (Jacobs & Wallach, 2021).

In the area of AI and ML, the term "autonomy" generally means the capacity of AI and ML agents or intelligent systems to operate independently without human intervention or guidance to take any decisions or actions. To invent these kinds of autonomous systems is the primary goal of these AI and ML fields. When AI and ML systems are exposed to unknown fields or areas of scope, they can learn how to handle sensor situations, adapt their behaviors, and act intelligently to solve any problems in the situation without changing their algorithms. In autonomous systems, AI and ML are when an application can study and develop from data or information and understanding, without being individually programmed to do so and with minimal or no human intervention (Steed & Caliskan, 2021).

The four elements that are the components of the autonomous systems are sensing, perceiving, understanding, analyzing, taking decisions, and obeying those decisions. The autonomous systems have healing, self-configuring, self-optimizing, and self-protecting characteristics. Too much autonomy in machines can also have a negative impact on the outcomes of organizational teams. Certainly, members of failed teams are concerned that too much autonomy raises team members' stress levels and keeps them under pressure to meet and exceed leadership expectations.

While developing these autonomous AI and ML systems, we need to concentrate on the following questions and objectives as well:

What do you consider to be AI, ML, and autonomous technologies?

Did you plan to use AI, ML, and autonomous technologies in your research and study?

How will these autonomous technologies affect the human teams in the organization?

What are the organizational standards and safety measures taken when developing these autonomous technologies?

What are the major impacts of implementing or developing these autonomous technologies?

What are the advantages and disadvantages of autonomous technologies?

What are the main hazards or challenges encountered while implementing these autonomous technologies?

It is very difficult to predict, ensure, and verify the predictability and reliability of autonomous technologies. These factors depend on the technical design and nature of the environment of the system, as well as the complexity of the action to be taken to solve any problem. Many AI and ML system functions make it difficult to test many impossible cases in order for the user to know whether these technologies will meet their expectations and produce the desired output. As a result of these factors, algorithm development is unpredictable, and they also become biased toward the relevant technology to develop (Steed & Caliskan, 2021).

Accountability

It is necessary to discuss some accountability issues while keeping the aspects of AI and ML and human society in mind. What are the challenges to accountability posed by AI and ML algorithmic systems? How can we protect accountability in algorithmic decision-making? From a public organizational perspective, what are the current challenges that can help human society and the limitations they pose for public accountability (Jacobs & Wallach, 2021; Steed & Caliskan, 2021)?

Accountability is an important part of human life, as well as in AI and ML for effective decision-making. The robots can take decisions effectively without human intervention. As humans can make decisions, robots can also make decisions, ask and answer debate questions, and so on. Many are arguing that AI and ML are of fundamental importance to the insertion, equality, and variety of both AI-based and human-prohibited communications, and that any human-facing interventions are planning to transform human development, performance, and knowledge. However, some argue that AI and ML are natural phenomena and that biases materialize the experimental and theoretical models of AI algorithms. All these materialized from experimental and theoretical models and are affecting human-controlled educational systems and interventions. The main differences between AI and ML models and human decision-making involve a large number of perspective-applicable judgments, individual flexibility, compassion, and complex ethical judgments that AI and ML lack. However, we contend that AI and ML models accurately reflect human decision-making and are thus critical to understanding intelligent systems. These kinds of understandings of human beings also predictably summarize the biases emerging from human intellectual and experimental limitations. With the aforementioned debate of people against AI and ML in relation to a specific outline, one can undeniably see a future for comprehensive and accountable government (Jacobs & Wallach, 2021; Steed & Caliskan, 2021).

AI and machine learning (ML) are currently receiving a lot of attention from social media and the press, both for their potential to handle challenges ranging from policing to healthcare to education and for the obvious threats they pose to human identity, independence, and future functioning. In the current view of AI and ML, there is a tension between human replacing machines (AI) and human assisting machines (IA).The human replaced this differentiation in the spirit of the questions about the implications of AI and ML for society and for the future of human independence, comfort, and safety (Jacobs & Wallach, 2021; Steed & Caliskan, 2021).

The current evolution of AI and ML from a purely scientific field or real-world applications has placed AI and ML at the heart of human decision making without the opportunity to employ the best understanding of the nature of those implications or to define the appropriate accountability procedures to monitor and protect against any problems or harms caused by AI and ML models to society. There is a need to direct the responsiveness in this case because current AI and ML systems have a proclivity to interpret and reinforce social inequalities and injustices (Jacobs & Wallach, 2021; Steed & Caliskan, 2021).

In a theoretical sense, accountability refers to being responsible for someone else and being compelled to clarify and substantiate action and function. Accountability is defined in this perspective as a relationship between a performer and a medium in which the performer is responsible for explaining and justifying his or her character, the medium can pose some questions and pass judgment, and the performer may face the consequences. The meaning of accountability practice is explained in three phases: information, explanation or justification, and consequences. These are the main effective requirements of accountability towards an external world of authority. To manage accountability effectively and efficiently, one needs, first and foremost, information. This serves to justify informational asymmetry by providing costly insight into performer decisions and actions (or functions). Accountability is mainly and closely related to answerability and decision-making, and a key part of it is the explanation or justification of how a human being can answer any question and answer naturally by thinking about his or her views. The political committee in Parliament is required to hear and submit their opinion about their societal improvements as organizational performers and be able to ask questions and look for explanations for their society's pragmatic failings. In this context, the information and justification requirements would serve as the fundamental foundation that allows the accountability environment to review and judge whether the decisions were appropriate and correct. For effective accountability to occur, the extent of failings must be identified, and the proper solution to the consequences must be extracted. Any negative judgment would result in a negative impact on society as well as on the human being. And in this regard, the performer or human needs to undertake some remedial actions to address the negative judgments, address the failures, and afford assistance to those relevant people adversely affected by the negative actions (Steed & Caliskan, 2021).

This discussion clearly states that the standards set by this AI and ML are always very clear and clean to society. The observation of this public accountability involves some of the standard trade-offs along with the challenging goals, claims, and normative decisive factors, as well as the exterior prospects or expectations of the human being. Accountable AI and ML will accord relevance and context to AI and ML algorithms that are useful in the public sector, especially from an accountability viewpoint given the confidence in non-habitual high-risk circumstances. When we speak of "performer" in an accountability sense, it is necessary to consider how the man is performing from a conventional perspective as a human performer and not as a robot. The man is able to perform, handle, or achieve very consciously and generously in any high-risk or sensitive situation. So, in spite of those extensively overestimated media stories, there has been some little noticeable progress towards "Artificial General Intelligence (AGI)" or "human level AI"—the responsibility to use algorithms, methods, and the latest technologies in the public sector essentially lies with human performers. The AI and ML providers, as well as public sector adopters and many users, would produce, acquire, and organize algorithmic system operation, techniques, methods, and suggestions (Jacobs & Wallach, 2021).

The accountability of AI and ML in the education sector: they are designed and used to assist learners and educators by

Providing relative security zones for learners will accommodate and even reduce any prominent differences or difficulties.
acting as a mirror in self-exploration and the development of self-regulation competencies
offering a medium for understanding and sharing individual viewpoints and individual experiences as the basis for development acceptance, consideration, and appropriately adapted educational support.

Transparency

AI and ML are intelligent system tools, and it is difficult to explain the machine learning's built-in processing. The AI and ML algorithms are unclear, even for the developers. This AI and ML restriction to the human's capability to identify with the technology leads to considerable information irregularities among AI and ML professionals and users. Trust is the foundation of all relationships, whether between humans or machines, and it is a prerequisite for real-world recognition (Jacobs & Wallach, 2021).

From a socioeconomic, legal, and scientific technology standpoint, transparency is linked in AI and ML. First, we will discuss the theoretical differentiation between transparency in AI and algorithmic transparency. Second, how transparency is used in different applications, i.e., across multiple disciplines, over time. Third, we'll talk about how the transparency expresses a theoretical image of more universal consequences, linked to positive associations that may have normative effects. Finally, we get a clear picture of a possible classification feature related to transparency (Jacobs & Wallach, 2021).

Theoretical transparency is an important feature of AI and ML, which are a combination of extremely interconnected systems and algorithmic transparency. The terms "algorithmic transparency" and "algorithmic decision-making" have developed into accepted terminologies in the significant study of AI and ML. On the other hand, there is a lack of transparency in computer science and technology, the law, and public observation. This is connected to the reality that intelligence alone is defined in at least 60 to 70 different ways. On the other side, ambiguity is also part of the algorithmic concept when considering its problematic nature in critical research. The algorithmic problem-solving approach in computer science and technology is a finite, step-by-step description of how to solve a particular set of problems that exist in the real world. As a result, the concept of algorithmic transparency becomes much narrower than the concept used in governance issues relating to accountability (Jacobs & Wallach, 2021).

In relation to the issues of unfair effects of algorithmic systems, it is frequently the case that the detailed algorithms and program code are very unintentionally intended to differentiate in a harmful path. Here, the challenge is that the relations between the data and the algorithms used to develop AI and ML systems are likely to be unidentifiable from the perspective of the program code. This is also a very tedious and important issue to be considered in the combinations of AI and ML algorithms, the required prepared or implemented data, and the decisions they inform. The main point here is to focus on who the AI-system or algorithmic decision-making should be more transparent for. There are so many digital platforms available around the world that we must focus on which data must be transparent, either qualitative data transparency or quantitative data transparency, which are primarily used by supervisory authorities to develop methods and algorithms for governance and defense (Jacobs & Wallach, 2021).

Because humans are unable to interpret the decision-making of machines due to the inbuilt code of AI and ML models, AI and ML models are evolving without human intervention, supervision, or assistance for decision-making. The big question and concern right now is whether humans can control AI and ML models. Preferably, humans can expect AI and ML models to imitate humans, or to do exactly what humans want them to do. Here is a challenge: if humans treat AI and ML models ethically, is it ethical for us to be able to control what actions they take and how they make decisions (Jacobs & Wallach, 2021)?

The metaphorical study of transparency has come to denote the future of modernized technologies, which are obviously complex and expanding towards social and legal challenges. That's why this concept became the accepted foundation that is necessary to highlight and needs to be discussed. Transparency focuses on openness and explainability, i.e., it is framed with positive values described by open data, open source, open algorithmic concepts, open technology, open access, and open science and is explainable and understandable to the society's open government. As a result, transparency primarily focuses on the policies and algorithms used to develop AI and ML systems, which are essentially open secrets to society, the government, and the public. Everyone can use these systems without fear of harm and with faith in their goodness. The AI and ML are there to build new technologies, not to harm the world in business, industry, business, technological, socioeconomic, human life, politics, law, or society (Jacobs & Wallach, 2021).

When we talk about the transparency of AI and ML systems, we're talking about both explainability and understandability. When these systems are assessing users' trust in applied AI and ML, an assumption is made that the challenge or issue of transparency is all about how ordinary people are able to understand the explanations of AI and ML systems. even how they are able to evaluate and trust their relationship to the service, product, or company that manufactured these systems. That is why explainable AI and ML are based on evidence that many AI and ML applications are not used in practice due to a lack of trust and proper explainability, similar to humans. To achieve a relational understanding of transparency, many studies based on social science, including law, have been conducted for a long time to build trust and its connections to transparency and its required conditions. Many legal, technological, and conceptual challenges are undertaken in social science. By drawing on research in law, the social sciences, and the humanities, a set of aspects of transparency are listed below (Jacobs & Wallach, 2021).

Legal aspects of proprietorship include the program code, data penetration in competitive markets, including trade secrets, and an aspect of international opacity.

The need to avoid misuse, too much openness of the program code, and openness can lead to misunderstandings about the purpose of AI and ML enabled processes. There are chance factors in system gaming and obstinate effects of confession that affect social media security and data distribution.

Data and algorithm user literacy, which indicates the ordinary human's basic understanding capability, has the undeviating cause of transparency when applied to AI and ML systems. This indicates the computational thinking of a normal human being and how much one is educated about using these AI and ML systems in the real world.

The mathematically founded algorithms for communication symbols and metaphors may be dependent on translations of human thinking and imagination in terms of language understandings .In other words, the decisions or user agreements made by the automated machines are easily understandable by the user. There is a lot of difference between machine explainability and human explainability in concern with sociology, politics, business, and every day contrastive, selective, and social decision-making.

The complexity of data ecosystems and markets trading in the stock market, called consumer data, has an unquestionable effect on transparency; it relates to how personal data can be obscured from its origins and how AI and ML systems are able to give an explanation in concern with transparency.

Now we have a look into how the transparency of AI and ML systems affects businesses. To ensure the accuracy and impartiality of intelligent systems, businesses must understand that AI and Ml systems make their decisions on their own or with the assistance of tools and techniques. Transparency in AI and ML is often used interchangeably with explainable AI. It concentrates on that model, which is open code and visible. As it comes to the transparency or interpretability of AI and ML systems, a data scientist and researcher are able to see the techniques and mechanisms that make these systems work efficiently and effectively by including the individual algorithms that are used to work and the data that are used to construct these systems (Jacobs & Wallach, 2021; Steed & Caliskan, 2021).

Transparency in AI and ML is critical for developing more trustworthy intelligent systems that can be applied to global markets and society at large. Here are the trust and issues of accountability that are taken into account in relation to the different values of the concept, including the deeper concept of transparency. The individual algorithms or components used in AI and ML systems are transparent. So, it is less unclear than the term "algorithmic transparency." Algorithmic transparency typically assists government organizations in providing clear data and information about the algorithmic tools they use and why they use them. It means being open about the tools and algorithms that support the systems (Jacobs & Wallach, 2021; Steed & Caliskan, 2021).

REFERENCES

Advantages and Disadvantages of Artificial Intelligence. (n.d.). https://www.javatpoint.com›advantages-and-disadvantages

Artificial Intelligence (AI) Ethics: Ethics of AI and Ethical AI. (2020.) *Journal of Database Management, 31(* 2), 74-87. doi:10.4018/JDM.2020040105

Barocas, S., Hardt, M., & Narayanan, A. (2022, Nov. 20). *Fairness and machine learning: Limitations and opportunities.* https://fairmlbook.org/pdf/fairmlbook.pdf

Computer hardware. (n.d.). In *Wikipedia.* https://en.wikipedia.org/wiki/Computer_hardware

Jacobs, & Wallach. (2021). Measurement and fairness. *Conference on Fairness, Accountability, and Transparency*, 375–385.

Kruse, T., Pandey, A. K., Alami, R., & Kirsch, A. (2013). Humanaware robot navigation: A survey. *Robotics and Autonomous Systems*, *61*(12), 1726–1743. doi:10.1016/j.robot.2013.05.007

Mavridis, N. (2015). A review of verbal and non-verbal human–robot interactive communication. *Robotics and Autonomous Systems*, *63*, 22–35. doi:10.1016/j.robot.2014.09.031

Sani, A. S., Yuan, D., Jin, J., Gao, L., Yu, S., & Dong, Z. Y. (2019). Cyber security framework for Internet of Things-based Energy Internet. *Future Generation Computer Systems*, *93*, 849–859. doi:10.1016/j.future.2018.01.029

Steed, R., & Caliskan, A. (2021). Image representations learned with unsupervised pre-training contain human-like biases. *Conference on Fairness, Accountability, and Transparency*, 701–713. 10.1145/3442188.3445932

Tutorials Point. (n.d.). http://www.tutorialspoint.com/computer_fundamentals/computer_quick_guide.htm

Chapter 8
Agricultural Social Network:
A New Direction Towards Sustainable Development

Subrata Paul
Brainware University, Barasat, India

Anirban Mitra
iD https://orcid.org/0000-0002-6639-4407
Amity University, Kolkata, India

ABSTRACT

India is one of the world's largest food producers, creating the sustainability of its agricultural system of global significance. More than 67% of the Indian population still depend on agriculture or its allied sectors for their livelihood. There lies a requirement for the discussion on balancing or enriching the agriculture production in order to bring in food security for the growing population. Agriculture in recent years is facing great downfall due to uncertain monsoons, decline of soil fertility, population pressure, lack of support services, and so on. To overcome these, there is a need for communication such as dissemination of right information on right time to the farmers, which would help them towards advancing their knowledge on agriculture. The growth of active internet users over the past few years shall make this task easier. The chapter shall make an in-depth analysis on the need for the development of an agricultural social network and shall also present a prototype of the proposed system.

1. INTRODUCTION

In past few years, Online Social Networks (OSNs) have cause complete influence on the daily lives. Communicating with others and communicating knowledge with individuals, organizations, and groups is beneficial. It is gaining enormous popularity and expanding quickly across the world. A social relationship that is either assumed or established between people, families, houses, villages, neighborhoods, territories, and other social units is referred to as a "social network." Connections or ties are the terms used to describe the connections between nodes in social networks. Connections or ties can be used to

DOI: 10.4018/978-1-6684-6821-0.ch008

symbolize resource transfers, affiliation, authority, economic exchange, and technical diffusion. Connections might be undirected like Facebook or LinkedIn or directed like Twitter.

Since two-thirds of the inhabitants relies on agriculture for a living either explicitly or implicitly, it plays a very significant role inside the economic development of a country like India. Producing food, fiber, or other plant or animal commodities utilizing farming practices that preserve the natural world, including the ecosystem, public health, human cultures, and animal welfare, is known as sustainable agriculture. With such a type of farming, it is possible to grow nutritious food without endangering the potential of coming generations doing the same.

Similar to human and physical capital, social capital is crucial for a nation's economic progress.

Since a large portion of our country's population relies on agriculture, there seems to be a deficit in information and knowledge sharing that is needed to create a sustainable agricultural ecosystem across the entire nation. Through OSN, a nationwide connectivity has been made possible by the usability of mobile and smart phones. There are numerous ways for using the OSNs to accomplish the goal. It is not merely a time- and money-saving option. Through extraction of data from the OSNs and evaluating the data through numerous Social Network Analysis (SNA) and Data Mining (DM) techniques, the OSNs is being used as a teaching and knowledge tool for farmers as well as stakeholders. SNA aids in a deeper understanding and utilization of social capital. An effective and sustainable agricultural supply chain can indeed be built with the aid of ICT (Information and Communication Technology (ICT) and SNA.

1.1 Agriculture in India

The bulk of the population in India still relies on agriculture as their primary source of income.

During recent years, this economy's reliance on agriculture has suffered a severe decline. In order to achieve food security, the agricultural sector must make significant progress. During past few years, the agriculture industry has experienced declines beyond just productivity. Throughout 1950 to 2015, this industry has experienced a significant decline in compared to any of the other manufacturing and service sectors. Merely 16 to 17 percent of the GDP would be produced by the sector where fifty percent of the labour force is employed, compared to 20 and 55 percent for the other two. Reduced soil fertility, productivity strain, poor land ownership, socioeconomic issues like subpar advertising, and an inadequate infrastructure are only a couple of minor causes of decreased productivity. The Prime Minister of India renamed the Department of Agriculture and Cooperation into Department of Agriculture, Cooperation, and Farmers Welfare on Independence Day 2015 in response to a unique development aim that focused on the welfare and prosperity of farmers. This would encourage agriculture and its related industries to become not just ecologically sustainable but also socioeconomically sustainable in aspects of farmer social welfare. (Welfare, 2016).

1.2 New Media Technologies and Development

The internet has created a number of opportunities for new media technologies to connect with people and reach them in many spheres of human life. The telephone is a piece of technology that has completely changed modern media. Mobile phone adoption is substantially higher in India, as it overcomes all skills gap hurdles and affects all demographics, including those in rural and urban areas. The idea of advancement that satisfies the needs of the present generation without jeopardizing those of the future is known as sustainable development. In order to feed the expanding world population and preserve the environment, sustainable agriculture must first establish stable rural economy. The essential players in overcoming this difficulty are the growers (First, 2019).

The modernization of agriculture is based on the adoption of new agricultural techniques. While the results of the government's extension activities are less than ideal in several emerging economies. Most landowners find it difficult to comprehend and use modern agriculture techniques, which reduce their effectiveness and slows down agricultural development. In actuality, a crucial element in farmers' embrace of agricultural technology has traditionally been disregarded. A social network is that. Recent research suggests that users' adoption of technology may be easily influenced by the actions of those in their social media network.

This chapter is organized as follows. In section 2, the authors have presented a review of the related works done in this area. In the next section a citation has been presented regarding the way social media has emerged as an efficient mode of communication. Further, a discussion has been made regarding the way social media can be leveraged to enhance businesses in present scenario. A discussion has been made regarding the particulars of the proposed system in the latter section of the paper. Finally, the chapter ends with a brief conclusion.

2. LITERATURE REVIEW

There has been various works over the past few years that have focused on the requirement of Social networks within the agricultural domain. Few of those researches have been discussed within the present section. Within the paper (Ramirez, 2013) authors have made an illustrative discussion on the collaborative efforts that occur inside social and professional groups, as well as tenure relationships. Research has shown that one of the most important factors affecting the implementation of irrigation techniques is membership in organizations. Technology is passed forward through tenant or familial relationships after being initially implemented by central farmers. The findings imply that ownership interest influences whether a farmer engages in organizations. An interdisciplinary technique within the research work has been done by (Zaveri *et al.*, 2016) for investigation of the climate change difficulties which confronts India's agricultural system, as well as the efficacy of massive water infrastructure projects aimed to address these difficulties. Demonstrations have provided on the development of agricultural production will demand rising volumes of unsustainable groundwater, even within regions where precipitation rises associated with climate change.

Further, the research by (Abid *et al.*, 2017) has discussed the report's results that discusses on the fact that farmers have noted an increase in pests and diseases as well as a decline in crop productivity as a result of climate change. Farmers' main actions include modifying crop kinds, sowing dates, input combinations, and tree planting. The primary adaption restrictions are an insufficient information, finances, and resources. Community-based groups mostly provide agricultural equipment and marketing advice to farmers, while private organizations provide weather prediction services. The network analysis has a weak representation of public bodies. Additionally, it was discovered that while agricultural financing, post-harvest services, and produce distribution dominated the financial support network but had poor connections, agricultural extension were important institutions in the network for adapting to climate change. It was also discovered that farmers migrate from low-cost, quick solutions to advanced solutions when the availability of solutions at the farm level increases. Related works has been done by (Chelladurai, 2020) which comprehends the ways in which new media has been used by farmers in Kancheepuram

District, Tamil Nadu, and discovered their perceptions of and obstacles to using new media. According to the research, the majority of farmers are more aware of and have access to new media. Additionally, it was discovered that media technology were extensively used for environmental information, market patterns, like pricing and stock availability, as well as weather forecasts and information connected to the environment. The Kancheepuram District's farmers have been found to have a favorable opinion of the role that new media can play in advancing agriculture.

(Bruce *et al.*, 2021) has discussed a case study that has offered a proof of robust social network structures, highlighting the significance of schools, transportation hubs, and cattle markets in establishing and sustaining these networks. The infrequent inclusion of these domains in agriculture policy emphasizes the necessity for a broader framing of questions. According to the research, social network analysis is an effective method for examining agricultural systems' adaptability since it can reveal previously undiscovered components. (Albizua *et al.*, 2021) has investigated farmers' views of the implications of their forest management, as well as the influence of social information flows on their management, using a case study in a farmer especially in Navarra, Spain, that is experiencing agricultural intensifying as a result of the use of large-scale irrigation. It was discovered that those that use contemporary technology are conscious that their management techniques frequently have adverse social-ecological effects; in comparison, more traditional farmers likely to be conscious of their favorable effects on intangible benefits including those connected with customs, cultural traditions, and climate regulation. It was also discovered that farmers' understanding of nature's connections to people's co-production, as well as their land management practices, influence the characteristics of social networks within the agricultural community. This has significant ramifications, including the fact that farmers generally are more conscious of their environmental impact—rely on intelligence which is managed by contemporary farmers—who are more intensive—and could endanger sustainable farming methods in this area. In addition to it, (Chaudhuri *et al.*, 2021) has pointed the prevailing viewpoints on the significance of social networking and learning among farmers in agricultural transformation, with a focus on India. In India, cyclical interconnections among water (irrigation), food (agricultural), and energy have caused severe socio-environmental disasters that call for targeted policy solutions, such as groundwater depletion, energy shortages, irrigation system failures, food insecurity, and loss of property. Participative action through farmers' social networks is a powerful tool to build resiliency in these situations. The study illustrates the importance of social learning for the adoption of new paradigms using examples from both India and around the globe (new technology, crops, cropping methods, etc.). The amount of farmer-to-farmer interaction (friendship or peer-advising network) has a direct impact on how quickly new information or concepts spread. The report also identifies important challenges to building functioning networks across farming communities. The Water Users' Association in India is given special attention in order to list the developing issues over farmers' participation in participative irrigation management systems. Ultimately, the study served as an appeal to the relevant agencies, research organizations, and stakeholders in India to establish meaningful partnerships for the generation of new knowledge in the principles and application of social networking and learning and to find contextualized ways to incorporate them into the advancement matrix.

The study by (Wolfram *et al.*, 2021) has employed Social Network Analysis (SNA) as a technique to find potential prospects for better weather and market advice distribution to rural areas, as well as to investigate the relationship among farmers' availability of information and output and selling price. As a case analysis, we used SNA to analyze weather and market information networks, as well as farmers' friendship networks, as prospective proxies for exchange of information. According to our findings, the friendship network in coastal Bangladesh was decentralized and interconnected, with a few isolated farmers, but the weather and market information systems relied on specific key sources of information. It was demonstrated that a number of social economic factors are highly connected with farmers' networks; nevertheless, there was minimal evidence of a connection among information availability and productivity and selling price. Works on (Bruce *et al.*, 2021) has leveraged interview sessions and social network analysis, to investigate a situational analysis of Orkney, Scotland, a relatively remote environment. This study provided proof of robust social network dynamics, highlighting the significance of schools, transportation hubs, and cattle markets in establishing and sustaining these networks. The infrequent inclusion of these disciplines in agriculture policy emphasizes the necessity for a broader framing of questions. According to the study, social network analysis has emerged as a useful method for examining agricultural systems' robustness since it can reveal previously undiscovered components.

3. USING SOCIAL NETWORKING FOR AGRICULTURAL DEVELOPMENT

Although social media has been used presently as an effective tool in variety of areas, the following advantages compels the use of social network within the agricultural domain:

i.   Fast Extension Advice
ii.   Agricultural Price Fluctuations
iii. Agricultural Innovations' Spread
iv.   Making Markets Available to Farmers
v.   collaborating among departments
vi.   connections to organizations and professionals
vii. responses from farmers (Sivaraj and Philip, 2017)

The mounting growth of Social media marketing within India has been due average the overall quantity of mobile subscribers in India that has upsurged to 952.34 million, which has bolstered the popularity of social media. In addition, the following elements also exist:

i.   At 88.45 percent, active mobile subscribers are now more prevalent (842 million).
ii.   Rural users made up 41.89 percent of all mobile subscribers, while urban consumers made up 58.11 percent of all urban subscribers.
iii. With 112 million users, Facebook (a sizable young population).
iv.   There are 70 million active WhatsApp users in the nation each month (Ramamritham, 2006).

In order to have a brief illustration on the fact of usage of Social Media, the following points further illustrates the view:

i.   Social media has served as a source of information for sustainable food production: For so-called "eco-consumers," or individuals who predominantly purchase sustainable products, platforms like Instagram, Facebook, have immensely emerged as an "information medium" and a source of information in the field of sustainable food production. By using social media, 41% of people aged 16 to 64 may find out about products from eco-consumers, according to the GlobalWebIndex

Table 1. Comparison of Traditional media with Social media

Characters	Traditional media	Social media
Effectiveness	Expensive and takes longer period	Time & cost effective
Literacy	Literacy of Client is mandatory	Can be easily accessed by Illiterate persons.
Feedback	It is single way procedure	Being a two-way procedure; feedback can be composed
Linkage	Weak linkage among agricultural allowance & farmers	Direct interaction among specialists & farmers
Need based technology	Absence of emphasis on location specific, target group necessities	It emphasizes on demand driven, underprivileged areas necessities

2019. The brands themselves come in second (34%) among these information sources, followed by video sites (25%) and self-governing evaluation sites and blogs (both with 22%). The pertinent target audience is largely searching online for details about sustainable food production!

ii. With good reason: WWW contains a wealth of information. Additionally, it is relatively simple to launch projects and campaigns via social media on subjects like politics and sustainability, for instance in the field of sustainable food production: A social media profile is solely required for the said purpose. The sharing features by themselves, along with the various hashtags and, of course, paid content, can reach thousands and millions of users with an engaging and planned topic. The concept will be a sure-fire accomplishment if the issue is being nailed, and in the ideal scenario, creation of the visible part of the budget and its distribute is not required. (Gugler, 2020).

iii. Content marketing for different channels: Social media is especially fascinating for complicated information in the context of content marketing, where subjects like ecological sustainability can be designated: Admittedly, there are other platforms for narrative, including in-depth YouTube videos, quick-moving images on TikTok and Instagram, and text-filled images on Facebook, Instagram, Pinterest, and TikTok. The intended audience can also be precisely narrowed down as per their areas of focus for sustainable food production with the aiming that is feasible via social media. When there is a lot of material, social media communication as part of a content marketing strategy gets intriguing in terms of providing challenging but important subjects like sustainable food production in a captivating and comprehensible way. A comprehensive, ecological, and moral perspective to agriculture that is motivated by the richness of distinctive ecosystems and geographies would be more appealing to younger consumers in general. Numerous "tales" about this segment can be found online by the relevant businesses!

iv. Social Media & Sustainability: Meanwhile, the concept of regenerative agriculture is gaining attraction, and its execution, alongside other major ideologies including climate protection and ecologically responsible food and beverage packaging, will be increasingly featured in blogs and on social media in the future. Regenerative agriculture begins with organic farming techniques and progresses to methods that enhance and reconstruct the soil and the environment (Gugler, 2020).

4. ADDITIONAL TECHNIQUES FOR IMPROVING FARM BUSINESS THROUGH SOCIAL MEDIA

In order to consider social media as a future prospect, there are 7 lessons that would be helpful if social media is to be considered from the business perspective during its working with farmers:

1) Have a Social Media Plan. Establishing the potential results is the first step in creating a successful social media strategy. Consequently, before choosing a certain social media platform, start by keeping the end in mind (s). What actions do you want people to do after reading the information you present, and how many people would you wish to reach? What metrics will you use to determine your performance (e.g., higher sales, more farmers attending your workshops, more YouTube views)? The 5 "Ws," or what, where, when, why, and who, can be used as a starting point for a social media strategy.

2) Focus on the Content. Initially, social media experts recommended mandates including x posts or tweets per day or week, but in reality, posting engaging and/or timely content should be the objective to be impactful (and prevent alienating people). It is best to remain silent in case there is nothing interesting to say.

3) Keep it Concise. Twitter's 140-character limit is a great trimming tool for limiting keyword density. Maintaining your message brief is crucial in the hectic world of social media. Less people choose to click the "see more" link. Coherent video material is key as well; according to YouTube analytics, the first 15 seconds (yes, seconds) of the video are crucial in determining whether people will watch it or not. Considerations are also done on the decision of watching a video which is to be watched if it is longer than 8 minutes.

4) Find Your Voice. Since social media is by definition "social," unlike "traditional" media, it is crucial to be personable in order to connect with your target demographic. It is very annoying to find people making false, artificial, or dry posts.

5) Use Photos and Numbered Lists. According to researchers, when text or oral knowledge is supplemented by an image, our brains recall that knowledge twice as well. This is built into our brains and probably developed as a result of survival strategies used in the savannah, when the majority of the important risks to human life were seen spatially. Numbered lists are particularly useful in social media since it appears that our brains also enjoy patterns. According to some experts, our memorization has a capability of just approximately seven informative units, so it's recommended to maintain lists between three and seven points in length.

6) Collaborate and Curate. These days, everyone is busy, so as a time management technique, consider ways to work with someone or edit your content on social media. Every six to eight weeks, someone from our colleague blogs while a pledge can be taken in in writing a blog article. Work is divided and distinct perspectives are being provided.

7) Measure your Work. Social media plan is checked and its performance is assessed. Many social media sites include built-in stats that let you know how many views, shares, etc. a post has received. If a particular social media platform isn't living up to your expectations, there could be ways to fix it (like some of the lessons mentioned above) or it might make sense to switch to another one. However, it can be difficult to make decisions if you don't track your efforts (Heleba, 2013).

The figure 1 mentioned below shows the mounting trend for the active internet users in India from 2015 to 2025. The figures shown in the future years are all projected figures.

Figure 1. Mounting trend for the active internet users in India

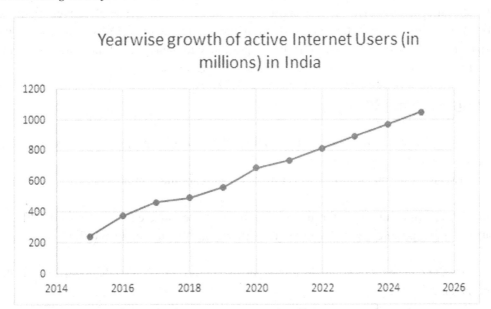

5. PARTICULARS OF THE PROPOSED SYSTEM

5.1 Objectives

The system's major goal is to research the connections between different assets being used promote sustainable agriculture in the social media spotlight before creating a knowledge base, learning platform, and agricultural worth in network for the assistance to society. The aims can be enumerated as following:

1)   Development of social learning platform for sustainable agricultural development

Establish a focused OSN opportunity to exchange knowledge and build connections between resources for sustainable agriculture, such as water, soil, seeds, weather, and other resources, and then use the network to educate farmers and stakeholders.

2)   Development of Knowledge base for the usage of SNA and numerous DM procedures

Obtain information out from OSN by following connections and sharing of information. Utilize various network analysis techniques, such as clustering algorithms, centrality analysis, and other data mining techniques, to analyze the retrieved data. Utilize the gathered data to create a pest control and disease prevention system. (To make improvements, GPS and image analysis methods could be applied.)

A long time information intermediary between the research and customer systems has been regarded as agricultural extension. In recent times, it has been conceived of as part of an Agricultural Knowledge and Information System (AKIS) which represents a variety of stakeholders with collaboration. A network of businesses and individuals connected by business, professional, or social ties makes up an agriculture knowledge and information system (AKIS) (Rollings, 1988).Networks for exchanging agricultural knowledge and information have become significantly more complex. The effectiveness of extension systems is severely threatened by this. Understanding the complexities of AKIS will require a powerful, cutting-edge analytical instrument. An amazing opportunity to analyze such intricate network systems is provided by social network analysis (SNA) (Wasserman & Faust, 1994).

5.2 Existing System Study

Employees conversing over the phone and via online chat. Emails and manual file management were used for the distribution of legal documents.

There are two ways for an employee to get in touch with another employee:

(1) Phone: When communicating through phone, the call is connected to the desired staff.
(2) Chat: When people become accustomed to online chat, it would be read online.

When sharing legal papers by email, an employee must upload a file and the receiver must download a file from the email.

As a result, file sharing chores in the current system are handled via email.

5.3 Project Definition

The company's varied employees to interact on social networking and bulletin boards, and they can also access the capabilities of the live community website

i.   Registration: It is simple to enroll in this application when employees desire to add to it.
ii.   Manage profile: Employees can quickly make the changes they want to their profiles.
iii. Employee searches are simple thanks to the availability of employee data.
iv.   Employees can search for other employees and then send an invite to participate and add their own account.
v.   Employees can send and receive scrap.
vi.   Employees can easily upload photographs to their personal employee accounts using the photo gallery.
vii. Chat: Interacting with online workers is simple with the use of chat.
viii. Feedback: If staff members wish to speak with other staff members, they would like to do so by sending an email to the administrator.

5.4 System Design of the Project

5.4.1 Data Flow diagram

Data-flow diagram provides a procedure for the illustration of the flow of data through a process or system. Alongside, it also arrange for information regarding the output and input of every entity and the process. It doesn't have any control flow, there doesn't exist any decision rules and loops.

Level 0 or the Context Diagram for the proposed system shall be demonstrated in the Figure 2 below.

Figure 2. Level 0 Data Flow Diagram

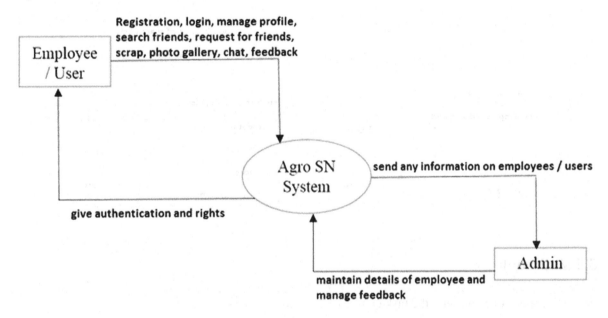

After getting a rough estimation of the data flow within the system, the authors tried in illustrating the information flow to a deeper extent through the Level 1 Data flow Diagram in figure 3.

5.4.2 Sequence Diagram for Search Employee or User

Sequence Diagrams are communication illustrations that features the way operations are carried out. They depict interactions among objects in the framework of an association. These illustrations are time focus and shows the instruction of the communication graphically with the use of vertical axis of the diagram to represent time what messages are sent and when. A sample sequence diagram for searching an employee or User has been depicted in figure 4.

Figure 3. Level 1 Data Flow Diagram

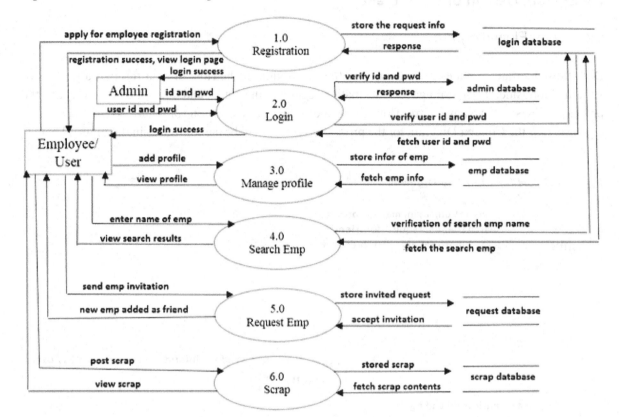

5.5 Methodology

For the purpose of Sampling, the task can be performed in three different ways:

- Location chosen at random which is also referred to as Purposive sampling This kind of selection, also known as "judgmental sampling," depends on the researcher's judgment when determining and choosing the people, situations, or events that can offer the most information to meet the study's goals. For the sake of work, the residential area of the author has been chosen as the area of sampling.
- Sampling of Institutions which is basically performed through stakeholder analysis, focus group discussion, Venn diagram. The Venn diagram can be expanded visually without the moderator or assistance moderator experiencing cognitive exhaustion. For instance, the moderator and assistant moderator could keep track of the responses from categories (e.g., gender, ethnicity). Alternately, the moderator or assistant mediator could monitor individual patterns by assigning each member of the focus group a different letter (for example, corresponding to the participant's name) or number (for example, corresponding to the seating chart), as opposed to observing subgroup response patterns. In addition, the number of distinct responses each focus group participant provided to a given question might be indicated by a subscript under each letter (or a superscript above each

Figure 4. Sequence diagram for searching an employee or User

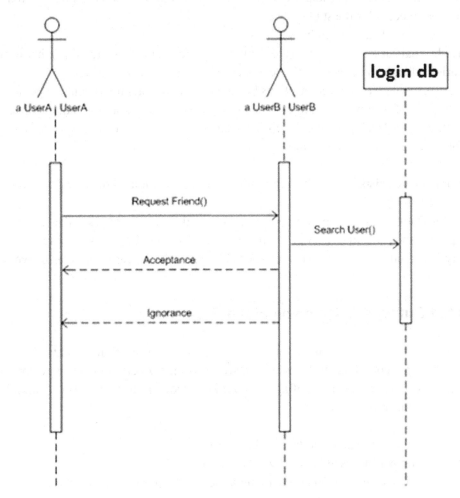

letter) (e.g., C4 = Member C made four individual contributions to the group's response to the question). 10 to 12 Institutions from the residential area of author was chosen for the said purpose.

- Snowball sampling will be used to sample ties, and egos will be chosen from an ego-centric network. This sampling strategy entails a primary data source proposing additional prospective data sources that could take part in the investigations. The only way a researcher can create a sample using the snowball sampling approach is through referrals. As a result, this technique is also known as the chain-referral sampling technique. When a population is unknown or rare and it is difficult to select participants to assemble them as study samples, the snowball sampling approach is frequently used. This sampling strategy can continue indefinitely, like a snowball growing in size (in this case, the sample size), until the researcher has access to sufficient data to analyze and come to definitive conclusions that can assist a company in making educated decisions. (Röling and Engel, 1990).

Considering the phase of Data Collection, the following points are to be considered:

- Comprehensive listing of participants is scheduled to be carried out within the desired workspace that shall be selected for the study.
- Two categories of data were gathered:
  - Traditional survey information (pertaining to performers' characteristics) that would include various details in concern with the actor being chosen for the study.
  - Network (relative to the connections between actors) evaluating relationships (for networks). This type of data would mainly focus on the actors with whom the main actor is concerned with so as to develop a relationship. This data would be used to develop a tie among the actor for the exchange of related information.

Whether or not a tie exists between two individuals or organizations is the most often utilized metric in SNA. (Yes=1, No=0)

The phase of Data Analysis is performed with the two different techniques that includes Standard survey data processing tools and SNA graph-theoretic approaches. Ucinet6-For comprehensive social network analysis (Freeman, 1994) or Net draw-For drawing networks can be used as network designing tool.

5.6 Expected Output and Outcome of the Proposal:

In terms of coverage size, density, number of ties, cliques, and centralization, the data is to be characterized. The usage of IR network centrality scale (degree/ closeness/ betweenness), key core institutions that are already involved in the spread of agricultural knowledge information were found. Each of the metrics are further illustrated as under:

i.   Network Size: total amount of nodes within a network
ii. Density: the number of ties alienated by the amount of pairs
iii. No of ties: total no of interconnection among nodes /actors/egos.
iv. Cliques: a network subset in which the actors are more closely and intensely associated to one additional than to other network members.
v.   Centralization: These network measures characterize the degree of inequality or alteration in our network as a percentage of that in a perfect "star network," the most inadequate kind of network.
vi. Degree Centrality is the complete quantity of ties a node has to supplementary nodes. A node is central, when it has the maximum number of ties.
vii. Betweenness centrality: the amount of times a node happens along the shortest path among two others.
viii. Closeness Centrality: "close" if a node lies a short distance from numerous additional nodes (as in being physically proximate) (Wasserman and Faust, 1994; Misra *et al.*, 2015).

If social networking should become commonplace in rural agriculture, significant obstacles must be addressed in the areas of infrastructure, sustainable revenue strategies, societal acceptance, and market connections. The degree to which an intervention meets the needs of those who will be most impacted ultimately determines the effectiveness of any development program. Social networks are created to provide their members a voice and may prove durable for huge development practices, despite the difficulties to scaling them.

Managers who are modernizers rely additionally on the evidences from exterior their communal (exogenous sources) than cash-renters who, as followers, rely mostly on information from within their group (endogenous sources). Information can be categorized as endogenous (internal) or exogenous (external) in association with the irrigation district's learning networks. Renters are probably linked to one powerful player (the landlord) and several other weaker actors (other renters). The farmers' learning networks are endogenous to this tenure-based grouping, which does not encourage access to new information. However, the link between an inventor and an imitator is what allows technology to spread. Learning from the experience of neighbor's supports the adoption decision although for innovators, first-hand information after membership in state and regional committees is crucial in their judgment.

6. CONCLUSION

Throughout the study, the authors have suggested the development of a research prototype for the development of an agricultural social network. Various formulations have been provided in the section of the detailed system design so as to demonstrate the way the data for the proposed is to be collected and the results that shall be generated based on the data. The framework shall enhance stakeholder networking through various types of partnerships and improved climate change adaption. The results that will be generated as an outcome of the system shall also provide a great scope for betterment of this system through efficient institutional arrangement. It will also demonstrate the possible mediators for quicker dissimilation of innovation within the chosen area. Finally the system shall make a way for better decision making, thus providing needed and timely information/ services/ materials through a better extension delivery system.

REFERENCES

Abid, M., Ngaruiya, G., Scheffran, J., & Zulfiqar, F. (2017). The Role of Social Networks in Agricultural Adaptation to Climate Change: Implications for Sustainable Agriculture in Pakistan. *Climate (Basel)*, *2017*(5), 85. doi:10.3390/cli5040085

Albizua, A., Bennett, E. M., Larocque, G., Krause, R. W., & Pascual, U. (2021). Social networks influence farming practices and agrarian sustainability. *PLoS One*, *16*(1), e0244619. doi:10.1371/journal.pone.0244619 PMID:33411756

Bruce, A., Jackson, C., & Lamprinopoulou, C. (2021). Social networks and farming resilience. *Outlook on Agriculture*, *50*(2), 196–205. Advance online publication. doi:10.1177/0030727020984812

Chaudhuri, S., Roy, M., McDonald, L. M., & Emendack, Y. (2021). Reflections on farmers' social networks: A means for sustainable agricultural development? *Environment, Development and Sustainability*, *23*(3), 2973–3008. doi:10.100710668-020-00762-6

Chelladurai, J. (2020). The Role of New Media towards sustainable agricultural development among farmer's of Kancheepuram District, Tamilnadu. *International Journal of Social Research Methodology*, *4*, 29-34. . doi:10.18231/2454-9150.2019.0227

First, F. (2019). *Sustainable Agriculture*. Retrieved February 2019, from Farmers First- A Global coalition for sustainable agricultural development: https://farmingfirst.org

Freeman, L. (2004). *The Development of Social Network Analysis: A Study in the Sociology of Science*. Empirical Press.

Gugler, J. (2020). *How social media influences sustainable food production*. https://www.austriajuice.com/news-blog/how-social-media-influences-sustainability

Heleba, D. (2013). *Making Social Media Work in Sustainable Agriculture: 7 Lessons Learned*. Women's Agricultural Network Blog. Available at: https://blog.uvm.edu/wagn/2013/12/11/making-social-media-work-in-sustainable-agriculture-7-lessons-learned/

Misra, S., Goswami, R., Khawas, T., & Basu, D. (2015). Application of Social Network Analysis for Studying Agricultural Knowledge and Information System: A Case Study in Kalimpong-I Block of West Bengal. Sustainable Agriculture for Food Security and Better Environment At: BCKV, Nadia, West Bengal, India.

Ramamritham, K. (2006). *Innovative ICT tools for information provisioning via agricultural extensions*. 1st IEEE/ACM International Conference on ICT4D, Berkeley, CA.

Ramirez, A. (2013). The Influence of Social Networks on Agricultural Technology Adoption. *Procedia - Social and Behavioral Sciences, 79*, 101-116. doi:10.1016/j.sbspro.2013.05.059

Röling, N., & Engel, P. G. H. (1990). Worldwide institutional evolution and forces for change. In W. Rivera & D. J. Gustafson (Eds.), *The Development of the Concept of Agricultural Knowledge Information Systems (AKIS): Implications for Extension*. Elsevier.

Sivaraj, P., & Philip, H. (2017). Social Networking for Agricultural and Rural Development -An Overview. In *5th Annual Agricultural Students Graduate Conference- Transforming Agriculture for Future*. Tamil Nadu Agricultural University.

Wasserman, S., & Faust, K. (1994). *Social Network Analysis*. Cambridge University Press. doi:10.1017/CBO9780511815478

Welfare, G. o. (2016). *State of Indian Agriculture 2015-16. Krishi Bhavan*. Government of India Ministry of Agriculture & Farmers Welfare.

Wolfram, J. S., Timothy, J. K., Norman, A.-G., Lucia, H., & Jeroen, C. J. G. (2021) Putting social networks to practical use: Improving last-mile dissemination systems for climate and market information services in developing countries. *Climate Services, 23*. doi:10.1016/j.cliser.2021.100248

Zaveri, E., Grogan, D., Fisher-Vanden, K., Frolking, S., Lammers, R., Wrenn, D., Proussevitch, A., & Nicholas, R. (2016). Invisible water, visible impact: Groundwater use and Indian agriculture under climate change. *Environmental Research Letters, 11*(8), 084005. doi:10.1088/1748-9326/11/8/084005

Chapter 9
Scope of Artificial Intelligence in Agriculture:
A Review on Futuristic Applications of Artificial Intelligence in Farming

Divya R.

B.S. Abdur Rahman Crescent Institute of Science and Technology, India

Karthikeyan Ramalingam

iD https://orcid.org/0000-0002-9334-427X

B.S. Abdur Rahman Crescent Institute of Science and Technology, India

Sneha Unnikrishnan

B.S. Abdur Rahman Crescent Institute of Science and Technology, India

ABSTRACT

The world population will increase by two billion in the year 2050 as per the United Nations Food and Agriculture Organization. To meet the needs of people, more efficient farming practices must be identified and implemented, which can increase the yield of crops in the field. A study shows that one in five deaths globally, equivalent to 11 million deaths, are because of poor diet and unavailability of food for the underprivileged. Automation in the agricultural field will not just ease the process but also increase the yield, helping many households to afford at least two meals a day. Implementation of artificial intelligence in agriculture can ease the process. Some countries like the United States, Singapore, etc. use AI in agriculture; they have reported a good impact on the yield of crops. The main objective of this work is to analyze the applications to implement artificial intelligence technology in farming, the advantages and disadvantages of artificial intelligence in agriculture, and the opportunity in India to implement these technologies in farming.

DOI: 10.4018/978-1-6684-6821-0.ch009

1. INTRODUCTION

Artificial intelligence was first termed by John McCarthy at the conference of Dartmouth, even before the term being coined there were a lot of experiments and studies that were carried out in the field. From the day they discovered it, it had brought about plenty of revolution in many fields. (McCarthy, 2006)

The history of machines replacing humans in agriculture falls back to the year 1794 when Eli Whitney invented Cotton Gin, which was used in removing seeds from the cotton fiber. It had made a great revolution in the cotton industry by increasing the speed of the removal of seeds from the cotton fiber collected the machine could remove seeds from 50 pounds of cotton seeds in a single day, computers in the 20th century started the visualization of the artificial intelligence-powered machine in Agricultural sector. (Woodbury, 1960)

At present, there are a lot of researches conducted in this field to find where Artificial intelligence can be implemented to improve agriculture. The government of various countries has provided support to the farmers to implement Artificial Intelligence in farming, as the Government of India in collaboration with IBM will conduct the pilot study with AI for weather forecast and to test soil moisture in Maharashtra, Madhya Pradesh, and Gujarat (Kumar et al., 2020).

There are a bunch of applications for agriculture that involves Artificial Intelligence, many countries have implemented and have seen the best results in the outcome. Artificial Intelligence assists in the weather forecast, soil monitoring, reducing pest infestation and reducing the number of pesticides used in the field, etc. (Talaviya et al., 2020)

2. OBJECTIVES

- To analyze the advantages and disadvantages of agricultural artificial intelligence.
- To analyze the application of agricultural artificial intelligence
- To analyze how the countries around the world is implementing agricultural Artificial Intelligence.

3. EFFECT OF AGRICULTURAL ARTIFICIAL INTELLIGENCE

These technologies improves the efficiency of farming in every field also assist to manage the problems encountered by various government and private sectors. It assists in the improvement of the crop yield in the agricultural field, watering of plants, identifying the content of the soil for efficient planting, crop follow up and management, weeds management in the field, and crop establishment. The AI-based technologies have enabled the farmers to ensure that they yield more production with less investment with high production; it ensures the farmers get profited in the market with the best price for their yield by analyzing the market. In the coming years, farmers will use 75 million connected devices for agriculture. By the year 2050 more millions of people will be benefited. There are several Methods that can benefit agriculture through Agricultural Artificial Intelligence (Talaviya et al., 2020).

3.1 Recognition and Perception of an Image

In recent years the pattern of importance to the unmanned aerial vehicle (UAV) that is drone had been observed and their favourable application for the agriculture field has been vast which includes recognition and surveillance of the crop, human body detection to detect random strangers entering the field, geo localization search and rescue. Because of their vast application and amazing imaging technology which helps in various fields like delivery of best service to photography of crops from which we can identify the pest and the plant's growth and feed the plant with fertilizer or killing the weeds and the pest with the help of pesticides with the amount required. The advantage of using it includes the ability to control the drones with the help of remote control; they are becoming very popular because of the distance from where they can fly by carrying out various applications (Talaviya et al., 2020).

3.2 Skills and Workforce

Artificial intelligence enables farmers to collect a huge proportion of data from the public and the government websites, inspect the data and come up with solutions to many enigmatic issues. Artificial intelligence provides a smarter way for watering plants using an automated irrigation system. Artificial intelligence in agriculture will be a revolutionary change for farmers it can decrease their losses and workloads. The farming field will drastically change in the upcoming years with the help of Artificial Intelligence paving a simple way for farmers to do sustainable farming (Talaviya et al., 2020).

3.3 Boost the Workforce

It is essential to select the best variety and excellent quality of the seed to increase the performance of any plant. The improved technology can help the farmers with this tedious process, by understanding the different factors that the crops depend on for growth like weather, different soil types, etc. Technologies enable farmers to collect information about the type of plant diseases and way to control it, it also educates them about the pest in the field and the way to eradicate. By implementing these technologies in agriculture they can meet the trends of the market, increases the yearly outcomes, satisfies the customer's needs thus with implementing technology farmers can manage the chaotic situations easily and generate good income through farming (Talaviya et al., 2020).

Figure 1. Classification of artificial intelligence

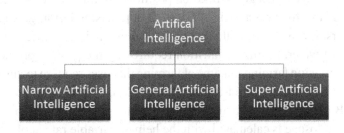

4. TYPES OF ARTIFICIAL INTELLIGENCE AND ITS APPLICATION IN FARMING

There are three types of artificial intelligence, based on the capabilities there are four types under the functionalities and they help in different applications for agriculture-

4.1 Narrow Artificial Intelligence

It is commonly called machine learning; they focus on one area and one problem at a time. This type of Artificial Intelligence is the common type of Artificial Intelligence that we can see in the market today for completing tasks like weather forecast prediction or for product recommendation. Narrow Artificial Intelligence can replicate and can sometimes surpass how humans can carry out tasks. The only type of Artificial Intelligence that is used presently around the world (Sarmah, 2019).

4.2 Artificial General Intelligence (AGI)

Artificial General Intelligence advanced to Narrow Artificial Intelligence, and it implies to Artificial Intelligence which has a "human level of cognitive function." For simulating just a second of neuro-activity the market-leading IBM took 40 minutes. It is hard to develop AGI systems, researchers are trying hard to develop the AGI system (Sarmah, 2019).

4.3 Artificial Super Intelligence (ASI)

This is the point where we think of science fiction. An Artificial Super Intelligence system can surpass any kind of human intelligence. It can make creative decisions, make rational decisions, build relationships, and can choose to be good or evil. If machines can come up with their concepts with AGI, a super-intelligent system will be the next logical step (Sarmah, 2019).

5. APPLICATION OF ARTIFICIAL INTELLIGENCE IN AGRICULTURE

5.1 Precision Farming

It uses information technology in agriculture. Back in the 1980s in the United States, the idea of precision farming began for the first time. The researchers created the first input recommendation for maps for the first time when they started a study on grid soil sampling. The satellite positioning system and electronic communication system can integrate time and position into all the procedures related to farming. Site-specific application of fertilizer is a basic application of precision farming; it also gears towards the best profit for the farmers. It can also be called satellite farming or site-specific farming (Searcy, 1997).

The precise amount of water, fertilizer, nutrition required by the plant is provided automatically in regular intervals. Thus precision farming is a type of farming that uses modern technologies at every stage as a management system. For applying seeds, pesticides, and fertilizers the computer, GPS navigators for the vehicles are used. Based on various factors digital field maps are made with the help of geospatial technology. The fertilizer dosage is calculated with the help of variable rate applications. The fields are monitored remotely with the help of drones and satellites. To detect weather, temperature, moisture, the

Figure 2. Systematic integration of precision farming into existing agricultural structures (Hermann Auernhammer, 2001)

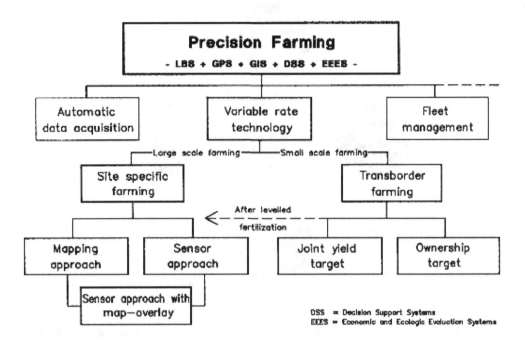

pressure of the field wireless weather sensor with other sensors is used. To analyze, maintain the documentation, and manage the farm efficiently mobile phones and computers are used (Auernhammer, 2001).

5.1.1 Technology Essential for Precision Farming

5.1.1.1 Geographical Information System (GIS)

This application is used for providing the tools to manipulate and display spatial data. It can be used for computerizing maps. Each data set is grouped in an overlay and a new set of data can be produced by combining overlays (like soil type, land ownership, etc). As the data is stored digitally it can be easily modified, copied, and reproduced whenever needed. The decision support systems a powerful management tool that can be constructed if the data sets are then combined with agronomic models (Blackmore, 1994).

5.1.1.2 Global Positioning System (GPS)

Helps in achieving high field accuracy and acts as the foundation for precision farming. It is mostly utilized for auto-steer systems and for preparing geo-reference information like yield mapping. GPS generally guides the machinery to drive along the field with repeatable pathways reduces the probable mistakes committed by the driver and making on-time performance possible for farm operations (Blackmore, 1994).

Satellite navigation is the best solution to enhance the precision, speed, and consistency of implementation. GPS also helps the farmers with keeping the machines in the same pattern of traffic it decreases the skips and overlaps.

Figure 3. GPS in precision farming

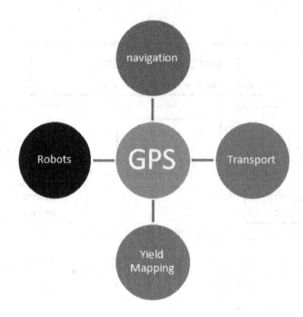

In addition to this it the movement of the machine around the field can be observed on a display screen, it is considered as the most important part of the GPS, this way the farmer has the information about the treated and untreated field surfaces (Blackmore, 1994).

Automated Steering System

The satellite navigation system also gives an alternative to manage the steering of the vehicle automatically. This can reduce errors and gives a better interface for the farmers to control the types of equipment. This provides the best field management. This minimizes the overlap of a row by following the edges of the field.

There are so many different types of automated steering systems that provide various precision levels of field operations. The centimeter system is the most accurate one it works based on the local station with real-time kinematic differential correction. This system needs a base station along with a data communication system. This system can be arranged in the machinery, it can also be used with the help of an electro-hydraulic steering system (Benson et al., 2001).

5.1.1.3 Variable Rate Technology (VRT)

Enables farmers to manage the quantity of input for instance seeds, fertilizers pesticides, and water. It can optimize the planting density and efficiency rate of the products for pest protection and nutrients with the help of VRT. This result in the reduction of cost in the farm, it also decreases the negative influence on the habitat.

This technology applies input at an accurate time along with the location by combining a variable rate technology command system with application equipment to achieve the site-responsive application rate of inputs (Blackmore, 1994).

Figure 4. Pictorial representation of the parts of the chemical applicator with VRT technology (Stephen Searcy.W., 1997)

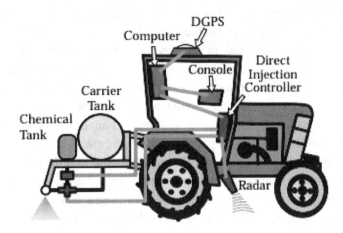

These are the three steps used by variable rate technology for spraying the fertilizers in the field

1. **Management Zones-** Management zones are the parts of the field separated based on where the different materials or chemicals must be applied. The variable rate application must be guided with the specific zones where the machines must apply the materials, or it may result in an error. The first step for applying fertilizer is setting the proper management zones because of its importance. It is very important to provide this information to the VRA system (Auernhammer, 2001).
2. **Atlas-Based and Detector-Based VRA** VRA can be either Atlas-based and detector-based VRA depending upon type of the application. The second step is to set up the application according to the form that is more viable for solving the problem. An atlas is created on the basis of topography and is provided to network as input before network has to perform the function in atlas. Sensors are integrated into variable rate application technology which will be able to find out the information automatically which help deciding what fertilizer to apply in the field in Sensor-based technology (Auernhammer, 2001).
3. **The Decision About Data and Imagery–**The next step after selecting sensor-based or map-based, is determining which type of data must be collected by the sensors and deciding the type of imagery for mapping the field. Some VRA technologies use drones and other imagery systems for detecting information about the field. With the help of sensors major information such as quality of soil and materials, the type of crop, information about the climate, and the speed of the vehicle that is used for applying the fertilizer (Auernhammer, 2001).

5.1.1.4 Geo-Mapping with Sensors and Remote Control

A technology that is used for creating maps for various conditions of soil and crop, like the soil nutrient levels, type of the soil, PH of the soil, occurrence of pest and for much more application the Geo-mapping is used. The soil maps are created by the detectors that are joined in the vehicle also done with help of the detectors joined to a vehicle with satellites, airplanes, or UAV's. The detectors obtain the information from the field for evaluating the condition of soil; crop health assigns the details for the specific fields (Puri et al., 2017).

The geographical atlas will be used by the farmer to accurately detect the events and the changes of the soil properties by providing a corresponding output.

Yield Mapping- Another technique that is very important in precision farming is yield mapping. Variability in the production will be predicted by yield mapping. For measuring and recording the quantity of grain harvesting of the field, in relation to the harvester an yield mapping system can be used. For producing a yield map, a receiver with the GPS technology and a detector for yield must be present with the farmer. Scale, flow meter can be used as a yield monitor. A detector is kept at the passage of the seeds when passing by harvester, while harvesting more grains. The passage rate, moisture content of the seed is measured by this type if system, it changes the measurement for matching the grains place where it was cut and divides passage rate by the machine's gathered area to get the yield per unit of area. The onboard computer receives the yield data and matches with the correct placing of field, information that was kept in the memory of the computer. Information can be transferred to a computer that is equipped with the information stored in the chip can be read with computer equipped with atlas software for production an yield map (Auernhammer, 2001) crop sensing, and analyzing the data collected (Puri et al., 2017).

5.1.1 Advantages of Precision Farming

With Satellite positioning, the field can be surveyed very easily and controlled by the farmer. The yield and soil can be mapped and characterized. The non-uniform fields can be partitioned into micro plots according to their accurate needs for the crop. It reduces the time required in traditional farming and provides a farmer with a feasible solution for the common problems (Blackmore, 1994). The resources can be managed in a better way in way to decrease the amount of wastage. Protects the environment and reduces the risk to the environment especially concerning nitrate leaching and groundwater management by reducing the contamination by optimizing the agrochemical products (Blackmore, 1994).

Precision farming assists farmers to get more yields and to get more profit from their field. This reduces the waste generally produced in the field in traditional farming also increases the quality of the yield. This also proves to be more cost-effective than other farming techniques used (Benson et al., 2001).

5.1.3 Disadvantages of Precision Farming

The techniques that are used for precision farming are still getting upgraded and developed every year so it is very essential to get guidance from a specialist before implanting it in the field, as it costs much to be implemented, if the technology is implemented without any knowledge then it will result in huge loss. The initial investment in precision farming is expensive but serves for the long term so this must be seen as a long-term investment. The implementation may take several years to analyze the data and collect the data according to the need and set everything in the right place. It demands expertise to understand the process of precision farming, for operating and maintaining the machines (Auernhammer, 2001).

5.2. Controlling Pest Infestation with the Help of Artificial Intelligence

Artificial intelligence helps in tracking pests. Artificial intelligence-based image recognition technique or technology is used for identification and eradication of the pest from the agricultural field. Pest can't be fully automated but this technology can assist in detecting the pest and treating the plants with the precise amount of pesticides and fertilizers this helps the farmers to increase the expected yield from their field. Few artificial intelligence-based apps allow the farmer to upload photos and information about the plant to get advice from the experts (Bestelmeye, n.d.). Some technologies are used commonly used around the world to control the pests they are:

5.2.1. Drones Used for Controlling the Pest.

Drones are developed to sense and assist farmers in detecting the pest infestation in the field, there are actuation drones that are developed to control the pest infestation at the hotspots of the infestation. The hotspots of the pest could be potentially directed with the help of a variable application rate of pesticides with a precise amount of the chemicals, this reduces the use of chemicals in the field (Puri et al., 2017).

For spraying pesticides, the aircraft have been used for decades, but the products used to cross the targeted areas and an enormous amount of pesticides get lost to drift. The chemicals used as pesticides can be harmful to the terrestrial along with the aquatic ecosystem; pesticides also prove to be harmful to human health. Whereas the usage of drones in this place can reduce the extra usage of pesticides in the field and can precisely act on the pest hotspots and help in controlling them from ruining the crops further and make the plant healthy (Puri et al., 2017).

5.2.2 AI-Enabled System to Detect Pests

The recent development in remotely sensed imagery and geospatial image processing allows the surveillance of insects and pests in the field. With the help of this technology, the pest in the plants can be easily detected. Researchers have developed technologies that can see the pictures and let the farmers know about the type of pest and how to control the infestation of the pest in the field. This gives about 90% of the accurate solution to the problem faced (Bestelmeye, n.d.).

5.3 Predictive Analytics in Agriculture

5.3.1 Monitoring the Environment and Plant With the Help of Predictive Analytics

With the developing technology, some task is very easy to analyze and is just a touch away the predictive analysis can be used for studying the soil type, climate, landscape, day-to-day market price and farmer's economy in managing the money earned by the farmer. With artificial intelligence, we can predict the suitable time for a crop and the suitable nutrition for a crop and also recommends the best fertilizer for it. Some software developed with the help of artificial intelligence can even suggest the best time for sowing crops (Pundru, 2019).

5.3.2 Predictive Analysis in Weather Forecasting

Machine learning is the basis for weather forecast, in the past, we had to feed in the instructions and it gives results. But now there is a machine learning algorithm we can give the input directly and it gives out the result to us directly. It just needs proper training with the help of data then it can produce the model and features. Using complex mathematical models the weather forecast is obtained. Artificial intelligence-based technologies are being used for the last three decades for weather forecasting is much better than Box-Cox modeling. The simple data-based A.I. model can simulate the entire year's weather condition around the world, which is quicker than the traditional weather models (Pundru, 2019).

5.3.3 Predictive Analytics to Study Soil Type

The type of soil is identified by analyzing the color and the moisture of soil with the help of the image of the field. The ratio of water mass in the soil is mentioned as the moisture of the soil. Two non-linear regression models are used for this process, a multilayer perceptron and support vector regression. Pixels are fed with the RGB pixels extracted from the digital images and identify the moisture content in the newly available images. It can detect the fertility of the soil by analyzing the soil's organic carbon. The random forest model is the frequently used machine learning algorithm for ease of use and variability. We can also estimate the soil erosion susceptibility of a field with the help of random forests (Viscarra Rossel et al., 2006).

5.4 Optimization of Irrigation with AI

About, 85% of the freshwater is consumed by the agricultural field across the world. With the increase in demand for food, the percentage of usage of water has also been growing. Thus the amount of water used must be optimized properly to save the water and to provide a sufficient amount of water for plant growth. The automatic scheduling techniques have replaced the manual irrigation method. To predict the amount of moisture and rainfall machine learning can be used. The economic implementation of the hardware can be done with the help of the internet of things. Smart irrigation is designed by inspecting the factors that are helpful to improve productivity like water level, soil temperature, nutrients, weather forecast (Arvind et al., 2017).

Machine-to-machine that was developed eases the way for transmission, information sharing with them, with server and to cloud by the main connection between all the junctions of the field of agriculture. To find out moisture content, temperature of Arduino in and Raspberry pi3 an automated robot model was developed by the researchers. At regular time intervals, the data is recorded and it's given to the Arduino's microcontroller that has edge level hardware connected. Input is converted to digital from analog. Raspberry pi3 receives signal which embedded with KNN algorithm. The signal sent to the automated model to begin the irrigation (Arvind et al., 2017).

Resource will supply the required water and then store the sensor values. Different sensors were developed in this approach like the soil moisture sensor for detecting the soil moisture, the temperature will be sensed by the temperature sensor, the pressure will be regulated by the pressure regulator sensor, molecular sensor increases growth of the crop. All outputs are then converted and sent as digital signal to a multiplexer by wireless network, hotspot, ZigBee (Arvind et al., 2017).

Subsurface drip irrigation process was the first technique that helped in minimizing the evaporation water loss due to evaporation, runoff since buried under the crop. Different sensors developed by researchers which were used for the detection of the need for field water supply; the soil humidity sensor, raindrop sensor instructed by the broadband and solar powered. Information collected reaches the farmer's phone as an SMS using the GSM module. With the help of this, the farmer can give an on or off command accordingly for the water supply in the field. Thus implementing this technology in the field the irrigation and watering process becomes easy for the farmer (Arvind et al., 2017).

5.5 Agricultural Robots

Robots are developed with the help of AI for some specialized work in the farming field. These robots are developed for different factors to be monitored in the field without reducing the work for a farmer. The agricultural robots perform works like the plucking of fruits, spraying pesticides, detecting and controlling disease and pests, and monitoring of plants in the field. Robots have been developed for various unique applications like orange harvester, lettuce bot, and weeder (Sistler, 1987).

The orange harvester is designed to pluck the oranges from the plant from any height and any site, a lettuce bot is capable to run through the field and plucking off the weeds from the field, and the weeder can remove the weeds and hoes the field by itself. The reducing number of labourers can be replaced with robots for reducing the work stress for the farmer and to manage the fieldwork in a smart way. There are a lot of advantages to engaging an agricultural robot in the field, they can work forever without getting tired or in pain, there is a very less amount of errors and they can do it in the very least amount of time (Dubey et al., 2016).

They can reduce the 80% usage of pesticides in the field and can protect people from the toxins of the pesticide, as they won't come in direct contact with the pesticides while spraying, they can operate it from a distant place too. It helps in increasing the yield and quality of the crops. The disadvantage of an agricultural robot is that the cost of the robot, is expensive for a farmer to afford; the maintenance cost is too high this can also reduce the labour that completely depends on farming for earning their livelihood (Sistler, 1987).

Chatbots

Chatbots are virtual assistants that can conversate interact automatically with the consumers and in this case the farmers. Chatbots powered with Artificial intelligence, can enable the people to know the language, can interact among the consumers in a customized way. Agriculture has used this facility to assist the farmers in receiving answers for their unanswered questions and to give advice to them and providing recommendations (Talaviya et al., 2020).

5.6 Application of Drones in Agriculture

Drones can also be called unmanned aerial vehicles/ systems. We can obtain a richer picture of the field with the help of drones; this will assist farmers in identifying crop growth, production, and quality. It promotes a sustainable agriculture pattern. The applications of drones in agriculture are crop scouting, field scouting, and precise data collection, with the data, collected maps are produced that can plot various data like the soil quality, field size, and plant health. The drones are 700-1400 gram; the wingspan is 5-10 m; it is built with water resistance and it can function under any weather conditions, and one flight can cover 12 Kilometres square (Puri et al., 2017).

Figure 5. Application of drones in agriculture (Tanha talaviya et al., 2020)

a. Planting Drone   b. Irrigation Drone   c. Soil Analysis Drone

d. Crop Monitoring Drone   e. Crop Spraying Drone   f. Health Assessment Drones

There are four types of drones single-rotor, multi-rotor, fixed-wing, and hybrid.

5.6.1 Single Rotor Drones

It has a single rotor; it is like a mini-helicopter and is more efficient than multi-rotor drones. Fuelled with a gas motor provides longer endurance for motor. According to the general rule of aerodynamics "the larger the rotor blade is, the slower it spins and the m ore efficient it is" the single rotor drones are powerful than the other drones. It can be used for spraying pesticides in the field. The disadvantages of this type of drone are the high cost and the ability of the drone to cause severe injuries if it hits a person, because of the big and sharp blades they can result in severe injuries in a person. There are several fa-

Figure 6. Single rotor drones (Chika Yinka-Banjo, et al, 2019)

talities recorded because of this issue. Also, they aren't stable when it comes to landing and due to the mechanical complexity; they require a lot of maintenance and care (Hassanalian & Abdelkefi, 2017).

5.6.2 Multi-Rotor Drones

Unlike single-motor drones, multi-rotor drones have two or more rotors in them. The thrust generated is greater than, equal to, or less than the forces of the gravity by changing the speed of the rotors and by drag acting on the drone; it can be moved in the direction we desire. This can be used in the field for various applications like spraying fertilizers and pesticides, surveillance of the field. The advantages of this type of drone are that it can be easily controlled, it has the ability to levitate, and it can take off easily and can land vertically also they are the most stable drones. The major limitations of this type of drone are that it has a flight time of 15-30 minutes only usually, they have very small payload capacities, along with that the major disadvantage is that the energy of the drone is drained on fighting the gravity and getting a balance in the air (Hassanalian & Abdelkefi, 2017).

Figure 7. Multi- rotor drone (Grác, Š., et al, 2020)

5.6.3 Drones with Fixed Wing

Drones with fixed wing like an airplane have a fixed-wing. The drone moves forward using the energy to move and is not static in a same place hence better than the other drones. They can cover enormous areas in a short time and map the field and can fly for a long time and monitor the field in a better way. They use the power source gas engines, if the fuel is provided with greater density, the drone could have a fly time of 16 hours or more. They can be used for long-time surveillance in the field (Hassanalian & Abdelkefi, 2017).

The disadvantage of this type of drone is that it can't hover in one place so it can't take a detailed photograph of the plants and can't identify the pest infestation and disease in plants as it needs detailed photography of the plant. Then the launching and landing is another disadvantage it may require runway, launcher for the flight. It needs skilled person to handle the device as it has a complex process to control this type of drone. In Australia, an eagle named wedge-tailed eagles attacks this drone especially. In addition to this, the cost of purchasing and maintaining the drone is too high (Puri et al., 2017).

Figure 8. Fixed wing drone- eBee (Mirzaeinia, A et al., 2019)

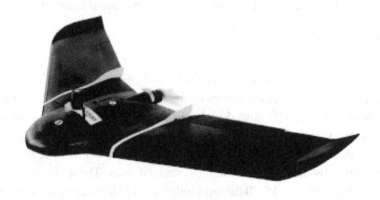

5.7 Artificial Intelligence in Hydroponics

5.7.1 Hydroponics IoT (Internet of Things)

IoT Internet of things) to connect persons around the world, World Wide Web, cloud data storage system help analyzing. Development encouraged farmers for automating the culture of hydroponics with the help of IoT. IoT helps to regulate light intensity, flow, water level, temperature and pH, a lot of research had been carried by engaging IoT for monitoring and controling of hydroponic system. Prototype of hydroponic based IoT was developed by Gosavi (2017) in this hydroponic prototype, in which the water luminosity, water conductivity, and pH are regulated with devices of meters for, and Lumens meter, pH meter, and Electrical conductivity meter (Gosavi, 2017). The message is sensed with the help of sensors and is transmitted to ARM 7 Microcontroller which helps the good growth of plants by monitoring continuously. In hydroponics plant has to be provided light for 16 hours and darkness for 8 hours. The Real-Time clock in the microcontroller controls lighting using the switch relay system. This LCD panel attached to the microcontroller displays valid information (Mehra et al., 2018).

5.7.2. Hydroponics Machine Learning

Artificial Intelligence (AI) Machine learning provides computers with the capacity to carry out their own actions as given in training a specialized work. For humanization of machine, the machine has to be educated as that of a human being. Human's brain learns past happenings, past data for which he is exposed on the basis people decides the future. The application of machine learning helps controlling the plant growth, optimization of electrical conductivity of nutrient solution (Mehra et al., 2018).

6. AGRICULTURAL ARTIFICIAL INTELLIGENCE AROUND WORLD.

The use of agricultural artificial intelligence gained importance during the year 2015 and it is still improving. North America and Europe have actively accepted Artificial Intelligence in Agriculture (Chamara et al., 2020). Farming is known for its hectic workload and labor-intensive work. World's technologically developed countries are working for implementing automation in agriculture and to implement robotics in agriculture many experimental models have been developed and many are used in the field (Sistler, 1987).

Citrus grading machines have been developed by the Sunkist cooperation, according to the color of the fruit, size of the fruit, blemishes, and scars on the fruit they are graded. Two of them are presently used in California. Each has a capacity of 480 fruit per minute (Sistler, 1987).

A lab-based model had been developed for transplanting seedling in the field in the agricultural engineering department of Louisiana. Transplanting needs one person per row in a conventional way of farming, the machine has the efficiency to pick up seed from vertical rotating trays series make a furrow into field and to drop the seed in the field and to press the soil on it covering the seed with the required amount of soil. They are programmed to do the work and they don't use any sensors. Development of planter is continuing, six plants per minute is transplanted by the prototype that is more than the rate of a human operator (Sistler, 1987).

Increasing efforts are made for developing the technology in agriculture and to implement Artificial intelligence in agriculture in Africa and Asia particularly in countries like Japan, India, and China. The market was valued at USD 545 million in the year 2017 for worldwide AI in agriculture and is estimated to be USD 2,075 million by the year 2024, at a Compound Annual Growth Rate (CAGR). But, there is a huge need to develop this technology to address some of the crucial issues related to getting a sufficient supply of food. Taking the environmental issues into concern as well (Chamara et al., 2020).

A survey was conducted in the USA by National Agricultural Statistics Service, in the year 2009, had revealed that in the year 2005, and in the total number of 51% of farmers using a computer and connected to the Internet, but 33% of the farmers was using the computer for their farm business. Computerized milking systems and feeding system were used by Only 5.3% of dairy farmers and 7.1% respectively. Ireland (2007) 56% of farming population in the country used computer, for farming purpose 35.8% of farmers used computers and farm management software was used by 15.2% of farmers (Chamara et al., 2020). The major development was made in the last 20 years for designing an accessible and friendly interface as a result, the expert systems are available for every person who can read and know use a keyboard and not only to the scientists the farmers were able to operate it with the basic knowledge as in the first stages of development. The common tools of human-computer interaction are text, images, sound files, and videos. Commercially available expert systems for agriculture that can be used via natural speaking language (Chamara et al., 2020) commands, this technology are not identified yet, it acquires a good amount of attention over time also the advancement of technology is appreciable, making it possible. There is already commercially available software that can recognize speech, text transcription from speech, the software can be used for controlling computers with voice and software can perform instant translations from a language to another language, so integrating these technologies in expert systems is just a matter of time (Chamara et al., 2020).

7. OPPORTUNITIES IN INDIA TO IMPLEMENT AI IN AGRICULTURE

NITI Aayog, (GOI) Government of India has collaborated with AI technology leading companies for implementing Agricultural AI projects. The Indian economy is based on the agricultural sector hence, requires several stakeholders with a several layered technology infusion, coordination; so it requires the government to play the leading role in the development of implementing the roadmap for Artificial

Intelligence in Indian agriculture. Agenda of the nation is to increase income of a farmer and government of India has attached importance to this; to boost productivity supply chain in agriculture, market development are essential (Kumar et al., 2020).

The cost of implementing Artificial Intelligence in agriculture is the only drawback, as many farmers in India will not be able to afford it. But the government of India is providing some schemes that may ease the way so that people may afford them easily. Some of the Indian agriculture technology start-ups are trying to integrate the technologies available for farming in the Indian farming field.

Indian agriculture faces a lot of challenges. Artificial Intelligence implementation is a must to improve insurance, credit, advisory, access to input and data to the farmers. Farmers can access the data directly from their phone. The data collected with the help of the sensors, IoT, photographs that are collected with the help of drones can help in developing predictive models which can enhance the decision about the seeds that must be sown, the conditions for planting seeds, fertilizer, and pesticides to be used. Most of these AI models are affordable and cheap but give a lot of value to the agricultural atmosphere (Kumar et al., 2020).

To provide real time advisory services to famers the government of India sought to AI-powered crop yield prediction with the help of industry. This can increase crop productivity; disease and pest warning save agricultural inputs from wastage, Indian Space Research Organization (ISRO) used remote sensing data which is used by the system. From the soil health cards of India Meteorological Department (IMD), weather prediction, temperature and analysis of soil moisture are collected. The project conducted in 10 districts around the country which includes the states of Bihar, Uttar Pradesh, Rajasthan, Maharashtra, Jharkhand, Madhya Pradesh, and Assam (Kumar et al., 2020).

The Indian Government is collecting data about the farmers from different states of the country through registration for the national level schemes provided by the Indian government. The details of the landholdings are being digitalized as well. To understand the status of the farmers and the crops they grow the government of India studies farm insurance, Kisan Credit Card and soil health card so as to give status of farmers, the plants they grow. To assist farmers around the country Pradhan Mantri Fasal Bima Yojana used modeling tools, remote sensing imagery and AI. Pradhan Mantri Fasal Bima Yojana covers almost 20 million farmers. There are many other projects related to artificial intelligence in agriculture for Indian agriculture, artificial intelligence is slowly gaining importance in Indian agriculture in the upcoming years farmers can easily access these technologies to ease their work at their farms (Kumar et al., 2020).

8. RISKS OF AI

There are several reasons why people are afraid to implement Artificial intelligence in any sector. It wastes away the experiences of the farmer, creating job losses for poor and down trodden due to agricultural AI, as AI systems grow in importance. Artificial Intelligence in agriculture can snatch away the jobs of several people who work in the agriculture field. It is expensive for a person to afford apart from this it can also the privacy of a farmer is always at risk as the data can leak easily (Cheatham, 2019).

Artificial Intelligence is programmed for doing something beneficial, for achieving goals it sometimes develops a destructive method this may happen when the AI's goals are not fully aligned with ours. Another risk of implementing artificial intelligence in the sector is that automation may cause job loss of people around the world which will increase the unemployment rate. Artificial intelligence can put privacy at risk; it can use an individual's information about their interest and the data without their knowledge. It can steal the data's that a farmer feeds, reduces the reliability of people on artificial intelligence. It can result in socio-economic inequality. Sometimes the automation can invite serious issues for farmers because of its complex programming and low transparency about the neural networks. (Cheatham, 2019)

9. CONCLUSION

In this paper the technologies available for smart farming and to solve the issues that are faced by the farmers in their field. The farming sector around the world faces a lot of issues like irrigation problems, weeds control, plant studies, controlling disease infestation, and weather prediction. With the help of artificial intelligence, performance can be increased and we can solve major issues faced by the farming sector. With the help of devices for soil humidity content detection, GPS assisted automatic irrigation. The weeding can be done with precision without losing lot of crops which is the major problem faced by the farmers. It has also reduced the number of pesticides and fertilizers used in the field as it uses the precise amount of chemicals for the plant. Monitoring of plants, drones technology the farmers can efficiently spray the chemicals in the field. Since the cost of implementing this technology is high, many farmers won't be able to afford it. Hence, for the betterment of the farming sector in the country, the country must support the farmers to implement this technology in their field by providing some schemes through which it will be easier for the farmers to implement artificial intelligence in their field.

ACKNOWLEDGMENT

I take this opportunity to thank the Almighty for providing me such a great platform for gaining knowledge in the field of my interest.

Firstly, I would like to thank each and every one who had helped me in every stage of this project.

My deep gratitude goes to my supervisor Dr. Karthikeyan Ramalingam, Dean (student affairs), Chief Proctor, Associate professor; school of life sciences, B.S. Abdur Rahman Crescent Institute of science and technology expertly guided me throughout the final year project with unconditional support, knowledge, and encouragement, with his unending support I was able to research in the field of my interest.

I would like to express my gratitude to Dr. S. Hemalatha, Professor and Dean, School of Life Sciences, B.S Abdur Rahman Crescent Institute of Science and Technology, for her support and motivation not only during my research work but throughout the period of my education in this institution.

It is indeed my pleasure to thank the research scholar, Sneha Unnikrishnan, for providing me with appropriate guidance throughout my research work.

Lastly, I would like to thank my family and friends for their unending moral support extended with love and constant encouragement throughout my project.

REFERENCES

Arvind, G., Athira, V. G., Haripriya, H., Rani, R. A., & Aravind, S. (2017). Automated irrigation with advanced seed germination and pest control. *IEEE Technological Innovations in ICT for Agriculture and Rural Development*, 64–67. Advance online publication. doi:10.1109/TIAR.2017.8273687

Auernhammer, H. (2001). Precision farming—The environmental challenge. *Computers and Electronics in Agriculture*, *30*(3), 31–43. doi:10.1016/S0168-1699(00)00153-8

Bendre, M. R., Thool, R. C., & Thool, V. R. (2015). Paper. *2015 1st International Conference on Next Generation Computing Technologies (NGCT)*, 744-750. 10.1109/NGCT.2015.7375220

Benson, Reid, & Zhang. (2001). *Machine Vision Based Steering System for Agricultural Combines*. doi:10.13031/2013.3446

Bestelmeye, B. (n.d.). Scaling Up Agricultural Research With Artificial Intelligence. *IT Professional*, *22*(3), 33-38. . doi:10.1109/MITP.2020.2986062

Blackmore, S. (1994). Precision Farming: An Introduction. *Outlook on Agriculture*, *23*(4), 275–280. doi:10.1177/003072709402300407

Chamara, R. M. S. R., Senevirathne, S. M. P., Samarasinghe, S. A. I. L. N., Premasiri, M. W. R. C., Sandaruwani, K. H. C., Dissanayake, D. M. N. N., De Silva, S. H. N. P., Ariyaratne, W. M. T. P., & Marambe, B. (2020). Role of artificial intelligence in achieving global food security: A promising technology for future. *Sri Lanka Journal of Food and Agriculture*, *6*(2), 43–70. doi:10.4038ljfa.v6i2.88

Cheatham, B. (2019). Confronting the risks of artificial intelligence. *The McKinsey Quarterly*, 1–9. https://www.healthindustryhub.com.au/wp-content/uploads/2019/05/Confronting-the-risks-of-AI-2019.pdf

Dubey, Manisha, Deep, & Singh. (2016). Robotics and Image Processing for Plucking of Fruits. In *Proceedings of Fifth International Conference on Soft Computing for Problem Solving. Advances in Intelligent Systems and Computing* (vol. 437). Springer. 10.1007/978-981-10-0451-3_69

Floridi, L., Cowls, J., Beltrametti, M., Chatila, R., Chazerand, P., Dignum, V., Luetge, C., Madelin, R., Pagallo, U., Rossi, F., Schafer, B., Valcke, P., & Vayena, E. (2018). AI4People—An Ethical Framework for a Good AI Society: Opportunities, Risks, Principles, and Recommendations. *Minds and Machines*, *28*(4), 689–707. doi:10.100711023-018-9482-5 PMID:30930541

Gosavi, J. V. (2017). Electrical conductivity and pH of the substrate solution in gerbera cultivars under fertigation. *Horticultura Brasileira*, *31*(3), 356–360. https://www.ijraset.com/fileserve.php?FID=8625

Hashimoto, Y., Murase, H., Morimoto, T., & Torii, T. (2001). Intelligent systems for agriculture in Japan. (2001). *IEEE Control Systems*, *21*(5), 71–85. doi:10.1109/37.954520

Hassanalian, M., & Abdelkefi, A. (2017). Classifications, applications, and design challenges of drones: A review. *Progress in Aerospace Sciences*, *91*, 99–131. doi:10.1016/j.paerosci.2017.04.003

Haupt, S. E., Cowie, J., Linden, S., McCandless, T., Kosovic, B., & Alessandrini, S. (2018). Machine Learning for Applied Weather Prediction. *2018 IEEE 14th International Conference on e-Science (e-Science)*, 276-277. 10.1109/eScience.2018.00047

Kumar, R., Yadav, S., Kumar, M., Kumar, J., & Kumar, M. (2020). Artificial Intelligence: New Technology to Improve Indian Agriculture. *International Journal of Chemical Studies*, *8*(2), 2999–3005. doi:10.22271/chemi.2020.v8.i2at.9208

McCarthy, J. (2006). A Proposal for the Dartmouth Summer Research Project on Artificial Intelligence. *AI Magazine*, *27*(4), 12–14. doi:10.1609/aimag.v27i4.1904

Mehra, M., Saxena, S., Sankaranarayanan, S., Tom, R. J., & Veeramanikandan, M. (2018). IoT based hydroponics system using Deep Neural Networks. *Computers and Electronics in Agriculture, 155*, 473–486. . doi:10.1016/j.compag.2018.10.015

Pham, X., & Stack, M. (2018). How data analytics is transforming agriculture. *Business Horizons*, *61*(1), 125–133. doi:10.1016/j.bushor.2017.09.011

Popa, C. (2011). Adoption of Artificial Intelligence in Agriculture. *Bulletin of Agricultural Sciences and Veterinary Medicine*, *68*(1), 284–293. doi:10.15835/buasvmcn-agr:6454

Pundru, C. S. R. (2019). *An Adaptive Model for Forecasting Seasonal Rainfall Using Predictive Analytics*. doi:10.22266/ijies2019.1031.03

Puri, V., Nayyar, A., & Raja, L. (2017). Agriculture drones: A modern breakthrough in precision agriculture. *Journal of Statistics and Management Systems*, *20*(4), 507–518. doi:10.1080/09720510.2017. 1395171

Reinecke, M., & Prinsloo, T. (2017). The influence of drone monitoring on crop health and harvest size. *2017 1st International Conference on Next Generation Computing Applications (NextComp)*, 5-10. 10.1109/NEXTCOMP.2017.8016168

Sarmah, S. (2019). *Concept of Artificial Intelligence, its Impact and Emerging Trends*. Retrieved from https://www.researchgate.net/publication/337704931

Searcy, S. W. (1997). *Precision Farming: A New Approach to Crop Management*. The Texas Agricultural Extension Service. Retrieved from http://agrilife.org/lubbock/files/2011/10/PrecisionFarmNew.pdf

Sistler, F. (1987). Robotics and intelligent machines in agriculture. *IEEE Journal on Robotics and Automation*, *3*(1), 3–6. doi:10.1109/JRA.1987.1087074

Talaviya, T., Shah, D., Patel, N., Yagnik, H., & Shah, M. (2020). Implementation of artificial intelligence in agriculture for optimisation of irrigation and application of pesticides and herbicides. *Artificial Intelligence in Agriculture*, *4*, 58–73. doi:10.1016/j.aiia.2020.04.002

Tsang, S. W., & Jim, C. Y. (2016). Applying artificial intelligence modeling to optimize green roof irrigation. *Energy and Building*, *127*, 360–369. doi:10.1016/j.enbuild.2016.06.005

van der Merwe, D., Burchfield, D. R., Witt, T. D., Price, K. P., & Sharda, A. (2020). Drones in agriculture. *Advances in Agronomy*, *162*, 1–30. doi:10.1016/bs.agron.2020.03.001

Viscarra Rossel, R. A., Minasny, B., Roudier, P., & McBratney, A. B. (2006). Colour space models for soil science. *Geoderma*, *133*(3-4), 320–337. doi:10.1016/j.geoderma.2005.07.017

Woodbury, R. (1960). The Legend of Eli Whitney and Interchangeable Parts. *Technology and Culture*, *1*(3), 235–253. doi:10.2307/3101392

LIST OF ABBREVIATIONS

IBM-: International Business Machines

AI-: Artificial Intelligence

UAV-: Unmanned Aerial Vehicle

DRONE- Dynamic Remotely Operated Navigation Equipment:

GPS-: Global Positioning System

VRT-: Variable Rate Technology

VRA-: Variable Rate Application

KNN-: K- nearest neighbor

pH-: power of Hydrogen

RGB-: Red Green Blue

IoT-: Internet of Things

SMS-: Short Message Service

GSM Model-: Global System for Mobile

Chapter 10
Internet of Things Integration in Renewable Energy Systems

Ghalia Nasserddine
https://orcid.org/0000-0001-9434-2914
Jinan University of Lebanon, Lebanon

Mohamed Nassereddine
University of Wollongong in Dubai, UAE

Amal Adel El Arid
https://orcid.org/0000-0001-5712-2138
Rafik Hariri University, Lebanon

ABSTRACT

Recently, with the birth of globalization, the world has witnessed a huge growth in its energy consumption. From an agricultural society, the world has transformed itself into an industrial and knowledge society. This transformation leads to a surge in energy consumption which led to an increase in carbon emission. For this reason, renewable energy systems with zero carbon emission has become a vital need for economic comfort and environmental security. However, the main disadvantage of renewable energy is its intermittency and prediction. Solar and wind generation are usually unpredictable, which leads to several problems if the network heavily relies on renewable energy as the primary source of electricity. This chapter describes the integration of the internet of things (IoT) with renewable energy systems to cover these problems. The authors will start with an introduction to renewable energy systems and their limitations. Then, they focus on the advantage of using IoT to enhance renewable systems.

INTRODUCTION

The world has witnessed extraordinary power generation and usage growth in the last decade. Today, power systems are essential components of modern human life. Numerous important tasks would have been impossible without electrical power at organizational and individual levels. The necessity of such

DOI: 10.4018/978-1-6684-6821-0.ch010

systems will grow with the ever-increasing world population. For this reason, renewable energy system assets are seen as alternatives to traditional energy sources (Allan, et al., 2015).

The three primary energy sources for generating electricity are fossil fuels (coal, natural gas, and petroleum), nuclear power, and renewable energy. Worldwide, most electricity is generated based on steam turbines that consist of fossil fuels, nuclear, biomass, or geothermal (Nehrir, et al., 2011). Some countries, such as the US, China, and France, recently used renewable energy (Solar and wind systems) to produce green energy (Panwar, et al., 2011). In 2015, one hundred ninety-six countries signed the Paris Agreement to reduce carbon emissions to zero by 2050. Many companies in these countries have started discovering new solutions to produce energy with zero carbon emissions. This goal can be achieved using appropriate energy sources and information technology tools like the Internet of Things (Al-Ali, 2016; Hamilton, et al., 2021).

The Internet of Things (IoT) is a revolutionary change in information technology (IT). The expression "Internet of Things" contains two main words. The first is the *Internet*, which refers to a global network that connects computers worldwide using the standard Internet protocol suite (TCP/IP). The second word is *Things*, which refers to any object or person which can be recognizable in the real world (Madakam & Lake, 2015). Therefore, IoT is defined as an open and broad network of intelligent objects capable of sharing information, arranging, and proceeding according to the current situations and status of the environment (Kosmatos, et al., 2011).

The key to sustainable energy transitions and climate change reduction is the optimization and integration of renewable energy. Automation, intelligent grids, electricity distribution management, greater efficiency, and other technological advancements are essential for this increase in efficiency. What is clear is that a significant step has been made in recent years to prepare for a future that will be increasingly connected and competitive. These advancements, led by the Internet of Things, are becoming a critical tool in the quest for greater efficiency in renewable energy, supporting an increasingly complex energy infrastructure capable of increasing the efficiency of consumption, energy distribution, and the installations themselves. Currently, IoT supports a vast number of applications in the energy sector. It can be used to enhance the energy efficiency, expand the allowance of renewable energy and reduce the impact of energy use on the environment (Al-Ali, 2016; Motlagh, et al. 2020).

This chapter comprises four sections: firstly, the different types of renewable energy systems are presented. Secondly, IoT will be presented briefly. The role of IoT in improving renewable energy systems is described in the next section. Finally, this chapter concludes on the importance of IoT in power systems.

RENEWABLE ENERGY SYSTEMS

Recently, electrical energy generation from renewable sources such as solar or wind energy and biofuels has gained strong momentum from many researchers, organizations, and countries. Indeed, relying on fossil fuels to support electrical demands increases the carbon emission into the atmosphere, leading to severe environmental and health consequences. For this reason, many countries, including the US, China, and France, have recently started using renewable energy systems such as solar and wind to produce green power with zero carbon emission (Hamilton, et al., 2021).

Renewable power systems can be organized according to the type of energy sources, such as wind, solar, geothermal, ocean, hydropower, and biomass waste (Guney, 2016). This section will briefly describe only renewable energy systems based on solar, wind, and geothermal.

Solar Energy System

Solar energy systems, also known as solar photovoltaic (PV) systems, convert sun radiation energy into electrical energy using silicon (SI) solar panels. These panels constitute arrays of PV cells connected in series and parallel to convert solar radiation into direct current electricity (Ali, 2021). A PV cell is an energy-gathering technology that transforms solar energy into electricity using the photovoltaic effect (see Figure 1).

Figure 1. A diagram showing the photovoltaic effect (Electrical, 2014)

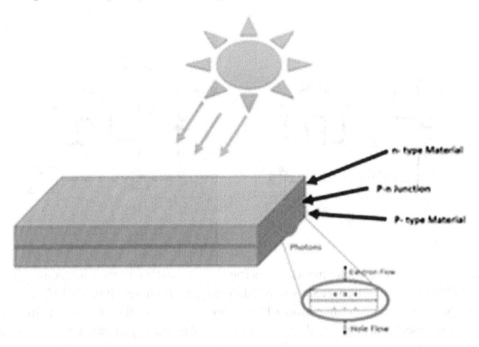

The photovoltaic effect is a procedure of generating an electric current in a PV cell from sunlight. Indeed, these cells contain two types of semiconductors (p-type and n-type) connected to produce a p-n junction. Therefore, an electric field may be generated at this junction as electrons move from the p-side to the n-side. Thus, this field pushes positively charged particles to move in one direction and negatively charged particles in another. Sunlight is composed of small bundles of energy called photons. When light with an acceptable wavelength covers these cells, energy from the photon is conducted to an electron of the semiconducting material, producing a higher energy state known as the conduction band. Therefore, these electrons can move through the material and create an electric current in the cell.

Generally, PV systems can be classified into two main groups (see Figure 2):

- On-Grid photovoltaic systems: These systems are designed to operate in synchronism with the national electrical grid. The goal of such a system is to supply electricity for the AC electrical loads directly during the sunlight period, where the grid is backup support to the PV system. In addition, the on-grid system can inject all excess generated energy from the PV into the grid (Figure 2 (b))

(Alkhalidi & Dulaimi, 2018). This injection of energy offers the system owner the opportunity to sell all surplus power to the local network service provider, which further reduces the electricity bills and the overall network emission.

- Off-Gird photovoltaic Systems: In these systems, solar panels are the sole source of electricity. The system design will consider the required PV energy to support the electrical load during the sunlight period and the energy required to support the energy storage (batteries) for outside sunlight period operation. Such systems provide an independent electricity supply to homes, farms, companies, and industries. They are widely used in rural areas (El-houari, et al., 2019; Ghafoor & Munir, 2015).

Figure 2. PV systems groups

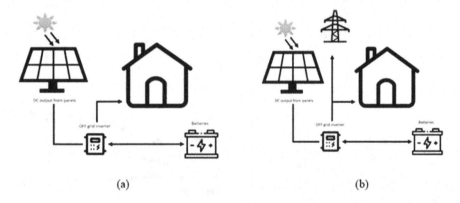

(a)   (b)

In addition, the increased deployments of electric vehicles (EV) and their integration within intelligent cities, along with the advancements in building integrated photovoltaic (BIPV) materials, force researchers, companies, and cities to consider PV energy as an essential part of smart cities. The BIPV material offers excellent housing or building features, simultaneously generating electricity and reducing carbon emissions and electricity bills. Furthermore, recent research showed that the deployments with PV systems and EVs reduce the burden on the local electrical network and offer a higher stability grid (Nassereddine, 2020).

Moreover, in agriculture industries, the advancement in power electronics opens the opportunity to run all irrigations system directly from the sun without the need for the grid and energy storage. The binding of PV and power electronics technologies opens broader land (lands that are far from cities Ann energy sources) for agriculture investment, which advances sustainable human life.

Solar Radiation

The PV system converts sunlight into electrical energy to support the electrical load. The design for an on-grid or off-grid system must consider the sun path, the house load, and the grid conditions. The sun's path changes throughout the day and months of the year. So it is vital to ensure the orientation and tilt of the sun are suitable for the optimum required output. Figure 3 shows the tilt and sun incident angle; it is clearly shown that changing the tilt will change the interception angle on the panel. Figure 4 shows the hourly sun radiation for different months for a system located in Australia. Figures 3 and 4 show the change in solar radiation throughout the day and year, reflecting the output-generated power.

The PV system can be located on top of the load, as shown in Figure 5; this layout advances the grid power, as explained in the following section.

Figure 3. The effect of Incidence Angle on PV Panel Efficiency (Rudisill, 2013)

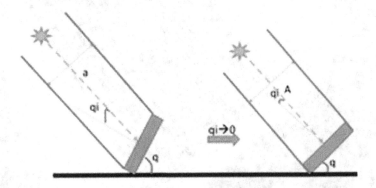

Figure 4. Hourly sun radiation during different months for a system located in Australia (Kabeel, et al., 2016)

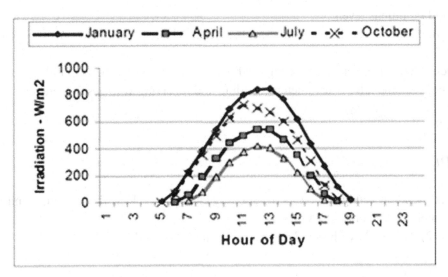

Electrical Grid and PV System

The power system comprises three main elements; generation, transmission, and load. Fossil fuels form the primary source of electrical power generation. The introduction of renewable energy alters the network to reflect the clean energy power station within the electrical network. Nowadays, the electrical power network contains a renewable energy power system close to the load point, which eliminates the requirements of the transmission line. The fossil fuel combustion generations are not suitable for residential properties due to the following reasons:

Figure 5. PV on the top of the house (Desai, 2020)

- Noise and pollutions levels
- Cost of fuels and oil for the residential-scale system. The return on investment cannot be justified

The power flow and losses can be computed using the ABCD matrix method, Eq. (1) shows the relationship between the ABCD parameters: sending and receiving voltages and currents.

$$V_S = AV_R + BI_R \tag{1-a}$$

$$I_S = CV_R + DI_R \tag{1-b}$$

Where V_S is the sending voltage (V), I_S is the sending current (A), V_R is the receiving end voltage (V), and I_R is the receiving end current (A).

Equations (2) and (3) show the sending and receiving power (Al-Ali, 2015).

$$S_{R3\varnothing} = \sqrt{3}V_{R(L-L)}I^*_{R(L-L)} \tag{2}$$

$$S_{S3\varnothing} = \sqrt{3}V_{S(L-L)}I^*_{S(L-L)} \tag{3}$$

The difference between the sending and receiving power represents the transmission line losses. Equation (4) illustrates the computation of the losses due to the transmission line system.

$$S_{L-S3\varnothing} = S_{S3\varnothing} - S_{R3\varnothing} \qquad (4)$$

The losses as per Eq. (4) are applicable for power transferred using transmission lines irrespective of the sources, green or fossil fuel power stations. Figure 6 illustrates the residential properties of the photovoltaic system with energy storage.

Figure 6. The residential properties of a photovoltaic system with energy storage

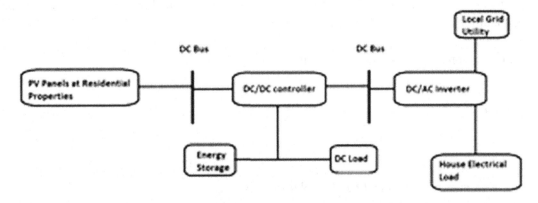

The house-installed system offers numerous advantages, which can be summarized as follows:

- The generation is at the load
- No transmission line is required to transmit the generated green energy
- No ground disturbance for PV system installations, the house infrastructure offers a free, suitable structure for PV systems
- Nowadays, numerous household equipment is operated on DC voltage which allows direct energy feed from the PV system without the inversion process
- Energy storage can be installed at the house to aid with the peak electrical demand during the evening and early hours of the night. As the batteries are installed, the load, with a good design and the connection resistance, is minimal, reflecting low losses. It is worth noting that installing a large-scale battery requires transmission of the power, which is reflected in losses and additional infrastructure.

Power Simulation

The works in this section cover the simulation of the city's required electric power using three sources, fossil fuels power stations, large PV stations, and micro-grid residential systems. In addition, the generated equations aid the designer in assessing the power flow from the three sources. Equation (5) shows the relation between the receiving electrical power from the three sources and the city's electrical demand.

$$S_{City} = S_{G-F} + S_{F-PV-S} + S_{G-M-G} \qquad (5)$$

Where:

- S_{City} is the total apparent power that the city requires
- S_{G-F} is the total power received from the fossil fuels generations. Equation (2) is used to compute S_{G-F}
- S_{F-PV-S} is the total apparent power received from the large PV power station. Equation (2) is used to compute S_{F-PV-S}
- S_{G-M-G} is the total apparent power received from the micro-grid system installed on residential properties. This power is usually consumed at the system-installed house under standard operating conditions.

The computation of S_{G-M-G} is completed using (6):

$$S_{G-M-G} = \sum_{i=0}^{n} S_{PV-i} \tag{6}$$

Where

- n is the number of houses that has *PV* solar system
- S_{PV-i} is the apparent power generated by the system at the house i

Equation (7) is generated from (5) and (6), aiming to determine the required receiving power from the transmission lines.

$$S_{G-F} + S_{F-PV-S} = S_{City} - \sum_{i=0}^{n} S_{PV-i} \tag{7}$$

The presence of the energy storage allows for the generation of (8):

$$S_{G-M-G} = \sum_{i=0}^{n} (S_{PVH-i} + S_{B-i}) \tag{8}$$

Where

- S_{PVH-i} is the generated energy from the *PV* system for the house i
- S_{B-i} is the battery power at the house i

When the battery is charging, the energy S_{B-i} has a negative sign; when the batter supports the load, S_{B-i} has a positive sign.

Equation (9) is generated to update Eq. (7) by reflecting (8) requirements:

$$S_{G\text{-}F} + S_{F\text{-}PV\text{-}S} = S_{City} - \sum_{i=0}^{n}(S_{PVH\text{-}i} + S_{B\text{-}i}) \tag{9}$$

Managing the power flow between the PV panels, battery, house load, and grid allows for optimum feed, reflecting positively on the transmission lines' receiving power. This management opens the door to an intelligent microgrid system. The micro-grid system has a load and control manager, which enables the following features:

1. Control the power to and from the battery storage. It has the ability to:
    a. Set the timing for charging and discharging,
    b. Set the power level of charging and discharging
2. Control the power to and from the utility grid. It can control the timing and power levels injected into the grid
3. Direct communication with utilities (with permission from the house owner) to control the system features set in steps 1 and 2.

Wind Power System

Another source of renewable power is the wind. The wind power system is composed of a wind turbine mounted on a tower to allow greater access to winds. Figure 7 shows the main components of the Wind electric system (Terciyanlı, et al., 2013).

Figure 7. Wind electric system components

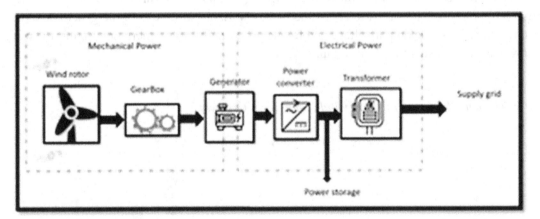

The wind turbine transforms wind energy into mechanical energy converted into electrical power using a generator. After that, electric energy is stored in the battery or transferred into the grid using a transformer and transmission lines. Typically, there are two different types of wind turbines: Vertical (see Figure 8(a)) and horizontal (see Figure 8 (b)) (Hiskens, 2011).

Figure 8. Types of Wind Turbines

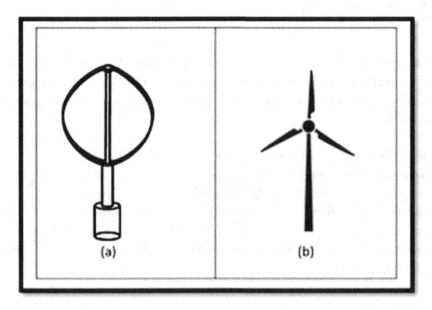

The horizontal type is most adapted due to its advanced suitability to aerodynamic performance and efficient mechanical balancing support. The wind turbine can be categorized into two main sections:

- Small types (lower power) utilize variable speed generators to convert mechanical energy into a variable voltage and frequency electrical power. This type must have a controller that converts the variable frequency and voltage into direct current (DC) power for further usage.
- Large types utilize a gearbox to adjust the blades' variable speed to suit the generator's synchronous speed for stable output voltage and frequency. In multi-pole generator systems, the use gearbox may not be required (Vieto & Sun, 2015)

Figure 9. The net addition to offshore wind capacity on Gigawatts

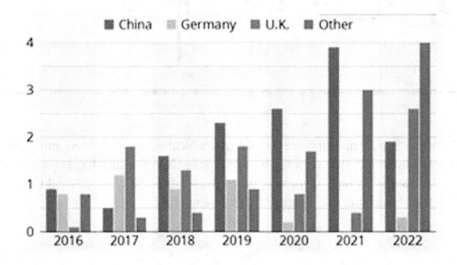

Figure 9 shows the number of net additions to offshore wind farm capacity by country in GigaWatts (Wood, 2022).

Geothermal Electric System

The United States of America is the first world country to generate electricity from the geothermal power system. IUSA generates yearly more than 3.5 gigawatts using geothermal plants. This electricity can cover more than three and a half million houses. The main components of a geothermal power plant are represented in Figure 10 (Huddlestone-Holmes & Hayward, 2011). The function of this plant can be summarized in five steps:

1. Hot water is driven from deep underground using high pressure.
2. When the water gets to the surface, it turns into a stream due to the release of the pressure.
3. The generated steam rotates the turbine, which is connected to a generator that produces electricity.
4. The cooling tower cools the stream and transforms it again to water.
5. The cooled water is injected back into the Earth, and the process starts again.

Figure 10. Geothermal power plant

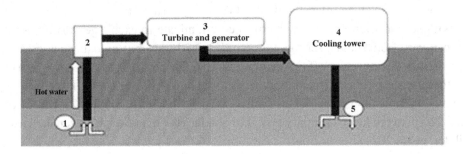

Recently, many countries have become highly dependent on geothermal power generations. Table 1 shows the total installed geothermal power generation capacity at year-end 2021. The total generation capacity using a geothermal plant becomes 15,854 MW, with an increase of 246 MW over 2020 (Richter, 2022).

INTERNET OF THINGS

The Internet of Things (IoT) consists of a real-objects network; these objects are known as things. Objects can be computing devices, digital equipment, mechanical machine, animals, and people. Each object has its Unique Identifiers called UIDs. In addition, objects are equipped with sensors, software, and other technologies that allow them to communicate information without requiring human-to-human or human-to-computer interaction. The concept of IoT was created in academic circles in 1998. However, most of its implementations are still in development (Khajenasiri, et al., 2017). Nowadays, more than seven billion devices are considered IoT devices (Soumyalatha, 2016).

Table 1. Top ten countries using geothermal power plants

Country	Current capacity	Increasing capacity over 2020
United States	3,722 MW	24.8 MW
Indonesia	2,276 MW	143 MW
Philippines	1,918 MW	-
Turkey	1,710 MW	22 MW
New Zealand	1,037 MW	32 MW
Mexico	962.7 MW	-
Italy	944 MW	-
Kenya	861 MW	-
Iceland	754 MW	300 KW
Japan	603 MW	-

Many organizations and industries are moving quickly to IoT to enhance operational efficiency, provide better customer service, and improve decision-making. Usually, an IoT ecosystem is composed of web-enabled intelligent devices that receive, send and behave according to their ecological status using embedded systems like central processing unit (CPU), sensors, and communication hardware (Soumyalatha, 2016). Indeed, an IoT network may take many forms. However, it should contain at least two devices with sensor layers that allow them to communicate to exchange information (see Figure 11). Sensors can vary from remote sensors for recording and transmitting data such as temperature to actuators used to turn devices on or off (Yaïci, et al., 2020). The network layer behaves as a communication channel that transfers data collected by sensors to other IoT devices. This layer can be performed using different communication technologies such as Wi-Fi, Bluetooth, Zigbee, Z-Wave, LoRa, cellular networks, etc. The network layer's primary task is to conduct the data flow between devices in the same network (Sikder, et al., 2021).

The data processing layer is the primary unit of IoT devices. It takes data collected in the sensor layer and analyses them to make the appropriate decisions or actions. In several IoT devices, such as a smartwatch, this layer retains the result of the previous analysis to enhance the user experience. In addition, the data processing layer may communicate its results with other connected devices using the network layer (Sikder, et al., 2021). The application layer executes and shows the results of the data processing layer to perform IoT devices' applications. The application layer is the fundamental user layer that executes all their tasks. Many IoT applications exist like intelligent transportation, smart home, personal care, healthcare, power systems, etc. (Atzori & Morabito, 2010; Soumyalatha, 2016).

The IoT has become one of the most relevant technologies in our life. It will continue to develop as long as humans benefit from it. Nowadays, many homes and offices worldwide are based on IoT technologies. Recently, numerous electronic devices such as lights, ovens, fans, heaters, and others are integrated with sensors and actuators that assist the efficiency of energy usage and monitor and control the amount of heating and level of light, which in turn minimizes the cost and increases energy saving (Whitmore, et al., 2015).

Figure 11. IoT architecture, consisting of four primary layers: Application, data processing, network layer, and perception layers

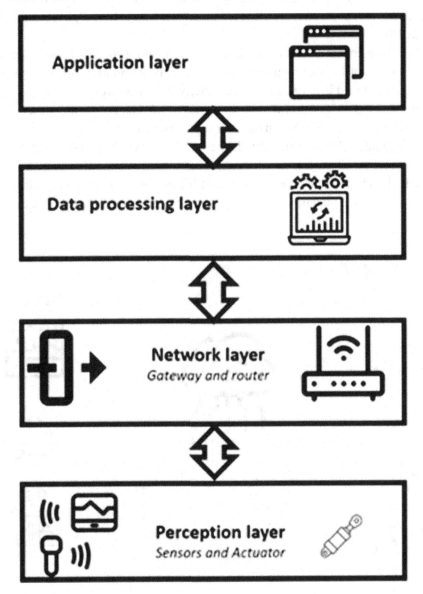

In addition, IoT is used in air quality monitoring. Indeed, embedded sensors are used to collect air component data like the amount of carbon monoxide (CO), nitrogen dioxide (NO2), temperature, and humidity levels. This data can provide information about the pollution level in the air and take precautions if it exceeds the standard level (Xiaojun, et al., 2015).

Lately, smart farming has become one of the IoT applications. Information such as temperature, solar intensity, plant wetness, and soil status may be collected and processed by IoT systems to send notifications to the farmers regarding water and treatment for the plants (Dagar, et al., 2018; Ratnaparkhi, et al., 2020).

The IoT enables healthcare providers like physicians to extend their capabilities outside their clinical location. Indeed, recently home monitoring systems have been used to allow patients and doctors to follow their health records and automatically recognize situations where a physical presence is needed (Kodali, et al., 2015).

Therefore, IoT represents the third revolution in information technology. However, the Internet of Energy (IoE) is a branch of IoT that combines information and communication technologies (ICT) and energy systems. A smart grid is defined as the electricity supply network that employs the ICT to perceive and behave to any changes in power usage. Recently, IoT has been widely used in smart grids to allow all components to share information through any communication network. IoT is central to smart grids, cities, and building schemes (Shahinzadeh, et al., 2019). Usually, the applications of IoT in the smart grid can be performed on four levels: generation, transmission, distribution, and consumption (See Figure 12). In this chapter, only the integration of IoT in energy generation levels will be discussed. Only power generation based on renewable energy resources such as wind, solar and thermal generation will be covered.

Figure 12. Integration of IoT in energy power system

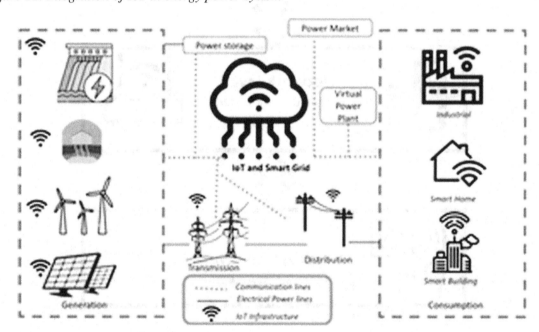

IOT IN RENEWABLE ENERGY SYSTEMS

In the last ten decades, the use of a renewable source in the generation of electric power has received enormous attention from industries and researchers. Indeed, the cost reduction of renewable energy components like solar photovoltaic panels and wind turbines promotes the use of these technologies worldwide. Most renewable system components are unreachable locations, such as rooftops, deserts, and others. Therefore, an advanced method is needed to monitor and control these components (Spanias,

2017). This section will explore the use of IoT technology to monitor and control the main components of renewable energy systems during the electricity generation step.

Long ago, power generation systems were managed using local controlling systems. A local operator must execute all control instructions.

Recently, the control of power generation systems has become much more considerable than evermore due to the following reasons:

- Electric vehicle usage dramatically affects power system generation scheduling
- The enormous penetration of renewable resources in power generation systems is uncertain and unpredictable
- The vast electricity consumption demand has been increasing recently with the uncertainty of hourly electricity prices (Al-Ali, 2015). Indeed, the hourly electricity price is correlated with instantaneous international fuel price (Lotfi & Khodaei, 2016).

For these reasons, the operator should treat the uncertainty and volatility of the electricity generation and consumption. In addition, he should deal with grid constraints that can conduct to shedding or curtailing load in some instances. IoT technology can facilitate managing these problems and challenges to maintain the generation power systems' security, stability, and environmental sustainability (Bedi et al., 2016; Shahinzadeh, et al., 2019). Table 2 shows the primary purpose of integrating IoT in generation power systems (Matsubara, 2020). The purposes mentioned in Table 2 will be explained in the following sections.

Table 2. Primary purposes for integrating IoT in generation power systems for each of the following power sources: solar, wind, and geothermal

Power source	Purpose
Solar	• Give a Stable operation of equipment • Maintain the efficiency of power generation • Reduce operational management costs • Improve the safety among the new participants in the industry
Wind	• Optimize and reduce the maintenance periods • Maintain the efficiency of power generation
Geothermal	• Improve the usage rate of equipment • Maintain the efficiency of power generation

IoT in Solar Energy

Due to global warming and environmental issues, non-fossil-based energy resources had taken more attention, starting in 1973. Nowadays, renewable energy resources should provide an enormous part of the world's energy demand. Solar energy is considered the first renewable source of energy used worldwide. Therefore, this source is viewed as the primary contributor to clean energy. Solar energy can be divided into radiant heat and sunlight. These two parts can be gathered using photovoltaic panel (PV) technologies and transformed into electrical energy (Shahinzadeh, et al., 2019). A PV system consists of an array of PV panels, wiring, switches, mounting system, and inverters. Sometimes this system can be accompanied by an energy storage system such as batteries. Recently, PV systems have been equipped with modern technologies like a maximum power point tracker (MPPT) controlling scheme, GPS solar tracker, solar irradiance sensors, anemometer, and other task-specific accessories (Spanias, 2017).

Moreover, the solar PV system's electrical power can be subject to many changes because the variable is solar radiance level, temperatures, snow, rain, and many other factors. Therefore, monitoring such systems becomes essential for providing a reliable electricity supplier (Woyte, et al., 2013). Recently, IoT devices have been widely used to monitor and control PV systems (Alhmoud & Al-Zoubi, 2019; Al-Ali, et al., 2019). Indeed, IoT can provide a real-time sharing of all data gathered from the PV sensors and remotely control the operation of solar units to avoid breakdown and fault detection and predict the need for preventive maintenance.

In addition, IoT infrastructure can provide grid-scale coordination between the energy storage system and the uncertain solar production to produce a reliable electrical power supply. Usually, Uncertainties depend on the solar resource evaluation and the performance of the PV system. Approximately 4% of the uncertainty depends on year-to-year climate variation. However, 2% is due to dirt and soiling, 1.5% is due to snow, 3% is related to the estimation of solar irradiation, and 5% is caused by other possible errors (Shahinzadeh, et al., 2019). In (Patil, et al., 2017), researchers propose an intelligent IoT system that provides real-time monitoring of solar PV systems based on raspberry pi using a flask framework (see Figure 13).

Figure 13. IoT system for monitoring PV Solar system

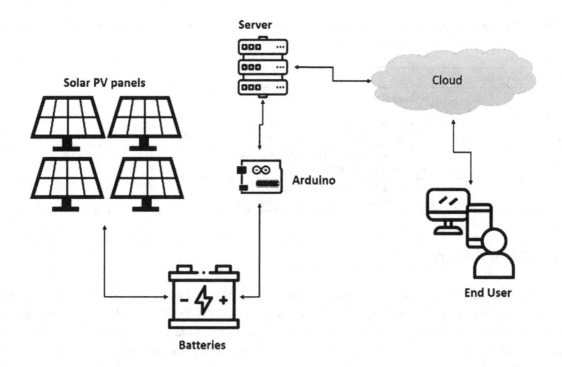

Bau et al. (2021) proposed a new system for monitoring solar PV systems based on IoT. Their system's voltage and current parameters have been stored and updated automatically. In addition, the daily or monthly study can be done using the continuous tracking of the solar photovoltaic system. Moreover, errors and ambiguity can be easily detected. Through tracking, the PV capacity can be computed accurately.

Nowadays, advancements in power technologies offer the power system an advanced monitoring platform to allow utilities to monitor the power flow and any system faults/malfunctions. The currently used monitoring apparatuses that provide the required data are (Tu, et al., 2017; Zhang & T. Huang, 2018):

- Phase measurement units (PMUs)
- Supervisory Control and Data Acquisition (SCADA)
- Electric meters
- Intelligent electric devices (IEDs)
- Digital fault recorder (DFR)
- Sequence even recorder (SER)

These technologies offer valuable data to utilities for system monitoring, operation, and maintenance. Data collected from these monitoring systems allow utilities to oversee the health conditions of the current electrical networks. However, the utilities are faced with significant issues related to the big data provided by these apparatuses. The collected data requires a platform to remove insufficient data, analyze the remaining data and issue recommendations based on the analyses. The collected data includes voltage, current, and power magnitudes and angles; their relationship is formulated in (1) and (2).

Al-Ali et al. (2019) proposed a new solar system based on IoT. Their system used IoT to operate remotely, monitor, and control s\distributed solar energy resources. Such systems are essential for areas that confront water lack and power shortage. This system used a single board system-on-a-chip controller (the controller hereafter) with built-in WiFi connectivity. It is connected to solar cells to deliver the necessary operating power. The soil moisture, humidity, and temperature sensors deliver data to the controller. However, the controller outputs suitable command signals to operate pumps. In addition, the underground water level is controlled by the controller. This task is fundamental to protect the pump motors from boiling because of the level in the water well. A prototype of this system was developed and tested.

In (Phung, et al., 2017), a responsible control system that directs and manages the energy discharge of renewable energy in solar panels was presented. This system is based on IoT and depends on data measurements collected from local sensors and meteorological data rescued in real-time from online sources. In addition, responsible controllers are designed to manage and optimize photovoltaic arrays' performance to catch solar radiation and support system stability and dependability in real-time. Experimental results show the performance of the proposed approach.

IoT in Wind Unit

In the last years, wind technologies have promptly progressed regarding efficiency and scale. The main complication of wind energy development is the unpredictable natural disruption of this resource. Therefore if the wind unit consists of a prominent part in the power generation system, that may lead to imbalance and threaten the overall system's security. Consequently, real-time control can prepare the rest of the generation power system to deal with this complication without experiencing costly gradients.

Additionally, cooperation with the energy storage system can be preserved if there is real-time data exchange between the wind and the energy storage units (Shahinzadeh, et al., 2017).

Singh et al. (2022) proposed a new wind emulation platform. The proposed platform is wind turbine-oriented, with improved traceability and efficiency compared to other systems. It was conducted with real-time wind velocity data fetched from nodes by using an IoT cloud application and programming interface. Indeed, data collected from IoT is transformed into information that studies and explores wind turbine performance. The proposed IoT approach with an associated prototype was tested and analyzed in a real-time environment.

Moreover, Yaqub, et al. (2019) proposed a new approach for integrating renewable technologies in conventional grids for powering desalination plants based on IoT technologies. The authors showed how to monitor and control renewable-based desalination plants using the Internet of things (IoT). The proposed system was a hybrid wind-solar energy-driven desalination plant. This system was controlled using the IoT perspective using CISCO Packet Tracer software. In addition, the plant was powered only by renewable sources. Furthermore, the motors are automatically managed based on the water level and demand, whereas the boiler is also controlled automatically by a thermostat. Also, there is a web platform for controlling the overall station by appropriate employees whose permission was granted.

Hence, each turbine within the farm is embedded with an IoT device to collect data and perform real-time controlling and monitoring of wind turbines. These devices collect the measured voltage output and create a power output model of the wind turbine (called the power curve). In addition, IoT nodes' battery lifetime is predicted using an energy model. Moreover, IoT devices help in wing electricity generation-related arguments, such as the interactivity between the farm wind turbines, inspection of further downwind analyses, and the periodic amelioration of yaw and pitch angles. Consequently, the Network Time Protocol (NTP) should be used. The NTP must run on both sides: IoT nodes and the web server (Srbinovski, et al., 2017).

In addition, to support a sustainable operation of the wind generation system, real-time monitoring of the wind turbine condition is mandatory to minimize human intervention as much as possible. IoT also provides a good solution by monitoring and controlling the sensors and actuators' operation within the turbine.

Moreover, IoT technologies and ICT infrastructures may accurately predict maintenance schedules, which help prevent enormous detriments. This scheduling can be based on machine learning and data mining techniques (Lotfi & Khodaei, 2016). Generally, a wind turbine consists of the following components: wind sensor, tower, blades, motor hub, drive shaft, high-speed shaft, brake system, gearbox, generator, power converter, transformer, and central controller. The controller usually contains various sensors and actuators. The primary role of the sensor is to report the state and performance of internal components. Besides, the control system processes the overall components using actuators. Typically, sensors are grouped into five groups (Rezamand, et al., 2020):

- Environmental: wind speed, humidity lighting, and icing sensors
- Mechanical: positions, angles, strains, and speed sensors
- Electrical: voltage, current, frequencies, and power factors sensors
- Temperature: detect the temperature in bearings, oil, winding, and electronic components
- Fluid: measure the pressure and flow levels

The sensor data are collected by the controller that analysis these data and sends electric, hydraulic, and mechanical instructions. The gearbox control system will execute these instructions, pitch angle control system, linkage control system, motors, magnets, switches, pistons, fans, and heaters. Hence, the wind turbines' physical layer should be connected to the cyber layer using network infrastructure to control the wind turbine components. The cyber layer groups the network system, condition-monitoring system, and SCADA. The network system represents a connection for data and control signals between the controller, other components, intelligent machines, and embedded devices in a wind farm (Shahinzadeh, et al., 2019). The network's job is to guarantee a real-time exchange of data and control signals between the controller, actuators, sensors, and data storage stations. Commonly, the design of a communication network is related to the local condition of the wind farms (Pettener, 2011). Each turbine must be embedded by a remote terminal unit (RTU), allowing it to connect to a local area network (LAN). The LAN network is connected with the SCADA system to a condition-monitoring system (CMS) at turbine and wind farm levels to control wind turbines and facilitate the earlier identification of breakdown or failures of wind turbines.

Accordingly, CMS can hold the stability using fault ride-through (FRT), under-voltage ride-through (UVRT), or low voltage ride-through (LVRT) Systems. These systems exchange the data with a central data center, including a cloud-based vast area network (WAN). All wind farm turbines hold an IoT-based device, distributed intelligence system, and wireless sensor networks (WSN). Thus, they can communicate using a cloud-based network, conducting the data using internet-enabled and open communication standards to the servers. These data can be analyzed and monitored by mobile human-machine interfaces (HMIs) (Shahinzadeh, et al., 2019).

Figure 14. IoT in wind energy generation

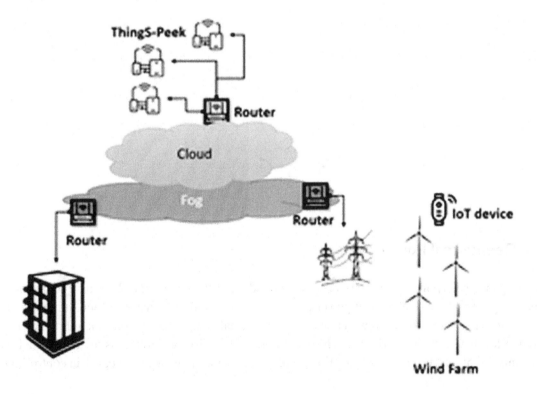

Figure 14 shows an IoT model for wind energy generation (Alhmoud & Al-Zoubi, 2019). This model is created to enhance the reliability of wind farms.

Each farm's wind turbine is embedded in this model with an IoT device, such as the Particle Electron, a cellular-connected microcontroller. The IoT device monitors wind turbine parameters such as wind velocity using an anemometer, voltage, current, vibration, humidity, and power using respective sensors. This device can be directly connected to a cellular network (considered here as the operator).

ThingS-peak (MathWorks, 2022) then stores and processes the collected wind data in the cloud. As a result, wind data can be retrieved, and wind turbines can be controlled from anywhere in the world via smartphones or computers. Indeed, an IoT integrated cloud portal aids in storing and analyzing data from measured real-time parameters with actual data determined by machine learning algorithms. These methods determine the fault and help make the appropriate decision (Kalyanraj, et al., 2016).

As seen before, the communication between wind turbines and the control center is usually done wirelessly; thus, this communication may be uncertain. The researchers (Noor-A-Rahim, et al., 2019) proposed an estimation of the state of a wind turbine to overcome this uncertainty. Moreover, they proposed an effective fusion algorithm to operate and combine the various data from different wind turbine sensors (see Figure 15).

Figure 15. Multi-sensor fusion for state estimation of wind turbine

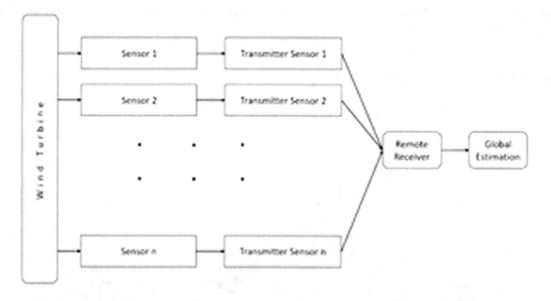

IoT in Geothermal Power System

Recently, geothermal power plants have been considered a powerful and clean alternative source of green power energy. In geothermal energy power plants, the steam and hot water are found underground to generate electricity via turbines. If well managed, geothermal energy may become an unlimited electricity source for home and industrial use. However, electricity power generated using geothermal plants covers only 1% of total electricity production globally for various reasons. Hence, IoT in controlling and monitoring geothermal plants has become an essential need. Thus, the temperature and vibration of the turbine generators can be detected using sensors. The data generated using these sensors can be collected and used to analyze and improve such power plants' efficiency. IoT devices provide remote management of the production and transmission of energy in real-time in power plants (Park & Ohan Shim, 2018). In addition, IoT can also improve the safety of power generation, as almost all geothermal power plants are located in earthquake-prone zones. Hence, the capability of management and monitoring power plants remotely is essential for employee safety (Yu & Zou, 2014).

Lately, the United Nations Industrial Development Organization (UNIDO) with Japan has started a new project to improve the efficiency of geothermal electricity production in South Africa. This project consists of integrating IoT technology with a geothermal power plant to get real-time control of all components in this plant. For this reason, sensors are embedded in power generators and turbines to collect data related to temperature and vibrations. These data can now be analyzed using IoT smart devices to increase the plants' efficiency. This process allows companies to remotely monitor and control the production and distribution of energy in real time. It also provides more safety for its workers (Pereira, 2020).

In (Park, et al., 2022), a geothermal monitoring system integrated with an open-source (IoT) system is developed. The objective of this system is to provide an economical alternative solution to existing commercial data collectors. In addition, it will give a solution for the limitation of existing data storage. Indeed, the proposed system is composed of hardware and software embedded with open-source support that assists in resolving the traditional limitations that the commercial system has. The developed system was a geothermal energy system deployed at a residential care facility for the elderly in Chuncheon, South Korea. It collected the data on temperature and fluid flow in real-time and for a prolonged period (i.e., years) at an affordable price compared to installing a conventional data-acquisition system. The real-time multi-year-long data helped confirm seasonality in heating and cooling. This system can be applied easily to other renewable energy systems to monitor temperature, pressure, wind speed, displacement, noise, and other factors.

In (Mona, et al., 2022), the authors propose a power generation system based on thermoelectric generator (TEG) modules and geothermal heat sources controlled by IoT devices. The IoT system was linked to temperature, humidity, and sulfur dioxide (SO_2) sensors to monitor and collect information about the hot spring. This information was monitored on mobile phones via the developed application. In addition, the IoT system collects data from the hot spring and stores them on cloud backup. The results of the prototype show the efficiency of this model.

CONCLUSION

Energy is one of the essential needs for the development of a nation. In the last ten decades, the rapid growth of the world population with the enormous development of technologies and other economic scenarios has increased the demand for energy consumption. As more than 80% of the generated energy comes from traditional sources such as fuel, finding a clean and reliable energy source becomes crucial. Lately, researchers have received significant attention from renewable sources like solar energy, wind, and geothermal. Many countries like the USA, Germany, and China have started producing a considerable part of their electrical energy consumption using renewable systems. However, usually, renewable power plants are located in inaccessible locations. Hence, the need for remote technologies that can monitor and control these plants has become essential. IoT represents the network of physical objects called things, equipped with sensors, software, and other technologies to communicate and exchange data using the Internet or other communication media. Recently, IoT has entered many applications, such as healthcare, business, smart cities, and many others. In this chapter, the role of IoT in renewable power systems has been presented. Three types of renewable systems have been described: wind, solar, and geothermal power systems. The importance of the use of IoT in such systems has been shown. Indeed, as the demand for clean energy increases, the need to monitor and control these power generation systems becomes essential. In addition, the IoT can detect any fault and predict the need for preventive maintenance. It may decrease the breakdown of the overall system. It appears that, in the future, the Internet of Things will be a tool with incalculable and limitless potential, which has already had and will continue to have a significant impact on energy production. Renewable energies will become more than just an option; they will be adaptable, resilient to setbacks, and, most importantly, much more sustainable and efficient. In short, an increase in possibilities is well observed, strengthening consumer confidence as energy production becomes sustainable and consumption becomes efficient. However, the proposed systems that integrate IoT in renewable power systems are compared to prove their performance. Therefore, future comparative studies should be performed on these systems. In addition, the role of IoT in the transmission, distribution, and consumption levels of power systems should be studied.

FUNDING AGENCY

This research received no specific grant from any funding agency in the public, commercial, or not-for-profit sectors.

REFERENCES

Al-Ali, A. (2016). Internet of Things Role in the Renewable Energy Resources. *Energy Procedia*, *100*, 34–38. doi:10.1016/j.egypro.2016.10.144

Al-Ali, A. R., & Aburukba, R. (2015). Role of Internet of things in the smart grid technology. *Journal of Computer and Communications*, *3*(5), 229–233. doi:10.4236/jcc.2015.35029

Al-Ali, A. R., Al Nabulsi, A., Mukhopadhyay, S., Awal, M. S., Fernandes, S., & Ailabouni, K. (2019). IoT-solar energy powered smart farm irrigation system. *Journal of Electronic Science and Technology*.

Alhmoud, L., & Al-Zoubi, H. (2019). IoT applications in wind energy conversion systems. *Open Engineering*, *9*(1), 490–499. doi:10.1515/eng-2019-0061

Ali, M., Rahim, A., & Ya'akub, S. R. (2021). Solar Energy System for Brunei Residence. *International Journal of Engineering Materials and Manufacture*, *6*(4), 312–318. doi:10.26776/ijemm.06.04.2021.07

Alkhalidi, A., & Dulaimi, N. H. (2018). *Design of an off-grid solar PV system for a rural shelter*. School of Natural Resources Engineering and Management, Department of Energy Engineering.

Allan, G., Eromenko, I., Gilmartin, M., Kockar, I., & McGregor, P. (2015). The economics of distributed energy generation: A literature review. *Renewable & Sustainable Energy Reviews*, *42*, 543–556. doi:10.1016/j.rser.2014.07.064

Atzori, L. I., & Morabito, G. (2010). The internet of things: A survey. *Computer Networks, 54*(15), 2787–2805. doi:10.1016/j.comnet.2010.05.010

Bedi, G., Venayagamoorthy, G. K., & Singh, R. (2016). Navigating the Challenges of Internet of Things (IoT) for Power and Energy Systems. In *Clemson University Power Systems Conference* (pp. 1-5). IEEE. 10.1109/PSC.2016.7462853

Bhau, G. V., Deshmukh, R. G., Chowdhury, S., Sesharao, Y., & Abilmazhinov, Y. (2021). IoT based solar energy monitoring system. *Materials Today: Proceedings*. Advance online publication. doi:10.1016/j.matpr.2021.07.364

Boyle, G. (2004). *Renewable Energy: Power for a Sustainable Future*. Academic Press.

Constantin, S., Moldoveanu, F., Campeanu, R., Baciu, I., Grigorescu, S. M., & Carstea, B. (2006). GPRS based system for atmospheric pollution monitoring and warning. In *International conference on automation, quality and testing, robotics* (vol. 2, pp. 193-198). IEEE. 10.1109/AQTR.2006.254630

Dagar, R., Som, S., & Khatri, S. K. (2018). Smart farming–IoT in agriculture. In *International Conference on Inventive Research in Computing Applications* (pp. 1052-1056). IEEE.

Desai, J. (2020, June 16). *Rooftop solar pv system: basic guide*. Retrieved June 27, 2022, from GharPedia: https://gharpedia.com/blog/rooftop-solar-pv-system-basic-guide/

El-houari, H., Allouhi, A., Rehman, S., Buker, M., Kousksou, T., Jamil, A., & El Amrani, B. (2019). Design, simulation, and economic optimization of an off-grid photovoltaic system for rural electrification. *Energies, 12*(24), 4735. doi:10.3390/en12244735

Electrical, E. (2014, August 15). *Created internally by a member of the Energy Education team. Adapted from: Ecogreen Electrical. Solar PV Systems.* Retrieved June 27, 2022, from ECOGREENELECTRICAL: http://ww1.ecogreenelectrical.com/

Geothermal. (2021, January 1). *Using the Earth to save the Earth*. Retrieved June 27, 2022, from Geothermal: https://geothermal.org/

Ghafoor, A., & Munir, A. (2015). Design and economics analysis of an off-grid PV system for household electrification. *Renewable & Sustainable Energy Reviews, 42*, 496–502. doi:10.1016/j.rser.2014.10.012

Guney, M. (2016). Solar power and application methods. *Renewable & Sustainable Energy Reviews, 57*, 776–785. doi:10.1016/j.rser.2015.12.055

Hamilton, I., Kennard, H. A., Höglund-Isaksso, L., Kiesewetter, G., Lott, M., & Watts, N. (2021). The public health implications of the Paris Agreement: A modelling study. *The Lancet. Planetary Health, 5*(2), e74–e83. doi:10.1016/S2542-5196(20)30249-7 PMID:33581069

Hiskens, I. (2011). Dynamics of type-3 wind turbine generator models. *IEEE Transactions on Power Systems, 27*(1), 465–474. doi:10.1109/TPWRS.2011.2161347

Huddlestone-Holmes, C., & Hayward, J. (2011). *The potential of geothermal energy*. CSIRO.

IEC. (2006). *IEC61400-25-1: Communications for monitoring and control of wind power plants – Overall description of principles and models*. International Electrotechnical Commission.

Kabeel, A., Abdelgaied, M., & Mahgoub, M. (2016). The performance of a modified solar still using hot air injection and PCM. *Desalination, 379*, 102–107. doi:10.1016/j.desal.2015.11.007

Kalyanraj, D., Prakash, S. L., & Sabareswar, S. (2016). *Wind turbine monitoring and control systems using Internet of Things. In 21st Century Energy Needs Materials.* Systems and Applications.

Khajenasiri, I., Estebsari, A., Verhelst, M., & Gielen, G. (2017). A review on Internet of Things solutions for intelligent energy control in buildings for smart city applications. *Energy Procedia, 111*, 770–779. doi:10.1016/j.egypro.2017.03.239

Kodali, R. K., Swamy, G., & Lakshmi, B. (2015). *An implementation of IoT for healthcare. In IEEE Recent Advances in Intelligent Computational Systems.* IEEE.

Kosmatos, E., Tselikas, N., & Boucouvalas, A. (2011). Integrating RFIDs and Smart Ob-jects into a Unified Internet of Things Architecture. *Advances in Internet of Things: Scientific Research, 1*(01), 5–12. doi:10.4236/ait.2011.11002

Lotfi, H., & Khodaei, A. (2016). *Levelized cost of energy calculations for microgrids. In IEEE power and energy society general meeting.* IEEE.

Madakam, S., & Lake, V. (2015). Internet of Things (IoT): A literature review. *Journal of Computer and Communications, 3*(5), 164–173. doi:10.4236/jcc.2015.35021

MathWorks. (2022, January 1). *ThingSpeak for IoT Projects.* Retrieved June 27, 2022, from ThingSpeak: https://thingspeak.com/

Matsubara, T. (2020). *Incorporating AI & IoT into Power-Generating Facilities: Status of Development and Challenges.* Academic Press.

Mona, Y., Do, T., Sekine, C., Suttakul, P., & Chaichana, C. (2022). Geothermal electricity generator using thermoelectric module for IoT monitoring. *Energy Reports, 8*, 347–352. doi:10.1016/j.egyr.2022.02.114

Motlagh, N. H., Mohammadrezaei, M., Hunt, J., & Zakeri, B. (2020). Internet of Things (IoT) and the energy sector. *Energies, 13*(2).

Nassereddine, M. (2020). Machine learning roles in advancing the power network stability due to deployments of renewable energies and electric vehicles. *International Journal of Emerging Electric Power Systems.*

Nehrir, M., Wang, C., Strunz, K., Aki, H., Ramakumar, R., Bing, J., Miao, Z., & Salameh, Z. (2011). A review of hybrid renewable/alternative energy systems for electric power generation. *IEEE Transactions on Sustainable Energy, 2*(4), 392–403. doi:10.1109/TSTE.2011.2157540

Noor-A-Rahim, M., Khyam, M. O., Li, X., & Pesch, D. (2019). Sensor fusion and state estimation of IoT enabled wind energy conversion system. *Sensors (Basel), 19*(7), 1566. doi:10.339019071566 PMID:30939747

Panwar, N., Kaushik, S., & Kothari, S. (2011). Role of renewable energy sources in environmental protection: A review. *Renewable & Sustainable Energy Reviews, 15*(3), 1513–1524. doi:10.1016/j.rser.2010.11.037

Park, C., Shim, B., & Park, J. (2022). Open-source IoT monitoring system of a shallow geothermal system for heating and cooling year-round in Korea. *Energy, 250*, 123782. doi:10.1016/j.energy.2022.123782

Park, C. H., & Ohan Shim, B. (2018). *Open Source IoT monitoring system of shallow geothermal energy integrated with OpenGeoSys*. EGU General Assembly Conference Abstracts.

Patil, S. M., Vijayalashmi, M., & Tapaskar, R. (2017). IoT based solar energy monitoring system. In *International Conference on Energy, Communication, Data Analytics and Soft Computing* (pp. 1574-1579). IEEE.

Pereira, D. D. (2020, March 13). *Using the "internet of things" to improve geothermal energy production in Africa*. Retrieved June 27, 2022, from Unido: https://www.unido.org/stories/using-internet-things-improve-geothermal-energy-production-africa

Pettener, A. L. (2011). SCADA and communication networks for large scale offshore wind power systems. In *IET Conference on Renewable Power Generation* (p. 11). 10.1049/cp.2011.0101

Philibert, C. (2005). The present and future use of solar thermal energy as a primary source of energy. International Energy Agency, 1-16.

Phung, M., Villefromoy, M. D., & Ha, Q. (2017). Management of solar energy in microgrids using IoT-based dependable control. *IEEE 20th international conference on electrical machines and systems (ICEMS)*, 1-6.

Ratnaparkhi, S., Khan, S., Arya, C., Khapre, S., Singh, P., Diwakar, M., & Shankar, A. (2020). Smart agriculture sensors in IOT: A review. *Materials Today: Proceedings*. Advance online publication. doi:10.1016/j.matpr.2020.11.138

Rezamand, M., Kordestani, M., Carriveau, R., Ting, D. S., Orchard, M. E., & Saif, M. (2020). Critical wind turbine components prognostics: A comprehensive review. *IEEE Transactions on Instrumentation and Measurement, 69*(12), 9306–9328. doi:10.1109/TIM.2020.3030165

Richter, A. (2022, January 10). *ThinkGeoEnergy*. Retrieved June 27, 2022, from Top 10 Geothermal Countries 2021 – installed power generation capacity (MWe): https://www.thinkgeoenergy.com/think-geoenergys-top-10-geothermal-countries-2021-installed-power-generation-capacity-mwe/

Rudisill, B. (2013, January 1). *The solar Ressource*. Retrieved June 27, 2022, from mcensustainableenergy: http://mcensustainableenergy.pbworks.com/w/page/20638192/The%20Solar%20Resource

Shahinzadeh, H., Gharehpetian, G. B., Moazzami, M., Moradi, J., & Hosseinian, S. H. (2017). Unit commitment in smart grids with wind farms using virus colony search algorithm and considering adopted bidding strategy. In *Smart Grid Conference* (pp. 1-9). IEEE. 10.1109/SGC.2017.8308892

Shahinzadeh, H., Moradi, J., Gharehpetian, G. B., Nafisi, H., & Abedi, M. (2019). IoT architecture for smart grids. In *International Conference on Protection and Automation of Power System* (pp. 22-30). IEEE.

Sikder, A. K., Petracca, G., Aksu, H., Jaeger, T., & Uluagac, A. S. (2021). A survey on sensor-based threats and attacks to smart devices and applications. *IEEE Communications Surveys and Tutorials, 23*(2), 1125–1159. doi:10.1109/COMST.2021.3064507

Singh, R. R., Banerjee, S., Manikandan, R., Kotecha, K., Indragandhi, V., & Vairavasundaram, S. (2022). Intelligent IoT Wind Emulation System Based on Real-Time Data Fetching Approach. *IEEE Access: Practical Innovations, Open Solutions, 10*, 78253–78267. doi:10.1109/ACCESS.2022.3193774

Soumyalatha, S. G. (2016). Study of IoT: understanding IoT architecture, applications, issues and challenges. *1st International Conference on Innovations in Computing & Net-working (ICICN16)*.

Spanias, A. S. (2017). Solar energy management as an Internet of Things (IoT) application. In *8th International Conference on Information, Intelligence, Systems & Applications* (pp. 1-4). IEEE. 10.1109/IISA.2017.8316460

Srbinovski, B., Conte, G., Morrison, A. P., Leahy, P., & Popovici, E. (2017). ECO: An IoT platform for wireless data collection, energy control and optimization of a miniaturized wind turbine cluster: Power analysis and battery life estimation of IoT platform. In *International conference on industrial technology* (pp. 412-417). IEEE. 10.1109/ICIT.2017.7913266

Terciyanlı, E., Demirci, T., Küçük, D., Sarac, M., Çadırcı, I., & Ermiş, M. (2013). Enhanced nationwide wind-electric power monitoring and forecast system. *IEEE Transactions on Industrial Informatics, 10*(2), 1171–1184. doi:10.1109/TII.2013.2294157

Tu, C., He, X., Shuai, Z., & Jiang, F. (2017). Big data issues in smart grid–A review. *Renewable & Sustainable Energy Reviews, 79*, 1099–1107. doi:10.1016/j.rser.2017.05.134

Vieto, I., & Sun, J. (2015). Small-signal impedance modelling of type-III wind turbine. *2015 IEEE Power & Energy Society General Meeting*.

Whitmore, A., Agarwal, A., & Da Xu, L. (2015). The Internet of Things—A survey of topics and trends. *Information Systems Frontiers, 17*(2), 261–274. doi:10.100710796-014-9489-2

Wood, J. (2022, March 29). *These are the countries bidding to become wind power superpowers.* Retrieved June 27, 2022, from Weforum: https://www.weforum.org/agenda/2022/03/offshore-onshore-wind-power-auction-capacity/

Woyte, A., Richter, M., Moser, D., Mau, S., Reich, N., & Jahn, U. (2013). Monitoring Of Photovoltaic Systems: Good Practices And Systematic Analysis. *Proc. 28th European Photovoltaic Solar Energy Conference*, 3686-3694.

Xiaojun, C., Xianpeng, L., & Peng, X. (2015). *IOT-based air pollution monitoring and forecasting system. In 2015 international conference on computer and computational sciences*. IEEE.

Yaïci, W., Krishnamurthy, K., Entchev, E., & Longo, M. (2020). Internet of things for power and energy systems applications in buildings: An overview. *2020 IEEE International Conference on Environment and Electrical Engineering*, 1-6. 10.1109/EEEIC/ICPSEurope49358.2020.9160522

Yaqub, U., Al-Nasser, A., & Sheltami, T. (2019). Implementation of a hybrid wind-solar desalination plant from an Internet of Things (IoT) perspective on a network simulation tool. *Applied Computing and Informatics*, 7-11.

Yu, Y., & Zou, Y. L. (2014). Application of technology of the Internet of Things on the monitoring of geothermal field. *Advanced Materials Research, 860*, 563–567.

Zhang, Y., Huang, T., & Bompard, E. F. (2018). Big data analytics in smart grids: A review. *Energy Informatics*, 1-24.

KEY TERMS AND DEFINITIONS

Actuator: A part of a machine that supervises movements and controls the system.

GearBox: It is a system of gears inside an engine or a vehicle.

Information Technology: The use of any electronic device such as computers, storage, networking and other physical devices in order to create, process, exchange and manage all kind of digital data or information.

Internet of Things: An open and broad network of intelligent objects capable of sharing and arranging information. Then, it acts according to the current situation and status of the environment.

Photovoltaic Effect: A process that generates electricity from a photovoltaic cell when it is exposed to solar radiation.

Photovoltaics: The process of converting light into electricity based on semiconducting materials and photovoltaic effect.

Renewable System: It uses renewable sources, including solar, wind, geothermal power, or ocean waves, to produce electricity.

Sensor: A device that detects and responds to some type of input from the physical environment.

Smart Device: An electronic gadget that can share, connect, and interact with users and other devices.

Chapter 11
Essentials of Internet of Things in Smart Agriculture:
Design Principles and Architectures for Its Application in Various Domains and Use Cases

Mitali Chugh

University of Petroleum and Energy Studies, India

Neeraj Chugh

University of Petroleum and Energy Studies, India

ABSTRACT

In the agricultural domain, the advent of IoT has paved the path for innovative research. Being promising yet at a budding stage, IoT must be extensively experimented upon to be applied widely in different agricultural applications. The rising demand for food has enhanced the necessity of industrialized progression and thorough production techniques in agricultural science. At the vanguard of the innovative farming age, an evolving internet of things (IoT) puts forward many innovative solutions. The agricultural parameters, such as environmental factors, soil conditions, etc., are traced in smart or precision agriculture to upsurge crop harvests, reduce costs, and sustain inputs for the process. Flourishing IoT technologies present several novel solutions and enhance growth prospects in the agricultural sector. To address the IoT's potential usage in the current scenario, this chapter looks at design principles, architectures, numerous challenges, and developments associated with smart agriculture. Also, a review of different perspectives on applications of IoT is conducted.

DOI: 10.4018/978-1-6684-6821-0.ch011

INTRODUCTION

The growing need for food and its enhanced quality and quantities has enhanced the requirement for industrial development and exhaustive agricultural production techniques. In this respect, the Internet of Things (IoT) (Gubbi et al., 2013; Ray, 2014), wireless ad-hoc and sensor networks (Ousmane et al., 2013), Radio Frequency Identifier (Pereira et al., 2011), cloud computing (Ojha et al., 2015), etc. technologies are becoming progressively more prevalent. At the spearhead of the novel agricultural epoch, there are evolving Internet of Things (IoT) practices that are suggestive of several innovative solutions.

Agriculture has been reformed by the diverse set of tools that IoT offers to cater to the challenges which farmers face in the field. Sensors are used to control various processes in farming. Farmers can also exploit IoT to keep up with the up-to-date situations of their farming land by a smartphone from everywhere in the world. Moreover, IoT-assisted technologies are significant in optimizing crop production costs and increasing land productivity. Hence, this chapter discusses at length some of the important roles of IoT in smart agriculture as water management, soil management, irrigation management, nutrient management, precision farming, etc.

Additionally, in various countries and organizations around the world, many IoT policies are implemented in farming. Though notable research has been conducted in the field of IoT there is still an excessive requirement for advanced research on the subject in the agricultural domain. When we consider the use of IoT in smart agriculture it is only the surface that the present computer applications are scratching. The complete strength of IoT to enhance agriculture is yet to be realized. Looking at the potential that IoT offers it is going to play a key role in various sectors of agriculture. It is due to the abilities of IoT as area-specific and remote data collection, analysis of intelligent information for cloud-based applications, and elementary communication framework (employing sensors, mobile devices, etc.) and facilitation in decision making. Such facilities can transform the agricultural industry which perhaps is one of the most significant spheres of our economic value chain at present.

The IoT technology became prominent in the year 2000 when Auto-ID was developed at MIT and was introduced in the consequent marketplace research reports. IoT is broadly perceived as the leading-edge technology with extensive relevance through nearly all facets of the marketplace, including the facility to escalate the incorporation of end products, methods, and services. IoT technologies are best for several systems and services, comprising healthcare services, transportation management, agricultural methods, and protection services.

ICT (Information and Communication Technologies) is present in traditional agricultural practices that support triggering the fourth farming revolution. The key technologies such as machine learning, Big Data Analytics, Remote Sensing, etc. have the competence to enhance farming practices to novel peaks. A wide range of agricultural factors, such as environmental parameters, soil state, irrigation water, herbicides, pesticides, and weed control, may perhaps be traced in smart agriculture to enhance yield, reduce costs, and retain process records. Smart agriculture along with reduced fertilizer utilization and pesticides in crops facilitates mitigating leaching problems, pollution, and climate variation effect, in smart agriculture (Walter et al., 2017).

There are various ongoing advances in research on IoT agriculture that consist of network engineering and applications, device design, and security challenges. In addition, in several countries and institutes worldwide, different IoT procedures and policies have been implemented in agriculture. Though notable research has been carried out in the field of IoT, there is a requirement for comprehensive further research on the topic in the domain of agriculture. This enhanced need for IoT for smart agriculture is the motivation behind this chapter.

In the present situation, the IoT-based solutions must be cost-effective to be reasonably priced thus facilitating end users for its use. Conversely, with the growing population, the requirement for food-cereal is rapidly escalating. The latest article notifies that the rise in the production of food grains is lesser when compared to population growth (Shi et al., 2015). Hence, research in this arena has been boosted to cope with the increasing demand by integrating cutting-edge technologies. This speed must be enhanced by including IoT for smart and definite agriculture.

To summarize the contributions of this book chapter, vital agricultural applications are emphasized, and IoT applications in the direction of upgraded performance and production have conversed. Features of IoT, Operational hardware platforms and IoT cloud services for agricultural applications are examined. Different sensor-based IoT systems emphasizing design principles and architectures are also listed in this chapter. The chapter concludes with a few case studies, analyzing the challenges and open research issues in smart agriculture.

Use of IoT in Smart Agriculture- An Overview

IoT is reforming agriculture by facilitating it with various tools that can address different challenges faced by farmers. IoT offers provision to farmers to connect with the fields and farms in nearly any part of the world by employing IoT-enabled technologies. IoT sensors, actuators, and wireless sensor networks are used for farming regulation and monitoring. Wireless cameras and sensors are used to create videos and take pictures for monitoring remotely, also smartphones help to keep up-to-date conditions of the agricultural land. Some of the key roles of IoT in smart agriculture are illustrated in Figure 1.

Figure 1. IoT in Smart Agriculture: Key roles

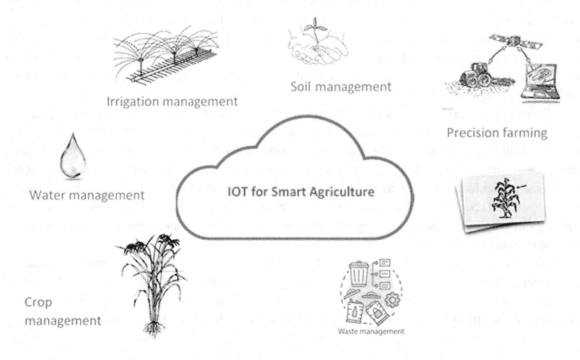

i.   **Water Management:** In a greenhouse to assess the water quantity required is most challenging (Wadekar et al., 2016). Thus, to prevent the wastage of water, smart sensors are used and function using a range of IoT techniques. The sensors monitor stored water amounts, and the cloud saves the related data using smartphone applications. The process is automated using IoT to operate the motor detecting the level of the water as low or high, thus making the motor functional or shutting it off. In conventional irrigation systems because of inadequacies approximately 50% of water is wasted (SHENG et al., 2013). The smart irrigation systems are designed to prevent water loss and overcome the problem of over-watering hence supporting the farmers to enhance the quality of the crop. Climate-based precision agriculture controllers keep track of and maintain irrigation programs following local weather statistics.

ii. **Irrigation Management:** is required for designing and maintaining irrigation systems. Irrigation system design needs to anticipate the water requirement based on the captured data and stimulate the flow of water without human intervention. Irrigation requirement is subject to soil properties such as moistness, temperature, and the crop type grown in the soil and smart irrigation systems use field-deployed sensors for monitoring all the stated factors. IoT also assists in tracing soil and weather conditions in a more sophisticated way by computing agricultural water needs. Ethernet and WIFI are all prototypes of how IoT technology tracks irrigation systems.

iii. **Soil Management:** IoT-based soil management includes technology to enable cultivators and producers to get the best crop production, lessen disease and improve resource utilization. The sensors efficiently measure the different parameters such as pH, moisture, temperature, photosynthetic radiation, NPK, and oxygen level of the soil. The sensors use IR technology to measure soil temperature and non-contact surface temperature. The soil moisture is also examined using electrodes. In soil science and hydrology, soil humidity plays a significant part in soil chemistry, plant growth, and the recharge of groundwater. In addition, IoT sensors measure various types of solar radiations (Solar – Photosynthetically active radiation, Solar – UV, Solar – Shortwave) as well which are useful for photosynthesis and plant growth. Nitrogen, Phosphorous, and Potassium (potash) sensors are quite novel to the marketplace however offer a means which by NPK nutrients can be measured using IoT sensors that uses TDR as the most prevalent method.

The captured data is stored centrally or in the cloud for analysis and visualization. The effective use of data and insights depends on your environment and application: Web-based dashboards can visualize data, and Mobile apps and mobile-optimized web pages can visualize data for mobile devices, Data can be imported or accessed using analytical tools such as Excel, PowerBI, or Tableau, Dashboard and monitoring systems can generate alerts if thresholds are exceeded (i.e., NPK levels, soil moisture, etc.). Following the results of the analysis for soil management farmers can take measures to improve plant breed, fertilization, and irrigation. If these kinds of difficulties are suitably addressed, farming patterns and practices can be followed with ease.

iv. **Precision Farming:** is an IoT-based technique that captures farming data (historical, ecological, and predictive modeling) to make the selection of appropriate crops with greater yield, optimize pest control, enhance environmental sustainability, foresee weather variations, and respond to them proactively. Agriculture business owners realize integrating technology into crop management as an approach to enhance the quality of decision-making, the return on investment (ROI), better crop protection, and the overall security of the site. The IoT technologies such as sensors, precision farming software, connectivity protocols, and location monitoring tools facilitate farmers for greater accuracy in data collection and analysis. IoT helps to monitor all activities of crop farming, reduces resource wastage, finds developing patterns and trends across all fields and the entire season, and gets a big-picture view of farm sites. Moreover, unmanned aerial vehicles (known as drones) tailored with hyperspectral and multispectral sensors support agriculturalists regulate the health of plants and measuring water stress levels. UAVs also assist in disaster management and risk reduction.

v. **Nutrient Management:** is the most effective use of crop nutrients in addition to preserving the environment. In nutrient management, a balance is maintained between the nutrients of the soil and crop needs. This is essential as an optimal amount of nutrients at right time facilitates enhancing crop yield. If the nutrient amount is too high may harm the environment and if it is too low constrains productivity. The improper use of nutrients (nitrogen, phosphorous, and ammonia) by crops can result in their leakage into underground or surface water vitiates its quality. Determining the nutrient concentration in the soil permits the choice of the best crop for many cropping cycles on the same land. Nutrients and technologies are vital for achieving sustainable agriculture when reducing ecological and commercial costs (Agrahari et al., 2021).

vi. **Waste Management:** The world produces 2.01 billion tons of municipal solid garbage annually, 33% of it not being controlled in a natural sound way. It is anticipated to rise to 3.40 billion tons by 2050 (The world bank, n.d.). One of the technologies that offer a waste clearance solution is IoT. Ultrasonic and proximity-based sensors are used to notify collection trucks when the trash cans are filled, assess segregation points, and find out at what locations drivers of collection trucks should stop or move on. Weight sensors can keep track of fill levels in bigger bins. The data generated by the different sensors is important to drive fleet operations and take rerouting decisions in real time. When this data is integrated with a scheduling engine, working groups may plan collection optimally and predict what to anticipate weeks ahead of time. The trash cans that are equipped with waste compactors can manage waste more efficiently by holding more garbage. IoT thus streamlines the waste management process by using smart dumpsters that can use optimized routes and utilize data for the garbage location and fill levels to avoid missed garbage pickups and schedule pickups to operate smoothly.

The IoT management systems have made it possible to optimize data with ease by using smart devices with different types of required data such as speed and frequency at which trash cans are filled, the shortest route to reach the filled trash can/bins, etc. can be gathered.

This data is precious because its utilization facilitates workforces and businesses to perform practical chores. However, disposal processes are a foremost shortcoming, then again with the usage of IoT technology, these difficulties are alleviated.

vii. **Crop Management:** Crop management includes evaluating and recording crop health. IoT sensors detect diseases in the crops and the related data can be collected from RFID tags and farmers can take preventive measures or essential steps to control pests, production tracking, and predict advantages for valued production decreasing losses. In a study conducted by Vitali et al. (2021), it emerges that the Internet of Things will draw attention to sensor quality and placement protocols, while machine learning should be oriented to produce understandable knowledge, which is also useful to enhance cropping system simulation systems (Vitali et al., 2021).

Background

In literature, various studies have suggested the significance of IoT in smart agriculture thereby emphasizing the benefits that the farmers and business houses can gain when IoT is employed for smart agriculture.

Nagaraj et al. (2019) have proposed a smart agriculture management system (SAMS) that facilitates farmers to enhance the production of crops and decreases the wastage of resources. The proposed system is equipped with various sensors to capture data related to environmental factors that affect the production of the crop and they also present the results using visual elements as graphs (Nagaraja et al., 2019). Mohapatra and Rath (2022) in their study show a twofold objective and propose an effective IoE-based smart agricultural model (IoESA) as a new AgriTech tool for efficient communication among all IoT-based devices and a sensor-based soil quality monitoring method called Soil-Smart Agriculture (SSA) that helps the farmers to get the current soil quality. The results show a framework for the system based on IoE for smart agriculture and data acquired related to soil is made available when required through IoESA-MIS (Mohapatra & Rath, 2022). Gupta et al. (2022) propose a framework that detects plant decay by using the smart croft algorithm. The study puts forward that the proposed framework can prevent huge damages and avoids the wastage of time and labor. The parameters that have been taken into consideration are humidity, moisture, temperature, and color of the leaf. The data from the sensors is sent to Arduino to Cloud which then analyzes the data and helps in identifying the plant decay (Gupta et al., 2022). Torky and Hassanein (2021) have recommended innovative Blockchain models which are an important solution for key challenges such as prolonged security and performance issues in IoT-based precision agricultural systems (Torky & Hassanien, 2020). Wicaksono et al. (2022) have suggested improving agricultural land productivity using an IoT-based solution. The outcome of this study is a fundamental loop diagram of internet-based system thinking that can be used as a recommendation for increasing land productivity (Galang et al., 2022).

Advanced IT techniques such as AI and cloud computing have been integrated to enhance the production of food. Particularly the technically sophisticated AI and DL models in the cloud layer are used to facilitate decisions as determining water amount for irrigation to improve crop growth (Bu & Wang, 2019). Wang et al. (2021) proposed an advanced Multilayer Perceptron (MLP) methodology to estimate the sugar quantity produced in IoT agriculture and the proposed algorithm has 99% accuracy (Wang et al., 2021). Lavanya et al. (2020) present an Internet of Things (IoT) based system by designing a novel Nitrogen-Phosphorus Potassium (NPK) sensor. The proposed model is validated for mountain soil, red soil, and desert soil (Lavanya et al., 2020). The results show that the developed IoT system facilitates farmers for increasing crop yield (Lavanya et al., 2020). Ouafiq et. al. (2022) has proposed big data, IoT, and knowledge-based system to address the issues of file handling in the agriculture industry related to computation performance. The proposed big data architecture-based solution has a data lake layer to manage the quality of data, as well as the incorporated data migration strategy, providing insights on data. In addition, to predict and forecast in smart farming analytics different ML algorithms are compared in the study(Ouafiq et al., 2022).

Thus, from the exhaustive review of the recent literature, we can identify the significance of IoT and a few other cutting-edge technologies in Smart agriculture. The researchers are exploring the potential of IoT in Smart agriculture to address the solutions for the diverse issues in farming such as increased crop yield, soil structure, prediction, forecasting, etc. In the following section, we discuss some of the prevalent IoT-based hardware, software, and applications that are used for Smart agriculture.

SOFTWARE, HARDWARE, AND APPLICATIONS FOR SMART AGRICULTURE

This section discusses the features of some apps, hardware, and software for Smart agriculture.

Smart Agriculture Applications

i.   Nutrient ROI calculator: this is an eKonimics product that is an enhanced version of the ROI calculator(Lindemann, 2019). It supports smart agriculture by yield optimization and integrates spatial uncertainty to give a facility of precise representation of predicted nutrient response. This helps them to take decisions about fertilizer use which results in more farm inputs thus finally providing more profit.
ii.   Sirrus: has the facility to provide data simply and supports the teamwork of farmers and agronomists (Chauhan, 2015). Sirrus Premium has a component of an advanced advice editor that enables consultation for farmers about the field modifications. It also provides the facilities for the change in fertilizer application rates, overall product prices, and costs.
iii. FieldAgent: has a feature for data collection that is used for representing health charts of the crops. It is also used in seed counting and weeds classification which are among its predominant features. This application has drone compatibility features i.e., it manages aspects of flying so that the users can focus only on the targeted map. The app helps to find the location of weeds, species of plants, and parameters for plant health quickly on the system (Hardcastle, 2019).
iv.   OpenIoT: helps to identify wheat varieties for plant breeders based on the calculation of humidity, air, temperature, and soil forecasts for irrigation schedules, harvest dates, etc. (Bhagat et al., 2019).
v.   Farmbot: is a robotic open-source hardware and uses open-source software for IoT in farming. It is centered on precision, regulated by the web, and accessible and suitable for small-scale operations. Farm Bot supports small-scale agriculture i.e., growing food with planting, soil testing, and weeding. It uses a Raspberry Pi, Arduino, and weather-resistant materials.

IoT Software for Smart Agriculture

The tools used in precision agriculture provide data-driven insights to maximize crop productivity and revenue. This software supports with facts such as the best planting plan, maintenance guidelines, and environmental aspects that may influence a particular crop. Precision agriculture software regularly deals with predictive analytics aspects such as estimated waste, yield size, and productivity related to market standards, permitting agriculturalists and farmers to select the best product option during each growth cycle.

Precision agriculture software usually connects with generally used controllers or specifically designed hardware in some cases. The software when used along with farm management systems and smart irrigation systems can make farming processes more efficient and decreases the effect of environmental factors and labor costs.

To include an app in the Precision Agriculture set, a product must:

1.   Identify sowing and harvesting plans built on data related to weather, production, etc.
2.   incorporate features such as calendar or syncing with outside calendars
3.   Mention specific crops for reaping grounded on conditions of market and environment.

4. Recommend different methods to enhance harvest and returns for the crop, such as sowing procedures and space utilization.

IoT with robotics, remote sensors, UAVs, and computer vision with persistently growing ML and computational software contribute to smart agriculture for crop tracking, field analysis, and surveys and offer farmers apt strategies to manage farms for saving time and cost.

Table 1 talks about some of the recognized IoT software employed in the domain of smart agriculture.

Table 1. IoT-based software for smart agriculture

Software	Description
Farm Works	1. Designed for modern livestock business to manage data for livestock management. 2. Has facility to ease the tracking of historical data and manage the upcoming events (vaccinations, breeding events, etc.) by use of the calendar. 3. Design simple and intricate prescription maps. 4. Customized reports are generated for viewing sales, by-products, etc.
SMS	1. Easy to use decision-making desktop software. 2. Assists in the collection of data related to fields that are later converted to smart management decisions. 3. Has different modes such as navigation, coverage, boundary, and sampling wizard. These can be used for planting, fertilizing, spraying, and harvesting-related decisions.
MapShots	1. Crop management software 2. Wireless data transfer. 3. Has a robust spreadsheet calculator for various variables and conditionals. 4. Real-time GPS functionality 5. Provides recommendations about nutrients using the nutrient script editor
AgDNA	1. Cloud-based web platform for the selection of tools by farmers. 2. Uses IoT for continuous data assimilation from in-field machinery. 3. Incorporates record-keeping features
Sentra	1. Used for crop health management. 2. Computer vision-based weed maps assist in the identification of the location and density of weeds. 3. Dynamic crop analysis tools support handlers to recognize strained zones by comparing plant health over time and regulating ideal input placement.
AgroSense	1. Comparison analysis tool 2. Has features such as-financial tracking reports, soil survey maps, harvest locator, nutrient management, and planning for targeted areas for fertilizers and pesticides.
AgroPal	Agro Pal, is a Free Farming Assistance Android App backed by Artificial Intelligence. Salient features include Crop Details Assistance, AI-backed Plant Disease Detection, Weather Prediction, Aggregation of useful Agro Information Web links, and Forum support to enable community discussion

IoT Hardware for Smart Agriculture

Table 2 shows the details of the hardware for smart agriculture

Table 2. IoT-based hardware for smart agriculture

Hardware	Description
ESP8266	The ESp8266 (Kumar & D, 2020) is a Wi-Fi module for connecting various IoT-based Smart agriculture components.
PIC Micro-controller	It is used in security, supervising gadgets, and household appliances frequently integrated into an EEPROM.
RTC module	It is useful for real-time clock adjustment and monitoring accurate time for operations of IoT systems (Kuo et al., 2021)
GSM module	This enables SIM to act as a smartphone in any GSM network provider. It has its contact number and uses RS-232 protocol to connect the controller (Saha et al., 2021)
LM35	The LM35 temperature sensor generates an analog O/P voltage equal to the measured temperature. It indicates the output voltage in Celsius (C). It is self-calibrating and does not involve external tuning circuitry.
DHT11	The DHT11 is a widely used sensor for measuring humidity and temperature. The DHT11 temperature and humidity sensor is a widely used component. The sensor is equipped with a specialized NTC for temperature measurement and an 8-bit microcontroller for serial data output [77]. Additionally, the sensor is factory-tuned, making communication with other chipsets easy.

Case Studies

i) Case study 1: IoT-cloud-based greenhouse service platform

Greenhouse serves the purpose of temperature management by absorbing solar energy during the daytime. This particularly assists in winter vegetable production in winter. There are five layers in the system perception and operating layer, data acquisition and control layer, network transport layer, portal service layer, background process, and service layer.

1. Layer 5 system perception and operating layer have temperature and humidity sensors, light sensors, carbon dioxide concentration sensors, soil temperature sensors, and PH sensors.
2. Layer 4 data acquisition and control layer has a light sensor, temperature, and humidity sensor.
3. network transport layer has a light sensor, temperature, and humidity sensor
4. portal service layer: SMS cat pool, voice server, and other terminal support devices; a 128 GB SSD
5. background process and service layer has PC clusters, cloud computing middleware, Hbase database system, and Linux operation system

At layer 5 the control of the system is based on the farmer's choice or a pre-set program. At layer 4 light intensity is controlled along with the control of temperature, humidity, and soil moisture. The greenhouse video data and the environment data are passed over ZigBee. At layer 3 connectivity with the internet, protocol conversion functions, data distribution, and control, encoding, and decoding exchange between the components are fulfilled to enable short-distance communication. At layer 2 information collection speed is enhanced using a voice server, SSD, terminal devices, and SMS cat pool. At layer 1 tenant management service, user management service, and data analysis service are performed. Pros: Multiple sensors are engaged. Cons: Cloud integration is not feasible.

ii) **Case Study 2:** A case study of issuing personalized agro advisories to groundnut farmers

HARITA (Harmonized Information of Agriculture, Revenue, and Irrigation for a Transformation Agenda) is an innovative project from the Government of Andhra Pradesh (AP). It is assigned to C-DAC and has the objective of irrigation, agriculture, and revenue data integration to safeguard timely, consistent, and efficient decision-making. In this project, real-time data for agriculture is acquired emphasizing the use of sensor-based technologies. The acquired data is employed for enhancing water management and customized agricultural expansion facilities. The prototype for the HARITA project is HARITA-PRIYA which aims at determining micro-climate information using WSNs that are useful for the issue of customized and location-specific advisories to agriculturalists using SMS. WSN nodes and gateways are installed in rural areas of Anantapur District in farmers' pastures farming groundnut for the period of the Kharif 2015 season. The system took about 450 acres of land in the pest and disease investigation system and about 710 agriculturalists of the involved villages were listed and received advisories for the period of the crop season of Kharif 2015.

The temperature, relative humidity, soil moisture, soil temperature, and leaf wetness are the five parameters that WSN nodes record and communicate the data regularly to a distant server, across a field installed with an internet-enabled WSN Gateway. Specific to each village there are WSN nodes that are associated with a WSN gateway and are relative to the area for groundnut cultivation. As discussed, decision support advisory prototypes are stored on the server for analysis of field data to produce warnings for pests and diseases.

FUTURE RESEARCH DIRECTIONS

In the last decade, we have seen substantial technological advancements that have contributed to improvising our routine lives by making resources available readily. Among the advancing technologies is IoT which has efficiently drawn a large community. IoT-based systems have sensors that collect real-time data to perform appropriate tasks by connecting to or internet. IoT as technology presents both challenges and opportunities. The four layers of the IoT-based system are the sensor (data gathering), the communication device (data transmission), the computational unit (data analysis), and the service layer (Just in time actions). The challenges related to IoT include:

i.   **Universal standards:** standards are significant when it relates to credibility. IoT has a range of heterogenous devices that poses problems in terms of interoperability and presents a need for diverse standards and protocols. Thus, the governing agencies as ETSI and IEEE are proposing standards and protocols for addressing the standardization issues so that it enables communication among millions and millions of IoT devices and facilitates interoperability at conceptual, technological, and organizational levels(Friha et al., 2021). Significant research is anticipated to be done to support open standards to enhance interoperability across IoT platforms.

ii. **IoT data:** Smart agriculture has voluminous data related to it. Thus, managing data uniformity, volume, and reliability are challenging. To manage data loss due to node failure or equipment failure, several researchers have put forward imputation approaches such as kernel smoothing, multiple mean matching, regression analysis, etc. This helps to maintain data uniformity.

The main causes of missing data in Smart agriculture are electricity or mechanical failure, weather conditions, or computation error. To ensure the reliability of data, data mining techniques have been implemented. These mining techniques assist in various dimensions of smart agriculture as pesticide reduction, irrigation prediction, etc.(F. Chen et al., 2015) (Y. A. Chen et al., 2021).In addition, noisy and abnormal data put forward substantial drawbacks to the effective application of data mining techniques in smart agriculture. Therefore, it is essential to handle noisy data by making use of proven techniques (Webster & Watson, 2002).

iii. **Regulatory issues:** The Internet of Things (IoT) involves legal and regulatory challenges, primarily in the domain of privacy and security. In addition, other regulatory challenges include technological difficulties, competitiveness, service provision, etc. (Y. A. Chen et al., 2021). Regulations can differ by country and distinct laws in various regions worldwide may have an impact on IoT applications in specific apps, such as agro-food supply.

iv **Security and Reliability** is an issue for IoT devices installed outdoors. The devices may be affected by environmental factors resulting in connectivity failures. To avoid such issues the IoT devices must be physically protected.

v. **Scalability:** In smart agriculture, a considerable number of linked devices and sensors are fitted, needing an intelligent IoT management framework to detect and control devices.

vi **Cost-Effectiveness:** In IoT deployment involved cost becomes a major concern. The researchers are working to find cost-effective solutions. Though the IoT-based systems have been deployed on farms internationally. However, the challenge remains to bring down the cost further. Therefore, such an area is purposely the need of the time.

vii **Energy Management:** Energy management is an extremely significant problem in IoT-based systems. The components of the system as network antennas, IoT devices, and additionally related passive modules and basic algorithms should suitably be readdressed when involved in energy harvesting. Otherwise, sources of energy harvesting solutions such as solar power, wind, biomass, and vibration cloud also are tested while designing IoT-based smart agriculture systems.

viii **Need for Real-Time Solution:** The majority of the IoT solutions that exist do not include real timeliness. However, to support precision agriculture, climatic information, and soil parameters be incorporated with the presently developed solutions.

CONCLUSION

IoT has developed progressively in past years and a range of IoT-based frameworks have been created in a diverse realm, specifically in agriculture. The present chapter is an effort to discuss the prevalent IoT status in agriculture examining existing IoT research trends common hardware and software, agriculture APPs, advantages & challenges. Regardless of many challenges, IoT is a pioneering revolution with expected exponential growth. The forthcoming studies, developments, and initiatives generally in the IoT-based smart agriculture field would enhance the living quality of farmers and cause significant advancements in the agricultural sector. Though, various questions must be answered to make things green for small and medium-scale growers. Cost, infrastructure, and Security are major concerns. We have also discussed case studies to better understand the applications of IoT for smart agriculture.

IoT solutions are focused on supporting agriculturalists to overcome the supply-demand gap thus some of the future trends of smart agriculture are the collection of data by smart agriculture sensors to anticipate the production output that assists to plan for improved product distribution, Agricultural drones for crop health assessment, crop monitoring, irrigation, planting, crop spraying, and soil and field analysis, Livestock tracking and geofencing, Smart Greenhouses, Predictive analytics for smart farming, other technological and deployment advancements. Particularly, low-cost, energy-efficient, interoperable, autonomous, standardized, and robust solutions with elements like AI and decision support systems and low maintenance are the need of smart agriculture. The underlying explanations of different facets of IoT must be dealt with in such a way that agriculture is smart and pervasive.

REFERENCES

Agrahari, R. K., Kobayashi, Y., Sonam, T., & Tanaka, T. (2021). Soil Science and Plant Nutrition Smart fertilizer management : The progress of imaging technologies and possible implementation of plant biomarkers in agriculture. *Soil Science and Plant Nutrition, 67*(3), 248–258. doi:10.1080/00380768.2 021.1897479

Bhagat, M., Kumar, D., & Kumar, D. (2019). Role of Internet of Things (IoT) in Smart Farming: A Brief Survey. *Proceedings of 3rd International Conference on 2019 Devices for Integrated Circuit, DevIC 2019*, 141–145. 10.1109/DEVIC.2019.8783800

Bu, F., & Wang, X. (2019). A smart agriculture IoT system based on deep reinforcement learning. *Future Generation Computer Systems, 99*, 500–507. doi:10.1016/j.future.2019.04.041

Chauhan, R. M. (2015). Advantages And Challenging in E Agriculture. *Oriental Journal of Computer Science & Technology, 8*(3), 228–233. www.computerscijournal.org

Chen, F., Deng, P., Wan, J., Zhang, D., Vasilakos, A. V., & Rong, X. (2015). Data mining for the internet of things: Literature review and challenges. *International Journal of Distributed Sensor Networks, 2015*(i). doi:10.1155/2015/431047

Chen, Y. A., Hsieh, W. H., Ko, Y. S., & Huang, N. F. (2021). An Ensemble Learning Model for Agricultural Irrigation Prediction. *International Conference on Information Networking*, 311–316. 10.1109/ICOIN50884.2021.9333852

Friha, O., Ferrag, M. A., Shu, L., Maglaras, L., & Wang, X. (2021). Internet of Things for the Future of Smart Agriculture: A Comprehensive Survey of Emerging Technologies. *IEEE/CAA Journal of Automatica Sinica, 8*(4), 718–752. doi:10.1109/JAS.2021.1003925

Galang, M., Wicaksono, S., Suryani, E., & Hendrawan, R. A. (2022). Increasing productivity of rice plants based on IoT (Internet Of Things) to realize Smart Agriculture using System Thinking approach. *Procedia Computer Science, 197*, 607–616. doi:10.1016/j.procs.2021.12.179

Gubbi, J., Buyya, R., Marusic, S., & Palaniswami, M. (2013). Internet of Things (IoT): A vision, architectural elements, and future directions. *Future Generation Computer Systems, 29*(7), 1645–1660. doi:10.1016/j.future.2013.01.010

Gupta, B., Madan, G., & Md, A. (2022). A smart agriculture framework for IoT-based plant decay detection using a smart croft algorithm. *Materials Today: Proceedings*, *62*, 4758–4763. doi:10.1016/j.matpr.2022.03.314

Hardcastle, T. L. (2019). *Field Agent-the iPhone app that pays you: Unlocking the door behind attracting, retaining, and bringing back past agents*. Academic Press.

Kumar, K. A. (2020). An Internet of Thing-based Agribot (IOT- Agribot) for Precision Agriculture and Farm Monitoring. *International Journal of Education and Management Engineering*, *10*(4), 33–39. doi:10.5815/ijeme.2020.04.04

Kuo, Y. W., Wen, W. L., Hu, X. F., Shen, Y. T., & Miao, S. Y. (2021). A lora-based multisensor IoT platform for agriculture monitoring and submersible pump control in a water bamboo field. *Processes (Basel, Switzerland)*, *9*(5), 1–17. doi:10.3390/pr9050813

Lavanya, G., Rani, C., & Ganeshkumar, P. (2020). An automated low-cost IoT-based Fertilizer Intimation System for smart agriculture. *Sustainable Computing : Informatics and Systems*, *28*, 1–12.

Lindemann, M. D. (2019). 169 awardee talk-nutrition from a risk management perspective. *Journal of Animal Science, 97*(Supplement_3), 174–175.

Mohapatra, H., & Rath, A. K. (2022). IoE-based framework for smart agriculture. *Journal of Ambient Intelligence and Humanized Computing*, *13*(1), 407–424. doi:10.100712652-021-02908-4

Nagaraja, G. S., A.B., S., Soumya, T., & Abhinith, A. (2019). IOT-based smart agriculture management system. *4th International Conference on Computational Systems and Information Technology for Sustainable Solution (CSITSS)*, 1–5.

Ojha, T., Bera, S., Misra, S., & Raghuwanshi, N. S. (2015). Dynamic duty scheduling for green sensor-cloud applications. *Proceedings of the International Conference on Cloud Computing Technology and Science, CloudCom,* 841–846. 10.1109/CloudCom.2014.169

Ouafiq, E. M., Saadane, R., & Chehri, A. (2022). Data Management and Integration of Low Power Consumption Embedded Devices IoT for Transforming Smart Agriculture into Actionable Knowledge. *Agriculture (Switzerland)*, *12*(3), 329. Advance online publication. doi:10.3390/agriculture12030329

Ousmane, D., Joel, J. P. C. R., Mbaye, S., & Jaime, L. (2013). Distributed Database Management Techniques for Wireless Sensor Networks. *Proceedings - 2013 International Conference on Computer, Electrical and Electronics Engineering: "Research Makes a Difference",* 548–553. 10.1109/ICCEEE.2013.6633999

Pereira, F. M. V., Milori, D. M. B. P., Pereira-Filho, E. R., Venâncio, A. L., Russo, M., Cardinali, M. C. B., Martins, P. K., & Freitas-Astúa, J. (2011). Laser-induced fluorescence imaging method to monitor citrus greening disease. *Computers and Electronics in Agriculture*, *79*(1), 90–93. doi:10.1016/j.compag.2011.08.002

Ray, P. P. (2014). Home Health Hub Internet of Things (H3IoT): An architectural framework for monitoring the health of elderly people. *2014 International Conference on Science Engineering and Management Research, ICSEMR 2014*, 31–33. 10.1109/ICSEMR.2014.7043542

Saha, H. N., Roy, R., Chakraborty, M., & Sarkar, C. (2021). Development of IoT-based smart security and monitoring devices for agriculture. *Agricultural Informatics: Automation Using the IoT and Machine Learning*, 147–169.

Sheng, Z., Yang, S., Yu, Y., Vasilakos, A. V., Mccann, J. A., & Leung, K. K. (2013). A Survey on the IETF Protocol Suite for the Internet of Things: Standards, Challenges, And Opportunities. Academic Press.

Shi, Y., Wang, Z., Wang, X., & Zhang, S. (2015). Internet of Things Application to Monitoring Plant Disease and Insect Pests. *Proceedings of the 2015 International Conference on Applied Science and Engineering Innovation, 12*. 10.2991/asei-15.2015.7

The World Bank. (n.d.). *What a Waste*. https://datatopics.worldbank.org/what-a-waste/

Torky, M., & Hassanien, A. E. (2020). Integrating Blockchain and the Internet of Things in Precision Agriculture : Analysis, Opportunities, and Challenges. *Computers and Electronics in Agriculture, 178*(May), 105476. Advance online publication. doi:10.1016/j.compag.2020.105476

Vitali, G., Francia, M., Golfarelli, M., & Canavari, M. (2021). Crop Management with the IoT : An Interdisciplinary Survey. *Agronomy (Basel), 11*(1), 1–18. doi:10.3390/agronomy11010181

Wadekar, S., Vakare, V., Prajapati, R., Yadav, S., & Yadav, V. (2016). Smart water management using IoT. In *5th International Conference on Wireless Networks and Embedded Systems (WECON)* (pp. 1-4). IEEE.

Walter, A., Finger, R., Huber, R., & Buchmann, N. (2017). Smart farming is key to developing sustainable agriculture. *Proceedings of the National Academy of Sciences of the United States of America, 114*(24), 6148–6150. doi:10.1073/pnas.1707462114 PMID:28611194

Wang, P., Aalipur, B., & Wang, D. (2021). Microprocessors and Microsystems An improved multilayer perceptron approach for detecting sugarcane yield production in IoT-based smart agriculture. *Microprocessors and Microsystems, 82*(November), 103822. doi:10.1016/j.micpro.2021.103822

Webster, J., & Watson, R. T. (2002). Analyzing The Past to Prepare for the future: Writing A Literature Review. *Management Information Systems Quarterly, 26*(2), 13–23.

Chapter 12
E–Waste Control and Its Recycling to Build Sustainable Society in the Global Context

Swatantra Kumar Jaiswal
National Institute of Technology, Raipur, India

Suraj Kumar Mukti
National Institute of Technology, Raipur, India

Kali Charan Rath
GIET University, India

ABSTRACT

Electrical and electronic equipment that has reached the end of its useful life produces e-waste for the society. It generates various problems for society sustainability. The time has come to take the remedial action for its preventive or recycle it for various usages. This chapter incorporates a correlation research of e-waste from distinct international locations and sufficiently illuminates the variables adding to the development of e-squander and its management structures. Accordingly, it gives reality to lower e-object usage at the customer facet and manipulates the estimate at the maker facet. Furthermore, it would be treasured by the leaders who are related to drafting India's future e-squander approach.

INTRODUCTION

When electrical and electronic equipment reached to the end of its useful life or is no longer suitable to use further then electronic trash, or e-wastes are produced. Computers, servers, workstations, displays, CDs, printers, scanners, copiers, minicomputers, fax machines, battery packs, PDAs, phones, TVs, iPods, medical equipment, clothes washers, coolers, and climate control systems are all included in such category of "e-waste" at the end of their life after use. Older devices that have been around for a while are replaced quickly by new one. As a result of this quantity of electronic waste increases. The effort of

DOI: 10.4018/978-1-6684-6821-0.ch012

administrative work that people do has gone up while expectations for the future have gone down. So, electrical and electronic contraptions that have been discarded.

E-waste is a name for electronic parts or components waste that are intended to be recycled, reused, or rescued. Handling electronic trash casually in immature nations can affect human wellbeing and the climate. Computer processors and other electronic waste may be hazardous. During the reuse and removal of old or damage components, the representatives and networks in immature nations are at risk. To stay away from dangerous openness in reuse exercises, extraordinary watchfulness should be taken. Care should be taken to stop the spillage of dangerous substances from landfills and cinders. The development of perilous waste is diminished by worldwide agreements. Despite the convention, E-waste are still being transported and unloaded. It has been observed that 50 million tons of electronic trashes were delivered in last few years. PCs, TVs, showcases, cell phones, and tablets make up half of this, with greater home machines and heating, ventilating, and air conditioning frameworks making up the rest. Just 20% of overall e-squander is reused yearly, which suggests that 40 million tons of e-wastes are either singed for asset recuperation or illicitly traded and handled in a shoddy way, regardless of 66% of the total populace being covered by e-squander regulation. E-wastes in various nations provide a negative effect on their environment which destroys the eco-friendly environment by the careless or nonexistent authorization of existing administrative structures, low level of attention to control the wastes.

To diminish natural pollution and wellbeing perils, non-industrial countries should make compelling techniques to advance reusing or revamping of e-wastes in expert offices. Starting around 2018, India has delivered north of 2,000,000 tons of e-waster yearly and has likewise imported a sizable measure of e-waste from different countries. It is common to see individuals unloading in open dump locales, which leads to issues like groundwater tainting, awful wellbeing, and the sky is the limit from there. According to the study Electronic Waste Management in India by the Associated Chambers of Commerce and Industry of India (ASSOCHAM) and KPMG, PC hardware accounts for nearly 70% of all e-waste, with the remainder coming from household sources like telephones (12%), electrical equipment (8%), and medical hardware (7%). The E-Waste (Management) Rules were released by the Ministry of Environment, Forests, and Climate Change. The public authority conducted EPR in accordance with the standards, which call for manufacturers to collect 40% to 70% of the electronic waste they generate.

Electronic products (like TV, computer, smart phones etc.) which are not in use or get discarded are called as e-waste. E-wastes calls a serious problem for the society and surroundings when these contents go beyond expectations. Some basic reasons behind increase of e-waste in large quantity is as follows:

Changing of technology
Shift towards new market electronic products
Poor and low grade finished products
Poor recycling facilities available

Environmental Effect of E-Waste

E-waste affects nearly every system in the human body due to presence of following components viz. mercury, lead, cadmium, barium, lithium, some plastic based products like PVC (Polyvinyl Chloride). It may cause some serious health issues on the main parts of the body, like: heart, brain, liver, kidney etc.. Persistent Bio Accumulative Toxins (PBTs) can create health and environmental issue when e-waste is not properly disposed. Such e-waste poor deposition may cause cancer-producing dioxins and can enter in our body with air. Environment get polluted when e-waste come in contact with air and water for a longer time. This will slowly enter to food chain system also and will create several problems for society.

So, for preventing such hazardous situation we should take preventive actions, such as:

Proper disposal of e-waste
Removal of toxic material as much as possible
Use of environmentally friendly electronic components

Current Challenge and May Become Future Opportunity of E-Waste

As system advances, wastes are also increased in same proportion. If we need to develop our work culture normal to smart, then we need good use of electronics products and components in day to day life use. Currently due to faster change in technologies, devices are also rapidly out of use and contribute in e-waste (Terazono et al. (2006)). This is very serious issue in developing countries where we use less finished products. Also due to growth in IT sector in India enhances the use of electronic products very quickly. So, India needs a strict forward e-waste (solid waste) management and legislature strategy to control various kinds of e-waste.

E-Waste Problem in India

On environmental performance index 2018 India ranks 177 out of 180 countries. This shows performance rating in e-waste disposal and declination of healthy environment. Though India as for report is 5th highest e-waste generating categories but India only can recycle 3% of total waste disposal.

Current Waste Management Opportunity in India

The ministry of environment, forest and climate change announces waste (management) rules in 2016 to reduce waste generating pollution and to increase recycling. In some countries waste are major source of metal production also. China recover approx one third of metal required by waste recycling. So same scenario we can also follow to reduce the dependency on ores for some metal availability. In short, we can use waste as great opportunity in near future.

The ASSOCHAM report 2017 suggests to draw out formal/standard operating procedures to reduce waste generation. The principle of EPR is applied for management of waste. So, waste cannot treat as simple solid waste management.

Some Waste Management Initiatives

As country progresses e-waste also increases. So strict action required for some effective policy to maintain the lower level of e-waste in India. Some techniques are called e-cycling. E-cycling is newest techniques to recycling with recovering. It also includes reduces greenhouse gas emission, reducing pollution and saving energy. It will help to promote green sound method to tackle toxic materials. We have to follow some other initiatives like e-marinara into-German based initiatives.

In some software firms in Karnataka, India, have agreements with e-Parisian. This is different technique than other because this follows some standard techniques in each part for e-waste disposal and recycling (Thakur & Kumar, (2021)). In dismantle line e-waste divided into plastic, rubber and metal sheet parts. Then proceed for further level of recycling these items . Delhi based company take initiative to collect e- waste by toll free number. This avoids people to mix e-waste with simple solid waste. Such initiatives should be taken in national level to facilitate easy e-waste collection in every state. Proper care must be taken by state Government for it's disposal.

E-Waste Classification

E-waste can classify on the basis of composition and components like ferrous and nonferrous metals, glasses, plastics and some others. Iron and steel are some major components which can be recycled in large proportion (Robinson (2009)). Second largest component which can be recycled is plastic with significant market value. Copper and aluminium are some other major metals which can be recovered by various technical procedures. On the basis of European Union there are 10 major categories as follows:

large electronics appliances: refrigerators, freezers, cooking stoves, electric fans etc.
small electronics appliances: vacuum cleaners, grinders.
IT and Telecommunication equipment's, mainframes, computers.
Consumer equipment's like radios, video camera, musical instruments.
Lightning equipment's: fluorescent lamps and discharge lamps.
Electrical and electronic tools: sewing machine, milling, grinder machine, drilling machine,
Toys equipment's: sporting goods with electrical equipment's.
Medical devices: cardiology, radiotherapy equipment's.
Monitoring and control instruments: smoke detectors, heating regulators.
Automatic dispensers: hot drinks, cold drinks.

The e-waste of such categories will be well taken care by the Government side through the environment control policy.

Components of Electronic Waste

E-waste has been categories mainly into 3 components:

Large household
IT and Telecom equipment's
Refrigerator and washing machines

On the basis of above machine and equipment's e-waste contains below mentioned materials:

Metals
Motors/compressors
Cooling, plastic
Insulation
Glass, LCD
Rubber, wiring/electrical

Transformers
Magnetrons
Textiles
Circuit boards
External electric cables
Ceramic fibers
Radioactive substances

Compositions of E-Waste in Mobile Phones

Composition of e-waste can be defined on the basis of equipment's we are talking about like smart phones, computers other electronic products. But in all types of electronic wastes some components are common like silicon, plastic, metals, non-metals etc.(Widmer et al. (2005)). Some components are in categories of hazardous and some in non-hazardous or called as nontoxic materials like metal, plastic, glass, wood, ceramics and printed circuit board. Few examples are iron and steel components are above 50%, Plastic approximately 21% and Nonferrous materials 13%

Some hazardous materials like mercury, lead, arsenic, cadmium is identified as toxic materials. These are also called as heavy metals with great density. Such toxic materials are valuable too. Here we have to see that how technically such materials can be recycled as much as possible. This will leads to decrease the load of metal production in country and requirements can come from recycling only. This becomes a source to conserve resources and can be used in near future for utilisation (Rautela et al. (2021)).

Mobile phone contains more than 40 elements.
Some base metals, some special metals and some precious metals.
Name of some base metals are copper and tin.
Name of some special's metals lithium, cobalt, indiums and antimony. Some precious metals are silver, gold and palladium.

Special treatment of such materials is can be treated as recovery of materials which is easy to recycle than extraction from ores. Circuit board contains most of the valuable materials like arsenic, cadmium, chromium, lead and mercury etc. These may be taken opportunity rather than treated as waste substance. 50 gram of lead solder can be obtaining in each square meter used in printed circuit boards. CRTs are one of the common sources of waste production (Vats & Singh, (2014)). Developed countries like US banned the direct disposal as land filling of CRTS. So in our country also needed some strong action against land filling of waste, that contaminates air in that area and also groundwater. Average lead find in CRTs are 1.2 to 1.5kgs. Because of toxic materials scientists and engineers have to accept this challenge with latest technology for manage waste. Disposal method and recycling technique can change the whole game of waste management scenario in India.

Due to poor e-waste disposal there are lot of problems arises for various heavy metals. Some of important lead metals with their health impacts are as follow:

Lead: Used in various electronic products like gaskets, computer monitors and in solders in printed circuit board. Lead causes damage to central and peripheral nervous system, blood systems, kidney and reproductive system in humans. Lead also can affect plants and their natural ability.

Figure 1. Components of e-waste

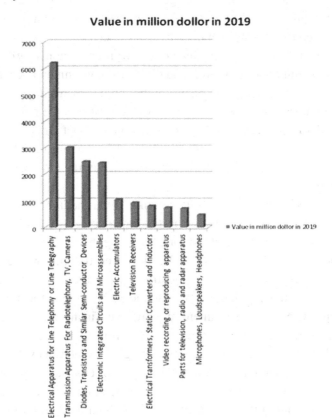

Cadmium Surface mounted devices (SMD) chip resisters, infra-red detectors, CRTS. Especially it effect s liver, kidneys, pancreas, thyroid.

Mercury: 22% of mercury yearly used in various electric and electronics equipment's. Mercury is used in thermostats, sensors, relays, switches, medical equipment's. Mercury directly effects respiratory system also add in food chain via fish.

Chromium: CR6 is used as corrosion protector of untreated and galvanized steel plants.CR6 can damage DNA and extremely toxic in the environment. Long term effects are skin sensitization and kidney damage.

Plastic PVC is one of the major components (approx. 26%) used as plastic in electronic components' components are found in cabling and computer housings.

LITERATURE REVIEW

The expression "electronic trash," is basically called as "e-wastes," alludes to different electric and electronic gadgets that are as of now not valuable to their proprietors (Osibanjo & Nnorom (2007)). Survey concentrated to analyze different five product categories, covering just 25% of the EU15's absolute WEEE stream: coolers, PCs, TVs, scanners, and little homegrown machines (Nnorom & Osibanjo

(2008)). Hence, these items match other WEEE gauges, which shift from 14 to 20 kg for every individual. Indeed, even yet, WEEE represents 8% of all metropolitan waste, making it one of the waste areas and remedial action can be taken to control (Plambeck & Wang (2009)).

In India, utilizing sustainable power is basically focused to progress monetary development, increment energy security, increment admittance to power, and dial back environmental change (Premalatha et al. (2014)). By utilizing supportable energy and ensuring that all occupants approach ability, trustworthy, manageable, and contemporary energy, economical advancement is made possible. The public authority has made liberal standards, programs, and an environment to tempt global venture and immediately advance the country in the sustainable power area (Sthiannopkao & Wong (2013)). In the next few years, it is planned to project that the homegrown work circumstance in the environmentally friendly power area will improve altogether.

It has been seen that e-waste is an issue for countries like China and India, because both are delivering locally and unlawfully imported. These material imports from squander streams furnish arising economies with a business opportunity as well as a method for addressing the requirement for reasonable utilized electrical and electronic hardware (Lu et al. (2015)). Moreover, the improvement of a semi-formal or casual area is being helped with industrializing countries by an absence of public guideline as well as lacking implementation of existing regulations. Around the exchanging, retouching, and recuperation of materials from old electronic contraptions, an entirely different financial area is creating.

According to the perspectives of asset efficiency and environmental safeguarding, the importance of managing electrical and electronic waste for domestic and global material cycles are increased (Kahhat et al. (2008)). With a give up intention to prevent the import of e-waste, China and India are one of a kind international locations as of overdue modified their general units of legal guidelines. In any case, considering the fact that they are full-size makers of EEE (China produces 90% of the sector's CRTs, for instance) (Singh & Zeng (2016)), these nations must recognize that it is far to their best advantage to close material cycles and get to the unrefined components found within the e-squander streams (Ilankoon et al. (2018)).

E-waste, electrical and electronic hardware (WEEE), or give up-of-life items are electrical and electronic equipment that has been deemed outdated or undesirable by the buyer (Patil et al. al. (2020)). The things, however, is misleading since it categorically labels used hardware (Islam et al. (2021)) as waste, even when some of the equipment in the streams may be reused through voluntarily accessible commercial enterprise sectors (Arya, & Kumar (2020); Forti et al. (2020)).

E-Waste Management Models Implemented in Various Countries

Our major focus will be on E-waste generated from mobile phones. India alone has 1026.37 million active mobile phone users according to TRAI's data few year back. Similarly, Australia has 18.6 million mobile phone users and Malaysia has 18.4 million users. So, it cannot be denied that mobile phones have huge contribution for E-waste generation of above-mentioned countries (Hossain et al. (2015)). The major reason of this tremendous amount of E-waste generation from mobile phones is because of their quick new model releases. The short life of mobile phones is causing them as major source of e-waste generation. As soon as they become outdated people carelessly throw them into dustbin and do not care if they are properly disposed, they should be properly sent to collection centers for recycling.

Africa has been divided into five regions East Africa, West Africa, North Africa, South Africa and Central Africa. As it is well known that Africa is one of the poor countries the major problems being faced are:

Lack of transportation facilities
Lack of communication

In a recent study (Patil& Ramakrishna (2020)) it is found that the disposal of such wastes in most of the African countries are informal and unregulated but as we know e-waste have toxic effects on health of human body. African officials have tried to manage informal sectors but they were unsuccessful. Most of the countries have still not build the proper framework for E-waste disposal. Well it is justifiable why people are using informal ways of disposal (Zhang et al. (2012)). It is also found that Kenya is the only country in East Africa that has proper framework for E-Waste management. Similarly in Southern Africa such facilities are came to frontier also.

The cause so found at the background work and found the major reasons as listed below:

Lack of proper disposal framework.
Lack of Government's policies and follow up
lack of E-waste recycling facilities.
Casualness for disposal of e-waste.

Action Plan by Various Countries to Deal With E-Waste

African government is still reliant on the old ways of E-waste disposal which include following

Burning openly
land filling
Informal e-waste recycling

The challenges being faced by them is self-created. Regulations and rules are lacking everywhere and government is also responsible for the same.

How Malaysia Deals With E-Waste

Like our country India, Malaysia is also a developing country producing huge amount of e- waste. Studies even suggest that the people there have capability of purchasing more than one handsets. Such issues have encouraged Government to establish legislation such as environmental quality released in 2005 which help Malaysia to control translation of e-waste. It also controls illegal import and export of e-waste to and from Malaysia. Still Malaysia transports lots of e-waste .

Figure 2. Total E-waste generated in Malaysia

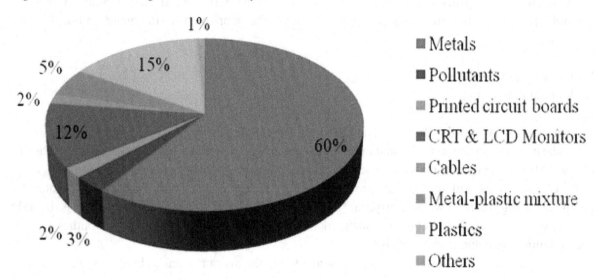

Total E-Waste Generated in Malaysia Year Wise in a Decade

Malaysia shows an increasing trend of e-waste between 2010 and 2020. In above figure it shows that total e-waste which was 6.5 lakh unit in 2010 becomes almost double in 2020. The major cause of this trend is increase in population as well as invent of technology.

Figure 3. E-waste generated due to TV in Malaysia

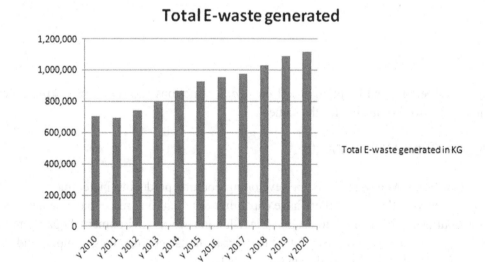

Television as an E-Waste in Malaysia

Television is a major contributor in e-waste in Malaysia which accounts 30% to 40% of total e-waste in initial years but percentage contribution decreased in upcoming years when other electrical and electronic commodities come into picture. No much variation is seen in decade.

Figure 4. E-waste generated due to computer in Malaysia

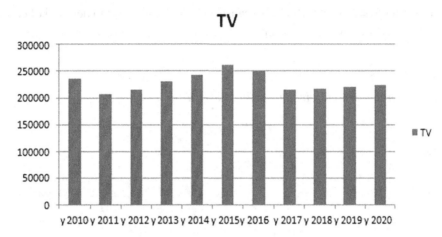

PC as an e-Waste in Malaysia

Pc or computers show a sharp increase in numbers approximately three fold in a single decade between the year 2010 to year 2020. The main reason is introduction of data collection at various places by using computers for e.g. Bank, govt. offices, colleges, hospitals etc.

Figure 5. E-waste generated due to cell phones in Malaysia

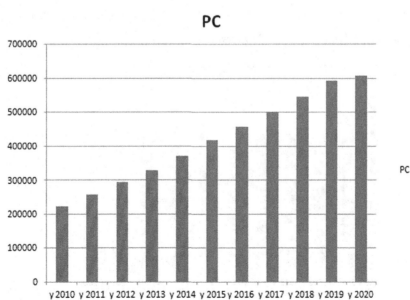

Cell Phones as an E-Waste in Malaysia

Like PCs cell phones have also seen a threefold increase in e-waste generation in last decade. It is a major concern among all the e-waste generated in the country. Dumping of Chinese phones in Malaysian markets is also a major cause because Chinese phones are cheaper with short lifespan. Cell phone demands are very high in developing countries. China is taking advantage of this fact. In current scenario all things are becoming online and cell phones are very essential to fulfill all communication requirements. Specially after invent of internet cell phones become very crucial in human life cycle.

Technology is growing day by day which can cause the exponential rise in demand of cell phones and other allied accessories. So we need to be prepared to combat such a large amount of e-waste generated by cell phone.

Figure 6. E-waste generated due to refrigerator in Malaysia

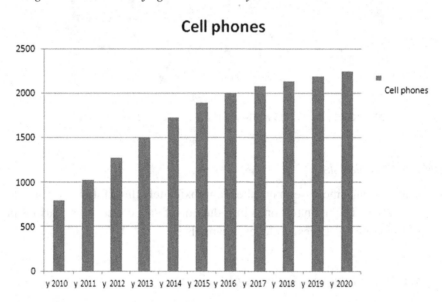

Figure 7. E-waste generated due to A/C in Malaysia

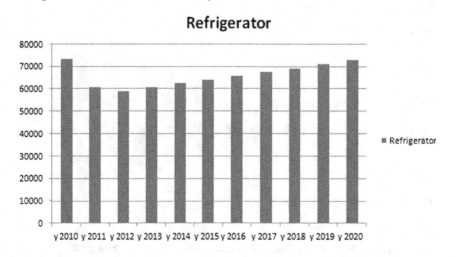

Figure 8. E-waste generated due to washing machine in Malaysia

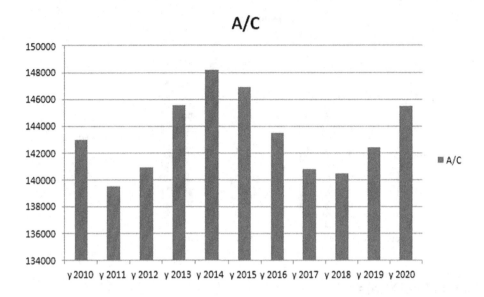

Figure 9. E-waste generated due to rechargeable batteries in Malaysia

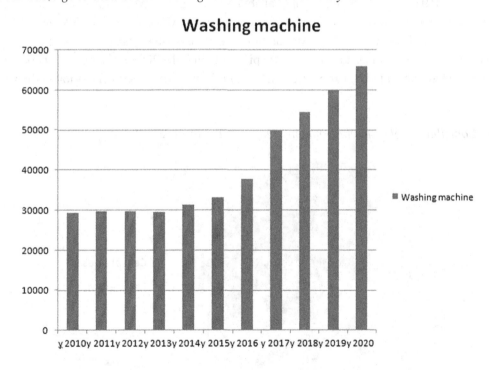

Comparisons are given that in a five-year span how composition or percentage contribution of all e-waste generating sources changed.

Figure 10. Contribution of different component in e-waste during the year 2010 -2015

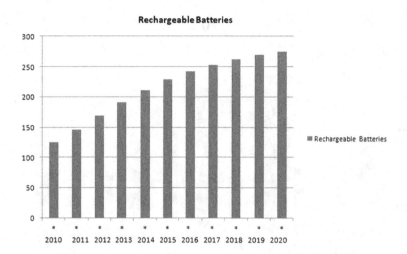

Comparison in Five Years

During the year 2010 to year 2015, the major contributor of e-waste in Malaysia was TV followed by PC or computers and Air conditioners. In 2015 PC or computers have surpassed the TV and becomes top contributor in e-waste followed by TV & Air conditioners. It also shows that how technology influenced the percentage composition and leads to a different pi-graph. In 2019 PC compressed other contributors at a large scale and have occupied 60 to 65 percentage of total share in e-waste generation in the year 2022.

Figure 11. Contribution of different component in e-waste in year 2019

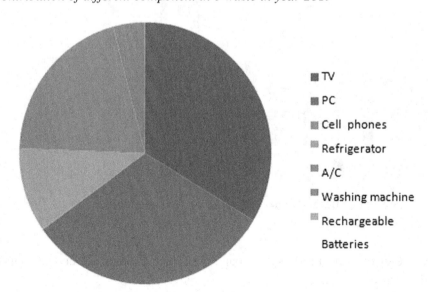

Figure 12. Contribution of different component in e-waste in year 2022

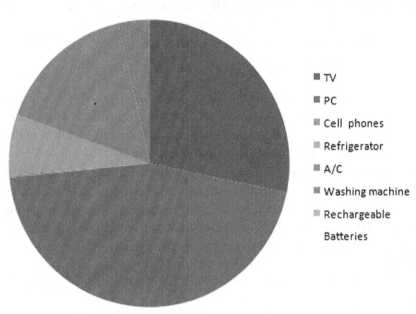

Figure 13. Contribution of different component in e-waste in last decade

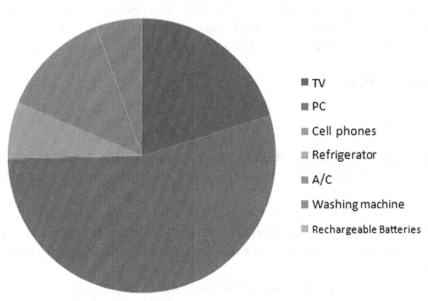

Recycling Factor

The recycling factors of the country depends on following factors

Awareness among citizens
Rules of Malaysian Government
Money back for E-waste

The major collection goes to Informal sectors because they offer much more money than offered by formal sectors. Studies depict that improper framework is leading to such low collection by formal sectors, they even tried putting various dustbin in respective localities.

There is a tie up between Department of Environment Malaysia and huge Brand names such as Nokia and Sony to enhance collection of e-waste through collection centers. Their service centers offers to take back scheme in lieu of obsolete mobile phones that encourages customer for giving their phones.

A study also implies that Malaysians are unaware of e-waste recycling and weak guidelines are imposed by Department of Environment causes no following of rules by Industries.

Malaysia is using:

Wet chemical process
Hydrometallurgical process
Electrolysis

Similar to India, Malaysia also has formal and informal two major sectors for material handling and treatment. Formal sector has all the facilities of recovery and recovering valuable material. They treat waste produced compulsorily. whereas informal sectors do not treat waste generated completely they use basic processes for the same which is inefficient.

Australia Deals With E-Waste

Problems faced by Australia:

88% of the four million computers and three million TV's purchased in Australia once a year can end up in landfill - this contributes to the 140,000+ tones of electronic waste generated by Australians once a year

Fewer than 1 Chronicles of TVs and around 100 pc of PCs and laptops are recycled Australia wide.

E-waste is to blame for 70th of the poisonous chemicals like lead, cadmium and mercury found in landfill - and 23,000 tons of CO_2 emissions would be saved if half the televisions discarded annually were recycled.

Electronic rubbish is growing at 3 times the speed of any other waste stream.

Discarded devices are stilt up round the world at a rate of 40 million annually.

98% of the elements in your pc or TV can be absolutely recycled.

There is a scheme called NATIONAL TELEVISION AND COMPUTER RECYCLING SCHEME which is basically available in every part of Australia even in the remote areas in addition to regional and metropolitan areas.

The NTCRS provides around 98% of Australia's population with reasonable access for collection services (televisions and computer parts). Location and opening times for recycling and collection services are determined by the organizations who manage them. This provides flexibility to suit local circumstances. Services may include a permanent collection site at a local waste transfer station or retail outlet, or one-off recycling events. These may be operated through local council or resource management centers. Services are free for households and small businesses, while charges may apply for larger businesses. Not all drop-off points in Australia are part of the scheme, and fees may be payable at some locations. Contact the providers below or your local council for details.

Four organizations have been approved to deliver recycling services under the scheme.

Technolect
Electronics Product Stewardship Australasia (EPSA)
E-Cycle Solutions

EPSA

EPSA is an approved co-regulatory arrangement partner below the National TV and pc recycling theme, offer free recycling for televisions, computers, printers and pc accessories.
Over 98 (by weight) of e-waste received by EPSA is diverted from landfill and recycled to be made into helpful raw materials.
EPSA is a company of Sims Lifecycle Services, the world leader in sustainable and responsible electronics recycling. Working with EPSA suggests that you're dealing directly with the recycler and not a 3rd party broker.
EPSA have assortment points accessible to households and tiny business's Australia wide.

Drop Zone

Drop zone is great initiative to attract common people for proper disposal of e-waste. It provides free recycling services for householders and a small business to dispose of unwanted televisions, computers and computer products (such as printers, keyboards and mice), regardless of their manufacturing date, brand, etc.. Such facilities should also have to implement in India to control various e-wastes.

E-Waste Control Management

To empower repair, reuse, and reuse over waste disposal inside the event that it's miles more conservative to do as such to decrease advent on the supply. To distinguish and facilitate each pastime alongside the waste management chain, laying out clearly defined jobs and duties for every one in every of them is important. The objectives of the waste management assessment are listed. I will assess the suggested activities and determine what kinds, what kinds, and how much trash I anticipate being produced; and I will examine any potential environmental effects that the location's production of rubbish may have. The 7R's Principle of waste management policy are:

Reduce.

Reuse.

Repair.

Recycle.

Re-gift.

Refuse.

Recover.

The CEO is eventually capable and answerable for waste the board inside the Business Administrations Association, and at the side of the Senior Supervisory institution, the man or woman will make certain that the BSO sees eye to eye to all lawful and felony commitments and instructions given by means of the DHSSPSNI via arrangements and methodology. The Waste Administration Controls Affirmation Standard has an Administrator appointed by the CEO. Setting up a detailing framework to bring relevant records to the senior crew is critical. All Directors should make sure that their group is aware of and follows all preparations of the waste management strategy, as it is proper to advance and empower a tradition of waste decrease, re-use, and fee investment budget inside their enterprise place.

Every worker has a responsibility to think about how their actions affect the environment. The Risk Management Steering Group is in charge of monitoring developments and assessing strategies for the control of waste, and they'll inform the CEO of their performance. Ensuring that waste generation is decreased to the greatest extent possible, and the risks associated when shipping, handling, and disposal are all handled properly, is one way to do that.

Policies to reduce and prevent the production of hazardous waste have been put in place by the government. There is a move of harmless to the system. The Local Foundation for English Speaking Nations (Africa Organization) advances the exchange of information about clean innovation and low-wastes creation. This will provide a good environment to society. The public authority hopes to get a lot from its cooperation. The Environmental Protection (Amendment) Act of 2008 has provisions for the polluter-pays principle. The Hazardous Waste Regulations require that hazardous waste be rendered harmless before disposal.

Prevention and reduction of waste will manage hazardous waste. The "cradle to grave" principle is taken into account when evaluating environmental impacts. There are no EIA procedures for the management of hazardous waste. The management, collection, processing, transport, treatment, storage, and disposal of hazardous waste are all governed by the Environment Protection (Standards for Hazardous Wastes) Regulations of 2001. According to the First Schedule of the Environment Protection (Amendment) Act of 2008, all stable wastes are situation to the "Incineration of Municipal Solid Waste, Quarantine" law. Part IV of the Act states that an EIA licence is vital for "Waste, Medical and Clinical Wastes," and "Landfill."

The directions should be discarded accurately and in the right holder. Waste paper should be discarded cautiously and securely. Isolation should be finished at the starting place if the suitable trash bin or container is used. Office trash bins should be open to work. All garbage sacks should be thrown away at the point when half full. Paper towels, flowers, and other non-toxic, non-hazardous garbage that cannot be recycled are domestic waste. The Landfill Directive requires all rubbish to undergo a segregation procedure. To comply with the Directive, the Trust removes all cardboard, office paper, recyclables, and food from the household waste stream. The Landfill Directive is intended to reduce the tendency of trash to affect the environment in a number of ways. The Environmental Permitting Regulations of 2010 are used to enforce the standards set forth in the Directive.

A similar national activity could be an aide for the proposed public interest plan/method. Every state, UT, and town must have a city or city-explicit interest plan in order to be made an itemized undertaking report. The Strong Waste Administration Rules, 2016 will be used to determine the gear, tool, and specialized decisions conditions, as a result of the Public Arrangement proposed in this record.

Local entities' readiness will be taken into account when assessing the nearby scenario. The state plan would offer guidance to nearby organizations and settle the information for establishing separate or incorporated waste processing and disposal facilities. A local or cluster method is needed for this. The monetary incentives and sanctions for nearby authorities entities needed to be dealt with by the State's policy.

How India Deals E-Waste

Recently during an Investigation performed by Central Pollution Control Board discovered that some numbers of e-waste industries operating in Uttar Pradesh . Union environment ministry and Pollution control board also reported that these companies were disposing all their remaining waste into the Ganga River causing irretrievable damage to watercourses and its surroundings, legal actions were taken against them. This is an example of how such activities are going silently in India. India had 310000000 users of mobile phones and now it has increased to 1026.37 million which is only behind one country China and is almost four times of mobile users compared to America. India belongs to top E-waste generator of world putting health of their people at risk.

Literature survey pointed out that in India 70% of E-wastages are generated through computers and around 12% are tele communication products. According to survey among metropolitan cities of India Mumbai generated highest amount of e-waste and is followed by Bangalore and Hyderabad. Most of the India belongs to slum so most of the e-waste generated are either disposed carelessly or filled into lands causing severe harm to nature and environment it is slowly creating toxic material.

Attainable Steps Towards E-Waste

We aim to recycle most of the E-waste generated . So, E-waste can be recycled by collecting them and expensive materials must have been planned to extract from the product by following the procedure of melting and segregating. According to a study 1.6% of total E-waste generated gets recycled in India. This shows how irresponsible are people here. people keep blaming each other rather than facing the real time issues.

Few companies are there which do not provide proper helmets and other required things for proper working in such environment. A great initiative is started in Bengaluru where two non- profitable organizations have been founded that they are trying to recycle e-waste.

Collectively it can be said that E-waste collection and disposal is becoming huge challenge for health of our people. In order to reduce illegal open burning improper landfills the government can try to concatenate informal and formal sectors. A supervised and improvised mechanism needs to be designed for the same. It can only have achieved by public awareness and urgent actions campaigns for proper education of E-waste handling. Similar to Malaysia mobile phone company Nokia has done great job in handling and collecting E-waste from India.

Just few years ago government suspended license of few companies who were illegally disposing E-waste generated by them and such decisions are appreciated.

Future of E-Waste in India

A new rule has been set by ministry of environment and climate change of India from 2016 which aims to reduce E-waste generation. The rule says that (the rules comes under Extended Producer Responsibility) the producer will be responsible for collection of 30% to 70% of the E-waste generated over next 7 years which is again great initiative. They are also trying to merge the Informal sector into formal so the process could be transparent. A new model suggests town wide collection system incorporating physical dismantling of waste and latest technologies, in order to gain higher revenue from the Printed Circuit boards. According to traditional method the recovery of gold is done by wet-chemical process to make it more efficient it will be now done by smelters and refineries. It will lead to safety of workers and higher revenue.

The composition of E-waste includes valuable metals such as silver and gold which can be brought back to their original form. If this is achieved than E-waste recycling will become money earning opportunity for a company as well as individual. Moreover, Government can try to pay informal E-waste collecting enterprises to attract them and integrate with formal sectors so as to elevate the recycling the E-waste efficiently. We should aim to increase the recycled E-waste from 1.6% to somewhere near 10-20%.

Chinese Cheaper and Low-Quality Product Impact on E-Waste Generation in India

China is a very prosperous country as compared to India in field of manufacturing electronic parts and accessories. China and India both are part of southern-eastern portion of Asia. Hence there are very low trade barriers like tariff and non-tariff barriers between both countries. India has an estimated population of 1.5 billion at present time which provides a very huge market to Chinese manufacturers. Economic distribution of wealth in India is a major cause which leads to the dumping of e- waste in India. A large population of India comes under lower middle income group and they have very less amount of money left in hands after fulfilment of basic requirement like food, clothes and shelter. So they can have spent very less amount of money for other purpose like purchase of mobile phones, electronic items & other electronic accessories. China provides all these at very cheap and economically affordable prices to Indian consumers. Due to low prices quality of products compromises and which leads to a very large amount of e-waste generation in India.

India becomes a dumping market for China and it also hamper the local Indian manufacturing units. So it is essential to develop a policy or framework by the government to reduce the burden of Chinese import in Indian markets. Government should have to promote local industries by providing them credit at lower interest rates and also provide tax rebate and tax benefits. For promotion of local industries there should be a proper law which backs these industries and support them by proper means of legislation.

Finally, it can be concluded that instead of collecting e-waste on large scale we should have to decrease the burden of e-waste by reducing Chinese low cost, poor quality and short life product import. The Below diagram shows pi-chart of composition of various electronic items export by china to India .

Figure 14. Chinese export to India of various electrical and electronics items

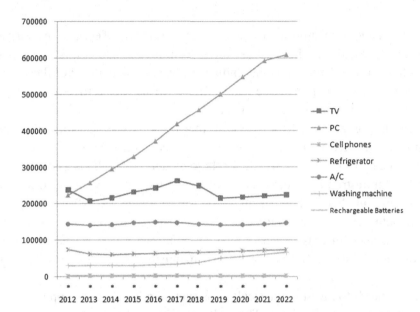

Figure 15. Chinese export to India of various electrical and electronics items

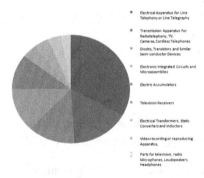

Results

The following outcomes are noted as a result from the above study:

Increase Tariff & non-tariff barriers so that domestic products can compete the cheaper Chinese products.

Initiatives needs to be taken in the direction of trade deficit. India needs to make a trade balance with China.

Promote local industries by providing them tax exemptions as well as credit loan at cheaper interest rates.

Provide support to newcomers in electronic & electrical industries.

Promote awareness about impact of Chinese products in Indian scenario.

Ease the labor laws & provide them social security.

Shifting of agricultural labors in manufacturing sector because agricultural sector is overburdened.

CONCLUSION

In country like India a large population contributes a very large amount of e-waste in total waste generated. Due to dumping of cheap and short life Chinese products in Indian market it is a very large contributor to the e-waste in India. Cause behind it is that India has a very large demand of these products. So it is required to produce electronic items on large scale in India and also needs to reduce dumping of Chinese product in Indian market by applying tariff barriers.

In this project we have gone through the case study of various countries and organizations in the world. Malaysia, Australian and African model of e-waste management are the very good example to tackle the problem and India needs to adopt a mixture of these models. Australia is a country having very less population and good infrastructure. So, in India Australian model can be applied in metropolitan and large cities like Delhi, Mumbai, Kolkata having good infrastructure and African model can be applied in the rural and remote areas of India. Malaysian model can also contribute some percent in this model.

For e-waste management there is no lack of methods & processes but we need physical infrastructure by cooperation of informal sector. Because, e-waste is mainly due to lack of proper segregation method at initial stage.

Government also needs to invest in physical infrastructure to generate a supply chain which can extract the e-waste from the grass root level. This will generate employment for the young generation of the society. Government also needs to run social awareness campaign at mass level so that citizens can aware about health impacts of e-waste and also needs to provide incentives for the e-waste collection promotion. Now time came to be alert for everyone to reduce e-waste and make the environment as an ecofriendly environment for life sustainability.

REFERENCES

Arya, S., & Kumar, S. (2020). E-waste in India at a glance: Current trends, regulations, challenges and management strategies. *Journal of Cleaner Production*, *271*, 122707. doi:10.1016/j.jclepro.2020.122707

Forti, V., Baldé, C. P., Kuehr, R., & Bel, G. (2020). The global e-waste monitor 2020. *Quantities, flows, and the circular economy potential*, 1-119.

Hossain, M. S., Al-Hamadani, S. M., & Rahman, M. T. (2015). E-waste: A challenge for sustainable development. *Journal of Health & Pollution*, *5*(9), 3–11. doi:10.5696/2156-9614-5-9.3 PMID:30524771

Ilankoon, I. M. S. K., Ghorbani, Y., Chong, M. N., Herath, G., Moyo, T., & Petersen, J. (2018). E-waste in the international context–A review of trade flows, regulations, hazards, waste management strategies and technologies for value recovery. *Waste Management (New York, N.Y.)*, *82*, 258–275. doi:10.1016/j. wasman.2018.10.018 PMID:30509588

Islam, M. T., Dias, P., & Huda, N. (2021). Young consumers' e-waste awareness, consumption, disposal, and recycling behavior: A case study of university students in Sydney, Australia. *Journal of Cleaner Production*, *282*, 124490. doi:10.1016/j.jclepro.2020.124490

Kahhat, R., Kim, J., Xu, M., Allenby, B., Williams, E., & Zhang, P. (2008). Exploring e-waste management systems in the United States. *Resources, Conservation and Recycling, 52*(7), 955–964. doi:10.1016/j.resconrec.2008.03.002

Lu, C., Zhang, L., Zhong, Y., Ren, W., Tobias, M., Mu, Z., & Xue, B. (2015). An overview of e-waste management in China. *Journal of Material Cycles and Waste Management, 17*(1), 1–12. doi:10.100710163-014-0256-8

Nnorom, I. C., & Osibanjo, O. (2008). Electronic waste (e-waste): Material flows and management practices in Nigeria. *Waste Management, 28*(8), 1472-1479.

Osibanjo, O., & Nnorom, I. C. (2007). The challenge of electronic waste (e-waste) management in developing countries. *Waste Management & Research, 25*(6), 489–501. doi:10.1177/0734242X07082028 PMID:18229743

Patil, R. A., & Ramakrishna, S. (2020). A comprehensive analysis of e-waste legislation worldwide. *Environmental Science and Pollution Research International, 27*(13), 14412–14431. doi:10.100711356-020-07992-1 PMID:32162230

Plambeck, E., & Wang, Q. (2009). Effects of e-waste regulation on new product introduction. *Management Science, 55*(3), 333–347. doi:10.1287/mnsc.1080.0970

Premalatha, M., Abbasi, T., & Abbasi, S. A. (2014). The generation, impact, and management of e-waste: State of the art. *Critical Reviews in Environmental Science and Technology, 44*(14), 1577–1678. doi:10.1080/10643389.2013.782171

Rautela, R., Arya, S., Vishwakarma, S., Lee, J., Kim, K. H., & Kumar, S. (2021). E-waste management and its effects on the environment and human health. *The Science of the Total Environment, 773*, 145623. doi:10.1016/j.scitotenv.2021.145623 PMID:33592459

Robinson, B. H. (2009). E-waste: An assessment of global production and environmental impacts. *The Science of the Total Environment, 408*(2), 183–191. doi:10.1016/j.scitotenv.2009.09.044 PMID:19846207

Singh, N., Li, J., & Zeng, X. (2016). Global responses for recycling waste CRTs in e-waste. *Waste Management (New York, N.Y.), 57*, 187–197. doi:10.1016/j.wasman.2016.03.013 PMID:27072617

Sthiannopkao, S., & Wong, M. H. (2013). Handling e-waste in developed and developing countries: Initiatives, practices, and consequences. *The Science of the Total Environment, 463*, 1147–1153. doi:10.1016/j.scitotenv.2012.06.088 PMID:22858354

Terazono, A., Murakami, S., Abe, N., Inanc, B., Moriguchi, Y., Sakai, S. I., & Williams, E. (2006). Current status and research on E-waste issues in Asia. *Journal of Material Cycles and Waste Management, 8*(1), 1–12. doi:10.100710163-005-0147-0

Thakur, P., & Kumar, S. (2021). Evaluation of e-waste status, management strategies, and legislations. *International Journal of Environmental Science and Technology*, 1–10.

Vats, M. C., & Singh, S. K. (2014). E-Waste characteristic and its disposal. *International Journal of Ecological Science and Environmental Engineering, 1*(2), 49-61.

Widmer, R., Oswald-Krapf, H., Sinha-Khetriwal, D., Schnellmann, M., & Böni, H. (2005). Global perspectives on e-waste. *Environmental Impact Assessment Review*, *25*(5), 436–458. doi:10.1016/j. eiar.2005.04.001

Zhang, K., Schnoor, J. L., & Zeng, E. Y. (2012). E-waste recycling: Where does it go from here? *Environmental Science & Technology*, *46*(20), 10861–10867. doi:10.1021/es303166s PMID:22998401

Chapter 13
An Entrenching Recommender System for Sustainable Transportation:
A Transit to Terminus

Prabhakar Yadlapalli
Koneru Lakshmaiah Education Foundation, India

Leela Rajani Myla
Koneru Lakshmaiah Education Foundation, India

Naga Venkata Sai Deekshitha Sandaka
Koneru Lakshmaiah Education Foundation, India

S. Gopal Krishna Patro
Koneru Lakshmaiah Education Foundation, India

ABSTRACT

Systems for course arranging help city sightseers and suburbanites in settling on the best course between two irregular focuses. Nonetheless, while prompting multi-modular courses, present day organizer calculations frequently don't consider client inclinations or the aggregate insight. Multimodal courses can be suggested in light of the assessments of purchasers with comparative preferences as per a method called cooperative separating (CF). In this chapter, the authors present a component—a portable recommender system for redid, multimodal courses—that consolidates CF with information-based ideas to improve the nature of course proposals. They give a full clarification of the crossover strategy and show the way things are integrated into a functioning model. The consequences of a client concentrated on show that the model, which joins CF, information-based, and well-known course suggestions, outflanks cutting-edge course organizers.

DOI: 10.4018/978-1-6684-6821-0.ch013

INTRODUCTION

Selecting the most efficient route for travel is a common occurrence in the daily lives of many people. There are numerous tools available for this use. Systems called route planners assist users in choosing the most efficient path to take to get to their destinations(Jiang et al., 2019; Li & She, 2017; Nayak & Panda, 2018; C. D. Wang et al., 2019). Multi-modal route planners incorporate various modes of transportation into one trip, including walking, car- and bicycle sharing, and private and public transportation. For instance, a commuter can use park and rides to transition from a private vehicle to public transportation and then use a bike-sharing Programme to get to work after exiting the subway(Yun et al., 2018). Modern route planning tools like Google Maps and Apple Maps typically ignore user preferences or the wisdom of the crowd when recommending multi-modal routes, instead only providing the quickest or shortest routes between two randomly chosen places. Route design should not be viewed as a classic shortest path problem, hence understanding this is crucial(Panda et al., 2020). Route planners could instead make the route recommendations more user-friendly. By incorporating user feedback into the route generating process, it may be possible to find routes that will leave users feeling the most satisfied in a certain situation(Hartatik et al., 2018; Herzog et al., 2017; Huang et al., 2019; H. Liu et al., 2019). Locals who frequently use public transportation are more knowledgeable about the best routes to take to get where they're going. This is especially useful when it's busy out, with congested streets and crowded public transportation. Having access to such information enables commuters to choose less congested routes and modes of transportation(Herzog et al., 2017; Huang et al., 2019). A possible approach to addressing the shortcomings of modern route planners is the integration of recommender systems (RSs). The information overload issue can be effectively solved by using RSs, which are software tools and processes that select objects like movies or restaurants that are most likely to be of interest to the user(Nakamura et al., 2014). Collaborative filtering (CF), which makes recommendations to users based on their shared characteristics with other users, is one of the most used RSs approaches(Bajaj et al., 2016; Y. Liu et al., 2021; Nakamura et al., 2014; Nawara & Kashef, 2020; J. Wang et al., 2018). CF is domain-free since it bases its suggestions exclusively on how frequently people provide the same feedback on products and engage with the system. In this chapter, we present, a unique mobile routing system-based recommender system (RS) for individualized, multimodal journeys. We demonstrate how applying CF to the wisdom of the crowd can improve the quality of route recommendations. Furthermore, we describe how to expand this strategy by adding a knowledge-based component to get around the pure CF recommendations with some future accessible imminent.

BACKGROUND

Vijay et al. (2018) (Vijay et al., 2018) studied about the personalized recommender system on travelling. Recent tendencies in net technology have created a large call for on line offerings with the unexpectedly developing customers. Travel recommender structures had been embraced through many researchers because of latest tendencies and full-size necessities with inside the e-tourism domain. Generating customized pointers with minimum interactions is a key mission and predicting customized listing of places with the to be had rankings on my own can't acquire powerful pointers. To cope with this issue, we expand a clever real-time user-precise tour recommender system (IRTUSTRS) via incorporating customers' social community profile and modern-day area through exploiting worldwide positioning system (GPS) information for tour advice generation. The proposed IRTUSTRS method facilitates stop customers via better tour pointers with advanced accuracy. The experimental assessment portrays the advanced overall performance of IRTUSTRS over baseline approaches. The offered paintings facilitates to apprehend the overall performance of recommender structures through utilizing on line social community profile of customers with the modern-day area via the GPS information.

Braunhofer et al. (2017) (Braunhofer & Ricci, 2017) learned about the particular travel recommender system. Setting cognizant recommender structures are realities separating and determination help programs that create hints through taking advantage of setting laid out shopper want information, incorporating scores expanded with the blueprint of the relevant situation recognized while the purchaser talented the thing. As a matter of fact, numerous logical components (e.g., climate, season, temper or friend) can likewise furthermore presumably affect the purchaser's revel in of a thing, yet at this point no longer they all are correspondingly basic for the recommender machine execution, or smooth to be precisely obtained. Thus, it's far basic to select and assemble best the ones components that just affect the shopper inclinations (scores) and could upgrade the adequacy of the clues figured through the recommender machine. Expanding our first work, on this paper, we suggest a novel strategy which adaptively evokes the most extreme helpful components from the customer upon score a thing. The proposed procedure considers a logical component as useful to be evoked while a buyer is scoring a thing, assuming it has an impact at the customer's expected score for that thing. The outcomes of our disconnected investigations, which we done on movement related score datasets, show that the proposed strategy plays higher than various stylish setting decision techniques.

Logesh et al. (2018) (Logesh et al., 2018) examined the hybrid recommender system for travel. Many academics have been drawn to the most recent studies in the field of recommender systems because of the increasing demand for such systems on a global scale. We offer hybrid guidance solutions in the e-Tourism field to bridge the gaps between the problems that customers have in the real world and the problems that researchers face inside the virtual world. In this essay, we have outlined the research challenges that exist within e-Tourism programmers and presented a workable method to obtain more individualized recommendations. By combining user-contextual data, they have advanced a PCAHTRS (Personalized Context-Aware Hybrid Travel Recommender System). Yelp and TripAdvisor's large-scale, real-time datasets are used to evaluate the proposed PCAHTRS. The results of the experiments show how much better the proposed method performs overall than more traditional ones. Future study directions are provided at the end of the publication to aid researchers in finding insightful solutions to information problems.

Shini et al. (2020) (Shini et al., 2020) learned about movement recommender systems. Consistently taking into account the beginning of civilization, venture for various reasons exists as an imperative piece of human ways of life all together excursion pointers, eleven however the early state of pointers had been the amassed examinations shared through the local area. Present day recommender structures created close by the blast of Data Innovation and are adding to all endeavor and transporter sections along with excursion and the travel industry. The experience started with regular recommender motors which gave way to customized recommender structures and also better than contextualized personalization with formation of manufactured insight. Current age is similarly seeing an expansion in virtual entertainment usage and the web-based entertainment huge data is showing up as a significant enter for various examination without an exemption for recommender structures. This paper data about the notice completed at the development of excursion recommender structures, their capabilities and state of the art set of limits. We also talk on the significant thing calculations getting utilized for class and counsel systems and measurements that might be utilized to survey the general exhibition of the calculations and in this manner the recommenders.

Choudhary et al.(2020) (Choudhury et al., 2020) studied about travel recommender systems. Travelling is a aggregate of journey, transportation, journey-time, accommodation, weather, events, and different elements which can be possibly to be skilled via way of means of maximum of the humans sooner or later of their life. To decorate such experience, we usually search for help in making plans a tour. Today, the data to be had on tourism-associated elements at the Internet is boundless and exploring appropriate journey bundle/product/carrier can be time-consuming. A recommender system (RS) can help for numerous tour-associated queries which includes pinnacle locations for summer time season vacation, most appropriate weather situations for tracking, the quickest manner to transport, or images help for unique locations. In this survey, we've got offered a pervasive overview on journey and related elements which includes hotels, restaurants, tourism bundle and making plans, and attractions; we've got additionally tailor-made guidelines on a tourist's various necessities which includes food, transportation, images, outfits, safety, and seasonal preferences. We have categorised journey-primarily based totally RSs and offered choice criteria, features, and technical elements with datasets, methods, and results. We have in short supplemented studies articles from various facets; numerous frameworks for a journey-primarily based totally RS are discussed. We agree with our survey might introduce a brand-new journey RS; it could be applied to remedy the prevailing boundaries and amplify its applicability.

Segota et al. (2019) (Baressi Šegota et al., 2019)studied about the recommender system on travelling. Travelling is a mixture of journey, transportation, journey-time, accommodation, weather, events, and different factors which might be possibly to be skilled via way of means of maximum of the human beings in some unspecified time in the future of their life. To beautify such experience, we typically search for help in making plans a tour. Today, the statistics to be had on tourism-associated factors at the Internet is boundless and exploring appropriate journey bundle/product/carrier can be time-consuming. A recommender system (RS) can help for diverse tour-associated queries along with pinnacle locations for summer time season vacation, greatest weather situations for tracking, the quickest manner to transport, or images help for unique locations. In this survey, we've supplied a pervasive evaluation on journey and related elements along with hotels, restaurants, tourism bundle and making plans, and attractions; we've additionally tailor-made pointers on a tourist's various necessities along with food, transportation, images, outfits, safety, and seasonal preferences. We have categorized journey-primarily based totally RSs and supplied choice criteria, features, and technical factors with datasets, methods, and results. We have in brief supplemented studies articles from various facets; diverse frameworks for a journey-primarily based totally RS are discussed. We accept as true with our survey might introduce a today's journey RS; it is able to be applied to remedy the prevailing boundaries and make bigger its applicability.

Khayati et al. (2021) (Khayati et al., 2021)studied about the portable recommender system in light of savvy city chart. Portable recommender structures have altered the way people find things, elements of interest, organizations, or perhaps new colleagues. The development at the rear of cell recommender structures has progressed to introduce client manners and social impacts. This paper acquaints an essential way with develop a cell exhortation gadget basically founded absolutely on smart town diagrams that appear subject highlights, individual profiles, and impacts got from social associations. It takes advantage of chart centrality measures to make greater specially crafted suggestions from the semantic records addressed with inside the diagram. The diagram shows and picks chart calculations for processing outline centrality this is the center of the cell recommender gadget are displayed. Semantic thoughts, for instance, semantic greatness and similarity measures, are acclimated to the diagram model. Use requesting circumstances looked to settle execution issues are also inspected.

Altulyan et.al (2021) (Altulyan et al., 2021) studied about the mobility Recommender system in smart cities. To date, there may be an extensive availability of instructional and industrial ICT proposals to enhance city mobility. Nevertheless, with inside the literature, there may be nonetheless a loss of appropriate answers for door-to-door routing assisting customers from their origins to locations and which includes the inspiration on in which to park. On the opposite hand, in an Internet-of Things (IoT) scenario, a whole lot of novel records re-assets will be exploited to compute greater green mobility answers to be proposed to the consumer. As an example, parking availability statistics will be effortlessly accrued and exploited to offer multimodal routes (i.e. routes with at the least unique approach of transportation) that encompass recommendations on in which to park and the way to attain the very last vacation spot. In this chapter, we describe a disbursed IoT structure closer to the definition of a Mobility Recommender System. In particular, we consciousness on a car-primarily based totally multimodality, in which the consumer constantly begins off evolved an experience with his/her non-public vehicle, however he/she also can depart the auto in Park-and-Ride infrastructures and attain the vacation spot with public transportation. This sort of routing on a much wider seek vicinity will end result to be greater costly, and thus, it's going to mainly advantage from a parallel computational architectural solution.

PROPOSED HYBRIDISED RECOMMENDER MECHANISM FOR ROLL-ON-ROLL-OFF TRANSPORTATION

As about the portable recommender system in light of savvy city chart. Portable recommender structures have altered the way people find things, elements of interest, organizations, or perhaps new colleagues. The development at the rear of cell recommender structures has progressed to introduce client manners and social impacts. This paper acquaints an essential way with develop a cell exhortation gadget basically founded absolutely on smart town diagrams that appear subject highlights, individual profiles, and impacts got from social associations. It takes advantage of chart centrality measures to make greater specially crafted suggestions from the semantic records addressed with inside the diagram. The diagram shows and picks chart calculations for processing outline centrality this is the centre of the cell recommender gadget are displayed. Semantic thoughts, for instance, semantic greatness and similarity measures, are acclimated to the diagram model. Use requesting circumstances looked to settle execution issues are also inspected.

APPLICATION OF COLLABORATIVE FILTERING IN THE PROPOSED MODEL

It is feasible to recognize model-based and memory-based CF calculations. Memory-based methods register the local arrangement of clients or things in view of a comparability metric by utilizing the total client thing dataset. The system produces suggestions in view of this local utilizing the number-crunching mean of evaluations or one more strategy for a comparative nature. In spite of the fact that it is costly to process, utilizing the total dataset brings about brilliant idea exactness. The model-based approach, then again, precomputes a model disconnected utilizing criticism data about the items and the customers. Rather than utilizing the whole dataset each time a proposal is asked, the precomputed model can then be utilized to develop the suggestions. This reduces the proposal age's run-time intricacy.

Figure 1. Diagrammatic representation of the proposed model

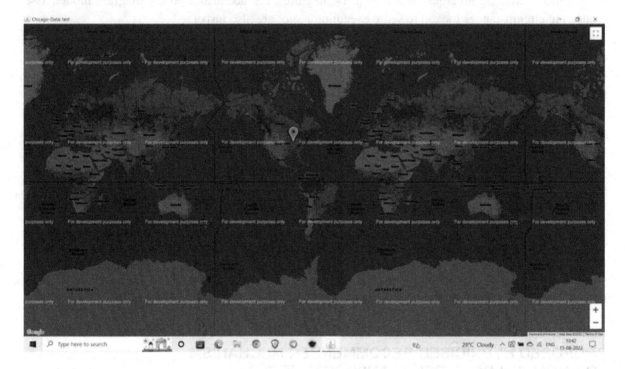

The open source, versatile AI library of Apache Flash fills in as the establishment for the recommended CF calculation. It shows the advantages of both memory-based and model-based methods. Moreover, the system precomputes a forecast model in light of any client conduct, whether understood or express. This resolves the issue of the client thing network's sparsity, which could be welcomed on by the shortfall of incessant unequivocal info. An item that is purchased or seen by everybody, for example, is presumably not a decent sign of taste. The program decides if co-events are sufficiently strange to comprise pointers and dispenses with the dreary co-events utilizing the Log Probability Proportion (LLR) test. Before a proposal is requested, all past displaying is now registered. The matrix of indication is multiplied by the user's history variable to determine the score of recommendation for a new user (Eqn.1).

$$\sigma = (H^I M)p\mu \tag{1}$$

Where $H^I M$ is the matrix of indication, σ is the score of recommendation values, and $p\mu$ is the previous history of user profile.

In our situation, a user can be recommended multi-modal routes using a wide range of interactions of customers along with their feedback. The algorithm shouldn't provide equal weight to each of these activities; for instance, preferring a certain route should be given more weight than merely viewing it. As a result, only one action is used by the algorithm as the major indicator of preference, and an LLR test is also used to determine whether the other indicators are correlated with this action. The final recommendation score is based on the matrices for each of the indicator can be stated as follows.

$$\sigma_n = \left(H^I M_1\right) p\mu_1 + \left(H^1 M_2\right) p\mu_2 + \ldots + \left(H^I M_n\right) p\mu_n \tag{2}$$

Where $(H^I M)p\mu$ is the value of recommendation of the principal action, and the right-side part of Eqn.2 represents respectively the recommendation values for pathways related to other actions for n number of users.

In this study, the major action revealing user preferences is the explicit input of loving an event. Viewing a route is an implicit feedback, another action that expresses a preference for a particular path. The most recent routes viewed are also a sign, as this is frequently the path which users choose to follow before quitting the programme.

CUSTOMER RECOMMENDATION STUDY

Twenty people took part in a user study we conducted (12 females and 8 males). For the study, we looked for volunteers with a range of backgrounds and levels of experience to represent prospective future participants. Almost all of the multi-modal route planners that are now commercially available demand that users select their mode of transportation before looking for routes. To be more like our prototype in that aspect, we sought a baseline that may suggest routes without this necessity. The Munich transit statistics were the ones we chose to have access to for the RS evaluation. This was a crucial requirement for us because Google Maps, the baseline application for the user study, uses the same data source for route planning as our prototype, thus at least some of the participants should be familiar with it. The Recommended travel mode tab on Google Maps for the web suggests routes to users regardless of their preferred method of transportation. The Google Maps mobile application does not have this capability. Google Maps serves as an excellent baseline application for our user study because the suggestions may be viewed as a pure knowledge-based RS without our CF modification. As previously mentioned, CF needs user ratings to produce suggestions. We built some pretend users because there weren't any users in our system prior to the study, and we only studied a small number of origin-destination combinations. This strategy gave us enough scores in the user-item rating matrix to test all the recommendations our suggested model offered.

RESULTS AND DISCUSSION

The user study was carried out as a lab experiment. Participants' main job was to interact with the baseline application and the suggested model application to complete a list of specified activities. Three stages made up the review of the applications: The initial step for the participants was to select their favourite recommended route from each application. The accuracy of the recommendations was determined using this route's ranking in the recommendation lists. Then, the participants were required to respond to two questionnaires to express their thoughts on the prototype's overall concept as well as other aspects of our suggested model and the base application. A final questionnaire was filled out by the participants to assess the user experience.

Our user study's findings demonstrate how tailored recommendations raise the calibre of route planning tools. Fig. 2 shows the screenshot of the code. The recommendations made by our suggested model, including those for popular routes and CF, were well received by the participants. Our suggested system proved to give more accurate recommendations, consumers were more pleased with the experience, and routes were located more easily when compared to a cutting-edge route planning system. Given that both the suggested model and Google Maps use the same route information, this is an intriguing discovery. Our suggested approach, however, is able to spot alternate routes that, although they might seem less evident, are actually a superior option for some people.

Figure 2. the overall representation of the code

The participants were able to enhance the recommendations by preferring pathways while engaging with the programme, however the collaborative recommendations in the suggested mechanism were primarily generated based on the ratings we created before to the user study. We experimented with a different method in this work. A comprehensive, multi-modal route represents the item advised to the user, as opposed to only one or a few sites. In comparison to cutting-edge route planners, our proposed model recommends routes that are not only the quickest and shortest or those that use a particular mode of transportation, but also taps into the wisdom of the crowd to find alternate routes that may not meet the requirements of current route planners but may be a better option for users. Our premise that CF should be utilised for path recommendations to get results that are more suited to the user's tastes in a particular context is confirmed by the input we gathered throughout the user study Fig.3 shows the user study graph. Our work's primary objective is to assist commuters who are familiar with a city, as well as visitors and other persons who are unfamiliar with the city's public transportation system. When we spoke with our participants and solicited their opinions, certain situations where our approach would be extremely useful emerged. Some believed it would be crucial in a nation where the information regarding traffic and public transportation is inaccurate. One instance was involving going to the airport.

Figure 3. graphical representation of the user study analysis

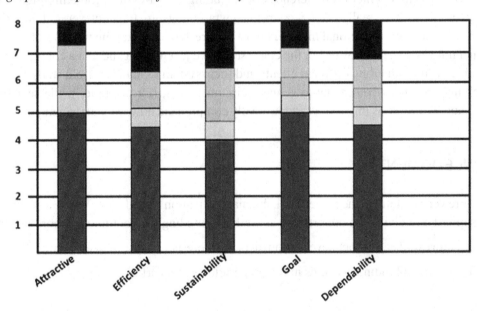

Most people who travel to the airport typically have luggage with them. The user study's findings demonstrate that our implementation can produce reliable results. It has been demonstrated, however, that suggestions given by friends can improve users' trust in those recommendations. To improve our system, we should only take the ratings of relevant people, such as friends, rather than all of the system's users.

SUSTAINABILITY

Our proposed model is sustainable as it restricts the information overload of the user's recommendation as well as shows the efficiency to protect a user from various problems in transportation system. It shows proper way in travel as well as the good choice for a new user to choose the right option.

CONCLUSION

We fostered a clever procedure for suggesting multimodal travel courses in this chapter. We assessed the viability of our cross-breed calculation and the convenience of the application in a client study with 20 members. As indicated by the outcomes, CF, information based, and popular course ideas supplement another more successfully than state of the art course organizer innovations. The Google Guides Programming interface empowers our application to offer seven elective excursion choices. To give further developed, multi-modular course proposals, future variants of our course organizer ought to incorporate extra methods of transportation like cabs, carsharing, and rental bicycles. In our procedure, the Like occasion was the most dependable indicator of course inclinations. Notwithstanding, the system might be changed to deal with counterfeit preferences by including a turn-by-turn route highlight that could survey whether clients have really taken a course. To wrap things up, to get cleverer client criticism, a bigger client overview with additional members must be directed. Our examination was planned as a lab try to get first information right away. For the client study, we just took a gander at a couple of beginning objective mixes while ridiculing different clients and their system remarks. A field study with genuine clients applying our prescribed model to genuine circumstances, (for example, while searching for a course from home to work) is important to additionally comprehend how well our technique capabilities.

ACKNOWLEDGMENT

The authors are very grateful to the Koneru Lakshmaiah Education Foundation, Vaddeswaram, India, for their kind support and giving the opportunity as well as providing the continuous laboratory facilities.

Conflicts of Interest: The authors have no conflicts of interests.

Funding: There are no funding agencies in the preparation of this article.

REFERENCES

Altulyan, M., Yao, L., Wang, X., Huang, C., Kanhere, S. S., & Sheng, Q. Z. (2021). A Survey on Recommender Systems for Internet of Things: Techniques, Applications and Future Directions. *The Computer Journal*. Advance online publication. doi:10.1093/comjnl/bxab049

Bajaj, G., Agarwal, R., Bouloukakis, G., Singh, P., Georgantas, N., & Issarny, V. (2016). Towards building real-time, convenient route recommendation system for public transit. *IEEE 2nd International Smart Cities Conference: Improving the Citizens Quality of Life, ISC2 2016 - Proceedings*. 10.1109/ISC2.2016.07580779

Baressi Šegota, S., Lorencin, I., Ohkura, K., & Car, Z. (2019). On the Traveling Salesman Problem in Nautical Environments: An Evolutionary Computing Approach to Optimization of Tourist Route Paths in Medulin, Croatia. *Journal of Maritime & Transportation Science*, *57*(1), 71–87. doi:10.18048/2019.57.05.

Braunhofer, M., & Ricci, F. (2017). Selective contextual information acquisition in travel recommender systems. *Information Technology & Tourism*, *17*(1), 5–29. doi:10.100740558-017-0075-6

Choudhury, T. T., Paul, S. K., Rahman, H. F., Jia, Z., & Shukla, N. (2020). A systematic literature review on the service supply chain: Research agenda and future research directions. *Production Planning and Control*, *31*(16), 1363–1384. doi:10.1080/09537287.2019.1709132

Hartatik, P., Purbayu, A., & Triyono, L. (2018). Dijkstra methode for optimalize recommendation system of garbage transportation time in Surakarta city. *IOP Conference Series. Materials Science and Engineering*, *333*(1), 012106. Advance online publication. doi:10.1088/1757-899X/333/1/012106

Herzog, D., Massoud, H., & Wörndl, W. (2017). Routeme: A mobile recommender system for personalized, multi-modal route planning. *UMAP 2017 - Proceedings of the 25th Conference on User Modeling, Adaptation and Personalization*, 67–75. 10.1145/3079628.3079680

Huang, Z., Shan, G., Cheng, J., & Sun, J. (2019). TRec: An efficient recommendation system for hunting passengers with deep neural networks. *Neural Computing & Applications*, *31*(S1), 209–222. doi:10.100700521-018-3728-2

Jiang, L., Cheng, Y., Yang, L., Li, J., Yan, H., & Wang, X. (2019). A trust-based collaborative filtering algorithm for E-commerce recommendation system. *Journal of Ambient Intelligence and Humanized Computing*, *10*(8), 3023–3034. doi:10.100712652-018-0928-7

Khayati, Y., Kang, J. E., Karwan, M., & Murray, C. (2021). Household use of autonomous vehicles with ride sourcing. *Transportation Research Part C: Emerging Technologies*, *125*(May), 102998. doi:10.1016/j.trc.2021.102998

Li, X., & She, J. (2017). Collaborative variational autoencoder for recommender systems. *Proceedings of the ACM SIGKDD International Conference on Knowledge Discovery and Data Mining, Part F1296*, 305–314. 10.1145/3097983.3098077

Liu, H., Tong, Y., Zhang, P., Lu, X., Duan, J., & Xiong, H. (2019). Hydra: A personalized and context-aware multi-modal transportation recommendation system. *Proceedings of the ACM SIGKDD International Conference on Knowledge Discovery and Data Mining*, 2314–2324. 10.1145/3292500.3330660

Liu, Y., Lyu, C., Liu, Z., & Cao, J. (2021). Exploring a large-scale multi-modal transportation recommendation system. *Transportation Research Part C: Emerging Technologies*, *126*(September), 103070. doi:10.1016/j.trc.2021.103070

Logesh, R., Subramaniyaswamy, V., Vijayakumar, V., Gao, X. Z., & Indragandhi, V. (2018). A hybrid quantum-induced swarm intelligence clustering for the urban trip recommendation in smart city. *Future Generation Computer Systems*, *83*, 653–673. doi:10.1016/j.future.2017.08.060

Nakamura, H., Gao, Y., Gao, H., Zhang, H., Kiyohiro, A., & Mine, T. (2014). Toward personalized public transportation recommendation system with adaptive user interface. *Proceedings - 2014 IIAI 3rd International Conference on Advanced Applied Informatics, IIAI-AAI 2014*, 103–108. 10.1109/IIAI-AAI.2014.31

Nawara, D., & Kashef, R. (2020). IoT-based recommendation systems - An overview. *IEMTRONICS 2020 - International IOT, Electronics and Mechatronics Conference, Proceedings*. 10.1109/IEMTRONICS51293.2020.9216391

Nayak, S. K., & Panda, S. K. (2018). A user-oriented collaborative filtering algorithm for recommender systems. *PDGC 2018 - 2018 5th International Conference on Parallel, Distributed and Grid Computing*, 374–380. 10.1109/PDGC.2018.8745892

Panda, S. K., Bhoi, S. K., & Singh, M. (2020). A collaborative filtering recommendation algorithm based on normalization approach. *Journal of Ambient Intelligence and Humanized Computing*, *11*(11), 4643–4665. doi:10.100712652-020-01711-x

Shini, S., Shini, A., & Bryden, W. L. (2020). Unravelling fatty liver haemorrhagic syndrome: 1. Oestrogen and inflammation. *Avian Pathology*, *49*(1), 87–98. doi:10.1080/03079457.2019.1674444 PMID:31565961

Vijay, D., Goetze, P., Wulf, R., & Gross, U. (2018). Homogenized and pore-scale analyses of forced convection through open cell foams. *International Journal of Heat and Mass Transfer*, *123*, 787–804. doi:10.1016/j.ijheatmasstransfer.2018.03.008

Wang, C. D., Deng, Z. H., Lai, J. H., & Yu, P. S. (2019). Serendipitous recommendation in e-commerce using innovator-based collaborative filtering. *IEEE Transactions on Cybernetics*, *49*(7), 2678–2692. doi:10.1109/TCYB.2018.2841924 PMID:29994495

Wang, J., Lu, Y., Wang, X., Dong, J., & Hu, X. (2018). SAR: A social-aware route recommendation system for intelligent transportation. *The Computer Journal*, *61*(7), 987–997. doi:10.1093/comjnl/bxy042

Yun, Y., Hooshyar, D., Jo, J., & Lim, H. (2018). Developing a hybrid collaborative filtering recommendation system with opinion mining on purchase review. *Journal of Information Science*, *44*(3), 331–344. doi:10.1177/0165551517692955

Chapter 14
Role of Quantum Computing in a Data Analytics Environment

B. K. Tripathy
Vellore Institute of Technology, India

Apoorv Singh
Vellore Institute of Technology, India

ABSTRACT

There is a strong consensus that quantum computers are likely to solve previously intractable problems, especially in data science and AI. Nowadays, processing power of machine learning algorithms is limited by that of conventional computers. Quantum computing (QC) is one of the digital trends with the quickest rate of growth, and it seems to provide an answer to large data problems. It is a combination of the fields of computer science, information theory, and quantum physics. Quantum computers use the ability of subatomic particles to exist in more than one state at once to solve complex problems. In spite of its recent origin, quantum computing is already being used in the field of data analytics. QC can process huge datasets at much quicker rates and can provide data to AI models. By comparing schemas to swiftly assess and comprehend the link between two counterparts, QC can also aid in the integration of data. The ability to perform more sophisticated analysis and build machine learning models is a benefit of employing quantum computers.

1. INTRODUCTION

Moore's law states that if technical advancements continue to improve performance, as they have over the past few decades, the transistor count per chip may double every eighteen months. Additionally, within the next ten years, processor clock frequencies could exceed 40 GHz (Williams & Clearwater, 1997). By that time, one atom might stand in for one bit (Williams & Clearwater, 1997). One of the potential issues could be that since quantum mechanics rather than classical physics describes electrons, this could lead to "quantum tunneling" on a chip. Electrons may escape from circuits in such circumstances.

DOI: 10.4018/978-1-6684-6821-0.ch014

Quantum computers have now been suggested as a possible solution, taking into consideration the quantum mechanical properties of single atom per bit level. Thus, certain computationally challenging issues that take a lot of processing time on classical computers can be solved using quantum computers. To assure the correct performance of quantum computers in the future, additional advancements will be required, but they appear attainable. There are currently certain algorithms that make use of the benefit of quantum computers. For example, Peter Shor (1994) suggested the polynomial-time approach for factoring a big integer with $O(n^3)$ time. Factoring is completed exponentially more quickly by this algorithm than by conventional computers. With a 1 GHz clock rate, this technique can factor a 512-bit product within just 3.5 hours (Oskin et al., 2002), while the traditional system would need 8400 MIPS years (Preneel, 2000). (A processor can process 1 MIPS of instructions at a rate of 1 million instructions per second.) Another well-known quantum technique was developed by Lov Grover and finds a single item in $O(\sqrt{N})$ time from a list of N unsorted elements (Grover, 1996).

The application of quantum mechanics is already exciting, but we suggest that having quicker algorithms is not the sole reason to explore quantum computing. Research into quantum computation may also provide substantial new information processing insights. For example, it can inspire concepts for safe data processing and analytics. It is undoubtedly intriguing to investigate how quantum machines can perform computations. Understanding the world's computational boundaries could result from this. Not to mention, multiple new classical algorithms have been developed as a result of the interaction between classical and quantum computing. Quantum computing holds the potential to significantly speed up complicated algorithms (Hidary, 2019). Because many algorithms still work in sequences that build on the outcomes of a preceding step, even supercomputers today struggle with tremendous algorithmic complexity. Of course, they employ massively parallel hardware and algorithms, but networking and the memory required to store the numerous combinations of real-world issues both have their limitations.

The field of quantum computing has transitioned from research to commercial use. Applications in industries like data science, pattern recognition, and cyber security will progress quickly as a result (Tripathy, 2017). The field of data analytics is already utilizing quantum computing, despite the fact that it is a relatively young technology.

Due to the growing amount of content on the web, the computer industry is constantly dealing with issues regarding storage of data and parallel processing (Tripathy & Deepthi, 2017a). People are interacting with data when they do anything in this data-driven age (Tripathy & Deboleena, 2018). Market research leans heavily on data analytics to find patterns, derive conclusions, and make forecasts (Tripathy, Sooraj, & Mohanty, 2018). Despite the abundance of big data analytical tools on the market, even the most sophisticated traditional computers are unable to answer some complex problems in time (Tripathy et al., 2021). The idea of quantum computing was created in order to give modern ordinary computers greater processing power.

2. QUANTUM THEORY & QUANTUM MECHANICS

It's critical to have a fundamental knowledge of quantum theory in order to comprehend quantum computing. A quantum is practically the lowest possible individual unit of a physical attribute, like energy, in physics.

In 1900, quantum theory first appeared. Max Plank put forward the idea that energy and matter are distinct, individual entities rather than continuous waves in a talk with the German Physical Society. According to this radical hypothesis, energy and matter can occasionally appear as particles or waves, and these tiny particles move erratically and inexplicably as a result. Problems arise when attempting to measure complementary quantities simultaneously, such as momentum or location; the closer one is observed, the more inaccurate the measurement of the other quantity will be (Pandey & Ramesh, 2015).

However, the development of quantum physics demonstrated that light is composed of minute, indivisible energy units, or quanta, that we refer to as photons.

It was astonishingly straightforward for a presentation that challenged the renowned Isaac Newton's theories regarding the nature of light. The double-slit experiment was first described by the English physicist Thomas Young to the representatives of the Royal Society of London in November of 1803. He had devised a sophisticated yet very rudimentary experiment to demonstrate the wavelike nature of light, disproving Newton's notion that light is composed of particles.

Young's experiment is a puzzle to behold and raises important issues regarding the very basis of reality when performed with singular photons or single matter particles like electrons and neutrons. A few have used it to support the claim that human awareness has an impact on the quantum world, giving our thoughts agency and a role in the study of the cosmos.

Schrödinger's idea of wave mechanics was another breakthrough in the development of quantum mechanics. Working concurrently with Heisenberg in late 1925 but wholly independently, Schrödinger developed a set of parameterized partial differential equations with solutions exclusively for a discrete range of parameter values. By selecting the suitable differential operators, Schrödinger showed that these equations could be used to model any physical system. Then he asserted that all conceivable energy values for a system were represented by the values of the discrete parameters for which the final equation had solutions after an operator had been correctly chosen to describe a specific system (Ananthaswamy, 2018).

Quantum theory has important practical applications in quantum computers, quantum optics, quantum chemistry, optical amplifiers, lasers, transistors, semiconductors, and imaging techniques like electron microscopes and imaging using magnetic resonance.

3. QUANTUM COMPUTING

3.1 What is Quantum Computing?

Even for anyone with a foundation in physics, the area involving quantum computing is often challenging to understand. Briefly stated, the goal of quantum computing is to create computer-based technologies that are based on quantum theory. The need for storage in society grows as more data is produced. As a result, there is now a high need for transistors that can handle such massive amounts of data. Since most traditional computers can only handle one task at a time, solving complicated issues can take an absurd quantity of time and resources. Intractable problems are those that go beyond the capabilities of conventional computers. Quantum computers were created expressly to deal with issues like these (Cohen, 2008).

3.2 Need for Quantum Computing

There are certain limitations to the use cases of classical computers. These can be greatly improved or enhanced by the use of quantum computers. Oftentimes, there are calculations that can be made by a classical computer, but it may require an absurd amount of time and resources in order to do so. This gives birth to the need for a new system, which is quantum computing in this case. There are a few examples where the limitations of classical computers are shown where quantum computers can be favored.

3.2.1 Cryptographic Systems with Public Keys and Classical Factorization of Large Integers

A sophisticated mathematical solution to the key distribution problem was found in 1970 in the form of "public key" systems. Before sending a message via one of these methods, users are not required to decide on a secret key. It works on the same idea as a safe that has two keys: a public key for locking the safe and a private key to open it. Anybody can put any information in the safe, but only a single person is able to take it out. Everyone possesses a key to close the safe, but only a single user has the key to open it again. The two keys actually consist of two big integer numbers. A private key can simply be converted into a public key, but not the other way around (Noble Desktop, 2022).

The approach takes advantage of the fact that some mathematical operations can be carried out more quickly in one way than the other, such as when multiplying numbers rather than factoring a huge number. The fundamental measure of a "quick" algorithm is not how long it actually takes to multiply a given pair of integers, but rather how slowly the time increases as we repeat the same procedure to ever-larger numbers. When we use the quicker trial division method to go from two three-digit numbers to two thirty-digit numbers, we can see that multiplication takes only a small amount of extra time because it takes roughly 1013 times as long or as much memory as factoring a three-digit number.

When we keep adding digits, factorization requires a significant amount of processing resources. In actuality, the key distribution problem might be avoided by public key cryptosystems. However, the stability of certain assumptions, like the complexity of factoring huge integers, is based on unproven mathematics. However, such a system is RSA, which makes electronic banking conceivable by presuming among banks and their clients that a successful forgery or phony financial transfer would take the fastest computer in the world thousands of years to complete. One more is the Data Encryption Standard (DES), which is not widely used but is nonetheless secure for the majority of routine commercial operations.

This approach was used in 1994 to factor a 129-digit value (referred to as RSA 129) on roughly 1600 workstations located all over the world. The factorization process took eight months. With the same computing power, it would take around 800,000 years just to factorize a 250-digit number, and a 1000-digit number would take 10^{25} years. For public key cryptography, like the 250-digit version used in banks, the challenge of factoring huge integers is essential.

To address the problem of the exponential rise as a function of L, the trial division approach for factorization requires $10L/2$ (=N) divisions. Let's say a computer makes 10 decisions every second. Because of this, a system can factor a number N in roughly 10^{40} seconds, which is far longer than the current estimate of the universe's age of 3.8×10^{17} seconds (12 billion years) (Noble Desktop, 2022).

3.2.2 Quantum Factoring

According to the analysis of the classical factoring of large integers, it appears that factoring large numbers will remain beyond the capability of any practical computing devices. Until scientists develop an effective factoring algorithm, public key cryptosystems will continue to be secure. However, the Classical Theory of Computation does not encompass all computations that are physically feasible. It does not specifically explain the calculations that can be carried out by quantum devices. Recent advances in quantum computation do really demonstrate that a quantum computer can factorize considerably faster than any classical computer.

According to Peter Shor's formula, factoring an integer on a quantum computer takes $O(\ln(N)2+E)$ steps, where E is small. With such a method, factoring a thousand-digit number would only take a few million steps because this is approximately quadratic in the size of the input. The implication is that factoring-based public key cryptosystems may be vulnerable (Noble Desktop, 2022).

3.2.3 Simulation of Quantum System by Classical Computer

Richard P. Feynman stated in 1982 that any quantum physical system consisting of N particles including its quantum probability cannot be replicated by a conventional computer without the simulation speeding up exponentially. However, a polynomial slowing can imitate an N-particle system in classical physics. This is primarily because quantum computers can avoid the slowness that occurs during the simulation of quantum systems because the descriptive size of one particle system is exponential in N as opposed to linear in N as it is in classical physics. A quantum system can be simulated using a probabilistic computer, however Feynman acknowledged that this is a challenging challenge because of interference effects (Noble Desktop, 2022).

3.2.4 Looking for an Item With a Particular Feature

Another issue that can be solved with incredible speed using a quantum logic-based algorithm is the search for an item with the necessary property among a set of N things. If we choose an object randomly from a group of N items, the probability of choosing the correct item is half as high as the probability of choosing the right one. So, on average, $N/2$ procedures are needed to retrieve the correct item. Nevertheless, Grover developed a quantum logic-based algorithm that completes the identical task on average in N operations (Noble Desktop, 2022).

4. QUANTUM COMPUTING SYSTEM

4.1 State of Superposition

In traditional computers, the 0 and 1 states are represented as one-bit information by electrical signals like voltages. The two bits represent four states 00, 01, 10, and 11, and n-bits represent a total of 2^n states. The one-bit information is represented inside the quantum computer by a quantum bit called a "qubit," which really is a two-state system. For instance, an electron can be used as a qubit in classical computers in place of an electrical signal. An electron can be in two states: spin-down and spin-up, or 1 and 0, respectively. A photon can also function as a qubit, with its horizontal and vertical polarizations serving as representations of both states. Quantum computers can carry out mathematical operations just like a conventional computer using qubits.

When we show the states 0 and 1 as state vectors $|\Psi\rangle$ and $|1\rangle$ respectively, this superposition state is then shown as a combination of $|0\rangle$ and $|1\rangle$.

Here, $|\Psi\rangle = a|0\rangle + b|1\rangle$; here '$a$' and '$b$' are probability amplitudes.

$|a|^2$ represents a probability which we get when $|\Psi\rangle = |0\rangle$ as a result of the measure of the qubit $|\Psi\rangle = a|0\rangle + b|1\rangle$. They satisfy $|a|^2 + |b|^2 = 1$. For instance, when the coefficients 'a' and 'b' are equal to $1/\sqrt{2}$, they can be expressed as state of superposition of 2 states:

$$|\Psi\rangle = (1/\sqrt{2})|0\rangle + (1/\sqrt{2})|1\rangle;$$

here vectors $|1\rangle = (0,\ 1)^T$ and $|0\rangle = (0,\ 1)^T$

Thus, when a state of $|\Psi\rangle$ is measured, it is figured $|0\rangle$ has a probability of $(1/\sqrt{2})^2 = 1/2$ and $|1\rangle$ has a probability of $(1/\sqrt{2})^2 = 1/2$.

Parallel processing in the true sense of the word is made feasible by this peculiar property of quantum computers. 4 states are represented by 2 qubits simultaneously, since each qubit can represent two states at once. In contrast to the 4 operations required by a conventional computer, when we employ 2 qubits that are superpositions of 1 and 0 states as the input for any operation, we can obtain the results of 4 operations for 4 inputs with just 1 computational step. The same is true when utilizing n qubits; we can create a superposition of 'n' states as input and then process them in a single step, as opposed to n steps for a classical computer. The same is true when utilizing n qubits; we can create a superposition of 'n' states as input and then analyze them in a single step, as opposed to n steps for a classical computer. Accordingly, after collecting the state of superposition of 'n' inputs, a quantum computer may compute 'n' inputs with just 1 processing step.

However, before we can make use of this incredibly useful property of quantum computers, a significant issue must be resolved. We obtain the superposition of the 4 results from a single superposition state, which represents 4 states as input and 1 processing step. Each output qubit will be viewed as either 1 or 0. This is because a qubit is a 2-state system when we assess the output qubits, which causes the superposition of quantum mechanics to collapse. Therefore, with the same probability, we only obtain one of the four outcomes: 00, 10, 01, or 11.

As a result, probability governs the superposition of qubits, and measurement is required to ascertain which of the potential states is represented. The use of quantum mechanical superposition causes this issue. But if we can create an algorithm that increases the likelihood of achieving the desired outcome, we can make use of the property of superposition of quantum mechanics.

4.2 Interference of States in Quantum Computation

Indisputable, Turing machine - a mathematical representation of a general computer - can simulate any classical computer. We first explain a processing tree utilizing a conventional "Probabilistic Turing Machine" (PTM) before discussing the Quantum Turing Machine (QTM).

A sample state transition diagram of PTM is shown in Fig. 1, and the PTM is derived as a computation tree in Fig. 2. Every vertex of the tree represents a machine state, and every edge represents the likelihood of a transition occurring (Kanamori et al., 2006).

Figure 1. State transition diagram of PTM

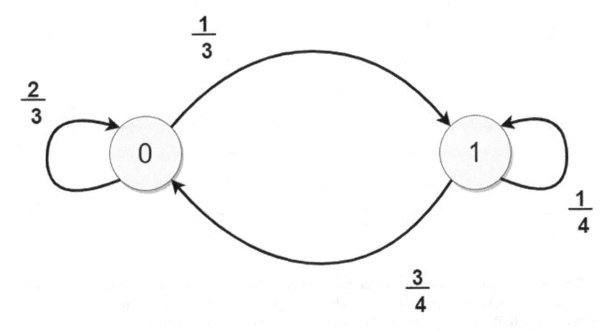

The starting state is represented by the tree's root, and every level of this tree stands for a calculation step. By adding the probabilities of these 2 potential routes to state 1 from the root, we can determine the likelihood that the transition 0 to 1 will occur after two calculation steps.

$$P(0 \rightarrow 1) = \left(\frac{2}{3} * \frac{1}{3}\right) + \left(\frac{1}{3} * \frac{1}{4}\right) = \frac{2}{9} + \frac{1}{12} = \frac{11}{36}$$

Similarly:

$$P(0 \rightarrow 0) = \left(\frac{2}{3} * \frac{2}{3}\right) + \left(\frac{1}{3} * \frac{3}{4}\right) = \frac{4}{9} + \frac{3}{12} = \frac{25}{36}$$

Figure 2. Computation tree of PTM

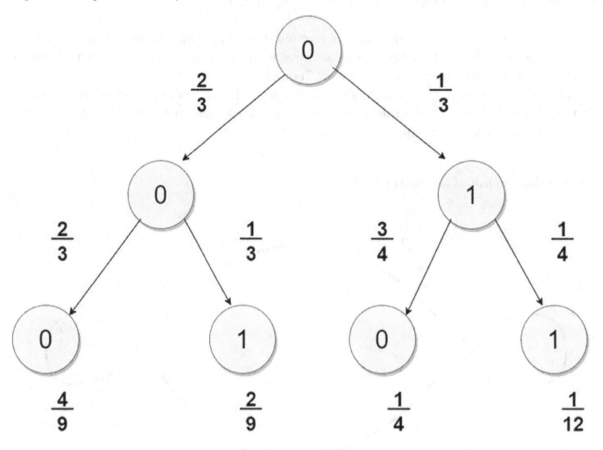

This outcome can be interpreted in the manner that follows. Starting from state 0, the PTM will move in two steps, having a probability of 11/36, it occupies state 1, and with a probability of 25/36, it occupies state 0. We will perform a QTM calculation utilizing the computation tree depicted in Fig. 3 and Fig. 4, similar to the PTM calculation. In the PTM, every edge denotes a transition probability, but in the QTM, every edge denotes a probability amplitude (Kanamori et al., 2006).

The PTM tree only allows for the simultaneous occurrence of one state at a time, but the QTM tree allows for the simultaneous occurrence of all states at the same level. The probability of 0 to 1 from the root in this case after one computing step is:

$$\left(-\frac{1}{\sqrt{2}}\right)^2 = \frac{1}{2}$$

And the probability of 0 → 0 from the root after one computational step is:

$$\left(-\frac{1}{\sqrt{2}}\right)^2 = \frac{1}{2}$$

Figure 3. QTM begins from state "0"

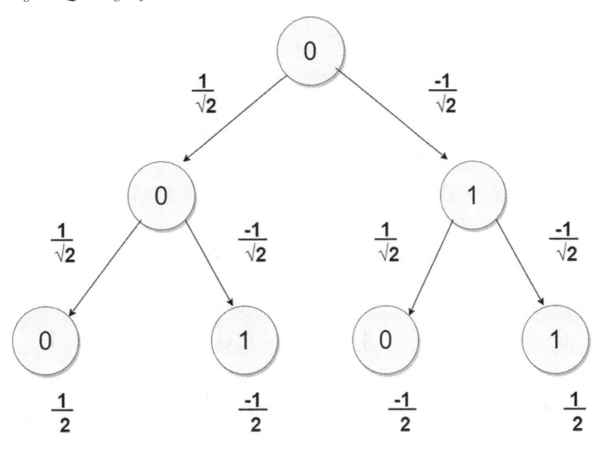

Let us compute the probability of transition 0→1 after the first two steps. First we need to find the probability amplitudes of two possible paths: $\Psi(0{\to}0{\to}1)$ and $\Psi(0{\to}1{\to}1)$:

$$\Psi(0 \to 0 \to 1) = \frac{1}{\sqrt{2}} \times \left(-\frac{1}{\sqrt{2}} \right) = -\frac{1}{2}$$

$$\Psi(0 \to 1 \to 1) = \left(-\frac{1}{\sqrt{2}} \right) \times \frac{1}{\sqrt{2}} = -\frac{1}{2}$$

We add both amplitudes:

$\Psi(0 \to 1$ after two steps$) = \Psi(0{\to}0{\to}1) + \Psi(0{\to}0{\to}1)$:

$$= \left(-\frac{1}{2} \right) + \left(-\frac{1}{2} \right) = -1$$

Figure 4. QTM begins from state "1"

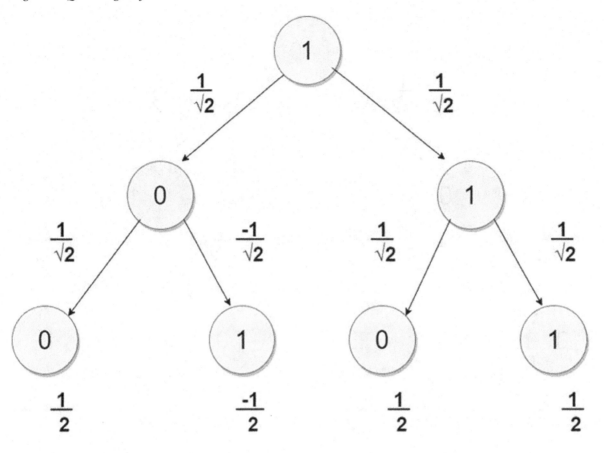

Thus, probability of transition $0 \rightarrow 1$ after two steps is:

P ($0\rightarrow1$ after two steps)

$= | \Psi (0 \rightarrow 1$ after two steps) $|^2$

$= |(-1)|^2= 1$

Similarly, we compute the probability of transition $0\rightarrow0$ after two steps:

$$\Psi(0 \rightarrow 0 \rightarrow 0) = \frac{1}{\sqrt{2}} \times \frac{1}{\sqrt{2}} = \frac{1}{2}$$

$$\Psi(0 \rightarrow 1 \rightarrow 0) = \left(-\frac{1}{\sqrt{2}}\right) \times \frac{1}{\sqrt{2}} = -\frac{1}{2}$$

$\Psi(0\rightarrow0)$after two steps:

$$= \Psi(0 \to 0 \to 0) + \Psi(0 \to 1 \to 0)$$

$$= \frac{1}{2} + \left(-\frac{1}{2}\right) = 0$$

P $((0 \to 0$ after two steps$) = | \Psi(0 \to 0)$ after two steps $|^2 = |0|^2 = 0$

The probabilities of $0 \to 1$ and $0 \to 0$ were both 1/2 after one computing step. The probability of $0 \to 1$ is 1, however, and the probability $0 \to 0$ is 0, after two computations from the same root. The probability amplitudes might have negative values, which leads to this outcome. This outcome, according to our interpretation, is the result of interference between the QTM's states. In other words, the situation of "$0 \to 1$ after two steps" had a constructive interference

$$\left[\left(-\frac{1}{2}\right) + \left(-\frac{1}{2}\right) = -1\right]$$

and the case of "$0 \to 0$ after two steps" had an interference

$$\left[\left(\frac{1}{2}\right) + \left(-\frac{1}{2}\right) = 0\right].$$

The superposition of 'n' output states is the outcome of a calculation requiring a superposition of 'n' input states. For factoring any 'n' digit binary number into 2 prime factors, 2^{n-1} integers must be tested under the worst-case scenario of Eratosthenes' sieve. Hence, a superposition must be created of 2^{n-1} integers as input and give the result of factoring as a superposition of 2^{n-1} outputs. The prime factors can be calculated with just one computational step as opposed to the traditional computer's 2^{n-1} steps, once we can develop a procedure such that the constructive interference happens at the expected output of the superposition of 2^{n-1} outputs whereas the destructive interference takes place at superfluous outputs.

The algorithm proposed by Shor performs factoring of big integers, although it's not a 1-step formula as presented. This algorithm has both types of processing: quantum and classical. The quantum processing part employs quantum interference, whereas the state of superposition determines the period 'r' of function $f_{x,n}(a) = x^a \bmod n$, where 'n' is the integer to be factored and 'x' is a random integer that is co-prime to 'n'. The classical part utilizes the findings from the classical number theory to calculate the factors of 'n' through 'x' and 'r' from the quantum part (Kanamori et al., 2006).

4.3 Quantum Gates and Quantum Circuits

Traditional logic gates change the form of conventional bits. For use with qubits, quantum gates are indeed the qubit equivalent of conventional logic gates. Quantum physics states that unitary transformations, such as unitary matrices, are also what quantum gates are. Quantum gates are often used in quantum circuits along with their corresponding connections to carry out quantum computation and manage quantum data. A quantum circuit is defined by the gates it contains and the results it produces, just like in the classical example, which is used like a computation model (Wang, 2022).

The traditional NOT gate maps 0 to 1 and 1 to 0 whereas the NOT gate of quantum form changes from $|1\rangle$ to $|0\rangle$ and $|0\rangle$ to $|1\rangle$. It then changes $|\Psi\rangle = \alpha_0 |0\rangle + \alpha_1 |1\rangle$ to $|\Psi\rangle = \alpha_1 |0\rangle + \alpha_0 |1\rangle$. Vectors and matrices might be used to represent quantum gates and qubits. Represented by C^2, vector space having every group of complex numbers (Nielsen & Chuang, 2010).

$|0\rangle$ and $|1\rangle$ are indicated by vectors $\begin{bmatrix} 1 \\ 0 \end{bmatrix}$ and $\begin{bmatrix} 1 \\ 0 \end{bmatrix}$ in C^2. $|\Psi\rangle$ is denoted by the vector $\begin{bmatrix} \alpha_0 \\ \alpha_1 \end{bmatrix}$ in C^2, and the quantum gate operating on $|\Psi\rangle$ indicates to the unitary matrix on C^2. For instance, a quantum NOT gate is represented by any matrix σ_x which satisfies (Wang, 2012):

$$\sigma_x \begin{bmatrix} \alpha_0 \\ \alpha_1 \end{bmatrix} = \begin{bmatrix} \alpha_1 \\ \alpha_0 \end{bmatrix},$$

Where,

$$\sigma_x = \begin{bmatrix} 0 & 1 \\ 1 & 0 \end{bmatrix}, \sigma_y = \begin{bmatrix} 1 & -\sqrt{-1} \\ \sqrt{-1} & -1 \end{bmatrix}, \sigma_x = \begin{bmatrix} 1 & 0 \\ 0 & -1 \end{bmatrix}$$

Here, σ_x, σ_y and σ_z are known as Pauli - x, y and z matrices respectively. The quantum gates involved with them are known as Pauli - x, y and z Pauli gates. Quantum NOT gate is the same as the Pauli-x gate (Wang & Song, 2020).

Quantum gates can actualize any classical gate, but the reverse is not true. Assume that two $\sqrt{NOT}$ gates are in a consecutive fashion to produce the $\sqrt{NOT}$ gate that is described as the gate signified by the letter $\sqrt{NOT}$. Due to the fact that the square root of the Pauli-x matrix appears within the complex domain but not in the real domain, despite the fact that this is classically impossible, there is a quantum $\sqrt{NOT}$ gate (Wilde, 2019). In reality, the following expression yields the square root of σ_x in the complex domain:

$$\sqrt{\sigma_x} = \begin{bmatrix} \dfrac{1}{2} + \dfrac{\sqrt{-1}}{2} & \dfrac{1}{2} - \dfrac{\sqrt{-1}}{2} \\ \dfrac{1}{2} - \dfrac{\sqrt{-1}}{2} & \dfrac{1}{2} + \dfrac{\sqrt{-1}}{2} \end{bmatrix}$$

4.4 Quantum Entanglement

When a set of particles are formed, interact, or share space in a way that prevents every particle's quantum state from being separately described from the states of all the others, even if the entities are isolated by a great distance, this is known as quantum entanglement.

It is possible to locate instances where observations of the entangled particles' characteristics, like momentum, position, polarization, and spin, are fully associated. For instance, if a couple of entangled particles are produced with a known zero spin but one particle is discovered to have a clockwise spin on the first axis, the other particle's spin, assessed on the same axis, is discovered to be the opposite. A measure of the particle's properties causes its wave function to fall irreversibly and alters its initial quantum state. This action, though, leads to outcomes that appear to be contradictory. With entangled particles, these measurements have an impact on the entire entangled system.

In 1935, Einstein, Podolsky and Rosen (Matson, 2012) published a paper on these events. Shortly afterward, Erwin Schrödinger published many articles on the subject, describing what is now called the EPR paradox (Einstein et al., 1935) (Schrödinger, 1935). Such conduct was deemed inconceivable by Einstein and others since it went against the local realism theory of causality, which led them to conclude that the current theory of quantum physics might not be complete.

In tests, though, where the spin or polarization of these entangled particles was detected at different locations, statistically defying Bell's inequality, the paradoxical implications of quantum physics were later confirmed (Bell & Bell, 2004) (Yin et al., 2013). In previous experiments, the possibility that the results at one location were gently conveyed to the distant point and influenced the results at the other location could not be completely discounted (Griffiths & Schroeter, 2018). Yet, the Bell was carried out in situations when the distances between sites were great enough for light-speed transmission to take more time, in an instance, thousands of times longer than the period between the observations (Bell & Bell, 2004) (Yin et al., 2013).

Despite their differences, all interpretations concur that entanglement causes correlations in the measurements and that it is feasible to use the correlation between the entangled particles, but that information transmission at rates faster than the speed of light is not achievable (Matson, 2012). Entanglement-based communication, computation, and quantum radar are all active research and development fields (Griffiths & Schroeter, 2018).

4.5 Quantum Annealing

Quantum annealing is the quantum equivalent of simulated annealing. It is basically the noisier variant of quantum adiabatically processed. For a faster convergence to the ideal state, quantum annealing introduces quantum fluctuations rather than thermal fluctuations (Nikolaev & Jacobson, 2010). A quantum annealing system can address separate optimization issues among its many other uses. "Quantum annealing machines," also known as "annealers," are expressly created for a particular function, such as optimization, ML, etc., in contrast to the gate circuit approach (Aharonov et al., 2008).

5. QUANTUM MACHINE LEARNING

5.1 What is Quantum Machine Learning?

Machine learning, a subset of artificial intelligence, derives its power from the ability to learn from history as well as make rational decisions in order to forecast the future, providing remarkable possibilities across a variety of industries. The current data environment poses a challenge to machine learning with its pace of "big data" incremental growth, which could become insurmountable for conventional computers. The current data environment poses a challenge to machine learning. Recently, quantum machine learning methods were put forth and are anticipated to be exponentially faster than traditional algorithms. Unsupervised and supervised learning are the two primary task kinds produced by machine learning (Mohri et al., 2018). A series of training samples with features expressed as high-dimensional vectors and accompanying labels for categorization are provided by supervised machine learning.

Rebentrost, Lloyd and Mohseni (Lloyd et al., 2013) demonstrated that quantum computers, which offer decent infrastructure for handling matrices and vectors, can provide an enormous increase in speed over their conventional counterparts in executing various ML algorithms requiring huge vectors. A quantum computer needs $O(\log(MN))$ time to allocate vectors of N-dimensions to one of 'K' clusters, with M samples for representation each.

The unprecedented speedup of the quantum machine learning algorithm and its potential for widespread applications looks promising in the application of quantum computers (Lloyd et al., 2013) (Aïmeur et al., 2006), along with Shor's algorithm for factoring (Shor, 1997) (Lucero et al., 2012), quantum simulation (Lloyd, 1996) (Houck et al., 2012), and quantum algorithm to solve linear equations (Harrow et al., 2009).

Lloyd used unsupervised and supervised quantum machine learning algorithms to perform cluster finding and assignment, and they presented that it can give a massive speed boost over traditional computers (Lloyd et al., 2013). A traditional computer takes $O(\text{poly}(MN))$ time to solve the most common classical problem of assigning N-dimensional vectors, whereas a quantum computer takes only $O(\log(MN))$ time.

Cai presented the entanglement focused on the categorization of two, four, and eight-dimensional vectors for separating clusters through the use of a small-scale photonic quantum computer, demonstrating the operation of unsupervised and supervised ML to categorize and modify high-dimensional vectors (Shaikh & Ali, 2016).

5.2 Pattern Classification Using Quantum Machine Learning

Using a set of data comprising events whose data is available, classification is a supervised learning method that establishes a group of classifications to which a new observation belongs (Duggar, 2022). Schuld in (2014) introduces a novel quantum pattern classification technique for binary feature vectors that is based on Trugenberger's suggestion for calculating the Hamming distance on a quantum computer and is comparable to the distance-weighted k-nearest neighbor approach. On a quantum computer, Schuld's (2016) provides a solution to the pattern classification problem by efficiently combining least-squares optimization with linear regression.

If the inputs are provided as quantum information, it executes in runtime logarithmic with dimensions "N" of the selected features and irrespective of the training set's size. The only requirement is that X*X can be approximated by a low rank estimation rather than that the sparsity of the matrix containing all training data X is required. To fill the void between ML and quantum processing, Lu examined the quantum form of the decision tree classifier in (Lu & Braunstein, 2014).

Liu (2013) presents a novel classifier based on quantum computation theory. Two separate datasets were used for the performance evaluation of QC, and the effectiveness of QC was compared to other traditional classification techniques like KNN (K Nearest Neighbor) and SVM (Support Vector Machine). According to the results, when there are fewer than 50 training samples, the QC performs better on small-sized training sets than KNN and SVM.

5.3 Use of Quantum SVM for Feature and Data Classification

Support vector machines are effective for linear as well as non-linear classification tasks (Tripathy, Raju, & Kaul, 2018). In linear SVM, the categorization criterion is to identify the largest margin hyperplane that separates those positions having $y_j=1$ from those with $y_j=-1$. The computer finds two parallel hyperplanes with normal vectors $\sim u$ separated by a distance as small as $1/|\sim u|$ that represent the two groups of training data.

Support vector machines were employed by Rebentrost (2014) to create an improved non-linear and linear classifier on quantum computers with massive speedups in vector size and training example count. The fundamental building block of the technique is a non-sparse matrix simulation algorithm to quickly execute the component analysis and matrix inversion to train the data kernel matrices.

Weinstein (2015) discusses Dynamic Quantum Clustering (DQC), a potent visual technique for handling large and highly complex datasets. Its hallmark is its ability to work with large, high-dimensional data sets by exploiting differences in the concentration of the information within feature sets and revealing feature subsets. The result of a DQC study is a video that demonstrates why and how data sets are genuinely categorized as constituents of simple clusters when they really display relationships between all measured variables.

Rebentrost (2003) described an efficient binary classifier that is implemented on a quantum computer and has logarithmic complexity in terms of vector size and training samples. Marghny (2007) proposed GEPSVM (Generalized Eigenvalue Proximal SVM) to solve the SVM complexity. In practical use, error or noise influences the data, making it difficult to work with.

6. DATA ANALYTICS AND QUANTUM COMPUTING

Despite being a relatively modern technology, Data Analytics is already utilizing Quantum Computing (Sharmila Banu & Tripathy, 2016). Below mentioned are some approaches where Quantum Computing is assisting big data experts:

- Quantum computing enables rapid detection, processing, merging, and diagnostic capabilities while working with huge, dispersed data sets.
- Quantum computers can concurrently view each object in a massive database, allowing them to swiftly find patterns in big, unordered sets of data (Tripathy, 2017).
- Quantum computers can do incredibly complex computations in a matter of seconds as opposed to traditional computers, which could take hundreds of years.
- Uses of A.I. employed nowadays are frequently used to manage huge data and assist in the analysis of datasets to find regularities (Tripathy & Banu, 2018).
- Despite the technology's rapid advancement, conventional computers are only capable of handling a finite amount of data. Contrarily, Quantum computers are unaffected by this restriction. The efficiency and power of Quantum computing are advantageous in data analytics and can be utilized in the following fields:
  - **Machine Learning:** Machine learning algorithms are put to use on a quantum computer using Quantum Machine learning. This innovative technology can access more computational power than a regular computer, resulting in significantly faster processing speeds.

◦ **Natural Language Processing:** The first NLP (Natural Language Processing) operation using quantum technology was completed in the year 2020. Grammatical statements have been successfully converted into quantum circuits by scientists. These algorithms were able to answer questions once they were executed on a quantum computer, which has significant implications for huge data.

◦ **Predictive Analytics:** From databases, A.I. systems can be utilized to extract important previous and contemporary information. Additional data is analyzed once quantum computing is integrated with it, producing pertinent data which can then be utilized to generate forecasts (Adate & Tripathy, 2022). However, any forecasting model, which must take into consideration multiple choices, features, and factors, may find the large volume of data accessible to be too abundant sometimes (Kaul et al., 2022). Quantum computing facilitates the development of far more flexible predictive models while minimizing operational delay.

The majority of quantum computers have obstacles that prevent them from reaching their maximum potential. These obstacles include the surroundings, which can lead to a condition of decoherence that renders them essentially unusable. Because of this, it might still be some time before quantum computing enters the majority of businesses or turns into a commonplace system for data analytics (Noble Desktop, 2022).

Quantum computing is indeed a fairly young concept in 2021. Machine learning techniques are constantly getting better thanks to developments in quantum computing. There is still a lot to be discovered about the potential of quantum computing and its implications.

7. CONCLUSION

Data science, especially data mining and statistical learning, has a lot of promise as a result of the benefits of quantum processing over classical computation. A theory of quantum learning is already being created in order to combine conventional knowledge and quantum computation as well as to better understand whether quantum resources can influence learning effectiveness and complexity for solving data science challenges. For example, quantum techniques can achieve improved efficiency in learning challenging operations or policies for particular machine learning tasks, whereas quantum machine learning could have significant computing gains over its conventional equivalent for tackling some machine learning issues.

Although it's common knowledge that quantum computers have the key to curing anything from fatal diseases to global warming. Although applying quantum computing to these problems may lead to novel, innovative solutions, none of us can tell with certainty what a quantum computer can or must be used for because the concept is still in its theoretical infancy. The tension seen between the future potential of quantum computing and its present limits. Not only is it absolutely feasible that quantum computing would only be useful in a small number of applications, but it's also conceivable that, given the pace of advancement, classical computing techniques will eventually surpass those of quantum computing.

It makes sense to assume that quantum computation will play a significant role in data science and that it has the power to completely transform both computing statistics and machine learning. As would be predicted, theoretical studies and experimental efforts into quantum computation and information are prevalent in the field of data science. There is a huge need to create better data science methodologies for quantum systems and information due to the sheer dynamic behavior of quantum physics and the advanced analytics involved in quantum experiments. Some specific themes demonstrated or hypothesized on potential areas of interaction between quantum physics and data science, as well as to promote the advancement of quantum data science.

Quantum certification was designed to establish protocols for verifying quantum equipment, including testing and evaluating its quantum capabilities. Data science is unquestionably required for the verification of quantum features to calibrate and validate them. Data analysis and explanatory approaches play a significant role in quantum supremacy. These findings imply that data science may provide practical solutions and insightful knowledge for quantum systems and quantum information. For instance, quantum entanglement in nonlinear games allows for greater correlations than are feasible in classical games. A subset of quantum algorithms is built on the quantum walk. As is well known, the quantum walk has a higher variance than the analogous conventional random walk. Because the techniques are unpredictable, the computational tasks they need might be viewed as statistical issues.

Despite the possibility that quantum speedup results from the use of quantum theory, the acceleration of recursion processes may be linked to certain mathematical techniques because accelerated techniques frequently use differential calculus of higher order. Whether the assets are described in terms of physical resources, digital data, or mathematical building blocks, the data science technique may result in the research of general resources for the computing speedup effect. In contrast to conventional computation and machine learning, quantum computing and data science must really work more in concert.

REFERENCES

Adate & Tripathy. (2022). A Survey on Deep Learning Methodologies of Recent Applications. In *Deep Learning in Data Analytics- Recent Techniques, Practices and Applications*. Springer. doi:10.1007/978-3-030-75855-4_9

Aharonov, D., Van Dam, W., Kempe, J., Landau, Z., Lloyd, S., & Regev, O. (2008). Adiabatic quantum computation is equivalent to standard quantum computation. *SIAM Review*, *50*(4), 755–787. doi:10.1137/080734479

Aïmeur, E., Brassard, G., & Gambs, S. (2006, June). Machine learning in a quantum world. In *Conference of the Canadian Society for Computational Studies of Intelligence* (pp. 431–442). Springer.

Aïmeur, E., Brassard, G., & Gambs, S. (2007, June). Quantum clustering algorithms. In *Proceedings of the 24th international conference on machine learning* (pp. 1-8). Academic Press.

Ananthaswamy, A. (2018). What Does Quantum Theory Actually Tell Us about Reality? Scientific American, Published online: 3 Sept 2018, URL: https://blogs.scientificamerican.com/observations/what-does-quantum-theory-actually-tell-us-about-reality/, Last Accessed on: 05 Feb 2023.

Anguita, D., Ridella, S., Rivieccio, F., & Zunino, R. (2003). Quantum optimization for training support vector machines. *Neural Networks, Elsevier, Vol, 16*(5-6), 763–770. doi:10.1016/S0893-6080(03)00087-X PMID:12850032

Bell, J. S., & Bell, J. S. (2004). *Speakable and unspeakable in quantum mechanics: Collected papers on quantum philosophy*. Cambridge University Press. doi:10.1017/CBO9780511815676

Cohen, M. L. (2008). Essay: Fifty Years of Condensed Matter Physics. *Physical Review Letters, 101*(25). doi:10.1103/PhysRevLett.101.250001

Duggar, D. (2022). Sarang Bang, B. K. Tripathy: Applications of Big Data Analytics in E-governance and other Aspects of Society. In *Encyclopedia of Data Science and Machine Learning*. IGI Publications.

Einstein, A., Podolsky, B., & Rosen, N. (1935). Can quantum-mechanical description of physical reality be considered complete? *Physical Review, 47*(10), 777–780. doi:10.1103/PhysRev.47.777

Griffiths, D. J., & Schroeter, D. F. (2018). *Introduction to quantum mechanics*. Cambridge University Press. doi:10.1017/9781316995433

Grover, L. K. (1996). A fast quantum mechanical algorithm for database search. *Proc. STOC*, 212–219. 10.1145/237814.237866

Harrow, A. W., Hassidim, A., & Lloyd, S. (2009). Quantum algorithm for linear systems of equations. *Physical Review Letters, 103*(15), 150502. doi:10.1103/PhysRevLett.103.150502 PMID:19905613

Hidary, J. D. (2019). *Quantum Computing: An Applied Approach*. Springer. doi:10.1007/978-3-030-23922-0

Houck, A. A., Türeci, H. E., & Koch, J. (2012). On-chip quantum simulation with superconducting circuits. *Nature Physics, 8*(4), 292–299. doi:10.1038/nphys2251

Kanamori, Y., Yoo, S. M., Pan, W. D., & Sheldon, F. T. (2006). A short survey on quantum computers. *International Journal of Computers and Applications, 28*(3), 227–233. doi:10.1080/120621 2X.2006.11441807

Kaul, D., Raju, H., & Tripathy, B. K. (2022). Deep Learning in Healthcare. In Deep Learning in Data Analytics. Springer. doi:10.1007/978-3-030-75855-4_6

Liu, D., Yang, X., & Jiang, M. (2013, August). A novel classifier based on quantum computation. In *Proceedings of the 51st Annual Meeting of the Association for Computational Linguistics (Volume 2: Short Papers)* (pp. 484-488). Academic Press.

Lloyd, S. (1996). Universal quantum simulators. *Science, 273*(5278), 1073–1078. doi:10.1126cience.273.5278.1073 PMID:8688088

Lloyd, S., Mohseni, M., & Rebentrost, P. (2013). *Quantum algorithms for supervised and unsupervised machine learning*. arXiv preprint arXiv:1307.0411.

Lu, S., & Braunstein, S. L. (2014). Quantum decision tree classifier. In Quantum Inf Process. Springer. doi:10.100711128-013-0687-5

Lucero, E., Barends, R., Chen, Y., Kelly, J., Mariantoni, M., Megrant, A., O'Malley, P., Sank, D., Vainsencher, A., Wenner, J., White, T., Yin, Y., Cleland, A. N., & Martinis, J. M. (2012). Computing prime factors with a Josephson phase qubit quantum processor. *Nature Physics, 8*(10), 719–723. doi:10.1038/nphys2385

Marghny, M. H., ElAziz, R. M. A., & Taloba, A. I. (2015). *Differential search algorithm-based parametric optimization of fuzzy generalized eigenvalue proximal support vector machine.* arXiv preprint arXiv:1501.00728.

Matson, J. (2012, August 13). Quantum teleportation achieved over record distances. *Nature.* https://www.nature.com/articles/nature.2012.11163

Mohri, M., Rostamizadeh, A., & Talwalkar, A. (2018). *Foundations of machine learning.* MIT Press.

Nielsen, M. A., & Chuang, I. L. (2010). *Computation and Quantum Information.* Academic Press.

Nikolaev, A. G., & Jacobson, S. H. (2010). Simulated annealing. In *Handbook of metaheuristics* (pp. 1–39). Springer. doi:10.1007/978-1-4419-1665-5_1

Noble Desktop. (2022). How is Quantum Computing Used in Data Analytics? Classes Near Me. published online: Jan 7, 2022, URL: https://www.nobledesktop.com/classes-near-me/blog/quantum-computing-in-data-analytics, Last Accessed on 05 Feb 2023.

Oskin, M., Chong, F. T., & Chuang, I. (2002). A practical architecture for reliable quantum computers. *IEEE Computer, 35*(January), 79–87. doi:10.1109/2.976922

Pandey, A., & Ramesh, V. (2015). Quantum computing for big data analysis. *Indian Journal of Science, 14*(43), 98–104.

Preneel, B. (Ed.). (2000). Lecture Notes in Computer Science: Vol. 1807. *Factorization of a 512-bit RSA modules.* Springer Verlag.

Rebentrost, P., Mohseni, M., & Lloyd, S. (2014). Quantum support vector machine for big data classification. *Physical Review Letters, 113*(13), 130503. doi:10.1103/PhysRevLett.113.130503 PMID:25302877

Schrödinger, E. (1935, October). Discussion of probability relations between separated systems. *Mathematical Proceedings of the Cambridge Philosophical Society, 31*(4), 555–563. doi:10.1017/S0305004100013554

Schuld, M., Sinayskiy, I., & Petruccione, F. (2014, December). Quantum computing for pattern classification. In *Pacific Rim International Conference on Artificial Intelligence* (pp. 208-220). Springer.

Schuld, M., Sinayskiy, I., & Petruccione, F. (2016). *Pattern classification with linear regression on a quantum computer.* arXiv preprint arXiv:1601.07823.

Shaikh, T. A., & Ali, R. (2016, December). Quantum computing in big data analytics: A survey. In *2016 IEEE international conference on computer and information technology (CIT)* (pp. 112-115). IEEE.

Sharmila Banu, K., & Tripathy, B. K. (2016). Data analytics in spatial epidemiology: A survey. Jurnal Technology, 78(10), 159-165.

Shor, P. W. (1994). Algorithm for quantum computation: Discrete logarithm and factoring. *Proc. 35th IEEE Annual Symp. on Foundations of Computer Science*, 24–34. 10.1109/SFCS.1994.365700

Shor, P. W. (1997). *Polynomial-Time Algorithms for Prime Factorization and Discrete Logarithms on a Quantum Computer (SIAM).* In *Quantum Physics.* Springer.

Tripathy & Banu. (2018). Neighborhood Rough Sets Based Spatial Data Analytics. In *Encyclopedia for Science and technology*. IGI Publications.

Tripathy, B. K. (2017). Rough set and neighbourhood systems in Big Data Analysis. In Computational Intelligence Applications in Business Intelligence and Big Data Analytics. CRC Press.

Tripathy, B. K., & Deboleena, D. (2018). Trustworthiness in the Social internet of Things (SIoT). In Big Data Analytics: A social network approach. Taylor and Francis.

Tripathy, B. K., & Deepthi, P. H. (2017a). An Investigation of Fuzzy Techniques in clustering of Big Data. In Computational Intelligence Applications in Business Intelligence and Big Data Analytics. CRC Press.

Tripathy, B. K., & Deepthi, P. H. (2017b). Quantum Inspired Computational Intelligent Techniques in Image Segmentation. In S. Bhattacharya, U. Maulik, & P. Dutta (Eds.), Quantum Inspired Computational Intelligence: Research and Applications (pp. 233–258). Elsevier.

Tripathy, B. K., Parimala, B., & Thippa Reddy, G. (2021). Prediction of Diseases using Innovative Classification and Regression Models. In *Data Analytics in Biomedical Engineering and Healthcare* (pp. 179–203). Academic Press. doi:10.1016/B978-0-12-819314-3.00012-4

Tripathy, B. K., Raju, H., & Kaul, D. (2018). Quantum Computing inspired algorithms in machine learning. In Quantum inspired intelligent systems for multimedia data analysis. IGI Publications.

Tripathy, B. K., Sooraj, T. R., & Mohanty, R. K. (2018). Data Mining Techniques in Big Data for Social Network. In Big Data Analytics: A social network approach. Taylor and Francis.

Wang, Y. (2012). Quantum computation and quantum information. *Statistical Science*, *27*(3), 373–394. doi:10.1214/11-STS378

Wang, Y. (2022). When Quantum Computation Meets Data Science: Making Data Science Quantum. *Harvard Data Science Review*, *4*(1). Advance online publication. doi:10.1162/99608f92.ef5d8928

Wang, Y., & Song, X. (2020). Quantum science and quantum technology. *Statistical Science*, *35*(1), 51–74. doi:10.1214/19-STS745

Wilde, M. M. (2019). *Quantum information theory* (2nd ed.). Cambridge University Press.

Williams, C. P., & Clearwater, S. H. (1997). *Exploration in quantum computing*. Springer-Verlag.

Williams, C. P., & Clearwater, S. H. (1998). *Explorations in quantum computing*. Springer.

Yin, J., Cao, Y., Yong, H. L., Ren, J. G., Liang, H., Liao, S. K., . . . Pan, J. W. (2013). *Bounding the speed of spooky action at a distance*. arXiv preprint arXiv:1303.0614.

Chapter 15
Biological Plant Recommendation System for Indoor Air Quality Improvement Using IoT

Ashish Anandrao Patil
KLE Institute of Technology, India

Manu T. M.
KLE Institute of Technology, India

Basavaraj S. Anami
KLE Institute of Technology, India

ABSTRACT

Various enforced rules on human beings due to pandemic have made them spend more time indoors. Hence, improving indoor air quality (IAQ) is significant so that people can work efficiently under good indoor ambience. There are various plants in nature that absorb harmful ingredients from indoor environments based on their biological properties. This chapter presents an internet of things (IoT)-based biological plant recommendation system to improve indoor air quality. This system monitors a particular indoor environment and measures the concentration of various gases at the front-end. In the back-end subsystem, the data received from the front-end subsystem is assessed and a suitable plant/s from the cloud database is recommended. This is a very handy and cost-effective system and can be easily implemented in any indoor environment.

DOI: 10.4018/978-1-6684-6821-0.ch015

1 INTRODUCTION

The advancements in technology in this era have led to the improvement in quality of life. After the pandemic, indoor air quality (IAQ) management is of prime importance and demands better ambience or environment in offices, homes and everywhere, to have a healthy life. One of the ways to achieve this goal is to improve the indoor air quality by purifying or removing harmful ingredients from the indoor air. This requires leveraging of natural resources and technology to develop IAQ monitoring system that helps people to obtain better air quality leading to good indoor environment.

Since air is one of the prime elements of humans' day-to-day life, it contains various gases and evidences of few rare elements. The bad air quality leads to some hazardous diseases such as asthma, nausea, breathing problems, heart diseases, lung cancer or deterioration of immunity. Most of the humans are indoor for longer hours during their day-to-day chores. Hence, the degradation of IAQ directly affects human health and working efficiency. Carbon dioxide (CO_2) concentration produced due to human respiration, the radiant energy released by indoor light sources and moisture present in the air are some of the factors which contaminate the indoor air.

Various studies have shown that indoor environment is more polluted than the outdoor environment. The excess CO_2 present in the indoor air may lead to dizziness, headache, nausea and few other symptoms as well. The allowed CO_2 concentration for indoor scenario varies depending on the size of the room and it ranges from 250 ppm to 1500 ppm across buildings. The radiant energy from various light sources inside the indoor environment directly affects the visibility of human eye. Based on the brightness and illumination of light sources the work ability of human depends in indoor ambience. The excess amount of moisture or humid indoor affects the health of some people. More moisture may lead to breathing difficulties and leads to serious health issues. As per the studies 30% to 60% relative humidity is considered to be most comfortable for average human being.

Different pollutants or gases or compounds present in indoor air cause variety of health issues. *Formaldehyde* present in air causes burning sensation in eyes, nose and throat, cough, skin irritation. Inhaling excess amount of *benzene* from air leads to dizziness, drowsiness, headache, irregular heartbeats and if the excess benzene is inhaled it can cause cancer or leukemia. *Nitrogen dioxide* causes damage to respiratory tract and increases susceptibility to respiratory diseases and asthma. *Carbon dioxide* causes breathing difficulty, increased blood pressure and heart rate, tiredness, sweating. *Carbon monoxide* causes harm by combining with hemoglobin in blood and reducing the Oxygen content from blood. *Xylene* causes irritation in throat, nose, eyes and skin, while *trichloroethylene* cause headache, dizziness, confusion and weakness. The furniture or electronics items in home emit different pollutants in the air, these pollutants are also harmful to human health as they can cause headache, dizziness and affect respiratory system. The high humidity or very less humidity causes serious of health issues.

There are various biological plants in the nature which relatively improve the moisture contents in the air, reduces some volatile organic compounds (VOCs) and also absorb CO_2 from the air and release Oxygen. Hence, this power of natural resources can be explored. When such multiple plants are used in the indoor environment, there will be improvement in IAQ. Various plants and their properties are summarized in Table X.1. The property of each plant, requirements for its growth, its average height and lifetime and its suitable location are given in Table X.1.

This chapter, presents IAQ management system developed with Internet of Things (IoT), and suggests a required remedy for the given environment. We have considered various plants useful in improvement of IAQ, these plants are chosen based on their properties given in Table X.1. We present both front end and back-end designs for the development of IAQ management system. The indoor sensing is carried out in front end, based on the sensors. The back-end system gives the remedy based on the data received from front-end system. The back-end is a cloud-based system and used to suggest the remedy through IoT technology. The back-end design uses the information on the required biological plants as well as some e-commerce websites and recommends their URLs to purchase those plants required by the customers for air purification.

2. LITERATURE SURVEY

From the literature survey, it is observed that researchers have worked in this area and its gist is presented in this section. F. Brili *et. al.* (2018) present a system, which considers cutting-edge technology and phytoremediation capacity of plants to improve IAQ with reduction in air consumption. This study focuses on the way in which the indoor air pollutants are removed through absorption or adsorption. Moya T. A. *et. al.* (2019) reviewed the plant systems and their effect on indoor environment. They have described how various properties or biological processes in plants help in controlling humidity, better health, air cooling, sound reduction. It is also suggested that green plants in combination with mechanical fans, the air cleaning speed is more than that of the potted plant systems. Tran V. V. *et. al.* (2020) reviewed and evaluated major emission sources of indoor pollutants and their effects on health. They have pointed out different strategies and methods for controlling and reducing concentration of pollutants and recent trends in improving IAQ are summarized by considering their potentials and advantages. The illness caused due to indoor pollutants is categorized as sick building syndrome (SBS) and building related illness (BRI). SBS is referred to a group of symptoms that are linked with specific building and their environment. These symptoms include eye, nose and throat irritation, reduced memory, headaches, tiredness, Asthma or Asthma-like symptoms, skin dryness or irritation etc. Identified and causative agents that are directly related to the cause of poor air quality in buildings and exposure to such environment leads to BRI. The common symptoms that fall under BRI are flu, hypersensitivity pneumonitis, humidified fever, lung or respiratory problems.

Table 1. Different biological plants suitable for indoor environment and their properties

Plant/biological name	Property	Requirements for growth	Average Height (inches)	Average Lifetime (Years)	Location in room
Aloe Vera (Aloe barbadensis miller)	Filters benzene and formaldehyde from air	Sunlight	35	12	Gallery/ Window
Spider plant (Chlorophytum comosum)	Removes formaldehyde	Grows in all conditions	15	20 - 50	corner
Snake plant (Dracaena trifasciata)	Filters formaldehyde, nitrogen dioxide and absorbs CO_2 at night	Very little sunlight and water	50 - 70	5 - 10	Corridor/ corner
Areca (bamboo) palm (Dypsis lutescens)	Humidifies the air	Shady area	90 - 240	70 - 100	Corridor/ corner

continues on following page

Table 1. Continued

Plant/biological name	Property	Requirements for growth	Average Height (inches)	Average Lifetime (Years)	Location in room
Gerbera (Transvaal daisy)	Absorbs carbon monoxide, releases oxygen in night	Shady areas/ Little sunlight	30	2 - 3	Bedroom
Golden Pothos (Epipremnum aureum)	Removes formaldehyde	Sunlight	150	5 - 10	Corridor/ Gallery/ window
Chrysanthemum	Combats with benzene, flower blooms for 6 weeks	Sunlight	12 - 36	3 - 4	Corridor/ Gallery/ window
Dragon tree (Dragon tree)	removes xylene, trichloroethylene and formaldehyde; poisonous	Sunlight	120	10 - 20	Corridor
Weeping fig (Ficus benjamina)	Removes benzene, formaldehyde and trichloroethylene	Sunlight and water	36 - 72	20	Corridor/ Gallery/ window
Dracaena	Removes VOCs, benzene, formaldehyde and trichloroethylene. Cools atmosphere	Shady areas/ Little sunlight	36 - 48	10	Corridor/ corner
Money Plant (Epipremnum aureum)	Romoves VOCs, Benzene, formaldehyde, xylene, Carbon Monoxide	Little sunlight and water	150	10	Gallery/ Window/ Bedroom/ Corridor
Peace Lily (Spathiphyllum)	Removes pollutants emitted by furniture, electronics, cleaning products etc.	Little/indirect sunlight	12 - 48	3 - 5	Corridor/ corner
Scarlet Star Bromeliad (Guzmania lingulate)	Removes VOCs	Humid environment, indirect sunlight	18	0.5	Bathroom
English Ivy (Hedera helix)	Air purification	Water, Indirect sunlight	6 – 8 (can climb up to 50 inches on wall)	50 - 100	Over the table/ cupboard/ bookcases
Boston Fern (Nephrolepis exaltata)	Purifies the air, improves humidity, restores moisture levels	Humid environment, indirect sunlight	100	100	Bathroom
Chinese Evergreen (Aglaonema modestum)	Purifies air by filtering indoor air pollutants and toxins	Low/medium lights	12 - 36	10	Darker corners of home
Corn Plant (Dracaena fragrans)	Removes VOCs, improves humidity,	Indirect sunlight	48 - 60	2 - 3	Corners/ Corridors
Janet Craig (Dracaena deremensis)	Removes VOCs, Improves humidity	Less water, little sunlight	40 - 80	10	Over the table
Broadleaf Lady Palm (Rhapis excelsa)	removes ammonia	Indirect sunlight, humidity	84	70 - 80	Kitchen/ Bathroom
Rubber Plant (Ficus elastica)	Purifies air, Anti-Inflammatory	Direct sunlight, water	600 - 1200	13	Corridor/ Gallery

IoT based air quality monitoring platform is demonstrated by JunHo Jo *et. al.* (2020), wherein IoT and cloud computing-based platform is used to monitor indoor air quality at anytime and anywhere. The monitoring is done remotely through a developed application, so that approved person monitors through application or through web server. The data acquisition, monitoring, processing and prediction for indoor as well as outdoor environment using Artificial Neural Network (ANN) is presented by B. Wang et. al. (2019) and this work is mainly focused on hazy and smoggy conditions, since data in these situations is non-linear. A two-layer prediction algorithm is presented using long short term memory (LSTM) neural network and gated recurrent unit (GRU) to analyze the non-linear data. Lai X. *et. al.* (2019), proposed a low-cost system to monitor air quality and real-time predictions through IoT and edge computing. Kalman filter-based algorithm is developed to improve the sensor accuracy and the concentration of six pollutants is immediately predicted using this system leading to for smart agriculture.

M. Ljubojevic *et. al.* (2016) addressed IAQ with respect to Context influence factors (CIF) by considering major contaminations. IoT based technique for objective assessment and continuous monitoring of IAQ is presented with the aim of improving design and accommodation of botanical purifiers to particular environment. As millions of people use subway tunnels during their way to office or home. Jo J. H. *et. al.* (2020) have evaluated and presented IoT based air quality monitoring system for subway tunnels. This system consists of smart air (air quality measurement device), a web server for cloud computing and IoT gateway to monitor the concentration of particulate matter (PM10), which is above the threshold. From various experiments and measurements, it is found that this system efficiently improves air quality in subway tunnels. S. Ali *et. al.* (2021) presents a low-cost novel sensor that measures particular matter (PM), CO, NO2, levels from the air through cost effective electrochemical sensors. It is also capable to work with low power, hence can be used over LoRaWAN network and effective short-range communications. In this chapter, a biological plant recommendation system using IoT is proposed that can suggest a particular plant/s for the given indoor environment.

3. BIOLOGICAL PLANT RECOMMENDATION SYSTEM

This section presents a model for biological plant recommendation system development through IoT. The model consists of two subsystems namely front-end subsystem and back-end subsystem as shown in figure 15.1. Indoor data collection and monitoring through various sensors is done under front-end subsystem and this collected data is further transferred to the back-end subsystem. The back-end subsystem assesses the received indoor air data and based on the concentrations of VOCs, various gases and humidity, it suggests the required plant/s for the given indoor environment.

Figure 15.2 shows a generalized block schematic diagram of the IoT based biological plant recommendation system. The controller system with CPU and memory is the main part of the front-end subsystem. The concentration of various elements in the indoor air is measured by different sensors and these sensors are connected to the controller through a multiplexer. This collected indoor information is processed at the back-end using cloud database with data assessment and plants' recommendation. The communication between front-end and back-end subsystems is done through a communication interface with Internet connectivity and the remedial plant suggestion by back-end system is done through Internet.

Figure 1. A simplified biological plant recommendation system

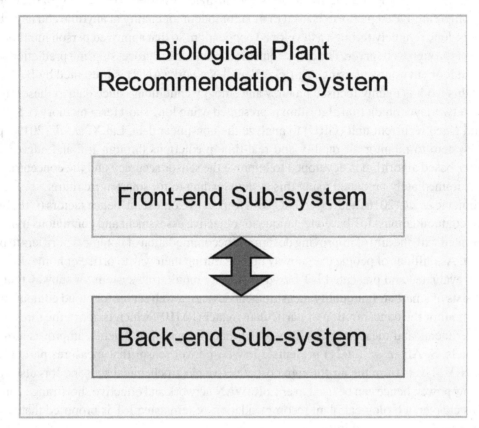

3.1 Front-End Subsystem

The front-end subsystem consists of sensors and multiplexer, controller unit and communication interface. The details of each are given below.

3.1.1 Sensors and Multiplexer

Different sensors, include CO_2, NO_2, CO, humidity, formaldehyde, Benzene, Ammonia, light intensity and UV radiation. All these sensors are compatible with Arduino and Raspberry-pi boards. There is scarce information about availability of xylene sensor and trichloroethylene sensor and their compatibility with different controllers. Yunsung Kang *et. al.* (2020) presented highly sensitive sensor module for xylene detection and Han, T. S *et.al.* (2002) presented flow injection microbial method for the detection of trichloroethylene. Multiplexer is used for data collection from default sensors, one sensor at a time. The data collection is scheduled periodically depending on the number of sensors interfaced with the controller. Following is a brief account of some sensors used in the model.

Figure 2. Block schematic model of IoT based biological plant recommendation system

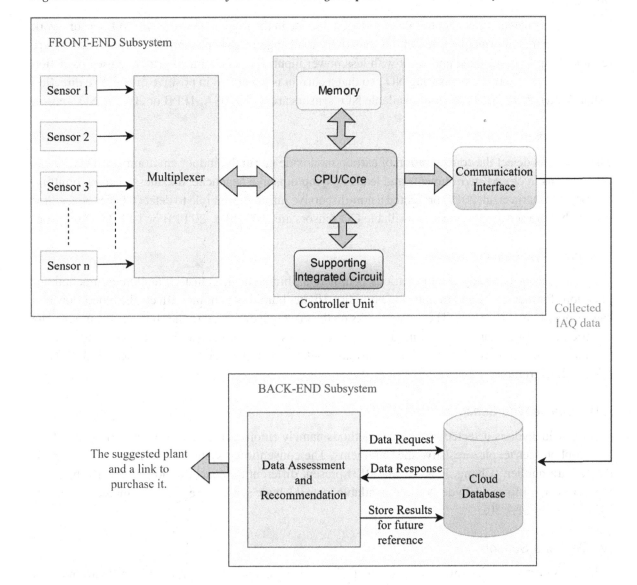

(i) CO_2 Sensor

These sensors detect the concentration of carbon dioxide in the indoor environment. Photoacoustic spectroscopy (PAS) based CO_2 sensors are one of the efficient, cost-effective and widely used sensors to detect and measure CO_2 (Qiao S *et. al.* 2019). The principle behind PAS is to pass infrared light pulses through an optical tunnel at CO_2 absorption wavelength (λ= 4.2 µm). CO_2 molecules absorb this light and the pressure is generated with each pulse due to shaking and this pressure change is converted into CO_2 concentration. Various available CO_2 sensors are, MQ-135, NDIR (non-dispersive infrared), Luxafor CO_2 monitor.

(ii) NO$_2$ Sensor

These sensors detect the concentration of nitrogen dioxide in the indoor environment. NO$_2$ sensors work on electrochemical principle due to high sensitivity to change in gas concentration. These sensors are reliable, long lasting, stable and work with less power input. Electrochemical principle used oxidation or reduction reactions for measuring NO$_2$, so that a current is generated in positive or negative direction (Khan MAH *et. al.* 2019). Various available NO$_2$ sensors are, DSO109A, 1PPB or 20 PPB NO$_2$ sensor.

(iii) CO Sensor

These sensors detect the concentration of carbon monoxide gas in the indoor environment. The CO gas is hazardous in closed environments and leads to symptoms like headache, dizziness, nausea, omitting etc. (Reza Diharja et. al. 2019) presented a non-dispersive infrared principle to detect CO gas concentration with more sensitivity. Various available CO sensors are, 100 PPM, 20 PPB or 1 PPB CO seonsor.

(iv) Humidity Sensor

Humidity sensor is widely used in various commercial, biomedical, industrial and environmental applications for measuring and monitoring humidity. Higher humidity at homes affects the blood flow and causes breathing difficulties. The sensor works on the principle of detecting the changes that modify the electric current or temperature. Humidity sensors are classified into capacitive, resistive and thermal conductivity-based (Farahani, H., 2014). Various available humidity sensors are, AcuRite 613, DHT22 AM2302, hygrometer.

(v) Formaldehyde Sensor

The formaldehyde is detected by various methods namely fluorometric, amperometric or conductive, spectrophotometric, piezoresistive measurements. The conventional systems that measure the formaldehyde are bulkier. (Chung, P. R. et. al. 2013) present different compact and low power methods for measurement of formaldehyde. Various available formaldehyde sensors are, Giner's ambient formaldehyde monitor, SFA 30.

(vi) Benzene Sensor

A highly selective and sensitive measurement of benzene gas into indoor and outdoor environment in presented in (Moon, Y. K. et. al. 2021). The sensitivity is achieved through a 2Rh-TiO$_2$/SnO$_2$ bilayer design and analyzed using proton transfer reaction-quadrupole mass spectrometer (PTR-QMS). This sensor helps in automatic monitoring of air pollutants and evaluate their impacts on human health. The easily available benzene sensor is MQ-135

(vii) Light Intensity Sensor

The light intensity sensor accurately measures the amount of solar radiation present in the environment. Higher UV index in the light is harmful to the human beings, this also causes routine fluctuations in the air quality. D. A. Hoang et. al. (2019) has introduced a stepper motor based rotating light sensor to measure the radiation in all directions in a normal workroom. Various available light intensity sensors are, LDR (Light detecting resistor), EM-light sensor, Photasgard RHKF-U.

Table 15.2 shows threshold values of various indoor air gases and ingredients. Concentration is represented in parts per million (ppm), parts per billion (ppb), microgram per volume ($\mu g/m^3$) and percentage.

Table 2. Various indoor gases and ingredients and their allowed concentration

Indoor Gases/Ingredients	Threshold Concentration
Carbon dioxide (CO_2)	400 ppm
Carbon monoxide (CO)	30 ppm
Nitrogen dioxide (NO_2)	40.0 $\mu g/m^3$
Formaldehyde	0.1 ppm
Benzene	5 $\mu g/m^3$
Xylene	5 ppm
Trichloroethylene	2 $\mu g/m^3$
Humidity	30% to 50%

3.1.2 Controller Unit

The controller unit is the heart of the front-end subsystem, it contains a central processing unit (CPU), memory and other supporting integrated circuits connected to CPU to perform external operations. The controller has internal memory, but to store and process more amount of data, external memory module is interfaced with the CPU. The widely used controller units are Arduino UNO, NodeMCU and Raspberry pi. These boards are helpful to start with small scale IoT based projects.

Arduino UNO is ATmega328P based microcontroller with 14 digital input/output pins. It has a power jack, USB port, a reset button, and ICSP header and a 16 MHz ceramic resonator. It has all required support of a microcontroller; we use it by directly connecting it to a computer and start tinkering it for required application (Arduino UNO R3, 2022). NodeMCU is an open-source firmware and development kit, which helps in developing IoT products with minimum code. It has same hardware structure for input-output like Arduino, event driven API for networking with the Nodejs style and it uses low cost wifi, which makes NodeMCU a highly suitable candidate for developing IoT based applications (NodeMCU, 2014-2018). Raspberry pi is a small computer board, which has a system on chip (SoC) with an integrated microcontroller. An operating system is installed on this board before using it and develop various IoT applications easily on this board (Raspberry pi).

The indoor air quality (IAQ) information received from indoor gas sensors is available with the controller unit and the same information is communicated to the cloud database with a suitable communication interface. Various communication modules such as UART, GSM, WiFi or LTE are example for the communication interfaces.

3.2 Back-End Subsystem

The back-end subsystem has a cloud database server, data assessment and recommendation units. The database containing various plants, their use and benefits is stored into a cloud server. This database is accessed through different databases such as MySQL, SQL and ORACLE, amongst these databases, MySQL is widely used due to its structured query processing capabilities (MySQL 2022). At back-end subsystem, the decision making about a particular plant is carried out by searching through database. The IAQ information received from controller unit is analyzed and the required plant/s for that particular indoor environment is suggested by the back-end subsystem. Figure 15.3 shows the working flow of back-end subsystem, where IAQ data received from front-end subsystem is input to this back-end subsystem. Based on the concentration of various gases in the given indoor environment, the back-end subsystem checks for the threshold levels of the received gases. If the concentration of all the gases is below the threshold value, system suggests that the particular indoor environment is having optimal concentration of gases. If some of the gases have higher concentrations than threshold, the system checks for required plant remedy for the given environment from the plant database. The back-end subsystem recommends the required plant/s for indoor environment along with the benefits and location of the plant. Further, advancement possible by directly suggesting different e-commerce websites to users for purchase of the particular plants. This IoT based biological plant recommendation system helps in improving indoor ambience and could eventually reduce the impact of various diseases caused due to different gases and humidity present indoor. Since, the indoor air is continuously monitored through this system, the plant replacement feature can also be added to this system based on the plant lifetime.

Figure 3. Working flow of back-end subsystem

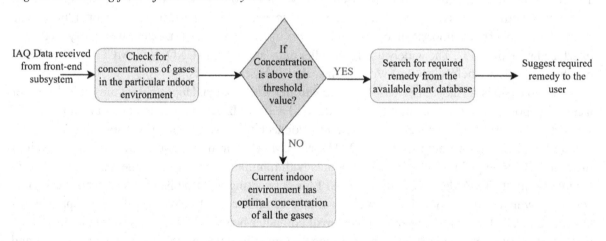

The biological plant recommendation system presented in this chapter is very attractive, portable, flexible and a low-cost that can be used to complement any engineering measures for most of the indoor environment. This system can be applied to any house, workplace or hospitals to maintain better indoor environment. The improved IAQ using biological plants is nature friendly solution to purify the air. The better IAQ will help people to breathe fresh air, which eventually keeps them healthy and active. This solution helps to overcome the diseases caused due to the contaminated air.

4 CONCLUSION

The lifestyle of people after pandemic have changed to some extent and it demands better air quality. The IoT based biological plant recommendation system presented in this chapter is one of the solutions suitable to improve indoor air quality. Since, average human being spends most of their time indoor and this system will help to achieve better indoor ambience or environment. This system can be implemented in any indoor environments such as offices, workplaces, classrooms, houses etc. Based on the lifetime of plant and its other properties further intelligence can also be added to this system, such as replacement of plants, addition of new plants, optimal positioning of plant etc.

REFERENCES

Ali, S., Glass, T., Parr, B., Potgieter, J., & Alam, F. (2021). Low-Cost Sensor With IoT LoRaWAN Connectivity and Machine Learning-Based Calibration for Air Pollution Monitoring. *IEEE Transactions on Instrumentation and Measurement, 70*, 1-11. Advance online publication. doi:10.1109/TIM.2020.3034109

ArduinoU. N. O. R3. (2022). https://docs.arduino.cc/hardware/uno-rev3

Brilli, F., Fares, S., Ghirardo, A., de Visser, P., Calatayud, V., Muñoz, A., Annesi-Maesano, I., Sebastiani, F., Alivernini, A., Varriale, V., & Menghini, F. (2018). Plants for sustainable improvement of indoor air quality. *Trends in Plant Science, 23*(6), 507–512. doi:10.1016/j.tplants.2018.03.004 PMID:29681504

Chung, P. R., Tzeng, C. T., Ke, M. T., & Lee, C. Y. (2013). Formaldehyde gas sensors: A review. *Sensors (Basel), 13*(4), 4468–4484. doi:10.3390130404468 PMID:23549368

Diharja, R., Rivai, M., Mujiono, T., & Pirngadi, H. (2019). Carbon Monoxide Sensor Based on Non-Dispersive Infrared Principle. *Journal of Physics: Conference Series, 1201*. 10.1088/1742-6596/1201/1/012012

Farahani, H., Wagiran, R., & Hamidon, M. N. (2014). Humidity sensors principle, mechanism, and fabrication technologies: A comprehensive review. *Sensors (Basel), 14*(5), 7881–7939. doi:10.3390140507881 PMID:24784036

Han, T. S., Sasaki, S., Yano, K., Ikebukuro, K., Kitayama, A., Nagamune, T., & Karube, I. (2002). Flow injection microbial trichloroethylene sensor. *Talanta, 57*(2), 271–276. doi:10.1016/S0039-9140(02)00027-9 PMID:18968627

Hoang, D. A., Tung, T. T., Nguyen, C. M., & Nguyen, K. P. (2019). Rotating Sensor for Multi-Direction Light Intensity Measurement. *International Conference on System Science and Engineering (ICSSE)*, 462-467. 10.1109/ICSSE.2019.8823447

Jo, Jo, Kim, Kim, & Han. (2020). Development of an IoT-Based Indoor Air Quality Monitoring Platform. *Journal of Sensors*. . doi:10.1155/2020/8749764

Jo, J. H., Jo, B., Kim, J. H., & Choi, I. (2020). Implementation of IoT-Based Air Quality Monitoring System for Investigating Particulate Matter (PM10) in Subway Tunnels. *International Journal of Environmental Research and Public Health, 17*(15), 5429. doi:10.3390/ijerph17155429 PMID:32731501

Kang, Y., Kim, K., Cho, B., Kwak, Y., & Kim, J. (2020). Highly Sensitive Detection of Benzene, Toluene, and Xylene Based on CoPP-Functionalized TiO2 Nanoparticles with Low Power Consumption. *ACS Sensors*, *5*(3), 754–763. doi:10.1021/acssensors.9b02310 PMID:32048833

Khan, M. A. H., Rao, M. V., & Li, Q. (2019). Recent Advances in Electrochemical Sensors for Detecting Toxic Gases: NO_2, SO_2 and H_2S. *Sensors (Basel)*, *19*(4), 905. doi:10.339019040905 PMID:30795591

Lai, X., Yang, T., Wang, Z., & Chen, P. (2019). IoT Implementation of Kalman Filter to Improve Accuracy of Air Quality Monitoring and Prediction. *Applied Sciences (Basel, Switzerland)*, *9*(9), 1831. doi:10.3390/app9091831

Ljubojevic, M., Simic, M., Babic, Z., & Zoric, M. (2016). Quality of life context influence factors improvement using houseplants and Internet of Things. *IEEE International Black Sea Conference on Communications and Networking (BlackSeaCom)*, 1-5. 10.1109/BlackSeaCom.2016.7901574

Moon, Y. K., Jeong, S.-Y., Jo, Y.-M., Jo, Y. K., Kang, Y. C., & Lee, J.-H. (2021). Highly Selective Detection of Benzene and Discrimination of Volatile Aromatic Compounds Using Oxide Chemiresistors with Tunable Rh-TiO_2 Catalytic Overlayers. *Advancement of Science*, *8*(6), 2004078. doi:10.1002/advs.202004078 PMID:33747750

Moya, T. A., van den Dobbelsteen, A., Ottelé, M., & Bluyssen, P. M. (2019). A review of green systems within the indoor environment. *Indoor and Built Environment*, *28*(3), 298–309. doi:10.1177/1420326X18783042

MySQL. (2022). https://www.mysql.com

NodeMcu. (n.d.). *Connect Things EASY (2014-2018)*. https://www.nodemcu.com/index_en

Qiao, S., Qu, Y., Ma, Y., He, Y., Wang, Y., Hu, Y., Yu, X., Zhang, Z., & Tittel, F. K. (2019). A Sensitive Carbon Dioxide Sensor Based On Photoacoustic Spectroscopy With A Fixed Wavelength Quantum Cascade Laser. *Sensors (Basel)*, *19*(19), 4187. doi:10.339019194187 PMID:31561611

Raspberry pi. (n.d.). https://www.raspberrypi.com/

Tran, V. V., Park, D., & Lee, Y. C. (2020). Indoor Air Pollution, Related Human Diseases, and Recent Trends in the Control and Improvement of Indoor Air Quality. *International Journal of Environmental Research and Public Health*, *17*(8), 2927. doi:10.3390/ijerph17082927 PMID:32340311

Wang, B., Kong, W., Guan, H., & Xiong, N. N. (2019). Air Quality Forecasting Based on Gated Recurrent Long Short-Term Memory Model in Internet of Things. *IEEE Access: Practical Innovations, Open Solutions*, *7*, 69524–69534. doi:10.1109/ACCESS.2019.2917277

Chapter 16
Digital Twins for Smart Grids:
Digital Transformation of Legacy Power Networks

K. S. Sastry Musti
https://orcid.org/0000-0003-4384-7933
Namibia University of Science and Technology, Nambia

Geetam Singh Tomar
Rajkiya Engineering College, Sonbhadra, India

ABSTRACT

The development of smart energy systems using the principles of Industry 4.0 to energize smart cities is of significant interest. On the other hand, digital twin systems are gaining popularity as they are expected to provide greater insights into the design, development, and maintenance processes of complex systems. This chapter first presents various salient operational requirements in energizing the smart cities through renewable energies, virtual power plants, and demand side management technologies. The tenets of digital twins and Industry 4.0 are the key drivers in the developmental process of cyber physical energy systems. The chapter illustrates the process of replicating the twins—physical and virtual systems—to function in synchronization for effective management. The digital transformation process of developing cyber physical systems from the conceptual living labs to the fully functional digital twins is presented.

INTRODUCTION

Smart cities are coming up in good numbers across the world and are expected to be equipped by smart technologies. They bring several concepts (Industry 4.0, Circular Economy etc.) and technologies (IIoT, Big data, Renewable energies) together and operate with digital platforms where information can be shared in a smart fashion for specific purposes (K.S. Sastry, 2020). One of the most essential aspects of smart cities is their energy consumption, which is higher than that of their conventional contemporaries. Smart cities are supposed to meet a significant portion of their energy demands on their own through renewable energies and efficient energy conservation processes. This aspect brings in Demand Side Management

DOI: 10.4018/978-1-6684-6821-0.ch016

(DSM), Renewable energies (REs), and circular economy (CE) (K. S. Sastry Musti, 2020). However, DSM and CE overlap in principles, objectivity and philosophies. Fundamentally smart cities are driven by fourth industrial revolution. Industry 4.0 advocates the use of Industrial Internet of Things (IIoT) that can combine measurement of data, analyzing the data through analytics and communication technologies and platforms. Dembski et. al(2020) presented various aspects of smart cities and provided foundation for the need of using digital twinning principles for their development (Ali et. al, 2021). Thus, it can be seen that using the concept of digital twins for smart cities is of significant interest. Energy consumption patterns of smart cities can be significantly higher and different when compared to legacy cities. Designing power distribution system networks for smart cities by itself is a challenging task. Laamarti et al (2020) has explained the ISO standards for developing smart cities based on digital twin approach. Yu et. al (2016) presented the need to establish cyber-physical systems for smart grids. A reliable and highly functional real-time measurement, monitoring and control system needs to be in place so that a typical smart city is able to efficiently a) conserve energy, b) serve consumers as per the quality standards c) manage energy resources etc. Hence, managing the energy related functions and services in a typical smart city are different from the regular non-smart cities (Onile et. al, 2021).

A well-defined smart grid can better serve a smart city to meet its energy demands. However, the challenge is that designing a new smart grid for an upcoming smart city; and/or transforming an existing non-automated power distribution network into smart grid. For instance, information on load consumption patterns is vital for determining type of DSM initiative. If the peak load is too high, then Time of Use tariff can be set to a high value so that consumers are forced to reduce the consumption to an extent. On the other hand, if the base load consumption is too low, power tariffs can be lowered to encourage consumers to increase the energy consumption. Similarly, DSM initiatives such as load shifting and valley filling etc., are heavily dependent energy consumption patterns which in turn can be obtained from precise measurements of data over the day in 30-minute intervals. Similarly, adoption of CE by smart cities can result in efficient energy conservation and thus make them more self-reliant; however, this requires significant monitoring of resources and even waste. Once a well-tested design model is available for typical a smart city that resolves above mentioned problems, then such model needs to be replicated elsewhere, in other words, the design needs to be replicated in the industry 4.0 era, following the principles of digital twinning Castelli et., al (2019).

Then another challenge comes in the form of power supply and/or distribution to the smart cities. In most countries, energy sector is deregulated, and power utilities no longer enjoy monopoly as in the past. This has resulted in decentralized production, network sharing and even new energy policies that mandate several aspects such as reduction of greenhouse gas emissions and high-quality energy supply. Hence, in the modern regime, a smart city can be supplied by different power companies besides their own generation. Even smart cities may encourage new, prospective investors to set up renewable energy plants to supply power. Such independent power producers (IPPs) need a lot of information and then also governed by the regulatory provisions of the state. IPPs may have to use existing transmission and distribution networks, which are generally owned by state utilities. These existing power distribution networks may generally lack industry 4.0 grade real-time measurement, monitoring and control facilities (K.S. Sastry et.al, 2020). Some of the other challenges that arise here are: A) how DSM is applied to manage the gap between energy supply and load. B) how to provide the information to the IPPs so that they can produce power when it is required most in tune with the load following power plant model? C) how to transform such legacy power distribution networks into smart grid so that some of the objectives of smart cities can be met? D) what are the various energy related information services that are typical to a smart city? E) how to provide information to the stakeholders and regulators?

This chapter takes up these questions and related discussion in detail. In doing so, a brief literature review on digital twins and digital transformation is provided. Then most critical aspects and operational issues in a typical power distribution system are explained. The chapter then focuses on how DSM can be used to manage the energy requirements and load consumptions. In the process, importance of data, computation and analytics will be presented. And then it makes a case for adopting the concept of digital twins to energy systems that power futuristic smart cities and also for transformation of existing, legacy networks. Various components of a typical cyber physical energy system are treated, followed by a systematic process for making a digital twin of the same (Orumwense et. al, 2019).

Background

In the recent past, researchers have treated the topic of digital twins and suggested as means to develop futuristic systems in the areas of farming, manufacturing, automotive industry and of course for smart cities as well (Tang Wenhu et al, 2020; John et. al, 2020; Perez et al (2020)). Basically, digital twins can help resolving several issues in automation and standardization where systems need to be replicated elsewhere. Digital twins can be very helpful in developing a full-scale replica of a physical system and then establish a proper synchronization between the two systems (Cioara et. al, 2021; Fernando et. al, 2018). This naturally assists in obtaining operational data, fault identification, maintenance automation and even overall system improvements. Specifically, aspects of maintenance using digital twins is explored by a few authors (Cioara et.al, 2021; You et.al, 2022; Errandonea et. al, 2020). Typically, electrical power systems are first designed, planned and then the physical projects are executed in the field. This has been the standard practice for decades and thus concepts of the twins is already in place. However, for the deeper discussion on digital twins for energizing smart cities, it is important to understand different areas including – synergies of smart cities, operational aspects of the smart cities and then the very digital twins themselves. K.S. Sastry et. al (2020) explained the need to establish a full-scale enterprise level management information system to implement DSM and related operations. One of the aspects of smart cities is to service futuristic population that essentially survives on smart environment. In fact, providing energy and related services to the consumers can be done in the best ways, if energy consumption patterns are known well-before; and this is possible with periodical energy audits (Sastry Musti K.S et al, 2021). Then, K. S. S. Musti (2020) illustrated the process of quantifying the overall demand in typical urban feeders, which is very important for planning the distribution systems for smart cities. K.S. Sastry (2020) provided the application of circular economy principles in energizing smart cities through implementation of DSM. Though the wide-ranging benefits of digital twins are well understood, details of key issues related operations in smart energy systems, digital transformation processes or evolution processes of digital twins in smart city context are not yet taken up.

Digital Twins for Smart Grids

Present From the above, it can be seen that there is a significant interest in general concepts of digital twins and their specific application to energy systems. However, most networks are in legacy state, as they may have been in operation for several years. Transformation of such networks into modern form to suit the upcoming smart city setting is the major challenge. And this aspect is not treated well so far and thus, is a clear gap in the research. In this context, this chapter makes an attempt to address development of energy systems for smart cities and also the transformation process of legacy networks as well. In accomplishing this objective, this chapter first considers the typical energy consumption patterns and aspects of DSM. The reason behind this is that the DSM is used in almost all over the world and the data will be readily available (Musti et. al, 2020). The next section explains the role and significance of data in designing a digital twin concept so that the same can be replicated whenever and wherever needed. The following section considers various reasons for applying the digital twins to energy systems so that design criteria is well established. The section also explains tfhe adoption of new technological development and challenges faced by legacy systems. Concepts such as DSM, energy efficiency and circularity are widely adopted (K. S. Sastry Musti, 2020). The challenges include increasing complexities in the network topologies, dealing with outages and servicing the consumers. Then the next section takes up the very application of digital twin concept to a typical smart energy system. The overall transformation from living labs to digital twins, developing multiple replicas (or twins) and rapid production processes are explained in the next section. Then opportunities for further research and scope are explored. Finally, conclusions are drawn.

ENERGY CONSUMPTION PATTERNS, OPERATIONS AND SERVICES

The conventional, fossil-fuel based generation and load consumption patterns are changing rapidly due to various reasons, but mostly due to the advent of smart infrastructure being put in the place, in the immediate past. And this is true for many countries even now, where little or no renewable energies are used. Typical (legacy) generation and load profile are shown in Fig 1. The hatched region indicates the power generated and/or supplied to the feeder at a constant level of 375kW throughout the day. Load is varying according to the consumption patterns of the consumers on the feeders. It can be seen that load consumption is not constant over any given day.

Figure 1. Daily load profile and energy supplied. Source: Authors (2022)

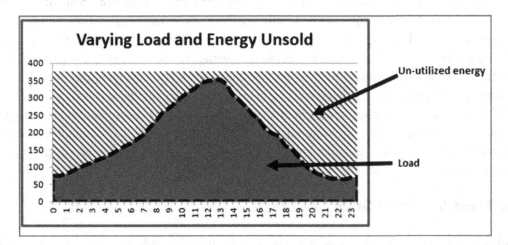

The hatched region indicates the energy that is supplied, but not consumed. Which means, utility did not earn any revenue for this energy that is supplied, but not sold. A few points should be noted here. 1. Generation levels are normally in mega-watts and this example has used kW only for illustration purposes. 2. Load profile can be visualized typically for a specific consumer, or for a feeder or even for an area such as a building or even a city. 3. Load profile can be visualized for a day or for a month (with average values) or for a year based on requirements. 4. Then consumption over the weekends and holidays differ significantly from that of weekdays due to obvious reasons. 5. The example uses a case of 11kV power distribution feeder with a limited number of consumers (peak load: 350kW) in a small area. 6. Generation sources, especially fossil-fuel based, base load generation facilities are from power distribution areas where the end-consumers are located. This means, there will be power loss over the transmission lines while transporting the energy, which generally varies, but can be safely assumed as 10% by taking the mix of high power and lower power distribution lines into consideration. This puts the un-sold energy to a tune of 5000kWh. 6. One important aspect about fossil fuel-based generation is that every plant normally will have different generator units and plant engineers do control the overall energy plant output based on the load forecast and power dispatch information that is available to them. Hence, it is possible to reduce the un-sold energy with proper management; albeit it requires a lot of real-time information and extensive computation. 7. In the modern regime, power sector in many countries have been de-regularized, which means the generation units may not be directly controlled (or owned) the power transmission and/or distribution company. Instead, utilities need to purchase energy from different plants and even from independent power producers (IPPs) to form their energy mix. Digital twins can help significantly as desktop simulations can be carried out to determine the appropriate portions of the energy mix.

Considering the most developed and developing nations, where renewable energies are now becoming the order of the day and time; utilities have more options in utilizing various resources and thus put up a pool of 'energy mix' that can be monitored and controlled in real-time. Solar, Wind and Biogas energies are most common. Particularly, energy resources based on solar, and biogas are usually located close to the end-consumer and thus reduce transmission losses. However, it is not possible to eliminate base load plants, as renewable energies do come with their own drawbacks. For instance, renewable energies suffer from issues such as varying outputs based on atmospheric/ weather conditions and/or other factors such as intermittency. As of today, utilities generally mix different form of energies to meet the varying patterns of load consumption.

From the above illustrations, it can be seen that the critical aspect is - to measure the load consumption for every 30 minutes or even 15 minutes; and then to communicate the readings to a central processing facility so that energy mix can be adjusted as needed. There is an imminent need for extensive computations towards load forecasting, estimation and energy dispatch. Engineers need the summarized information with a lot of details in tables and wide-ranging visualizations. Once all the information is taken into account, then engineers can perform the control actions. In summary, the most critical engineering tasks viz., measure, communicate, compute, visualize, control usually assist operational engineers in any utility and thus form a continuous routine in engineering management of power distribution. Fourth industrial revolution and specifically the IIoT apparatus and systems are capable of managing these vital tasks independently with very less or no supervision. This indeed is the basis for the 'smart systems'.

Smart meters did not exist 15 years or two decades back. Advances in micro-electronics, sensor technologies and particularly with the advent of IoT, smart meters are being deployed gradually almost in every country. Smart meters are one of the important products of industry 4.0. With different types, wide-ranging features and abilities, smart meters in energy sector have come a long way through the ages. Thus, the impact of smart meters on power distribution networks is quite significant. Five basic parameters viz., Voltage, Current, Power factor, Active and Reactive powers from every node in a power distribution network are important and are required to measured for various purposes. Now, from figure 1, it can be seen that the energy consumption needs to be measured for every 15- or 30-minute interval.

Similarly, other four parameters (besides parameters) also need to be measured, but detailed discussion on various parameters is avoided to keep the focus on the energy consumption related operations so that foundation can be provided for digital twins.

DSM in the Context of Futuristic Smart Cities

Though, the expectations of are ever growing in general; smart cities are expected to manage their energy requirements within their own purview. Many residents are encouraged to setup their own energy production and storage facilities, thus turning them into 'prosumers' in a bid to reduce or even eliminate the dependency on energy resources that are external to the smart city itself (Musti and Kapali, 2021). In the modern times of renewable energies, energy mix and prosumers the energy management in smart cities is essentially carried out by a local command center, what is called as 'virtual power plant' that exclusively manages the energy requirements of the smart city. Most popular energy resources within the smart cities are roof-top solar PV, small and medium biogas plants and battery storage systems, if not small-scale wind-turbines, subjected to abundant availability of wind resource (K.S.S. Musti, 2020). It is important to note that the overall energy demands of the smart cities far higher than that of a legacy townships or towns. Hence energy management requires a proper application of DSM to manage the overall load through reducing and/or influencing the energy consumption patterns of residents. Several aspects such as energy mix, energy tariffs, reduction and/or avoiding energy consumption, district heating systems and importantly Time of use tariffs etc., come under the umbrella of DSM. As the overall in-house energy supplies of a smart may not be entirely adequate to meet the overall demand, DSM comes in handy to answer the most important questions – how and when the energy is consumed, how much energy need to be purchased from outside? Who is paying for what? Who is contributing to what? Let us examine a typical load curve in detail. The figure 2 shows a daily load profile with a peak of 352.2 kW and a minimum of 62.6kW.

Energy consumpton typically goes up when the power distribution feeder has mix of industrial, commercial and residential consumers. Usually energy consumption peaks during mid day, though there may be exceptions. For instance, if the feeder has only domestic consumers and majority of those may be full time employees, then peaks may occur after 5pm in the day. There is no one standard pattern or formula to ascertain the nature of load profile over day and it depends on socio-economic backgrounds and nature of consumers connected to the feeder. From the figure 2, it can be seen that operating temperatures of all the power apparatus (lines, circuit breakers and transformers etc) of the utility (or that of the smart city) increase as the energy consumption peaks.

Thus, there is a risk to the infrastructure due to electrical and thermal stresses. Also, higher amounts of energy may not be available internally and thus needs to purchased from external sources. DSM provides ToU mechanism to the system operators so that higher tariffs can be applied for different time zones in the day and the consumers are left to their descretion to use the energy based on their energy requirements and financial abilities to pay. In essence, to accomplish the above complex tasks of Energy mix and Demand side management, virtual power plants have come into existence. Some consumers may want to invest in roof-top solar or battery storage systems and/or start a business with a small-scale biogas plant within the smart city since policy in general is to encourage energy capacity addition internally. On the hindsight, advising such consumers may appear trivial or the related computations may appear simple. However, a greater analysis is required to understand the existing energy consumption of that specific consumer, current tariff structures, cost of investments towards the energy system itself, safety apparatus and other components involved. Usually, payback period for the investments is the most

Figure 2. Typical load profile over the day. Source: Authors (2022)

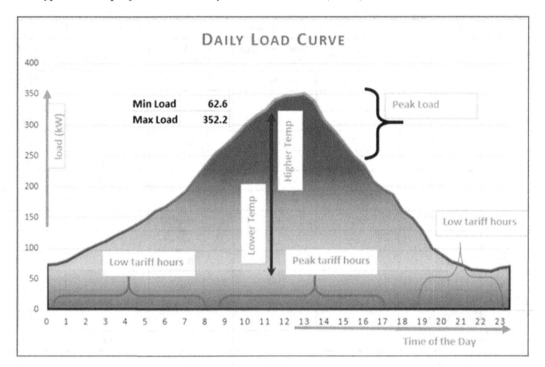

important indicator for the consumer to decide and hence this aspect needs a lot of input data which normally cannot be obtained in legacy setting. Some prosumers may want to add/ modify or upgrade their existing energy systems. Some industrial and/or commercial category consumers want to audit their energy bills in detail for the last financial year.

With several prosumers with different scales of internally distributed energy sources will be feeding into the smart grid of the smart city. Since all the systems are interconnected, there are high chances for some of the uneventful technical faults/ electrical failures may cause damage to the main smart grid of the city itself. In this case, important information on the cause, source and the exact time stamp of the fault needs to be extracted from the existing apparatus to determine the impact and financial value of the damages and costs towards restoring the system to previous safe operating conditions. It needs to be noted even the legacy protection systems are gradually being replaced by IoT/ smart apparatus. Thus, modern smart grids can provide more protection to most common faults and also can provide more precise information in the event of a fault; when compared to that of legacy systems. If there is a legal proceeding, then the information extracted from the modern smart grids will be of great value.

DATA DRIVEN COMPUTATIONS AND SERVICES

Now, one of the interesting aspects is to design the overall strategies and processes for the utilities to determine the ToU tariffs. K.S. Sastry et al(2020) and K.S. Sastry (2020) illustrated various aspects and the wider scope for using ToUs to control (or to reduce) the energy consumption by the consumers. Besides ToU framework, other tools such as load shedding (simply switching off the supply from the substation); ripple control (switching off selected loads at the consumer premises during a specific

Table 1. Daily load and Energy Profile for morning times

Load Profile		Generation Profile				
Time of the day	Load (kW)	Time of the day	Coal based Gen (kW)	Solar PV Gen (kW)	Total (Gen)	Excess / Deficit Energy
0	73.5	0	150	0	150	76.5
0.5	74.4	0.5	150	0	150	75.6
1	79.6	1	150	0	150	70.4
1.5	88.6	1.5	150	0	150	61.4
2	97.3	2	150	0	150	52.7
2.5	105.1	2.5	150	0	150	44.9
3	111.3	3	175	0	175	63.7
3.5	120.5	3.5	175	0	175	54.5
4	128.2	4	175	0	175	46.8
4.5	136.7	4.5	175	0	175	38.3
5	147.3	5	175	0	175	27.7
5.5	159.9	5.5	200	0	200	40.1
6	168.2	6	200	0	200	31.8
6.5	179.2	6.5	200	0	200	20.8
7	192.4	7	200	0	200	7.6
7.5	214.3	7.5	250	0	250	35.7
8	232.4	8	250	5	255	22.6
8.5	253.6	8.5	250	10	260	6.4

time period with prior intimation) and paying incentives or compensating the consumers directly for switching off their bulk loads; do exist. As stated earlier, computational processes may look trivial, but really it requires a deeper understanding of load profile in the first place and then a several other factors. Smart cities are predominantly powered by data and information. To effectively illustrate the aspects of complex processes and the need to have data on hand; the following numerical example is set up.

Tables 1, 2 and 3 present a typical daily load profile of a feeder with 30minute interval readings of the load (active power) consumed in kW, external and internal power supply (active power) in kW are provided. In addition, the last columns of the tables show surplus/ deficit of the power for that interval. The data is presented in 3 tables to show lower tariff (or lower load consumption) regions, higher tariff (high/ or peak consumption) regions as opposed to a single and long table to avoid cluttering. However, the distribution losses within the system are not shown, but need to be considered. Let us safely assume that the distribution losses are 15% of the total energy consumed for each interval. With taking the losses into consideration, it can be seen that energy supply to the system is adequate only some parts of the day and in deficit over other parts of the day.

Now, several aspects can be seen from the three tables. The highlighted section of the Table 1 indicates the duration from 4am to 8.30am in the morning when the application of ripple control is most effective. Usually this is the time when most consumers are likely to switch on their electrical heaters and thus utility wants to moderate or avoid this pattern. It should be that this situation is assumed along

Table 2. Daily load and Energy Profile during peak hours

Load Profile		Generation Profile			Difference
Time of the day	Load (kW)	Time of the day	Coal based Gen (kW)	Solar PV Gen (kW)	Total (Gen)	Excess / Deficit Energy
9	267.5	9	250	15	265	-2.5
9.5	282.5	9.5	250	20	270	-12.5
10	300.7	10	250	25	275	-25.7
10.5	314.4	10.5	250	30	280	-34.4
11	325.5	11	250	35	285	-40.5
11.5	342.1	11.5	250	40	290	-52.1
12	348	12	250	45	295	-53
12.5	349.5	12.5	250	50	300	-49.5
13	352.2	13	250	50	300	-52.2
13.5	339.4	13.5	250	45	295	-44.4
14	308.6	14	250	40	290	-18.6
14.5	292.1	14.5	250	35	285	-7.1
15	271.8	15	250	30	280	8.2
15.5	250.2	15.5	250	25	275	24.8
16	235.8	16	250	20	270	34.2

with the data of tables 1, 2 and 3 only illustrate various implications and thus providing a ground for need to smart systems and then make a case for designing a process that can be replicated to feed into the concept of the digital twin. Now, this aspect brings a few more questions. How to switch off selected (for instance water heaters in showers) consumer loads for a specific duration? This aspect is answered by Ripple control switching systems that can do the task provided internal and external electrical wiring systems are uniformly designed and implemented.

The word 'uniformly' needs to be taken into consideration, as this is one of the indicators for replicating or digitally (or physically) twinning the systems. Ripple control also assumes that electrical wirings are securely designed, and consumers will not be tampering with. Any physical interference or tampering needs to be picked by the ripple control system itself and relay the information promptly to the operators for necessary action. It is now clear that ripple control requires physical hardware that controls network elements on a pre-set time zones of the day; and do come with built-in communication and security protocols. These features are essentially smart and do not exist in legacy systems. The other question is about the actions of consumers to use or abstain from using the hot water for showers at least in this case of illustration. A few consumers may use gas or their own, separate electric heaters that can be plugged in other power outlets and still continue to consume power during the same time. However, generally such numbers (or instances) will be lesser as most consumers try to alter their morning routines before leaving for work as they are aware of the ripple control being in effect. Sastry Musti K.S. et. al. (2021) emphasized on the need to conduct routine energy audits to understand consumer actions and the power consumption patterns. Thus, the very objective of DSM in influencing the energy consumption patterns is served.

Table 3. Daily load and Energy Profile during evening to night

Load Profile		Generation Profile				
Time of the day	Load (kW)	Time of the day	Coal based Gen (kW)	Solar PV Gen (kW)	Total (Gen)	Excess / Deficit Energy
16.5	208.6	16.5	250	15	265	56.4
17	196.4	17	250	10	260	63.6
17.5	187.1	17.5	250	0	250	62.9
18	162.1	18	200	0	200	37.9
18.5	149.3	18.5	200	0	200	50.7
19	128.4	19	200	0	200	71.6
19.5	100.3	19.5	150	0	150	49.7
20	89.6	20	150	0	150	60.4
20.5	78.4	20.5	150	0	150	71.6
21	72.9	21	150	0	150	77.1
21.5	66.2	21.5	150	0	150	83.8
22	64.8	22	100	0	100	35.2
22.5	62.6	22.5	100	0	100	37.4
23	68.1	23	100	0	100	31.9
23.5	70.2	23.5	100	0	100	29.8

Furthering the above discussion, a little; power pilferage is one of the widely discussed aspect in both legacy and smart power grids. It is interesting to note that smart power distribution systems of the industry 4.0 grade identify any tampering with meters and/or other forms of pilfering the power in no time. This is one of the important advantages and even convivence for the utility engineers to track down the elements of threat to the system. On the other hand, regulators (and citizens in general) need to know about the reduction of greenhouse gases in a month or in a year. Reduction in power consumption, Addition of more Renewable energies; and replacing peak loads with battery or wind or biogas energy. It is possible if and only if the electrical energy consumption is monitored and analyzed. In all the above cases, the modern smart grids act acting as an automated cyber physical system. Fundamentally, a cyber physical system, with its chief components of measurement, communication, computation, control and visualization will be able to offer appropriate services to the end users (Martin Molnár and István Vokony, 2019, Orumwense, 2019). Here, several opportunities for B2C and B2B commercial processes and services.

Continuing the discussion for the Tables 2, it is evident that the energy supply is not adequate. For this duration, the operators in the virtual power plant need to purchase the power from external suppliers. Such power purchases can vary in their terms. It is possible to buy power on the spot or for a period of a week or a month depending on the nature and protocols of energy trade in place locally. This is another aspect of modern era energy systems; and obviously require a sophisticated measurement and monitoring apparatus needs to be in place to determine the energy flows and revenues in real time. On the other hand, DSM application in the form of high ToU tariff during that peak load duration is a simple strategy and in fact will work as a cost-effective measure. With high tariffs in place, load consumptions will be reduced. Loads that can be shifted to other zones (such as washing and cleaning) will migrate and thus improving the base load consumption in other zones, which are otherwise provide lesser revenue to the utility. In this case, the operators need effective computational tools with friendly visualizations to investigate various approaches to determine suitable ToU tariff structures. Obviously, such tools need a lot of measured data and information that is made possible by modern smart systems, and of course not in the legacy regimes. With the induction of ToU tariffs, energy bills need to be computed carefully for consumers on individual basis taking into the standard interval of obtaining the readings, usually 30 minutes. In addition to the ToU tariffs, there will be additional charges (or penalties) if peak load consumption of a specific (industrial /commercial) consumer goes beyond a designated value.

Another important aspect of a virtual power plant is that a full-fledged digital power distribution system is expected to be in place and in operation that too in tandem with the physical power distribution network. For instance, power networks are displayed to the operators through assorted visualizations in various formats such as line, raster and vector. For instance, load shedding is carried out in the physical network, the same action is shown to the operators within the virtual power plant. This is accomplished by IoT sensors doing their detection of the status of breaker and then communicating the information to the 'digital twin' counterpart of the physical system. The design and evolution process of a typical digital twin for a physical power distribution network is taken up in later sections after providing the necessary foundations and establishing the rationale for a digital twin for power networks.

Why Digital Twins for Power Distribution Systems?

Digital twinning in energy systems can be done in different ways at different levels. Firstly, distribution networks can be digitally simulated on the computers. Several software solutions exist to represent the networks in graphical manner so that users can identify various network elements and even the consumers along with their locations. Then several simulations such as load flows and short circuit studies on those networks can be carried. As of now, power systems are typically designed and planned on the computers much before the actual infrastructure procurement and deployment happens. Thus, the physical system after the project completion, is actually a replica of the simulated system. This is a good example of digital twinning in the area of power system. One of the advantages is - whatever the changes contemplated on the physical system can be first simulated on its digital twin which is located on the computer to understand the implications (Granacher et. al, 2022). Next level is the real-time operation. It is possible to keep the digital version and the physical system in synchronization to execute the operations in real-time. This is nothing but a fully grown Supervisory Control and Data Acquisition (SCADA) system. Another level is to understand the policy changes and their implications. A well-designed digital twin can help understanding the policy implications as well. Even the maintenance processes can be standardized to greater extent. Identification or/and of faulty equipment, avoiding network faults based on the maintenance history (from information gathered and periodical studies) and especially in planning the capacity addition as this needs a significant capex.

However, the big challenge is that the majority of the power systems are in legacy mode. Removing obsolete apparatus and digital transformation of legacy systems towards industry 4.0 standards is the most required aspect in in every sector and energy sector is not an exception (Fernando et al, 2018). From the above section, it can be seen that the injection of renewable energies, locally monitored and controlled settings of smart cities and information driven societies are already becoming the order of the day. However, it should be noted that except for a few energy systems that are established in the immediate past; a majority of the downstream power distribution networks from the substation to the end consumer still operate in legacy segment. Which means, older power networks do not have smart

Figure 3. Energy channeled through virtual power plant to a smart city. Source: Authors (2022)

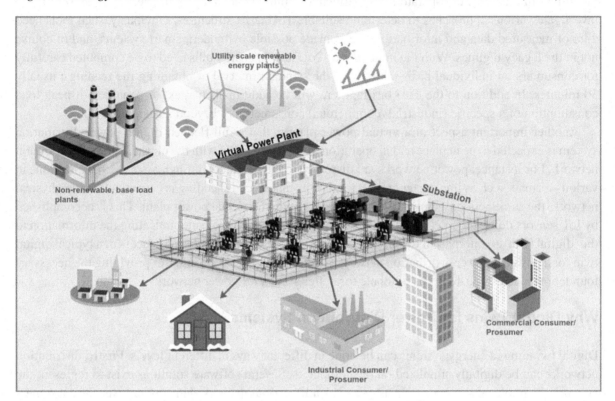

apparatus and thus need digital transformation through a systematic process so that they can as well participate in industry 4.0 revolution. On the other hand, some urban distribution networks may have mixed type of infrastructure comprising non-smart and smart apparatus. Figure 3 shows a representative arrangement of a typical system that may have both non-smart and smart infrastructure.

From the above, it is clear that both renewable and non-renewable energies feeding different consumers (may be or may not be a part of smart city) through a virtual power plant. Essentially in this case, the energy plants are either utility owned, or the plants owned and operated by independent power producers. Such energy plants are typically industry grade in both in standards and scale. However, inside the smart city, the arrangement can be slightly different, with internal solar-PV generation, small-sized wind turbines and battery storage systems- all owned by various prosumers. In addition, DSM will be in effect both with ToU tariffs and control measures such as ripple control etc. to balance and/or match the load to energy supply. This setting is illustrated in the figure 4.

It is important to note that the phenomenal rise of Electrical Vehicles (EVs) has a significant impact on existing power networks and in fact on overall energy requirements of any state for that matter. Transports systems in smart cities do have a separate and illustrious treatment both in literature as well as on the real-world setting. Smart cities do cater to the needs of smart transport systems that include EVs, charging stations, onsite battery replacement services, faster turnaround times for even major repairs, and energy efficient bulk transport systems etc. Though this may sound all is well, on the costs for powering up the energy to the modern and smart infrastructure part of the smart cities will go up significantly. This means, smart cities do require significant capacity addition and that too from renewable segment to fulfil the core objectives and expectations smart cities in energy efficiency segment. Charging stations

Figure 4. Distributed Energy Resources owned by prosumers in a smart city. Source: Authors(2022)

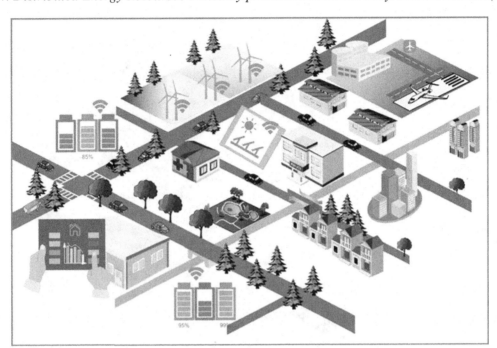

require smart grid, sophisticated communication systems, precise location services and of course, IoT based infrastructure. For all these different infrastructures are independent and yet need to coexist and work in tandem to deliver various services to the residents and operators of the smart cities. Naturally, there will be hardware, software and other IoT based measuring and control equipment – all essentially come from fourth industrial revolution. These factors make a good case for applying digital twins for replicating power distribution systems (Godoy. 2019).

Based on the discussion, there are essentially three major possible situations. Fist one is that a legacy system is in the need of a digital transformation through a structured approach. Second is that a semi-automated system that needs a smooth transition into a smart system. Third case is that a new system needs design and development from the beginning. In case of semi-automated energy systems, data about 30minute energy consumption may be available and thus it will be easy to upgrade the same to a smart system that has pre-set objectives and well-defined specifications. In any case, energy systems comprise of several power distribution networks that have more or less same components, but serve in different regions, and may have different distribution capacities. Protective switchgear in 11kV or 33kV in a given area will be more or less having same specifications for the same class and type of apparatus (S.MKS, 2005). Consumer requirements, services offered/ or expected and related computational processes too more or less same, albeit numerical quantities, scale and volumes may be different. In other words, most of the components, tasks and infrastructure can be (and need to be) replicated to serve different parts of smart city systems. For instance, there may be 10 substations each having 3 or 4 different feeders. If a smart cyber physical system that is highly scalable, replicable and its constituents can be repeated with or without minor modification, then such a system can be used elsewhere as is. For example, a well-designed cyber physical system for a typical EV charging station can be replicated and installed in different locations. This is the very concept of digitally twinning the systems. Also, consider the case of large building (such as a shopping mall or an airport) that may have several different wings with dif-

Figure 5. Various layers in a cyber physical system. Source: Molnár and Vokony (2019)

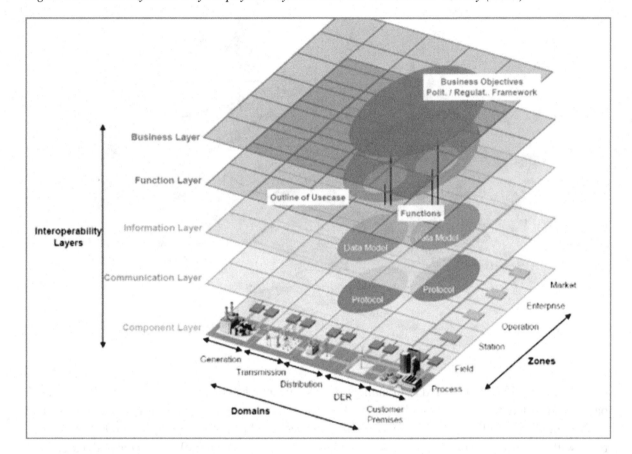

ferent establishments inside. Each wing or section normally requires its own internal power network. It makes a lot of sense to deploy a scalable and replicable cyber physical infrastructure with proven design effectiveness if readily available (Orumwense et. al, 2019, Sigrist, 2018). In all, modern smart energy systems do need digital twin framework so that they can effectively serve the energy needs of smart cities. On financial and budgetary front, about a third of overall expenditure goes towards establishing and managing energy infrastructure. In the light of all the above discussion it is imperative that digital twin framework be adopted to energy systems in smart cities. Now this brings several questions - what exactly specifies a digital twin for a smart energy system? How is this created or developed in general?

Digital Twin for a Smart Energy System

Molnár and Vokony (2019) specified that a cyber physical system consists of different layers, such as IoT equipment layer, Communication infrastructure layer, Information layer, Functional and Business layers. The overall arrangement of these layers of a typical cyber physical system is shown in figure 5. Component layer consists of mostly the physical infrastructure including Distributed Energy Resources (DER), Power Generating stations, transmission and distribution networks and several other components. However, the diagram does not indicate the presence of digital twin of this layer. Hence, a complete cyber physical system is a combination of digital twin or digital version of the physical network and all above layers. There are several works that have reported on the design and development processes of power systems with digital counterparts so that various tasks such as real time monitoring and control, information analysis and system enhancement students etc can be carried out. To put it in other words, there will be several online tasks as well as off-line tasks (design simulations) that have to be carried as per the requirements. In fact, these activities are very routine tasks for control room (virtual power plant) engineers and operators. It is also important to keep the database of the digital network systems up to date with the latest information so that engineers can get the recent state of the system for any corrective action during the emergencies. These digital counterparts are referred as 'test beds' in the literature and mostly described as the digital version of the physical systems; and it mimics all the characteristics and properties of its physical version in real time. This justifies the application of framework of digital twin to a cyber physical energy system.

Table 4. Layers and the need for twinning

Layer	Rationale for standardization to create a similar or a twin
IoT devices, apparatus and infrastructure	There are several different devices, versions and brands. This area is very rapidly developing and in fact, breakout IoT components are very common. It is for this reason; a standardized set of a system needs to be developed before replicating. Otherwise, there will be too many different systems in a single eco system leading to confusion; especially during maintenance. A properly designed layer with IoT apparatus is very much desirable.
Communication apparatus and infrastructure	Same as above. Standardized and scalable solution is desirable
Information layer	This consists of data aggregation, analysing and computational processes, visualization frameworks. Predominantly this layer consists of software, but the data itself resides in servers. Communication layer takes care of data transfers. Like other layers, this too needs the standardization framework.
Functional and Business layers	It is in fact, an extension to the information layer. Just as information layer, this too needs standardization.
Security layer	Cyber security is the most challenging aspect of cyber physical systems. Of course, this needs standardization.

Power distribution feeders provide energy to different types of consumers located in different geographical locations. It is a well-known that these feeders experience outages (or also known as downtimes) due to wide ranging reasons such as – flooding, lightening, vehicular accidents, excess tree growth around the conductors and mechanical failures of the support systems etc (M.K.S. Sastry, 2007). Majority of the incidents result in a short circuit which is also termed as a fault in general. Consumers experience power outage following a fault and naturally the utility needs to first identify the fault, clear that fault and then re-energize the network. However, identification of fault location and clearing are time consuming and labor intense in nature. Consumers usually lodge complaints either through phone calls and/or through websites. Though outage management systems are well matured over the years, restoration of power to the end consumer is still a time-consuming process. Digital twins can offer interesting solutions in outage management, especially when a failed device such as a transformer needs to be replaced (M.K.S Sastry, 2007, Sigrist, 2018). When feeders are designed, installed and operated through digital twin principles, most components will have the same size, same technical specifications and ratings. This results in managing the inventory and the supply chain. In summary, digital twins provide a lot of similarity, familiarity and simplicity as nature, end-use, applicability of all components are more or less fixed. Over the years, service personnel get familiar with all the components, and this results in improved service to the consumers.

Relaying systems that protect distribution networks need to be set properly so that they function in coordination with one another (S.MKS, 2005). However, this determination of relay settings is a complicated task especially in modern urban networks due various aspects such as – complex network configurations composed of mesh and radial systems, changing load, intermittent nature of newer generation injections duck curve phenomenon and dynamic changes in the network configuration due to switching during maintenance etc (G. M. Pitra and K. S. S. Musti, 2021). Normally relay coordination studies require capturing network topological information and execution of computer programs. And then relays need to be set either digitally and/or manually. And this can be cumbersome due to the repetitive nature of the process itself. If major parts of distribution networks are transformed using the concepts of digital twins, then relay settings can be adopted uniformly in different feeders and this minimized the complexity, improves quality of operation and saves a lot of time as well (S.MKS, 2005).

DISCUSSION

From the above sections, it can be seen that that with their salient features the digital twins can provide excellent solutions. Especially they bring in a lot of simplicity, similarity and ample savings in both time and costs. This section explains the possibilities of creating the concept of a digital twin in the form of a living lab and then transforming into a fully operational cyber physical energy systems. Also, table 4 points to the fact that a cyber physical energy system is indeed a System of Systems (SoS). Such a complex SoS needs greater care and thoughts in conceptualizing right from their design and planning stages (Abdelali et al, 2021). It is for this reason; prototype testbeds need to be designed in living labs to further develop the system. Several of testbeds need to be created to ascertain overall efficacy, functionality and to validate the design process. Once the prototype passes rigorous testing regime, then it needs to be converted into a testbed to further its development by adding more complicated layers such as cyber security and real time operational capabilities. Then the testbed needs to be furthered into a cyber physical system that can be integrated with a physical smart grid. Then it needs to be subjected further full-scale, onsite testing under real-world operating conditions. At this stage, the SoS can be considered as successful and thus it can be considered as ready for the twinning process. In other words, fully matured system can be replicated to deploy elsewhere with proper scaling and adjustments.

FUTURE RESEARCH DIRECTIONS

Though new concepts such as circularity, energy efficiency and DSM in energy systems may appear to provide a lot of savings; power utilities may not be able to appreciate in long term (K. S. Sastry Musti, 2020). Under the circularity and DSM policies, consumers tend to use solar water heaters and even their own solar PV units(Musti and Kapali, 2021). These approaches definitely are known to save energy on the load side and thus revenue from the consumers will be reduced. This impacts the utility operations since systems are planned based on the load and there may not be adequate provisions to accommodate the revenue losses when consumers adopt the modern concepts of circularity, energy efficiency and DSM. The only way out for the utilities to find new consumers in the same vicinity so that a portion of the saved energy can be consumed. Digital twin applications in design and/or transformation processes do not result in revenue losses and thus can be considered by the utilities for wider adoption.

Future works may be carried out in several areas of operation and maintenance of distribution networks with digital twin concepts. For instance, relay coordination studies need to be done on legacy distribution system and then on a transformed network after applying digital twin concepts. Outcomes from before and after scenarios need to be compared to study the effectiveness of using digital transformation and digital twin concepts. Similarly, outage management studies, overall operation and maintenance costs of distribution systems need to be studied before and after applying digital twin principles. Further studies are also required to determine the revenue losses if any, with the adoption of digital twin concepts design and/or transformation processes of the power distribution systems.

CONCLUSION

The process of adopting the principles of Digital Twins is explained in this chapter. Digital twins can be applied in several areas of power distribution systems. This chapter has considered design, computations and operational aspects of energy systems of the smart cities for their transformation. Advantages, particularly in planning and designing new power distribution systems; maintenance and/or replacement of existing smart power distribution systems; and in upgrading legacy systems into smart systems through digital transformation process have been illustrated. As smart cities need several feeders, EV charging station and different information services, digital twinning provides effective means and solutions. In summary, digitally twinning the development process of smart energy systems for futuristic smart cities is essential for various benefits in the areas of operation and maintenance.

REFERENCES

Agouzoul, Tabaa, Chegari, Simeu, & Dandache. (2021). Towards a Digital Twin model for Building Energy Management: Case of Morocco. Procedia Computer Science, 184, 404-410. doi:10.1016/j.procs.2021.03

Ardebili, Longo, & Ficarella. (2021). Digital Twin (DT) in Smart Energy Systems - Systematic Literature Review of DT as a growing solution for Energy Internet of the Things (EioT). *E3S Web of Conferences, 312*, 09002

Castelli. (2019). Urban Intelligence: a Modular, Fully Integrated, and Evolving Model for Cities Digital Twinning. *IEEE 16th Int. conf. on Smart Cities: Improving Quality of Life Using ICT & IoT and AI (HONET-ICT),* 33-37. 10.1109/HONET.2019.8907962

Cioara, T., Anghel, I., Antal, M., Salomie, I., Antal, C.D., & Ioan, A.G. (2021). *An Overview of Digital Twins Application Domains in Smart Energy Grid.* ArXiv, doi: abs/2104.07904.

Dembski, F., Wössner, U., Letzgus, M., Ruddat, M., & Yamu, C. (2020). Urban Digital Twins for Smart Cities and Citizens: The Case Study of Herrenberg. Journal of Sustainability, 12(6).

Erkoyuncu, J. A., Fernández del Amo, I., Ariansyah, D., Bulka, D., Vrabič, R., & Roy, R. (2020). A design framework for adaptive digital twins. *CIRP Annals, 69*(1), 145–148. doi:10.1016/j.cirp.2020.04.086

Errandonea, I., Beltrán, S., & Arrizabalaga, S. (2020). Digital Twin for maintenance: A literature review. *Computers in Industry, 123*, 103316. doi:10.1016/j.compind.2020.103316

Fernando, L., Dur, C. S., Haag, S., Anderl, R., Sch, K., & Zancul, E. (2018). Digital Twin Requirements in the Context of Industry 4.0. In *Product Lifecycle Management to Support Industry 4.0.* doi:10.1007/978-3-030-01614-2

Godoy, A. J. C. (2019). Design and Implementation of Smart Micro-Grid and Its Digital Replica: First Steps. *16th Int. Conf. on Informatics in Control, Automation and Robotics*, 715-721. 10.5220/0007923707150721

Granacher, J., Nguyen, T.-V., Castro-Amoedo, R., & Maréchal, F. (2022). Overcoming decision paralysis—A digital twin for decision making in energy system design. *Applied Energy, 306*, 117954. doi:10.1016/j.apenergy.2021.117954

Laamarti, F., Badawi, H., Ding, Y., Arafsha, F., & Hafidh, B. (2020). *An ISO / IEEE 11073 Standardized Digital Twin Framework for Health and Well-being in Smart Cities*. doi:10.1109/ACCESS.2020.2999871

Mks, S. (2005). Simplified algorithm to determine break point realys & relay coordination based on network topology. *2005 IEEE International Symposium on Circuits and Systems (ISCAS)*, 772-775. 10.1109/ISCAS.2005.1464702

Molnár, M., & Vokony, I. (2019). The Cyber-Physical Security of the Power Grid. *2015 International Conference on Computational Intelligence and Communication Networks (CICN)*, 832-838. 10.1109/CICN.2015.169

Musti, K. S., & Kapali, D. (2021). Digital Transformation of SMEs in the Energy Sector to Survive in a Post-COVID-19 Era. In N. Baporikar (Ed.), *Handbook of Research on Strategies and Interventions to Mitigate COVID-19 Impact on SMEs* (pp. 186–207). IGI Global. doi:10.4018/978-1-7998-7436-2.ch009

Musti, K. S. S. (2020). Quantification of Demand Response in Smart Grids. *IEEE Int. Conf. INDISCON*, 278-282. 10.1109/INDISCON50162.2020.00063

Onile, A., Machlev, R., Petlenkov, E., Levron, Y., & Belikov, J. (2021). Uses of the digital twins concept for energy services, intelligent recommendation systems, and demand side management: A review. *Energy Reports, 7*, 997–1015. doi:10.1016/j.egyr.2021.01.090

Orumwense, E. F., Abo-al-ez, K., Orumwense, E. F., & Abo-al-ez, K. (2019). A systematic review to aligning research paths: Energy cyber-physical systems. *Cogent Engineering, 6*(1), 1700738. Advance online publication. doi:10.1080/23311916.2019.1700738

Pérez, L., Espeche, J., Loureiro, T., & Kavgić, A. (2020). DRIvE Project Unlocks Demand Response Potential with Digital Twins. Proceedings, 65, 1-14. doi:10.3390/proceedings2020065014

Pitra, G. M., & Musti, K. S. S. (2021). Duck Curve with Renewable Energies and Storage Technologies. *13th International Conference on Computational Intelligence and Communication Networks (CICN)*, 66-71. 10.1109/CICN51697.2021.9574671

Ramkhelawan, R., & Sastry, M. (2019). Power System Load Flow Analysis using Microsoft Excel – Version 2. *Spreadsheets in Education, 12*(1).

Sastry, M. K., Bridge, J., Brown, A., & Williams, R. (2013, February). *Biomass Briquettes: A Sustainable and Environment Friendly Energy Option for the Caribbean*. In Fifth International Symposium on Energy, Laccei, Puerto Rico.

Sastry, M. K. S. (2007). Integrated Outage Management System: An effective solution for power utilities to address customer grievances. *International Journal of Electronic Customer Relationship Management, 1*(1), 30–40. doi:10.1504/IJECRM.2007.014424

Sastry Musti, K. S. (2020). *Industry 4.0-Based Enterprise Information System for Demand-Side Management and Energy Efficiency*. In Novel Approaches to Information Systems Design. doi:10.4018/978-1-7998-2975-1.ch007

Sastry Musti, K. S. (2020). *Circular Economy in Energizing Smart Cities*. In Handbook of Research on Entrepreneurship Development and Opportunities in Circular Economy. doi:10.4018/978-1-7998-5116-5.ch013

Sastry Musti, K. S., Paulus, G. N. T., & Katende, J. (2021). *A Novel Framework for Energy Audit Based on Crowdsourcing Principles*. Springer. doi:10.1007/978-3-030-77841-5_11

Sigrist, L., May, K., Morch, A., Verboven, P., Vingerhoets, P., & Rouco, L. (2018). *On Scalability and Replicability of Smart Grid Projects — A Case Study*. doi:10.3390/en9030195

Tang, W., Chen, X., Tong, Q., Gang, L., Li, M., & Li, L. (2020). Technologies and Applications of Digital Twin for Developing Smart Energy Systems. *Strategic Study of Chinese Academy of Engineering*, 2(4), 74. Advance online publication. doi:10.15302/J-SSCAE-2020.04.010

You, Y., Chen, C., Hu, F., Liu, Y., & Ji, Z. (2022). Advances of Digital Twins for Predictive Maintenance. *Procedia Computer Science*, *200*, 1471–1480. doi:10.1016/j.procs.2022.01.348

Yu, X., & Xue, Y. (2016). Smart Grids: A Cyber – Physical Systems Perspective. *Proceedings of the IEEE*, *104*(5), 1058–1070. doi:10.1109/JPROC.2015.2503119

KEY TERMS AND DEFINITIONS

Circular Economy: A system that operates on the 4R principles – Reuse, Reduce, Repair, and Recycling and thus results in significant direct savings in energy and finances. Circular economy is also known for creating new range of employment prospects in semi-formal services, especially in recycling and repair sectors.

Cyber Physical System: A composite system that consists of both hardware and software. It is used to automate most of the monitoring and control large industrial and organizational processes.

Digital Transformation: A systematic process for converting legacy, un-automated systems into fully automated digital systems. Digital transformation process generally involves significant improvements to existing system especially provides the industry 4.0 capabilities such as sensors to identify the changes, communication for information exchange and real-time control, and the combinations of these capabilities.

Digital Twin: A virtual model of a physical system that can function in tandem with the physical system (or the twin) in real-time. This facilitates several simulations for different case scenarios to study the behavior and thus paving the way for improvements in design and operation.

Duck Curve Phenomenon: A graph that represents the difference between the load and the electricity generation typically over a given day. Duck curve also illustrates the instance where excess solar energy generation can lead to either loss of load or capacity.

Living Lab: A conceptual framework for developing innovative products and ecosystems. Typically, the development is expected to be carried out through open and transparent processes and using real-life environments. The development cycle depends on the continuous testing and feedback in order to produce a long lasting and sustainable product(s).

Smart City: An urban environment that is setup to provide modern and futuristic features and services to the residents. Smart cities are typically capable of meeting the energy demands on their own and thus do not depend much on the external sources. Information visualization, automated facilities and services, environmentally friendly living spaces are key elements in a smart city.

Chapter 17
Digital Transformation:
Towards Smart and Sustainable City Services

Hanène Babay
Faculty of Monastir, Tunisia

Nozha Erragcha
Higher Business School of Tunisia, Tunisia

ABSTRACT

Several reasons seem to justify the development trend of smart cities. Indeed, humanity is facing several challenges such as an increasing environmental impact, enormous difficulties in living in congested cities, and ever-increasing running costs. These challenges threaten the quality of life, especially in times of crisis, which has drawn attention to the relevance of using ICTs for governance purposes and has proliferated the awareness of stakeholders (authorities, citizens, civil society, etc.) to act in favor of the implementation of the mechanisms necessary for a new way of governing. This chapter presents the concept of smart cities and identifies the issues related to their development as well as the technologies that can intervene in the conversion of cities into smart and sustainable cities.

INTRODUCTION

Technological advancement and its interventions in daily processes have led to the emergence of intelligent ecosystems where all aspects of daily life are automated in one way or another. Services related to transport, agriculture, logistics, maintenance, education and healthcare are now accessible remotely but also controlled and managed using smart devices. The smart city is a promising project that aims to make the lives of residents more convenient and more inclusive. On a practical level, this smart city idea is slowly but surely taking shape in many countries around the world. These countries offer their own smart city model using cutting-edge technologies such as artificial intelligence (AI), Internet of Things (IoT), machine learning (ML), deep learning (DL), cognitive Computing and Big data analytics. These

DOI: 10.4018/978-1-6684-6821-0.ch017

technologies have greatly contributed to the rise of these smart cities (Obaidat & Nicopolitidis, 2016) as a new generation of cities facing ICTs.

In addition, apart from being connected, these "smart cities" lend themselves to responding to the injunctions of "sustainable development". Indeed, according to Daptardar and Gore (2019), a multitude of projects in India are intended to fuel the growth of this country while improving the well-being of its citizens. These projects are currently in different stages of deployment and aim to make India a highly productive and sustainable nation (Daptardar and Gore, 2019).

In this perspective, this chapter sets out to identify the main challenges associated with the development of smart cities and to explore to what extent AI and related technologies can serve as tools to overcome these challenges.

To do this, the authors will first define the concept of smart cities and present the challenges relating to their development. Next, they will review the branches of AI-related technologies that are used to develop smart cities. Finally, they will come back to the key points for converting a city to a smart city and present the experiences of the smartest cities in the world to inspire other cities wanting to embark on this path.

SMART CITIES: DEFINITIONS AND MAIN CHALLENGES RELATED TO THEIR DEVELOPMENT

Why Would it be Interesting to Develop Smart Cities?

Urbanization is a phenomenon characterized by the growth of urban areas to the detriment of rural areas. This growth is manifested by a greater density of population in the cities and consequently a physical extension of these agglomerations, which could generate important repercussions on the quality of life in these areas (Son et al., 2017). According to OECD estimates, around 70% of the world's population will live in urban areas by 2050. This density is likely to increase the pollution rate in these areas, will increase the scarcity of resources (water and energy) and make their daily and long-term management more difficult. The situation can thus become alarming, especially since, originally, 75% of world energy production is consumed in capital cities, which generates 80% of greenhouse gas emissions. Faced with this reality, developing smart cities can help us avoid many of these negative repercussions of increased urbanization by putting in place solutions intended to combat pollution, better manage scarce resources and increase the well-being of inhabitants of these areas (Dameri, 2013).

In addition, it should be remembered that during a period of crisis, many cities were subjected to severe tests, which highlighted the need to change the way these cities operate through greater digitization. It is now commonly accepted that digital innovation would certainly have mitigated the consequences of this health crisis if the authorities were careful to integrate it in time into their governance policies. For all these reasons, the city development project remains promising and deserves to be promoted to push further for its adoption.

What is Smart City?

The concept of "smart city" initially referred to projects that aim to harness new information and communication technologies to improve the efficiency of urban services and generate new economic opportunities. Nevertheless, despite its attractiveness, the smart city concept is considered to be always on the move and several considerations keep it a subject of debate.

Indeed, the definitions of smart cities seem to vary between countries and OECD institutions, notably depending on the geopolitical context and the specific problems of each country. These considerations have guided the debate towards a relevant question, that of asking whether the development initiatives of smart cities based on digital innovation manage to improve the quality of life, that is to say the level of citizens' well-being.

In response to this dilemma, a human-centered approach is more than necessary to make a city smarter. This search for a compromise appears clearly in the definition of smart city adopted by the OECD according to which smart cities are based on "initiatives or approaches that effectively exploit digitization to improve the well-being of citizens and provide services and more efficient, sustainable and inclusive urban environments as part of a collaborative, multi-stakeholder process"(OECD, 2018).

This definition therefore emphasizes four essential points:

- The need to link efforts geared towards the development of smart cities to improving the lives of citizens in all areas of intervention;
- Stakeholders (public, private, citizens, etc.) must be involved in local governance and collaborative partnerships must be built to achieve the objectives of this project.
- Public access to open data could be decisive for successfully carrying out construction projects and policies, particularly with the participation of the private sector in decision-making;
- The need for an integrated and holistic approach to address urban challenges through digital innovation in city governance, planning and infrastructure investments.

The word "smart" refers to the adoption of an automated mechanism in order to perform a desired activity in an optimized manner (Abdul Ahad et al., 2020). Thus, the "Smart City" is a city that has optimized its operation in several directions, in particular in terms of governance, production or provision of urban services adapted to the needs of the population (Douay and Henriot, 2016).

In practice, this concept is essentially based on the use of digital technology and technological innovations to improve the functioning and security of urban systems as well as the quality of life of inhabitants and their involvement in urban development. It also aims to create a friendly urban environment tha combats pollution and reduces the consumption of natural resources. The smart city is a concept based on an interdisciplinary approach using technical, social and environmental data to develop knowledge-based city management (Anthopoulos, 2015).

According to Rudolf Giffinger, expert in urban development in Vienna, a smart city is a city whose performance is ensured by the combination of strengths coming from six levers revolving around the economy, mobility, the environment, the population, the habitat and governance. This combination certainly heralds a new arrangement, but not a new paradigm.

According to Giffinger et al., (2007), these levers make it possible to identify and classify smart cities according to whether they have an "intelligent economy", "intelligent mobility", an "intelligent environment", "intelligent inhabitants", a "mode intelligent life "and" intelligent administration ". They are also in harmony with the pillars of sustainable development: the economy, the social and the environment. However, in order to materialize these different dimensions, it is necessary to face a set of technical, environmental and socio-economic challenges. In what follows, the authors of this chapter will return to these challenges and then attempt to explore solutions to overcome them.

Figure 1. Diagram of the six levers of a smart city (Inspired by: Giffinger et. Al. 2007)

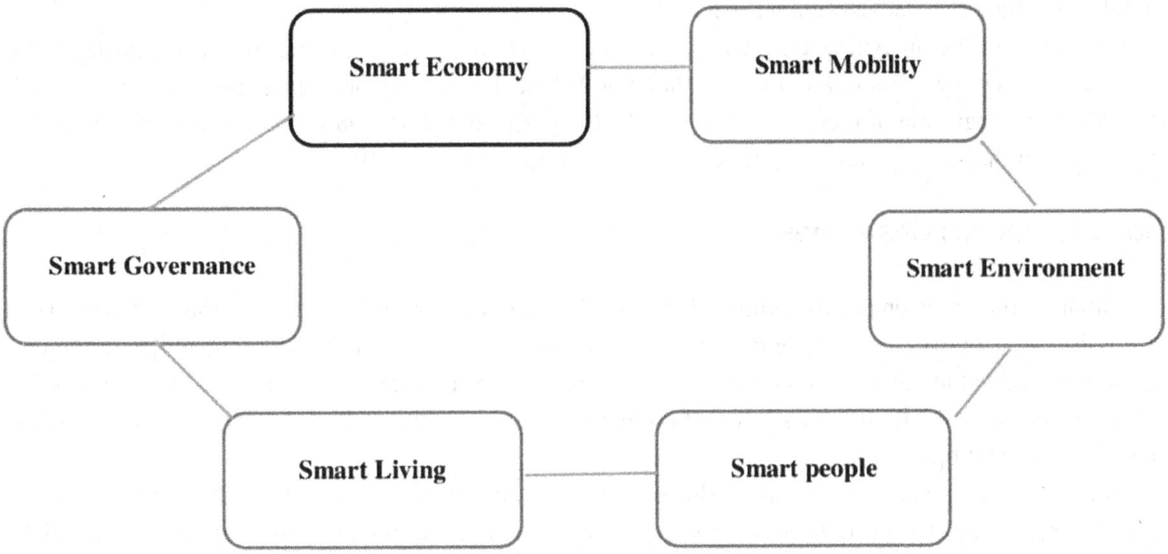

Main Challenges Related to The Development of Smart Cities

Today, developing a smart city seems to face significant and varied challenges. These challenges are a priori classified into three categories:

Technical Challenges

Data security is the main concern of actors in a smart city. Indeed, these cities are complex environments where billions of interconnected devices and processes generate enormous amounts of data (Georgescu and Popescul, 2016). Most of this data must be collected and manipulated in real time, which brings real threats to the accessibility, integrity and confidentiality of this data.

In the literature, five main vulnerabilities of digital technologies in the smart city have been identified:

Poor security of data encryption software,
Insecure legacy systems and poor maintenance,
A domino effect due to the interdependencies between smart technologies and urban systems,
Numerous large and complex interdependencies with the attack surfaces,
Human errors and deliberate misdeeds of current or disgruntled former employees (Kitchin and Dodge, 2017).

These vulnerabilities are increased by interrelated causes such as the lack of financial resources in the public sector, the lack of ICT specialists in communities and public services (these are more motivated to work in private companies), the lack of contingency plans for cyber-attacks and the lack of culture or strategic vision in this area.

The authorities must also present a clear regulatory framework and inform providers and citizens about the obligations and associated risks.

Nevertheless, by analyzing the literature on the smart city, it emerges that the technical-technical approach is giving way more and more to the approach centered more on human capital. Indeed, in addition to the integration of technology in the city, the premise of this smart city development project is to strengthen the socio-cultural capital of citizens (Gil-Garcia et al., 2015).

Socio-Economic Challenges

The smart economy is one of the pillars of the development of a smart city. Indeed, thanks to NICTs, it is possible to establish an intelligent economy, based on innovation, and which contributes to the creation of added value but also of sustainable jobs. The entrepreneurial spirit put forward in this type of economy, combined with the possibility of collecting and analyzing multiple and varied data, generate new development opportunities.

In addition, companies operating in this entrepreneurial universe will undoubtedly acquire significant flexibility and the ability to transform and conquer the international market (Giffinger et al., 2104; Giffinger et al.,2007). Thus, the smart economy is likely to positively influence the prosperity and attractiveness of the city on the international scene (Harrison and Donnelly, 2011). Thus, building a smart and efficient economy is one of the biggest challenges for smart cities.

Socially, for the successful development of a smart city, it is essential that users (especially citizens) accept the resulting changes and support the implementation of digital services for the benefits they provide. Thus, the involvement of citizens is also an important challenge that could condition the successful implementation of smart solutions. Indeed, according to Craglia and Granell (2014), smart cities are not only referred to by the use of ICTs, energy optimization and improved transport infrastructure, they are reflected in the behavior of citizens. participating constructively in the daily governance of their city and who are involved in the protection of the environment and the achievement of global well-being. However, if this involvement is insufficient then a social inclusion program is needed in order to encourage the assimilation of the changes and to commit to the achievement of the expected objectives more quickly and more effectively. Smart services will now be accessible to all and public programs will have a positive impact on their social and economic life (Khan, 2006; Visvizi et al., 2018).

In addition, one point must be considered with great care here, that of the possibility of designing intelligent solutions in line with the socio-economic and cultural conditions of the city concerned. Indeed, each city has its own characteristics in terms of size, built environment, fiscal resources, etc. This data will affect the ability of cities to adopt smart technologies and manage large projects. Moreover, successful experiences studied in large cities may be inapplicable in small towns. Another problem concerns the digital divide within the same city. For example, in Detroit (United States), 29.71% of the population does not have access to any type of broadband (National Digital Inclusion Alliance, 2019). Thus, it is clear that there is no digital formula that can be applied in all cities, smart city development projects must match local conditions to proliferate gains. Diagnostics should be carried out in order to understand where each city is located, to encourage dialogue between stakeholders with a view to devising suitable solutions to the problems observed and to decide in which direction the city should take.

Environmental Challenges

Today, the effects of urbanization on the environment are manifold, inevitable but also fatal for health. Human beings live in an increasingly unhealthy environment, which has multiplied the interest of communities in preserving the environment and combating the dangers caused by urbanization. Indeed, the density of the population in urban areas is at the origin of a growing pollution rate manifested in particular by a greenhouse gas emission rate of up to 80%, a volume of huge amount of waste that can be directly or indirectly dangerous, an exponential consumption of energy, etc. This is at the origin of several dangers and diseases affecting the urban population (chronic respiratory diseases, psychosocial disorders, dangers linked to traffic, dangers caused by toxic substances existing in the air, water and food, noise pollution resulting from traffic, industrial activity and overcrowding of housing which can reduce the time required for sleep and cause hearing problems; etc.)

Faced with these challenges, an ecological transition is required to establish sustainable ecosystems. The smart sustainable city today presents a point of convergence between ecological transition and digital transition. It is forced to rely on the levers of sustainable development to make significant contributions on more than one level (waste management, building management, road mobility, etc.).

ARTIFICIAL INTELLIGENCE: BRANCHES AND APPLICATIONS

Artificial Intelligence, Machine Learning And Deep Learning `

Artificial Intelligence

Artificial intelligence (AI) is a promising and attractive concept for the development of smart cities. Indeed, AI encompasses a set of technologies that can contribute to improving the lives of citizens, developing the economy and the competitiveness of businesses as well as improving environmental conditions.

Generally speaking, artificial intelligence is based on a set of algorithms that can be constantly fed with data to provide solutions to a given problem. It makes it possible to achieve a very high level of autonomy by reducing human intervention. Indeed, taking advantage of the accessibility of information (now possible thanks to NICT), AI makes it possible to base decision-making on a reproduction of knowledge and human behavior (Gretzel, 2011) and goes so far as to anticipate needs, predict behavior and develop preventive solutions.

Through process modeling, AI attempts to deliver human skills to machines and computers. For example, cars are now able to detect objects and obstacles on the road. The principle is to design computer systems from algorithms in order to sort, store and process information and develop solutions. The information processing is done in the form of simulations dealing with several scenarios of a problem, in order to create a form of intelligence for the machines allowing them to process specific cases or a change in data. Machines are no longer limited to the passive execution of pre-programming. They begin to learn, hence the birth of concepts such as "Machine Learning" and "Deep Learning". In what follows, the authors will present these two branches of artificial intelligence and then return to the fields of application of these new technologies as well as their main contributions.

Machine Learning

Being a branch of artificial intelligence, machine learning aims to make computers capable of dealing with problems without having already been programmed but by proliferating learning on the basis of previously treated examples or experiences (Sarker, 2021). The principle of machine learning is to study several examples of the same problem to allow the algorithm to create correspondences between the inputs and the outputs.

When the learning is done, the algorithms become able to process new data and suggest predictions as shown in the following figure:

Figure 2. How machine learning works

Phase 1 : Training

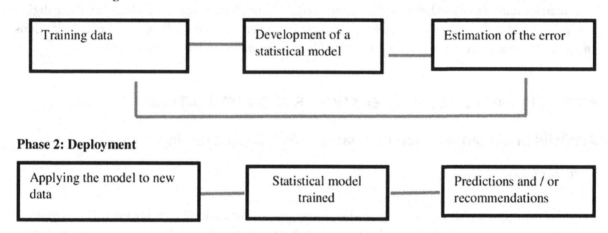

Phase 2: Deployment

Applied, for example, to an e-commerce site, this model makes it possible to predict the volume of purchases that could be made from the processing of data relating to the behavior of visitors to this site. In this example, the input data relates to the visit schedule and the outputs reveal the number of items purchased. Simulations in terms of correspondences made between the input data and those of the outputs will allow the algorithms to develop a machine learning capable of predicting new input and output values as shown in the table opposite:

Table 1. Machine learning algorithm

Entry data: Visit schedule		Output: Number of items purchased
H1: 9 a.m	---------------------------------	N1: 0
H2: 10 a.m	---------------------------------	N2: 2
H3: 11 a.m	---------------------------------	N 3: 30
⋮	---------------------------------	⋮
Hn: 9 p.m	---------------------------------	Nn': 15

In accordance with this operation, a machine learning type system would be very different from conventional computer programs based on compliance with previously defined instructions. This process will work based on the learning that is built from previous experiences. The performance of such a process is likely to improve as the algorithm trains on larger amounts of data.

Deep Learning

Deep Learning is a derivative of Machine Learning (Sarker, 2021). It is based on a network of artificial neurons connected to each other like neurons in the human brain (Aggarwal, 2018). An artificial neuron is likely to match multiple inputs and multiple outputs while involving other parameters that help solve the problem. The more neurons the network contains, the deeper and more complicated it is considered. The combination of several neurons within the same network makes the system capable of storing a very large volume of information. Among the main applications of Deep Learning, there is facial and / or voice recognition (Dargan et al., 2020). Indeed, Deep Learning is likely to identify one aspect or part of an image relative to each layer of neurons and then link all of the identified aspects to reconstruct the complete image or photo. If we use deep learning to recognize, for example, a cat in photos, the neural network should be able to recognize cats of all types and in all possible shots and angles. This recognition is the result of training that occurs on a set of photos that may or may not contain the image of a cat. As the system processes different images, it gains more experience and it becomes more efficient.

Artificial Intelligence: Advantages and Application's Fields

New technologies now make important contributions to problem solving and entity management. Indeed, on the basis of data provided by Big Data, these technologies ensure the processing and sharing of data and facilitate the relevant and rapid design of solutions. Cloud computing, for example, ensures the timely sharing of information between the various departments of an entity, and artificial intelligence uses its algorithms to model and execute appropriate solutions not only quickly but also with impending capacity of self-study. As a result, the companies that use it benefit from greater agility and flexibility to cope with sudden, complex and uncertain changes and are now able to make the best decisions on time.

Better yet, artificial intelligence allows decision-makers to implement forward-looking approaches, which allows companies to be less vulnerable and more competitive (Villani, 2018; Aghion, 2017). Artificial intelligence helps promote economic growth and support business activity, particularly through the optimization of resources and the proliferation of innovations (Mc Afree, 2011; Vieira, 2015).

The contributions of artificial intelligence are manifold. They are not limited to a specific sector. Indeed, in the field of health, artificial intelligence has made it possible to develop an intelligent diagnosis for thousands of patients, to carry out genetic sequencing to meet the needs of scientific research and treatment of pathologies, to create new molecules in order to develop new drugs, etc.

In the transport sector, artificial intelligence is helping to proliferate more safety and comfort for drivers, in particular through the design of fully autonomous vehicles and systems for detecting driver fatigue.

In the industrial sector, AI has also made it possible to generate languages that can be decoded by robots and to undertake predictive maintenance of machines. From a legal standpoint, AI has made it possible to search case law for arguments suitable for a legal questioning as well as to estimate the probability of winning a dispute or the amount of compensation expected. It also makes it possible to assess the quality of contracts to be signed, etc.

In the marketing context, AI makes it possible to process large volumes of data, which gives managers the possibility of carrying out more relevant analyzes of the market and of optimizing their marketing campaigns based on better customer knowledge and by anticipating industry trends (Davenport et al, 2020; Verma et al., 2021). AI also helps improve customer relationship management and better manage website traffic (Kumar et al., 2019).

The IA contributions cited in this section are neither exhaustive nor complete. This technology is capable of contributing to the management of many other sectors and aspects of human life and will continue to improve to provide more innovative maneuvers in the service of science and humanity. Nonetheless, the authors are interested, in this case, in describing the key points to be capitalized on in order to develop smart cities and the contributions that artificial intelligence could make to this end. It is, in fact, to answer the specific question: to what extent could AI be at the service of the development of smart cities?

ARTIFICIAL INTELLIGENCES SERVING THE CONVERSION OF CITIES INTO SMART CITIES

Points Of Conversion of a City Into A Smart City

ICTs are the backbone of the smart city development project. Nevertheless, there is a need to act on a set of key points that make it possible to place a city in the sphere of smart cities. These key points revolve around:

Building Automation and Control

One aspect of converting a city into a smart city is to operate and maintain buildings in an automated, secure and sustainable manner. Indeed, building automation is manifested by intelligent building management according to which it is necessary to reduce the operating costs of these buildings and to optimize energy consumption, in particular by effectively controlling the elevators, air conditioning, lighting, water, etc.

It can be applied for all kinds of buildings like office buildings, hotels, hospitals, schools, museums, train stations and airports. Several gains have resulted from this automation, including:

- Optimize lighting and prevent damage to exterior window blinds by lowering and raising them automatically depending on weather conditions
- Provide optimal heating and air conditioning of rooms by capturing indoor and outdoor temperatures
- Avoid operating errors and detect any malfunctions early.
- Effectively monitor access to buildings and allow intelligent routing of passenger flows for better organization of access, especially when there are events

In this regard, success stories bear witness to the importance of this smart building management and its contribution towards the development of a smart and sustainable city. Indeed, in Alba Iulia, the first Romanian smart city, where thanks to 150 lighting and water sensors, the city has saved between 50% and 70% of electricity for street lights while maintaining the same level of lighting for the inhabitants.

Another example dates from 2007 when the first smart and sustainable town hall was opened in Belgium in the City of Gembloux in Wallonia. This project is part of the city's sustainable development strategy and Gembloux 2020 objectives. Its objective is to contribute to the revitalization of the city center. To do this, the project has ensured that the criteria set by the "Smart Cities & Sustainable Development" financing program which was launched by Belfius Bank and the European Investment Bank (EIB) were strictly respected. The project truly demonstrates a strategic, integrated, innovative and sustainable approach. It ensures accessibility to people with reduced mobility, energy performance, insulation and airtightness, limitation of the risk of overheating, good energy savings through optimized lighting, a water recovery system rain, photovoltaic solar panels, etc. Thus, this project has enabled the city of Gembloux to be an example to follow for other agglomerations.

Efficient Urban Planning

In terms of urban planning, one of the challenges facing the authorities is its obsolescence. Indeed, adopting an urban planning plan (PLU) can easily take many years of study. However, as soon as this plan enters into force, we realize that it has already become obsolete, that is to say that it must be amended to take into account the socio-economic developments that have occurred. There is also the risk of overlaps within this plan between different projects or different levels of planning. This being so, because in reality it is not a plan but development plans, each corresponding to a level of public decision. In this regard, it is important to remember that the development of a smart city is closely linked to the establishment of a new governance based on intelligent data management (Bibri & Krogstie, 2020).

Indeed, thanks to NICTs, data on transport, energy consumption, waste management and others are first collected and analyzed in real time for better management of the means and devices for the current management of a city. These data are also used to plan the needs for means, devices and future projects according to the predictions made on the development of the density of the urban population. City management is now more efficient thanks to this intelligent data management, which makes it possible, among other things, to plan urban plans based on up-to-date data and allowing timely predictions to be made.

Urban Mobility and Sustainable Public Transport

To cope with increasing population density in urban areas, authorities tend to consider extensive growth of road or rail networks. However, many of these solutions of this type come up against constraints of the budgetary and / or environmental type. Thus, intelligent mobility is considered as an alternative aiming to optimize and make profitable the existing networks and this, by designing IT solutions allowing to ensure a more sustainable and efficient mobility system and to reduce congestion and other problems are associated.

Indeed, integrating AI into smart city mobility systems makes it possible to generate real-time reports on traffic saturation and traffic accidents (Hawi et al., 2015). It also makes it possible to predict traffic jams and immediately resolve complex traffic problems (Agarwal et al., 2015).

As an indication, ANNs make it possible to supervise urban traffic and therefore to find the most suitable alternatives to solve traffic problems (Hawi et al., 2015). Solutions like IBM's Twende-Twende project can educate citizens about the possibility of taking an alternate route to bypass traffic jams or avoid toll roads. This information is sent directly to users on mobile phones (Hawi et al., 2015).

Use Of Digital Technologies in Education

The smart city must be a vehicle for education and offer accessible and effective educational services to its citizens. NICTs now promote remote access to education. Thus, by leveraging these digital means, education would be universally accessible and would contribute to the development of a smart and constructive city. From this perspective, AI helps to expand access to the education system and increases the diversity of the learner population. This flexibility has therefore generated a more diversified training portfolio by integrating non-traditional learners such as people with disabilities. AI has also made it possible to increase the involvement of learners and teachers and to develop a more engaging education process (Popenici and Kerr, 2017) through the use of robots.

Indeed, these robots have the merit of attracting the attention of learners and providing personalized teaching experiences (Timms, 2016). The use of AI has generated practical and innovative teaching methods and materials like MOOCs. Thus, AI has contributed to the improvement of learning outcomes "(Fauvel and Yu, 2016).

Use Of Digital Technologies for Health

Developing a smart city undoubtedly requires the provision of adequate and accessible medical services on a daily basis as well as in times of crisis. It is about ensuring the well-being of citizens in terms of physical, mental and psychological health.

The services rendered by the use of new technologies do not strictly concern the management of consultations and the archiving of medical records which were produced manually, but tend to improve the well-being of the community by involving citizens in this process of collective benevolence. There is no shortage of ideas to do so. In this context, the city "Aizuwakamatsu" in Japan is a good example. This city has adopted the latest technologies to improve the well-being of its inhabitants. Indeed, as part of a health project, Japanese citizens are called upon to provide data on their physical condition to the regional community through a system called Opt-in.

To this information is added the data held by the hospital. All of this information is then analyzed by the region, which will make recommendations to those concerned to help them take care of their health.

The platform used by the Japanese community is based on the involvement of citizens in this project since it could not be fed without their agreement and conviction. The involvement of citizens is crucial, but also beneficial for them as well as for the community, because the more information they provide, the more they could benefit from services that are adapted to them. This data can also be useful for conducting scientific research or for providing the community with advice on improving the lifestyle. Sharing experiences and information can be very beneficial in creating positive behaviors in the community. Indeed, statistics have shown that 89% of people who have used these services have changed their behavior vis-à-vis their health.

Another interesting experience in this respect is that of the city of ARAO, which tested an intelligent mirror capable of analyzing the well-being of individuals by analyzing information on their pulse, sex, age, smile and indicating a score on the health and level of cheerfulness of the person. This mirror, functioning through an artificial intelligence algorithm, is capable of making recommendations to the person who is exposed to it, such as playing sports or relaxing. The aim is to help citizens to maintain good physical and psychological health and to live happier and longer lives.

An Electronic Commerce System

Electronic commerce is expanding. This boom is believed to bring about changes in the conventional spatial structure of a city. Its role in the implementation of a smart city is not yet sufficiently explored by researchers. This role is meant to manifest on more than one plane. Indeed, the literature so far has focused on the effect of e-commerce on mobility, traffic volume, logistics dynamics and operational strategies.

However, it is also interesting to highlight the influence of e-commerce on the conventional spatial structure of a city, the intertwined relationship between the city center, the periphery and the rural areas as well as to shed additional light on the role of electronic commerce in building smart cities by considering all possible facets of this role. Studies call for an ideological shift in the conceptualization of a smart city from a concept to a process (Nahiduzzaman et al, 2021).

The rise of e-commerce and its increased adoption by citizens could lead to a decrease in dependence on cars and a transition to a sustainable city (Pettersson et al. 2016). This emerging process of transformation must be taken into account in the planning and management practices of dynamic urban structures. Particular attention should be paid to studying the consumption habits of citizens and the changes that have occurred with the rise of electronic commerce, depending on the category of products and the characteristics of customers.

Nevertheless, some studies have already revealed that ICTs have affected the consumption behavior of leisure activities by generating several virtual activities and thereby affected the travel habits of citizens (Lila and Anjaneyulu 2016).

The technological advancement applied to the generation of exciting and thrilling virtual consumption experience as well as the success of digital marketing and social media marketing have already left a considerable mark on the change in consumption habits, this which suggests that electronic commerce is likely to be a vector for the development of smart sustainable cities.

On the other hand, this e-commerce alternative has also been beneficial in times of health crisis and has allowed many merchants to continue their activities remotely when they need to lower their curtains. It also allowed confined citizens to obtain supplies without endangering themselves. This also applies to all those who have difficulty moving even outside times of crisis.

Transparency, Security, Protection and Sharing of Data

The governance of smart cities is about adopting new forms of human collaboration by using ICTs to establish more open governance processes and consequently achieve better performance. It is about leveraging the sharing of data that could transfer experiences or useful information for the community. Governing smart cities is based on the idea of making this governance more participatory and more inclusive. To do this, users of these platforms are invited to disclose their personal information transparently, so as not to distort the decisions and measures taken on the basis of this data. In addition, the recommended sharing of data does not exclude the importance of managing this data securely. In this regard, AI can help overcome security and privacy concerns.

The use of AI and its derivatives helps reduce the time required to resolve a cybersecurity problem. ML, image recognition or NLP have been used to detect fraud (Necula, 2017) and prevent network intrusions (Roy et al., 2017), etc. The integration of AI is really relevant here since anomalies and vulnerabilities must be identified on large volumes of data. These large amounts of data, in turn, help improve the efficiency of the learning and action capacity of these computer models.

Smart Waste Management

According to the World Bank, the planet produces more than 2 billion tonnes of urban solid waste each year. Globally, only 13.5% of waste is recycled and 5.5% of garbage is composted. A large part of waste is still incinerated or buried and a lot of waste still escapes our trash cans and ends its life in nature, forests and rivers, which has negative consequences on the environment and on health (Vergara & Tchobanoglous, 2012). These numbers are not only alarming but tend to amplify as the population grows. Thus, intelligent waste management is essential. This management takes place in the form of a process which attempts a smarter treatment of waste but which also relies on efforts to minimize waste production, particularly through bulk sales, reuse or even upcycling. This includes all initiatives that allow us to discover the possibility of cities without garbage cans.

In waste sorting, smart waste management can be undertaken by mobilizing connected assistants or decision support services to help households and businesses sort their waste. In Gironde, the case of Trizzy is a good example. This is a chatbot that supports communities by talking to them about the waste they want to throw away. These communities are thus directed to the right centers or informed about the best sorting and recycling practices. This concept is currently being tested by cities such as Poitiers and Angoulême.

In the same vein, startups like Urbyn and its waste management platform for businesses have been created to optimize professional waste flows. Others have designed real connected bins, like the R3D3 model offered by the French startup green creative. These bins can automatically recognize beverage packaging to sort them according to their composition. The concept of connected bins seems to be booming. Indeed, digital innovation is being exploited to develop intelligent functionalities that now make it possible to improve the sorting and collection of waste by providing relevant services and indicators.

This is the case with the redesign of trash cans based on the IoT with its sensors and data analysis engines. Connected trash cans are also equipped with alert systems to inform municipal teams about the level of the trash cans to consider efficient and timely collection. This practice has been tested for years, particularly in the city of Copenhagen and Rennes. The data collected is used to better analyze the uses and flows in the city, in order to identify, for example, the areas where the bins are used the most, those which remain most often empty, the average frequency of filling, the most active days, etc.

In addition, another concept deserves to be mentioned, that of pneumatic waste collection, which offers a different concept of waste collection and transport. This collection practice is based on the provision of waste holders who suck up the waste that is poured into it. This waste is then collected at a central point, then sent to the waste management channels. This system has the advantage of being available 24 hours a day and of limiting noise and odor nuisance, but it has a high investment cost and consumes a lot of energy to supply the waste suction network.

Environmental, Economic, Political and Social Sustainability

On the basis of the three levers of sustainable development, the concept of sustainability acquires an inherent importance within the framework of the development project of smart and sustainable cities. Indeed, a city that wants to be smart and sustainable must ensure:

Environmental sustainability which refers to the ability to maintain biological aspects in their productivity and diversity over time. It is about preserving natural resources by creating a conscious responsibility on the ecological level which must not be altered by the concern of development.

Economic sustainability which refers to the ability to produce enough wealth in different areas in order to build a solvent population capable of solving its economic problems. This includes strengthening production and consumption in the money-producing sectors without destroying the balance between man and nature, that is, without losing sight of the interests of future generations.

Political sustainability that focuses on the establishment of a political system capable of distributing political power in such a way as to strengthen democracy and respect for the population. It is about adopting to put in place a secure and stable government as well as a legal framework protecting the rights of communities against unfair measures, with a view to promoting solidarity between communities and regions and '' improve the quality of life.

Social sustainability which refers to maneuvers and practices intended to promote the well-being of people in the places where they live and work. Social sustainability includes putting in place the right infrastructure to support social and cultural life, systems of citizen engagement, and space for people and places to evolve. It aims to promote:

§ Equity

It is about identifying disadvantages within a target group, looking for their causes and ways to reduce them. The principle of equity aims to meet the needs of any particularly disadvantaged and marginalized person within a target group.

§ Diversity

This involves identifying the various groups within a target group with a view to recognizing cultural, ethnic and racial diversity and seeking ways to meet the particular needs of each group. The objective being to take into consideration the diversity of points of view, beliefs and values, to promote understanding and tolerance within a diverse community

§ Social Cohesion

It is about acting in order to develop a feeling of belonging to the community at large, in particular by increasing the participation of individuals in the social activities of a target group, by building links between the target group and other groups in the community, encouraging the target group to contribute to the community or support others.

§ Life Quality

This is to improve affordable and appropriate housing opportunities for the target group, their physical and mental health outcomes as well as education, training and skills development opportunities offered within the target group.

Sustainable Smart Cities: Success Stories

In this section, the authors propose to present the experiences and achievements of the smartest cities in the world. This is the city of:

Hong Kong

Hong Kong is one of the most influential cities in Southeast Asia. Its experience in the smart city conversion plan is attractive. Indeed, in terms of:

Smart Mobility: the city has developed a traffic data analysis system and created a "Smart Traffic Fund" to promote research and the application of vehicle-related technology to ensure intelligent mobility

§ Smart Living: the city has created an iAM Smart digital platform to streamline driving license allocation services; use telehealth, especially for the elderly, adopt videoconferencing and remote medical consultation; use blockchain technology to improve the traceability of pharmaceutical products. It also considered the early detection of fires in natural parks.

§ Smart Environment: As part of the "Climate Action Plan 2030+", the city of Hong Kong is on the path to reducing carbon intensity from 65% to 70% by 2030 and '' achieve carbon neutrality before 2050; it launched a residential building subsidy program for the installation of charging stations for electric vehicles. It also adopted sludge pretreatment technology to turn waste into energy and implemented a smart recycling system for the community.

§ Smart People: IT innovation laboratories and the establishment of science, technology, engineering and mathematics education programs have been created in schools.

§ Smart Government: an electronic platform for processing construction plans has been created; customs clearance is now faster via the Smart Customs Blueprint; an association with the private sector was carried out in order to develop new technological solutions via the Smart Government Innovation Lab, etc.

In times of health crisis, many smart initiatives have been decided and implemented in Hong Kong to fight COVID-19, which is cited as keeping a dashboard with COVID-19 statistics; a "StayHomeSafe" home quarantine monitoring application with a connected electronic bracelet; a LeaveHomeSafe trip tracking application; the use of contactless payments in the markets; the use of robots for baggage handling, cleaning and disinfection at the airport; a new HA Go mobile application for booking consultations in public hospitals; the use of antimicrobial technologies to disinfect public transport, etc.

Amsterdam

Amsterdam has been praised both in Europe and on the world stage for its smart projects. This city has attracted attention with its technological advances, its international reach and its urban planning. Indeed, the city has joined in partnership projects with local businesses and organizations to test sustainable alternatives for "Utrechtsestraat", the city's largest shopping district. The "Climate Street" projects have also helped save energy on lighting, reduce pollution and reduce tram stops.

Barcelona

This city has been praised so many times for implementing projects based on smart technologies. Among these projects is the feat achieved in saving the economy which suffered serious difficulties in the 1980s when textile factories and others shriveled up. In 2011, the city hosted the first Smart City Exposition and World Congress to encourage a self-sufficient city with thriving communities within a large hyper-connected zero-emission city. In Spain, the second largest city is now full of LED sensors that monitor traffic, air quality, pedestrian movement and noise. These sensors can also automatically dim or turn off the lights. In addition, in the city of Barcelona there are a lot of smart dustbins with vacuum cleaners for removing garbage to underground storage. This innovation minimizes disgusting odors and reduces the need for trucks to haul garbage. The city has also implemented a bicycle commuting program to minimize the use of vehicles, especially in high traffic areas.

New York

Local authorities in New York have stepped up to make the Big Apple one of the smart and sustainable cities. The projects carried out for this purpose have been carried out by the public and private sectors. Advanced technologies have been used to improve the efficiency of governance in the city. For example, sensors have been installed both at traffic lights and in buses to clear traffic in this city.

London

By promoting collaboration between the public, technological and academic sectors, the London Public Innovation Challenge has enabled startups to design solutions to several urban challenges. The city has become fully connected with 5G access under the initiative of a project called "Connected London" requiring additional infrastructure that can provide sufficient fiber optic coverage. Officials have used the drones to locate spaces where cellular antennas need to be mounted. In the same perspective, another program has been implemented to provide free access to Wi-Fi in government facilities as well as on the streets.

Oslo

Oslo has taken solid steps in its conversion to a smart sustainable city, focusing on the development of a sustainable and environmentally friendly atmosphere. The city now has 650,000 LED lights, all connected to a surveillance hub. These smart lights automatically change the lighting to the amount needed to meet needs. Oslo is also mobilizing license plate detectors to avoid traffic jams. It is on the way to completely rehabilitating its transport system in the years to come.

Boston

The city of Boston was one of the first cities to adopt smart innovations, especially in its seaport. It has also capitalized on the involvement of its citizens by introducing a series of apps that provide parking information and allow their users to report service issues and communicate with each other. Citizens can also follow a school bus or even report graffiti anywhere in the city's many neighborhoods. Considerable efforts have been made to deal with traffic problems and facilitate mobility in the city. A digital kiosk has also been installed to provide real-time details on buses and trains. It also provides information on carpooling, bike sharing and other related services.

Copenhagen

The Danish capital has implemented radical environmental measures to convert into a smart city. The Copenhagen Solutions Lab system was among the measures undertaken and winning an award in 2017 for its ability to monitor traffic, air quality, waste management and energy consumption. It also integrates parking networks, traffic lights, smart meters and charging systems for electric vehicles, in order to facilitate traffic in real time. The system also optimizes energy consumption by taking into account the cost of fuel, traffic flow and weather conditions.

Dubai

The Smart Dubai 2021 program has put the city of Dubai on the path to smart cities. This program includes a multitude of projects relating to transport, telecommunications, energy, financial services and plans to digitize all government services through the DubaiNow application. As a result of the implementation of these projects, local authorities estimate that they will save approximately $ 245 million. They also plan to eliminate paper transfers once the program ends. According to the Road and Transit Authority, a device for tracking bus drivers using artificial intelligence has significantly reduced road accidents due to fatigue.

Singapore

Singapore is the second most densely populated city in the world. It registered around 8,000 people per square kilometer. Yet it has secured the first place among the most innovative and intelligent Smart Cities in the world. His government continues to seek effective ways to integrate digital advancements and increase productivity by starting with the digital collection of critical city information through the Singapore Smart Nation program. The development of "Virtual Singapore" has also led to the design of a dynamic 3D city model that acts as a collaborative data platform. Public housing, which accommodates 80% of the city's inhabitants, is continuously fueled by advanced innovations in water management and systems for monitoring and assisting the elderly. By 2022, the city government plans to roll out smart, energy-efficient lighting in all city streets and build 6,000 solar panels on the roofs of city buildings.

CONCLUSION

By 2050, nearly seven in ten people worldwide will live in cities. This trend towards increased and very rapid urbanization continues to create enormous challenges including worsening social inequalities, suffocating traffic jams, alarming pollution rates, etc. The consequences of these challenges will now be inestimable and will visibly affect the quality of life. Aware of the gravity of the situation, governments and municipalities have made a commitment to convert their cities into smart sustainable cities and henceforth equip themselves with an intelligent mode of governance in order to overcome all these challenges. To do this, these authorities have chosen to use NICTs and other technologies in order to implement these promising projects. This chapter has defined what is a smart and sustainable city, shed light on the main challenges facing development projects in these cities. He also presented the main aspects on which action must be taken to convert a city into a smart sustainable city as well as the main technologies used to implement these projects.

Moreover, although there are not yet cities where all urban services are connected, several cities around the world have, as indicated in the last part of this chapter, put themselves on the right track to become smart and sustainable cities. These cities are based on new technologies to save on energy consumption, review their management of urban waste, improve building management, ensure health care at the same level of efficiency for all social categories, optimize traffic management and road safety, etc. These experiences have already achieved many gains, thereby inspiring cities that have not yet embarked on this path.

REFERENCES

Abdul Ahad, M., Paiva, S., Tripathi, G., & Feroz, N. (2020). Enabling Technologies and Sustainable Smart Cities. *Sustainable Cities and Society*, *61*(102301).

Aggarwal, C. C. (2018). Neural networks and deep learning. Springer. doi:10.1007/978-3-319-94463-0

Aghion, P., Jones, B., & Jones, C. (2017). *Artificial Intelligence and Economic Growth*. NBER Working Paper N° 23928. doi:10.6/w23928

Anthopoulos, L. (2015). *Defining Smart City Architecture for Sustainability* [Paper presentation]. 4th IFIP Electronic Government (EGOV) and 7th Electronic Participation (ePart) Conference. 10.3233/978-1-61499-570-8-140

Bibri, S. E., & Krogstie, J. (2020). The emerging data–driven Smart City and its innovative applied solutions for sustainability: The cases of London and Barcelona. *Energy Informatics*, *3*(1), 1–42. doi:10.118642162-020-00108-6

Craglia, M., & Granell, C. (2014). *Citizen Science and Smart Cities*. Number EUR 26652 EN; Publications Office of the European Union.

Dameri, R. P. (2013). Searching for smart city definition: A comprehensive proposal. *International Journal of Computers and Technology*, *11*(5), 2544–2551. doi:10.24297/ijct.v11i5.1142

Daptardar, V., & Gore, M. (2019). Smart Cities for Sustainable Development in India: Opportunities and Challenges. *European Journal of Sustainable Development*, *8*(3), 133. doi:10.14207/ejsd.2019.v8n3p133

Dargan, S., Kumar, M., Ayyagari, M. R., & Kumar, G. (2020). A survey of deep learning and its applications: A new paradigm to machine learning. *Archives of Computational Methods in Engineering*, *27*(4), 1071–1092. doi:10.100711831-019-09344-w

Davenport, T., Guha, A., Grewal, D., & Bressgott, T. (2020). How artificial intelligence will change the future of marketing. *Journal of the Academy of Marketing Science*, *48*(1), 24–42. doi:10.100711747-019-00696-0

Douay, N., & Henriot, C. (2016). La Chine à l'heure des villes intelligentes. *L'Information Geographique*, *80*(3), 89–104. doi:10.3917/lig.803.0089

Fauvel, S., & Yu, H. (2016). *A Survey on Artificial Intelligence and Data Mining for MOOCs.* https://images-insite.sgp1.digitaloceanspaces.com/dunia_buku/koleksi-buku-lainnya/a-survey-on-artificial-intelligence-and-data-mining-for-moocs-pdfdrivecom-10781581695980.pdf

Georgescu, M., & Popescul, D. (2016). The Importance of Internet of Things Security for Smart Cities. In Smart Cities Technologies (pp. 3-18). InTech. doi:10.5772/65206

Giffinger, R., Fertner, C., Kramar, H., Meijers, E., & Pichler-Milanović, N. (2007). *Ranking of European medium-sized cities.* Final Report. www.researchgate.net/publication/261367640_Smart_cities_-_Ranking_of_European_medium-sized_cities

Giffinger, R., Haindlmaier, G., & Strohmayer, F. (2014). *Typology of cities, Planning for Energy Efficient Cities.* https://publik.tuwien.ac.at/files/PubDat_240139.pdf

Gil-Garcia, J. R., Pardo, T. A., & Nam, T. (2015). What makes a city smart? Identifying core components and proposing an integrative and comprehensive conceptualization. *Information Polity, 20*(1), 61–87. doi:10.3233/IP-150354

Gretzel, U. (2011). Intelligent systems in tourism: A Social Science Perspective. *Annals of Tourism Research, 38*(3), 757–779. doi:10.1016/j.annals.2011.04.014

Harrison, C., & Donnelly, I. A. (2011). A Theory of Smart Cities. *Proceedings of the 55th Annual Meeting of the ISSS, 55*(1). Retrieved from https://journals.isss.org/index.php/proceedings55th/article/view/1703

Hawi, R. O., Alkhodary, D., & Hashem, T. (2015). Managerial Competencies and Organizations Performance. *Research Academy of Social Sciences, 5*(11), 723–735.

Khan, K. (2006). How IT governance is changing. *Journal of Corporate Finance, 17*(5), 21–25.

Kitchin, R., & Dodge, M. (2017). The (in) security of smart cities: Vulnerabilities, risks, mitigation and prevention. *Journal of Urban Technology, 26*(2), 47–65. doi:10.1080/10630732.2017.1408002

Kumar, V., Rajan, B., Venkatesan, R., & Lecinski, J. (2019). Understanding the role of artificial intelligence in personalized engagement marketing. *California Management Review, 61*(4), 135–155. doi:10.1177/0008125619859317

Lila, P. C., & Anjaneyulu, M. V. L. R. (2016). Modeling the Impact of ICT on the Activity and Travel Behaviour of Urban Dwellers in Indian Context. *Transportation Research Procedia, 17,* 418–427. doi:10.1016/j.trpro.2016.11.083

McAfee, R. P. (2011). The design of advertising exchanges. *Review of Industrial Organization, 39*(3), 169–185. doi:10.100711151-011-9300-1

Nahiduzzaman, K. M., Holland, M. E., Sikder, S., Shaw, P., Hewage, K., & Sadiq, R. (2021). Urban Transformation Toward a Smart City: An E-Commerce–Induced Path-Dependent Analysis. *Journal of Urban Planning and Development, 147*(1), 04020060. doi:10.1061/(ASCE)UP.1943-5444.0000648

Necula, S.-C. (2017). Deep Learning for Distribution Channels' Management. *Informações Econômicas, 21*(4), 73–84. doi:10.12948/issn14531305/21.4.2017.06

Obaidat, M. S., & Nicopolitidis, P. (2016). *Smart cities and homes: Key enabling technologies* (1st ed.). Kindle Edition.

OECD. (2018). *Mieux tirer parti de la transition numérique pour les villes intelligentes du futur.* https://www.oecd.org/cfe/cities/MIEUX-TIRER-PARTI-DE-LA-TRANSITION-NUM%C3%89RIQUE-POUR-LES-VILLES%20INTELLIGENTES%20DU%20FUTUR.pdf?fbclid=IwAR0CY4mup9H9JBq5a54R2-t_AhQTnwUr7mUOoRG4ChhX1kEv5HQJ_Ib8Txk

Popenici, S. A. D., & Kerr, S. (2017). Exploring the impact of artificial intelligence on teaching and learning in higher education. *Research and Practice in Technology Enhanced Learning*, *12*(22), 1–13. doi:10.118641039-017-0062-8 PMID:30595727

Sarker, I. H. (2021). Machine learning: Algorithms, real-world applications and research directions. *SN Computer Science*, *2*(3), 1–21. doi:10.100742979-021-00592-x PMID:33778771

Son, Chen, C.-F., Chen, C.-R., Thanh, B.-X., & Vuong, T.-H. (2017). Assessment of urbanization and urban heat islands in Ho Chi Minh City, Vietnam using Landsat data. *Sustainable Cities and Society*, *30*, 150–161. doi:10.1016/j.scs.2017.01.009

Vergara, S. E., & Tchobanoglous, G. (2012). Municipal solid waste and the environment: A global perspective. *Annual Review of Environment and Resources*, *37*(1), 277–309. doi:10.1146/annurev-environ-050511-122532

Verma, S., Sharma, R., Deb, S., & Maitra, D. (2021). Artificial intelligence in marketing: Systematic review and future research direction. *International Journal of Information Management Data Insights*, *1*(1), 100002. doi:10.1016/j.jjimei.2020.100002

Vieira, A. (2015). *Predicting online user behaviour using deep learning algorithms*. Academic Press.

Villani, C. (2018). *Pour une intelligence artificielle significative. Vers une stratégie française et européenne*. Une mission parlementaire du 8 septembre 2017 au 8 mars 2018. https://www.aiforhumanity.fr/pdfs/ MissionVillani_Report_ENG-VF.pdf

Visvizi, A., Lytras, M. D., & Mudri, G. (2018). Smart Villages in the EU and Beyond. Emerald Publishing Limited.

Chapter 18
Digital Twins–Enabling Technologies Including AI, Sensors, Cloud, and Edge Computing

Tumburu Chandhana
Vellore Institute of Technology, India

Anuhya Balija
Vellore Institute of Technology, India

Siva R R Kumaran
Vellore Institute of Technology, India

Brijendra Singh
ⓘ https://orcid.org/0000-0003-2608-3388
Vellore Institute of Technology, India

ABSTRACT

Digital twin technology is starting to receive interest in the industry and, more recently, in academics. The digital twin is best described as the seamless integration of data between a physical and virtual system in either direction. The internet of things (IoT), cloud computing, edge computing, digital twins, and artificial intelligence all bring challenges, applications, and enabling technologies. Despite the fact that the idea of the "digital twin" has been well established over the past few years, there are still many different interpretations that result from varied professional viewpoints. The digital twin is primarily introduced in this chapter, along with its advantages and practical applications in different sectors. The authors have presented a detailed review of the artificial intelligence-driven digital twin, sensor-driven digital twin, cloud-driven digital twin, and edge computing-driven digital twin. It looks at the architectures, enabling technologies, potential obstacles, and challenges of current research on digital twins.

DOI: 10.4018/978-1-6684-6821-0.ch018

1. INTRODUCTION

Digital twin is a digital representations of physical objects, processes, or services. A digital twin can be a digital replica of an object in the physical world, such as a jet engine or wind farm, or even larger items such as buildings or even whole cities. A digital twin is, in essence, a computer program that uses real-world data to create simulations that can predict how a product or process will perform. Before actual devices are manufactured and deployed, data scientists and IT specialists can run simulations on digital twins, which are virtual replicas of physical devices. Real-time IoT data can also be used by digital twins to optimize performance using AI and data analytics. Essential technologies for implementing a cyber-physical system (CPS) are thought to be digital twin technology. By fully using physical models, sensor updates, operation histories, and other data, simulation technology incorporates interdisciplinary, multi-physical quantity, multi-scale, and multi-probability information. It is a mapping technology that allows for the virtualization of the entire lifecycle of a piece of physical equipment (A. Fuller et.al., 2020).

When considered in the context of the digital twin's beginnings and current development, its applications predominantly center on the stages of product design, operation, and maintenance (Khajavi,2019). However, with the fast and easy adaptation of innovative information and communication technologies like big data, the Internet of Things, mobile Internet, and cloud computing, the digital twin has expanded beyond the conventional stages of product design and operation. This section defines digital twin technology to make it easier to comprehend.

In essence, a digital twin is computer software that represents how a process or product would work using data from the real world (A. Fuller et.al., 2020).To enhance accuracy, these systems can incorporate software analytics and the internet of things artificial intelligence. These virtual models have become a mainstay in contemporary engineering to spur innovation and boost efficiency.

1.1 Benefits of Digital Twin Technology

Digital twin technology provides massive advantages to society. Developing a digital twin enables the advancement of major technological trends; prevent expensive breakdowns in physical items, and test processes and services leveraging enhanced analytical, monitoring, and predictive skills. Digital Twin optimizes performance and efficiency, choices may be made quickly and more effectively using simulations, actionable insights, and an integrated picture of all online and offline data. It enables a full view of all historical data and real-time data in one location, data centers can be eliminated and unlock the value throughout a project's lifecycle (Khajavi et al., 2019). Maintenance and operations are greatly enhanced using real-time sensor data and predictive recommendations are made by machine learning and artificial intelligence. The value from operations, the amount of development effort, and the time it comes to the market is all immensely improved by creating digital twins of complex assets, factories, and processes.

1.2 Importance of Digital Twin Technology

Digital twins are effective for boosting performance and innovation. Think of it as your most talented product technicians equipped with the most cutting-edge monitoring, analytical, and predictive tools. Within the next five years, digital twins will represent billions of items. Physical world product specialists and data scientists, whose employment is to comprehend what data says us about operations, will have new chances to collaborate as a result of these proxies for the physical world (Marr. B,2017). For a better understanding of consumer demands, d eloping improvements to current products, operations, and services, and even driving the innovation of new businesses, digital twin technology aids businesses in enhancing the customer experience.

The organization of the rest of this book chapter is as follows. The second section presents the literature review on digital twin. Section 3 presents digital twin driven architecture. In section 4 we present artificial intelligence-driven digital twins with their applications and challenges in different sectors. Section 5 presents sensor-driven digital twin technologies. We present cloud and edge-driven digital twin technologies with their challenges in section 6. Finally, the conclusion is presented in the last section.

2. LITERATURE REVIEW

A network load balancing and spatial-temporal graph convolution network-based prediction model for autonomous vehicles is proposed (Chen, D., & Lv, Z.,2022) using Digital twins. Additionally, through simulation, the accuracy, precision, recall, and F1-score performance of this model are examined. The experimental findings show that, in a comparison examination, this model's prediction accuracy is 92.70% which is 2.92% greater than previous research. The model achieves a lower average delay time than other comparative models, according to an investigation of the security performance of network data transmission. Additionally, both the message delivery and leakage rates are essentially consistent at 80% and 10%, respectively. As a result, the prediction model for autonomous vehicles developed in this paper not only guarantees low delay but also has high network security performance, allowing more effective information interaction. The research findings could serve as an experimental foundation for smart city transportation development and performance enhancement in terms of safety.

Manufacturers will be able to reduce costs, improve customer service, and discover new income streams by using the digital twin (Kumar, S., et al., 2020). Manufacturers may provide value across the whole lifespan of a piece of machinery, from design to maintenance. The connecting of sensors to the equipment, machine-to-machine communication, real-time monitoring, advanced analytics, preventive maintenance, etc. are now being researched in the framework of Industry 4.0. In a nutshell, the paper states that Digital Twin integrates many methods that let consumers comprehend, anticipate, and optimize performance. One of the important topics that other sectors and scholars are concentrating on is predictive maintenance (PdM). It may be used with many different kinds of machinery to lessen unanticipated downtimes. For the manufacturing industry, the combination of artificial intelligence and digital twins has the potential to open up several prospects. Generating simulated data is one of Digital Twin's powers. Infinite cycles of situations must be run through a simulation environment. A novice AI model may then be successfully trained on a variety of parts of the manufacturing processes using the generated simulated data. By doing this, the AI model can learn to recognize probable real-world circumstances that would be exceedingly challenging to find otherwise. Another name for this is reinforcement learning. The capacity to find, plan and test new characteristics that may be utilized to improve data operations in a machine learning process is the digital twin's feature.

The concept of mirror worlds, which has only lately been expanded upon and developed in the context of multi-agent systems, serves as the foundation for the agent-based Digital Twins concept that the authors propose in this work (Croatti, A., et al.,2020). A mirror world is a digital layer that is controlled by software agents and is related to a physical environment in both directions, giving any relevant physical entities—including users—a digital counterpart in the mirror that agents may see and interact with. It is possible to construct intelligent settings where mirror worlds offer many types of augmentations for people working in or living there, including cognitive, social, and temporal augmentations, by taking advantage of this connection between the digital and physical layers.

The construction of agent-based smart environments designed as mirror worlds is considered as being facilitated by the digital twin in the healthcare industry. Any pertinent assets in a healthcare context may have a digital twin modeled as a component of the environment that software agents may sense and respond to.

By doing this, the agent's perception of the observable state of the digital twin is coupled with that of the physical twin, and the particular model used would depend on the desired level of abstraction. Physical assets that are modeled as part of the MAS environment can either be atomic, like a patient, equipment that monitors vital signs, or a car, or composite, like a structure that has links to other, independent digital twins, like a hospital with rooms, staff members, patients, and so on. Assets can relate to both specific items and processes.

In the context of smart manufacturing, digital twins can help machine tools conduct their monitoring and troubleshooting jobs autonomously (Ghosh, A., et al., 2021). This requires the development and integration of a unique kind of twin known as a sensor signal-based twin into cyber-physical systems. The twin must, among other things, machine-learn the necessary information from past sensor signal datasets, seamlessly interact with real-time sensor signals, handle datasets that have been semantically tagged and are stored in clouds, and account for data transmission delays. Such twin development has not yet been thoroughly investigated. By addressing sensor signal-based digital twin generation for intelligent machine tools, this research closes this gap. It is suggested to build and adjust the twin using two computerized systems known as the Digital Twin Construction System (DTCS) and Digital Twin Adaptation System (DTAS), respectively. The suggested DTCS and DTAS modular architectures are discussed in detail. For both systems, the real-time responses and delay-related computational architectures are also explained. The systems are also created using a platform that is based on JavaTM. The effectiveness of DTCS and DTAS is illustrated via milling torque signals. In light of smart manufacturing, this work advances the development of intelligent machine tools.

To create digital twins—exact replicas of the actual world in cyberspace—for the cutting-edge manufacturing systems known as Industry 4.0, this research uses hidden Markov models (Ghosh, A., et al., 2019). The model component and the simulation component make up the suggested digital twin. The model element uses some discrete states and associated transition probabilities to create a Markov chain that captures the dynamics underlying the phenomenon. The Monte Carlo simulation method is used in the simulation component to replicate the phenomenon. An example case study that describes the digital twin of the surface roughness of a surface made by sequential grinding operations demonstrates the effectiveness of the suggested digital twin-building process. The findings of this study will be useful to those who create cyber-physical systems because these systems require computerized virtual abstractions of manufacturing phenomena to address problems related to the maturity index of futuristic manufacturing systems (i.e., understand, predict, decide, and adopt).

A cardiovascular digital twin platform to model how exercise affects key heart parameters that are significant from a medical standpoint has been proposed (Roy, D., et al., 2021). To calculate cardiac variables such as left ventricular dynamics, cardiac output, ejection fraction, mean arterial pressure, etc. of a person while they are exercising, the model incorporates the real-time ECG signal from the body-worn sensors. The unique contribution of this work is to estimate systemic resistance from the knowledge about the exercise level of a specific person engaged in physical activity and to estimate cardiac compliances from the morphology of the single-lead ECG signal. The simulation findings are obtained using an open-source database called Troika, and they display patterns in all the derived cardiac variables that are recognized by the medical community. The suggested approach can help patients with cardiac co-morbidity gradually track their cardiovascular performance during exercise and serve as a personalized therapy roadmap in a continuum of care situation.

A new approach is required to enhance the management and coordination of cars and cargo due to the increasing volume of seaborne trade and the associated traffic burden on the road infrastructure in port districts (Hofmann, W., & Branding, F., 2019). Since the digital twin is implemented as a cloud-based service, scaling and easy implementation are both possible. Using simulation-based performance projections, a digital twin for truck dispatching operator assistance is described in this contribution, allowing for the selection of the best-dispatched policies. Three key obstacles stand in the way of developing digital twin applications for logistics systems: proprietary modeling software with constrained interfaces, application deployment in demanding industrial environments, and the incorporation of real-time sensor data. Therefore, for simple integration of real-time data, our system leverages an extensible open-source simulation package combined with an IoT platform.

A Digital Twin framework (Dang, H. V., et al, 2021) for structural health monitoring based on cloud computing and deep learning is suggested to effectively carry out real-time monitoring and preventative maintenance. Because it enables the convergence of the physical structure and its digital counterpart across each of their complete life cycles, digital twin technology has recently gained traction in engineering circles. With the quick advancement of enabling technologies like machine learning, 5G/6G, cloud computing, and the Internet of Things, the concept of the digital twin has been gradually transitioning from theory to practice. The framework is made up of structural elements, device measurements, and digital models that were created by fusing several sub-models, such as those based on mathematics, finite elements, and machine learning. Case studies of damage detection on the model bridges and real bridge structures using deep learning algorithms, with high accuracy of 92%, show the viability of the proposed framework.

One of the use cases intended by the fourth industrial revolution (Industry 4.0), which will provide improved automation and remote controlling capabilities through the digitization of robotic systems is the Digital Twin (Girletti, L., et al., 2020). Based on this idea, this research suggests a method for creating an Edge-based Digital Twin for robotic systems that makes use of the continuum between the cloud and things to transfer computation and intelligence from the robots to the network. This places strict constraints on communication technology, and the suggested approach satisfies those criteria by depending on 5G. A series of experimental assessments are used to implement and validate this method in an E2E scenario. Results indicate that when backed by 5G connectivity, outsourcing the robot's functions to the edge is possible. Additionally, the advantages of introducing automation and intelligence are also evaluated.

3. DIGITAL TWIN ARCHITECTURE

Cloud and Sensor Driven Digital Twin Architecture is shown in Figure 1. It shows that the digital twin consists of two layers namely the industrial layer and the application layer. The application layer consists of two divisions one is for sensor-driven and another for cloud-driven processes. The application layer and the industrial layer are communicated through Wireless Enterprise Communication Protocols. The

Sensor- Driven process consists of internal IoT-related processes like Knowledge Data Base, Rules Engine for Data, and IoT Gateway. IoT architectures in one sense encourage connectivity between multiple levels and components making it reliable and secure. Interactions with actual intelligent objects and physical systems are performed. IoT gateways and other components when coupled can provide user-friendly virtual representations and deliver systems data analytics that is efficient, embedded, and smart tools and algorithms. Then the Cloud-driven framework consists of cloud features such as storing Data, Data representation, Data analysis, and applications in software companies. Many cloud computing service providers, including Amazon, Microsoft Azure, and Oracle, had suggested frameworks for the creation and deployment of digital twins.

Figure 1. Cloud and sensor-driven digital twin architecture

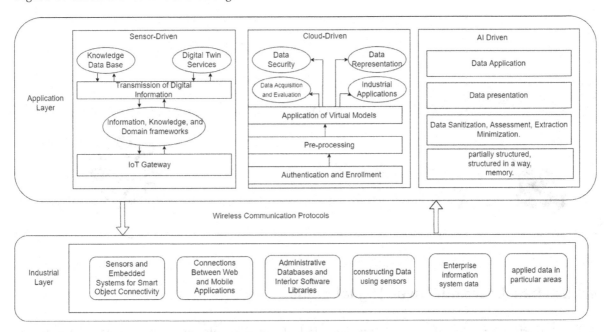

4. ARTIFICIAL INTELLIGENCE-DRIVEN DIGITAL TWIN TECHNOLOGY

Artificial intelligence techniques and digital twins relate to and enhance each other. For most complex systems, a data-driven approach is required to construct a digital twin and these approaches include machine learning and partial explicit manual modeling which hopefully results in a powerful digital object that can be used to optimize the physical world and improve operational performance.

The chronology of creating a digital twin using Artificial Intelligence is shown in Figure 2. The above figure shows that a digital twin design is made by gathering data and creating a model that represents the underlying object to test and determine the accuracy of the model. The process includes data collection from sensors on the physical devices which are responsible for data acquisition pipelines. The sensor data which is collected is fed to the historians for being processed. The chronology also leverages engineering models to process the principles that underlie the physical processes. On the other hand, the digital world takes the data and presents it for monitoring purposes using big data pipelines. AI and Machine Learning aggregate the data from these pipelines.

Figure 2. Chronology of creating a digital twin using artificial intelligence

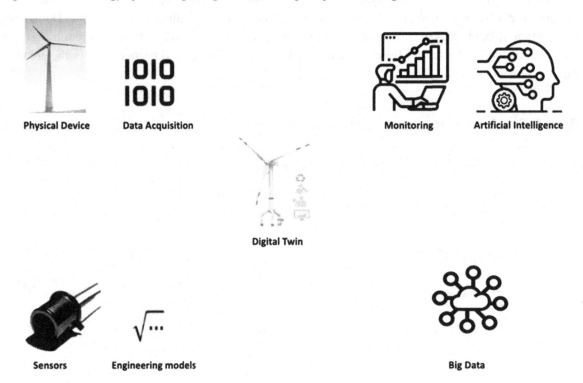

4.1 Machine Learning-Driven Digital Twins

Machine learning and digital twins are two notable features of developing technologies. Each stage of the life cycle may be made more responsive, predictable, and adaptive by using these two technologies in the whole life cycle analysis of complex equipment. Various research papers propose a technical system that incorporates machine learning models into digital twins. Predictive maintenance of diesel locomotives by combining machine learning with a digital twin is discussed(S.A. Shah et al., 2021) The machine learning-based diagnostic, prognostic methodologies, and algorithms help to enhance system performance, reliability, and the future digital twin technology for LEDs lifetime analysis(Ibrahim et al., 2020).

Machine Learning Algorithms are being employed more frequently as efficient methods for processing vibration data generated from sophisticated industrial machinery. In the past, the diagnosis of rotating machines using automatic fault detection algorithms has primarily relied on historical operating data sets, which has limited the diagnostic accuracy of devices with a long operational history. Furthermore, the circumstances of data gathering and the particular items for which they were recorded limit physically collected data frequently. A strong tool that can produce a ton of training data for MLAs is the digital twin (DT)(Mohamed Habib Farhat et al., 2021). To replace the tests, the DT model must be precise enough. By utilizing simulation-driven machine learning algorithms based on the multifactorial analysis of fault indicators linked to a DT, this work seeks to circumvent the experience requirement. A rotor-ball bearing system numerical model is designed to realize this strategy. Based on a comparison between the pertinent characteristics of the experimentally recorded signals and the signals simulated by the model, is revised under the parameter update strategy (Mohamed Habib Farhat et al., 2021).

Figure 3. Simulation-driven Machine Learning Algorithm (MLA)

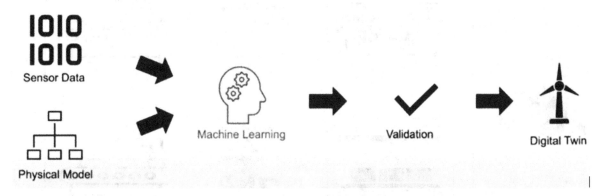

Simulation-driven Machine Learning Algorithm (MLA) is shown in Figure 3. The Figure defines the design of a simulation-driven Machine Learning Algorithm which is employed on the sensor data collected from the physical model integrated into an algorithm that is validated by Digital twin.

4.1.1 Applications in Various Sectors

4.1.1.1 Manufacturing

Implementations of the Digital Twin (DT) can advance smart manufacturing by fusing the physical and digital worlds. Applications of machine learning-based artificial intelligence (AI) are commonly regarded as promising technologies in the industrial sector. However, ML techniques need a lot of high-quality training datasets, and manual labeling of such datasets is frequently necessary for supervised ML. Especially in a highly complicated and dynamic manufacturing environment, such a method is expensive, labor and time-intensive, and prone to mistakes (Alexopoulos et al., 2020).

Smart Manufacturing using Predictive Models and Physical Assets is shown in Figure 4. The above figure shows a cyber-physical system (CPS) in which a mechanism is monitored and controlled by computer-based algorithms. In this CPS the machine learning frameworks monitor the cyber world where the digital twin is employed. CPS in manufacturing is used to seamlessly integrate computational machine learning algorithms with the physical world by leveraging physical assets in the industry.

4.1.1.1 Medical Sector

Digital twin models, which forecast the full paths of patient health data, have the potential to advance clinical trials and patient management. A population of patients with ischemia is used in the procedure, and they are treated with a digital twin model built on a variation auto-encoder. The ability of the digital twin to simulate patient clinical features was assessed regarding its capacity to forecast clinical measurement trajectories before the onset of the acute medical event and beyond using the International Classification of Diseases (ICD) codes for ischemic stroke and lab values as inputs (Allen et al., 2021).

Figure 4. Smart Manufacturing using predictive models and physical assets

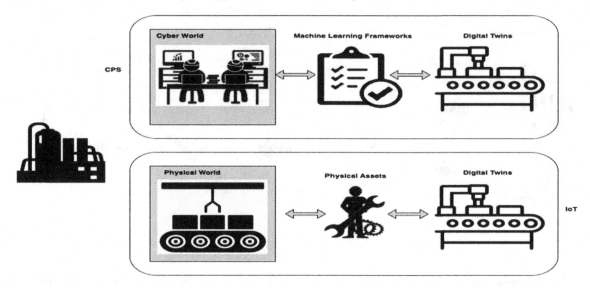

4.1.1.2 Risk Estimation

Pipelines are still a viable option in the oil business today, but the risk probability rate is rising and the maintenance system is becoming more challenging due to the early detection of accident risks by undertaking the complete pipeline (Priyanka et al., 2022). To study and forecast the risk probability rate of an oil pipeline system, the existing work aims to provide the structural system of a digital twin based on prognostics and machine learning techniques. By assessing the risk condition concerning the pressure data and evaluating the remaining usable life, prognostics focuses on the identification of a failure precursor (RUL) (Priyanka et al., 2022).

4.1.1.3 Prediction

Prediction of future patterns is possible by using digital twins for multi-timescale dynamical systems. The method combines a data-based strategy with system physics. For monitoring the temporal evolution of system parameters, ME-GP is offered. This method can correctly forecast future replies (Chakraborty, S et al., 2021)

4.1.2 Challenges

4.1.2.1 Data Quality and Imbalance

Data not being up to date without accuracy and has different values for different users which leads to no situational awareness.

Applications of ML to Data Quality:

- Recognize false data
- Determine the incomplete data
- Recognize sensitive information for compliance (maybe, PII identification)
- Utilizing fuzzy matching techniques for data reduplications
- Binning with historical trends and missing data
- Alert on probable service-level agreement violation using past data
- Assistance in effectively creating new business regulations (defining apt thresholds) (Jyoti Dhiman ., 2021)

4.1.2.2 Continuous Adaptation and Concept Drift

Predictive models are being used more often in smart manufacturing to manage industrial facilities. This leads to the requirement for long-term model performance monitoring and model evolution if the environment changes and the target prediction accuracy is no longer achieved. The diverse array of corporate systems, hardware-restricted IIoT platforms, machine learning frameworks, and application scenarios necessitate adaptable, reliable, and error-tolerant solutions that permit automatic model adaption(Bachinger et al., 2021).

4.1.2.3 System-Level Digital Twins and Interoperability

Use cases that call for information interchange between many organizations are impeded by the absence of interoperability between the digital twins of different firms. Digital twin interoperability necessitates converting the provided data to different forms (Platenius-Mohr et al., 2020)

4.1.2.4 Data Analytics

Digital Twins for decision-making heavily include AI algorithms for data analytics. It might be difficult to choose a specific model from hundreds of ML models with specialized settings. Depending on the applications and datasets, each AI technique has a varied level of accuracy and efficiency (feature set). On the other hand, efficiency on the contrary may be impacted by accuracy. Therefore, choosing the right ML algorithm and features is difficult since it depends on the purpose and application of a DT. Additionally, there are greater difficulties because there are fewer real-world applications of AI approaches for digital twinning in the literature(Tom Kevan,2020).

4.2 Deep Learning-Driven Digital Twin Technology

Neural networks are needed for decision-making enhancement and workflow optimization. Artificial neural networks (ANN) are used in manufacturing to create intricate digital twin models and resolve regression issues. Continuous training is performed to adapt to new difficulties in real time and optimize daily operations, the use of neural networks enhances the digital twin's ability for decision-making (Alexopoulos et al., 2020).

Digital Twin Software has event simulation and integrated assistance for the design and training of neural network models, enhancing decision-making, complex problem analysis, and improving industrial processes. There is a multitude of features being created that enable users to utilize neural networks in different ways, as presented below:

- Development of feed-forward neural networks without the requirement of programming algorithms, making it easier to integrate AI into digital twins.
- Embedded Trainer that enables ongoing supervised and unsupervised training of neural networks to boost the network's accuracy.
- Deep Learning makes it possible to automate processes for further scheduling, planning, and decision-making in industrial facilities(Eric Howard,2022).

Enterprises looking to optimize routine operations have access to improved analytical skills because of simulation and digital twin models. Planning and scheduling, preventive maintenance, remote monitoring, data-driven plant optimization, validation, and teg, etc. are all areas where the applications of these models are possible (Eric Howard,2022). The addition of neural networks establishes a mutually beneficial link between AI and simulation. In simulation and digital twin models, neural networks automate procedures and make it easier to create sophisticated logic. A productive environment for creating synthetic training data, training neural networks, and assessing their performance is provided via simulation and digital twins. By creating artificial training data, testing and training neural networks are feasible (Eric Howard,2022).

4.2.1 Applications in Various Sectors

4.2.1.1 Human-Machine Interaction

Deep learning technology is used in the digital twin to materialize and enhance Human-machine interaction (HMI) while examining physical and virtual data. Convolutional neural networks (CNN) are employed for the analysis of visual data. Two CNN models—Visual Geometry Group Network (VGG) and Residual Network (ResNet)—are used to handle the HMI job in DT. Modified 3D-VGG and 3D-ResNet models are put forth as an advance over the current VGG and ResNet models. The models concentrate on data related to humans in videos that are recorded using the sensors of the HMI system. The information comprises the movement and positioning of the human skeleton and may be viewed as digital twin data(Tian Wang et al., 2021). When it comes to recognizing human movements, the models work accurately. The model is capable of efficiently producing skeletal data from video input. With the help of digital twin data analysis, humans and computers can communicate with the generated information effectively (Tian Wang et al., 2021).

The 3D-ResNet model is shown in Figure 5. It shows the working visualization of the 3D-ResNet model and depiction of various layers in the convolution block where the input is fed to the Model 3D-ResNet which has a convolutional layer, batch normalization layer, activation layer, Pooling layer, and Dropout layer. Once the layers are applied to the input video the output is demonstrated as actions. In human-machine interaction, the videos are recorded using sensors of the HMI system.

Figure 5. 3D-ResNet model

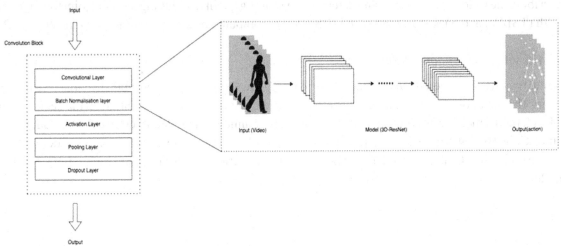

4.2.2.2 Network Slicing

To deliver an assortment of services in 5G networks and resources specifically suited for Industry 4.0, network slicing has emerged as a potential networking architecture. However, because of the virtualized architecture and strict quality-of-service requirements, the increasing network complexity presents a significant problem in network administration. The use of digital twin (DT) technology paves the way for cost-effective and performance-optimal management by digitally simulating the behavior of slicing-enabled networks and forecasting their time-varying performance. To capture the entangled interactions among slices and track their end-to-end (E2E) metrics in a variety of network contexts, a scalable DT of network slicing is used(H. Wang et al., 2022).

Graph neural network model can directly retrieve insights from slicing-enabled networks defined by non-Euclidean graph topologies, and is utilized by the DT. The DT can precisely mimic network behavior and forecast E2E latency in a range of topologies and uncharted situations(H. Wang et al., 2022).

4.2.1.3 Personalized Healthcare

To provide tailored medication, digital twins can be utilized to simulate a person's genomic makeup, physiological traits, and lifestyle. The existing method offers a more individualized focus than precision medicine, which often includes particular groups within a larger population, it is expected to disrupt clinical practice. The human body may be twined to assist in several fields such as therapy evaluation, follow-up monitoring, preventative medicine, and diagnostics [24].

4.2.1.4 Manufacturing

In welding manufacturing, A deep learning-enabled digital twin is created as a virtual digital replica of mechanical welding for joint growth monitoring and penetration control(Qiyue Wang et al.,2020). In such a system, pulsed gas tungsten arc welding gathers the data immediately available from sensors, such as weld pool pictures, arc images, welding current, and arc voltage. By using conventional image processing techniques and deep convolutional neural networks (CNNs), the predominant information describing the weld joint geometry and determining welding quality, including the weld joint top-side bead width (TSBW) and back-side bead width (BSBW), is computed or estimated (Qiyue Wang et al.,2020).

4.2.1.5 Visual Communication

Digital twins (DTs) have a strong virtual simulation, high real-time interaction, and virtuality-reality symbiosis. The sector of education has also benefited from expanded applications. Based on the deep learning (DL) method a model is used to enhance the visual communication (Viscom) course design(Guan-Chen Liu & Chih-Hsiang Ko, 2022). By integrating DL into Viscom courses, instructors may deliver more diverse and sophisticated visual data while increasing the effectiveness of their teachings(Q. Paletta et al., 2021)

4.2.2 Challenges

4.2.2.1 Generalization

The Digital Twin Network must be capable of operating effectively under various unanticipated network conditions. Because training a DTN model takes time and is impractical with each network change, generalization is crucial. Link failure is one such example. It is impossible to restart the training procedure since these changes take place quickly (e.g., in vehicular networks). Modern networks are enormous, making it challenging to simulate them or reproduce them on a test bed to collect the data required to train the DTN model. Because of this, the DTN model may be trained on smaller network versions and then applied to larger real-world networks without suffering much from performance loss(Almasan. P et al., 2022).

4.2.2.2 Flow-Based Operation

To effectively model a network, it is necessary to comprehend the network traffic at a low level. However, the sheer volume of flows in networks creates scaling problems for ML-based approaches(T. Benson et al., 2010). Instead of attempting to simulate each flow, some network systems address the scalability issue using sampling or aggregation approaches. To control how indicative the samples will be, the network operator can adjust the sampling granularity. The majority of the flows, however, are brief and may be invisible to the flow sample method (Almasan. P et al., 2022).

4.2.2.3 Operation with Large Neural Networks

The DTN faces a scaling difficulty due to the efficient functioning of large-scale networks. In these cases, performance and inference costs should increase in step with the network size (bigger topologies necessitate larger DTN models, which have higher inference costs) (Almasan. P et al., 2022).As larger situations are intrinsically more complicated and demand more training time, the training procedure should also scale effectively with the network. The benefits over conventional simulations are lost if a DTN is used on a bigger network and its performance declines or it requires more time to run or train.

4.2.2.4 Data Collection and Storage

Data processing and collecting are difficult and expensive processes. Only useful data is valued, which is often accomplished by employing a standard data format or labeling. However, data in real-world networks originates from many sources and is formatted in various ways. In order to create a common representation that is unrelated to the original data source, the data-gathering process must aggregate or alter the original data. To do this, it is necessary to collect pertinent network-related data using standard telemetry systems(Almasan. P et al., 2022).

The need for enormous amounts of storage is one of the drawbacks of collecting network-related data. For instance, the bulk of flows in production-scale data centers (on the order of thousands of servers) are brief flows or flows with a relatively short life(T. Benson et al., 2010). Keeping track of all flows' data would need hundreds of GB of storage space, which would be difficult to maintain and manage (T. Benson et al., 2010). This necessitates network compression techniques research and a solution to the problem of data size reduction.

4.3 Transfer Learning-Driven Digital Twin Technology

Digital twins have been touted as efficient in various contexts, including fault prediction, virtual commissioning, and reconfiguration planning. Cross-phase industrial transfer learning is one of the many useful applications that may be substantially expanded or made possible by giving Digital Twins artificial intelligence features. Transfer learning is a collection of strategies that improves learning new tasks based on previously learned information in machine learning. Information is moved from one phase of the lifecycle to another to cut down on the size of the data or training time required for a machine learning algorithm(Maschler Benjamin et al., 2021)

To decrease the volume of data or the amount of time required to train a machine learning algorithm, information is transferred from one lifecycle step to another. Adopting this idea will provide various benefits when considering typical obstacles in developing and deploying industrial gear with deep learning functionalities: Learning algorithms are created, programmed, and tested using an intelligent Digital Twin during the design process before the physical system is in place and actual data can be gathered(Benjamin Maschler et al., 2021).

4.3.1 Applications in Various Sectors

4.3.1.1 Fault Diagnosis

A new IT transition is being formed due to the rapid evolution to provide intelligent manufacturing. The stages of the product lifetime include process planning and maintenance for the early detection of potential system faults and proactive management. Big data, the cloud, and the Internet of Things are examples of technological breakthroughs that have adapted digital twins to industrial practice. The automation of the machinery process entails the use of trustworthy technologies to assess the machinery's state and identify faults (Hong Xiao et al., 2021).

A digital twin-assisted defect diagnosis uses deep transfer learning to understand the operational circumstances of machining gear. A k-type thermocouple and a cloud data collecting system through the WiFi module are also included in the intelligent tool holder that has been designed for this system(Hong Xiao et al., 2021).

4.3.1.2 Diagnostic Analysis

Transfer learning is combined with DT in magnetic resonance imaging enhancement. By evaluating the application state of DTs in the medical field and the fundamentals of MRI imaging, a solution for MRI image enhancement based on meta-material composite technology is developed. MRI super-resolution deep neural network structure is built based on deep transfer learning(J. Wang et al., 2022).

4.3.1.3 Renewable Energy systems

A transfer learning framework is proposed after identifying the fundamental problems with power fore-casting and anomaly detection in the context of renewable energy systems. Missing sensor data is the major challenge that is addressed by using an embedding strategy. In the context of organic computing, the suggested TL methods assist in increasing a system's autonomy (Nivarthi, C. P, 2022).

4.3.2 Challenges

4.3.2.1 Negative Transfer

The most challenging part of transfer learning is negative transfer. Transfer learning can only be effective if the initial and target circumstances are sufficiently comparable for the first round of training to be applicable. Developers are free to make logical judgments about what training is "similar enough" to the goal, but the algorithm need not concur. The model could perform worse if it is not trained at all before. There are now no established guidelines for determining whether training programs are properly connected to one another (Naveen Joshi, 2020)

4.3.2.2 Overfitting

Developers cannot eliminate the network layers in transfer learning to identify the best AI models. The dense layers will be impacted if the initial layers are removed because a change in the number of trainable parameters will occur. Dense layers can also be a useful starting point for layer reduction, but determining how many layers and neurons to keep is necessary to prevent the model from overfitting takes time and is difficult. The major drawback of practically all prediction methods is overfitting. One of the prevalent biases in large data is this one. However, overfitting occurs in the context of transfer learning when the new model picks up features and noises from training data that have a detrimental influence on its results(Naveen Joshi, 2020).

5 SENSORS-DRIVEN DIGITAL TWIN TECHNOLOGY

A wide range of sensors and monitors made possible by the Internet of Things has given rise to smart home amenities as well as more efficient and safe business operations. The way that digital and physical worlds interact is evolving because of the Internet of Things and digital twins. Digital twins, which are digital models that virtually replicate their physical counterparts, are interconnected with IoT to enable connection and access to intelligence in the actual world. The rapid growth of IoT sensors contributes to the development of digital twins. In addition, as IoT devices advance, digital-twin scenarios might incorporate simpler, less sophisticated things, providing businesses with even more advantages.

Digital twins can frequently be used to optimize an IoT deployment for optimal efficiency, as well as to assist designers in determining where objects should go or how they should function before they are physically installed. The more accurately a digital twin can represent a physical object, the more likely that the performance and other advantages can be found. IoT serves as the anchor for beacons and sensors and as the archive for isolated data. Workplace management systems, serve as the framework. Without digital twins, the Internet of Things would require far more networking between data origin and use points. Digital twins consolidate all of the company's data, just like your office does.

5.1 Applications in Various Sectors

5.1.1 Education Sector

As students advance through their education, they increasingly struggle to image massive, complex pieces of equipment, which has led to the long-standing idea of using digital twin simulations in instruction. Based on these simulations, it may be expanded to include the simulation of chemical experiments. Early education and demonstrations can be carried out by digital twin simulation as chemical labs become riskier and require frequent adherence to multiple protections.

5.1.2 Aerospace Sector

A digital twin of the spacecraft design can help with design and planning when it is made and restricted to the various external factors that affect the safety of the spacecraft. Using Industry 4.0's digital twin technology, a spacecraft might be created that can endure harsh environments while spending less on R&D.

5.1.3 Health Sector

The process of creating new medications includes time-consuming and expensive clinical studies. Numerous regulations must be followed, and costs keep rising. Additionally, finding and keeping new patients are serious issues. A digital twin could be a great solution.

Digital twins enable the collecting and use of essential data (such as blood pressure, oxygen levels, etc.) at the individual level, allowing people to track persistent diseases and, as a result, their priorities and contacts with doctors by offering fundamental information. As a result, clinical trials and laboratory research data are built on such customized data.

5.1.4 Production and Manufacturing Sector

Digital twins can help simulate unforeseen supply surges and troughs to meet industrial demands and speed up the process overall. Digital twins can help duplicate these abrupt highs and lows in supplies to help meet production demands and streamline the process.

5.2 Challenges

The possibilities of what you can accomplish with digital twin technology are only limited by your imagination, given how quickly Internet of Things (IoT) technology is developing and how much computing power is becoming readily available to enterprises of all kinds. Implementing a digital twin demand are a significant investment of time, money, and engineering power, and just like any project of this size, there are several common risks to avoid.

5.2.1 Using the Same Platform for Several Applications

While it may be tempting to attempt and repurpose a digital twin platform, doing so can, at best, lead to inaccuracy data and, at worst, catastrophic errors. Since each digital twin is entirely specific to a particular part or machine, assets with different operating environments and configurations cannot use the same digital twin platforms.

5.2.2 Large and Rapid Expansion

It is a mistake to try and deploy digital twins for every piece of equipment or program at once. In the long run, a digital twin duplicate of your entire manufacturing line or building is feasible and might offer tremendous insights. Large and Rapid expansion might be expensive and risk you missing important information and setups along the road. Instead of trying to complete everything all at once, focus on perfecting a few key pieces of equipment first, then build upon that foundation.

5.2.3 Lack of Reliable Data Sources

Data collected in the field may contain inaccuracies or duplicate entries brought about by human error. Your digital twin's insights are only as valuable as the data it uses to operate. Because of this, it is crucial to standardize data-gathering procedures across your company and to frequently clean your data of duplicates and mistakes.

5.2.4 Device Communication Protocols Are Not Standardized

Miscommunications can complicate your processes and jeopardize your digital twin endeavor if your IoT devices do not share a common language. Create an IT infrastructure that enables efficient connection between your IoT devices to assure success.

5.2.5 Not Gaining User Acceptance

Users from all points along the value chain of your product are involved in an effective digital twin strategy. It is crucial that your users comprehend and value the benefits that your digital twin offers both to them personally and to your company as a whole. A lack of user participation can obstruct all of your efforts if there is a lack of buy-in brought on by uncertainty, lack of confidence, or opposition.

6 CLOUD AND EDGE COMPUTING DRIVEN DIGITAL TWINS

Digital twins are the preferred method for integrating and achieving interoperability across real and virtual domains. Digital twins can be categorized into three levels: unit level, system level, and system of systems level (SoS) from a hierarchical standpoint. Edge computing and cloud computing are introduced to integrate with Digital twins at various levels for function enhancement to meet the practical needs of smart manufacturing.

In a process of value generation, smart manufacturing involves many different parties. The Digital twins can be separated into different levels, depending on the diverse data magnitudes in smart manufacturing and the various temporal sensitivities of smart applications. Status perception, data analysis, decision-making, and execution are all included in each level's data closed loop. But because different levels have different functions and infrastructures, a key problem is how to establish multiple levels of digital twins for smart manufacturing.

Solutions to the problem could be found in edge computing and cloud computing. Cloud computing offers pervasive, accessible, on-demand network access to a shared resource pool. Cloud computing is the ideal technology solution for the SoS-level Digital twin due to on-demand resource sharing, high computation and storage capabilities, and low costs.

By using edge computing, data processing can be done closer to the data sources. The edge can be described as the point where data providers and consumers meet. Edge computing will be quite helpful for the unit-level Digital twin.

6.1 Three-Level Digital Twin Framework

Manufacturers are dealing with data growth that is exploding due to the increasing applications of New IT in manufacturing. The fundamental idea behind a Digital twin is to use sensors to collect data from physical objects and the environment, compute that data in a virtual environment, and then use that analysis to control the physical objects and surroundings. The contact and fusion between the physical space and the virtual space are created as a result, creating the data closed loop. There are distinct needs for data processing and data circulation at different levels of Digital twins in manufacturing, including latency, bandwidth Digital twin, security, etc. The implementation of the unit-level, system-level, and SoS-level Digital twins is given new concepts and approaches by edge computing and cloud computing with complementing qualities. Digital twins deployed at the unit level based on edge computing and at the SoS level based on cloud computing can achieve asset control, management, optimization, and business optimization from the perspective of resource efficiency (Tao et al., 2019).

Three level digital twin Framework is shown in Figure 6. The Three-level digital twin framework depicts the structure of the three-level digital twin which includes computing models at each level as edge computing is implemented at the unit level likewise fog computing at the system level and cloud computing at the system of system level. The Figure explains the working of the systems at different levels which leads to the working of the digital twin. At the System of system level, all the sensor data concerning their network connections are stored in the customized cloud storage and analysis of enterprises that operate those sensors that are embedded in the physical devices at the unit level, whereas the system level is a processing level in which all the data received from the end devices (sensors) is processed and organized.

Figure 6. Three level digital twin Framework

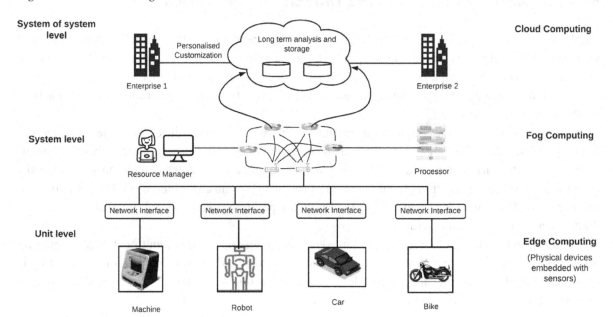

6.2 Edge Computing Driven Digital Twin

The fundamental conditions that must be fulfilled to build a unit-level Digital twin are state awareness, computation and data processing, and control of physical things. Edge computing is an architecture that brings cloud computing, networking, and storage capabilities to the edge, enabling object perception, computation, and control through data processing in edge nodes. The unit level Digital twin is made up of the production resources (machine, robot, component, AGV, etc.) along with physical components (machine body, spindle, tools, etc.) and cyber components (embedded system, a sensing device, etc.).

The physical devices can be controlled by the cyber parts using an actuator that can take control commands, and the cyber parts can monitor and perceive information from the physical devices. Edge computing can be implemented on the unit-level Digital twin, which is a type of edge node, thanks to its observation, data analysis, and control capabilities. Edge computing can use smaller apps to help deliver better real-time responses because of the data that is circulating on the unit device.

Applications for real-time processing and analysis of sensory input, data buffering, high-performance real-time control, actuator monitoring, defect detection, health feature extraction, cycle count accumulation, fault handling, and safe shutdown are all provided by edge computing at the unit level. For instance, sensors are employed on a machine tool or robot arm to determine whether certain failures may provide a safety risk. Delay is intolerable in this situation. The response time can be excessively long if the data is transferred to the cloud. However, because the data is close to the data source, edge computing reduces the time delay, enabling judgments to be made instantly. The unit-level Digital twin benefits from the edge computing architecture's lack of reliance on an Internet connection.

6.3 Cloud Computing Driven Digital Twin

By creating a smart service platform, it is possible to optimize several system-level Digital twins together. An SOS-level Digital twin is therefore made up of several system-level Digital twins. A smart cloud service platform, for instance, enables collaboration between several production lines or factories, ensuring enterprise-wide system integration throughout the product lifecycle. The SOS-level Digital twin involves a variety of individuals and resources, some of which may be scattered geographically. The SOS-level Digital twin's data is richer and more varied. Therefore, in order to fulfill the requirements for the SoS-level Digital twin, it is necessary to provide distributed data processing and storage as well as data and smart services for enterprise collaboration. The organization and control of numerous linked devices, as well as the combining and integration of an enterprise's internal and external data, are all made possible by the cloud computing architecture.

Through the application software, various types of storage devices can collaborate in the cloud computing architecture to jointly provide data storage and business access for organizations. Additionally, the distributed processing and virtualization technologies that are typical of cloud computing must facilitate big data mining. SoS-level Digital twin analysis and long-term, huge data storage are both best suited for cloud computing as a technology. Additionally, services that exhibit interoperability open the door for system-level Digital twin collaboration. Because of the cloud design, different unit-level Digital twins or system-level Digital twins can be packaged as services and shared by other participants as plug-and-play components. In this method, manufacturers can use a variety of resources pay-as-you-go and conveniently supply their services to their cooperative stakeholders.

In conclusion, the cloud computing architecture offers greater architectural flexibility and increased use of outside data for new product development and value creation. Understanding the aggregate data view can be useful for supply chain applications and product modification, for instance.

Cloud and Edge Driven Digital Twins with Sensors are shown in Figure -7. IoT can generally benefit from the almost limitless capabilities and resources of the Cloud to make up for its technological limitations (e.g., storage, processing, and communication). To name a few, the cloud can provide a practical solution for IoT service composition and management, as well as for building programs and services that make use of the objects or the data they generate. On the other hand, IoT can help the cloud by broadening its application to interact with real-world objects in a more distributed and dynamic way and by enabling the delivery of new services in a variety of real-life circumstances. Many times, the cloud might act as an intermediary layer, masking all the complexity and features required to create the apps (A.Botta et al., 2016)

6.4 Applications in Different Sectors

A future unlike anything we've ever experienced might be made possible by the fusion of e-tools and gadgets. Computer applications can be used to optimize a future day. People anthropomorphize edge computing and virtual twin-powered device when they first hear about this concept, which gives the idea a poor reputation. However, given that edge computing can quickly minimize risk, this couldn't be further from the truth. Digital twins are of huge value to the business and daily life because of their capacity to accurately forecast future events.

Figure 7. Cloud and Edge Driven Digital Twin with Sensors

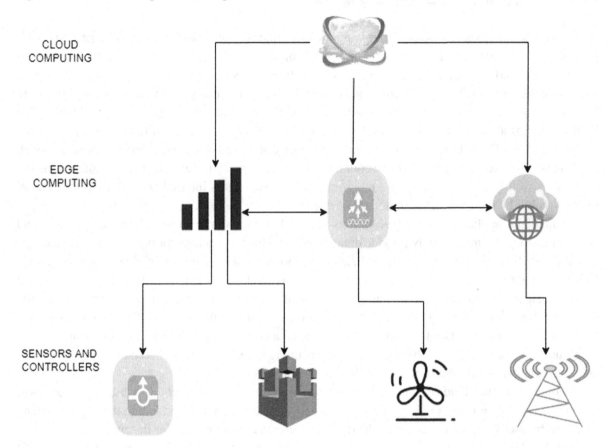

6.4.1 The Automobile Sector

The automobile industry has seen substantial change in the past 10 years as a result of the public's quick acceptance of electric vehicles. Edge computing and simulations can help shrink the gap and usher in the age of self-driving cars even if there is still a long way to go before electric cars can drive themselves.

In contrast to cloud-based computing, which is a data transformation technique that helps store data remotely, edge computing enables the speedy movement of data because the data storage unit is located locally. This implies that, in contrast to cloud-based vehicles, cars using this technology might make judgments significantly more quickly (Q. Qi et al., 2018) regarding whether to brake, start driving, make turns, etc.

A constantly expanding consciousness field can be created by the technology to help our vehicles navigate the terrain and avoid collisions by scanning potential roadblocks (such as other vehicles, humans crossing the road, etc.) and using edge computing to determine whether to stop, slow down, or outsmart them. This can be combined with Digital twin technology, which has the ability to simulate future reality.When it comes to Digital twins, the automotive business is unique. Technology has a lot of profit-making potential. We are holding a symposium on improving digital twin computing in order to assist manufacturers in lowering development costs, increasing productivity, and dramatically increasing sustainability in the automotive industry.

6.4.2 Reduce Industrial Injuries

Together, these two technologies will provide steadily safer and more secure workplaces. If edge computing technology is combined with online platform-based simulations, the ongoing issue of work-related injuries can be solved. If the digital twin technology is combined with edge computing, the workspace environment might be monitored in real-time by successfully integrating digital twin technology into work environments and creating completely constructed digital replicas of offices and buildings. This implies that danger-posing workplace dangers and hazards can be avoided before they occur.

6.4.3 Use of Digital Twins to Enhance Edge Computing

Though designed to model future events, ascertain context, and create a chain of consequences, digital twin technology can also help edge computing with real-time algorithm improvement, making the world a little bit safer every single second. For instance, having a developed digital twin of the terrain and the vehicle can help computing technologies predict what changes it needs to execute and make the journey safe and successful if a self-driven vehicle encounters drastic weather changes, newly generated traffic jams, or course changes.

6.5 Challenges

To give employees the chance to interact with the "digital twin" and make decisions in real-time, connectivity must be quick, assured, and available throughout the various locations where the organization is based. Unfortunately, in many Italian realities, this infrastructure condition cannot still be taken for granted(Farsagli, S, 2019).

Hardware, or computer power, is needed to handle the vital sensors attached to the digital twin effectively and to enable real-time processing of the data that is already available. Long life cycles, or building the digital twin while keeping in mind that many of the assets for which this technology is utilized have a long-life cycle that typically goes well beyond the usefulness of the proprietary software used for their design, simulation, or analytics (W.[Shi et al., 2016). This prompts us to think about the technology chosen as a success element while taking into consideration its longevity.

Data collection from various sources, intellectual capital, and hence value for enterprises, security, which has become transversal to numerous business sectors, is also evoked and poses a challenge. Security must be secured to prevent any harm to the company. The creation and administration of this technology will be aided by human resources, which are also at the core of the Digital Twin (W.Shi et al., 2016).

7 CONCLUSION

In two important ways, digital twins can promote sustainability. Currently, they are mostly used to collect, organize, and present data in order to provide a realistic representation of the outside world. This can assist us in comprehending and quantifying what is occurring and in combining data from many sources to determine the effects of our decisions. However, the digital model can also be employed as a foresight tool. This can demonstrate what is likely to occur in the future, contrast potential outcomes, and predict the results of certain decisions before they are made. These qualities may provide substantial advantages in a number of different industries. The dynamic nature of the modeling makes it useful for topics like crowd and traffic management and logistics optimization in addition to asset management. Importantly for sustainability, twinning can also assist with electricity grid balancing, water network flow forecasting, and resilience-building in the face of climate change impacts. To maximize the advantages, digital twins must be expanded from concentrating solely on individual assets to include entire processes, even entire businesses or cities.

Recent years have witnessed a change in the rise of the use of digital twins, which has been aided by an increase in the number of papers published and significant investments in the technology's development by key players in various sectors. Digital twin plays an important role in replicating the instances of physical assets. With the development of IoT, big data, and deep learning it gain more popularity in different sectors. In this book chapter, we have presented an overview of digital twin technologies and their applications in different sectors. Digital twin architecture based on cloud and sensor technologies is presented. We found that the manufacturing sector is the focus of the majority of Digital Twin research. The number of publications covering Digital Twins for smart cities and healthcare is substantially lower than the number of papers discussing manufacturing, indicating research needs in these fields. Digital twins for healthcare and smart cities are two more topics of growing attention, according to the analysis done above. As a result, the chapter adds to a comprehensive evaluation that covers not just manufacturing but also healthcare and smart cities. The limitations of this chapter are that various architectures were not much explored based on different technologies. Challenges in the implementation of digital twins are identified as an investment of time, computational resources, capturing of physical properties of objects accurately, automatic updates on real data, communication between physical and digital things, conflict detection, and its resolution to name a few. A categorical review of recent studies is produced after a review of publications on digital twins enabling technologies. Even though the concept of the Digital twin has come into the picture in recent years, there are still a variety of interpretations. We have also introduced the digital twin and its benefits as well as its importance in real-life situations. An overview of artificial intelligence-driven digital twin, Sensor driven digital twin, and cloud, edge computing-driven digital twin has been provided with its challenges. This chapter facilitates researchers to understand and analyze the challenges in different sectors and provide cost-effective solutions.

REFERENCES

Alexopoulos, K., Nikolakis, N., & Chryssolouris, G. (2020). Digital twin-driven supervised machine learning for the development of artificial intelligence applications in manufacturing. *International Journal of Computer Integrated Manufacturing*, *33*(5), 1–11. doi:10.1080/0951192X.2020.1747642

Allen, A., Siefkas, A., Pellegrini, E., Burdick, H., Barnes, G., Calvert, J., Mao, Q., & Das, R. (2021). A Digital Twins Machine Learning Model for Forecasting Disease Progression in Stroke Patients. *Applied Sciences (Basel, Switzerland)*, *11*(12), 5576. doi:10.3390/app11125576

AlmasanP.GalmésM.F.PaillisséJ.Suárez-VarelaJ.PerinoD.LópezD.R.PeralesA.A.HarveyP.CiavagliaL.WongL.RamV.R.XiaoS.ShiX.ChengX.Cabellos-AparicioA.Barlet-RosP. (2022).

Bachinger Bachinger, F., Kronberger, G., & Affenzeller, M. (2021). Continuous improvement and adaptation of predictive models in smart manufacturing and model management. *IET Collab. Intell. Manuf*, *3*(1), 48–63. doi:10.1049/cim2.12009

Benson, T., Akella, A., & Maltz, D. A. (2010). Network traffic characteristics of data centers in the wild. *Proc. of the ACM SIGCOMM Conf. on Internet Measure., ser. IMC '10*. 10.1145/1879141.1879175

Botta, A., De Donato, W., Persico, V., & Pescapé, A. (2016). Integration of cloud computing and internet of things: A survey. *Future Generation Computer Systems*, *56*, 684700. doi:10.1016/j.future.2015.09.021

Chakraborty, S., & Adhikari, S. (2021). Machine learning-based digital twin for dynamical systems with multiple time scales. *Computers & Structures, 243*, 106410.

Chen, D., & Lv, Z. (2022). Artificial intelligence-enabled Digital Twins for training autonomous cars. *Internet of Things and Cyber-Physical Systems*, *2*, 31–41. doi:10.1016/j.iotcps.2022.05.001

Croatti, A., Gabellini, M., Montagna, S., & Ricci, A. (2020). On the integration of agents and digital twins in healthcare. *Journal of Medical Systems*, *44*(9), 1–8. doi:10.100710916-020-01623-5 PMID:32748066

Dang, H. V., Tatipamula, M., & Nguyen, H. X. (2021). Cloud-based digital twinning for structural health monitoring using deep learning. *IEEE Transactions on Industrial Informatics*, *18*(6), 3820–3830. doi:10.1109/TII.2021.3115119

Dhiman, J. (2021, August 22). *Is Machine Learning the future of Data Quality?* Academic Press.

Farsagli, S. (2019, August 20). *What are the developments, challenges, and opportunities for businesses provided by Digital Twin?* Ingenium.

Fuller, A., Fan, Z., Day, C., & Barlow, C. (2020). Digital Twin: Enabling Technologies, Challenges, and Open Research. *IEEE Access: Practical Innovations, Open Solutions*, *8*, 108952–108971. doi:10.1109/ACCESS.2020.2998358

Ghosh, A. K., Ullah, A. S., & Kubo, A. (2019). Hidden Markov model-based digital twin construction for futuristic manufacturing systems. *Artificial Intelligence for Engineering Design, Analysis and Manufacturing*, *33*(3), 317–331. doi:10.1017/S089006041900012X

Ghosh, A. K., Ullah, A. S., Teti, R., & Kubo, A. (2021). Developing sensor signal-based digital twins for intelligent machine tools. *Journal of Industrial Information Integration*, *24*, 100242. doi:10.1016/j.jii.2021.100242

Girletti, L., Groshev, M., Guimarães, C., Bernardos, C. J., & de la Oliva, A. (2020, December). An intelligent edge-based digital twin for robotics. In 2020 IEEE Globecom Workshops (GC Wkshps) (pp. 1-6). IEEE. doi:10.1109/GCWkshps50303.2020.9367549

Hofmann, W., & Branding, F. (2019). Implementation of an IoT-and cloud-based digital twin for real-time decision support in port operations. *IFAC-PapersOnLine*, *52*(13), 2104–2109. doi:10.1016/j.ifacol.2019.11.516

Howard. (2022, January 21). *5 Advantages of Integrating Neural Networks into Your Digital Twins.* Academic Press.

Ibrahim, M. S., Fan, J., Yung, W. K. C., Prisacaru, A., Driel, W., Fan, X., & Zhang, G. (2020). Machine Learning and Digital Twin Driven Diagnostics and Prognostics of Light-Emitting Diodes. *Laser & Photonics Reviews*, *14*(12), 2000254. doi:10.1002/lpor.202000254

Joshi, N. (2020). *Exploring the limits of transfer learning.* https://www.bbntimes.com/technology/exploring-the-limits-of-transfer-learning

Kevan. (2020, January 31). *AI Rewrites the Possibilities of Digital Twin.* DE247 Digital Engineering.

Khajavi, S. H., Motlagh, N. H., Jaribion, A., Werner, L. C., & Holmström, J. (2019). Digital twin: Vision, benefits, boundaries, and creation for buildings. *IEEE Access : Practical Innovations, Open Solutions*, *7*, 147406–147419.

Kumar, S., Bongale, A., Patil, S., Bongale, A. M., Kamat, P., & Kotecha, K. (2020). Demystifying Artificial Intelligence based Digital Twins in Manufacturing-A Bibliometric Analysis of Trends and Techniques. *Libr. Philos. Pract*, *2020*, 1–21.

Liu, G.-C., & Chih-Hsiang, K. (2022). Exploring Multiple Application Scenarios of Visual Communication Course Using Deep Learning Under the Digital Twins. *Computational Intelligence and Neuroscience*, *2022*, 5844290. doi:10.1155/2022/5844290 PMID:35211166

Marr, B. (2017). What is digital twin technology-and why is it so important? *Forbes*, *6*(March), 2017.

Maschler, Braun, Jazdi, & Weyrich. (2021). Transfer learning as an enabler of the intelligent digital twin. *Procedia CIRP, 100*, 127-132.

Maschler, B., Braun, D., Jazdi, N., & Weyrich, M. (2021). Transfer learning as an enabler of the intelligent digital twin. *Procedia CIRP*, *100*, 127–132. doi:10.1016/j.procir.2021.05.020

Nivarthi, C. P. (2022). Transfer Learning as an Essential Tool for Digital Twins in Renewable Energy Systems. In S. Tomforde & C. Krupitzer (Ed.), *Organic Computing -- Doctoral Dissertation Colloquium 2021* (pp. 47-59). Kassel University Press.

Paletta, Q., Arbod, G., & Lasenby, J. (2021). Benchmarking of deep learning irradiance forecasting models from sky images - an in-depth analysis. *Solar Energy*, *224*, 855–867. doi:10.1016/j.solener.2021.05.056

Platenius-Mohr, M., Malakuti, S., Grüner, S., Schmitt, J., & Goldschmidt, T. (2020). File- and API-based interoperability of digital twins by model transformation: An IIoT case study using asset administration shell. *Future Generation Computer Systems*, *113*, 94–105. Advance online publication. doi:10.1016/j.future.2020.07.004

Priyanka, E. B., Thangavel, S., Gao, X. Z., & Sivakumar, N. S. (2022). Digital twin for oil pipeline risk estimation using prognostic and machine learning techniques. *Journal of Industrial Information Integration*, *26*, 100272. doi:10.1016/j.jii.2021.100272

Qi, Q., Tao, F., Zuo, Y., & Zhao, D. (2018). Digital twin service towards smart manufacturing. *Procedia CIRP*, *72*, 237242. doi:10.1016/j.procir.2018.03.103

Roy, D., Mazumder, O., Khandelwal, S., & Sinha, A. (2021, June). Wearable sensor-driven Cardiac model to derive hemodynamic insights during exercise. In *Proceedings of the Workshop on Body-Centric Computing Systems* (pp. 30-35). 10.1145/3469260.3469670

Shah, S. A., Shukla, D., Bentafat, E., & Bakiras, S. (2021). The Role of AI, Machine Learning, and Big Data in Digital Twinning: A Systematic Literature Review, Challenges, and Opportunities. *IEEE Access: Practical Innovations, Open Solutions*, 9, 32030–32052. doi:10.1109/ACCESS.2021.3060863

Shi, W., Cao, J., Zhang, Q., Li, Y., & Xu, L. (2016). Edge computing: Vision and challenges. *IEEE Internet of Things Journal*, 3(5), 637646. doi:10.1109/JIOT.2016.2579198

Tao, F., Zhang, M., & Nee, A. (2019). *Digital Twin and Cloud*. Fog, Edge Computing., doi:10.1016/B978-0-12-817630-6.00008-4

Wang, H., Wu, Y., Min, G., & Miao, W. (2022, February). A Graph Neural Network-Based Digital Twin for Network Slicing Management. *IEEE Transactions on Industrial Informatics*, 18(2), 1367–1376. doi:10.1109/TII.2020.3047843

Wang, J., Qiao, L., Lv, H., & Lv, Z. (2022). Deep Transfer Learning-based Multi-modal Digital Twins for Enhancement and Diagnostic Analysis of Brain MRI Image. IEEE/ACM Transactions on Computational Biology and Bioinformatics. doi:10.1109/TCBB.2022.3168189

Wang, Q., Jiao, W., & Zhang, Y. M. (2020). Deep learning-empowered digital twin for visualized weld joint growth monitoring and penetration control. *Journal of Manufacturing Systems, 57*, 429-439.

Wang, T., Li, J., Deng, Y., Wang, C., Snoussi, H., & Tao, F. (2021). Digital twin for human-machine interaction with a convolutional neural network. Issue 7-8: Digital Twin-enabled Smart Industrial Systems. *Recent Developments and Future Perspectives, 34*, 888–897.

Xiao, H., Zeng, H., Jiang, W., Zhou, Y., & Tu, X. (2022, December). HMM-TCN-based health assessment and state prediction for robot mechanical axis. *International Journal of Intelligent Systems*, 37(12), 10476–10494. Advance online publication. doi:10.1002/int.22621

Yang, C., Li, Y., Yang, Y., Liu, Z., & Liao, M. (2022). Transfer Learning-enabled Modelling Framework for Digital Twin. *IEEE 25th International Conference on Computer Supported Cooperative Work in Design (CSCWD)*, 113-118. 10.1109/CSCWD54268.2022.9776083

Chapter 19
Digital Twin Understanding, Current Progressions, and Future Perspectives

Megha Gupta
MSCW, University of Delhi, India

Nida Khan
J.C. Bose University of Science and Technology, YMCA, India

ABSTRACT

The digital twin is a burgeoning technology that has just recently gained popularity. The term "digital twin" refers to a virtual twin that is put on site with sensors that collect real-time data. Hard real-time embedded operating systems are required for operating systems that enable digital twins, which use real-time data. Digital twin indicates a virtual replica that takes into account both device dynamics and individual component parts. The digital twin's primary dynamic is represented by each and every component or gadget. Regardless of the gadget's physical, internal, or functional aspects, the physical device handles them all. The use of digital twins has grown around the globe. Different technologies, such as IoT, AI, ML, data mining, cloud computing, and others, benefit from this technique. This chapter presented the detailed view of this rapidly expanding field of study along with several digital twins application fields, emerging concerns, and future prospects. Also, this chapter discussed the relation between digital twin and latest technologies such as IoT, AI, etc.

1. INTRODUCTION

The digital twin is a burgeoning technology that has just recently gained popularity. The term "digital twin" refers to a virtual twin that is put on site with sensors that collect real-time data. Hard real-time embedded operating systems are required for operating systems that enable digital twins, which use real-time data. Digital twin indicates to a virtual replica that takes into account both device dynamics and individual component parts. The digital twin's primary dynamic is represented by each and every

DOI: 10.4018/978-1-6684-6821-0.ch019

component or gadget. Regardless of the gadget's physical, internal, or functional aspects, the physical device handles them all. Two decades ago, for the first time, the notion was introduced to the industrial business. ANSYS, IBM, Microsoft, SAP, PTC, and Oracle are just a few of the big names using digital twin technologies now-a-days. Growth in technology is a good indicator of how far a location has come in the recent past. The use of digital twins has grown around the globe. Some current locations where digital twins are serving include the United States, Canada, Germany and the United Kingdom as well as many more countries. In the digital world, a digital twin is a virtual representation or system that resembles its real-world counterpart. Different technologies, such as Internet of Things, Artificial Intelligence, Machine Learning, Data Mining, Cloud Computing, and others, benefit from this technique. The topic of IoT is one that is both exciting and rapidly expanding. To a large extent, sensor-based modelling is at the heart of it. Devices with digital twins are being developed and deployed to keep track of every aspect of the gadget. Machine learning is critical to the success of digital twins. In machine learning, a computer learns from the data it collects via sensors. Cloud computing and data mining are only two examples of the many technologies that make up digital twining.

As it has grown in popularity, this cutting-edge technology has encroached on almost every industry. Manufacturing, healthcare, astronomical, retail, and transportation are all examples of these industries. Production may be increased significantly by using digital twins. For example, digital technology is having a significant impact on the healthcare industry. Patient monitoring and disease dissemination by touch are both made easier with the assistance of digital twins. In the astronomy business, NASA was the first to collaborate with digital twin technology. When it comes to anticipating severe catastrophes, a digital doppelganger is being built for Earth. Closed-loop analysis of the in-store purchasing experience using digital twins has revolutionized retail. Transport is a critical area for the establishment of any new technology. Using real-time data generated by the digital twin, traffic controllers are able to better manage the flow of traffic. Automatons have a variety of characteristics that allow them to thrive in a constantly evolving environment of information exchange, processing, and functioning. In addition to affinity, division of functionality, computerized footprints, and sharp and amalgamated changes, digital twins also have certain key traits.

Affinity is the driving force behind digital twin technology. In order to use this method, you must have some kind of network connection. The actual and virtual twins are linked in some way. Additionally, digital twins allow for functional segmentation, which is another benefit. This simplifies the process of creating a doppelgänger in the desired setting. Customization is another benefit of segmentation. When a digital twin is used to solve a problem, it leaves behind specific traces or footprints. By recording the footprints that are utilized to handle the downs that are connected to the previously travelled issue, this is done. Digital twins have been proven to be much improved. Digital twins are employed in Internet of Things-based smart devices. A reprogrammable domain is produced by all smart devices' digital twins. Thus, it is possible to radically alter the virtual copy. One of the best features of digital twin technology is its ability to amalgamate. It is often referred to as the physical mixing of information. Information is combined to create a digital twin. Even though digital twin has been there for more than two decades, it is still making a name for itself on the worldwide market for technological growth. The digital twin market is expected to grow to $13,020 in revenue by 2027. The ominous technology will see an increase in demand. There was a dramatic increase in the development of this technology with the outbreak of Covid-19. Benefits in the digital twin are projected to be extended in the near future. As digital twins use real-time data, the person may somehow be linked to their actions.

Nowadays this subject is the focus of a great deal of investigation. The work (Nee & Ong, 2021) gives broad view about the role of Digital twin in industrial market. This paper details the recent success of digital twins in the industrial department. For financial services, John Blicq underlines the role of digital twins in his work (Blicq, 2021). The use of digital twins to transform financial services is the focus of this short book. Digital twins may help extend the life of equipment in use, according to the authors (Armendia et al., 2019). Herwig et al. (2021) published the first book on digital twins and bioprocessing. Authors studied about digital twin in bioprocessing and also explains how to use smart manufacturing in a cost-effective manner.

The work (Evangeline, 2021) illustrates the various disciplines and systems that are getting developed recently by including digital twin mechanism. Digital twin works with various latest technology is demonstrated in their work. Yeh et al. (2019) examines the background of various models that uses digital twin for manufacturing in IoT devices that provides smart manufacturing services. The benefits of healthcare and digital twin technologies are well-documented in (El Saddik, 2022), as are the difficulties that may arise during implementation. Raghunathan and Barma (2019) provides an in-depth look of digital twin technology, covering every nuance down to the architecture. Anand Iyer (2017) explores almost every possible use of digital twin technology. Multi-media applications of twin technology are the focus of the book (Shanmuganathan et al., 2022). For a variety of reasons, using the most recent technology and multi-media data is critical.

This chapter serves as an introduction for academics and practitioners who are interested in learning about essential parts of the new and quickly increasing field of research on Digital Twins. It is divided into following sub-sections:

- Attributes of Digital Twins
- Digital Twins & Others Technologies
- Digital Twins Application Domains
- Digital Twins Issues and Challenges
- Digital Twins Future Prospective

2. ATTRIBUTES OF DIGITAL TWINS

A digital twin is a detailed representation of an actual physical thing. We can envision what could happen to actual assets in the future with the aid of digital twins.

What is a digital twin? A digital twin is a virtual representation of a physical thing that uses simulation, machine learning, and intelligence to assist in decision-making. A digital twin may also be a system that lasts the life of the object and is constantly updated with new data (Armstrong, 2020). It wasn't until 2010 that NASA defined a digital twin for spacecraft physical-model simulation, although Michael Grieves of the University of Michigan presented the concept of a digital twin back in 2002.

Additionally, digital twins are frequently referred to as being able to represent a counterpart from the actual world in a highly intricate virtual replica. The digital twin is taking into account all of the actual object's dynamic aspects. Figure 1 depicts how it imprints the overall existential trajectory of the device's design, foundation, and operation. It's important to examine the ground engineering tools, which include the materials needed to build structures and all of the bit aspects, during the actual design process. As we go forward, our primary focus will be on formulating real results. An emphasis here is placed on achieving the desired outcome while maintaining tight tolerances. The device's output is handled in the last phase of operation, which is known as the functioning phase. Feedback generated in this phase helps the product age and improves programming in the earlier stages. As seen in Figure 2, there are just a few key traits that have made digital twins so sought after in the previous two decades. The following is a breakdown of the digital twin's high-quality qualities (Takyar, n.d.)

1. Affinity

Affinity is one of the main reasons why digital twins are so difficult to create. A physical asset in the deployment region is used to link the virtual copy. Sensor data may be sent in real-time with the help of this feature. This is a critical element for expanding the scope of any technology's potential applications. Connectivity to the data source is required for analysis in today's environment since data is such an important topic. Data is really critical as one has to implement certain in order to manage large amounts of data. Affinity become a really important element in digital. The digital twin is associated with a technology that handles real-time data. Real-time data is highly critical and vast to manage at a go. Affinity enables users to connect with data in real-time. Increased connection to data reduces the risk of data errors. It is a prominent aspect of the digital twin.

Figure 1. Lifecycle of a Device

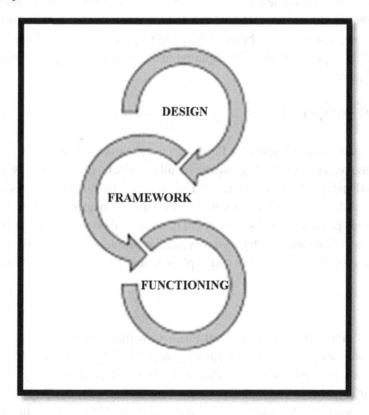

Figure 2. Characteristics of Digital twin

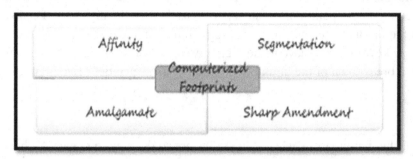

2. Functionality Segmentation

Digital twin technology has a key element of functional segmentation. Using this function, a large work may be broken down into smaller ones, making it much easier to do. This method ensures that the digital twin is able to carry out the prescribed work in an appropriate way. The technology of this kind benefits greatly from modularity. When a job is broken down into smaller modules, the overall issue is more effectively handled. Modules are created via digital twin technology. Various functions are handled by each of the other modules. The operational burden is reduced through segmentation. Even the odds of seeing mistakes are made easier. Also handling and managing modules becomes easier as bugs and defects are easier to tackle in such cases. Adding a new feature is not a complex task to manage with as modularity gives ease of re-useability. Segmenting a particular task is beneficial as digital twin technology is extremely large and wide to be captured in a module or two. It requires a mechanism that handles sub-divided tasks efficiently.

3. Computerized Footprints

Another benefit of digital twin technology is the ability to save traces of previously solved problems. If an issue arises before it can be resolved, it may be readily confronted. This is only feasible if the issue has already happened and has been documented. Using digital twin technology, you may take use of this incredible functionality. Now, this feature makes digital twin majorly applicable in major domains. In this outcome of some particular inputs or problem is saved. This saved result is used to progressively handle the problem associated with such previously similar problem. This one-of-a-kind characteristic is the ability to store a solution to one issue and apply it to another that has a similar structure.

4. Amalgamate

The ability to utilize information in its physical form is another crucial characteristic of digital twin technology. The homogeneity of data or information in physical form might lead to the creation of a digital twin. This means that data is accumulated and may be utilized in its physical form in a digital twin at the most basic level of the concept. Before any models are built, this physical data is fine-tuned. Block chain technology can be considered as a popular use case for following up the policy of digital twin which is amalgamation (Taylor, n.d.). Amalgating is somewhat related to blending. Digital twin when sort of linked with block chain turns several advantages. These perks majorly comprises of the decentralized infrastructure and reliable resources.

5. Sharp Amendment

IoT devices that can be reprogrammed and deliver smart services are the primary focus of digital twins. Technology for creating digital twins has been greatly improved. As a result, smart gadgets are better able to carry out their tasks. Digital twin technology podcasts are available for the whole lifecycle of any Internet of Things (IoT) gadget that incorporates it. Digital twin technology is a major legacy of the Internet of Things (IoT). When it comes to achieving desired outcomes, IoT relies on clever technologies. All intended outcomes of real-time challenges may be achieved with the help of digital twins that can be reprogrammed and sharpened using smart technology. Digital twin have impact on almost major domain of development. One of them which easy finds to adapt this feature of the technology is manufacturing. Sharp amendment is crucial aspect of the technology. It's highly responsible for certain major functionality related to the manufacturing industry (Friedericha et al., 2022). Smart manufacturing with digital twin is excellent in terms of advancement in traditional manufacturing industry as well as the better outcome. This some way gives an ease of managing industry so well and efficiently.

3. DIGITAL TWINS & OTHERS TECHNOLOGIES

Technology like the Internet of Things (IoT), Artificial Intelligence (AI), Machine Learning (ML), Data Mining (DM), Cloud Computing (CC) all help digital twins.

1. DT & IoT

A digital twin is a virtual version of a real asset, equipment, vehicle, or gadget on the Internet of Things platform. It represents data, procedures, operational status, and assets in a digital form. With the help of digital twins in industries, airports, machine shops etc., you can eliminate any risk of data loss or missing information. When it comes to smart gadgets, this function attracts a lot of attention. Transparency between the user and the device service provider is becoming vital with the advent of smart gadgets. Further accuracy in forecasting and trend analysis may be achieved by using data obtained. Digital twin technology may be used to build pre-defined models based on raw data. It's the last and most beneficial phase of an operation, and it helps the customer make changes to their marketing plan based on the latest trends. Documentation and communication are the only things the client cares about. Documentation produced by a smart device implementer based on analysis and prediction is the main concern of the client. With the ever-expanding IoT services, digital twin technology may be used to integrate several systems. IoT devices may now be found in a variety of settings. With the use of Internet of Things (IoT) devices, digital twin technology may be made smart and programmable. As a result, the automation of the digital twin has been greatly improved. Presently using Oracle Internet of Things cloud service to build applications (Oracle, n.d.).

2. DT & AI

As digital twins and artificial intelligence come together, we will see transformations on a scale we have never seen before (Zhihan & Xie, 2021). The use of artificial intelligence in digital twin technology makes it easier to integrate this technology into a system based on digital twin technology. When it comes to making predictions and conducting searches, artificial intelligence relies on a standard algorithm. On the basis of traditional AI, there are several algorithms accessible in artificial intelligence. Artificial intelligence is a critical component of digital twin technology for achieving certain goals. In order to create an intelligent system, the purpose of combining the most recent technology is to develop such algorithms. Further research is needed to determine whether or not this approach is truly being utilized to make predictions about outcomes. This calculation is pooled if the previous analysis was correct. Any future issue with comparable plots will be digitally traced back in order to forecast desired outcomes. Digital tracing, a key element of digital twin technology, may be used to save computation repetition via intelligent systems.

3. DT & ML

Digital twin technology is benefiting greatly from the coordinated efforts of machine learning and artificial intelligence. Analyzing data is the cornerstone of digital twin technology's programming. Predefined machine learning models offer better analysis. Unsupervised, supervised, and reinforced methods may all be used to get the best possible results, but only one can be used at a time. To make sense of the information, machine learning algorithms are used to crunch the numbers. The goal of machine learning is to find the best possible model that can accurately predict the result.

4. DT & DM

By leveraging a preexisting data mining technique, data preparation is made possible. Using data mining, retailers may better understand their customers' attitudes about purchasing decisions by not just preprocessing the data but also creating patterns from it. Patterns that are concealed in the acquired data may now be discovered thanks to this new technology. Digital twin employs data mining to ensure that the sensors' data is error-free. Data refinement is a primary goal of data mining, which makes heavy use of digital twin technology. The acquired data is really being used to power the digital twin technology. It is possible to identify specific correlations between the data gathered and utilized for prediction and analysis by using particular data mining methods. The customer may now provide services based on current trends once again.

5. DT & CC

In recent years, there have been a number of cloud service providers on the market. This technique necessitates the use of cloud computing to store and process the data. Microsoft azure is the primary cloud computing service provider in digital twin technology. This much-heralded technology is used by Microsoft Azure, the company's cloud computing platform. With Microsoft, you're getting a world-class cloud computing platform from the best. A number of services are available via Microsoft Azure, including SAAS, IAAS, and PAAS. Azure is often used in conjunction with digital twin technology, which allows it to deal with real-time data. There are a number of cloud service companies working hard to implement digital twin technologies. Another cloud service provider is Oracle.

Technologies such as data virtualization, edge computing, and statistical analysis are all increasingly utilized in digital twin technology. Digital twins are always being updated to take advantage of the most recent advances in technology. Several more technologies are continually being changed and linked in order to provide better installation results.

4. DIGITAL TWINS APPLICATION DOMAINS

Manufacturing, healthcare, astronomy, retail, and transportation are just a few of the industries benefiting from digital twin technologies.

Manufacturing - Digital twins are virtual representations of real-world objects, products, people, processes, supply chains, or whole business ecosystems (Crawford, 2021). There are seven ways in which digital twin technology may help the industrial business. 1. Product design 2. Process Optimization 3. Quality management 4. Supply chain management 5. Predictive Maintenance 6. Cross-Discipline Collaboration 7. Analyze the Customer Experience Digital twins in manufacturing have a promising future. As a result of this technology's vast range of applications, this industry will benefit greatly.

Healthcare - Over the next three years, 66% of healthcare experts expect to see an increase in the number of advanced twins being studied. Because sophisticated twins promote healthcare organization execution, identify ranges for improvement, provide customization and personalization of medicine, and enable the development of contemporary medication equipment, this occurs often.

Retail - The usage of digital twins allows firms to realize previously unimagined benefits, such as the ability to upgrade production lines while also enabling a shorter time-to-market (Hazem, 2022). Incorporating digital twins into the retail business provides five essential features. 1. Prediction Propagation 2. Real-time Farther Monitoring 3. Better Team-participation 4. Adequate Monetary Choice Making 5. Accelerated Chance Evaluation and Generation Time

Transport - By incorporating digital twins into the transportation management system, both the transportation infrastructure and the traffic management system have improved. According to Dasgupta et al. (2021), the old transport system is less efficient than a digital twin-based transport management system.

5. DIGITAL TWINS CHALLENGES AND FUTURE TRENDS

There are various lows to every technology. These issues must be addressed if the process is to work well in any industry. The aim of the digital twin association may be achieved by ensuring that issues are effectively addressed. Challenges of digital twin technology are shown in Figure 3.

1. Privacy

Every industry that utilizes digital twins demands privacy as a major problem for the system. Analyses are conducted using the data that has been obtained. There are concerns that data leaks might have serious ramifications for the healthcare business. Data loss and leakage are unacceptable in systems using digital twin technology; hence privacy is a big problem.

Figure 3. Challenges for Digital twin technology

2. Data Handling

Another problem that digital twins have to deal with is the management of data. The sensors collect data. However, data is lacking at the ground level, and the search is left unanswered on occasion. It is impossible to guarantee that the data gathered is always correct. Data may go lost or be misplaced at any moment. In order to correctly handle data, it is necessary to manage this search and lack of information.

3. Security

Privacy and security are served one after the other. Once system developed assures privacy, security is granted automatically after that. By security we not only mean security of data but also ensures that physical system deployed at the site is also secured. Security prevents breaching of data. It also avoids system from getting hacked.

4. Manifest and Interpretability

The manifest of any system or technology is required. There is a direct correlation between increased openness and increased technological complexity. Many people believe that digital twin technology is underwhelming. Proper risk management is required to get over this stumbling block, which forces the system to be opaque. It's important to have ideas that can be interpreted in a variety of ways. Digital twins aren't always a supporter of this. It's possible to get around this problem, though, by using cutting-edge tools like machine learning.

5. Requirement for a Training Team

Because creating a virtual replica of an already-deployed system is both difficult and complicated, creating a digital twin is a worthwhile endeavor. Maintaining a workforce that can work well with digital twins is thus strongly advised. This group is made up of highly skilled professionals. To maximize the system's economic benefits, this team has to be well-versed in every aspect of the creation process. It's a challenge to put up a team that can both work and educate current employees in the field about a complicated model. That doesn't imply, though, that this squad can't be put together. Interest in building and understanding a digital twin team is growing because of the rapid growth of digital twin technologies in recent years.

Future Trend - Recent years have seen a rapid rise in the demand for digital twins. Product creation and development, inventory management, business optimization, predictive maintenance and performance monitoring are just a few of the areas where digital twins will have a bright future (KBV Research, 2021). A CAGR of 39.1 percent is expected from 2022 to 2030 for the worldwide digital twin market, which was valued at USD 7.48 billion in the year 2021 (Grand View Research, n.d.). Many countries, mostly in North America, have embraced the concept of the digital twin. Several new uses for this technology were made possible in the UK as a result of the covid-19 outbreak. Digital twins have a bright future in the near future, according to a recent trends analysis.

6. CONCLUSION

The digital twin is a technology that is evolving. The implementation of digital twin technology is being heavily subsidized by several countries. The integrated sensors in digital twins primarily capture real-time data. Data from that source is utilized by this technology to do particular analysis and forecasting. When we need it the most, this technology has risen to the occasion. It is quite difficult to put it into practice in order to improve performance in any field. The retail purchase may be taken to the next level by forecasting and relating specific features to data patterns of market need and demand. However, a great amount of effort is being made to incorporate digital twin technology into other industries, such as healthcare, IoT devices, retail, and so on. In the industrial area, digital twins have shown to be quite effective. Efforts are being made to incorporate digital twins into a wide variety of industries. Digital twin mechanization is unique in that it may be used to a wide range of fields due to a number of essential properties.

Artificial intelligence, machine learning, the internet of things, data mining, cloud computing, and edge computing are just a few of the areas that digital twins need to be prepared for. The field of artificial intelligence is advancing at a rapid pace these days. Algorithms are used by AI to make decisions and predictions. Digital twin technology is already supported by a wide range of algorithms in a typical arrangement. Digital twin technology relies heavily on machine learning. Machine learning has preset models that are used to analyze and forecast. Data mining and machine learning work together to get more exact results. When it comes to digital twin mechanisms, IoT devices wield a lot of sway. Each and every part of an IoT gadget is examined by digital twins. The dynamics of a chunk or a physical piece of information may be thrown onto the complete realm of a digital twin. In addition to digital twins, cloud computing is a big part of this. In the world of cloud computing, the main purpose of purchasing a cloud is to store sensor data.

In order for digital twin technology to advance at a good pace in the future market, the challenges connected with the technology must be counterbalanced. To prepare for the challenges of this next twin automation, ongoing study is taking place. Digital twin has to do additional effort to enhance the current system and implement or deploy it in more new fields. The problems of this freshly established area will be sparked in a unique manner. Future work that incorporates other cutting-edge technologies is likewise highly regarded.

REFERENCES

Armendia, Ghassempouri, Ozturk, & Peysson. (Eds.). (2019). Twin-Control: A Digital Twin Approach to Improve Machine Tools Lifecycle. Springer.

Armstrong, M. M. (2020). *Cheat sheet: What is Digital Twin? Here's your quick guide to digital twins, what they are and why they matter for your organization.* https://www.ibm.com/blogs/internet-of-things/iot-cheat-sheet-digital-twin/

Blicq. (2021). *Digital Twins: The Next Human Revolution That Will Disrupt the Financial Services Industry.* Innovations Accelerated.

Crawford, M. (2021). *7 Digital Twin Applications for Manufacturing.* https://www.asme.org/topics-resources/content/7-digital-twin-applications-for-manufacturing

Dasgupta, Rahman, Lidbe, Lu, & Jones. (2021). *A Transportation Digital-Twin Approach for Adaptive Traffic Control Systems.* Cornell University.

El Saddik, A. (2022). *Digital Twin for Healthcare: Design, Challenges, and Solutions.* Elsevier.

Evangeline, P. (Ed.). (2021). The Digital Twin Paradigm for Smarter Systems and Environments: The Industry Use Cases. Elsevier.

Friedericha, Francisb, Lazarova-Molnara, & Mohamedc. (2022). A framework for data-driven digital twins of smart manufacturing systems. *Computers in Industry, 136.* doi:10.1016/j.compind.2021.103586

Grand View Research. (n.d.). https://www.grandviewresearch.com/industry-analysis/digital-twin-market

Hazem. (2022, Jan. 6). *What Is A Digital Twin? How Is It Useful In The Retail Industry?* https://thinkpalm.com/blogs/what-is-a-digital-twin-how-is-it-useful-in-the-retail-industry/

Herwig, Pörtner, & Möller. (2021). *Digital Twins: Applications to the Design and Optimization of Bioprocesses.* Springer Nature.

Iyer, A. (2017). *Digital Twin: Possibilities of the new Digital twin technology.* Independently Published.

KBV Research. (2021). https://www.kbvresearch.com/digital-twin-market/

Lv & Xie. (2021). *Artificial intelligence in the digital twins: State of the art, challenges, and future research topics.* https://digitaltwin1.org/articles/1-12

Nee, A. Y. C., & Ong, S. K. (Eds.). (2021). Digital Twins in Industry. Applied Sciences, 11(14), 6437.

Oracle. (n.d.). *Developing Applications with Oracle Internet of Things Cloud Service*. https://docs.oracle.com/en/cloud/paas/iot-cloud/iotgs/iot-digital-twin-framework.html

Raghunathan & Barma. (2019). *Digital Twin: A Complete Guide For The Complete Beginner*. Independently Published.

Shanmuganathan, Kadry, Vijayalakshmi, Pasupathi, & River. (2022). *Deep Learning for Video Analytics Using Digital Twin*. River Publishers.

Takyar, A. (n.d.). *A Complete Knowledge Guide On Digital Twins*. LeewayHertz. https://www.leewayhertz.com/digital-twin/

Yeh, Nee, Tao, & Zhang. (2019). *Digital Twin Driven Smart Manufacturing*. Academic Press.

Taylor, K. (n.d.). *Blockchain and Digital Twins: Amalgamating the Technologies*. HiTechNectar. https://www.hitechnectar.com/blogs/blockchain-and-digital-twins-amalgamating-the-two-technologies/

Chapter 20
Sustainable Development Using Digital Twin Technology With Image Processing

Kunal Dhibar
Bengal College of Engineering and Technology, India

Prasenjit Maji
iD https://orcid.org/0000-0001-8057-6963
Bengal College of Engineering and Technology, India

Shiv Prasad
Bengal College of Engineering and Technology, India

Moumita Pal
JIS College of Engineering, India

ABSTRACT

Numerous industries have embraced cutting-edge computer technology as digitalization has progressed, including big data, artificial intelligence (AI), cloud computing, digital twins, and edge computing. In order to analyze the state of the application of digital twins in conjunction with AI, this chapter looks at the research findings of recently published literature. It then evaluates the applications and futures of AI in digital twins. High-fidelity computer simulations are used in modern engineering practice for the design and research of complex engineering systems. In the field of mechanical and aeronautical engineering, computational simulations have long been used to support conceptual design, prototyping, manufacturing, production, test-data correlation, and safety evaluation. In the last 10 years, there has been a change in how computational simulations are used to give assistance across the whole product life cycle.

DOI: 10.4018/978-1-6684-6821-0.ch020

INTRODUCTION

Digital twin technology is computer software that permits simulating the effects of various influences on a certain system or object. To generate a digital replica of a product or gadget, digital twins are used. With the help of this service, businesses may gain invaluable insights on how to enhance operations, boost efficiency, save expenses, or identify problems or errors before they arise. One must understand that it is more than simply a representation of the actual item. IoT sensors assist digital twins, allowing the twin to receive ongoing, real-time data from the physical object. You can thus really see how your items respond and behave. And all of that information is shown on his/her screen!

In the field of digital manufacturing, digital twins are quite important. Here, developing the product, manufacturing method, and assets is crucial before anything else. It's a huge simplification, but according to Arthur Haponik (2020), the procedure normally goes like this:

Digital twin Item -> Production of Digital Twins -> Digital Twin Possessions

Examine digital twins' use in the four domains of aerospace, on-site smart manufacturing, unmanned aerial vehicles, and smart city transportation while evaluating current and future issues. The use of digital twins and AI in the aerospace sector has been shown to have significant effects on error alerts, aircraft development, and even unmanned flying. By combining data analytics, digital twins, and computer vision in this way, asset and production control may be better understood. As a result, producers might reduce expenses and enhance their goods. The actual road environment is reproduced with smart city traffic, and traffic accidents are simulated to guarantee clear and efficient traffic conditions and enable quick and precise urban traffic management. We will conclude by using the development of digital twins and artificial intelligence as a guide for future studies in related areas.

Digital Twins (DTs) were motivated primarily by the requirement for interaction between genuine physical systems and the digital cyberspace model (Tao, Fei & Qi, Qinglin & Wang, Lihui & Nee, Andrew, 2019). In cyberspace, people attempt to replicate real-world events. Only cyclic feedback in conjunction with whole-life monitoring captures the whole life cycle. This method makes it possible to properly ensure digital reality throughout the whole cycle. It can be tested using various simulations, analyses, data keeping, mining, and artificial intelligence applications to see if it works with real-world physical systems. To determine an intelligent system's intelligence, one must first observe, model, research, and reason. The real production system must be accurately modeled by the digital twins for the intelligent manufacturing system to be put into practice. Usage of Digital Twin technology in various fields and organizations can be understood from the Figure 1 graph (Karin, July 3, 2019).

LITERATURE REVIEW

In many industries, the use of digital twins has improved, and there are promising application possibilities in the future, according to research done by academics. This has also been supported by several recent studies. Recent developments in computer pipelines, Multiphysics solvers, AI, big data cybernetics, data processing, and management tools have made digital twins highly useful.

Figure 1. Usage of Digital Twin Technology.

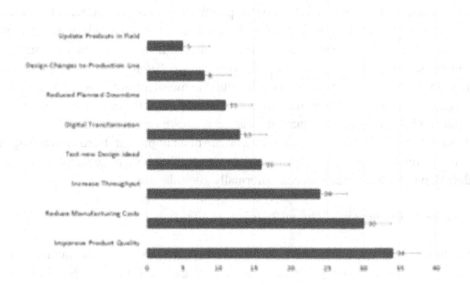

In a variety of applications, digital twins are currently a significant rising trend. Also known as synchronizing virtual prototypes, device shadows, mirrored systems, avatars, and computing huge models. In addition to revolutionizing the design and operation of cyber-physical intelligent systems, digital twins also support the modularization of multidisciplinary systems and help us get past fundamental challenges. A digital twin is "an integrated Multiphysics, multiscale, probabilistic simulation of a complex product that serves to replicate the life of its corresponding twin," according to Glaessgen, Edward H., Stargel, D. S., 2013. A digital twin is made up of the physical product, the virtual product, and the link between the physical and virtual products. Although they are not currently very popular, digital twin applications offer a lot of potentials. At the end of 2016, the renowned IT research and consulting company Gartner (Marc Kerremans, Tushar Srivastava, 2021), said that "hundreds of millions of things will soon be represented by digital twins" in its list of the "Top 10 Trends for 2017". A key area of artificial intelligence is picture object identification, which is the process of identifying various patterns in both the target and object technologies. A mature field that has reached numerous technical apex stages and is presently progressively stabilizing is image recognition technology. The White Paper on the Judicial Application of Internet Technological published by the Beijing Internet Court in 2019 lists it as one of the ten common technology applications (Guo, J., Lv, Z., 2020).

Digital Twins were first put out by University of Michigan professor Dr. Michael Grieves in 2003. It goes under several names, such as virtual mirroring and computerized mapping. It is a technique for physical or digital expression in the actual world. It is obvious and simple to comprehend that it is there in the virtual world. The idea of authentic items being duplicated in the actual world goes beyond realism. It is a digital simulation technique that integrates a variety of disciplines, physical quantities, scales, and probabilities using physical models, sensor technology, and historical operational data. According to Gartner, one of the top ten significant technical developments for 2019 was the digital twin. By 2020, More than 20 billion sensors and terminals will be expected to be connected, and the digital twin will connect billions of real things to replicate the state of the physical world as exactly as possible in the virtual one. The authors anticipate that more sensors and terminal equipment will be used in this technology once this prediction is confirmed in 2021. (Singh, Maulshree & Fuenmayor, Evert & Hinchy, Eoin & Qiao, Yuansong & Murray, Niall & Devine, 2021). Due to the growing popularity of their benefits, digital twins have a wide range of study topics related to them, particularly in the field of computer-integrated manufacturing. As seen in Figure 2 below, the development process has gone through several stages.

Figure 2. Digital Twin Technology's Development Cycle.

The field of artificial intelligence (AI) has altered not only our life but also other sectors. To develop a new sophisticated computer that can respond in a way comparable to human intelligence, it aims to understand the foundations of intellectual capacity. Some of the subject topics covered in this field include robotics, language recognition, picture identification, natural language processing, and knowledge-based systems. Artificial intelligence is used in computers, automation, politics and economic decision-making, control mechanisms, and simulation systems (AI). Figure 3 demonstrates how technology is progressively altering our way of life. Our cleaning robot can efficiently clean a large duplex house, our smart watches can monitor and predict health issues, and the robots in our homes can read stories to our children in the voices of our parents. When driving, we can use map software to avoid traffic. Digital twins and artificial intelligence will transform every element of our life in unfathomable ways. Additionally, this has been validated by several recent research.

Wan et al. (2021) examined the potential of semi-supervised support vector machines (SVM) for feature recognition, diagnosis, and prediction in digital twins of merged brain images (Liu, Zhansheng & Jiang, Antong & Zhang, Anshan & Xing, Zezhong & Du, Xiuli, 2021).

It is proposed to use a semi-supervised SVM that uses both labeled and unlabelled data to manage the sizable amount of unlabeled data found in brain images. The research also describes how the AlexNet model is enhanced and how the digital twin model is used to transform the actual brain image into the virtual one.

Even though images of brain tumors have complicated edge structures, artifacts, offset fields, and other problems that affect image segmentation, it is not difficult to see how the use of digital twins in the medical field brings about the necessary actions for an accurate diagnosis of brain tumors that truly satisfy clinical needs. For the clinical follow-up screening and treatment of brain tumors, it is essential. Finally, a simulation and analysis of the built-in model are possible. The approach displays outstanding advantages in convergence rate and impact, as well as great robustness. The study offered fresh proof that the development of the aviation industry depends on internet technology.

Digital twins, which are precise virtual replicas of devices or systems, Tao et al. (2021) shown, are transforming the market. These intricate computer models, which are driven by real-time data gathered from sensors, represent nearly every element of goods, practices, or services. Digital twins have been employed by several sizable businesses to identify issues and boost productivity. By 2021, an expert believes that half of the organizations may be utilizing them (Tao, F., Cheng, J., 2018).

APPLICATION / USAGE

There are several uses for digital twins that have theoretical and technological underpinnings in the areas of product design, equipment manufacture, medical analysis, aerospace, and other fields. In China right now, engineering construction has the broadest application, and the area of research which has drawn the most enthusiasm is intelligent manufacturing. The papers assembled were chosen using specified search strategies and parameters, and they were evaluated to offer a state-of-the-art review on Virtual Twins, the basic Digital Twin architectural, kinds of Digital Twins, assimilation stages, and a maturity evaluation approach.

Utilizing Digital Twins in The Aerospace Sector- the aerospace sector was the first to argue for the use of digital twins. Digital twins are used, for instance, to manage and ensure the quality of flight simulators and other aerospace aviation equipment. When the digital space and sensors are combined, the true airplane model is established (L. Li, S. Aslam, A. Wileman, and S. Perinpanayagam, 2022). The status of the virtual aircraft and the actual flying aircraft are in sync.

This enables the simulation and recording of each aircraft's takeoff and landing operations. Through the analysis of digital space data, it can determine whether the aircraft requires repair and whether it can continue to the next voyage. Concerning the issues with the quality deviation control system for civil aircraft, the quality analysis of data and quality discrepancy regulate Fusion System's complete absence of closed-loop cyber physics, and the performance deviation control data is distributed across various management systems, making it impossible to collect quality data-related information gathered from the aforementioned aircraft's entire life cycle. In the aerospace industry, the digital twin may be utilized for a range of tasks, including digitally recreating aircraft flight patterns, rapidly reporting problems and maintenance, and assessing the performance of autonomous aerial vehicles, in accordance with the mentioned discussions. In these areas, significant advancements have been made. Figure 3 below shows the utilization of Digital Twin in the aerospace field.

The Evolution of Automatic Driving Through The Use Of Digital Twins - Applications are growing swiftly as big data analysis and deep learning technologies progress. The advancement of autonomous driving systems requires the application of AI algorithms. Instances of how autonomous driving technologies are being applied in the real world include fewer traffic accidents, more effective use of time, space, and many other commodities, and even improved driving availability for those with disabilities. Despite this, due to the rapid changes in the technological environment of autonomous vehicles, the need for digital twins to replicate mobility in a virtual environment has become a critical step. Self-driving vehicles must pass stringent virtual simulation testing before they are allowed on the road to assure their safety (Ashfaq, Niaz & Muhammad Usman, Shoukat & Jia, Yanbing & Khan, Samiullah & Niaz, Fahim & Raza, Muhammad, 2021).

In the conventional virtual simulation test environment, HTL (High Threshold Logic) equipment is frequently used for security and preventative performance tuning. However, in this type of test, only the controller is used; the driver, the gearbox, the power, the atmosphere, and the road conditions are all practically simulated. The performance of the tested automobile item is less precise because of the current low processing level, which prevents the simulation platform from being set up too complexly, and the classification performance does have some variation (Ferdousi, Rahatara & Laamarti, Fedwa & Hossain, M. & Yang, Chunsheng & El Saddik, Abdulmotaleb, 2021). Figure 4 shows a basic autonomous driving architecture.

Figure 3. Digital Twin Technology used in Aerospace flight life.

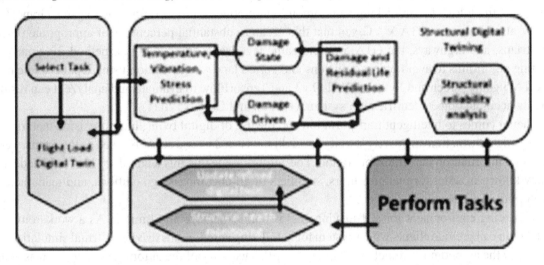

Figure 4. Digital twins are used in a simple automated driving architecture.

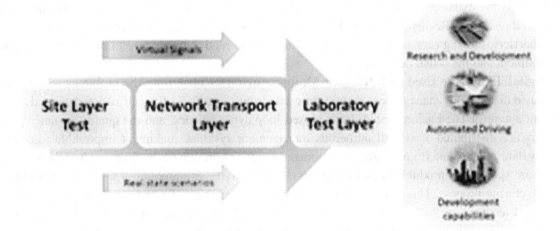

Testing in a real setting is the ideal solution, but because of several physical restrictions, it might be difficult to create a consistent test scenario each time. Thus, it is proposed to establish a test assessment system that integrates computerized mobility simulation testing based on digital twin technology with existing road conditions.

To ensure that there are no communication barriers between any of the components, the method chosen is to use the International Organization for Standardization's joint Internet of Things platform and the oneM2M interconnection platform in the Internet of Things domain. Digital twins in self-driving automobiles have been modified to make use of the benefits of the digital era. Additionally, maintaining the security of self-driving vehicles can significantly lower the frequency of traffic accidents (Bottani, Eleonora & Assunta, Cammardella & Murino, Teresa & Vespoli, Silvestro, 2017).

Additionally, there are several advantages to maintaining a safe distance when driving. Making a simulation environment that accurately mimics the conditions on the road, however, demands a lot of labor and has very low cost-effectiveness since so many aspects need to be included. The research presented a methodology for mimicking autonomous automobiles with the online video game Grand Theft Auto V also known as "GTA V". Given that this offers a substantial percentage of appropriate objects, pedestrians, and highways, the GTA 5 online game is a useful computational method for simulation. Creating algorithms to avoid object collisions and varied lane categorization using OpenCV to capture the GTA 5 game screen and Python's YOLO v3 and TensorFlow to evaluate and analyze it can result in a highly accurate object identification system. (H. Yun and D. Park, 2021).

When it comes to intelligent transportation and the use of digital twins, high-precision material that can provide information on the city- or city-level digital twin datasets could be used as the primary environmental information for vehicle operation. The authors argue that this technology has to be made more widely known in order for manufacturers, suppliers of all-encompassing solutions, and manufacturers of autopilot equipment to utilize it.

The testing environment for self-driving cars is both expensive and limited, As a workaround, the digital twin can provide clients with a system for simulating autonomous driving. Virtual simulation may be used by the autonomous vehicle system to verify the accuracy of the automobile algorithm as well as the performance of the sensors. On the other hand, in the real world of autonomous vehicles, it may be utilized as a component of the mapping software. The digital test field allows automakers to electronically assess the dynamics, convenience, and endurance of their automobiles. Testing takes place on a simulated test track. Realistic elements like stationary cars, traffic signs, bystanders, pedestrian crossings, barriers, moving cars, and the number of lanes on the road must be present in both the simulated environment and the actual occurrences.

Digital Twins Are Used in Intelligent Manufacturing - Concerning the problems with the performance discrepancy management system for civil aircraft, analysis of performance data, and quality deviation control The Fusion System lacks closed-loop cyber physics, and the quality variance packet headers are distributed across all numerous management systems, making it impossible to compile quality data-related data from the aforementioned aircraft's entire life cycle. As a result of their customers' more specialized product needs, businesses deal with a massive amount of information during the manufacturing process. This makes it difficult for businesses to handle and assess data. The efficient and rapid feedback of the utilization condition of the production workshop equipment, as well as the early detection of flaws, are thus critical issues in the modern intelligent manufacturing sector (Dietmar, P., F., Möller., Hamid, Vakilzadian., Weyan, Hou, 2021). Workshops for creating digital twins are an essential part of intelligent production. The virtual workshop, which consists of a physical workshop, a virtual workshop, a workbench support system, and workshop twin data, is their core element. Along with additional aspects, such as the use of digital complex geometries to depict the employees, tools, and goods in the workplace, three main perspectives are employed to build a virtual workshop. Simulations of the workshop equipment's operational condition, as well as the workshop equipment's speed trajectory and other production instructions, are a few examples of behavior elements. Rule components use the actual workshop environment to assess, analyze, forecast, and improve the production system to create a virtual workplace. Recurring mechanical problems throughout the actual manufacturing process influence the project's timeline and budget. When repairs are made after an issue has already developed, fault screening is sometimes challenging and expensive to do. As a result, it's essential to set up early warning mechanisms for equipment malfunction and equipment service life. Investigations are conducted on the interplay between digital twins and real-time 3D workspace visualization. A real-time data-driven virtual workshop, as well as a multi-level 3D visualisation monitoring mode, are recommended.

In-depth explanations of geometrical workplace modeling, and real-time workshop information management, this article discusses multi-level workshop 3D visualization monitoring and the creation of workshop status panels. A virtual architectural model of the intelligent workshop could be built, and workshop commodities could be produced under real-world applications. Job shop scheduling is always critical to the manufacturing process and one of the most important factors influencing manufacturing productivity (Zhang, Qing & Chen, Hao & Zhu, YuGe & Wang, JiaYin & Zhou, ChangZhong, 2021).

Figure 5. Equipment Failure detection using Digital Twin.

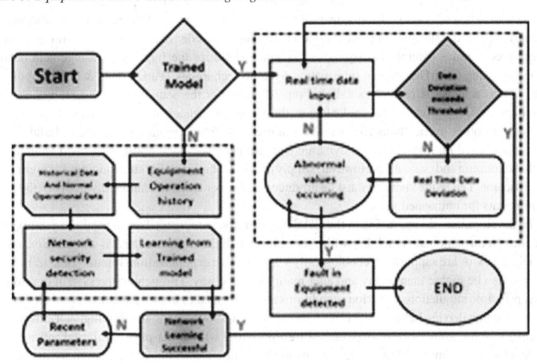

According to the research, digital twins have advanced the field of manufacturing systems, particularly through the use of virtual workshops. These workshops can help staff make specific qualifications to the overall workshop scheduling and increase the efficiency of equipment production. Utilizing digital twin technology, manufacturing companies may improve the effectiveness of product development and production by creating virtual simulations of items, manufacturing techniques, and even a comprehensive facility. A virtual, three-dimensional space can also be utilized to create items. Product geometry confirmation work, assembly practicality assessment work, and workplace management can all be made considerably simpler by altering the products and components of different sizes and assembly relationships. The iterative approach significantly reduces manufacturing costs, times, and prices associated with making physical prototypes. The digital twin-based intelligent equipment failure detection is shown in Figure 5.

Smart Cities' Usage of Digital Twins - Simply mapping people, objects, relationships, and activities from the real world towards the virtual one is the core tenet of digital twins. After that, researchers may understand the investigation and management of real-world goods by viewing and evaluating the digital twin in virtual space. The primary goals of the urban functional management department are to restrict or regulate the proper land use and lay the groundwork for the efficient utilization of urban space. Urban planning is fundamentally based on pertinent indicators, such as the carrying capacity of the region's natural resources and the environment, the concentration statistics of the current infrastructure investment, and the likelihood of future regional growth. By utilizing GIS (Geographic Information System) technology, architects may more effectively optimize the functional organization of metropolitan areas. In order to create a digital representation of the actual traffic system, smart transportation uses surveillance footage, a fusion of millimeter-wave radars, motorized vehicle holographic perception, vehicles, pedestrians, and other traffic elements. The primary goal of urban functional area management is to limit or regulate proper land use and to lay the groundwork for efficient urban space use. Urban planning is primarily based on relevant indicators, including the available capacity of the region's environment and natural resources the statistics of present regional development's density, and the possibilities for future emerging economies. Architects may more efficiently optimize the functional arrangement of urban regions by using GIS (Geographic Information System) technology (Park, Jiman & Yang, Byungyun, 2020). Smart transportation creates a digital representation of the actual traffic system by combining surveillance video, millimeter-wave radar fusion, the holographic vision of pedestrians and non-motorized vehicles, and other traffic characteristics. We can use twin data to replicate a scenario, build a digital twin model based on how static and dynamic data are perceived, and assist unmanned vehicles with simulated training and evaluation. However, simply providing high-fidelity surroundings for digital twins is insufficient. The twin situations must be produced and generalized to continually improve the testing environments for unmanned vehicles.

The development and upgrading of the CITS (Cooperative Intelligent Transportation System), which combines (semi-)automated mobility with cyber-physical digital infrastructure, is a notable example of this. Digital twins are supported technologically via derivative generalization. It must come from reality, but must also be higher than reality and alter reality in some way. Throughout the system development phase, principle simulations of various conditions are performed to improve the observation of weather changes, human driving behaviors, and scenario settings. CITS (Cooperative Intelligent Transportation System), which combines (semi-)automated transportation with cyber-physical digital infrastructure, was developed and improved as an excellent example of this. The technical foundation for digital twins is a derivative generalization. It must be derived from reality, but it must also be greater than reality and, in some way, alter reality. Throughout the system development phase, principle simulations of various scenarios are also performed to improve the observation of weather variations, human driving habits, and scenario settings. By gradually implementing certain intelligent traffic management approaches, These centers are now addressing the primary issues with the transportation network. They can maximize the potential of modern traffic control by utilizing digital twins and AI (Saifutdinov, Farid & Jackson, Ilya & Zmanovska, Tatjana & Tolujew, Juri, 2020). To aid in the development of visual guiding mechanisms, It was suggested that a novel sensor merging technique be used, which includes cloud-based camera images and digital twin knowledge. Using the results of the target detector operating on the vehicle and the cloud location information, the bounding box of the specific vehicle is created and matched. Monitoring and discovery are prioritized. A closed loop of data collecting and administration may be established using the digital twin technology, and the entire procedure may be managed.

To assist in the creation of visual guidance mechanisms, A novel sensor merging approach based on cloud camera images and digital twin data has been presented. The results of the target detector working on the vehicle and the cloud location information are combined to build and match the bounding box of the target vehicle. Identification and observation come first. It is feasible to control the entire procedure and set up a feedback circuit for data gathering using the digital twin system. To summarise, digital twins are widely used in smart urban transportation. Making use of digital twin technology, which includes elements of engineering principles, topographical knowledge, existing road scenes, and real three-dimensional situations, urban information models are created. Global data management and operations governance, connectivity, lightweight computation, visualization, and application are at the heart of it. The visual representation of the urban environment makes urban traffic administration easier, more efficient, faster, and more precise.

Application Of Digital Twin in Image Extraction: Image feature points are filtered and extracted using a system based on digital twins. Its novelty is the analysis of the picture's inherent structural similarity and image smoothing. Target key points in the original image are identified based on the optimization of the denoised image by digital twinning, aberrant, and split local features are then deleted, and the orientation of images texture feature points is allocated. It not only resolves the issue of ambiguous feature extraction boundaries brought on by noise and aberrant data, but it also enhances the challenging feature point recognition at edge places. This technique has a great impact on the experimental sample tree's surface texture feature extraction process. To achieve effective image extraction of features, the developed image texture feature extraction technology based on the digital twin has clear picture saturation and steady processing amplitude. Shape and texture data augmentation is investigated and some results are produced using the designed technology (R. Tamilkodi and G. R. Nesakumari, 2021). The identification of texture feature indexes is a challenging problem since the majority of texture pictures acquired in various engineering fields have wrinkled and deformed appearances then instead of flat smoothness. This may be examined in more detail in the study that follows.

DISCUSSION

Digital Twin to enhance production process; Particularly in these three fields of digital production, digital twins are used:

- Engineering: The most effective and efficient way to enhance goods, equipment, and procedures is to use virtual representations of them.
- Customization: It might be challenging to integrate client input into a standard production process. It may be expensive and time-consuming. But not with digital twin technology, which makes it straightforward to further customize the current products and add additional customization options. In addition to assisting with product adaptation, digital twins can provide a more complete view of patterns in consumer demand. Processing client use data allows you to fully comprehend how bespoke setups impact your sales success.

- Operations: In digital manufacturing, producers first develop a digital image of a good or asset. They then collect data from it, which provides them with a more thorough understanding of the actual manufacturing performance and operational circumstances.

Machine vision is typically considered to be a part of computer vision. They are based on cameras, radars, sensors, lights, and software, exactly like computer vision, but this technology is tailored to the demands of the industrial industry. Algorithms for machine vision are capable of:

- Automatically identifying deviations and launching remedial measures.
- Identifying quality issues
- Visual information is processed considerably more quickly

Digital twins and computer vision use cases both have important roles to play in the current digital manufacturing process. Monitoring the entire process and identifying possible trouble spots are made easier with the use of computer vision (Deac, Crina & Popa, Cicerone Laurentiu & Ghinea, Mihalache & Cotet, 2017). Compared to human workers, this technology is a lot faster and more efficient. By giving a far greater grasp of the finished product, its manufacturing process, and any possible hiccups or problems that could be noticed through routine usage, digital twins assist enhance the final product. Manufacturers may make improvements to their products before they hit the market, saving them a significant amount of capital expenditure. Artificial Intelligence and Digital Twin can be used to simulate ecological analysis which can be understood in Figure 6.

Digital twins and the challenges of artificial intelligence:

Testing Flexibility Issues - Cameras, lidar, millimeter-wave radars, and other sensors, computers, and controllers are all included in the auto-driving system of autos. The virtual test environment must now accommodate the needs of several automotive driving test systems and is no longer just one scenario. As a result, to ensure that no traffic accidents happen, the test environment must be capable of supporting not just a single car test but also numerous automobiles operating concurrently. Higher standards for the test environment are proposed as a result of the accident (Guo, Jiapeng & Zhao, Ning & Sun, Lin & Saipeng, Zhang, 2019).

Testing Cost Issue - Although the existing method for testing autonomous vehicles is not yet comprehensive, it has already resulted in hefty test costs. The difficulty here is enormous for the car industry. How to maximize advantages and reduce costs is the most crucial concern for automakers. To lower test costs, it is crucial to build an effective and affordable testing environment, an organized testing procedure, and a robust testing standard (Fuller, Aidan & Fan, Zhong & Day, Charles, 2020).

The Test System Advances Without Difficulty - Future modifications and advancements to automotive autonomous driving technology solutions are unavoidable. The test system must, above all, be flexible enough to accommodate new technological advancements. Vehicles, pedestrians, the state of the roads, traffic signals, etc. must all be kept steady and orderly during the test. Naturally, it must also be examined following the test. The quantity of items increases, and various automobile kinds sometimes get system updates (R. Ganguli, S. Adhikari, 2020). Graph from Figure 7 gives the intensity of problems faced by Digital Twin technology.

Figure 6. Ecological Simulation analysis using Digital Twin with Artificial Intelligence.

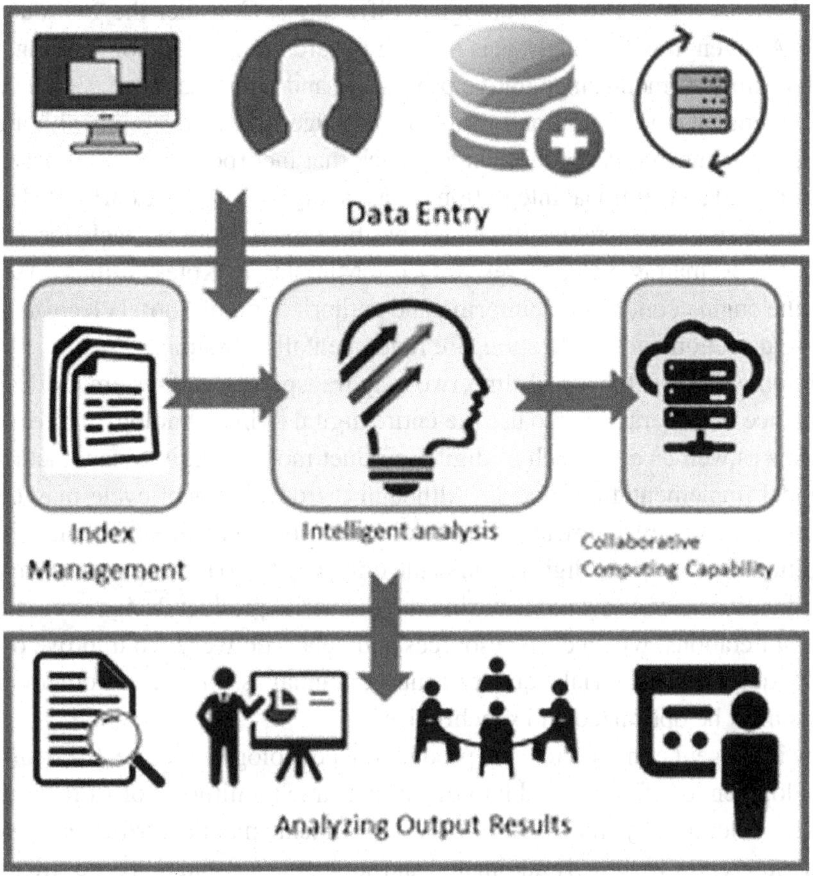

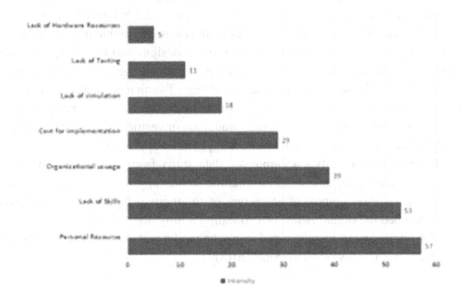

Figure 7. Problems faced implementing Digital Twin Technology.

Although there has been much study on the use of digital twins in artificial intelligence in the aerospace industry, there are still certain technological difficulties. Consider the gas route system seen in aviation engines. Aero-engine data analysis is moving toward being all-encompassing, multi-level, and visual as a result of improvements in cognitive processing and industrial level. Engine components, the engine as a whole, engine condition monitoring, and management of overall health are all included in the study of engine parameters. A digital twin approach that incorporates a lot of data, methodologies, and models has replaced conventional integration in data analysis. There are currently few tools available for determining the engine's general health, which has become a major obstacle for academics all over the world (Bambura, Roman & Šolc, Marek & Dado, Miroslav & Kotek, Lubos, 2020). At this time, the detection of the engine condition monitoring and authorization of digital electronic control system, as well as damage detection and localization, are fundamentally possible.

Therefore, the only way to achieve real-time, two-way, transparent, and systematic design, manufacturing, and performance consideration is to use the entire digital twin technology to create a large number of fantastic models as well as data, such as digital product models, digital manufacturing models, and performance model implementation models. Although the development cycle may be controlled and shortened, as research and development get more difficult, there is a greater chance that delivery will be delayed. Additionally, complete digitization is the only way to do rid of the performance design constraint. If no digital assistance is available during the industrial product design process, a product must go through several iterations, which costs resources and delays delivery. To improve overall efficiency, several pieces of equipment, materials, quality control, manual assembly, and other connections based on accurate beats must be optimized and synchronized.

Even as many intelligent construction and production technologies mature, the main area of research remains the development of effective and intelligent real-time monitoring of workshop equipment production processes. Additionally, the application of intelligent manufacturing technology is growing. Industrial production is now extremely automated and sophisticated, but there are still a lot of issues that need to be fixed and optimized. A few examples include inadequate data management, inconsistent data standards, a large number of information islands, and many factories with various stages of information system development. Incomplete paths exist between the systems as well. The facility creates a number of highly specialized and faulty products in particular (Cupek, Rafał & Drewniak, Marek & Ziębiński, Adam & Fojcik, Marcin, 2019). This presents significant issues for production, sourcing, storage, and quality as well as leading to regular adjustments to product designs and manufacturing procedures. If there is no digital assistance available during the industrial product design process, a product will require several iterations, which will cost resources and delay delivery. To enhance total efficiency, several pieces of equipment, materials, quality control, manual assembly, and other linkages based on accurate beats must be optimized and synchronized. The manual simulation or verification on an actual manufacturing line are the only options available for the conventional planning approach.

Under conditions where the city's accumulated data shifts from quantitative to significant shift and in light of significant advancements in information technology, such as perception modeling and artificial intelligence, the development of a new type of smart city is being pursued using a brand-new technological path called the digital twins' city. Building a fully digital model is an essential first step since the city of the digital twin is constructed using the model and data (Werner Kritzinger, Matthias Karner, Georg Traar, Jan Henjes, Wilfried Sihn, 2018).

There is still data fragmentation in many industries from the standpoint of the present traditional smart city development. The housing and urban-rural construction system, the spatial and temporal big data platform led by natural resources and land planning, and the city base map for urban security and complete and accurate democratic accountability based on public security politics and the law are the three bases that are typically present in most cities. Every base map develops its system, and it frequently only supports the apps that the system provides. It cannot be used whenever or however other departments see fit. It is difficult to pass up and incorporate the data because it was gathered over a long period. This makes the urban traffic simulation method difficult to implement.

SUMMARY

The act for use of digital twins has already been demonstrated to provide various advantages in the aerospace industry. It is possible to achieve unprecedented economic safety and reliability by reducing the number and duration of aircraft certification tests, the number of unintentional cracks and failures, and the number of unintentional cracks and failures, as well as the number and frequency of maintenance inspections for the aircraft's general structure, using physical entity models and relevant data. There is still much to learn about how to enhance digital twin models in the future, and the technology of digital twins does not yet have a comprehensive, global reference model. Digital twins will develop further in the integration and simulation directions. Future studies will equally focus on these two. The success of their industrial use hinges on twins, which allow for the virtualization of the digital item while maintaining its integrity. Every physical model has a commonly used model that is unique to it. These models include thermodynamics, applied mechanics, fatigue damage, material state evolution models, and fluid and structural mechanics. The connection of several models and their representation in the twin model in real-time will be crucial for the implementation of digital twin technology in the future.

Digital twin manufacturing will rise in the next years. Digital twin technology is being used by more and more companies to automate processes, provide real-time database assessments, and start looking into prospects to update novel services, products, and business models. The industrial sector will be the one to spearhead the implementation of electronic twin technology initially. Manufacturing businesses will imitate early adopters if they can demonstrate first-mover advantages in other fields. Long-term system and data integration may be required to fully realize the potential of digital twin technology. Create a thorough digital reproduction of the client life cycle or supply chain, as well as an intelligent macro-operational picture that includes first-tier suppliers and their suppliers. But external elements must still be a part of the internal digital ecosystem. The ongoing advancement of information technology will aid in the development of the digital twin intelligent transportation system, the establishment of commercial networks, the gradual improvement of 5G standards, as well as network performance with large bandwidth, high speed, and low latency. On the one hand, the 5G ultra-high-speed network performance enables vehicle-to-vehicle collaborative automated driving, vehicle formation automated driving, and remote automated driving while permitting safe and dependable communication during high-speed movement. Figure 8 provides a summary of what we discovered concerning digital twins.

Figure 8. Digital Twin concept in Layman's Language.

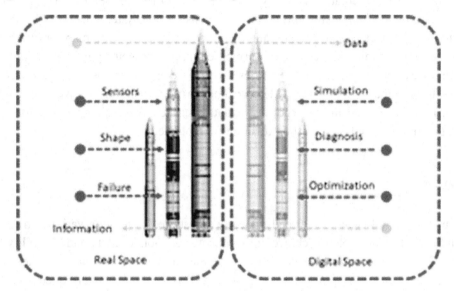

CONCLUSION

Digital twins are widely used as a cutting-edge technology in many facets of life as big data, IoT, industrial internet, and advanced control technologies all increase quickly. The perfect link between the material realm of manufacturing and the digital virtual world has emerged, and it is known as a digital twin. They are an effective technical method of establishing the collaboration and interaction between the real and virtual worlds. Using historical data, real-time data, and computer simulations, a digital twin reconstructs a physical object so that it may be imitated, verified, forecasted, and controlled during its entire life cycle.

Digital twins can be used to build models, gather data, analyze it, forecast it, and simulate it to enable industrial digitalization, digital industrialization, and the merging of digital and real economies. They are an essential technological component and an essential tool for increasing productivity. Digitization, knowledge mechanisms, and other technologies are used to create digital twins, Internet of Things (IoT) and other technologies for converting physical data and information into general data; and an amalgamation of AR/VR/MR/GIS (Augmented Reality/Virtual Reality/Mediated Reality/Geographic Information System) and other technologies are being developed to precisely replicate physical objects in the digital world.

This enables the use of common applications across a range of vertical sectors, such as digital twin description, diagnostic pre-adjustment/prediction, and intelligent decision-making using technologies such as AI, big data, and cloud computing. Unquestionably, one of the fundamental technologies supporting the ecosystem of digital twins is artificial intelligence. The vast data handling and system self-optimization that form the digital twin ecosystem's brain and provide planned and intelligent cloud transfer are perhaps the best examples of its importance. For the current stage of research, the two must be combined, and future research will provide different levels of cognitive conversion to different companies.

REFERENCES

Ashfaq, & Usman, Jia, Khan, Niaz, & Raza. (2021). Autonomous Driving Test Method Based on Digital Twin. *Survey (London, England)*, 1–7. doi:10.1109/ICECube53880.2021.9628341

Bambura, R., Šolc, M., Dado, M., & Kotek, L. (2020). Implementation of Digital Twin for Engine Block Manufacturing Processes. *Applied Sciences (Basel, Switzerland)*, *10*, 6578. doi:10.3390/app10186578

Bottani, Assunta, Murino, & Vespoli. (2017). *From the Cyber-Physical System to the Digital Twin: the process development for behaviour modelling of a Cyber Guided Vehicle in M2M logic*. Academic Press.

Cupek, Drewniak, Ziębiński, & Fojcik. (2019). *"Digital Twins" for Highly Customized Electronic Devices – Case Study on a Rework Operation*. IEEE Access. . doi:10.1109/ACCESS.2019.2950955

Deac, C., Popa, C. L., & Ghinea, M. (2017). Machine Vision in Manufacturing Processes and the Digital Twin of Manufacturing Architectures. doi:10.2507/28th.daaam.proceedings.103

Dietmar, P. (2021). Intelligent Manufacturing with Digital Twin. doi:10.1109/EIT51626.2021.9491874

Ferdousi, & Laamarti, Hossain, Yang, & El Saddik. (2021). Digital twins for well-being: An overview. *Digital Twin.*, *1*, 7. doi:10.12688/digitaltwin.17475.1

Fuller, A., Fan, Z., Day, C., & Barlow, C. (2020). Digital Twin: Enabling Technologies, Challenges and Open Research. *IEEE Access: Practical Innovations, Open Solutions*, *8*, 108952–108971. doi:10.1109/ACCESS.2020.2998358

Ganguli, R., & Adhikari, S. (2020). The digital twin of discrete dynamic systems: Initial approaches and future challenges. *Applied Mathematical Modelling*, *77*(2), 1110-1128. https://doi.org/ doi:10.1016/j.apm.2019.09.036

Glaessgen, E. H., & Stargel, D. S. (2013, August 25). *The Digital Twin Paradigm for Future NASA and U.S. Air Force Vehicles - NASA Technical Reports Server (NTRS)*. Retrieved September 21, 2022, from https://ntrs.nasa.gov/citations/20120008178

Guo, H., Zhu, Y., Zhang, Y., Ren, Y., Chen, M., & Zhang, R. (2021). A digital twin-based layout optimization method for discrete manufacturing workshop. *International Journal of Advanced Manufacturing Technology*, *112*, 1–12. doi:10.100700170-020-06568-0

Guo, J., & Lv, Z. (2022). *Application of Digital Twins in multiple fields*. Multimed Tools Appl. doi:10.100711042-022-12536-5

Guo, J., Zhao, N., Sun, L., & Saipeng, Z. (2019). Modular based flexible digital twin for factory design. *Journal of Ambient Intelligence and Humanized Computing*, *10*. Advance online publication. doi:10.100712652-018-0953-6

Haponik, A. (2020, October 16). *Addepto*. Retrieved July 20, 2022, from https://addepto.com/blog/digital-twin-computer-vision-use-case/

Kerremans, M., & Srivastava, T. (2021, July 13). *Market Guide for Technologies Supporting a Digital Twin of an Organization*. Gartner. Retrieved July 21, 2022, from https://www.gartner.com/en/documents/4003512

Kritzinger, W., Karner, M., Traar, G., Henjes, J., & Sihn, W. (2018). Digital Twin in manufacturing: A categorical literature review and classification. *IFAC-Papers Online, 51*(11), 1016-1022. https://doi.org/10.1016/j.ifacol.2018.08.474

Li, L., Aslam, S., Wileman, A., & Perinpanayagam, S. (2022). Digital Twin in Aerospace Industry: A Gentle Introduction. *IEEE Access: Practical Innovations, Open Solutions, 10*, 9543–9562. doi:10.1109/ACCESS.2021.3136458

Liu, Z., Jiang, A., Zhang, A., Xing, Z., & Du, X. (2021). Intelligent Prediction Method for Operation and Maintenance Safety of Prestressed Steel Structure Based on Digital Twin Technology. *Advances in Civil Engineering, 2021*. Advance online publication. doi:10.1155/2021/6640198

Park, J., & Yang, B. (2020). GIS-Enabled Digital Twin System for Sustainable Evaluation of Carbon Emissions: A Case Study of Jeonju City, South Korea. *Sustainability, 12*, 9186. doi:10.3390u12219186

Saifutdinov, Jackson, Zmanovska, & Tolujew. (2020). *Digital Twin as a Decision Support Tool for Airport Traffic Control.* . doi:10.1109/ITMS51158.2020.9259294

Singh, M., Fuenmayor, E., Hinchy, E., Qiao, Y., Murray, N., & Devine, D. (2021). Digital Twin: Origin to Future. *Applied System Innovation., 4*, 36. doi:10.3390/asi4020036

Tamilkodi, R., & Nesakumari, G. R. (2021). Image retrieval system based on multi feature extraction and its performance assessment. *International Journal of Information Technology, 14*(2), 1161–1173.

Tao, F., Cheng, J., & Qi, Q. (2018). Digital twin-driven product design, manufacturing and service with big data. *International Journal of Advanced Manufacturing Technology, 94*, 3563–3576. doi:10.100700170-017-0233-1

Tao, F., Qi, Q., Wang, L., & Nee, A. (2019). Digital Twins and Cyber-Physical Systems toward Smart Manufacturing and Industry 4.0: Correlation and Comparison. *Engineering., 5*, 653–661. doi:10.1016/j.eng.2019.01.014

Yun, H., & Park, D. (2021). Simulation of Self-driving System by implementing Digital Twin with GTA5. *2021 International Conference on Electronics, Information, and Communication (ICEIC)*, 1-2. doi: 10.1109/ICEIC51217.2021.9369807

Zhang, & Chen, Zhu, Yu, Yin & Zhou. (2021). Digital Twin Based on 3D Visualization and Computer Image Recognition Technology in Coal Preparation Plant. *Journal of Physics: Conference Series, 2083*, 042068. doi:10.1088/1742-6596/2083/4/042068

Chapter 21
E-Commerce:
Revolution of Personalized Filtering to Resolve the Unraveled Cold-Start Problem

Abhishek Kumar Sinha
GIET University, India

S Gopal Krishna Patro
Koneru Lakshmaiah Education Foundation, India

Amrutashree Hota
GIET University, India

ABSTRACT

The recommendation system works on an idea of suggesting or recommending items, products, books, movies, etc. by analyzing and using some filtering to find the user's interest. To maximize the growth of business and profit gain, users need to be recommended with products belonging to their area of interest. To fulfill this requirement, the recommendation system has been implemented. In this study, the discussion is over recommendation system and how different concepts come to work out individually as well as together for recommendation. In this analysis, the focus is on recommending the method of e-commerce. In that scenario, "cold start problem" comes into consideration. Cold start problems are also studied, and a purposed idea has also been highlighted to reduce cold start problem to some extent. 'LCW Aspect' is going to execute and analyze user's culture, weather, local scarcity, and focused on solving recommendation problems for new emerging users.

INTRODUCTION

Since last few decades, it has been observed that, the sheer information analysis is growing massively just like weeds in a field. The number of movies, web series, books, CD, and online products are seen to be getting uncountable day by day with rapid increase in their volume. This volume of amount and varieties in products is relatively very confusing for people to filter or to select the best which matches

DOI: 10.4018/978-1-6684-6821-0.ch021

for them. People have to handle the information of their own effort and sometime get the good one. But many time customer or people not able to get the product of their own choices because either the product is not accessible or not visible to them. There is a lot number of things are done to filter, to give customer what they needed.

For example, newspaper editor selects what are the paper or article are most liked by people and accordingly put them or print them. Book keepers have to give effort of their own to decide what books to carry so that people would like them to buy. These take a great effort and time. However, the emergence of electronic information age, this barrier becomes less and makes easy to suggest everyone with less effort. With the help of information, now it is easy to recommend customer products, items of their choices and interests (Selvi & Sivasankar, 2019). The first paper on collaborative system was published in mid-1990, since then the Recommendation system has become able to fix a crucial role in Research Area (C. D. Wang et al., 2019).

The Recommendation system helps the user, customer and clients to select the items, products which are of that user's interest. Basically, the Recommendation system works on two methods. The first one is "Content based" system and the second one is "Collaborating filtering" system. The content-based system works on the principle of user's past purchased, likes, rating etc. The second Collaborating system works by suggesting users on the basis of similar preference (Tahmasebi et al., 2021). In today's date, many e-commerce websites are being operating which are serving customized recommendation to user. Amazon.com is a great example of that. It recommends products, items, movies, web-series, books, kindle books etc. Like that, Netflix recommendation system suggests movies, web-series to users according to their past clicks, type of movies recently watched, and their area of interest in past (Nilashi et al., 2018).

Recent recommendation system basically works on the rating predictions, which are given by the customers when they buy and use any product. These rating may include (a) how many customers rated as good to any specific product (b) each user can able to rate only once (c) the data of rating should be static. However, these assumptions of rating may be violated at many scenarios. For example, it will violet the assumptions when a particular customer buy product in multiple purchases and given rating every time, these products includes food, grocery, daily needs items etc. Similarly, this also effects negatively in rating based recommendation system (Lv et al., 2019). The recommender system logically works on the past data of user, purchases, ratings etc. For example, if a customer buys or clicks or searches any product, then whenever that user again logins, then he would be given many recommendations related to that category or interest as shown in Figure 1.

But this recommendation system does not work effectively when it comes to new user. One of the most difficult and challenging task is to recommend something to a new user, which has never seen previously(Kumar et al., 2019; Natarajan et al., 2020; Tahmasebi et al., 2021). This problem is known as "Cold Start Problem". This also includes new items which are recently added to website or app and those are not rated yet. So, that becomes one difficult, though common problem to recommend that product to any customer. However, it can be only recommended on basis of similarities among products which has been bought by any customer, buy this is not the effective method(Ranjbar Kermany & Alizadeh, 2017; Razia Sulthana & Ramasamy, 2019; Selvi & Sivasankar, 2019). The cold start problem generates a great practical impact as because of two reasons. Firstly, in modern online age, thousands of items are published on daily basis on different online platforms and its essential to recommend to user to keep the system going. Secondly, the collaborative filtering is the backbone of most of the recommendation engines; they have to be make itself more advanced and have to overcome the problem of Cold start problem (Bhatia et al., 2020; Hosseinzadeh Aghdam, 2019; Huitzil et al., 2020; Kumar & Thakur, 2018).

To overcome this problem up to some extent, it is important to exchange information between domains about the customer interest (Nassar et al., 2020).

The main idea of this study is to improvise the recommendation system efficiency by reducing the impact of cold start problem by means of introducing a new approach of recommendation for new users on the basis of their location, logged in device, whether, season, gender, age, country, culture etc. These areas can be used to provide a set of recommendation to a new user. In this way the efficiency will be good even a new user arrives.

Figure 1. Recommendation System

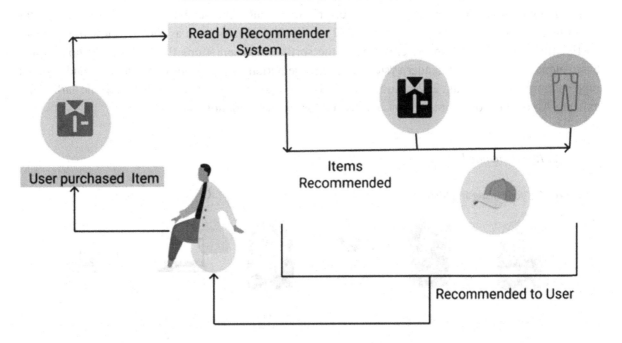

2. LITERATURE REVIEW

The Recommendation system is helping a large number of customers by recommending them the best choice for them. Web has a collection of large amount product information and also its keep updating on daily basis, which makes a great challenge for both customers as well as online business co-operates in e-commerce(Jeong et al., 2017). In recent years, the line of boundary between social media and e-commerce sites is fading away. E-commerce websites like eBay, introduced many features that of social networks. This feature allows both users and business persons to communicate over chatting online and from their only they can buy any products they like. Many products are also recommended them as well as they can have used this for social networking up to some extent (Jiang et al., 2019; Natarajan et al., 2020; K. Wang et al., 2020). Most basic formulation of any recommender systems to do prediction of products that have never been seen by user. On the basis of this prediction it recommends the new products to user(Iwanaga et al., 2019; Katarya & Verma, 2017; Peng et al., 2017; Son & Kim, 2017). Secondly, recommender system analysis the user's past ratings, user's location their profiles, item details and many more things as well as recommends the products accordingly.

In above Figure 2 and Figure 3 many products are recommended to the users on the basis of their past purchased, liked, disliked, and clicked items. These websites like Amazon.com, flipkart.com use personalized recommendation method and analyze as well as recommend every user along with showing items of their specific interest only.

But when there is no information about user i.e. that is a new user, then it goes to a condition called "Cold start problem". System doesn't know what to recommend to that new user or item because it doesn't have enough information about that user to do any analysis or recommendation. For example: when a new user visits to Booking.com for the first time (Miranda et al., 2020; Rui Zhang, Alexander Shapiro & H., 2019). Like, if someone visits to Bookmyshow.com website then that unable to recommended movies user's interest movies as it doesn't have any information about user's interest. Only after selecting location its show some recommended movies based on location as shown below in Figure 4.

Existing recommendation systems uses some sort of representations that commonly holds three basic elements in a recommender system-user representation, transaction representation and product representation(Huitzil et al., 2020; Kumar & Thakur, 2018; Oluwagbemi et al., 2016). Some earlier and existing Algorithms or techniques are being used for recommendation system.

Figure 2. Recommended products by amazon.com

Figure 3. Recommended products by flipkart.com

Figure 4. Recommended movies by Bookmyshow.com to a new user based on location

2.1. Content-Based Filtering

Content based recommendation system basically works with profiles of users, these profiles are created in the beginning of the new user. This profile contains information about user as well as it analyses his taste or interest of items. These tastes depend on many factors such as user's likes, dislikes, rating etc. These files are kept updated every time when that particular user goes through the website or that channel (Hwangbo et al., 2018).

Figure 5. Content based filtering

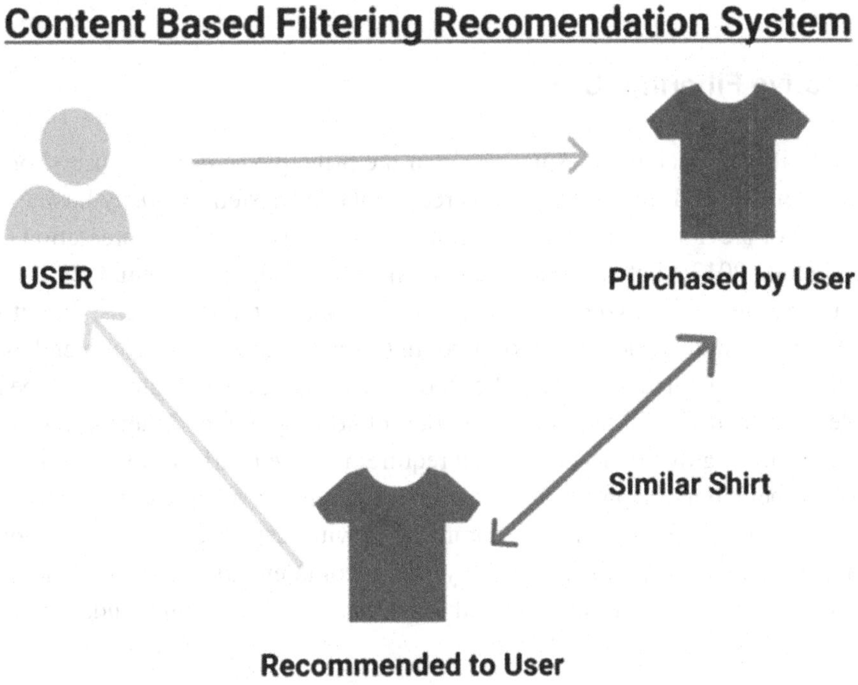

Like in Figure 5, a user purchases a red shirt. The recommender system analyzed that this user likes shirt and purchases it. So the recommender system picks that content of user and recommends him another similar shirt he may like and eager to purchase.

Figure 6 and Figure 7 show that a user has recently watched some movies on his taste and after watching, he rated the movies out of 10. This particular information analyzed and stored in user profile by recommender system and then when user next time login or comes back again it used content to give him recommendations with the list of similar movies. Like here user watched type of movies i.e. Spiderman: Action movie Anabella which is horror movie, and Lost in Space: Fiction movie. And also, he rated conjuring 9 out of 10. So, the system analyses that the user like theses 3 types of movies more and out of them he likes horror movies the most as he rated 9 out of 10. So, the system recommends movies like Anabella and Conjuring 3 which are again horror based movies and also recommends movies of types he also watched along them.

Figure 6. Movies watched by user recently and rating given

Movies	Spider-man	Conjuring	Lost in Space	Dark Matter
Rating	6	9	5	Not Rated

Figure 7. Movies are recommended to user, based on ratings

Recommended Movies	Anabella: Creation	Conjuring 3	Spiderman: Homecoming	Red planet	Spiderman: No way Home

2.2. Collaborative Filtering (CF)

The collaborative filtering method does not work on the principle of previous users, or items. That is why it is most commonly and frequently used as recommended system by many businesses for recommendation. Instead of previous user's knowledge, it works on past user-item interaction (Aher & Lobo, 2013; Bobadilla et al., 2013; Ji et al., 2019; Yang et al., 2018). The idea behind CF is that it creates a community of users. Suppose if two users have same or similar interest of items, then it keeps them in a single community or simply called neighborhood. In this way a user gets recommendation of items he never rated by that has been rated by his neighborhood having same area of interest (Gope & Jain, 2017).

For example, a U1 and U2 are two users making online shopping and their interests are similar to each other. After analyzing that their interest and requirement are nearly similar, recommendation system makes them as neighbors. Suppose at some user U1 purchased a leather jacket and rated as a good product. At the same time user U2 will be recommended with leather jackets as recombination even if he never rated or searched that product. Basically, this recommendation comes because his neighbors have rated it and as their interest of items is similar, that has become recommendation for user U2.

Figure 8. Collaborative Filtering

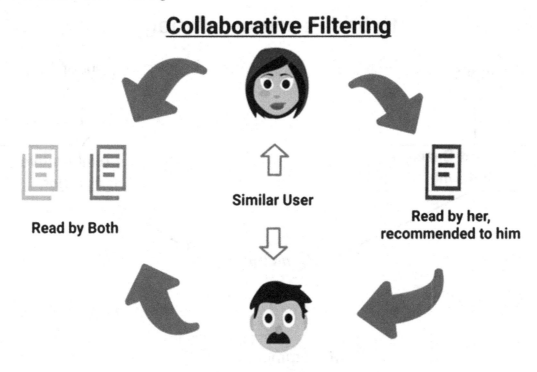

2.3. Hybrid Recommendation Approach

"Hybrid" means combination of two or more approaches. Here hybrid recommendation approach combines both contents based filtering and collaborative filtering to generate recommendation for users. Using this approach, it is able to provide a better recommendation to users by making recommendation system more effective. Also, by this approach recommender system can be able to avoid cold start problem up to some extent. The combination of two approaches to make hybrid can be done in many methods (Cai et al., 2018; Jeong et al., 2017; Patro et al., 2020)as mentioned below.

(i)   Implementing both filtering separately, and later combining them.
(ii) Making uses of some rules from both filtering systems.
(iii) Making use of a set of rules of content-based filtering in CF.
(iv) A new recommender system must be created which used both filtering together.

3. EARLY YEARS RECOMMENDATION APPROACH

The people are changing with time and along with them the gadgets, devices and technologies are also changing swiftly. In some years back, the people used to get recommendation from of products on the TVs or from radio based on their channel language and based on other perspectives which are not so affective. That time has not so advanced gadgets and resulting of that the recommendation system are also not able to develop because there was not advanced medium to reach out the customers. But as

Figure 9. Hybrid recommendation approach

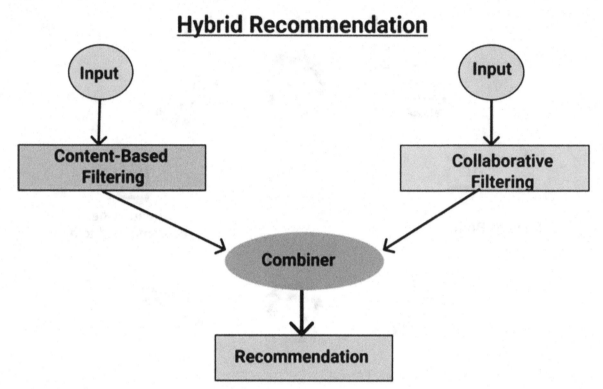

per today's scenario, almost every person has gadgets, devices which are rich in advancement. Today's peoples are using smartphones, laptops, desktops, tablets, etc. for daily uses and for their browsing. Based on this is becomes easy for companies to develop more advanced recommender system as now they have the medium to reach out the customer easily and effectively.

It is clearly noticeable in Fig.9 that few years back, in 2009, the peoples are very familiar only with flat-screen TVs and conventional TVs more frequently. The uses of tablets, laptops, desktops are less as compared to TVs. Also, the use of mobile phones is not so high. Because at that time the smart phones or mobiles are not so much developed and advanced. Also, it is not easy for each and every normal people to get mobiles. People used to sit and watch TVs in home, and whatever recommendation about new products, or items shown in that TVs, on that only people are attracted. But this method was not so effective because the advertiser or recommender not able to reach every customer. Also, maybe customer is suggested with right products, but it not every time easy for that customer to get that product because of availability of that products nearby him, or lack of knowledge from where to get it. Although, people were using desktop computer and laptops, but that were not accessible anywhere. Whenever user sits to operate at a particular place, he can be recommended with products. But those products were not handy, which anyone can carry everywhere in pockets.

3.1. Existing Recommendation Approach

Mobiles are the devices which are handy, can be accessible anywhere, anytime. As in Fig. 9 the uses of mobiles are increased intensively in a very short time. In 2020, the phones are not only phones, these becomes smartphones. The uses and advancement of these smartphones in future will be on the top most priority by users as well as per business developers. So, most customers are equipped with smartphones by now, so it becomes easy to recommend them effectively. The location of the user can be taken into consideration for recommendation, also the age, gender can be requested from users for proper recommendation. Although, doing this many thing, the unbreakable rock, "cold start problem" gets into the path.

In this paper, a new method is proposed in order to break some stone from that unbreakable rock, "cold start problem". So, with the help of this devices they can get customer's locations, their person details like age, name and gender.

Figure 10. Pie chart on change of Devices uses as per 2009 and 2020

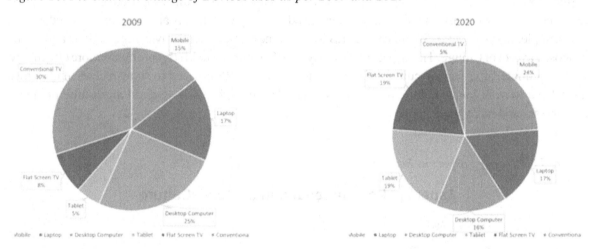

To overcome this cold start problem to further level of extent, a method is proposed called "Personalized Filtering". Till 2020 the percentage of people switched to smart phones has increased vastly, and by 2030 this percentage will reach up to 50% for sure. So, in this personalized filtering methods, the feature and capabilities of smartphones are used to purify the recommendation more precisely and supply a proper and personalized recommendation. Smart phones have features and specialties to able to identify user's exact location, their activities, culture, and current weather from where they belong to. In this method, these features of a smart phone are being used and merged with content-based filtering to deliver a more accurate recommendation to the users. Here, the user's current weather, exact location and their culture in being requested from user in the form of location access, weather access etc. And then those data are being used for the freshly new user for recommendation purpose. In this way, the cold start problem can be crushed up to further some extent. The methodologies' aspects are discussing below:

3.1.1. Aspect in Recommendation System: Culture

Anywhere, Culture is known as the characteristics or information or knowledge of a specific bundle of peoples. This bundle may be encircled by language, arts, tradition, norms, festivals, architecture, food, clothes, taste, color, odor, texture and some other categories(Cordero et al., 2020; Parvatikar & Parasar, 2021). There are many cultures are followed worldwide like Indian culture, Italian culture, French, Spaniards, Chinese, UK, Greece, Swedish culture and many more. As shown in Fig. 10.1, with the help of user's mobile location, there activity and then mixing up them with previous aspects, system can predict user's culture. According to user's culture, then recommendation system can generate recommendation for that specific user. This makes feel user most delight and comfortable to select recommended products easily, as user is already pre-adjusted with a specific culture(Miranda et al., 2020; Rui Zhang, Alexander Shapiro & H., 2019). The recommender system only has to analyses and predicts user's culture and recommended related to that only.

For example, in fig. 10.1, a new user emerges into a shopping app. In this case, the recommender system doesn't have any previous purchase data about that user. So, in this proposed aspect the RS first feed in user's previous aspects like country, age, gender, along with that is also feed in proposed aspect, for example, Indian culture. So, this makes RS to recommend user affectively using previous aspect and proposed aspect of Culture. This aspect makes easy for RS to prevent cold start problems more effectively. In this example, after feeding culture of user as Indian culture, RS proceed to show recommends which are related to or in Indian culture like Indian culture dresses, spices, cheap and long-lasting products, silk dresses and many more.

Figure 11. Proposed aspect in Recommendation System: Culture

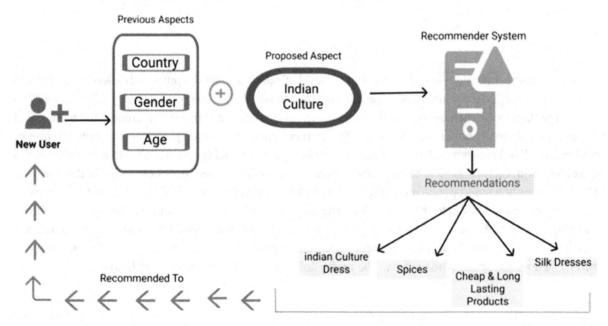

3.1.2. Aspect in Recommendation System: Local Scarcity

Local Scarcity simply implies that the lack of sufficient products or items in a specific place or in local area. This lack of sufficient number of products in known as scarcity. Using this aspect of Local Scarcity, this problem can be solved. Along with previous aspect and proposed culture aspect, this aspect can be added to perform better recommendation. The scarcity usually occurs in places either demand is more or reach is not constructed. This aspect can be implemented by knowing the exact location of a user. Again, that can have done using the collaboration with smart phone location access permission. But in this location, system has to determine user's exact location. On that basis system can predict the number and type of products which is lack in sufficient amount in a specific area or location.

For example, in fig 10.2, when a new user joins and start shopping, RS feed in previous aspect, proposed culture aspect and proposed local scarcity aspect parallel. This set of data goes to the RS. After analyzing the set of that personalized user, RS decided from what type of area the user belongs to. If user belongs to rural area then RS may suggest middle level products, if from urban area then RS may suggest high level products, if from big city then RS may suggest latest products, and if from any other places, RS accordingly recommend then products.

Figure 12. Proposed aspect in Recommendation System: Local Scarcity

Aspect in Recommendation System : Local Scarcity

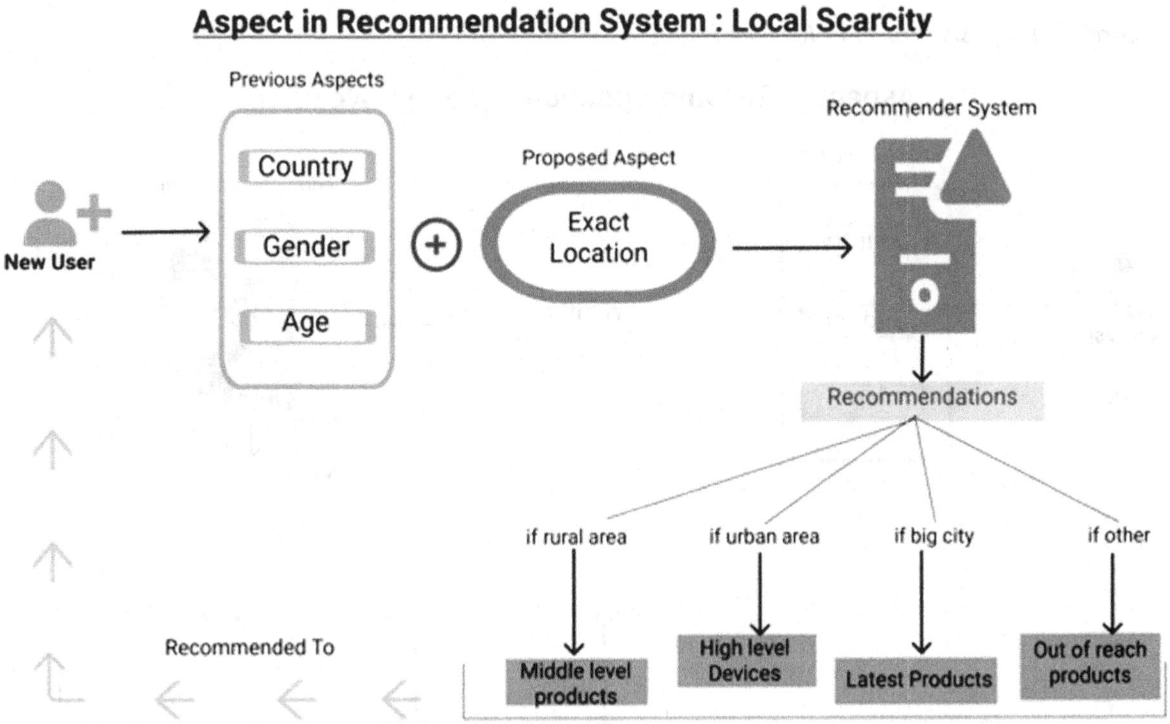

3.1.3. Aspect in Recommendation System: Weather

Weather is factor which has which plays a crucial role in recommendation system. But this aspect is not taken in consideration deeply. Till now the weather is only counted on the basis of months changing i.e. winter, summer, rainy, spring etc. Here, in this aspect, the weather aspect is taken into consideration so deeply. In this method, the weather is not counted on basis of months, but the weather is counted on basis of live changing weather for a personalized user. That means, it will be counted and analyzed every week and according to that the personalized recommendation of products is given to user. For this the RS need to access user's location as well as it need to do any collaboration with someone which do live weather broadcast. In this method, the RS analyses whether the weather is cloudy winter or cloudy summer or winter, summer, rainy, cloudy etc.

For example, in Figure 13, when a new user enters into system, the RS feed in user's previous aspects, plus proposed weather aspect. After that RS gets data from collaborated live weather broadcaster, and accordingly generate personalized recommendations for user. If the weather is cloudy winter then RS may recommend light jackets, if weather is winter then RS may suggest heavy jackets, if weather is cloudy summer then RS may suggest simple T-shirts, similarly if weather is rainy then RS may suggest Umbrella or raincoat. In this way RS can analyses the current week weather and show personalized recommendations to user.

Figure 13. Proposed aspect in Recommendation System: Weather

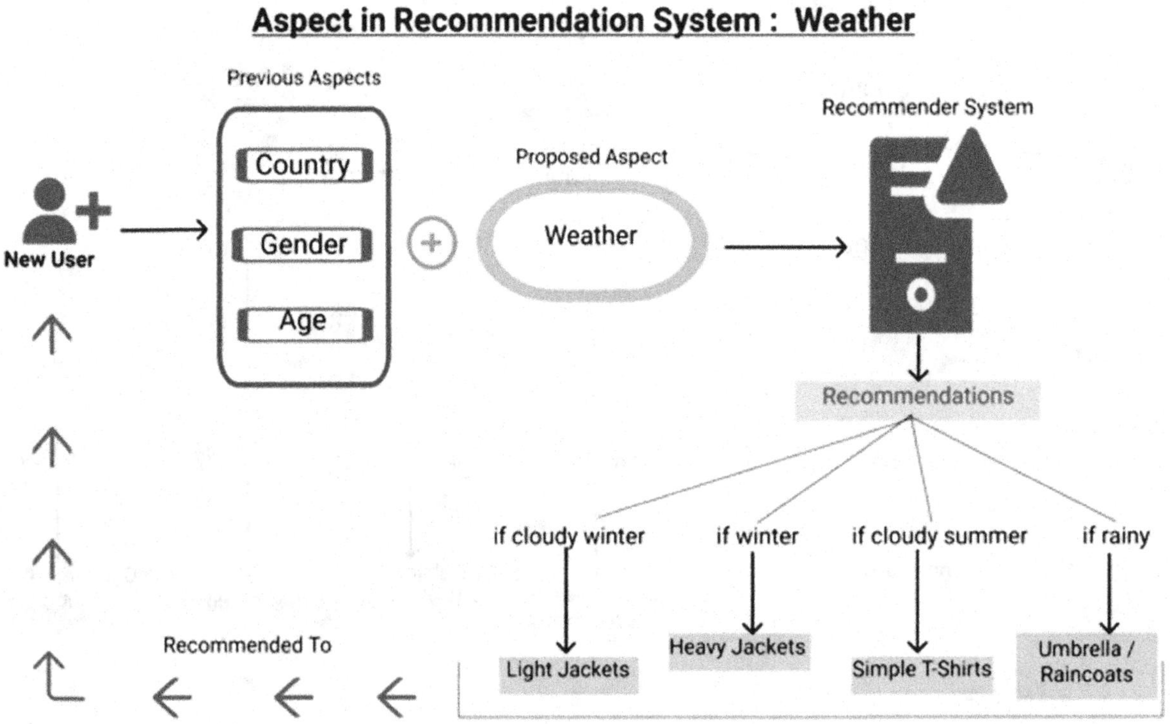

3.2. Personalized Filtering in Recommendation System: LCW Aspect

The above proposed aspects are introduced in this paper. Personalized filtering method foundationally works by adding previous aspects of age, gender, location, along with that is created a bundled of aspects which consist of **L**ocal scarcity aspect, **C**ulture aspect, and **W**eather aspect. Using the above three aspects, the personalized filtering technique is proposed. These three aspects conjointly termed as "LCW Aspect". In this method the RS works by reading and analyzing all three in parallelism, along with previous aspects, which is clearly shown in fig 11. In this personalized filtering the RS feed in new user set of data on basis of these three personalized aspects and in last by analyzing three of them, RS generates recommendation for user.

Figure 14. Personalized Filtering in Recommendation System

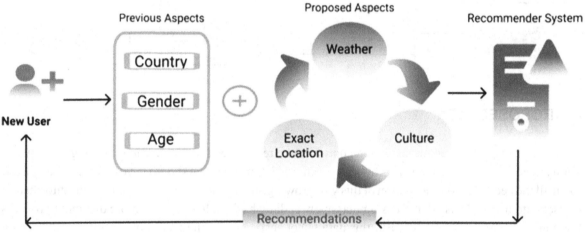

By using personalized filtering method, RS can gain mainly advantages. Like:

Ø   Cold start problem can be resolved up to some further level.
Ø   Users can be recommended with personalized recommendations.
Ø   RS can be able work more efficiently.
Ø   As recommendation system is suggesting in a more personalized way, user can rely on the recommendation system.

This personalized filtering system in recommendation system is smoothly adaptive. This method can be combined with other available methods in recommendation system till now. This can work efficiently anywhere, with every other method. The theoretically working of Personalized recommendation system can be deeply understood by the below flowchart (Figure 15).

Figure 15. Flow chart of personalized filtering

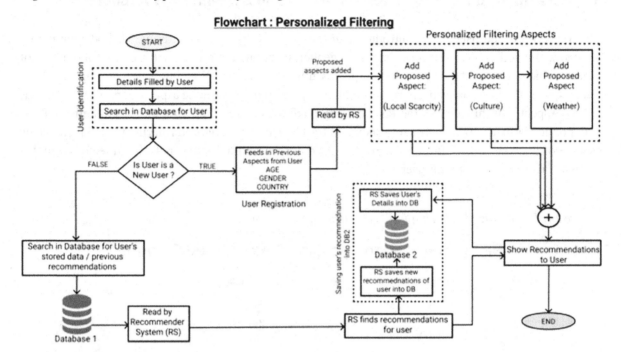

4. PROPOSED IDEA

Although using hybrid recommendation approach, the recommender system can't able to give its workability up to a satisfactory level. This hybrid recommendation approach should have to be upgrading itself to fulfill the need of recommendation of this vast growing and developing online fashion. The information of users, items, products are increasing massively at daily basis, it has become more difficult to process them and give recommendation. But this data is not sufficient for the recommendation system in case of a new users or to solve cold start problem. Besides using similar user's interest, location, gender, age and their profiles, that is also not enough to recommend a more effective suggestion.

To overcome this cold start problem up to some level, an idea is being proposed. This idea is the modification of personalized filtering method. Using this approach, the recommendation system can be used to recommend more effectively by collecting data about a new user like their location, country, culture, along with the current whether, culture and exact location. In this manner system can recommend more precisely and efficiently. For example, analyzing user's culture, it can recommend them especially about that culture, by collecting information about their whether, it can make suggestion whether wise like winter clothes or summer clothes etc.

5 PROPOSED METHODOLOGY

In content-based filtering the customers are suggested with items, products on the basis of customer's purchased record in past time. This system at the earliest finds customer's past searched, purchased, liked data on this database. Then RS finds matches for the same products as customer's area of field and after that makes the implementation of recommendation. This method of filtering is used by many Recommendation System (RS), but there are some stumbling blocks in this method. They are:

Ø   Cold start problem: the main problem comes into consideration when a new user comes into that system. As system has no customer's past purchased record, it foundationally fails to suggest items.
Ø   Here, the current scenario of user's location is not taken into consideration for recommendation.
Ø   Customer's likes, related to which no purchased hasn't done, is not mentioned in suggestions.
Ø   When this RS filtering doesn't find any data, it by default forced to show recommendation to user, which may detest for the customer.
Ø   This RS filtering fails, if an existing user try to browse on any other device with another's id or another's phone.

In collaborative filtering methods the customers are suggested by the help of their interest as well as based on other's customer who possess a like interest. Here the RS use this technique and finds the customers, which are called neighbor of a customer who have ever purchased or have interest on same type of objects which were previous ordered or like by that customer. In this way, this technique created a user and neighbor relationship. This relationship technique is used by the recommender system for suggesting more precisely. By this method, customer used to receive suggestions more precisely than content-based filtering. But this filtering also has some drawbacks. The drawbacks are:

Ø   Cold start problem: this filtering also can't halt cold start problem. When new users come, system doesn't have any data of that user as well as not able to recommend then products on the basis of any of him neighbor, as till that time that new user has no neighbor generated by the system.
Ø   If user changes device, this filtering can't recognize and recommend products.
Ø   If a neighbor is generated on basis of same interests, but in future neighbor interest are shifted to very new fields, the system recommends that type of products to that user. So, that product maybe be detest for that particular user.
Ø   Sometimes, maybe, that neighbor may left that system, so the system has again to make a new neighbor of that system. So, sometimes it may engage more times, which is again a demerit.

Looking into the Hybrid concept filtering for recommendation, this technique, puzzle out the problem of Cold start problem up to some extent. But even though, it is not effectively work to smash cold start problem. Even though it uses Content based and collaborative filtering, the new users are getting lack of adaptive recommendation from system.

5. RESULT AND ANALYSIS

Personalized filtering in recommendation (LCW Aspect) system provides a better and personalized method for recommendation. This personalized filtering will surely make difference in user's shopping experience as well as the business will also grow. It will help users to get recommendation which are specially made for them on basis of their interest. Users don't have to face any cold start problem, bad recommendation. RS system also work efficiently with effectively tackling cold start problem more rigidly. RS don't have to reply on other user i.e. neighbor user to recommend the user, which was happening in collaborative filtering.

Fig. 13 shows an analysis growth on smartphone user through year. This shows that the growth of smartphone user is massively increasing year by year. The analysis is done from year 2016 to the prediction up to year 2026. The users who are switching to smartphones is always increasing and will always increase in future. And the personalized filtering is using the smart phones of user for recommendation precisely, so in future the personalized filtering method is going to works more advance and will able to catch maximum percentage of users. With the growth of technology of smartphones, personalized filtering method can greatly use in future for recommendation. Also trend of recommendation will shift from non-personalized to personalized.

Also, in personalized filtering the users will always get connected to their culture as here the aspect of culture in being used. in this way, the user's culture and tradition will always be reminded. This feature of personalized filtering in recommender system makes it unique from other techniques. Users also will be satisfied with personalized filtering which provides more accurate recommendation as well as connecting to their cultures.

Figure 16. Smart Phone users in billion over years (2016 to 2026)

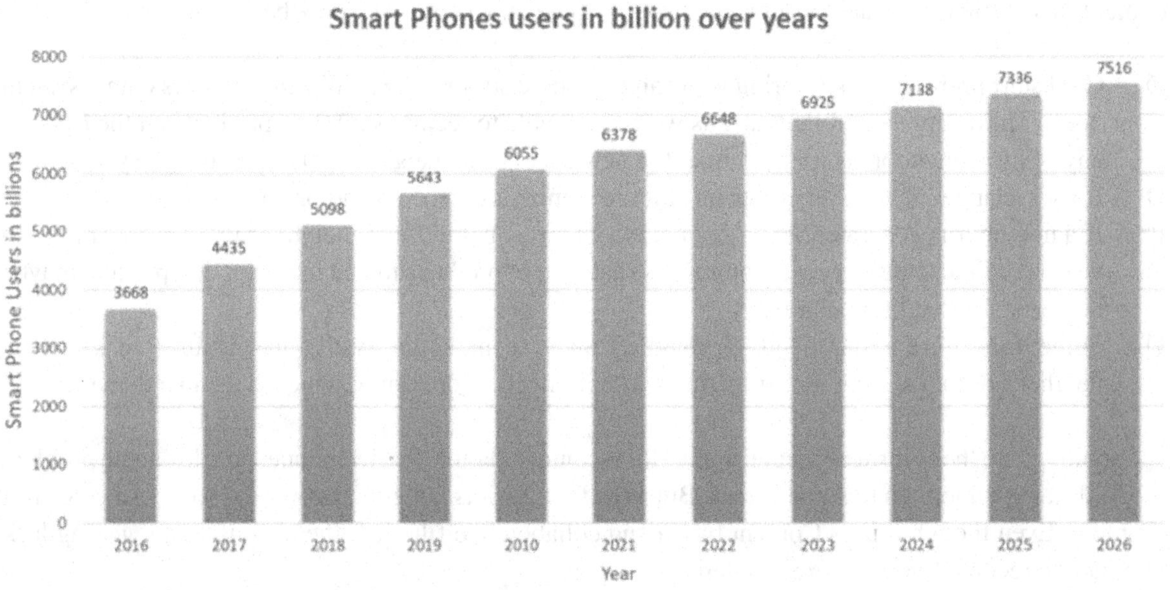

6. CONCLUSION

In this article, the focus is on exploring and understanding the recommendation system. Basically, the recommender mechanism is used to create and suggest recommendations for users so that new customers get several items of their own interests. Recommendation system uses content-based filtering, collaborative filtering and some used hybrid recommendation approach. But these techniques are somehow not impressive for the users when they come in action, which is basically known as "cold start problem". In this study, a number of papers is being studied to overcome this cold start problem using in backend using diagrams of every filtering approach. The content-based filtering method uses past rated, liked, and disliked comments to create a proper suggestion/recommendation. On the other hand, collaborative filtering, analyzes the rating of users with similar interest and accordingly recommends items/ products which are rated or liked by any other user. Hybrid recommendation approach uses both the filtering system to provide more filtered suggestion for users. Recommender system frequently uses user's past likes, dislikes, rated items, browsed products, share items, etc. to analyses and recommendations along with using the user's location to make things analyzed. The online shopping era of modern society accepts the E-commerce system massively using recommender mechanism. These recommendations are widely given in the form on advertisements over variety of web pages to a vast gain user base. As in e-commerce, number of products keep on adding in every fraction of seconds along with a joining of large number of new users. To manage this large amount of user's profile as well as new items, a high-profile recommender system is highly needed. Also, it needs to tackle the "cold start problem" which generally arises when a new user signs up not having any kind of past information. To overcome such problems, a new model is being proposed called as Personalized Filtering, which works on "LCW Aspect". Here, along with age, gender, location, RS also analyze user's Local scarcity, culture and whether to suggest recommendation. In future, this approach can be further improvised by adding more criteria to give accurate recommendation.

ACKNOWLEDGMENT

The authors are very grateful to the GIET University, Gunupur, India, for their kind support and giving the opportunity as well as providing the continuous laboratory facilities.

Conflicts of interest: The authors have no conflicts of interests.

Funding: There are no funding agencies in the preparation of this article.

REFERENCES

Aher, S. B., & Lobo, L. M. R. J. (2013). Combination of machine learning algorithms for recommendation of courses in E-Learning System based on historical data. *Knowledge-Based Systems*, *51*, 1–14. doi:10.1016/j.knosys.2013.04.015

Bhatia, M., Sood, S. K., & Kumari, R. (2020). Fuzzy-inspired decision making for dependability recommendation in e-commerce industry. *Intelligent Decision Technologies*, *14*(2), 181–197. doi:10.3233/IDT-190143

Bobadilla, J., Ortega, F., Hernando, A., & Gutiérrez, A. (2013). Knowledge-Based Systems Recommender systems survey. *Knowledge-Based Systems*, *46*, 109–132. doi:10.1016/j.knosys.2013.03.012

Cai, J., Wang, Y., Liu, Y., Luo, J. Z., Wei, W., & Xu, X. (2018). Enhancing network capacity by weakening community structure in scale-free network. *Future Generation Computer Systems*, *87*, 765–771. doi:10.1016/j.future.2017.08.014

Cordero, P., Enciso, M., López, D., & Mora, A. (2020). A conversational recommender system for diagnosis using fuzzy rules. *Expert Systems with Applications*, *154*, 113449. Advance online publication. doi:10.1016/j.eswa.2020.113449

Gope, J., & Jain, S. K. (2017). A survey on solving cold start problem in recommender systems. *Proceeding - IEEE International Conference on Computing, Communication and Automation, ICCCA 2017*, 133–138. 10.1109/CCAA.2017.8229786

Hosseinzadeh Aghdam, M. (2019). Context-aware recommender systems using hierarchical hidden Markov model. *Physica A*, *518*, 89–98. doi:10.1016/j.physa.2018.11.037

Huitzil, I., Alegre, F., & Bobillo, F. (2020). GimmeHop: A recommender system for mobile devices using ontology reasoners and fuzzy logic. *Fuzzy Sets and Systems*, *401*, 55–77. doi:10.1016/j.fss.2019.12.001

Hwangbo, H., Kim, Y. S., & Cha, K. J. (2018). Recommendation system development for fashion retail e-commerce. *Electronic Commerce Research and Applications*, *28*, 94–101. doi:10.1016/j.elerap.2018.01.012

Iwanaga, J., Nishimura, N., Sukegawa, N., & Takano, Y. (2019). Improving collaborative filtering recommendations by estimating user preferences from clickstream data. *Electronic Commerce Research and Applications*, *37*, 100877. doi:10.1016/j.elerap.2019.100877

Jeong, H. Y., Park, K. M., Lee, M. J., Yang, D. H., Kim, S. H., & Lee, S. Y. (2017). Vitamin D and hypertension. *Electrolyte & Blood Pressure*, *15*(1), 1–11. doi:10.5049/EBP.2017.15.1.1 PMID:29042901

Ji, Z., Pi, H., Wei, W., Xiong, B., Wozniak, M., & Damasevicius, R. (2019). Recommendation Based on Review Texts and Social Communities: A Hybrid Model. *IEEE Access: Practical Innovations, Open Solutions*, *7*, 40416–40427. doi:10.1109/ACCESS.2019.2897586

Jiang, L., Cheng, Y., Yang, L., Li, J., Yan, H., & Wang, X. (2019). A trust-based collaborative filtering algorithm for E-commerce recommendation system. *Journal of Ambient Intelligence and Humanized Computing*, *10*(8), 3023–3034. doi:10.100712652-018-0928-7

Katarya, R., & Verma, O. P. (2017). An effective web page recommender system with fuzzy c-mean clustering. *Multimedia Tools and Applications*, *76*(20), 21481–21496. doi:10.100711042-016-4078-7

Kumar, P., Kumar, V., & Thakur, R. S. (2019). A new approach for rating prediction system using collaborative filtering. *Iran Journal of Computer Science*, *2*(2), 81–87. doi:10.100742044-018-00028-5

Kumar, P., & Thakur, R. S. (2018). Recommendation system techniques and related issues: A survey. *International Journal of Information Technology (Singapore)*, *10*(4), 495–501. doi:10.100741870-018-0138-8

Lv, J., Song, B., Guo, J., Du, X., & Guizani, M. (2019). Interest-Related Item Similarity Model Based on Multimodal Data for Top-N Recommendation. *IEEE Access: Practical Innovations, Open Solutions*, *7*(c), 12809–12821. doi:10.1109/ACCESS.2019.2893355

Miranda, L., Viterbo, J., & Miranda, L. (2020). Association for Information Systems AIS Electronic Library (AISeL) Towards the Use of Clustering Algorithms in Recommender Systems Towards the Use of Clustering Algorithms in Recommender Systems. *Association for Information Systems AIS*, 0–10.

Nassar, N., Jafar, A., & Rahhal, Y. (2020). A novel deep multi-criteria collaborative filtering model for recommendation system. *Knowledge-Based Systems*, *187*, 104811. Advance online publication. doi:10.1016/j.knosys.2019.06.019

Natarajan, S., Vairavasundaram, S., Natarajan, S., & Gandomi, A. H. (2020). Resolving data sparsity and cold start problem in collaborative filtering recommender system using Linked Open Data. *Expert Systems with Applications*, *149*, 113248. doi:10.1016/j.eswa.2020.113248

Nilashi, M., Ibrahim, O., & Bagherifard, K. (2018). A recommender system based on collaborative filtering using ontology and dimensionality reduction techniques. *Expert Systems with Applications*, *92*, 507–520. doi:10.1016/j.eswa.2017.09.058

Oluwagbemi, O., Oluwagbemi, F., & Abimbola, O. (2016). Ebinformatics: Ebola fuzzy informatics systems on the diagnosis, prediction and recommendation of appropriate treatments for Ebola virus disease (EVD). *Informatics in Medicine Unlocked*, *2*, 12–37. doi:10.1016/j.imu.2015.12.001

Parvatikar, S., & Parasar, D. (2021). Recommendation system using machine learning. *International Journal of Artificial Intelligence and Machine Learning*, *1*(1), 24. doi:10.51483/IJAIML.1.1.2021.24-30

Patro, S. G. K., Mishra, B. K., Panda, S. K., Kumar, R., Long, H. V., Taniar, D., & Priyadarshini, I. (2020). A Hybrid Action-Related K-Nearest Neighbour (HAR-KNN) Approach for Recommendation Systems. *IEEE Access: Practical Innovations, Open Solutions*, *8*, 90978–90991. doi:10.1109/ACCESS.2020.2994056

Peng, T., Liu, Q., Meng, D., & Wang, G. (2017). Collaborative trajectory privacy preserving scheme in location-based services. *Information Sciences*, *387*, 165–179. doi:10.1016/j.ins.2016.08.010

Ranjbar Kermany, N., & Alizadeh, S. H. (2017). A hybrid multi-criteria recommender system using ontology and neuro-fuzzy techniques. *Electronic Commerce Research and Applications*, *21*, 50–64. doi:10.1016/j.elerap.2016.12.005

Razia Sulthana, A., & Ramasamy, S. (2019). Ontology and context based recommendation system using Neuro-Fuzzy Classification. *Computers & Electrical Engineering*, *74*, 498–510. doi:10.1016/j.compeleceng.2018.01.034

Selvi, C., & Sivasankar, E. (2019). A novel Adaptive Genetic Neural Network (AGNN) model for recommender systems using modified k-means clustering approach. *Multimedia Tools and Applications*, *78*(11), 14303–14330. doi:10.100711042-018-6790-y

Son, J., & Kim, S. B. (2017). Content-based filtering for recommendation systems using multiattribute networks. *Expert Systems with Applications*, *89*, 404–412. doi:10.1016/j.eswa.2017.08.008

Tahmasebi, F., Meghdadi, M., Ahmadian, S., & Valiallahi, K. (2021). A hybrid recommendation system based on profile expansion technique to alleviate cold start problem. *Multimedia Tools and Applications*, *80*(2), 2339–2354. doi:10.100711042-020-09768-8

Wang, C. D., Deng, Z. H., Lai, J. H., & Yu, P. S. (2019). Serendipitous recommendation in e-commerce using innovator-based collaborative filtering. *IEEE Transactions on Cybernetics*, *49*(7), 2678–2692. doi:10.1109/TCYB.2018.2841924 PMID:29994495

Wang, K., Zhang, T., Xue, T., Lu, Y., & Na, S. G. (2020). E-commerce personalized recommendation analysis by deeply-learned clustering. *Journal of Visual Communication and Image Representation, 71,* 102735. Advance online publication. doi:10.1016/j.jvcir.2019.102735

Yang, Z., Sun, Q., & Zhang, B. (2018). Evaluating prediction error for anomaly detection by exploiting matrix factorization in rating systems. *IEEE Access: Practical Innovations, Open Solutions, 6,* 50014–50029. doi:10.1109/ACCESS.2018.2869271

Zhang, Rui, & Alexander Shapiro, Y. X., & H. (2019). Stastical Rank Selection for Incomplete Low-rank Matrices. *IEEE Access: Practical Innovations, Open Solutions, 3,* 2912–2916.

Chapter 22
A Survey of Weed Identification Using Convolutional Neural Networks

Neha Shekhawat
Banasthali Vidyapith, India

Seema Verma
Banasthali Vidyapith, India

Ankit Vijayvargiya
Swami Keshvanand Institute of Technology, Management, and Gramothan, India

Manisha Agarwal
Banasthali Vidyapith, India

Manisha Jailia
Banasthali Vidyapith, India

ABSTRACT

Weeds are the major source of concern for farmers, who anticipate that weeds may lower crop productivity. Thus, it is essential and vital to detect weeds. Traditional weed classification methods such as hand cultivation with hoes have many hindrances such as labour cost and time consumption. Currently, weed reduction farmers are using herbicides, but they have a negative impact on farmer health as well as on the environment. So, farmers want to lower the use of herbicides. Precise spraying is one of the methods in present-day agriculture to lower the usage of herbicides and to destroy the weeds with the assistance of new technologies. Deep learning approaches are already being employed in a variety of agricultural and farming applications and gave better results. This chapter uses convolution neural networks to provide a short overview of some significant agricultural research endeavours. Different architectures of CNN for classification and detection were used. In the sector of agriculture, the authors have outlined the notion of CNNs.

DOI: 10.4018/978-1-6684-6821-0.ch022

INTRODUCTION

The population of the world is currently around 7.7 billion people, and it is predicted to expand to around 9.7 billion by 2050. To meet the demands of a rapidly growing global population, agricultural productivity must quadruple. So, for this, it is essential to increase the crop yield in the agricultural field. However, agriculture faces enormous challenges including water scarcity, changing climate as well as reducing the crop yield and food quality. Weeds are the major problem faced by the farmers in the agricultural sector. There are numerous definitions for weeds, Weeds are unwanted plants that compete for sunshine, soil, nutrients, space, and water with crops for growth (Iqbal, N., et al., n.d.). Weeds are the tough competitors of crop, their seedling process is faster than the crops. Weeds not only reduce the crop yields but also sometimes can be poisonous and can taint the food and crops. Weeds have to remove before they get mature. To reduce the impact of weeds, there are some strategies, which are categorized into 5 main types: 'preventive'(prevent weeds from being initiated), 'cultural'(by maintaining conditions), 'mechanical'(involves the use of farm equipment eg: mowing and tillage), 'biological'(use of natural enemies of weeds e.g: gazing and insects), 'chemical'(use of herbicides). But all these approaches have their drawbacks. These methods are too tedious, insufficient, high labor cost, and time-consuming. In modern agriculture, spraying chemicals such as herbicides and pesticides are used to control the weeds (Harker, K.N., & O'Donovan, J.T, 2013). However, the continuous use of chemicals may concern the environment and affect the soil, animals, and the health of farmers (Bah, M.D., et.al 2018). Therefore, one of the modern approaches is to use precision spraying i.e. to spray where it is needed, but it's also challenging because herbicide use must be minimized while crop yields must be enhanced. Therefore, there is a need for an automatic weed identification system. The precision farming technique monitors the crops and weeds and only attacks the weeds with herbicides. For precision farming, we need automatic weed detection in the field (Stafford, J.V., & Benlloch, J.V., 1997). To develop an automatic weed detection system we need to detect weeds correctly. Sometimes, this task can be challenging as the weeds and crops can be of the same shapes, textures, and colors.

There are some challenges in detecting and classifying weeds and crops such as shadows of plants in natural light, occlusion, color, and texture are similar.

With the traditional Machine Learning methods, it is difficult to extract and discriminate patterns as there is a similarity in crops and weeds. Deep Learning has the advantage of automatic feature extraction. This survey is presented to highlight the great potential of different deep learning techniques for classifying, localizing and detecting the weeds. An overview of different deep learning methods to detect and classify weeds was presented.

In this study, CNN's achievements in the field of agriculture were discussed. In section II, introduction of Deep learning was discussed. In section III, a general overview of the CNN model was discussed. In section IV, different CNN models based on classification tasks were discussed with their application in weed and crop classification tasks. In section V, various CNN models based on detection tasks were discussed with their tasks of weed and crop detection.

DEEP LEARNING

The most significant approach of Machine Learning is deep learning. Both the technologies are applied to identification and detection of weeds. Deep learning is more resilient than machine learning, Deep Learning-based approaches has the ability to learn patterns from an image automatically. In a variety of fields, deep learning has shown the major advances, including object detection (Girshick, R, 2014), speech recognition (Hinton, G et.al, 2012), segmentation [Song, S. et.al, 2015], video classification (Karpathy, A. et al, 2014) and in many other fields.

Several Deep Learning architectures have been presented in the recent decade. Currently, the main networks are Convolutional Neural Networks, Recurrent Neural Network (RNN) and Multilayer Perceptron. The architecture of Convolutional Neural Networks is particularly useful for image processing (Girshick, R, 2014; Zelier, M.D, 2014; Guo, Y, 2016). Convolutional Neural Networks are Artificial Neural Networks (ANNs) that have 3 layers: convolution, pooling, activation layer and fully connected. In 2012, AlexNet (Krizhevsky, A, et.al, 2012) proposed by Krizhevsky, performed outstanding at ImageNet Large Scale Visual Recognition Challenge (ILSVRC) (Russakovsky, O, et.al, 2015). Later on, Convolutional Neural Networks gained popularity for Image Classification. In agriculture, for weed classification (Peteinatos, G et.al, 2020) and weed detection (Sa, I et.al, 2017) CNN-based approaches have been used.

Recently, deep learning move forward in automatic feature extraction from image (Hinton, G et.al, 2012). A.S.M Mahmudul Hasan (Hasan, A.S.M et.al, 2021) detect and classify weeds using technique called deep learning. Chunying Wang (Wang, C et.al, 2021) made an analysis on deep learning to hyperspectral images in agriculture. They include variety classification, remote sensing image classification, ripeness and component prediction and plant disease detection.

Aichen Wang (Wang, A et.al, 2019) summarized the current state of weed identification systems based on ground-based machine vision and imaging processing. Kenneth Li-Minn Ang (Ang, K.L.M., & Seng, J.K.P., 2021) proposed a way to use big data in agricultural remote sensing research was evaluated. Syamasudha Veeragandham and H Santhi (Veeragandham, S, & Santhi, H, 2021) made comparison review on different architectures of CNN. Jinzhu Lu (Lu, J et.al, 2021) summarized the most recent CNN network for identifying plant leaf disease, as well as DL principles for detecting plant leaf disease.

BACKGROUND OF CONVOLUTIONAL NEURAL NETWORKS

Convolutional Neural Networks are a kind of multilayer neural network that is particularly remarkable. The mechanism of living creatures' visual systems was used to design the well-known CNN architecture. In 1959, Hubal and Weisel (Hubel, D.H., & Wiesel, T.N., 1968) proposed that animal visual cortex cells are accountable for perceiving light in a restricted receptive field. Kunihiko Fukushima was motivated by this work and postulated the neocognitron in 1980(Hu, J, et.al, 2018). In this, first hierarchical structure is used to process the images. The very first CNN was propound by Yann LeCun et.al in 1998(LeCun, Y et.al., 1998), referred as LeNet-5 which is used to recognize the handwritten digits. However, at that time there is no huge amount of training data and computational capacity, so their network cannot perform well. CNN sprang to prominence in 2012 after winning the ImageNet Large Scale Visual Recognition Challenge (ILSVRC) (Russakovsky, O et.al, 2015) is AlexNet (Krizhevsky, A et.al, 2012).

CONVOLUTIONAL NEURAL NETWORKS

Convolutional Neural Networks are a commonly utilized architecture in the discipline of computer vision. Convolutional Neural Networks are good at selecting patterns from input images such as lines, edges, gradients, and even faces. Without much pre-processing a raw input image can be operated directly in a convolutional neural network. Convolutional neural networks have 3 layers: input layer, hidden layer, and output layer. There is convolution, pooling, and fully connected layers in the hidden layer. The convolution layer and pooling layer were used to extract the patterns from an input image, and the use of a fully connected layer is to map the extracted pattern into a final output like classification. The CNN design is made up of several blocks or stages with basic components such as: kernel, convolution layer, pooling layer, and non-linearity activation function. Each phase represents patterns as a set of arrays called activation maps. The figure 1 shows the CNN architecture composed of the stack of convolution blocks and one or more fully connected layers.

Figure 1. Convolutional Neural Networks model.

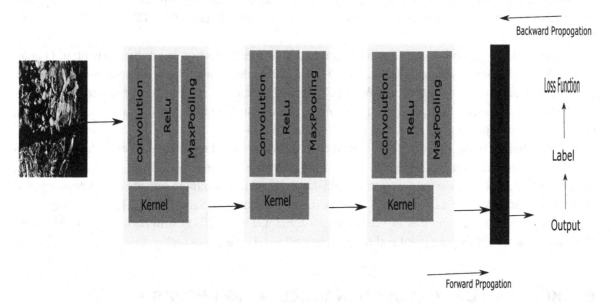

Filter or Kernel: The patterns of an input image are extracted using a kernel or a filter. It's an integer matrix that traverses across the input image. The filter's size taken is smaller than the input image's size.

Convolution layer: The center of the Convolution Neural Networks (CNNs) is the convolution layer, this layer performs convolution operation. For pattern extraction a linear operation is used which is called convolution. In this layer, as for the input we use 2D image (I) which is convolved with the 2D kernel matrix (K), then the mathematical equation formed is given in[26]:

$$S_{ij} = \left(I * K \right)_{ij} = \sum_{m} \sum_{n} I_{ij} . K_{i-m,j-n} \tag{1}$$

In convolution layer, a small matrix called kernel or filter sliding throughout the image. At every location, it computes the dot product between each weight of kernel and the corresponding element of input image. This process is repeated until the filter has passed throughout the image, and for every filter a feature map is generated.

Activation Layer: After the feature maps are created they forward to the next layer, the activation layer. In order to make network to learn complex pattern from the data there is need to add non-linearity in activation layer. In this layer non-linear activation function is put in Equation (1) to produce activation maps, where only triggered features can move forward to the next layer. Then for the activation function, the mathematical definition is as follows:

$$\phi\left(Y_i^{(l)}\right) = f(B_i^{(l)} + \sum_{j-1}^{m_i^{(l-1)}} k_{ij}^l * Y_j^{(l-1)}) \tag{2}$$

There is different type of activation functions.

Sigmoid: This function takes any real values between [0, 1] so, it is used for probability-based output. The curve for this function looks like the S-shape (Goodfellow, I, et.al, 2016). Mathematical definition is as follows:

$$f(x) = \frac{1}{1 + e^{-2x}} - 1 \tag{3}$$

Tanh (Hyperbolic tangent) function: The shape of tanh function is also S-shaped which is identical to the Sigmoid function (Goodfellow, I, et.al, 2016), but it ranges from [-1,1]. The benefit of tanh is that the negative values will be mapped strongly negative and the zero values will be mapped near to zero. It is zero centered function. The mathematical definition for this function is as follows:

$$f(x) = \frac{2}{1 + e^{-2x}} - 1 \tag{4}$$

Rectified Linear Unit function (ReLU): In convolution layer the ReLU is widely used activation function. The main catch here is that in ReLU all the neurons are not activated at the same time. The neurons will only deactivate only when the output of linear transformation is zero (Sharma, S, et.al, 2017). The mathematical definition is as follows:

$$F(x) = \max(0, x) \tag{5}$$

Pooling Layer: With the help of pooling layer, each activation maps that are created by the output of the convolutional operation can be downsampled. It has two primary functions: Firstly, to limit the number of parameters and the other is to prevent overfitting. Each activation map is treated separately by the pooling layer (Yamashita, R et.al, 2018). There are various approaches to pooling. Here are some common approaches:

Max Pooling: The layer uses the activation map supplied by the convolutional layer with the most significant feature in max-pooling (Gholamalinezhad, H & Khosravi, H, 2020).

Min Pooling: In this layer the most non-prominent patterns of activation map are provided by the convolutional layer.

Average Pooling: This layer uses the activation map which is the output of the convolutional layer with the average values of each region (Yamashita, R et.al, 2018).

Global Average Pooling: A global average pooling is a sort of extreme downsampling in which a activation map is downsampled into a 1x1 array by simply averaging all the components in each activation map while keeping the activation maps' depth (Gholamalinezhad, H & Khosravi, H, 2020).

Fully Connected (FC) Layer: The output from the final convolutional or pooling Layer is converted into a 1-Dimensional array of numbers and then fed into the fully linked layer as the input. The FC layers process and use them to classify the image into a label, just like a regular neural network (i.e., class). In the last layer there is an activation function which computes the final probabilities for each class and is chosen based on the task. Number of output nodes is same as number of classes in the last fully connected layer.

REVIEW OF WEED CLASSIFICATION USING CNN MODELS

LeNet

Concept: In 1998, very first convolutional neural network was proposed by Yann LeCun et.al (LeCun, Y, 1998) which uses for Handwriting and character recognition, called LeNet. Without counting the input, LeNet-5 has seven layers, each of which contains parameters (weights). The image's input size is 32x32 pixels. 3 convolutional layers, 2 subsampling layers, 1 fully connected layer (F6), and a single output layer make up the model. LeNet-5's architecture is depicted in Figure 2. The LeNet-5 layers are shown in figure 2:

Figure 2. Simple model of LeNet-5 (LeCun, Y, 1998).

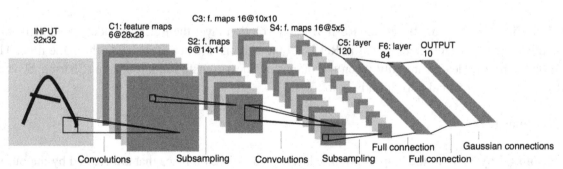

For the first layer (C1), the size input image is 32x32 gray scale pictures. The first convolutional layer, which consists of six activation maps or filters with a size of 5x5 and with stride 1, processes this image. The size of the image transforms from 32x32x1 to 28x28x6 pixels. Subsampling is the second layer (S2), which results in six 14x14 activation graphs. Each activation map cell is linked to two 2x2 neighborhoods in C1. The second convolution layer (C3) includes 16 activation maps, each of which is 5x5 in size and has a stride of 1. The fourth layer (S4), is also a subsampling (Pooling layer) layer, this time with a stride of 2 and a filter size of 2x2. This layer is identical to the second layer (S2) except that it contains 16 activation mappings, resulting in a 5x5x16 output. C5, the fifth layer, is fully linked convolutional layer with 120 5x5 activation maps. Each cell in S4's 16 activation graphs is associated with the 5*5 neighborhood. With 84 units, the sixth layer (F6) is the fully connected layer. F6 layer is completely connected to the C5 layer. There are total 10164 parameters that can be trained. The output layer is the final layer which has 10 neurons and uses softmax function.

Application: Nawmee Razia Rahman et al. (Rahman, N.R et.al, 2020) compare LeNet-5, VGG16, ResNet50 and DenseNet121 for weed classification. There are twelve species to classify and ResNet50 outperformed. Cordova-Cruzatty Andrea et.al(Andrea, C.C, et.al, 2017) compares LeNet, ALexNet, CNet and SNet architectures for classification of Weeds and Maize. Among which CNet performed better with the 97.23% accuracy. Syamasudha Veeragandham et al. (Veeragandham, S & Santhi, H, 2021) compare the performances of LeNet, AlexNet, CNEt and SNet for weed classification among which CNet gave better results.

AlexNet

Concept: AlexNet was propound by Alex Krizhevsky et al. (Krizhevsky, A et.al., 2012), this is a convolutional neural network, which won the first place in the ImageNet Large Scale Visual Recognition Challenge (ILSVRC) competition (Russakovsky, O et.al., 2015) in 2012. AlexNet contain eight layers: 5 convolutional layers and 3 fully linked layers. The architecture of AlexNet is very much similar to LeNet but it is much deeper than LeNet. ReLU activation function was used for non-linearity and it is noted that the speed of training process is increased by 6 times. Dropout was used to reduce the overfitting although the training time was increased, and also Normalization was also used. The architecture of AlexNet is shown in figure 3.

Figure 3. Architecture of AlexNet (Krizhevsky, A et.al, 2012).

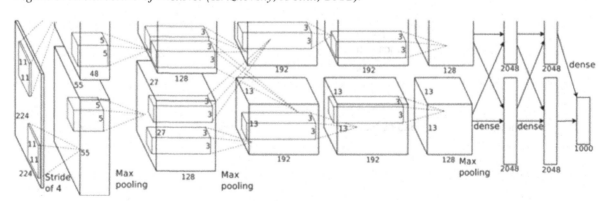

Applications: Trupti R.Chavan and Abhijeet V.Nandedkar (Chavan, T.R., Nandedkar, A.V et.al, 2018) uses AgroAVNET which is acquire from AlexNet and VGGNet for weed classification. The filter's depth picked from VGGNet whereas the normalization concept is taken from AlexNet. The performance of AgroAVNET is performed better compared to AlexNet and VGGNet. A. Subeesh et al. (Subeesh, A et.al, 2022) compares 4 deep learning models i.e. AlexNet, GoogLeNet, Inceptionv3, and Xception to classify weeds. Jizhan Liu et al. (Liu, J et.al, 2021) use AlexNet, GoogLeNet and VGG16 for weed classification in strawberry field. Among these VGG16 perform better. Dr. E.Gothai et al. (Gothai, E et.al, 2020) adopt VGG16, ZFNet and AlexNet along with four-layered, six-layered, eight-layered and thirteen-layered architecture among which eight-layered architecture out perform with 96.53% accuracy. Cordova-Cruzatty Andrea et al. (Andrea, C.C, et.al, 2017) compares LeNet, ALexNet, CNet and SNet architectures for classification of Weeds and Maize. Among which CNet performed better with the 97.23% accuracy. Yogesh Beeharry et al. (Beehary, Y., Bassoo, V, 2020) compare the performances of ANN and ALexNet for weed classification and among which ALexNet outperformed. Syamasudha Veeragandham et al. (Veeragandham, S & Santhi, H, 2021) compare the performances of LeNet, AlexNet, CNEt and SNet for weed classification among which CNEt gave better results.

Google Net

Concept: Szegedy et al. (Szegedy, C, 2015) proposed architecture of GooLeNet, winner of ILSVRC 2014. They used parallel filters called inception module to increase the number of units in each layer (Szegedy, C, 2015) of size 1×1, 3×3 and 5×5 in each convolution layer. This network has 22 layers but has less parameters about 5 million. Deep neural networks are time-consuming to compute. To make it efficient, the authors include an extra 1x1 convolution before the 3x3 and 5x5 convolutions to decrease the number of input channels. ReLu layer was used for non-linearity and in place of fully connected layer, they make use of global average pooling layer. To solve the overfitting and vanishing gradient problem they use small auxiliary classifier, which is smaller CNNs. Inception module, naïve version is shown in figure 4 and inception module with dimension reduction is shown in figure 5.

Figure 4. Inception module, naïve version (Szegedy, C, 2015).

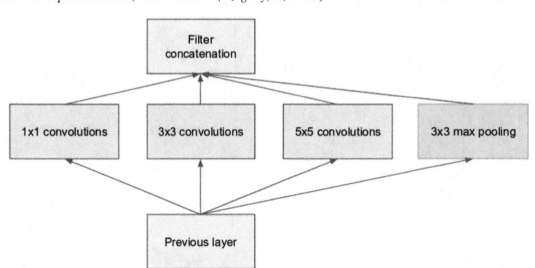

Figure 5. Inception modules with dimension reduction (Szegedy, C, 2015).

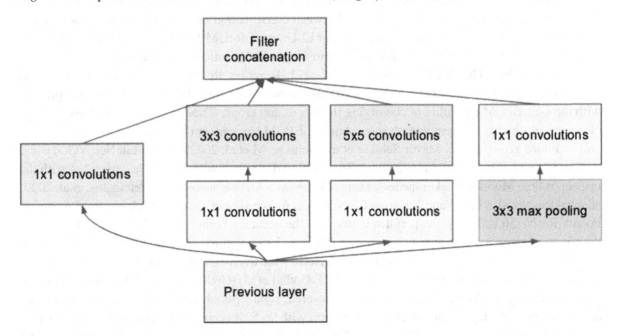

Application: A. Subeesh et al. (Subeesh, A et.al, 2022) compares 4 deep learning models i.e. AlexNet, GoogLeNet, Inceptionv3, and Xception to classify weeds. Jizhan Liu et al. (Liu, Jizhan et.al, 2021) use AlexNet, GoogLeNet and VGG16 for weed classification in strawberry field. Among these VGG16 perform better. Martinson Ofori and Omar El-Gayar (Ofori, M & Gayar, O.F et.al, 2020) conduct three experiments: train model with scratch with random weight initialization, fine-tuning the model and use pre-trained model. VGG16, Inceptionv3, DenseNet121, Xception, ResNet151v2 are used in this work. Alex Olsen et al. (Olsen, A et.al, 2019) use Inceptionv3 and ResNet50 architecture to classify eight weed species from Australian rangeland and ResNet50 gives the better results. Vi Nguyen Thanh Le et al. (Le, V.N.T et.al, 2020) compares VGG16, VGG19, ResNet50, and Inceptionv3 with the k-FLBPCM algorithm in classifying the weeds and crops. CNN models require large number of images of plant at different growth stages but k-FLBPCM can perform with small leaf shapes of second and third growth stage.

VGG Net

Concept: K. Simonyan and A. Zisserman, proposed VGG-Network (Simonyan, K & Zisserman, A, 2014) in 2015, runnerup in the ImageNet Large Scale Visual Recognition Challenge (ILSVRC) (Russakovsky, O et.al, 2015). VGG stands for Visual Geometric Group. This network is same as AlexNet which means it also have huge number of features. It has 138 million parameters. The size of input for the network is 224x224 RBG image. VGG-Net uses small receptive field of 3x3. To perform a linear transformation of input there is 1x1 convolution filter before a ReLU unit is applied. VGG-Net has 3 fully connected layers, the first two has 4096 units each and the last layer had 1000 units, for each class.

Application: Trupti R.Chavan and Abhijeet V.Nandedkar (Chavan, T. R & Nandekar, A.V et.al, 2018) uses AgroAVNET which is acquire from AlexNet and VGGNet for weed classification. The filter's depth picked from VGGNet whereas the normalization concept is taken from AlexNet. The performance of AgroAVNET is performed better compared to AlexNet and VGGNet. Jizhan Liu et al. (Lu, J et.al, 2021) use AlexNet, GoogLeNet and VGG16 for weed classification in strawberry field. Among these VGG16 perform better. Martinson Ofori and Omar El-Gayar (Ofori, M & Gayar, O, 2020) conduct three experiments: train model with scratch with random weight initialization, fine-tuning the model and use pre-trained model. VGG16, Inceptionv3, DenseNet121, Xception, ResNet151v2 are used in this work. Vi Nguyen Thanh Le et al. (Thanh, V.N et.al, 2020) compares VGG16, VGG19, ResNet50, Inceptionv3 with the k-FLBPCM algorithm in classifying the weeds and crops. CNN models require large number of images of plant at different growth stages but kFLBPCM can perform with small leaf shapes of second and third growth stage. Mayur Selukar et al. (Selukar, M et.al, 2022) use MobileNet, VGG16 and ResNet50 to identify weeds. Among which ResNet50 perform well with 91.94% accuracy but with the respect of time MobileNet takes the lesser time. Gerassimos G. Peteinatos et al. (Peteinatos, et.al, 2020) adapted ResNet50, VGG16 and Xception CNN models for weed classification in Maize, Sunflower and Potato. ResNet50 and Xception perform better with the accuracy higher than 97%. As for the VGG16 there is some misclassification between species. Nawmee Razia Rahman et al. (Rahman, N.R et.al, 2020) compare LeNet-5, VGG16, ResNet50 and DenseNet121 for weed classification. There are twelve species to classify and ResNet50 outperformed. Dr. E.Gothai et al. (Gothai, E et.al, 2020) adopt VGG16, ZFNet and AlexNet along with four-layered, six-layered, eight-layered and thirteen-layered architecture among which eight-layered architecture outperform with 96.53% accuracy. Martinson Ofori and Omar El-Gayar (Omar M & Ofori M, 2020) use VGG16 and EfficientNetB1 to classify weeds and crops. Belal A.M. Ashqar et al. (Ashqar, B.A.M et.al, 2019) use VGG16 architecture to classify 12 species of weed and crops.

ResNet

Concept: He et al. (Kaiming H et.al 2016) proposed ResNet, or Deep Residual Network, won the ImageNet competition in 2015, surpassing human accuracy error for the first time with a rate of 3.6 percent. The network is quite complex, the one that was presented during the challenge has 152 layers. A vanishing gradient problem occurs when a deeper CNN is stacked with more layers. To overcome this problem, they used skip connections where the input of layer and the output of layer are directly connected. Residual block is shown in figure 6.

Without the skip connection:

$$H(x) = F(x) \tag{6}$$

Using skip connection:

$$F(x) = H(x) - x \tag{7}$$

$$H(x) = F(x) + x \tag{8}$$

In the ILSVRC 2014 competition, they used various depths of ResNet (34, 50, 101, and 152). For CNNs with depths greater than 50, they used a 'bottleneck' layer to reduce dimensionality. Convolution layers 1x1, 3x3, and 1x1 make up their bottleneck design.

Figure 6. Residual block (Kaiming H et.al 2016).

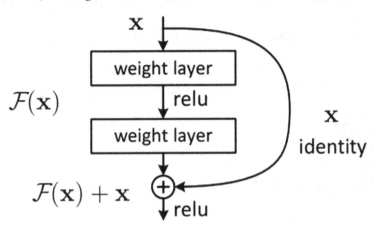

Application: Martinson Ofori and Omar El-Gayar (Omar M & Ofori M, 2020) conduct three experiments: train model with scratch with random weight initialization, fine-tuning the model and use pretrained model. VGG16, Inceptionv3, DenseNet121, Xception, ResNet151v2 are used in this work. Alex Olsen et al. (olsen, A et.al., 2019) uses Inceptionv3 and ResNet50 architecture to classify eight weed species from Australian rangeland and ResNet50 gives the better results. Vi Nguyen Thanh Le et al. (Le, V.N.T et.al, 2020) compares VGG16, VGG19, ResNet50, and Inceptionv3 with the k-FLBPCM algorithm in classifying the weeds and crops. CNN models require large number of images of plant at different growth stages but kFLBPCM can perform with small leaf shapes of second and third growth stage. Mayur Selukar et al. (Selukar, S et.al, 2022) use MobileNet, VGG16 and ResNet50 to identify weeds. Among which ResNet50 perform well with 91.94% accuracy but with the respect of time MobileNet takes the lesser time. Gerassimos G. Peteinatos et al. (Peteinatos, G.G et.al, 2020) adapted ResNet50, VGG16 and Xception CNN models for weed classification in Maize, Sunflower and Potato. ResNet50 and Xception perform better with the accuracy higher than 97%. As for the VGG16 there is some misclassification between species. Nawmee Razia Rahman et al. (Rahman, N.R et.al, 2020) compare LeNet-5, VGG16, ResNet50 and DenseNet121 for weed classification. There are twelve species to classify and ResNet50 outperformed. Abdel-Aziz Binguitcha-Fare and Prince Sharma (Sharma, P & Binguitcha-Fare, A.A, 2019) uses ResNet101 to classify twelve species of weeds and crops and achieve accuracy on validation set 98.47% and on testing set 96.04%. Namratha Makanapura et al. (Makanapura, N et.al, 2022) uses three different CNN architectures (MobileNetv2, ResNet50v2, EfficientNetB0) to classify weeds and plant species and EfficientNetB0 model outperformed with the accuracy of 96.52%.

DenseNet

Concept: DenseNets are the next step toward improving the depth of deep convolutional networks. Huang et al. (Huang, G et.al, 2017) introduced DenseNet, a network that includes dense blocks in traditional networks. Classical neural networks output is connected of the layer to the next layer after applying a composite of operations. ResNets improved on this behavior by adding the skip connection function. The first distinction between DenseNets and ResNets is made at this point. Rather than adding the output activation maps of the layer to the input activation maps, DenseNets concatenates them. Each layer reuses the previous layer's features, which enhances feature propagation and reduce the problem of vanishing gradient.

DenseNet Architecture with 5 blocks is shown in figure 7.

Figure 7. DenseNet with 5 blocks (Huang, G et.al, 2017).

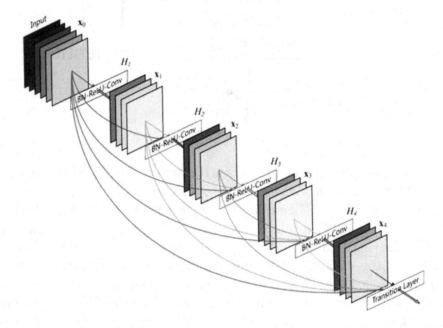

Application: Nawmee Razia Rahman et al. (Rahman, N.R et.al, 2020) compare LeNet-5, VGG16, ResNet50 and DenseNet121 for weed classification. There are twelve species to classify and ResNet50 outperformed. Martinson Ofori and Omar El-Gayar (Omar M & Ofori M, 2020) conduct three experiments: train model with scratch with random weight initialization, fine-tuning the model and use pretrained model. VGG16, Inceptionv3, DenseNet121, Xception, ResNet151v2 are used in this work.

ZFNet

Concept: ZFNet (Zeiler, M.D & Fergus, R, 2014) is the winner of ILSVRC (ImageNet Large Scale Visual Recognition Competition) 2013; this is the revised version of ALexNet. The important difference between ALexNet and ZFNet is that, ZFNet uses 7x7 filters instead of 11x11 filters. The premise is that by deploying larger filters, we lose a lot of pixel information, which we can keep by utilizing smaller filter sizes in the early conv layers. Architecture of ZFNet shown in figure 8.

Application: Dr. E.Gothai et al. (Gothai, E.G et.al., 2020) adopt VGG16, ZFNet and AlexNet along with four-layered, six-layered, eight-layered and thirteen-layered architecture among which eight-layered architecture outperform with 96.53% accuracy.

Figure 8. Model of ZFNet (Zeiler, M.D & Fergus, R, 2014).

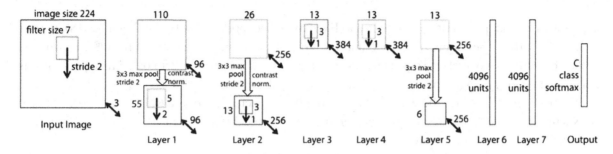

CapsNet

Concept: CNNs suffer from two problems. The first one is subsampling, where the spatial information loses between-higher level features. Second one is that it has a hard time extrapolating to novel viewpoints. To overcome these problems G.Hinton proposed CapsNet (Hinton, G. E et.al, 2017) in 2017. The idea behind this is to add capsules where the output is the vector with direction. CapsNet architecture consists of encoder and decoder. Model of CapsNet is shown in figure 9.

Figure 9. Model of CapsNet (Hinton, G. E et.al, 2017).

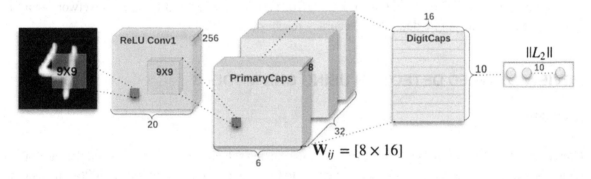

Encoder has 3 layers. First is convolutional layer has 256, 9x9 kernels with stride 1 and ReLU activation function is used. The input for the primary capsule layer is the input of previous layer. There are 32 primary capsules in the next convolutional layer which is called primary capsule layer. Each capsule has dimension 6x6 with shared weights. Thus, the output of this layer is 32x6x6. The next layer is DigitCaps layer which consists of 6D capsule per digit class. The output of this is inserted into the decoder network. The decoder contains 3 fully connected layers. Layer one contains total 512 neurons. Next layer consists of 1024 neurons in total. Lastly, it is sigmoid layer that contains 784 neurons.

Application: Yu Li1 et al. (Li, Y et.al, 2019) uses capsule network for recognition of crop of rice using UAV images.

SENet

Concept: Hu et al. put forward "Squeeze and Excitation Network" (SENet) (Hu, J et.al, 2018), winner of ILSVRC-2017. The "Squeeze-and-Excitation" block is shown in figure below. Ftr: X ⊗ U, where Ftr is the convolutional operator. To produce 1x1xC dimensional channel descriptor average pooling was performed on every single channel of activation map by the squeeze function (Fsq). Fex is the simple gating mechanism, in which there are 3 layers: two fully connected layers and ReLU is applied. To make SENet the SE block should be stacked together to generalize the different data set. The Block of Squeeze and Excitation is shown in figure 10.

Figure 10. Block of Squeeze and Excitation (Hu, J et.al, 2018).

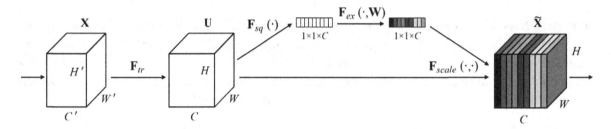

Application: Junde Chen et al.(Chen, J et.al., 2021) uses Squeeze and Excitation Network in agricultural field with the public dataset the accuracy reaches to 99.88%.

REVIEW OF WEED DETECTION USING CNN MODELS

R-CNN

Concept: R-CNN extracts 2000 regions from an image using selective search method and they are called region proposals. These region proposals are feed into CNN and as output it produces 4096-dimensional vector. CNN acts as a pattern extractor so the extracted patterns are fed into SVM classifier to classify the objects. The diagram of R-CNN is shown in figure 11.

The problem with the R-CNN is that per image it has to classify 2000 region proposals so it takes huge amount of time to train.

Application: M. Vaidhehi and C. Malathy [64] segment the weeds using RCNN. R-CNN was compared with CNN, RF, SVM, MCS-1, and MCS-2 and the R-CNN perform better. Shahbaz Khan et al. (Khan, S et.al., 2021) compares KNN, SVM, YOLOv3 and Faster R-CNN in two different fields i.e. strawberry and pea.

Figure 11. R-CNN (Girchick, R et.al, 2014).

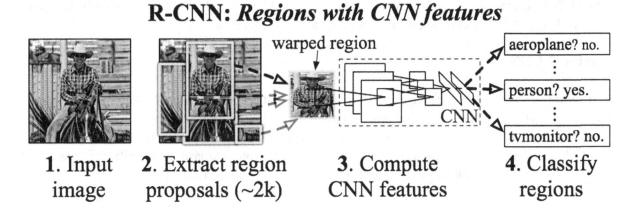

Fast R-CNN

Concept: Fast R-CNN overcomes the downside of R-CNN. The approach is same as R-CNN but in this method instead of region proposals, the input image is feed into convolutional neural network to trigger the convolutional activation map. From this activation maps region of proposals are extracted. Next, by using ROI Pooling layer all the region of proposals are modify into a particular size and fed into the fully connected network. On top of fully connected layer softmax layer is applied which is used to predict the class score and to predict bounding boxes of detected objects. The diagram of Fast R-CNN is shown in figure 12.

Figure 12. Fast R-CNN (Girshick, R, 2015).

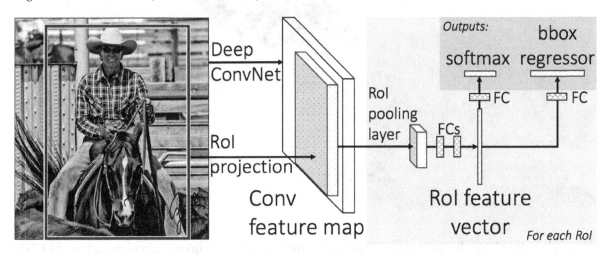

The speed of Fast R-CNN is increased as compared to the R-CNN because in this there is no requirement to feed 2000 region proposals in CNN every time.

Application: Mahmoud Abdulsalam et al. (Mahmoud A & Aouf, N, 2020) uses fused version of YOLOv2- ResNet50, Faster RCNN for weed detection and Fast RCNN. YOLOv2-ResNet50 is faster than the Faster RCNN and also performed better in terms of accuracy also.

Faster R-CNN

Concept: In Faster R-CNN the image is fed into convolutional neural network but instead of using selective search method for creating region proposal a sub network called Region Proposal Network is used to learn and produce proposals. After that ROI Layer will be applied to reshape all the region proposals at fixed size. And then these proposals are fed to the fully connected layer to identify the objects in proposed region. The architecture of Faster R-CNN is shown in figure 13.

Figure 13. Architecture of Faster R-CNN (Shaoqing R et.al 2015).

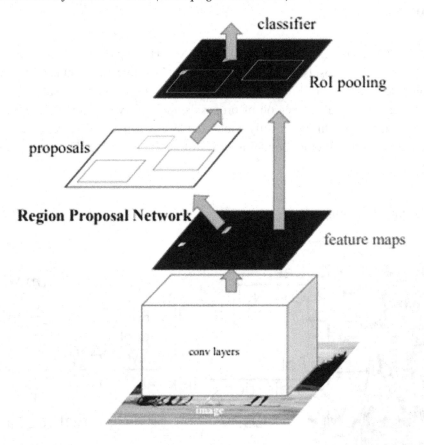

Application: Longzhe Quan et.al (Quan, L et.al, 2019) detect weed in maize field using Faster RCNN with VGG19. Their work compares the YOLOv2, Faster R-CNN and Faster R-CNN with VGG19 and best results given by Faster R-CNN with VGG19. Mahmoud Abdulsalam et al. (Mahmoud, A et.al, 2020) uses fused version of YOLOv2-ResNet50 and Faster RCNN for weed detection. YOLOv2-ResNet50 is faster than the Faster RCNN and also performed better in terms of accuracy also. Karthik Buddha et al.

(Buddha, K et.al, 2019) detect weeds and crops through Faster R-CNN for precision agriculture. Muhammad Taufiq Pratama et al. (Muhammad, T.P et.al, 2020) compare the results for weed detection in the fields of Soybean of RetinaNet, Faster R-CNN and Cascade R-CNN architectures and among which Cascade R-CNN outperformed.

Mask R-CNN

Concept: Mask R-CNN is an object detection algorithm which is developed by Facebook AI researchers in 2017. This model can detect object as well as it generates a mask for each instance in an image. For each object there are two outputs in Faster R-CNN i.e. a class label and a bounding-box offset but in Mask R-CNN there is third output also which object mask is. The diagram of Mask R-CNN shown in figure 14.

Figure 14. Mask R-CNN (He, K et.al, 2017).

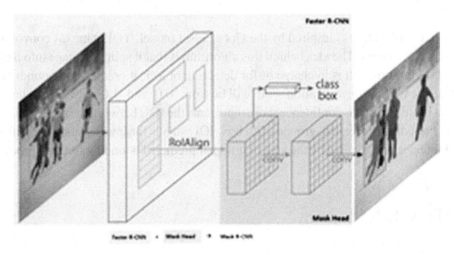

Mask R-CNN is the extension of Faster R-CNN and it follows the same two stage approach but at second stage ROI Pool is replaced by ROIAlign which is used to convert all generated feature maps into fixed size.

Application: Sanjay Patidar et al. (Patidar, S et.al, 2020) uses Mask R-CNN for weed detection as it is much faster algorithm for detection.

YOLO

Concept: In 2015 Joseph Redmond et al. proposed YOLO and it stands for You Only Look Once deals with object detection problem in real time. As by the title, the algorithm only look once at the image and it need only one forward propagation pass to make predictions. The architecture of YOLO is shown in figure 15.

Figure 15. Architecture of YOLO (Redmon, J et.al, 2016).

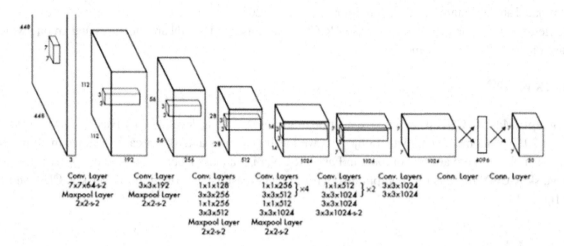

The architecture of YOLO is inspired by the GoogLeNet model. YOLO has 24 convolutional layers and 2 fully connected layers. The idea behind this algorithm is that it split the image into SxS dimension of square grid. Every grid cell is in charge of for detecting object. It predicts the bounding boxes with their confidence score. The classification score will be from '0.0' and '1.0'. The lowest level is the '0.0' and the highest is the '1.0'. This confidence score represents the IOU between the predicted bounding box and the actual bounding box called, ground truth box. IOU stands for Intersection over Union is defined as the area of intersection, divided by the area of union of predicted bounding box and ground-truth box.

$$IOU = \frac{area\left(B_p \cap B_{gt}\right)}{area\left(B_p \cup B_{gt}\right)}$$

Application: Shahbaz Khan et al. (Khan, S et.al, 2021) compares KNN, SVM, YOLOv3 and Faster R-CNN in two different fields i.e. strawberry and pea. Brahim Jabir and Noureddine Falih (Jabir, B & Falih, N, 2022) uses YOLO to detect weeds in wheat field. This model is implemented in Raspberry based system, there is no need to spray one herbicide all over the plot but it is decide by the system to spray right herbicide depending upon weed detect. Longzhe Quan et al. (Quan, L et.al, 2019) detect weed in maize field using Faster R-CNN with VGG19. Their work compares the YOLOv2, Faster R-CNN and Faster R-CNN with VGG19 and best results given by Faster R-CNN with VGG19. Mahmoud Abdulsalam et al. ()Mahmoud, A et.al., 2020 uses fused version of YOLOv2- ResNet50 and Faster RCNN for weed detection. YOLOv2-ResNet50 is faster than the Faster RCNN and also performed better in terms of accuracy also.

CONCLUSION

Weeds are the tough competitors for crops, it is essential to remove them. If weeds are not removed at their early stages then they overlap with crops at their grown stages, making conventional weed detection systems impossible to identify. With the advancement in deep learning, automated weed detection system are showing promising performance. This review summarized the current status of different deep learning techniques for classifying and detecting weeds in crops their applications. First, fundamental blocks of convolutional neural networks including activation functions, pooling layers, convolutional layer, fully connected layer and filters was discussed. Secondly, review of weed classification using different convolutional neural networks models and their applications was summarized. Thirdly, review of weed detection using different convolutional neural networks and their application was discussed.

With the combination of deep learning techniques and image processing, this became very promising real-time weed detection system in fields.

ACKNOWLEDGMENT

The authors are thankful for the support by DST under ASEAN-India Collaborative Research and Development scheme for carrying out this work.

REFERENCES

Abdulsalam, M., & Aouf, N. (2020). Deep weed detector/classifier network for precision agriculture. In *2020 28th Mediterranean Conference on Control and Automation (MED)*. IEEE. 10.1109/MED48518.2020.9183325

Ang, K. L.-M., & Jasmine, K. P. S. (2021). Big data and machine learning with hyperspectral information in agriculture. *IEEE Access: Practical Innovations, Open Solutions*, *9*, 36699–36718. doi:10.1109/ACCESS.2021.3051196

Beeharry, Y., & Bassoo, V. (2020). Performance of ANN and AlexNet for weed detection using UAV-based images. In *2020 3rd International Conference on Emerging Trends in Electrical, Electronic and Communications Engineering (ELECOM)*. IEEE. 10.1109/ELECOM49001.2020.9296994

Buddha, K. (2019). Weed Detection and Classification in High Altitude Aerial Images for Robot-Based Precision Agriculture. In *2019 27th Mediterranean Conference on Control and Automation (MED)*. IEEE. 10.1109/MED.2019.8798582

C ordova-Cruzatty, Barreno Barreno, & J acome. (2017). Precise weed and maize classification through convolutional neuronal networks. In *2017 IEEE Second Ecuador Technical Chapters Meeting (ETCM)*. IEEE.

Chavan, T. R., & Nandedkar, A. V. (2018). AgroAVNET for crops and weeds classification: A step forward in automatic farming. *Computers and Electronics in Agriculture*, *154*, 361–372. doi:10.1016/j.compag.2018.09.021

Chen, J. (n.d.). *Identification of plant disease images via a squeeze-and excitation MobileNet model and twice transfer learning.* doi:10.1049/ipr2.12090

Dian Bah, M. (2018). Deep learning with unsupervised data labeling for weed detection in line crops in UAV images. *Remote Sensing, 10*(11), 1690. doi:10.3390/rs10111690

Gholamalinezhad, H., & Khosravi, H. (2020). *Pooling methods in deep neural networks, a review.* arXiv preprint arXiv:2009.07485.

Girshick, R. (2014). Rich feature hierarchies for accurate object detection and semantic segmentation. *Proceedings of the IEEE conference on computer vision and pattern recognition,* 580–587. 10.1109/CVPR.2014.81

Girshick, R. (2015). Fast r-cnn. *Proceedings of the IEEE international conference on computer vision,* 1440–1448.

Goodfellow, I., Bengio, Y., & Courville, A. (2016). *Deep learning.* MIT Press.

Gothai, E. (2020). Weed Identification using Convolutional Neural Network and Convolutional Neural Network Architectures. In *2020 Fourth International Conference on Computing Methodologies and Communication (ICCMC).* IEEE. 10.1109/ICCMC48092.2020.ICCMC-000178

Guo, Y., Liu, Y., Oerlemans, A., Lao, S., Wu, S., & Lew, M. S. (2016). Deep learning for visual understanding: A review. *Neurocomputing, 187,* 27–48. doi:10.1016/j.neucom.2015.09.116

He, K. (2016). Deep residual learning for image recognition. *Proceedings of the IEEE conference on computer vision and pattern recognition,* 770–778.

He, K. (2017). Mask r-cnn. *Proceedings of the IEEE international conference on computer vision,* 2961–2969.

Hinton, G., Deng, L., Yu, D., Dahl, G., Mohamed, A., Jaitly, N., Senior, A., Vanhoucke, V., Nguyen, P., Sainath, T., & Kingsbury, B. (2012). Deep neural networks for acoustic modeling in speech recognition: The shared views of four research groups. *IEEE Signal Processing Magazine, 29*(6), 82–97. doi:10.1109/MSP.2012.2205597

Hinton, G., Deng, L., Yu, D., Dahl, G., Mohamed, A., Jaitly, N., Senior, A., Vanhoucke, V., Nguyen, P., Sainath, T., & Kingsbury, B. (2012). Deep neural networks for acoustic modeling in speech recognition: The shared views of four research groups. *IEEE Signal Processing Magazine, 29*(6), 82–97. doi:10.1109/MSP.2012.2205597

Hu, J., Shen, L., & Sun, G. (2018). Squeeze-and-excitation networks. *Proceedings of the IEEE conference on computer vision and pattern recognition,* 7132–7141.

Huang, G. (2017). Densely connected convolutional networks. Proceedings of the IEEE conference on computer vision and pattern recognition, 4700–4708. doi:10.1109/CVPR.2017.243

Hubel, D. H., & Wiesel, T. N. (1968). Receptive fields and functional architecture of monkey striate cortex. *The Journal of Physiology, 195*(1), 215–243. doi:10.1113/jphysiol.1968.sp008455 PMID:4966457

Iqbal, N. (2019). Investigation of alternate herbicides for effective weed management in glyphosate-tolerant cotton. Archives of Agronomy and Soil Science. doi:10.1080/03650340.2019.1579904

Jabir, B., & Falih, N. (2022). Deep learning-based decision support system for weeds detection in wheat fields. *Iranian Journal of Electrical and Computer Engineering*, *12*(1), 816. doi:10.11591/ijece.v12i1.pp816-825

Karpathy, A. (2014). Large-scale video classification with convolutional neural networks. *Proceedings of the IEEE conference on Computer Vision and Pattern Recognition*, 1725–1732. 10.1109/CVPR.2014.223

Khan, S., Tufail, M., Khan, M. T., Khan, Z. A., & Anwar, S. (2021). Deep learning-based identification system of weeds and crops in strawberry and pea fields for a precision agriculture sprayer. *Precision Agriculture*, *22*(6), 1711–1727. doi:10.100711119-021-09808-9

Krizhevsky, Sutskever, & Hinton. (2012). Imagenet classification with deep convolutional neural networks. *Advances in Neural Information Processing Systems, 25*.

LeCun, Y., Bottou, L., Bengio, Y., & Haffner, P. (1998). Gradient-based learning applied to document recognition. *Proceedings of the IEEE*, *86*(11), 2278–2324. doi:10.1109/5.726791

Li, Y., Qian, M., Liu, P., Cai, Q., Li, X., Guo, J., Yan, H., Yu, F., Yuan, K., Yu, J., Qin, L., Liu, H., Wu, W., Xiao, P., & Zhou, Z. (2019). The recognition of rice images by UAV based on capsule network. *Cluster Computing*, *22*(4), 9515–9524. doi:10.100710586-018-2482-7

Liu, J., Abbas, I., & Noor, R. S. (2021). Development of Deep Learning-Based Variable Rate Agrochemical Spraying System for Targeted Weeds Control in Strawberry Crop. *Agronomy (Basel)*, *11*(8), 1480. doi:10.3390/agronomy11081480

Lu, J., Tan, L., & Jiang, H. (2021). Review on convolutional neural network (CNN) applied to plant leaf disease classification. *Agriculture*, *11*(8), 707. doi:10.3390/agriculture11080707

Mahmudul Hasan, A. S. M. (2021). A survey of deep learning techniques for weed detection from images. *Computers and Electronics in Agriculture*, *184*, 106067. doi:10.1016/j.compag.2021.106067

Makanapura, N. (2022). Classification of plant seedlings using deep convolutional neural network architectures. Journal of Physics: Conference Series, 2161. doi:10.1088/1742-6596/2161/1/012006

Neil Harker, K., & John, T. (2013). Recent weed control, weed management, and integrated weed management. *Weed Technology*, *27*(1), 1–11. doi:10.1614/WT-D-12-00109.1

Ofori & El-Gayar. (2020). *Towards deep learning for weed detection: Deep convolutional neural network architectures for plant seedling classification*. Academic Press.

Olsen, A., Konovalov, D. A., Philippa, B., Ridd, P., Wood, J. C., Johns, J., Banks, W., Girgenti, B., Kenny, O., Whinney, J., Calvert, B., Azghadi, M. R., & White, R. D. (2019). DeepWeeds: A multiclass weed species image dataset for deep learning. *Scientific Reports*, *9*(1), 1–12. doi:10.103841598-018-38343-3 PMID:30765729

Patidar, S., Singh, U., & Sharma, S. K. (2020). Weed seedling detection using mask regional convolutional neural network. In *2020 International Conference on Electronics and Sustainable Communication Systems (ICESC)*. IEEE. 10.1109/ICESC48915.2020.9155701

Peteinatos, G. G., Reichel, P., Karouta, J., Andújar, D., & Gerhards, R. (2020). Weed identification in maize, sunflower, and potatoes with the aid of Convolutional Neural Networks. *Remote Sensing*, *12*(24), 4185. doi:10.3390/rs12244185

Pratama, M. T. (2020). Deep Learning-based Object Detection for Crop Monitoring in Soybean Fields. In *2020 International Joint Conference on Neural Networks (IJCNN)*. IEEE. 10.1109/IJCNN48605.2020.9207400

Quan, L., Feng, H., Lv, Y., Wang, Q., Zhang, C., Liu, J., & Yuan, Z. (2019). Maize seedling detection under different growth stages and complex field environments based on an improved Faster R–CNN. *Biosystems Engineering*, *184*, 1–23. doi:10.1016/j.biosystemseng.2019.05.002

Rahman, N. R., Md, A. M. H., & Shin, J. (2020). Performance Comparison of Different Convolutional Neural Network Architectures for Plant Seedling Classification. In *2020 2nd International Conference on Advanced Information and Communication Technology (ICAICT)*. IEEE. 10.1109/ICAICT51780.2020.9333468

Redmon, J. (2016). You only look once: Unified, real-time object detection. *Proceedings of the IEEE conference on computer vision and pattern recognition*, 779–788. 10.1109/CVPR.2016.91

Ren, S. (2015). Advances in neural information processing systems: Vol. 28. Faster r-cnn: Towards real-time object detection with region proposal networks. Academic Press.

Russakovsky, O., Deng, J., Su, H., Krause, J., Satheesh, S., Ma, S., Huang, Z., Karpathy, A., Khosla, A., Bernstein, M., Berg, A. C., & Fei-Fei, L. (2015). Imagenet large scale visual recognition challenge. *International Journal of Computer Vision*, *115*(3), 211–252. doi:10.100711263-015-0816-y

Sa, I., Chen, Z., Popovic, M., Khanna, R., Liebisch, F., Nieto, J., & Siegwart, R. (2017). weednet: Dense semantic weed classification using multispectral images and mav for smart farming. *IEEE Robotics and Automation Letters*, *3*(1), 588–595. doi:10.1109/LRA.2017.2774979

Selukar, M., Jain, P., & Kumar, T. (2022). A device for effective weed removal for smart agriculture using convolutional neural network. International Journal of System Assurance Engineering and Management, 13(1), 397–404. doi:10.100713198-021-01441-z

Sharma, P. (2019). Crops and weeds classification using Convolutional Neural Networks via optimization of transfer learning parameters. International Journal of Engineering and Advanced Technology.

Sharma, S., Sharma, S., & Athaiya, A. (2017). Activation functions in neural networks. Towards Data Science, 6(12), 310–316.

Simonyan, K., & Zisserman, A. (2014). *Very deep convolutional networks for large-scale image recognition*. arXiv preprint arXiv:1409.1556.

Song, Lichtenberg, & Xiao. (2015). Sun rgb-d: A rgb-d scene understanding benchmark suite. *Proceedings of the IEEE conference on computer vision and pattern recognition*, 567–576.

Stafford, J. V., & Benlloch, J. V. (1997). Machine-assisted detection of weeds and weed patches. In *Precision agriculture'97: papers presented at the first European Conference on Precision Agriculture, Warwick University Conference Centre, UK, 7-10 September 1997*. BIOS Scientific Pub.

Subeesh, A. (2022). Deep convolutional neural network models for weed detection in polyhouse grown bell peppers. Artificial Intelligence in Agriculture, 6, 47–54. doi:10.1016/j.aiia.2022.01.002

Szegedy, C. (2015). Going deeper with convolutions. *Proceedings of the IEEE conference on computer vision and pattern recognition*, 1–9.

True, J. (2022). Weed detection in soybean crops using custom lightweight deep learning models. Journal of Agriculture and Food Research, 100308.

Veeragandham, S., & Santhi, H. (2021). A Detailed Review on Challenges and Imperatives of Various CNN Algorithms in Weed Detection. In *2021 International Conference on Artificial Intelligence and Smart Systems (ICAIS)*. IEEE. 10.1109/ICAIS50930.2021.9395986

Vi, N. T. L., Ahderom, S., & Alameh, K. (2020). Performances of the lbp based algorithm over cnn models for detecting crops and weeds with similar morphologies. *Sensors (Basel)*, *20*(8), 2193. doi:10.339020082193 PMID:32295097

Wang, A., Zhang, W., & Wei, X. (2019). A review on weed detection using ground-based machine vision and image processing techniques. *Computers and Electronics in Agriculture*, *158*, 226–240. doi:10.1016/j.compag.2019.02.005

Wang, C., Liu, B., Liu, L., Zhu, Y., Hou, J., Liu, P., & Li, X. (2021). A review of deep learning used in the hyperspectral image analysis for agriculture. *Artificial Intelligence Review*, *54*(7), 5205–5253. doi:10.100710462-021-10018-y

Yamashita, R., Nishio, M., Do, R. K. G., & Togashi, K. (2018). Convolutional neural networks: An overview and application in radiology. *Insights Into Imaging*, *9*(4), 611–629. doi:10.100713244-018-0639-9 PMID:29934920

Zeiler & Fergus. (2014). Visualizing and understanding convolutional networks. In *European conference on computer vision*. Springer.

Chapter 23
Medication Discovery Using Neural Networks

Akshay Mendon
Thakur College of Engineering and Technology, India

Bhavya Manoj Votavat
School of Computer Science and Engineering, VIT Bhopal University, India

Vighnesh Hegde
Thakur College of Engineering and Technology, India

Megharani Patil
Thakur College of Engineering and Technology, India

ABSTRACT

The genesis of artificial intelligence (AI) has subsequently led to many machine learning algorithms being used for purposes like drug discovery. The strategies for developing drug targets and medication revelation have joined forces with AI and deep learning algorithms to improve the effectiveness, adequacy, and nature of created yields. Drug discovery is a very difficult endeavor as its success depends on data from several fields, yet it is very crucial and beneficial for us in the long run. In this chapter, the applications that have created novel techniques and produced significant yield in this field are reviewed.

INTRODUCTION

It is a challenging endeavor to discover new medicines because it necessitates data from several organic and synthetic fields, yet it is crucial to preserving, enhancing, or increasing human existence. Artificial intelligence (AI) is widely used in business and academia. In many domains, including the information age and research, AI (ML), an important subset of AI, has been integrated. Natural frameworks function generally through the real collaboration of particles. hence essential for the discovery of novel medications and for expanding the understanding of science. At the time when subatomic restricting occurred. Proteins are the most versatile natural particles because they may perform tasks ranging from underlying

DOI: 10.4018/978-1-6684-6821-0.ch023

scaffolding to dynamic freight transit, passing through enzymatic research, protein folding supervision, correspondence, photochemical detection, and other calculation-based approaches, like ML, which call for a strong numerical and computational premise. The traditional technique that is based on complete therapy is the foundation of medication revelation. Clinical organizations all across the world started using an allopathic approach to therapy and recovery. With this development, ailments were successfully fought, but the high expense of medications that followed created problems with medical treatment. The era of "current" medications begins around the turn of the nineteenth century. The need to treat a disease or other condition affecting people for whom there is currently no effective therapy in place or where existing medications are insufficient drives the discovery and enhancement of medications. To apply medicine to treat the sickness—a process called target revelation—it is unquestionably necessary that the bodily systems by which the illness is caused are understood. Above all else, malignant growth is a genetic disease. Girl cells get acquired base-pair alterations in their genomes when environmental mutagens or insufficient DNA repair mechanisms produce explicit mutations in the DNA of a normal typical cell. Such alterations may be positive (such as "traveler changes") or may only exacerbate the dangerous modification of the cell (such as "driver changes''). While the most effective anti-cancer medications, fortunately, were discovered and effective through the inhibition of cell division on a living being wide scale, new atomic specialists are being developed gradually to specifically hinder the ability of individual subatomic targets driving tumor development. In the 1970s and 1980s, the first of these atomically targeted cancer treatments were developed. About these "focused therapies," Gleevec (for BCR-ABL positive leukemia), Herceptin (for Erbb2 intensified breast cancer), and Tamoxifen are just a few notable instances of how they have helped patients overcome obstacles (for ER-positive bosom disease). In any case, computational approaches, such as machine learning (ML), might advance the following three steps of early pharmaceutical improvement: Target ID from written information mining, a structure-based plan for drugs that are intended to irritate a target, as well as simplification of the standards for assessing small atom or biologic inhibitors. structure-based planning of drugs anticipated to interfere with a goal, and improvement of standards for assessing small atom or biologic inhibitors.

To assist with these issues, the authors offer AtomNet as another forward-thinking architecture. AtomNet is innovative in two ways: The primary deep convolutional neural network for predicting sub-atomic limiting partiality is called atonement. It is also the main deep learning framework that combines fundamental information about the goal to create its expectations. For speech and vision, deep convolutional neural networks (DCNN) currently produce the best predictive models. The spatial and ephemeral building of its region must be used in the model design of the DCNN (Korotkov A, Tkachenko V, Russo DP, Ekins S.2017) a class of deep neural networks. For instance, a small, spatially-general set of pixels might depict a low-level image, such as an edge. By "tying the loads" of the finder neurons, such a component indicator can distribute evidence over the whole receptive field as the recognition of the edge is independent of its location inside an image. By reducing the number of model boundaries, overfitting is reduced and the appearance of generalizable highlights is enhanced. The network then gradually transforms neighborhood low-level highlights into larger, unexpected spotlights. According to the theory, biochemical relationships are often close by and should be demonstrated by similarly limited AI schemes. Even though these atoms are general to one another, the spatial organization and holding of diverse particles in space depict compound gatherings. The level of their shock or interest may differ depending on their kind, distance, and point precisely when complex social events partner, such as through hydrogen holding or -bond stacking, although these are primarily local effects. Given that even in these situations eliminated particles only occasionally interact with one another, the maintained region of a DCNN is reasonable, it is possible to depict perplexing bioactivity features by taking into account neighboring packs that strengthen or weaken a particular affiliation. Additionally, the applicability of a marker for, say, hydrogen holding or -bond stacking is invariant throughout the response field when using edge finders in DCNNs for photos. Then, using dynamic characteristics, these local biochemical relationship locators may be transformed into more complex representations of the erratic and nonlinear marvel of sub-nuclear confinement. The primary significant neural association for a structure-based limited proclivity gauge is AtomNet, notwithstanding the introduction of the DCNN design for biochemical segment divulgence (Zhou, Zhenpeng & Li, Xiaocheng & Zare, Richard, 2017).

For QSAR and ligand-based virtual screening, deep neural networks recently seemed to outperform erratic timberlands and SVMs. The Merck Molecular Activity Kaggle Challenge's top per-shaping design involved carrying out several tasks on a sophisticated neural network (MT-DNN). They carry out many activities to create a single neural network with many yield neurons, each of which expects the activity of the information atom differently. Particles are frequently tested in a variety of ways, thus the MT-DNN design may combine gathering evidence with similar expectation tasks. This demonstrated that the MT-DNN method was scalable to very large biochemical databases, such as PubChem Bioassays and ChEMBL.(Coley CW el at . 2017)

Ligand-based systems, such as MT-DNN, have a few drawbacks. They cannot produce predictions for novel targets since they are limited to locations for which significant amounts of historical data are currently accessible. When everything is taken into account, this creates a perplexing dynamic—these perceptive models provide the most assistance to the targets who least need it. It is also challenging to demonstrate that an association is "fitting for the proper reasons" because of the de-irregularity of recognized unique ligands; relics in the arrangement data, such as fundamental inclination, also make it challenging to accurately measure precision and generalizability. Second, nuclear fingerprints, like ECFP, are used as data in current key neural linkages for ligand-based models. Such data encoding eliminates the capacity to identify emotional aspects and restricts the disclosure of features to plans of the pre-shown sub-nuclear developments depicted during the fingerprinting cycle. Third, the model cannot explain which possible participations are left unfulfilled by a molecule since it is careless with relation to the evenhanded. This restricts the possible heading that may be used to aid scientists in modifying the molecule.(Chang P et al. 2018)

AtomNet combines information about the ligand and information about the advancement to overcome these limitations. Although ligand-based techniques of reasoning do not consider the domains of every particle in the confinement site of the aim, our style of thinking does. Acceptance of this information interacts with the model to get daring subatomic highlights.

In this chapter the author uses convolutional neural networks to demonstrate the prediction of bioactivity of small molecules. Followed by applying local convolutional filters to structural target input information. As the biochemical interactions are local by nature, hence they should be well-handled by these sparse machine learning architectures.(Sakellaropoulos et al.2019)

LITERATURE REVIEW

In (Manallack, D & Livingstone D. 1999),throughout the past ten years, neural networks have become a proficient strategy for information examination in the field of medication revelation. The early issues experienced with neural networks, for example, overfitting and overtraining, have tended to bring about a strategy that outperforms conventional measurable techniques. Neural Networks have along these lines to a great extent satisfied their commitment, which was to beat QSAR statistical issues. The next revolution in QSAR will almost certainly include research into delivering better descriptors utilized in these investigations to work on our capacity to relate the synthetic design to the organic movement. This survey centers around the utilization of brain network techniques and their improvement over recent years

Throughout the review of (Baskin II, Winkler D, Tetko IV . 2016) the authors examine traditional drug disclosure methods as well as newly emerging neural network methods. They emphasize back-propagating neural networks and their variations, self-sorting out maps and related strategies, as well as a moderately new strategy, deep learning. It is discussed how to prevent overfitting through regularization, how to group and perform multiple tasks, and how to assess relevance space. There are several aspects to involving neural networks in drug discovery: predicting drug selectivity, toxicity profiles, ADMET, and physicochemical properties; characteristics of drug delivery systems; and virtual screening.

In (Xu Y, Yao H & Lin K. Dec 2018), the artificial intelligence systems based on neural networks (NNs) track rules for drug discovery based on preparing particles, and atoms in particular should be taken into account. The use of molecular descriptors and fingerprints as contributions to artificial neural networks (ANNs) has been around for quite some time, while other ways of representing particles are used exclusively for storing and introducing atoms. Variations of ANNs are now able to utilize various types of data sources, which allow analysts to make more decisions about drugs. Regions covered: The creators give a short outline of the uses of NNs in drug revelation. Joined with the attributes of various ways for portraying atoms, relating strategies in view of NNs give new decisions to tranquilize revelation, including once more medication plan, ligand-based drug plan, and receptor-based drug plan. Well-qualified assessment: Different ways of depicting atoms can be contributions of NN-based models, and these models accomplish agreeable outcomes in measurements. Albeit the vast majority of the models have not been broadly applied and tried and by, they can be the reason for programmed drug revelation later on

In (H. M. R. Afzal et al. 2020), A issue of critical relevance for several computer vision fields, including face analysis and face recognition, whose applications are continuously expanding, is the ability to reliably recreate 3D faces from 2D pictures. 3D face data are less impacted by lighting and position than 2D facial photos are. Convolutional neural networks (CNNs) may now be used to create 3D facial reconstructions from 2D facial photos thanks to recent developments in the field of computer vision. The 3D facial reconstruction approach proposed in this study uses two facial images—one taken from the front and one from the side—which are frequently accessible to law enforcement organizations. The method is based on CNN (LEAs).The suggested CNN was honed using both fake and actual face data. We demonstrate that the proposed network outperformed the present state-of-the-art in its ability to predict 3D faces in the MICC Florence dataset. Additionally, a method for employing the suggested network when just one facial picture is available is also provided. To do this, a new network is added, whose job it is to create a rotated version of the original picture, which, along with the original face image, forms the image pair utilized for the prior technique of reconstruction.

METHODOLOGY

The authors begin by outlining the evolution of the test benchmarks that they used to evaluate their system. They show their information encoding and their sophisticated convolutional network's design.

1. Ml Algorithms Used in Drug Discovery

Drug development has considerably progressed thanks to ML algorithms. The use of various ML computations for drug discovery has substantially benefited pharma organizations. Different models for predicting the synthetic, organic, and physical properties of combinations in drug discovery have been developed using ML computations. All phases of the pharmaceutical disclosure cycle can use ML computations. For instance, ML computations have been used to identify unauthorized drug use, predict drug-protein interactions, identify drug viability, ensure the existence of security biomarkers, and increase the bioactivity of atoms. ML computations that have been extensively used in drug discovery include:

The methods and algorithms used in ML are not a homogenous, homogeneous subset of AI. Supervised and solo learning are the two main types of ML computations. In managed learning, names for new examples are chosen for tests that have already been prepared with realized names. Without any assistance, learning takes in patterns in a variety of tests, usually without any feedback for the instances. To recognize designs in high-dimensional information, the information is often transformed into a lower measurement via unassisted learning calculations first. Measurement reduction is advantageous not just because unassisted learning is more successful in a smaller measurement space, but also because the seen example can be understood more clearly. Semi-managed and support realizing, which combines managed and unassisted learning and allows for the utilization of the two capabilities for various knowledge sets, may be used to describe both types of learning. Large amounts of data are necessary for the creation, advancement, and applicability of efficient ML calculations at each stage of the drug revelation measure. The need for extensive, high-quality data and well-known, clearly outlined preparation sets is increasingly essential for precise medication and treatment inside drug disclosure. To develop potent personalized drugs, accuracy medication necessitates a thorough depiction of all relevant omic data, including genomic, transcriptomic, proteomic, and other associated data. . The advancements in information analysis have successfully attempted to display and interpret the produced information. This project, supported by ML techniques and coordinated data sets using various programming/web devices, is presently routinely used for all methods in drug discovery. Repositioning, target revelation, tiny particle disclosure, amalgamation, and other applications have shown the value of new information examination's ability to work in concert with established procedures and older ideas to develop unique hypotheses and models. Multidimensional data is generated in the clinical and multi-omic sectors. The information is frequently noisy and comes from a variety of sources. It may be possible to solve the problems of analysis and translation of multi-dimensional information by using ML approaches, as summarized in direct models using NB. Regression, clustering, regularization, neural networks (NNs), decision trees, dimensionality reduction, ensemble approaches, rule-based methods, and instance-based methods are further ML techniques and models frequently utilized in these study fields(Patel L et al.2020)(Chen H et al.2018).

2. Datasets

The authors have demonstrated the use of the AtomNet model on three realistic and testable benchmarks: the Directory of Useful Decoys Enhanced (DUDE) benchmark, the DUDE-like benchmark, and a benchmark containing tentatively proven inert particles. Each of these metrics provides a different and complementary evaluation of the presentation; the advantages of each are summarized here and are shown in more detail below. DUDE enables direct connections with other construction-based restricted affection prediction systems since it serves as the industry benchmark. The authors ensured that there is no cover between the preparation and test particles by creating the DUDE-like benchmark because, regrettably, DUDE only selects a test set without identifying a different preparing set. Finally, since fundamentally comparable particles might have different names, precisely describing tentatively tested dynamic and dormant atoms is a testing test. Due to the divergence requirement to assume baits are idle, such scenarios are disqualified from benchmarks using property-coordinated fakes.

A. **DUDE:** A prominent reference point for methods of structure-based virtual screening is the DUDE. For the time being, the benchmark is constructed by first putting together various configurations of dynamic particles for several target proteins. By removing comparable activities, the simple tendency is alleviated. Model actives are then selected from each group after first grouping the actives based on platform proximity. Every dynamic particle is then mixed with several property-coordinated baits at that instant (PMD). Regarding various 1-dimensional physicochemical characteristics (such as atomic weight), PMD is chosen to be similar to one another and to know activities while being topologically diverse and dependent on particular 2D fingerprints (e.g., ECFP). The recognition of the topological difference supports the hypothesis that the imitations will most likely be inactive since they are purposefully altered from any recognized dynamic. The benchmark consists of 102 goals, 22,886 actives (with 224 actives on average for each objective), and 50 PMD for each dynamic. The remaining 72 focuses were designated as the preparation set, and they arbitrarily selected 30 of them as the test set.

B. **ChEMBL-20 PMD** They created a dataset akin to DUDE using ChEMBL form 20.
They took into account all-action estimates that crossed the following channels:

    i.   Affinity units that are less than 1M and approximated in IC50 or Ki.

    ii.   The target certainty was higher than or equal to 6.

    iii.   Target has an aim of 2.5A and a restricted location that is specified in the scPDB information base.

    iv.   Ligands met the wantonness and PAINS filing requirements.

Before eliminating targets with less than 10 dynamic ligands, the authors first constructed target affinities using their UniProt quality name prefix. This cycle of sifting produced 123,102 actives and 348 targets in total. Second, 30 PMD were selected from the ZINC data collection to match every dynamic. By initially grouping the dynamic ligands for each target based on their Bemis-Murcko platforms and selecting ligands that were at least 3 M apart as the bunch models, they divided the data into preparation, approval, and testing sets. Under-10-model bundles were discarded. Fourth, they defined the test as being composed of 50 randomly selected foci and the associated activities and lures. The preparation set was then divided across the bunches into sets with a 5-crease cross-approval. The most recent dataset contains 290 targets, 2,367,120 baits, and 78,904 activities.

Benchmarks reliant on PMD are constrained in that they must avoid baits that resemble dynamic particles. This strategy is intended to support the assumption that, even in the absence of test approval, selected distractions will likely be ineffective. In some difficult situations where active and dormant particles are particularly similar, this implemented difference between actives and fakes suggests that PMD benchmarks fall short. By substituting fakes with particles that have been conditionally allowed to be idle, they integrated these challenging scenarios. The authors created a benchmark that is similar to the ChEMBL-20 PMD test, except they replaced PMD with latent particles. If an atom's purposeful movement is higher than 30 M, they classified it as latent. In the end, they had a collection of 78,904 active, 363,187 latent, and 290 targets that were divided up into sets that received approval over the Bemis-Murcko groups using 3-overlap. Targets with fewer than ten clusters weren't ever included in the validation set. As a result, there were 149 targets in the validation sets.

3. Structure-Based Deep-Convolutional Neural Network

An input layer, several 3D-convolutional and entirely related layers, and a computed expenditure layer that distributes probabilities across the dynamic and dormant classes make up the network structure. The ReLU enactment work is used to execute all units in hidden layers.

The objective proteins and small particles are co-constructed over vectorized adaptations of 1A 3D frameworks that are examined inside the limiting site of the objective. First, they use a flooding calculation developed by a bound ligand explained in the scPDB knowledge source to characterize the limiting site. Second, starting from the focal point of mass of the limiting site, they shifted the facilitation of the co-edifices to a 3D Cartesian framework. Third, they evaluated a variety of gifts inside the pit of the limiting site. The mathematical data is then cropped to fit inside an appropriate bounding box in step four. In this investigation, they employed a 20A 3D form that was centered on the source. Fifth, using 1A splitting, they translate the incoming data into a fixed-size framework. Each matrix cell has a value that indicates whether or not there is any significant underlying highlights present there. Basic main highlights can vary from straightforward chemical type identification to more erratic protein-ligand descriptors like SPLIF, Filter, or APIF. The 3D framework is then unfolded into a 1D skimming point vector(H. M. R. Afzal et al. 2020).

Figure 1. Example of an architectural structure of neural networks

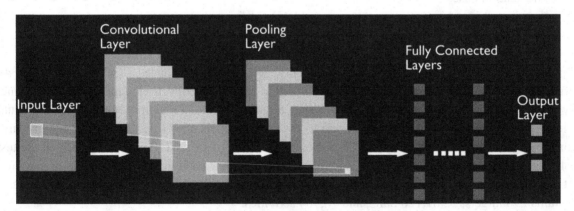

To assist with boundaries, such as channel size, 3D convolutional layers were used. They used the information layer organization scheme shown above, followed by four convolutional layers of 12853, 25633, and 25633, and two fully related layers with 1024 secret units each, followed by a strategic relapse cost layer across two movement classes. Figure 1 is an example of the architecture of a convolutional neural network.

The AdaDelta flexible learning approach, the backpropagation computation, and tiny groups of 768 models for each slope step were used to complete the model. Apart from the limitation of fitting the model into a GPU memory, no effort was taken to increase meta-boundaries. Six Nvidia-K10 GPUs took around seven days to prepare.

For the SB assessment, they started with Smina, an AutoDock Vina fork. Smina, which is accessible for free under the GPLv2 license, provides an enhanced empirical scoring function and reduction methods over its predecessor.

RESULTS AND DISCUSSIONS

To report absurd results, they operate inside the collector working trademark (AUC) and logAUC. The area under the curve (AUC) of the real positive rate vs the fake positive rate quantifies how well the arrangement (or positioned request) performed. When the AUC value is 1.0, it indicates excellent detachment, whereas when it is 0.5, it denotes arbitrary division. By giving greater weight to the beginning of the bend, LogAUC, a similar estimate to AUC, emphasizes early enhancing execution. As a result, instances that are successfully described at the top of the position requested rundown contribute more to the score than later examples do. They used a logarithmic base of 10 in this case, which means that the weight of the top 1% of the results is equal to the weight of the bottom 10%. Since a logAUC value is difficult to interpret due to its nonlinearity, they subtract the area under the log-scaled irregular bend (0.14462) from it to obtain a modified logAUC. As a result, although negative adjusted logIC esteems indicate more regret than irregular execution, positive ones indicate better than irregular execution. For the rest of this composition, they will just use altered logAUC and logAUC in reverse.

Table 1 and Figure 2 to 4 present a summary of the results for the three different benchmarks. On each of the four assessment informational indices, AtomNet significantly outperforms Smina at a level of accuracy that is beneficial for drug discovery. The results of the AUC and log AUC tests for different execution limitations are shown in Tables 2 and 3. AtomNet achieves or surpasses 0.9 AUC on 59 targets (or 57.8%) throughout the whole DUDE collection. Smina recently met the benchmark, or about 0.9 AUC, for a single goal (wee1). Smina only achieves 0.8 or greater AUC for 17 targets (16.7%), compared to AtomNet's 88 (86.3%). %). When they restrict the evaluation to the DUDE's 30 held-out goal subset, AtomNet achieves AUC values of 0.9 and 0.8 for 14 targets (46.7%) and 22 targets (73.3%), respectively. Smina achieves a comparable level of precision for 5 targets (16.7%) and 1 objective (3.3%), individually. On the held-out set, AtomNet achieves a mean and middle AUC of 0.855 and 0.875 compared to 0.7 and 0.694 achieved by Smina, reducing the mean blunder by 51.6%. True to habit, Smina's execution doesn't change, but AtomNet's exhibition somewhat declines for its held-out models.

AtomNet and Smina both achieve an AUC of 0.9 or greater for 10 held-out targets (20% of the set) on the ChEMBL-20-PMD dataset, although AtomNet only does so for one target. When they lowered the bar for accuracy to an AUC of 0.8 or higher, AtomNet wins on 25 targets (the equivalent of 50%), but Smina only wins on one target (2%). According to all accounts, the third benchmark is more challenging than the previous two since it uses inactive rather than imitations with the coordinated property. Smina wins at zero, but AtomNet predicts an AUC at or greater than 0.9 for 10 targets (6.7%). AtomNet wins for 45 targets (30.2%) and Smina wins for 4 (2.7%) for reaching or above 0.8 AUC. AtomNet still significantly outperforms Smina in overall and early advancement demonstrations, even if both Atomnet and Smina perform less admirably than on previous benchmarks. This benchmark includes evaluating order examples of atoms that are similar but have different marks since it uses inactive. Due to the notion that fakes must be primarily different to presume they may be designated as latent; these situations are disqualified from benchmarks using PMD.

Additionally, AtomNet has excellent early advancement performance, as shown by the extremely precise logAUC values. In terms of initial enhancement, AtomNet outperforms Smina, achieving a mean logAUC of 0.321 compared to 0.153 for Smina on the DUDE-30 benchmark. The contrast between the AUC and logAUC estimates for the early advances is defined by picturing the ROC bends. For instance, the AUC incentive for target 1m9m is 0.66 in Figure 4, which suggests that average execution was achieved. However, the logAUC for that target shows an early improvement of 0.25, which suggests that many activities should be gathered at the real top of the results for the position sought. A log-scale figure suggests that 35% of target 1qzy's activities are gathered at the real top of the position request list, where logAUC is 0.44, even though target 1qzy has an AUC estimation of 0.76.

Table 1. Mean and Median of AUC and Adjusted logAUC

		AUC		Adjusted logAUC	
		Mean	**Median**	**Mean**	**Median**
ChEMBL-20 PMD	AtomNet	0.781	0.792	0.317	0.328
	Smina	0.552	0.544	0.04	0.021
DUDE-30	AtomNet	0.855	0.875	0.321	0.355
	Smina	0.7	0.694	0.153	0.139
DUDE-102	AtomNet	0.895	0.915	0.385	0.38
	Smina	0.696	0.707	0.138	0.132
ChEMBL-20 inactives	AtomNet	0.745	0.737	0.145	0.133
	Smina	0.607	0.607	0.054	0.044

On the DUDE, ChEMBL-20-PMD, and ChEMBL-20-inactive benchmarks, comparisons between AtomNet and Smina were made. In contrast to DUDE-102, which refers to the whole dataset, DUDE-30 refers to the held-out collection of 30 targets.

Filter visualization Convolutional layers are made up of several channels that learn to distinguish explicitly private highlights by applying these channels consistently over the wide field. One might imagine these channels while handling images to validate that the model is capable of picking out important highlights. shown, for instance, that channels in the model's first convolutional layer could recognize lines, edges, and shading inclinations. However, because the channels are 3-dimensional and the information channels are discrete, they were unable to clearly see the channels in our case. For instance, two similar RGB values will result in two similar tones even if carbon is not physically closer to nitrogen than it is to oxygen. In other words, equivalent capabilities are not implied by comparable attributes.

ChEMBL-20 PMD Benchmark Results

Figure 2. Distribution of AUC and logAUC values of 50 ChEMBL-20-PMD targets for AtomNet and Smina.

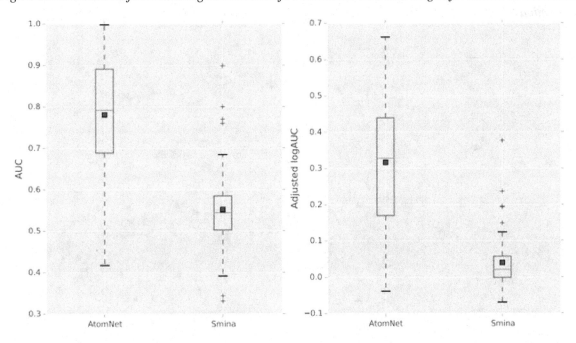

DUDE Benchmark Results

Figure 3. Distribution of AUC and logAUC values of 102 DUDE targets for AtomNet and Smina

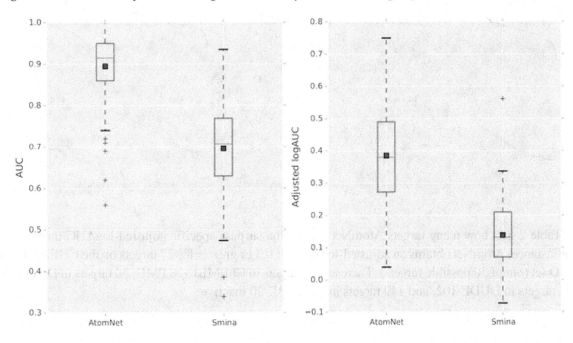

ChEMBL-20 with Inactives Benchmark Results

Figure 4. Distribution of AUC and logAUC values of 149 ChEMBL-20-inactives targets for AtomNet and Smina

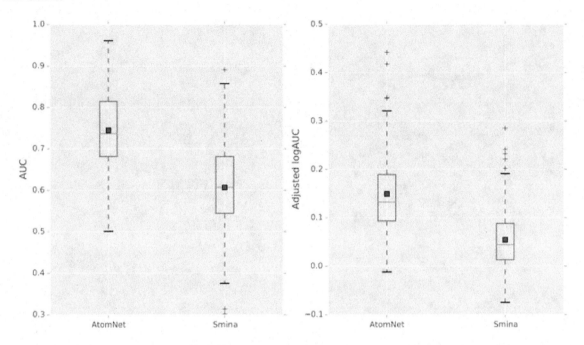

Figure 5. An illustration of the differences between the AUC and logAUC measurements with respect to the early enrichment.

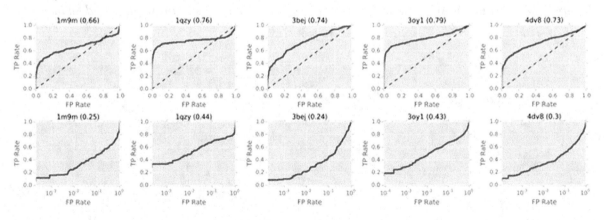

Table 2 lists how many targets AtomNet and Smina surpass specific adjusted-logAUC thresholds. For instance, AtomNet obtains an adjusted-logAUC of 0.3 or greater for 27 targets on the CHEMBL-20 PMD set (out of 50 possible targets). There are 50 targets in ChEMBL-20 PMD, 30 targets in DUDE30, 102 targets in DUDE-102, and 149 targets in ChEMBL-20 inactive .

Table 2. Comparison of Atomnet and Smina on surpassing specific adjusted-logAUC thresholds

AUC		> 0.5	> 0.6	> 0.7	> 0.8	> 0.9
ChEMBL-20 PMD	AtomNet	49	44	36	26	10
	Smina	38	10	4	1	0
DUDE-30	AtomNet	30	29	27	22	14
	Smina	29	25	14	5	1
DUDE-102	AtomNet	102	101	99	88	59
	Smina	96	84	53	17	1
ChEMBL-20 inactives	AtomNet	149	136	105	45	10
	Smina	129	81	31	4	0

Table 3. Comparison of Atomnet and Smina on surpassing specific adjusted-logAUC thresholds less than 0.5

AUC		> 0.0	> 0.1	> 0.2	> 0.3	> 0.4
ChEMBL-20 PMD	AtomNet	49	44	36	27	10
	Smina	35	8	2	1	0
DUDE-30	AtomNet	30	27	22	17	10
	Smina	29	19	8	2	1
DUDE-102	AtomNet	102	99	88	69	43
	Smina	94	65	28	5	1
ChEMBL-20 inactives	AtomNet	147	107	36	10	2
	Smina	123	35	5	0	0

Table 3 justifies that instead of just envisioning channels to understand their specialty, the used channels to enter information and examine the region where they fire most effectively. They could map out passageways to accommodate different material capacities using this technique. Figure 5, for instance, shows the 3D regions in which a particular channel from the first convolutional layer fires. A visual examination of the dynamic regions of that channel reveals that it functions as a sulfonyl/sulfonamide indicator. This demonstrates the model's ability to distinguish complicated compound highlights from less complex ones. With no artificially created prior knowledge, the channel has inferred a considerable geographical plan of information for this case.

Relationship to other construction-based tactics Instead of focusing just on correlations with previous design-based methodologies, the purpose of this study is to offer a unique application of deep convolutional neural organizations to bioactivity predictions. The authors used the popular application Smina as a baseline perspective to create the setting. Smina offers practical advantages since it is rapid, free, and adaptable to changing conditions, thus they believe it is suited for researching large benchmarks in a practical, economical manner. By comparing AtomNet with other business docking calculations described in the article, they may provide a more comprehensive setting by using distributed labor. The most common benchmark is DUDE, which, like Smina, is widely available and used. They do so by presenting the following connections with recently shown results:

- Surflex-Dock was assessed using a collection of 10 agent-focused agents from the DUDE. Surflex-average Dock's unit of comparison (AUC) was 0.76 as opposed to AtomNet's 0.93.

- Completely computerized ridiculous Fella benchmark evaluation of DOCK3.7. In comparison to the AUC of 0.895 and logAUC of 0.385, they achieved a mean AUC of 0.696 and logAUC of 0.174.

- AtomNet's AUC of 0.852 was compared to a detailed mean AUC of 0.72 on 5 DUDE targets using Dock6.7.

Figure 6. Sulfonyl/sulfonamide detection with autonomously trained convolutional filters

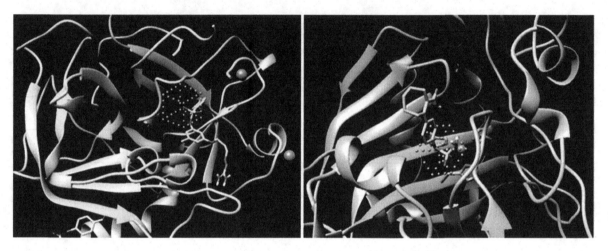

CONCLUSION AND FUTURE SCOPE

To predict the bioactivity of small atoms for drug disclosure applications, they proposed AtomNet, the primary construction-based profound convolutional neural organization. By gradually transforming common basic compound features into more perplexing ones, the privately mandated deep convolutional engineering enables the framework to demonstrate the delicate, asymmetric marvel of atomic limitation. AtomNet can predict new dynamic particles for foci with no known modulators by combining main objective data. In contrast to previous docking methods, AtomNet achieves an AUC greater than 0.9 on 57.8% of the DUDE benchmark's objectives, demonstrating exceptional results on a widely used design-based benchmark. Here, neural networks will carry out tasks like branching certain medications, which will aid in the diverse medications' drug development. Additionally, in the Machine Learning mode, neural networks in the form of DCNN will be employed. Drug revelation attempts conclusively require sustaining the suitable mentality and culture of the various partners in order to make trust and the proper environment empowering the improvement of new prescriptions. Over the course of the last 50 years, wonderful advances have been made in drug revelation and development as a field. However, assuming we consider novel information about diseases and the utilization of present day advances and all methodologies, by 2050, one would expect that numerous diseases will be better analyzed, forestalled, relieved, or ultimately managed now and again with nonpharmacological intercessions.

REFERENCES

Afzal, H. M. R., Luo, S., Afzal, M. K., Chaudhary, G., Khari, M., & Kumar, S. A. P. (2020). 3D Face Reconstruction From Single 2D Image Using Distinctive Features. *IEEE Access: Practical Innovations, Open Solutions, 8*, 180681–180689. doi:10.1109/ACCESS.2020.3028106

Baskin, I. I., Winkler, D., & Tetko, I. V. (2016, August). A renaissance of neural networks in drug discovery. *Expert Opinion on Drug Discovery, 11*(8), 785–795. doi:10.1080/17460441.2016.120126 2 PMID:27295548

Chan, H. C. S., Shan, H., Dahoun, T., Vogel, H., & Yuan, S. (2019, August). Advancing Drug Discovery via Artificial Intelligence. *Trends in Pharmacological Sciences, 40*(8), 592–604. doi:10.1016/j.tips.2019.06.004 PMID:31320117

Chang, P., Grinband, J., Weinberg, B. D., Bardis, M., Khy, M., Cadena, G., Su, M. Y., Cha, S., Filippi, C. G., Bota, D., Baldi, P., Poisson, L. M., Jain, R., & Chow, D. (2018, July). Deep-Learning Convolutional Neural Networks Accurately Classify Genetic Mutations in Gliomas. *AJNR. American Journal of Neuroradiology, 39*(7), 1201–1207. doi:10.3174/ajnr.A5667 PMID:29748206

Chen, H., Engkvist, O., Wang, Y., Olivecrona, M., & Blaschke, T. (2018, June). The rise of deep learning in drug discovery. *Drug Discovery Today, 23*(6), 1241–1250. doi:10.1016/j.drudis.2018.01.039 PMID:29366762

Coley, C. W., Barzilay, R., Jaakkola, T. S., Green, W. H., & Jensen, K. F. (2017, May 24). Prediction of Organic Reaction Outcomes Using Machine Learning. *ACS Central Science, 3*(5), 434–443. doi:10.1021/acscentsci.7b00064 PMID:28573205

Ghasemi, F., Mehridehnavi, A., Pérez-Garrido, A., & Pérez-Sánchez, H. (2018, October). Neural network and deep-learning algorithms used in QSAR studies: Merits and drawbacks. *Drug Discovery Today, 23*(10), 1784–1790. doi:10.1016/j.drudis.2018.06.016 PMID:29936244

Korotkov, A., Tkachenko, V., Russo, D. P., & Ekins, S. (2017, December 4). Comparison of Deep Learning With Multiple Machine Learning Methods and Metrics Using Diverse Drug Discovery Data Sets. *Molecular Pharmaceutics, 14*(12), 4462–4475. doi:10.1021/acs.molpharmaceut.7b00578 PMID:29096442

Manallack, D., & Livingstone, D. (1999). Neural networks in drug discovery: Have they lived up to their promise? *European Journal of Medicinal Chemistry, 34*(3), 195–208. doi:10.1016/S0223-5234(99)80052-X

Patel, L., Shukla, T., Huang, X., Ussery, D. W., & Wang, S. (2020, November 12). Machine Learning Methods in Drug Discovery. *Molecules (Basel, Switzerland), 25*(22), 5277. doi:10.3390/molecules25225277 PMID:33198233

Rossi, G. P. (2003, Spring). Dual ACE and NEP inhibitors: A review of the pharmacological properties of MDL 100240. *Cardiovascular Drug Reviews, 21*(1), 51–66. doi:10.1111/j.1527-3466.2003.tb00105.x PMID:12595917

Sakellaropoulos, T., Vougas, K., Narang, S., Koinis, F., Kotsinas, A., Polyzos, A., Moss, T. J., Piha-Paul, S., Zhou, H., Kardala, E., Damianidou, E., Alexopoulos, L. G., Aifantis, I., Townsend, P. A., Panayiotidis, M. I., Sfikakis, P., Bartek, J., Fitzgerald, R. C., Thanos, D., ... Gorgoulis, V. G. (2019, December 10). A Deep Learning Framework for Predicting Response to Therapy in Cancer. *Cell Reports*, *29*(11), 3367–3373.e4. doi:10.1016/j.celrep.2019.11.017 PMID:31825821

Segler, M. H. S., Kogej, T., Tyrchan, C., & Waller, M. P. (2018, January 24). Generating Focused Molecule Libraries for Drug Discovery with Recurrent Neural Networks. *ACS Central Science*, *4*(1), 120–131. doi:10.1021/acscentsci.7b00512 PMID:29392184

Xu, Y., Yao, H., & Lin, K. (2018, December). An overview of neural networks for drug discovery and the inputs used. *Expert Opinion on Drug Discovery*, *13*(12), 1091–1102. doi:10.1080/17460441.2018.1547278 PMID:30449189

Zhou, Z., Li, X., & Zare, R. (2017). Optimizing Chemical Reactions with Deep Reinforcement Learning. *ACS Central Science*, *3*(12), 1337–1344. Advance online publication. doi:10.1021/acscentsci.7b00492 PMID:29296675

KEY TERMS AND DEFINITIONS

Artificial Intelligence: The hypothesis and advancement of PC frameworks ready to perform undertakings typically requiring human knowledge, for example, visual insight, speech recognition, decision making, and interpretation between dialects.

AtomNet: It is an innovative principal on drug discovery calculation to utilize a profound convolutional brain organization. This sort of organization came to conspicuousness a couple of years prior and has a novel property: it succeeds at grasping complex ideas as a blend of increasingly small snippets of data.

Drug Discovery: It is the cycle through which potential new remedial substances are distinguished, utilizing a blend of computational, exploratory, translational, and clinical models.

Neural Network: A neural network is a progression of calculations that perceive essential connections in a data set, a process that imitates the manner in which the human cerebrum works. In this sense, brain networks allude to frameworks of neurons, either natural or fake.

Chapter 24
Global Cost of Living in Different Geographical Areas Using the Concept of NLP

Meenu Vijarania
K.R. Mangalam University, India

Milind Udbhav
K.R. Mangalam University, India

Swati Gupta
K.R. Mangalam University, India

Robin Kumar
K.R. Mangalam University, India

Akshat Agarwal
Amity University, Gurgaon, India

ABSTRACT

Cost of living affects the maintenance if a certain standard of living, which includes housing, food, taxes, healthcare, etc. To overcome this issue, the project aims to analyze the amount of money needed to survive in different geographical areas and compare the cost of living in different areas. The analysis of the cheapest and most expensive places in the world is done for proper categorization. For getting proper data there is a need of extracting the latitude and longitude of all different locations. The comparison of expenses in different countries based on different parameters gives an idea about the living standards in different countries. Analyzing different parameters also helps to decide the lifestyle of people in different countries and whether their expenses will be high or low in the particular country. One major type of analysis, which is geospatial analysis, is also used here to study the entities using different topological or geographical properties. The project deals with real-life scenarios people face in day-to-day life when there is a need to decide the lifestyle of living.

DOI: 10.4018/978-1-6684-6821-0.ch024

1. INTRODUCTION

The sum of money required by a particular person for a particular area and time to pay for his necessities which includes housing, food, taxes, and medical care is known as his cost of living. The cost of living can be explained by comparing how expensive, it is to live in one city or another. In contrast, a high wage may not appear adequate in a pricey metropolis like New York. The cost-of-living index compares a major city's cost of living to that of an equivalent metropolitan area. The index includes the cost of several living costs to produce an overall measurement that new workers can use as a benchmark. The index offers a useful overview of housing, transportation, and grocery prices as recent graduates examine their employment options and people looking for a new job contemplate relocating. This study looks into the relationship between the cost and standard of living. It also lists the factors that affect how much something costs to live. Knowing which comes first—the level of living causing the expense of living or the other way around—is crucial. The standard of living is a measurement of a person's quality of life or degree of material success. Quality of life is defined as including personal advancements, a healthy lifestyle, access to and freedom to pursue knowledge, and achieving a standard of living that exceeds the satisfaction of an individual's basic and psychological needs to achieve a level of social well-being consistent with national aspirations. Contrarily, the cost of living is what is required to sustain some minimally essential standard of living at a given period. It is also referred to as the price of purchasing sufficient amounts of various goods to maintain a certain basic level of living. The economic definition of the cost of living can be "what is the minimum cost of this month's prices to reach the actual level of unity achieved in that base period of the time," according to the office for the National Statistics (ONS) present in the United Kingdom. There are different meanings and definitions given by different people from various places and areas. As the living conditions and the amount of money earned are also different from their expenses. The way of thinking also varies from place to place and person to person so there is no certainty about expenses also the conditions also cost money as the good living environment with the excellent condition would also cost due to these reasons expenses vary as well as the conditions and people too.

Cost of living helps one in keeping a certain standard of living for oneself which includes house, food, taxes, healthcare and etc. To overcome this issue the project aims to analyse the amount of money needed to survive in different geographical areas and compare the cost of living in different areas. The analysis of the cheapest and most expensive places in the world is done for proper categorization. For getting data there is a need of extracting the latitude and longitude of all distinct locations. Create new features from existing ones, feature engineering is used to increase the overall performance of the model. After feature engineering, there is a need of grouping countries to find out the lifestyle factor by the use of different shades of colour. Knowing the expense of food, education, travelling, living, lifestyle, e, etc., comparing expensive and inexpensive countries is done to get meaningful insights. The comparison of expenses in different countries based on different parameters gives an idea about the living standards in different countries. Analyzing different parameters also helps to decide the lifestyle of people in different countries and whether their expenses will be high or low in the particular country. One major type of analysis which is geospatial analysis is also used here to study the entities using different topological, or geographical properties. The methods use the concept of geographical maps by using latitudes and longitudes to find out different parameters in different countries to find out the real-life tracking of parameters required for getting proper database records. Technological advancement also helps to decide the overall value and its growth generating numerous opportunities for people and can be ranked based on the cost of living. Ranking helps to decide the chances of survival based on food, cost, travel, living, income, lifestyle, education, and income. Majorly the cost of essential items plays a vital role as it is used in day-to-day life and may vary from place to place, country to country, the analysis of the database also helps people to save money by knowing the basic needs. The cost-of-living project helps people to analyze the quality of life in the city which is preferred by people to visit or live whether it has a better health care system and low crime rates or not. The project keeps the understanding of data to suggest better places to live based on certain lifestyle factors. For people who move frequently, the project makes understanding expenses and lifestyles easy for them. The project deals with real-life scenarios people face in day-to-day life when there is a need to decide the lifestyle of living.

2. LITERATURE SURVEY

Cost of living helps by maintaining a kind of certain standards of living which include house, food, taxes, healthcare and etc as mentioned by (Barbieri,et al.2005). The cost-of-living project helps people to analyse the quality of life in the city which is preferred by people to visit or live whether it has a better health care system and low crime rates or not as described by (Hassan,et al.2005). The project keeps the understanding of data to suggest better places to live based on certain lifestyle factors. For the people who relocate frequently, the project makes understanding expenses and lifestyles easy for them. The project deals with real-life scenarios people face in day-to-day life when there is a need to decide the lifestyle of living. As seen by comparison between several countries and places also no one has done it on a global scale but only on a small scale for which they have not used many perimeters but only a number of them were used like living conditions, environmental conditions, population, geographical conditions, human well beings, condition of the food, living expenses and other factor as well. But the perimeters and other conditions used in the project are completely different as the comparison is done between a lot of countries and on a lot of different bases like location which is further expanded into what type of location it is and how the environment, living conditions, rent, travel, food, etc are present or not with how it is for settlement. How the lifestyle of the people living there are they happy or not and also income sources as described in (Dalton,et al.2008). The comparison done is also like which country is cheaper compared to others and which is the expensive one. Also, where food and lifestyle are good, where is food and lifestyle are just average and where it is just bad in condition. The project aims to analyse the amount of money needed to survive in different geographical areas and compare the cost of living in different areas. The analysis of the cheapest and most expensive places in the world is done for proper categorization. For getting proper data there is a need of extracting the latitude and longitude of all separate locations. Creating e new features from existing features, feature engineering is used for increasing the overall performance of the model. After feature engineering, there is a need of grouping countries to find out the lifestyle factor by the use of different shades of colour. Knowing the expense of food, education, travelling, living, lifestyle, etc, the comparison of expensive and inexpensive countries is done to get meaningful insights. The comparison of expenses in different countries based on different parameters gives an idea about the living standards in different countries. Analysing different parameters also helps to decide the lifestyle of people in different countries and whether their expenses will be high or low in a particular country as described in(Walsh,et al.2001). One major type of analysis which is geospatial analysis is also used here to study the entities using different topological, or geographical properties. The methods use the concept of geographical maps by using latitudes and longitudes to find out different parameters in different countries to find out the real-life taking of parameters required for getting proper database records as mentioned in(keyfitz,et al.1989). The distinct factors used in the project also helps to identify the relationship and similarity between them to identify some trends and pattern which helps in improving the predicting process. Education, Travel, Income, Food, Living, and Lifestyle have been seen as important points for comparison of the cost of living globally by people.

3. TECHNOLOGIES AND METHODOLOGIES USED IN THE GLOBAL COST OF LIVING

3.1 Artificial Intelligence (AI)

Artificial intelligence is the capability of machines, especially computer systems, to execute tasks that would normally require human intelligence. AI applications include expert systems, machine learning, natural language processing, speech recognition, and machine vision. Simply said, AI enhances key business processes by boosting the speed as well as the accuracy of strategic decision-making processes, enabling firms to make better judgments. In the future years and decades, artificial intelligence (AI), a genuinely ground-breaking achievement by computer science, had developed into a crucial component of all contemporary software. This presents as a threat but also an opportunity at the same. Both defensive and offensive cyber operations would be supported by artificial intelligence (AI). In addition, cyberattack methods will be created to take advantage of AI's technical shortcomings. Finally, AI's voracious appetite for vast quantities of data training would increase the value of the data and redefine how must we think about data protection. This guarantees that this era-defining technology will lead to broadly shared safety and prosperity, and prudent global governance will be necessary. In general terms, AI refers to computational tools that can be used to substitute for human intelligence in the performance of certain tasks. Similar to the exponential expansion that database technology witnessed in the latter part of the 20th century, this technology is currently developing at a breakneck rate. The foundational technology that powers enterprise-level software is now databases. Similar to this, during the next few decades, it is anticipated that AI will account for the majority of new value added to the software. Automating tasks that formerly required human intelligence is one of the primary goals of artificial intelligence (AI). Gained efficiency can be made by reducing the number of labour resources an organisation has to use on a project or the amount of time a person needs to spend on repetitive chores. For instance, medical assistant AI can be used to detect diseases based on a patient's symptoms while chatbots might be employed to respond to customer service inquiries. Some of the classic objectives of AI research are names such as reasoning, knowledge representation, planning, learning, natural language processing, sensing, and the capacity to move and manipulate objects which are the classic objectives of AI research. One of the long-term objectives of the area in intelligence, or the capacity to solve any of problems. Artificial intelligence is already changing our environment in a variety of ways and playing an increasingly significant task in our daily lives and economy. The US and Asia have emerged as the world's leaders in the heated struggles for the enjoyment of their benefits. A lot of people have started to believe that AI will boost productivity as well as their economy. Analysing massive amounts of data, which can increase productivity and significantly enhance the decision-making process. It can also help to lead the development of new markets, industries, products, and services, which would definitely increase consumer demand and open up new sources of income. AI could, however, potentially has a profoundly disruptive impact on society and the economy together. A little caution that it might result in the formation of super companies, which are known as the centres of wealth and knowledge, which might have a negative impact on the larger economy all together. Additionally, it can expand the skill gap between developed as well as developing nations and may increase the demand for the particular types of workers while displacing the others; the latter tendency might have a significant impact on the labour market as well. Experts caution against it because it might lead to greater inequality, lower wages, and a smaller tax base altogether. These worries are still legitimate, but it's unclear whether and how much the associated risks will come to pass. They are not a given, and a well-crafted policy might encourage the advancement of AI while limiting its negative implications. The EU has the chance to strengthen its position in the global race and steer AI in a direction that helps its people and economy. It must first decide on a common strategy that would play to its advantages and allow for the most efficient use of the resources of the Member States. The majority of research highlights the enormous economic impact that AI would achieve. By 2035, AI could quadruple the yearly global economic growth rates, according to the research conducted by consultancy firms. Accenture and spanning twelve industrialised economies that together account for more than 0.5% of the global economic production. This increase will automatically be fuelled by the AI in three keyways. Firstly, it will result in a significant rise in labour productivity by up to 40% as a result of innovative technology which makes workforce-related time management more effective as compared to before. Secondly, the AI will develop a brand-new virtual workforce that is capable of problem-solving as well as self-learning at the same time. This workforce is referred to as "intelligent automation" in the research done. Thirdly, the economy will gain from the spread of innovation, which would have an impact on various industries and also opens up new revenue streams altogether. So far, artificial intelligence has had a positive type of effect on society, making life easier for us humans by improving our daily routines with virtual and at-home helpers and by effectively storing as well as analysing data all across different industries altogether.

3.2 Natural language Processing (NLP)

Natural language (NL) refers to people's way to communicate(talk) with each other in the form of speech and text. The process includes the verbal written form of communication, which carries a huge amount of information. In day-to-day topics which are chosen by humans, their tone, their selection of words, everything adds up to some type of information that can be interpreted, and its value can be extracted from the given form of data. In simple words, the machines are given the ability to read, understand and derive meaning from human language by NLP which is a field of artificial intelligence (AI). With the help of NLP, humans can communicate with computers using a natural language such as English. In today's world NLP is booming with the advancements in access to the data and increase in computational power. NLP is immensely helpful in areas like healthcare, media, and finance. Today, millions of data are generated through conversations, declarations, or tweets and these data are unstructured data this data do not fit in the row and column structure which makes them difficult to analyze and manipulate. With the help of NLP, the machines can detect figures of speeches like irony and even perform sentiment analysis. Data can be contained in the form of numbers all the time as to deal with textual data, NLP can easily take raw language as input and derive meaningful insights from it. The demand for NLP is high in the market today. None of the companies wants to ignore the digital transformation. Every business is trying to leverage the power of A.I. The text data forms a substantial portion of unstructured data which is analyzed by companies to identify patterns and make data-driven decisions. Professionally skilled people in NLP are in high demand for projects involving textual analytics. The recognition and prediction of diseases are done based on electronic health records present as well as a patient's speech with the help of NLP. Organizations can be determined by what the customers review on the products by the identification and extraction of information from them. Sentimental Analysis can tell a lot about the customer's choices and their decision drivers. Amazon's Alexa and Apple's Siri are examples of intelligent voice-driven interfaces which use NLP to respond to vocal prompts and do everything. NLP is also used in both the search as well as the selection phase of talent recruitment by identifying the skills of potential hires. The autocorrect and autocomplete also use the NLP technology to show correct items and outcomes. To solve NLP-based problems first step is to gather data. Gathering textual data from emails, posts, and tweets are its an example. The second step is to allow the model to learn meaningful features and not overfitting of irrelevant noise. Also, remove all the irrelevant characters. The steps involve tokenizing the word by separating it into different words. The last part of the second step is to convert all characters to lower case and combine misspelt or spelt words into a single representation. Now, comes the last step is to change textual data into numbers from which the algorithm can understand and derive insights from it. Also, the process involves inspection and classification for better results. By using these steps an NLP based problems are solved. By using NLP, the process of automation and discovery of new emerging technologies can be easily done.

3.3 Machine Learning

Software programmes that, with the use of machine learning (ML), a subset of artificial intelligence (AI), are better able to predict outcomes without being explicitly instructed to do so. Machine learning algorithms forecast new output values using historical data as input. Machine learning is frequently used in recommendation engines. Business process automation (BPA), predictive maintenance, spam filtering, malware threat detection, and fraud detection are some further common uses. Machine learning is important because it helps with the creation of new products and gives organisations an understanding of patterns in consumer behaviour and corporate operations. A significant portion of the operations of Facebook, Google, and Uber, revolve around machine learning. For many businesses, machine learning has become a key to competitive differentiation. Machine learning has been used for a range of purposes, from predicting consumer behaviour to creating the operating system for self-driving automobiles. Benefit-wise, machine learning can help companies understand their customers better. By collecting customer data and comparing it with behaviour over time, machine learning algorithms may help teams identify relationships and support them in tailoring product development and marketing campaigns to customer demand. For business models, some businesses heavily rely on machine learning. For instance, Uber uses algorithms to pair drivers with passengers. To surface the ride advertisements in searches google uses machine learning. More data than humans can be accessed and stored by machines with machine learning and artificial intelligence, including mind-blogging statistics. Machines can detect the patterns and utilize that information to generate solutions to any kind of environmental problem whether we recognize it or not, machine learning affects how we live our daily lives. It determines what we see when we browse Facebook, what we see when we go to a business website, and how we engage with brands online. Simply put, a cost function measures how inaccurate the model is at estimating the relationship between X and y. The difference or distance between the projected value and the actual value is often used to express this. The cost function (you may also see this referred to as loss or error.) The method for assessing "the performance of our algorithm/model" is the cost function. Calculating how much of the model was in its forecast, considers both the model's projected and actual outputs. If our forecasts and the actual numbers differ significantly, it produces a greater number. ML is the concept of teaching computers to spot patterns in data and use them to solve specific issues. Iterative machine learning or IML is crucial because it allows models to independently adjust to new data when it is presented to them. Machine learning allows the examination of enormous amounts of data and can supply a quicker, more correct result that can assist in finding lucrative opportunities and risky situations. The following ones use or employ machine learning as their base for working Internet search engines, spam-filtering email software, websites that offer personalized recommendations, banking software that spots suspicious transactions, and many phone apps like speech recognition all employ machine learning as their base.

3.4 Data Science

Data science is the study of how to extract useful information from data for business decision-making, strategic planning, and other purposes by using innovative analytics tools and scientific concepts. Virtually all facets of corporate operations and strategies heavily involve data science. For instance, it provides data on clients that businesses may use to develop effective marketing campaigns and target advertisements to boost product sales. In factories and other industrial settings, it helps to manage financial risks, uncover fraudulent activity, and stop equipment problems. It aids in thwarting cyberattacks and additional security risks in IT systems. Its applications in healthcare include disease diagnosis, picture analysis, therapy planning, and scientific study. Data science is used by academic institutions to monitor student performance and enhance their recruitment efforts. Data science is used by sports teams to monitor player performance and formulate game plans. Other significant users include public policy organisations and governmental bodies. Generally speaking, the ability to empower and support better decision-making is one of data science's main advantages. When making business judgments, organisations that invest in it can use measurable, data-based proof. Such data-driven decisions should result in improved business performance, cost savings, and workflow efficiency. Depending on the organization and industry, data science has different distinct business advantages. Data science, for instance, aids in identifying and enhancing target audiences in firms that deal with customers To increase conversion rates and develop individualised marketing campaigns and promotional offers that boost sales, marketing and sales teams might mine customer data. Data scientists frequently work on modelling, pattern identification, anomaly detection, classification, categorization, and sentiment analysis. Additionally, they create artificial intelligence (AI) tools like chatbots, autonomous vehicles, and machines, as well as technology like recommendation engines, personalization systems, and these. Due to the sophisticated analyses, it uses, data science is inherently difficult. The enormous amounts of data that are frequently evaluated increase project complexity and lengthen completion times. The analytics process is further complicated by the fact that data scientists frequently work with massive data pools that contain a variety of structured, unstructured, and semi-structured data. Data scientists' main responsibility is to analyse data, frequently large amounts of it, to identify information that can be shared with business leaders, managers, and employees, as well as with government officials, medical professionals, researchers, and many other groups. Additionally, data scientists develop AI tools and technologies that are used in a variety of applications. In both situations, they collect data, create analytical models, train, test, and apply the models to the data. Machine learning algorithms play an important role in data science. In machine learning, data sets are learned about, and then algorithms search for patterns, anomalies, or insights in them. It combines supervised, unsupervised, semi-supervised, and reinforcement learning techniques, with the algorithms receiving varying degrees of data scientist training and supervision. Deep learning is another branch of machine learning that is more complex and focuses on using artificial neural networks to evaluate massive amounts of unlabelled data. Predictive models are another core data science technology.

By using machine learning, data mining, and statistical algorithms for the data sets to forecast business scenarios as well as anticipated outcomes or behaviour, data scientists develop them. In predictive modelling and other advanced analytics applications, data sampling techniques—a data mining approach intended to speed up and simplify the analytics process—are frequently used to evaluate a representative subset of data. Both fields have strong statistical underpinnings, emphasise modelling to address quantitative issues, and demand adept analytical abilities. Additionally, data science is transforming several of the fields economists work in, such as banking, finance, public policy, and consulting. In conclusion, data science has had a significant impact on how businesses operate in the modern world. Data science not only gives organisations the ability to understand their customers' data but also enables them to locate important data about their own. Economic data analysis has typically concentrated on providing causal explanations. Although not always the case, many of the most important problems in empirical economics are causal. Examples include the short-term and long-term effects of educational decisions on laboratory results and the effects of economic policies on outcome distributions. As a result, they are conceptually different from predictive problems, which numerous recently developed machine learning algorithms are primarily intended to address. Data enables businesses to identify issues' root causes more precisely. To visualise connections between events occurring in various places, departments, and systems the organizations use the data.

4. TECHNIQUES USED FOR REAL-LIFE IMPLEMENTATION AND WORKING ON THE GLOBAL COST OF LIVING

a. Geospatial Analysis

When used with geographic models, geospatial analysis is the collection, visualisation, and modification of imagery, GPS, satellite imagery, and historical data that is either explicitly described in terms of geographic coordinates or implicitly described in terms of a street address, postal code, or forest stand identifier. Organizations can anticipate potential changes brought on by shifting spatial conditions or location-based events and prepare using geospatial analytics. Decision-makers can better understand why solutions that succeed in one place frequently fail in another by using location-based data. Geospatial analytics integrates data from various sources, such as satellite imaging, GPS, position sensors, social media, and mobile devices, to create data visualisations for comprehending events and recognising trends in complex relationships between people and places. Almost any event on Earth can be applied to this geo-referenced data. Maps, graphs, statistics, and cartograms that depict recent and historical trends are examples of visualizations. This can make predictions easier and more correct. With the addition of timing and location to traditional sources of data, geospatial analytics may provide a more comprehensive view of events. Images and patterns that are simple to discover provide insights that would have been buried in a massive spreadsheet. Massive amounts of geographic and geometric data may be processed instantaneously by geospatial analytics firms. Thus, users can explore geographical representations in real-time and interact with billions of mapped places. Users may rapidly see how something has evolved from days to years by examining data across time and geography. Geospatial data analytics began in the 1960s when Canada used the first geographic information systems (GIS) to catalogue natural resources. Geospatial analysis is being utilized to collect data to analyze everything from sales patterns to population forecasts and weather modelling. Data is visually arranged by time and geography using geospatial big data analytics, which frees it from the infinite rows and columns of a standard spreadsheet. This method makes it simpler for the human brain to assimilate information. Geospatial data analytics makes it possible to see hidden patterns in huge datasets, such as proximity, contiguity, affiliation, and distance. It is also simpler to notice how things change over time and where the change is most obvious when spatial data is visualised. Examples of spatial analysis include calculating lengths and angles, planning routes and tracking vehicles, and establishing relationships between things by comparing their locations to geographic coordinates. Organizations can anticipate and get ready for potential changes caused by shifting spatial conditions or location-based events with the aid of geospatial analytics. By using location-based data, decision-makers can better understand why solutions that work in one region usually fail in another. The point cloud, which stores geographic data as a collection of points in three-dimensional space, is an emerging third type of model (latitude, longitude, and elevation). Lidar, an airborne laser scanning method, is frequently used to capture point clouds. In the project latitudes and longitudes are used to find places and extract their data as a useful resource to measure the living conditions, the condition of the food, as well as the environmental issues that may affect the economy of the person that may be able to raise the price of the place or decrease it in case of the issues that might arise from time to time.

b. Feature Engineering

Feature engineering is a machine learning method that uses data to create new variables that are not present in the training set. In addition to accelerating and streamlining data transformations, it can create novel features that boost model precision for both supervised and unsupervised learning. Through the creation of an input data set that perfectly complements the algorithm, feature engineering seeks to optimise the performance of machine learning models. Adding new variables or features to your dataset to increase the efficiency and precision of your machine learning models is known as feature engineering. The foundation of the most efficient feature engineering is a thorough understanding of the business issue and your data sources The four main steps in feature engineering in machine learning are feature creation, feature transformations, feature extraction, and feature selection. The process of constructing, transforming, extracting, and choosing features—also referred to as variables—that are most helpful in developing a precise ML algorithm is known as feature engineering.

c. Feature Creation

In feature engineering, the first stage is the identification of all pertinent predictor variables to be included in the model. Finding these variables is a theoretical exercise rather than a practical one that can be accomplished by looking through pertinent literature, speaking with subject-matter experts, and brainstorming.

d. Feature Transformation

A predictor variable may be feature transformed to enhance its performance in the predictive model.

Feature Extraction

Transformations that take part in creating a new variable by the manipulation of one of the variables in one way or another. The creation of variables by the extraction from some other data by them is called feature extraction.

e. Feature Selection

The choice of which predictor variables to include in a model is known as feature selection. It can seem straightforward to a beginner to incorporate all of the elements into the model. Let the prediction model decide which ones are appropriate after that. Sadly, in practice, it is not quite that easy. When all the potential predictor variables are chosen, the computer you are using occasionally crashes. Sometimes it's possible that the algorithm being used wasn't intended to utilise every accessible variable. If you were to incorporate every attribute a model might have, the model might end up discovering fictitious relationships. In actual reality, choosing features for a predictive model includes a blend of intuition, theory, and assessing how well various feature combinations perform. Feature engineering requires deep technical skills, detailed knowledge of data engineering, and the way ML algorithms work. It demands a specific skillset including programming and understanding of how to work with databases. Most feature engineering techniques require Python coding skills Feature engineering is the process of transforming raw data into features that may be used to construct a prediction model using deep learning or statistical modelling.

Raw data is transformed into features through the pre-processing stage of machine learning known as feature engineering, which may then be used to create prediction models by either machine learning or statistical modelling. The engineering of machine learning features aims to improve model performance. The "skill" of creating meaningful features from existing data following the learning aim and the applied machine learning model is known as feature engineering. It entails changing data into forms that more closely connect to the fundamental goal that must be learned. Adding new variables or features to your dataset to increase the efficiency and precision of your machine learning models is known as feature engineering. The best feature engineering is built on a solid understanding of the business issue and the data sources you have access to.

f. Geographical Properties

Geographic features, often known as places, sites, areas, or regions, are elements of a planet. On Earth, there are both natural and abstract geographic features, as well as manufactured geographic features. Hills, streams, gulches, canyons, streambeds, or channels—whether they are flowing or dry—as well as natural bridges, lakes, monuments, mesas, deserts, woodlands, springs, water holes, cliffs, and other similar natural features, are examples of geographic features. The five main topics of geography are as follows location, place, human-environment interaction, movement, and region. Geographical characteristics influence the rise of civilizations. For these civilizations to succeed, they had to adapt to their surroundings. Explore how the globe as we know it now was shaped by the mountains, lakes, rivers, and forests throughout your journey. Topography, climate, soils, and hydrology are some of the physical features they possess. Human traits include things like language one speaks, the religion one follow, political and economic structures, and population distribution of the area. There is a significant difference in the cost of living in various places with different environments, conditions of life, economic stability, food cost as well as clothing and many other things cost varies from place to place so does the cost of living varies. In addition to measures of financial resources, the cost of living may also specifically contribute to family stress. Two families may appear to have comparable incomes, but the family in the more expensive neighbourhood may be under considerably more strain trying to provide for their kids. Because the same goods and services (including rent, childcare, and extracurricular activities) cost more in higher-cost places, living there adds stress that is not accounted for by income. Living in a more expensive place may also make it more difficult for a family to meet their basic needs because things like food and shelter are more expensive. The stress associated with living in a high-cost area is lost when the expense of living is not expressly considered and is replaced by unexplained statistical noise. It is a contextual factor that pervades every financial choice made by families in a certain geographic location and is constant for all families there (although all families may not be influenced equally). Parents are unable to simply select or control their cost of living, which makes it distinct from other costs of living. When choosing a place to live, parents frequently consider things like employment availability and accessibility to social networks. The cost of living may play a secondary role, but only to a limited amount because it frequently correlates with nearby places. In summary, the cost of living has a special impact on a child's development since it is a context-specific aspect of the family that affects all financial decisions while also being a component that many families are powerless to change.

g. Topological Properties

A topological property, also known as a topological invariant, is a property of a topological space that is invariant under homeomorphisms in topology and related mathematical fields. A valid class of topological spaces that are closed under homeomorphisms is what is referred to as a topological quality. The characteristics of spaces that are unaffected by continuous deformation are studied in topology. As the objects can be stretched and contracted like rubber sheets without breaking so it is frequently referred to as "rubber-sheet geometry". A topological space is a set that has a topological structure that enables the specification of continuous subspace deformation and, more broadly, all kinds of continuity. Euclidean spaces and, more broadly, metric spaces are instances of topological spaces, topology is defined by metric or distance.

5. VISUAL REPRESENTATION OF THE OUTCOMES OF THE GLOBAL COST OF LIVING

In the Figure 1, it is described the most expensive countries from the ones taken the currency taken for the comparison is EURO. The comparison is done by taking the food, lifestyle, education, travel, income and living into account. The comparison done here explains the details about the countries that which one is good for which criteria like Switzerland in the food section, the United

Kingdom in the Travel section, Singapore in Living, Iceland in Lifestyle, NY in Education and Switzerland in Income ones these are shown in the above graph in figure 1.0.

In the Figure 2, it is described the least expensive countries from the ones taken the currency taken for the comparison is EURO. The comparison is done by taking the food, lifestyle, education, travel, income and living into account. The comparison done here explains the details about the countries that which one is good for which criteria.

Figure 1. Graph for the Most Expensive Countries (Expenses in Euro)

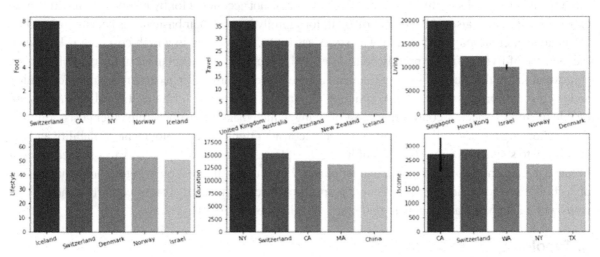

Figure 2. Graph for the Least Expensive Countries (Expenses in Euro)

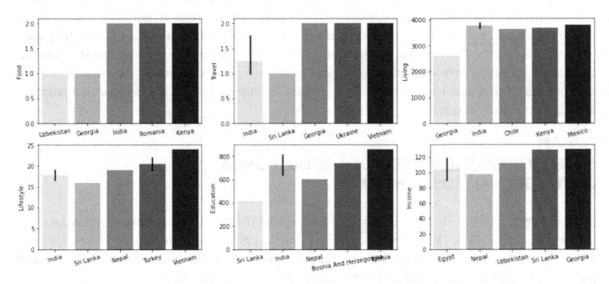

As shown in the Figure 3 price of education is shown all over the world as a base of comparison between different countries and their cities are also used in this comparison. By analysing the above figure, we can see and compare where the price of education is more and where it is less as well as where we can get a good education as compared to other places with the expensive and cheap ones for the choice of our one for where to go and for which one is to be left alone. Above it has been explained clearly.

As shown in Figure 4 given above explains the price of travel for where the travel is expensive and where it is least expensive. Travelling from one place to another cost a lot but sometimes going somewhere nice also cost a lot but above it explains where it is expensive to travel and where we can go for the least expensive and have fun. Here the comparison is not only done between the countries only but also between their respective cities so that the decision-making can be done easily, and no problem may arise.

Figure 3. Map showing the price of education globally

Figure 4. Map showing the price of Travel globally

As shown in Figure 5 mentioned above it is shown the countries and their cities where the income is more, and settlement can be done for a good income. With a good income source, it is easy and comfortable to live a good life. Here the comparison is not done only between the countries only but also their respective cities too for easy comparison and also to make the decision easier for others.

As shown in Figure 6 mentioned above it is explained that the food of which place is most expensive, and for which place it is least expensive. By this, it can be concurred for where to travel for the most expensive food and for where to travel for the least expensive food. Here the comparison is not done only between the countries but also their cities too for helping the people to choose wisely and easily.

Figure 5. Map showing the price of Income globally

Figure 6. Map showing the price of Food globally

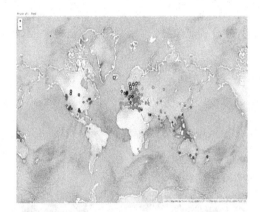

As shown in figure: - 7 mentioned above the price of living is shown in different countries and their cities. It is shown where the price of living is most expensive and where it is least expensive.

As shown in Figure 8 mentioned above the price of lifestyle is shown for different countries in different regions as well as their respective cities lifestyle price is compared to one another to find the most expensive ones and the least expensive ones by comparing their lifestyle prices with each other.

Figure 7. Map showing the price of Living globally

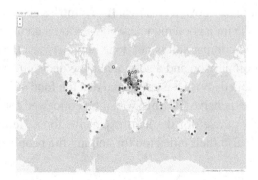

Figure 8. Map showing the price of Lifestyle globally

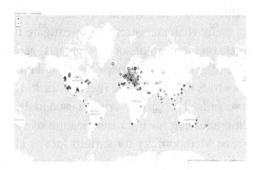

The above-mentioned figure: - 9 it is shown the comparison between the cities of India named Chandigarh, Gurgaon, Ahmedabad, Hyderabad, Chennai, Pune, Noida, Bangalore, Kolkata, Mumbai and Delhi on the bases of Travel, Living, Lifestyle, Education and Income. It is explained which city of India is best of which and where to go on the bases of the comparison done and shown in the above graph.

Figure 9. Comparison of Indian Cities

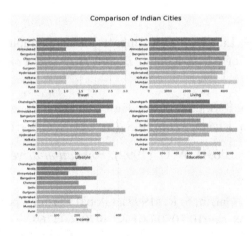

6. CONCLUSION

Highlighting the importance of the cost of living is the objective of the research. A certain standard of life including house, food, taxes, healthcare, etc are maintained by the cost of living. The analysis of the amount of money needed to survive in different geographical areas is the major aim of the analysis. A comparison of the cost of living in different areas gives a brief about the brief of different parameters essential for living. The global cost of living also helps to analyze the cheapest and the most expensive places in the world. The project uses technologies like artificial intelligence, machine learning, and NLP for real-time working analysis. With the use of modern technologies real-time prediction has become easy rather than getting an accuracy score, the use of modern technologies helps to improve from past parameters and give accurate outcomes in the form of visualization which are easy to understand and interpret. The project makes it simple for those who frequently shift to comprehend cost and way of life.

The project is concerned with actual situations that people encounter daily when deciding on a way of life. A person's lifestyle and whether or not they would have high or low expenses in a certain country can be determined by analyzing many characteristics. To investigate the entities utilizing various topological or geographical qualities, one important sort of analysis, geospatial analysis, is also applied here. The approaches use the idea of geographical maps by using latitudes and longitudes to find out various parameters in various countries to find out the real-life tracking of parameters which is necessary for getting correct database records. The various criteria used in the project also aid in determining their relationships and similarities, allowing for the identification of some trends and patterns that aid in enhancing the prediction process. Methodology for various factors also aids people. By understanding the necessities, database study also assists people to save money. The price of necessities, which are used in everyday life and might differ from location to location and country to country, often plays a significant impact. In terms of the quality of life in the city that people prefer to visit or call home, the cost-of-living project helps determine whether a city has a good healthcare system and a low crime rate—or not. The program recommends better places to live using data based on specific lifestyle factors. With the help of the research, the paper aims to help people with day-to-day issues which people face while establishing careers and living lifestyles.

REFERENCES

An, L., He, G., Liang, Z., & Liu, J. (2006). Impacts of demographic and socioeconomic factors on Spatio-temporal dynamics of panda habitat. *Biodiversity and Conservation*, *15*(8), 2343–2363. doi:10.100710531-004-1064-6

Barbieri, A. F., & Soares-Filho, B. S. (2005). Population and land use effects on malaria prevalence in the southern Brazilian Amazon. *Human Ecology*, *33*(6), 847–874. doi:10.100710745-005-8213-8

Bilsborrow, R. E., & Okoth Ogendo, H. W. O. (1992). *Population-driven changes in land use in developing countries*. Ambio.

Bongaarts, J., O'Neill, B. C., & Gaffin, S. R. (1997). Global warming policy: Population left out in the cold. *Environment*, *39*(9), 40–48. doi:10.1080/00139159709604769

Bühlmann, P., & Van De Geer, S. (2011). *Statistics for high-dimensional data: methods, theory and applications*. Springer Science & Business Media. doi:10.1007/978-3-642-20192-9

Campbell-Lendrum, D., & Woodruff, R. (2006). Comparative risk assessment of the burden of disease from climate change. *Environmental Health Perspectives*, *114*(12), 1935–1941. doi:10.1289/ehp.8432 PMID:17185288

Carr, D. L., & Bilsborrow, R. E. (2001). Population and land use/cover change: A regional comparison between Central America and South America. *Journal of Geography Education*, *43*(8), 7–16.

Cassen, R. (Ed.). (1994). *Population and Development: Old debates, new conclusions* (Vol. 19). Transaction Publishers.

Dalton, M., O'Neill, B., Prskawetz, A., Jiang, L., & Pitkin, J. (2008). Population ageing and future carbon emissions in the United States. *Energy Economics*, *30*(2), 642–675. doi:10.1016/j.eneco.2006.07.002

Dasgupta, P. (2000). Population and resources: An exploration of reproductive and environmental externalities. *Population and Development Review, 26*(4), 643–689. doi:10.1111/j.1728-4457.2000.00643.x

Eswaran, H., Lal, R., & Reich, P. F. (2019). Land degradation: An overview. *Response to land degradation*, 20-35.

Harikrishnan, V. K., Vijarania, M., & Gambhir, A. (2020). Diabetic retinopathy identification using autoML. *Computational Intelligence and Its Applications in Healthcare*, 175.

Hassan, R., Scholes, R., & Ash, N. (2005). Ecosystems and human well-being: current state and trends. Academic Press.

Hecht, S. B. (2005). Soybeans, development and conservation on the Amazon frontier. *Development and Change, 36*(2), 375–404. doi:10.1111/j.0012-155X.2005.00415.x

Huesemann, M. H. (2006). Can advances in science and technology prevent global warming? *Mitigation and Adaptation Strategies for Global Change, 11*(3), 539–577. doi:10.100711027-006-2166-0

Jiang, L., & O'Neill, B. C. (2004). The energy transition in rural China. *International Journal of Global Energy Issues, 21*(1-2), 2–26. doi:10.1504/IJGEI.2004.004691

Keyfitz, N. (1989). The growing human population. *Scientific American, 261*(3), 118–127. doi:10.1038cientificamerican0989-118 PMID:2772607

Lepers, E., Lambin, E. F., Janetos, A. C., DeFries, R., Achard, F., Ramankutty, N., & Scholes, R. J. (2005). A synthesis of information on rapid land-cover change for the period 1981–2000. *Bioscience, 55*(2), 115–124. doi:10.1641/0006-3568(2005)055[0115:ASOIOR]2.0.CO;2

Lutz, W., Sanderson, W. C., & Scherbov, S. (2001). The end of world population growth. *Nature, 412*(6846), 543–545. doi:10.1038/35087589 PMID:11484054

Marcoux, A. (1999). *Population and environmental change: from linkages to policy issues*. Academic Press.

Martinez, W. L., Martinez, A. R., & Solka, J. L. (2017). *Exploratory data analysis with MATLAB*. Chapman and Hall/CRC.

Meyerson, F. A. (1998). Population, carbon emissions, and global warming: The forgotten relationship at Kyoto. *Population and Development Review, 24*(1), 115–130. doi:10.2307/2808124

Myers, N. (1999). Environmental scientists: Advocates as well. *Environmental Conservation, 26*(3), 163–165. doi:10.1017/S0376892999000235

Nakicenovic, N., Alcamo, J., Davis, G., Vries, B. D., Fenhann, J., Gaffin, S., ... Zhou, D. (2000). *Special report on emissions scenarios*. Academic Press.

Neumayer, E. (2002). Can natural factors explain any cross-country differences in carbon dioxide emissions? *Energy Policy, 30*(1), 7–12. doi:10.1016/S0301-4215(01)00045-3

Neumayer, E. (2004). National carbon dioxide emissions: Geography matters. *Area, 36*(1), 33–40. doi:10.1111/j.0004-0894.2004.00317.x

Sanjay, A., Vijarania, M., & Jaglan, V. (2021). Security Surveillance and Home Automation System using IoT. *EAI Endorsed Transactions on Smart Cities*, 5(15), e1–e1.

Turner, B. L. II, Matson, P. A., McCarthy, J. J., Corell, R. W., Christensen, L., Eckley, N., Hovelsrud-Broda, G. K., Kasperson, J. X., Kasperson, R. E., Luers, A., Martello, M. L., Mathiesen, S., Naylor, R., Polsky, C., Pulsipher, A., Schiller, A., Selin, H., & Tyler, N. (2003). Illustrating the coupled human-environment system for vulnerability analysis: Three case studies. *Proceedings of the National Academy of Sciences of the United States of America*, 100(14), 8080–8085. doi:10.1073/pnas.1231334100 PMID:12815106

Udhbav, M., Kumar, R., Kumar, N., Kumar, R., Vijarania, D., & Gupta, S. (2022, May 27). Prediction of Home Loan Status Eligibility using Machine Learning. Swati, Prediction of Home Loan Status Eligibility using. *Machine Learning*.

Vatcheva, I., De Jong, H., & Mars, N. J. (2000, August). Selection of perturbation experiments for model discrimination. In ECAI (pp. 191-198). Academic Press.

Walsh, S. J., Crawford, T. W., Welsh, W. F., & Crews-Meyer, K. A. (2001). A multiscale analysis of LULC and NDVI variation in Nang Rong district, northeast Thailand. *Agriculture, Ecosystems & Environment*, 85(1-3), 47–64. doi:10.1016/S0167-8809(01)00202-X

Chapter 25
The Convergence of Digital Twin, Internet of Things, and Artificial Intelligence:
Digital Smart Farming

Shipra Shivkumar Yadav
IICC Nagpur, India

ABSTRACT

An agricultural digital twin is presented in this research using technologies from the sensing change and smart water management platform projects. Unlike the sensing change project, which created a soil probe, an internet of things is now being developed by the SWAMP project platform for managing water. The authors come to the conclusion that this system is capable of collecting data from the soil probe and displaying it in a dashboard, allowing for the deployment of additional soil probes, as well as other monitoring and controlling devices, to create a fully functional digital twin

I INRODUCTION

Many nations' development depends heavily on agriculture, which is also essential to achieving Sustainable Development Goal 2 of "Zero Hunger" (United Nations, n.d.).). To fulfil the demands of a projected population of 10 billion people by 2050, the Food and Agriculture Organization (FAO) estimates that agricultural output must rise by 40% between 2012 and 2050 (). The creative application of technologies like drones, applications, and machines coupled with social, organizational, and institutional shifts is one strategy for enhancing production.

70% of the fresh water consumed globally is used for agriculture (). This makes a strong case for the development of technologies like the internet of things (IoT) to increase the amount of food produced on farms while reducing the amount of water required in agriculture.

DOI: 10.4018/978-1-6684-6821-0.ch025

Irrigation systems utilize the majority of the fresh water that is present on Earth, and 40 percent of the fresh water used in developing nations was wasted due to leaks and over irrigation (Panchard et al., 2007). The availability of fresh water has become a global concern due to factors including climate change and population growth, specifically in rainfall.

regions of scarcity (Gonzalez Perea et al., 2019) that call for a different viewpoint on irrigation systems and their optimization to guarantee food security for the expanding population (Pulido-Velazquez & Ward, 2020). In agriculture, appropriate irrigation that is managed by field sensors is crucial since inadequate or excessive watering reduces crop output (). Artificial intelligence (AI) can improve the farming process in this context by collecting data on plant conditions and computing it with high performance and low cost (Athan & Tejeshwar, 2017), maintaining crop yield at normal standards, reducing water waste, and ultimately increasing the availability of potable water (Pulido-Velazquez & Ward, 2020).

A digital twin model based on the internet of things can be applied in farms to effectively recognize their current environment in order to capitalize on this worldwide concern. This means that a virtual representation of a farm should be able to behave depending on the systems' analyses and judgments as well as gather information from the farm. The fundamental creation of a digital twin for smart farming using the Internet of Things to regulate an irrigation system based on a farmer's and/or AI choice is presented in this Chapter. Section 2 of this article provides examples of IoT applications in agriculture, Section 3 introduces the idea of a digital twin in the context of agriculture, Section 4 details the creation of the digital twin, Section 5 describes the initial findings and analysis, and Section 6 concludes.

II INTERNET OF THINGS IN AGRICULTURE

The majority of the literature on the development of IoT technologies in agriculture consists of exploratory research that demonstrate systems in small pilot projects (Verdouw, 2016). The development of equipment and devices used on farms to gather information about the soil, crop quality, weather conditions, and other factors can be divided into two categories when it comes to the use of IoT in agriculture (Agale, 2017; Krishna et al., 2017). The second category includes the development of platforms that are used to store, organize, analyze, and visualize data to help with decision-making (Jayaraman et al., 2016).

The term "smart farming" appears while reading the literature on the application of information and communication technologies (ICT) in agriculture. Although the term "smart farming" has been in use for some time, there is still a need for a comprehensive definition of the term that encompasses the technology now employed in the agriculture industry. In order to integrate information and communication technologies in the cyber-physical farm management cycle, smart farming entails integrating them into machinery, equipment, and sensors. (Pivoto et al., 2018), (Wolfert et al., 2017).

Several technologies, including IoT, Big Data, Artificial Intelligence (AI), Process Management, etc., are perceived as being included in this notion. According to the literature, ICT usage in agriculture is a developing field that currently faces some obstacles, but there are also many advantages associated with its use.

III DIGITAL TEIN SMART FARMING

According to the research of (Kritzinger et al., 2018), a digital twin model is one in which data transfer between a physical and digital entity occurs automatically, as seen in figure 1. By utilizing technologies like big data, IoT, AI, etc., a digital twin is able to link information about the farm and business and is able to act depending on a choice made automatically by the system.

By extending the idea of smart farming, a digital twin for a smart farm or a digital smart farm is suggested. Building discrete services to understand the data of a specific system, such as an irrigation system, a seeding system, etc., and bringing them together in a cyber-physical system is how a digital smart farm is executed. This makes it possible to combine various systems and gives farmers a thorough understanding of how their crops are doing. It is possible to adjust the farm to changes in the environment, weather, markets, water limitations, etc. by employing a digital smart farm.

Figure 1. Digital Twin Concept (Kritzinger et al., 2018).

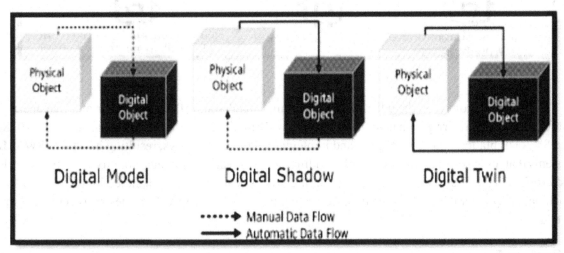

IV DIGITAL SMART FARMING SYSTEM

This section, which is separated as follows, describes a digital smart farm based on two initiatives (The Sensing Change and SWAMP projects): The previous two projects are summarized in subsection A, the system design is described in subsection B together with its hardware and devices, and the system architecture is shown in subsection C along with cloud services and other components.

A. Sensing Change and SWAMP programmers are related works.

The Sensing Change project's approach was based on the idea that it could be applied to any type of agricultural activity and that it could make use of low-cost commercial tools and supplies (Maia & Tran, 2017). Three key parts make up the system: the monitoring station, the smart phone app, and the cloud system (Figure. 2). This project created an information-gathering and information-analysis monitoring system for a farm. However, it was the farmers who made the decisions and took the necessary steps.

Figure 2. Sensing change system diagram (Maia & Tran, 2017)

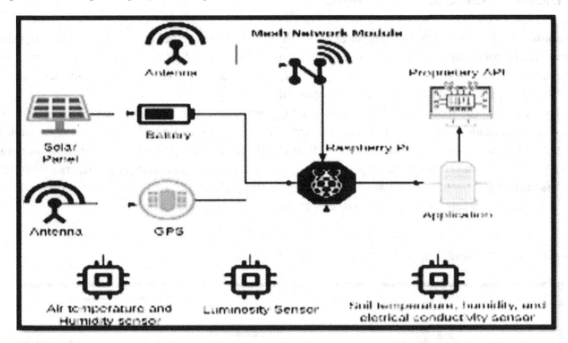

The SWAMP project, on the other hand, is creating a hands-on, IoT-based smart water management platform for precision irrigation in four locations across Brazil, Italy, and Spain (Kamienski et al., 2018). The SWAMP platform can be designed and implemented in various ways, resulting in several SWAMP Systems that are tailored to meet the needs and limitations of various settings, countries, climates, soils, and crops. This indicates that the decision-making process can be entirely handled by the farmer, by a machine, or by a combination of the two. According to Figure. 3, the SWAMP design is separated into five layers.

A System Design

The system comprises of a field-installed probe that measures ground temperature at 7 cm depth (DS18B20), soil moisture at depths of 7 cm, 28 cm, 50 cm, and 72 cm, ambient light, and geographical position (CSMv1.2). The Raspberry Pi-3 module receives probe signals via the I2C bus (CSM v1.2 and BH1750), GPIO (DHT22), serial bus (Venus GPS), and One-Wire bus (DS18B20). a module for ADS1115 is also employed for the conversion of the CSMv1.2 A/D signal. This data is read by the Raspberry module using a Python script, which displays numbers as percentages of soil moisture. The script then generates a payload including all probe data and delivers it to the Orion broker for subscription via the IoT agent. A prototype of the system utilized for laboratory testing can be shown in Figure 4. The final model of the probe that can be seen in the figure will be used in the field.

Figure 3. SWAMP project architecture layers

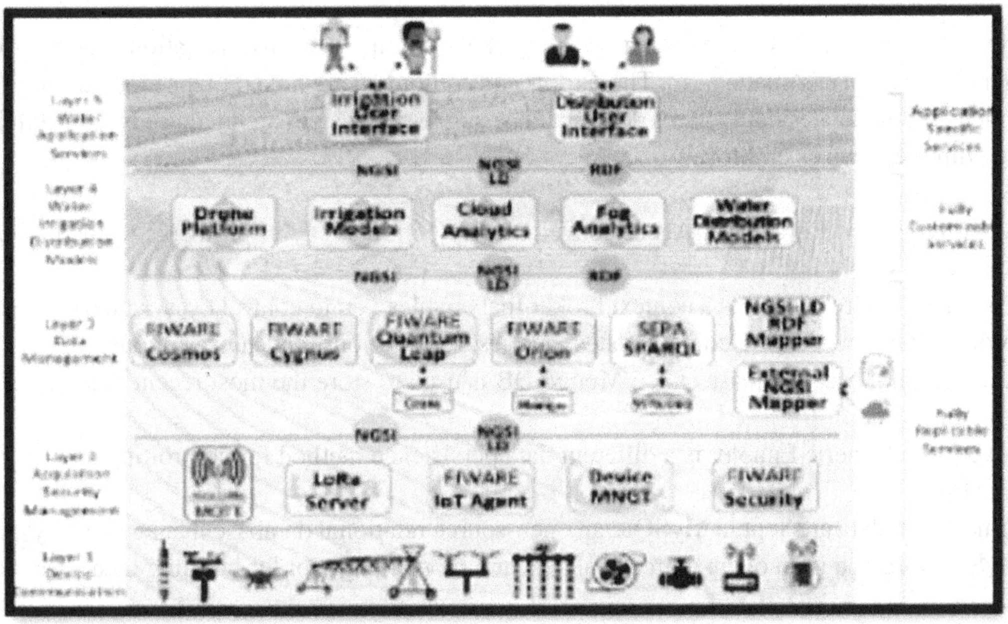

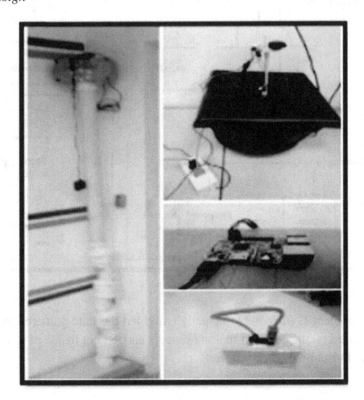

Figure 4. System design

System Architecture

Numerous equipment and systems, such as soil probes, weather stations, irrigation systems, seeders, harvesters, etc., are in use on the farm. These tools and equipment are linked to the cloud through a gateway, which communicates data to an IoT Agent. The suggested system architecture is shown in Figure. 5, along with the services employed.

- A service called Fiware IoT Agent converts many communication protocols to the cloud-based standard.
- The term "fiware" Orion is a context broker that enables you to control every stage of the context information lifecycle, including updates, queries, registrations, and subscriptions.
- A document-based database called Mongo DB is used to store the most recent data in a complex structure.
- Draco: is a Generic Enabler is a different data persistence method for controlling context history. citeDraco
- Time-series data are kept in MySQL, an open-source relational database management system. cite
- MySQL Grafana is an open-source analytics and monitoring tool for building data dashboards.

Figure 5. System Architecture

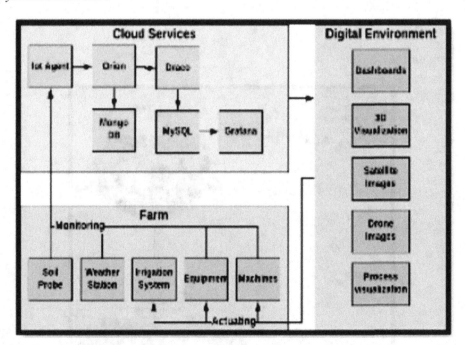

This digital environment is intended to visually enlighten the data gathered by IoT and to deliver data to the systems based on the decision-making process carried out inside of it. Information can only currently be displayed visually on dashboards.

However, all of the other settings must be built in an integrated manner in order to properly construct the digital smart farm. The information gathered and analyzed in the cloud and represented digitally should be entered into the physical system via the cloud or by integrating Programmable Logic Controllers (PLCs) into the machinery, equipment, and irrigation system.

V FIRST RESULT AND ANALYSIS

The system's initial testbed findings are shown in Fig 6 in our laboratory. On the basis of the thermogavimetric data, the soil moisture sensor was calibrated (Robinson et al., 2008). This initial test shows that the probe can send data to the cloud and that it is possible to display that data in a dashboard that updates in real time. It is obvious that the air temperature and humidity have dropped abnormally, which suggests a hardware or communication issue that has to be further investigated.

Figure 7 displays field data that was gathered using a nearby weather station. The Penman-Monteith equation can be used to extract the reference evapotranspiration (ETo) using data from this meteorological station, including air temperature and humidity, wind velocity and direction, rainfall solar radiation, dew point, rain forecast, and rain chance (Allen et al., 1998). The crop evapotranspiration is calculated by multiplying the ETo by the crop factor (Kc) for the specified crop. The ETo stands for the amount of water, in mm, that the reference crop uses (Doorenbos & Pruitt, 1977).

Figure 6. Dashboard with probe data

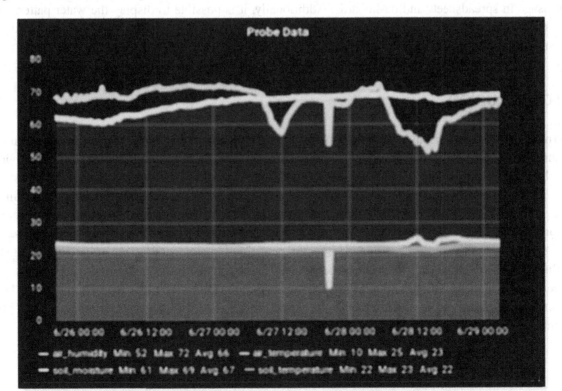

Figure 7. Field data collected

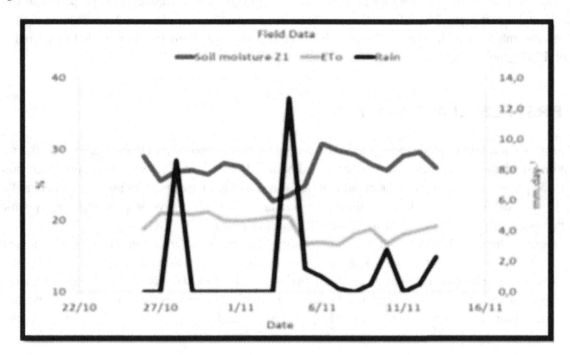

The initial findings show that the technology is functional and capable of uploading data to the cloud for usage in spreadsheets and dashboards. Additionally, it is possible to display the water patterns in the soil and extract ETo using the nearby weather station. It is clear from Fig. 7 that during periods of drought, the soil moisture reduces and increases after each rainfall.

VI CONCLUSION

Farmers can connect various assets and systems utilizing the digital twin concept and internet of things technology to have a better understanding of the various factors and elements that affect the farm's behavior, final yield production, and resource use. This essential component helps farmers make wiser decisions and lessen their influence on the environment's water, land, and soil resources. This chapter outlines the preliminary steps in creating a digital smart farm. However, numerous systems must work together in order to represent all of the farm's functions before a digital smart farm can be fully implemented.

According to this study, the system architecture and cloud implementation are effective and may be utilised for the deployment of the subsequent steps, which include the creation of IA algorithms and other digital contexts. Once the complete system is operational, it will be feasible to comprehend how farms use resources and how that affects agricultural productivity. This promotes sustainable development and raises food security for everyone on the planet.

REFERENCES

Agale, R. R. (2017). Automated Irrigation and Crop Security System in Agriculture Using Internet of Things. *International Conference on Computing, Communication, Control and Automation (ICCUBEA)*, (pp. 1–5). IEEE. 10.1109/ICCUBEA.2017.8463726

Allen, R., Pereira, L., Raes, D., Smith, M., & Ab, W. (1998). Guidelines for computing crop water requirements-FAO Irrigation and drainage document 56. *Crop Evapotranspiration*, pp. 1–15

Athani, S. & Tejeshwar, C. (2017). *Proceedings of the International Conference on IoT in Social, Mobile, Analytics and Cloud, I-SMAC 2017*. IEEE.

Charles, A., Names, A., & Rodrigues, P. (2017). Comparison of data mining methods applied to a surface meteorological station. *Rbrh, 22*.

Doorenbos, J. & Pruitt, W. (1977). Guidelines for forecasting crop water requirements. FAO Irrigation and Drainage Paper, *24*, 144.

dos Santos, F., Fernandes, P., Rockett, F., & de Oliveira, A. (2017). *The State of Food and Agriculture: Leveraging Food Systems for Inclusive Rural Transformation, (vol. 2, no. 7929)*. Food and Agriculture Organization of the United Nations. http://www.fao.org/3/a- I7658e.pdfpercentApercent5Cn https://www.ncbi.nlm.nih.gov/pubmed/24897208

FAO. (2016). *Aquastat*. FAO. https://www.fao.org/nr/water/aquastat/waterusage

Gonzalez Perea, R., Camacho Poyato, E., Montesinos, P., & Rodriguez D'az, J. A. (2019). Optimization of water demand forecasting by artificial intelligence with short data sets. *Biosystems Engineering, 177*, 59–66. doi:10.1016/j.biosystemseng.2018.03.011

Jayaraman, P Yavari, A Georgakopoulous, D Morshed, A Zaslavsky, A. (2016). Internet of Things Platform for Smart Farming: Experiences and Lessons Learned. *Sensors (Basel), 16*(11), 1–17.

Kamienski, J., Soininen, M., Taumberger, S., Fernandes, A., Toscano, T. S., Cinotti, R., Maia, F., & Neto, A. (2018). Swamp: an iot-based smart water management platform for precision irrigation in agriculture. In *2018 Global Internet of Things Summit (GIoTS)*, (pp. 1-6). MDPI.

Krishna, K., Silver, O., Malende, W., Anuradha, K. (2017). Internet of Things application for implementation of smart agriculture system. *Proceedings of the International Conference on IoT in Social, Mobile, Analytics and Cloud, I-SMAC* (pp. 54–59). Semantic Scholar.

Kritzinger, W., Karner, M., Traar, G., Henjes, J., & Sihn, W. (2018). Digital Twin in Manufacturing: A Categorical Literature Review and Classification. IFAC-Papers OnLine, *51*(11), 1016–1022. . doi:10.1016/j.ifacol.2018.08.474

Maia, R. & Tran, A. (2017). Precision agriculture employing remote monitoring systems in Brazil. *IEEE Global Humanitarian Technology Conference, Proceedings*, (pp. 1-6). IEEE.

Panchard, J., Rao, S., Prabhakar, T., Hubaux, J., & Jamadagni, H. (2007). Common Sense Net: A Wireless Sensor Network for Resource-Poor Agriculture in the Semi-Arid Areas of Developing Countries. *Information Technologies and International Development, 4*, 51–67.

Pivoto, D., Waquil, D., Talamini, E., Finocchio, C., Corte, V., & Mores, G. (2018). Scientific development of smart agricultural technologies and their implementation in Brazil. Information Processing in Agriculture, *5*(1), 21–32. https://linkinghub.elsevier.com/retrieve/pii/S2214317316301184

Pulido-Velazquez, M., & Ward, F. A. (2020). Water conservation in irrigation can improve water use. *Proceedings of the National Academy of Sciences of the United States of America*, (vol. 105, no. 47, pp. 18 215–18 220).

Robinson, D. A., Campbell, C. S., Hopmans, J. W., Hornbuckle, B. K., Jones, S. B., Knight, R., Ogden, F., Selker, J., & Wendroth, O. (2008). Soil moisture measurement for ecological and hydrological watershed-scale observatories: A review *Vadose Zone Journal*, *7*(1), 358–389. doi:10.2136/vzj2007.0143

Suakanto, S., Engel, V., Hutagalung, M., & Angela, D. (2016). *Sensor networks data gathering and job management for decision support of smart farming. International Conference on Information Technology.* Information Processing in Agriculture. https://linkinghub.elsevier.com/retrieve/pii/S2214317316301184

United Nations. (n.d.). *Goal 2: Zero Hunger.* United Nations. https://www.un.org/sustainabledevelopment/hunger/

Verdouw, C. (2016). Internet of Things in agriculture. *CAB Reviews: Perspectives in Agriculture, Veterinary Science, Nutrition, and Natural Resources*, 11(35). http://www.cabi.org/cabreviews/review/20163379897

Wolfert, S., Ge, L., Verdouw, C., & Bogaardt, M.-J. (2017). Big Data in Smart Farming - A review *Agricultural Systems*, *153*, 69–80. doi:10.1016/j.agsy.2017.01.023

Chapter 26
Taxonomy of Ethical Dilemmas in Artificial Intelligence

Fredrick Romanus Ishengoma

https://orcid.org/0000-0002-3337-6210

The University of Dodoma, Tanzania

ABSTRACT

As artificial intelligence (AI) gets more prevalent in our everyday lives, the issue of ethical concerns related to AI inevitably needs to be addressed. Currently ethical issues surrounding AI have been fragmented, and there is lack of studies that have provided a comprehensive taxonomy. While most existing research focuses on a single application domain (e.g., health or autonomous vehicles), AI ethics is currently a cross-disciplinary issue. This chapter presents a state-of-the-art argument and discussion on ethical dilemmas associated with AI advancement, thereby generating new research agendas within AI and ethics domain. Moreover, the taxonomy of AI ethical dilemmas is presented along with recommendations.

INTRODUCTION

Artificial intelligence (AI) is reshaping every aspect of our lives. Its usage is becoming ubiquitous in various applications, from smartphones to self-driving cars (Liu et al., 2021; Saxena et al., 2021). As algorithms become more sophisticated and autonomous, we have trusted them to make crucial decisions on our behalf (Candrian & Schere, 2022). AI technology is already capable of automating decisions, such as medical diagnostics and smart manufacturing, that humans would typically do (Bohr, & Memarzadeh, 2020; Arnold, 2021).

It has been suggested that humanity's future will depend on the implementation of solid moral standards in AI systems, given that these systems may, at some point, either match or supersede human capabilities (Torresen, 2018). Nevertheless, the fast adoption of AI has created new ethical dilemmas for researchers, governments, and users (Goyal et al., 2021). Thus, we are entering a new frontier for AI ethics, whereby discussion between researchers, industry, and the government is needed to develop AI ethical standards in an AI-driven world.

DOI: 10.4018/978-1-6684-6821-0.ch026

The AI dilemmas stem from growing fears that AI results in job losses, economic disparity, sparking widespread social unrest, to more significant and philosophical concerns such as weaponized AI drones (Sujan et al., 2021). Almost every significant corporation presently has AI systems and considers deploying AI a critical component of their business operations. Private firms also use AI to make decisions in multidisciplinary issues, including healthcare, job recruitment, credit risk, and even criminology (Verdicchio & Perin, 2022).

With much deployment of AI in our daily lives, ethical dilemmas need to be addressed. For instance, AI biasness is an active ethical issue of concern that needs more research and debate (Tjoa et al., 2021). Consequently, there are currently no widely accepted guidelines or accountability frameworks, despite witnessing the rampant use of drones, facial recognition technology, fingerprint scanners, driverless cars, and other notable AI advancements that pose severe ethical concerns (Hagendorff, 2020). What's more concerning is when governments use AI and machine learning to make policy and legislative decisions, such as using these technologies in crime decision-making and the justice system (Bohr et al., 2020).

Since AI is so complex, determining liability isn't trivial. This is especially true when AI has severe implications for human lives, like piloting vehicles, determining prison sentences, or automating university admissions (Toth et al., 2022). These decisions will affect real people for the rest of their lives, and it's unrealistic to expect AI will never make a mistake.

It's within the arguments mentioned above that this chapter presents and discusses the current issues on AI ethical concerns to stimulate more research in this domain. We must understand the ethical and societal considerations of the technology so that we can develop trustworthy systems that include assurances of transparency, explainability, and fair AI systems.

In summary, this chapter's contributions can be summarized as follows: (1) provide a state of art discussion on areas of ethical dilemma in AI, (2) presents a comprehensive taxonomy of the ethical dilemmas of AI, and (3) present a discussion on how to deal with ethics in AI effectively and (4) introduce open issues and specific areas where more research is needed when incorporating ethics in AI. The chapter is structured as follows: Section 2 presents the initiatives toward AI ethical standards. Section 3 presents the taxonomy of ethical dilemmas in AI. The study recommendations on how to deal with AI ethical dilemmas are discussed in section 4, and the chapter concludes with conclusions in section 6.

INITIATIVES TOWARDS AI ETHICAL STANDARDS

In computer terms, we can say ethics are the right and wrong of machine actions. Humans have a variety of cognitive biases, including recency and confirmation bias, which are manifested in our actions and, consequently, in our data. Thus, we must design research and computations with this in mind because data is the basis for all machine learning techniques (Bryson et al., 2017). Artificial intelligence has the power to magnify and expand these human biases at an extraordinary rate. Therefore, using AI as a technology is neither morally right nor wrong. Instead, developers, scientists, governments, and researchers must set up guidelines or frameworks to ensure they employ AI systems safely and ethically while preventing AI abuse (Bruschi & Diomede, 2022).

The good news is that several initiatives are underway exploring how ethics can be incorporated into ongoing AI development. Leading AI businesses have a stake in establishing these standards since they have already begun to feel the repercussions of neglecting to adhere to ethical standards in their services (De Laat, 2021). Governments and regulators have already begun to play a crucial role in establishing policies and guidelines to tackle AI-related ethical issues (Stahl, 2021). For instance, since 2016, the US, UK, and European Union have conducted large-scale public inquiries which have grappled with the question of what a good and just AI society would look like (Cath et al., 2018). Moreover, the recently introduced European Union General Data Protection Regulation (GDPR) requires organizations to be able to explain decisions made by their algorithms (Wulf & Seizov, 2022).

Though most of these efforts are in initial phases and do not impose binding requirements on companies (with GDPR a prominent exception), they signal growing urgency about AI ethical issues (Quinn, 2021; Alfrink et al., 2022). Moreover, regarding the AI standards and guidelines, more debate has been rising on what's right and wrong in AI ethics. Universities and research institutions are playing an important role as well. Not only do they educate those who design and develop AI-based solutions but they are also researching ethical questions and auditing algorithms for the public good (Tsamados et al., 2022). Some universities, including Carnegie Mellon and MIT, have launched courses dealing specifically with AI and ethics. MIT also created the Moral Machine platform to crowdsource data and effectively train self-driving cars to respond to life-threatening scenarios (Awad et al., 2018). Moreover, academics are getting seats on AI governance teams at many technology companies and other enterprises as external advisers to help guide the responsible development of ethical AI applications.

Consortia and think tanks are bringing together technology companies, governments, nonprofit organizations, and academia to collaborate on a complex and evolving set of AI-related ethical issues, leverage each other's expertise and capabilities, and simultaneously build the AI ecosystem. Thus, there are initiatives around the globe with the common aim of addressing the ethical dilemmas in AI. This work discusses a taxonomy that depicts the ethical concerns against AI. This work can serve as a steppingstone toward creating a holistic ethical dilemma framework and comprehensively addressing several ethical issues.

Taxonomy of Ethical Dilemmas in AI

In this chapter section, various ethical dilemmas are presented and discussed.

Bias and Fairness in AI Algorithms

One critical ethical concern related to AI is bias and fairness. Unfair systems have a disparate impact on different groups of people and are especially concerning when results disproportionately impact and reinforce existing patterns of group marginalization (Roselli et al., 2019). These unfair systems are often the result of bias.

Algorithms can become biased in an assortment of ways. Even when sensitive factors like gender, ethnicity, or sexual preference are omitted, AI systems are trained to make conclusions relying on training data that may contain biased judgements or replicate historical or social injustices (Zhou et al., 2022). One such area that has voiced issues about bias is the employment of AI systems in legal judgements and healthcare settings (Roselli et al., 2019). Instances like race rectification in clinical algorithms, clinical trial recruitment, and adverse drug events tracking have highlighted how bias and inequities along the axes of race, age, and gender affect health care accessibility and healthcare service provision (Panch et al., 2019; Ntoutsi et al., 2020).

It is critical to guarantee that decisions made by AI systems do not exhibit discriminatory acts toward specific groups or populations since these systems have the potential to be employed in many sensitive contexts to make significant and life-changing judgments. The inability to purposefully challenge and quickly detect potential biases risks escalating existing social divisions and unequally distributing AI benefits across society's segments (Johnson et al., 2020).

Moreover, the definition and measurement of "fairness" is among the most challenging with ongoing research in this domain. Some academics have created technical definitions of fairness to ensure that models have similar predictive value or false positive and false negative rates across groupings. Multiple fairness criteria typically cannot be fulfilled simultaneously at the same time, which is a considerable challenge.

Data Privacy and Security

Governments worldwide are implementing sophisticated AI surveillance technologies to track, follow, and manage people to achieve a variety of policy goals, some of which are legal, some of which violate human rights, and some in murky areas (Saheb, 2022). Questions about how surveillance technologies fit with ethical and social norms have been highlighted by their growing proliferation. Particularly in facial recognition, trade-offs between privacy, security, and justifiable tracking and tracing demands much attention and debate.

A lot of citizens' private information is gathered to enhance AI-enabled operations. Recommender systems, virtual assistants, and search algorithms are just a few examples of applications that incorporate AI and are built on massive quantities of actual user data. However, AI can potentially use personal data in ways that could violate privacy and security concerns by enhancing the speed and capability of personal information analysis (Kosta, 2022). Data that has been anonymized also runs the danger of being deanonymized (via AI) or not being appropriately anonymized in the first place (Borealer et al., 2019). This brings up the ethical and legal dilemma of protecting user privacy while getting and processing the data businesses require to fuel AI applications.

For instance, both legitimate and fraudulent query traffic lights-CCTV cameras can purport to quantify the number of persons who pass by each hour while monitoring a video feed of city junctions. The goal of a maliciously motivated query may be to hunt down a few particular people by keeping an eye out for their faces, as opposed to a legitimate query from an urban planning agency that may wish to tally pedestrian counts to improve pedestrian crossings.

Unemployment

There is no doubt AI is disrupting the labor market by automating a significant number of existing jobs. Indeed, the automation of industry with AI has been a major contributing factor in job losses since the beginning of the industrial revolution (Diamoli et al., 2021). AI will extend this trend to more fields, including fields traditionally thought safer from automation, such as law, medicine, and education (Frey & Osborne, 2017). Consequently. It is unclear what new careers unemployed people will ultimately be able to transition into (Deranty & Corbin, 2022).

Discussions regarding how AI will affect employment typically center on the expected quantitative impact or how much AI would likely result in computers taking over jobs from people. When enormous amounts of data can be analyzed to detect patterns, make judgments depending on those trends, and works by enhancing or productivity rewards, like in the banking and financial industries, task-oriented, routine situations are where AI technology is most effective (Petropoulos, 2018). For these grounds, it appears reasonable to compare the impact of AI to the initial wave of automation brought on by computerization. That is to say, AI will replace many occupations and regular tasks that are frequently done manually and only require a trim level of knowledge; classic examples include the hospitality and tourism industries (Huang et al., 2021).

The companies that are spending the most on AI development today have a lot of money to spend. A primary ethical concern is AI will only serve to centralize wealth further. If an employer can lay off workers and replace them with unpaid AI, it can generate the same profit without paying employees. Machines will create wealth more than ever in the economy of the future. Governments and corporations should start thinking about how we redistribute that wealth so everyone can participate in the AI-powered economy.

Weaponized AI

Lethal autonomous weapons systems, also known as "killer robots" or "slaughterbots," are weapons that employ artificial intelligence (AI) to locate, choose, and execute targets without the assistance of a human. Regarding autonomous weaponry, AI algorithms are the only thing that decides who lives and dies, unlike unmanned military drones, which are controlled remotely by a human operator. While AI has brought advances and efficiency in many areas of our society, like recreation, aviation, and medicine, numerous concerns are expressed regarding the ability of armed AI machines to operate without human involvement. It's possible to imagine a scenario where a bad actor takes over the AI model that controls a city's water supply, power grid, or traffic signals. However, the weaponization of AI is scarier, where robots learn to fight, and drones can fly autonomously into combat, targeting a particular ethnicity using AI-powered facial recognition.

Some of the rising ethical concerns involve the issues of misidentification. For instance, can autonomous weapons distinguish between armed soldiers and a 12-year boy playing with a toy gun when choosing a target? Distinguish between displaced people leaving a battle scene and insurgents conducting a strategic retreat? The issue goes beyond the fact that AI systems frequently make mistakes. The problem is that when they make mistakes, their creators frequently don't understand why they did and how to fix them – the Blackbox dilemma. Thus, it is nearly hard to trust that weaponized AI systems can be ethically responsible due to the black box dilemma of AI.

Another scenario is what will happen when the weaponized AI violates the International Laws of Armed Conflict (LOAC) and International Humanitarian Law (IHL). The laws are based on the notion that humans will be held responsible for their deeds even in times of conflict and that killing combatants does not grant the right to execute civilians. Can autonomous weapons be made responsible? Who is at fault when a robot commits atrocities? Who would be the defendant? The combatant? The weapon? The weapon's superiors? The companies that produced the weapon? International law specialists are concerned that using autonomous weapons may result in a significant responsibility gap.

Autonomous Vehicles

Whereas many authors have acknowledged the potential advantages of self-driving cars—including enhanced road safety, more efficient fuel use, and better-coordinated traffic—researchers have also highlighted the concerns for ethical dilemmas (Hansson et al., 2021; Lui et al., 2021). For instance, when a driver hits on the brakes to avoid colliding with a pedestrian crossing the road illegally, she makes a moral choice that alters the risk away from the road user and toward the passengers in the car. A fully autonomous driven car will face an ethical dilemma in a moment in time if a child leaps from the curb into the car's path. There is no time for a pause. What happens, then? Did the veer leave into oncoming traffic, posing a danger to the vehicle's occupants? Veer directly onto the sidewalk, possibly causing injury to pedestrians? Proceed straight ahead, perhaps colliding with the child? Consequently, its time for self-driving cars needs to make such ethical judgments independently (Lui et al., 2021).

The ethical dilemma question is how self-driving cars should be programmed to act in the event of an unavoidable accident. For instance, the scenario of a car avoiding a crash with a motorcycle by driving into a wall considers that the chance of survival is higher for the driver of the car than for the rider of the motorcycle (Ryan, 2020; Evans et al., 2020). The discussion is fundamentally relevant to all autonomous agents with a large degree of freedom in making decisions, both human and non-human (Lin, 2016). One example from the medical domain would be a robot performing a Caesarean operation confronted with a scenario in which any decision it could make will lead to the death of either the mother or the child. The answer to these ethical dilemmas cannot be found by employing humans' ability of ethical reasoning alone because the assignment of blame to the human programmer or black-box AI processes might be too complex to answer for human beings alone. This is still an open research agenda that needs to be researched further.

AI, Art, and Copyright

Creativity is understood as the capacity to produce new and original content through imagination or invention and plays a central role in our society. For this reason, the impact of AI on human creativity deserves careful attention. While AI is a powerful tool for creation, it raises crucial questions about art's future, artists' rights and remuneration, and the integrity of the creative value chain (Hristov, 2017). For instance, what is the case for copyright when AI can create works of art itself? To what extent can copyrights be attributed if machines and algorithms replace a human author?

Can and should an algorithm be recognized as an author and enjoy the same rights as an artist? A work of art produced by AI requires a new definition of what it means to be an "author" to do justice to the creative work of both the "original" author and the AI algorithms that produced the work of art itself (Gerald, 2019). We need to develop new frameworks to recognize the value of AI creative work in our creations. These frameworks are needed to avoid not recognizing and differentiating between the AI algorithm work and human creativity, ensuring adequate remuneration and recognition for artists (Ch'ng, 2019).

One of the most hotly contested topics in contemporary practical philosophy and legal theory is the moral and ethical status of robots and in, especially the position of AI robotic systems (Schröder, 2021). Such issues become more urgent as robots get more complex and engineers mix tool-like capabilities with what appear to be psychological abilities once assumed to be human-only. Debates are characterized by a distinct dividing line: what some find desirable, such as "robot rights" and "legal personality" for AI systems, others regard repulsive (Miller, 2015). This is true even though some people are predisposed to see robots as more than simply machines. We must structure human-robot interactions by moral and legal standards that maximize benefit and reduce damage to both parties (Gordon, 2021).

Some researchers have wondered whether AIs might eventually become self-conscious, attain their own volition, or otherwise deserve recognition as persons like ourselves. Morally speaking, we can anticipate that technologists will attempt to make the most human-like AIs and robots possible, and perhaps someday, they will be such good imitations that we will wonder if they might be conscious and deserve rights—and we might not be able to determine this conclusively (Liu, 2020). If future humans conclude that AIs and robots might be worthy of moral status, then we should err on ethics.

Ethics in Deep Fakes

Deepfakes are one type of cybercrime fueled by AI. A deepfake, a derivation of "deep learning" and "fake," can be employed to imitate individuals by merging several facial angles, copying their gestures and speech behaviors, and manipulating features and vocals. Creating a false narrative using deepfakes can harm people's trust in the media. This mistrust is dangerous for societies considering that mass media is still governments' number one option to inform people on emergency events (e.g., pandemics).

The proliferation of fake news generated by AI-bots and its transmission on platforms such as YouTube, Twitter, Facebook, and Instagram, as well as the data manipulation to influence political elections and referendums, have eroded public confidence in the integrity of our central government systems and increased anxiety about who should be believed and trusted.

AI in Judicial Systems

AI methods can potentially significantly impact many areas, from the legal professions and the judiciary to aiding the decision-making of legislative and administrative public bodies. For example, they can increase the efficiency and accuracy of lawyers in both counseling and litigation, with benefits to lawyers, their clients, and society as a whole.

Existing software systems for judges can be complemented and enhanced through AI tools to support them in drafting new decisions. This trend toward the ever-increasing use of autonomous systems has been described as the automatization of justice. Some argue that AI could help create a fairer criminal judicial system, in which machines could evaluate and weigh relevant factors better than humans, taking advantage of its speed and significant data ingestion. Therefore, AI would make decisions based on informed decisions devoid of bias and subjectivity. But there are many ethical challenges, including AI decisions are not always intelligible to humans, AI-based decisions are susceptible to inaccuracies, discriminatory outcomes, embedded or inserted bias, concerns for fairness, and risk for human rights and other fundamental values. So, would one want to be judged by a AI in a court of law? Even if we are not sure how it reaches its conclusions? Questions like these are some dilemmas that need to be addressed in AI automatization of justice.

Figure 1. Taxonomy of Ethical Dillemas in AI

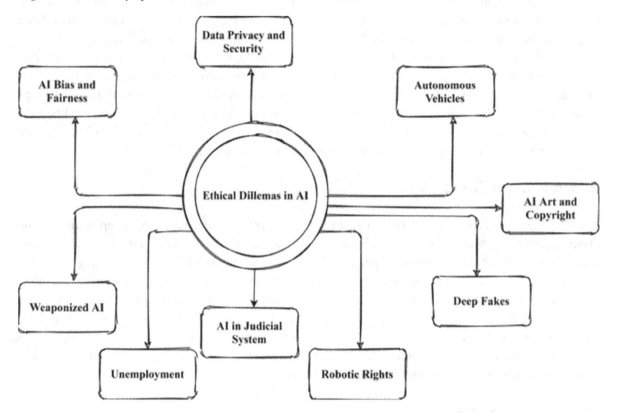

DEALING WITH AI ETHICS

Several suggestions for intervention emanate on effectively dealing with bias and fairness in AI algorithms. First, we must wisely use the many ways that AI may supplement our current human decision-making approaches. Machine learning algorithms ignore factors that inaccurately predict results. On the other hand, humans could exaggerate or not even be aware of why they decided to hire or reject a particular job prospect. Inexplicable as deep learning models may be, the human brain is the quintessential "black box," making it possible for biases that had gone undiscovered or unverified to be revealed by computers. Applying AI fairly and unbiasedly in decision-making is sought to help historically underprivileged communities.

When considering AI use in health, for instance, it is vital to use technology that utilizes strategies and techniques such as homomorphic encryption, techniques that separate data from identifying information about individuals, and techniques that protect against tampering, misuse, or hacking. Ultimately, these protection techniques available today will enhance the privacy and security of a patient's data while enabling actionable insights for the researcher and clinician.

In the case of AI creating unemployment, while technology has made many jobs redundant, it has always created more jobs than it destroys and will typically reallocate and enable rather than displace jobs. Automating tasks to be done more quickly and/or cheaply will typically accelerate business expansion and increase demand for human workers to do other manual tasks that support new technology.

Regarding AI biasness, we need to comprehend that AI takes on the biases of the dataset it learns from. This means that if researchers train an AI on skewed data for race, gender, education, wealth, or any other point of bias, the AI will also adapt that bias. Of course, the challenge with AI training is that there's no perfect dataset. There will always be under- and overrepresentation in any sample. These are not problems that can be addressed quickly. Mitigating bias in training data and providing equal treatment from AI is a primary key to developing ethical AI.

Consequently, research and collaboration among industry, government, and academia is needed to develop ethical AI systems and application guidelines. To promote fairness and inclusivity, engineers, developers, and coders should not only practice inclusive behaviors but also come from diverse backgrounds with varied experiences. Moreover, data feeding the AI system and the data collection process, regardless of the technique, should be developed from reliable data collected. This is an ongoing research domain that researchers are working on introducing multiple techniques that can mitigate bias in AI.

Another debate is on, should robots have rights? If we think of a robot as an advanced washing machine, then no. However, the answer is unclear if robots could have emotions or feelings. Some researchers believe there is no fundamental difference between humans and machines and that general AI rights won't be possible unless robots have self-conscious emotions. A suggestion in the debate around robot rights is that robots should be granted the right to exist and perform their mission, which should be linked to the duty of serving humans. In the case of weaponized AI, governments and international organizations need to develop standards and ethical guidelines on how to operationalize the weapons.

Ethical norms regarding the uses of AI and our ability to regulate them intelligently and beneficially should keep pace with the fast-changing technological capabilities. By identifying research gaps where it would help developers make ethical design choices, decision-makers can allocate resources to studies that address immediate needs. That is why we need AI researchers to actively involve ethicists in their work and address ethical issues with the same AI pace.

The critical question is: How do we ensure there are more good AIs and not bad AIs? It will come down to two major factors (in no particular order) – 1) government regulation and 2) market components. Regulations will need to make sure the proper rules are in place to shut down by court order an AI breaking the law. The owner, manufacturer, or trainer can be penalized as well.

Businesses will need to have an AI ethics code or have refreshed existing governance protocols to outline what the machine is expected to do and its limitations. Ideally, these should be shared with customers, so they can make informed choices about who they are doing business. To reassure those affected, AI algorithms will need to be designed so that they can be reviewed by a third party to avoid manipulation or bias.

It's evident that technological progress tends to outpace regulatory change, which is undoubtedly true in AI. But organizations may not want to wait for AI-related regulations to catch up. To protect their stakeholders and adhere to ethical AI systems, standardized ethical guidelines must be developed and implemented globally. This study proposes the following guiding principle to mitigate ethical dilemmas in the AI industry.

1. AI developers and businesses need to explain how their algorithms arrive at their predictions to overcome ethical issues arising from inaccurate, biased, and unfair predictions. Developers should be able to describe how their system will function in the field, including the objectives it aims to achieve and the tasks it will undertake, how it will do it, the technologies it will rely on to do so, and the technical, legal, and ethical risks inherent to using AI systems.

2. Proposing standardized ethical AI frameworks at both country and international levels (e.g., UN) will clarify the path to ethical AI development. Pioneering companies should spearhead these efforts to create clarity for the industry.

3. Increasing AI community diversity is key to improving model quality and reducing bias. This can help solve unemployment and discrimination that automated decision-making systems can cause.

4. AI systems should be accompanied by ethical documentation highlighting possible points of failure and research gaps to ensure that non-technical audiences understand the legal and ethical risks and benefits of new AI-enabled systems.

5. As updates to AI system designs occur and recur, legal and ethical implications should continuously be proposed, reexamined, and evaluated.

6. Companies should advise employees on how AI may affect their jobs in the future. This could include retaining workers whose tasks are expected to get automated or whose work will likely entail using automated systems or giving them time to seek new employment.

7. Law and ethics researchers should analyze AI data sets, algorithmic weighting, system outputs, and human inputs to identify bias throughout the design process and serve as sounding boards for developers and subject matter experts.

CONCLUSION

The discussion around AI and ethics has grown far more urgent recently, and many initiatives to tackle ethical questions surrounding AI are ongoing. This chapter has presented a comprehensive state of art taxonomy of the AI ethical dilemmas. The proposed taxonomy supports identifying significant categories of ethical challenges that come in the way of AI development and implementation and that challenges AI integration in society. With this study, stakeholders can use the taxonomy to consider the discussed ethical issues that affect the implementation of AI systems and respond accordingly.

In addition, researchers can use the taxonomy to 1) understand the existing research gaps and agenda to be addressed in the AI and ethics domain and; 2) develop new and innovative research, for instance, how to code AI systems ethically. Policymakers can use this study when planning and designing AI strategies and policies by considering the identified AI ethical dilemmas. Moreover, policymakers can propose possible solutions to those dilemmas, facilitating the smooth use and adoption of AI systems in society.

ACKNOWLEDGMENT

This research received no specific grant from any funding agency in the public, commercial, or not-for-profit sectors.

REFERENCES

Arnold, M. H. (2021). Teasing out Artificial Intelligence in Medicine: An Ethical Critique of Artificial Intelligence and Machine Learning in Medicine. *Bioethical Inquiry*, *18*(1), 121–139. doi:10.100711673-020-10080-1 PMID:33415596

Awad, E., Dsouza, S., Kim, R., Schulz, J., Henrich, J., Shariff, A., Bonnefon, J. F., & Rahwan, I. (2018, November). The Moral Machine experiment. *Nature*, *563*(7729), 59–64. doi:10.103841586-018-0637-6 PMID:30356211

Bohr, A., & Memarzadeh, K. (2020). The rise of artificial intelligence in healthcare applications. *Artificial Intelligence in Healthcare*, 25–60. doi:10.1016/B978-0-12-818438-7.00002-2

Boreale, Michele & Corradi, Fabio & Viscardi, Cecilia. (2019). Relative Privacy Threats and Learning From Anonymized Data. *IEEE Transactions on Information Forensics and Security*. IEEE. . doi:10.1109/TIFS.2019.2937640

Bruschi, D., Diomede. (2022). N. A framework for assessing AI ethics with applications to cybersecurity. *AI Ethics*. doi:10.1007/s43681-022-00162-8

Bryson, J., & Winfield, A. (2017). Standardizing Ethical Design for Artificial Intelligence and Autonomous Systems. *Computer*, *50*(5), 116–119. doi:10.1109/MC.2017.154

Candrian, C., & Scherer, A. (2022). Rise of the machines: Delegating decisions to autonomous AI. *Computers in Human Behavior*, *134*, 107308. doi:10.1016/j.chb.2022.107308

Cath, C., Wachter, S., Mittelstadt, B., Taddeo, M., & Floridi, L. (2018). Artificial Intelligence and the 'Good Society': The US, EU, and UK approach. *Science and Engineering Ethics*, *24*. doi:10.100711948-017-9901-7 PMID:28353045

Ch'ng, E. (2019). Art by computing machinery: Is machine art acceptable in the artworld. *ACM Transactions on Multimedia Computing Communications and Applications*, *15*(2s), 1–17. doi:10.1145/3326338

Damioli, G., Van Roy, V., & Vertesy, D. (2021). The impact of artificial intelligence on labor productivity. *Eurasian Bus Rev*, *11*(1), 1–25. doi:10.100740821-020-00172-8

De Laat, P. (2021). Companies Committed to Responsible AI: From Principles towards Implementation and Regulation? *Philosophy & Technology*, *34*(4), 1135–1193. doi:10.100713347-021-00474-3 PMID:34631392

Deranty, J. P., & Corbin, T. (2022). Artificial intelligence and work: A critical review of recent research from the social sciences. *AI & Society*. doi:10.100700146-022-01496-x

Evans, K., de Moura, N., Chauvier, S., Chatila, R., & Dogan, E. (2020). Ethical Decision Making in Autonomous Vehicles: The AV Ethics Project. *Science and Engineering Ethics*, *26*(6), 3285–3312. doi:10.100711948-020-00272-8 PMID:33048325

Frey, C., & Osborne, M. (2017). The future of employment: How susceptible are jobs to computerization? *Technological Forecasting and Social Change*, *114*, 254–280. doi:10.1016/j.techfore.2016.08.019

Gerald, Spindler. (2019). *Copyright Law and Artificial Intelligence*. IIC - International Review of Intellectual Property and Competition Law. . doi:10.1007/s40319-019-00879-w

Gordon, J. S., & Pasvenskiene, A. (2021). Pasvenskiene, A. Human rights for robots? A literature review. *AI Ethics*, *1*(4), 579–591. doi:10.100743681-021-00050-7

Gries, T., & Naudé, W. (2022). Modelling artificial intelligence in economics. *Journal for Labour Market Research*, *56*(1), 12. doi:10.118612651-022-00319-2

Hagendorff, T. (2020). The Ethics of AI Ethics: An Evaluation of Guidelines. *Minds and Machines*, *30*(1), 99–120. doi:10.100711023-020-09517-8

Hansson, S. O., Belin, M. Å., & Lundgren, B. (2021). Self-Driving Vehicles—An Ethical Overview. *Philosophy & Technology*, *34*(4), 1383–1408. doi:10.100713347-021-00464-5

. Hristov, Kalin. (2017). Artificial Intelligence and the Copyright Dilemma. *IDEA - The Journal of the Franklin Pierce Center for Intellectual Property, 57*, 431.

Huang, A., Chao, Y., de la Mora Velasco, E., Bilgihan, A., & Wei, W. (2021). *When artificial intelligence meets the hospitality and tourism industry: An assessment framework to inform theory and management.* J Hosp Tour Insights.

Kosta, E. (2022). Algorithmic state surveillance: Challenging the notion of agency in human rights. *Regulation & Governance*, *16*(1), 212–224. doi:10.1111/rego.12331

Lin, P. (2016). Why Ethics Matters for Autonomous Cars. In M. Maurer, J. Gerdes, B. Lenz, & H. Winner (Eds.), *Autonomous Driving*. Springer. doi:10.1007/978-3-662-48847-8_4

Liu, H.-Y., & Zawieska, K. (2020). From responsible robotics towards a human rights regime oriented to the challenges of robotics and artificial intelligence. *Ethics and Information Technology*, *22*(4), 321–333. doi:10.100710676-017-9443-3

Liu, N., Shapira, P., & Yue, X. (2021). Tracking developments in artificial intelligence research: Constructing and applying a new search strategy. *Scientometrics*, *126*(4), 3153–3192. doi:10.100711192-021-03868-4 PMID:34720254

Miller, L. F. (2015). Granting automata human rights: Challenge to a basis of full-rights privilege. *Human Rights Review (Piscataway, N.J.)*, *16*(4), 369–391. doi:10.100712142-015-0387-x

Ntoutsi, E, Fafalios, P, & Gadiraju, U. (2020). Bias in data-driven artificial intelligence systems—An introductory survey. *WIREs Data Mining Knowl Discov*, *10,* e1356. doi:. doi:10.1002/widm.1356ry

Panch, T., Mattie, H., & Atun, R. (2019). Artificial intelligence and algorithmic bias: Implications for health systems. *Journal of Global Health*, *9*(2), 010318. doi:10.7189/jogh.09.020318 PMID:31788229

Petropoulos, G. (2018). The impact of artificial intelligence on employment. *Praise for Work in the Digital Age*, 119.

Quinn, P. (2021). Research under the GDPR – a level playing field for public and private sector research? *Life Sciences, Society and Policy*, *17*(1), 4. doi:10.118640504-021-00111-z PMID:33648586

Roselli, D., Matthews, J., & Talagala, N. (2019). Managing Bias in AI. WWW '19: *Companion Proceedings of the 2019 World Wide Web Conference,* (pp. 539-544). ACM. 10.1145/3308560.3317590

Ryan, M. (2020). The future of transportation: Ethical, legal, social and economic impacts of self-driving vehicles in the year 2025. *Science and Engineering Ethics*, *26*(3), 1185–1208. doi:10.100711948-019-00130-2 PMID:31482471

Saheb, T. (202). Ethically contentious aspects of artificial intelligence surveillance: a social science perspective. *AI Ethics*. doi:10.1007/s43681-022-00196-y

Sarker, S., Jamal, L., Ahmed, S. F., & Irtisam, N. (2021). Robotics and artificial intelligence in healthcare during COVID-19 pandemic: A systematic review. *Robotics and Autonomous Systems*, *146*, 103902. doi:10.1016/j.robot.2021.103902 PMID:34629751

Saxena, A., Brault, N., & Rashid, S. (2021). *Big Data and Artificial Intelligence for Healthcare Applications* (1st ed.). CRC Press. doi:10.1201/9781003093770

Schröder, W. M. (2021). Robots and Rights: Reviewing Recent Positions in Legal Philosophy and Ethics. In: von Braun, J., S. Archer, M., Reichberg, G.M., Sánchez Sorondo, M. (eds) Robotics, AI, and Humanity. Springer. doi:10.1007/978-3-030-54173-6_16

Stahl, B. C. (2021). Addressing Ethical Issues in AI. In *Artificial Intelligence for a Better Future. Briefs in Research and Innovation Governance*. Springer., doi:10.1007/978-3-030-69978-9_5

Torresen, J. (2018). A Review of Future and Ethical Perspectives of Robotics and AI. *Frontiers in Robotics and AI*, *4*, 75. Advance online publication. doi:10.3389/frobt.2017.00075

Tóth, Z., Caruana, R., Gruber, T., & Loebbecke, C. (2022). The Dawn of the AI Robots: Towards a New Framework of AI Robot Accountability. *Journal of Business Ethics*, *178*(4), 895–916. doi:10.100710551-022-05050-z

Tsamados, A., Aggarwal, N., Cowls, J., Morley, J., Roberts, H., Taddeo, M., & Floridi, L. (2022). The ethics of algorithms: Key problems and solutions. *AI & Society*, *37*(1), 215–230. doi:10.100700146-021-01154-8

Verdicchio, M., & Perin, A. (2022). When Doctors and AI Interact: On Human Responsibility for Artificial Risks. *Philosophy & Technology*, *35*(1), 11. doi:10.100713347-022-00506-6 PMID:35223383

Wulf, A. J., & Seizov, O. (2022). Please understand we cannot provide further information": Evaluating content and transparency of GDPR-mandated AI disclosures. *AI & Society*. doi:10.100700146-022-01424-z

Zhou, N., Zhang, Z., Nair, V. N., Singhal, H., Chen, J., & Sudjianto, A. (2022). Bias, Fairness and Accountability with Artificial Intelligence and Machine Learning Algorithms. *International Statistical Review*, *90*(3), 468–480. doi:10.1111/insr.12492

KEY TERMS AND DEFINITIONS

Artificial Intelligence: Artificial intelligence (AI) refers to the simulation of human intelligence in machines that are programmed to think like humans and mimic their actions

Ethics: Ethics is the discipline concerned with what is morally good and bad and morally right and wrong.

Deep Fakes: Deep fakes are a type of artificial intelligence used to create convincing images, audio, and video hoaxes

Robotics: Robotics is a branch of engineering that involves the conception, design, manufacture, and operation of robots

Autonomous Vehicle: The autonomous vehicle is the vehicle capable of sensing its environment and operating without human involvement.

Data Privacy: Data privacy is a discipline that keeps data safe against improper access, theft or loss.

Data Security: Data security is the practice of protecting digital information from unauthorized access, corruption, or theft throughout its entire lifecycle.

Chapter 27
Digital Twins and Sustainable Developments in the Tourism and Hospitality Industry

Ali Yuce

https://orcid.org/0000-0003-4700-2006

Cappadocia University, Turkey

ABSTRACT

As information and communication technologies have had such a profound impact on every part of our lives, the globe has undergone significant transformation. This impact will not only increase productivity and efficiency, but will also have a substantial positive impact on all aspects of sustainable development. Recent developments in technologies that convey dynamic and real-time data, like the digital twin, have the great potential to revolutionize our concept of sustainability in smart manufacturing and monitoring natural resources. With the use of digital twin technology, one may decrease and potentially eliminate possible energy waste, maintenance expenses, and time waste by making quick predictions and taking prompt remedial action during the manufacturing process. This conceptual paper contends that digital twin can significantly boost an organization's productivity and profitability while enhancing destinations' values, including distinctive natural, cultural, and environmental resources, without endangering the lives of the next generation.

INTRODUCTION

The age we are currently living in is called "digital" which makes everything possible everywhere with the click of our finger. The way businesses work, from creating products to creating marketing strategies, has undergone a substantial paradigm shift as a result of advanced technology in the decades past. The convergence of Artificial Intelligence (AI) with large data and sensors has led to the emergence of digital twins. As stated by Marai, Taleb, and Song (2021), these technologies are interrelated and help one another in many ways. Digital twins have great potential to provide more accurate, dynamic, and prompt predictions based on the data they gather in real-time from these technologies (Kantaros, Piro-

DOI: 10.4018/978-1-6684-6821-0.ch027

malis, Tsaramirsis, Papageorgas, & Tamimi, 2022; Li et al., 2022; Qi, Tao, & Nee, 2022). The digital twins serve a variety of purposes, including enhancing productivity and efficiency and assisting in the identification of failure points during cyber replication. (Tao, Zhang, Liu, & Nee, 2019).

Digital twins, in contrast to many other modern technologies, give the tourism industry a number of important benefits. In contrast to many other contemporary technologies, digital twins offer the tourism sector a number of significant advantages. Although there is a lack of evidence-based information in the current literature on tourism and hospitality, it is anticipated that in the near future, based on multidisciplinary literature from the service industry, healthcare, manufacturing, development of smart cities, and construction, digital twins will be used in the industry's various segments (Aheleroff, Xu, Zhong, & Lu, 2021; Allam & Jones, 2021; James, 2021; Mylonas et al., 2021; Opoku, Perera, Osei-Kyei, & Rashidi, 2021). In this context, adopting digital twins technology in this situation can enhance staff productivity and increase business efficiency in the fiercely competitive travel and tourism sector.

This study argues that once digital twins evolve even more significantly, they will have a big impact on tourism industry in a variety of ways. Firstly, based on real-time data collecting and analysis procedures, digital twins have the potential to increase companies' effectiveness and enable sustainable development with regard to the ecosystem. Secondly, due to ongoing monitoring and evaluation of the digital representation of the real thing, digital twins also offer functionality that checks the products before they are ever acquired or made (based on the possible scenario). Thirdly, using computer-generated simulations to actively monitor, measure, and reflect the actual dynamics of the organization, the convergence of digital twins with artificial intelligence (AI) and huge databases has the potential to save maintenance costs and increase overall operational effectiveness. Furthermore, digital twins can aid in the abolition of dubious and foreboding marketing strategies that jeopardize the viability and endurance of the destinations' priceless resources, reputation, and integrity. Last but not least, the deployment of sensors in actual locations allows digital twins to save the unique cultural heritage sites and essential natural resources for future generations.

Technology has a huge impact on the tourism industry's transformation in a number of ways, including by advertising the attractions and locations and assisting with every stage of an organization's commercial operations (Allam & Jones, 2021; Buhalis & O'Connor, 2005; Yuce, 2022c). For the past three decades, tourism has been expanding at an even quicker rate, particularly since the introduction of the most cutting-edge creative technologies like immersive and AI (Huang, Backman, Backman, & Chang, 2016; Pirker, Loria, Safikhani, Künz, & Rosmann, 2022). However, although being a relatively new idea in social sciences, digital twins technology also presents a potentially game-changing opportunity for the tourism and hospitality sector to obtain a competitive edge and helps for the long-term viability of its valuable resources (Qi et al., 2022; Shubenkova, Valiev, Shepelev, Tsiulin, & Reinau, 2018). As previously mentioned, if it reaches its full potential, digital twins' characteristics have the potential to improve businesses' operational effectiveness while minimizing and even avoiding the problems with organization's overall carbon footprint that have a detrimental impact on ecological balances and pose significant risk of jeopardizing future life forms.

Despite the fact that tourism has a huge positive socioeconomic impact on communities all over the world (Ibănescu, Stoleriu, Munteanu, & Iațu, 2018), destinations and organizations must fight to remain viable in the face of fierce competition. (Cronjé & du Plessis, 2020; Nyanga, Pansiri, & Chatibura, 2020). Tourism-related locations and businesses have been dealing with a variety of problems, including tourism development paradoxes, marketing dilemmas and overcrowding as well as social and health crises and ever-changing customer behavior (Namberger, Jackisch, Schmude, & Karl, 2019; Pillai, Haldorai,

Seo, & Kim, 2021). In this context, a number of significant stakeholders, particularly local populations, have been assessing whether tourism, especially mass tourism, improves or degrades the socioeconomic and environmental conditions of the host communities (Adie, Falk, & Savioli, 2020; Khan, Hassan, Fahad, & Naushad, 2020). Even though the majority of the existing research emphasizes the industry's benefits to society, some studies highlight the negative effects of tourism operations, particularly when they are not under control, (Khan et al., 2020). Recent studies have also placed a strong emphasis on the use of digital twins to create healthier and more sustainable methods of reversing the detrimental effects of urban expansion (Darwish & Hassanien, 2022; Qi et al., 2022). In addition, research show that the construction of digital twins can be utilized to intervene when city or tourism development plans are poorly created, developed and executed in the destinations in addition to promoting smart production for industry. (Chang & Jang, 2021; Li et al., 2022).

Digital twins and other cutting-edge technology, as was mentioned before, may enable the preservation of cultural artifacts. (Darwish & Hassanien, 2022). This chapter makes the case that creating and utilizing newer technology can aid in reducing or even eliminating the negative effects of tourism-related activities and create more environmentally and socioeconomically responsible tourist practices. Furthermore, this paper claims that appropriate and useful technologies can significantly increase an organization's efficiency and profitability when they are developed, deployed and used in a responsible manner. Among the numerous new technologies, artificial intelligence (AI), big data, and digital twins are the two primary pillars for enhancing the value of cultural heritage sites and preventing negative consequences caused by insufficient or nonexistent destination management organizations. Digital twin technology, on the other hand, enables businesses to adopt smarter and more effective sustainable management strategies to reduce waste of the touristic operations through active location monitoring. Although, there is conclusive empirical data (Chia, Yuen, & Woon, 2022) that clarifies the relationship between digital twins and overall equipment effectiveness (OEE) in terms of carrying Intelligent Production Planning to explore whether it maximizes the production flow or not within 24 hours period (Chia et al., 2022). The researchers found that the output was six times higher than the regular production method (Chia et al., 2022). Despite the increased academic interest in this area, there is less data to support scholarly discussion about how digital twin technology may affect the tourism sector. Therefore, this study will assess the most recent literature and provide in-depth information in order to broaden our vision and lay a firm foundation for future researchers in the field of the tourism sector.

BACKGROUND AND RELATED WORK

Comparing the last 30 years, digitalization has had a significant impact on every aspect of our lives (Mkrttchian & Voronin, 2021; Qi et al., 2022). We can now instantaneously send messages and emails to others using digital tools like cellphones as opposed to the conventional mail and analogue landlines that we used to utilize communications. Historically, engineers and architects would laboriously develop equipment or buildings for weeks at a time (Kantaros et al., 2022). What's worse is that they wouldn't know if they would have any major problems until the job was finished. However, technology developers now have the chance to design and manufacture intelligent 'things', such as smart homes, smart cities, smart transportation, smart services, and smart manufacturing, thanks to the digital age (Allam & Jones, 2021; Chang & Jang, 2021; Kantaros et al., 2022; Mylonas et al., 2021).

Digital twins as one of these latest technologies has ability to offer significant advancements across industries in myriad of ways. The capability of real-time monitoring and the capacity to make prompt decisions based on a virtual representation of the objects or dynamics set digital twins apart from earlier technologies. Due to real-time monitoring and intelligent decision-making processes, the digital twins enable the ability to foresee how they will appear before they are actually used or created. In other words, as they will have a clearer and more plain comprehension of product information and modifications, developers and investors have influence over the products even throughout the development phases (Grieves, 2015). This cutting-edge capability will save costs, speed up manufacturing, and improve product quality (Chang & Jang, 2021; Grieves, 2015; Hribernik, Cabri, Mandreoli, & Mentzas, 2021).

Additionally, the deployment of digital twin technologies can have a positive impact on the ecological system. Using the most current technologies, such as Virtual Reality, AI, big data, digital twins, IoT, Data visualization, cloud computing and blockchain technology, digital twins will also help add to actual efficacy during energy transmission, according to one of the most recent research (Kantaros et al., 2022; Li et al., 2022). Since excessive energy consumption and lack of efficient maintenance exacerbate environmental deterioration while constantly increase operational costs, smart use of technology has also potential to reduce it.

Without cutting-edge technologies, the travel business, like the rest of it, cannot operate efficiently. The development of smart or digital tourism is just one illustration of how digital innovation has been an important scientific field that has applications in numerous industries (Marai et al., 2021; Qi et al., 2022). Since technology and tourism are intertwined at every level of the sector, tourism's output has been increasing and is having an impact on the economic development of many nations (Nyanga et al., 2020). Numerous studies show that technology is responsible for a wide range of positive effects, including employment and the creation of foreign exchange as well as improving bonds between host communities and the tourism sector (Yuce, 2022c). The ability to provide services and manufacturing procedures have been dramatically impacted by technology (Qi et al., 2022). Researchers have provided numerous examples of how developing technologies are transforming the tourist sector in ways that have never been seen before, particularly in tourism literature (Buhalis & O'Connor, 2005; Yuce, 2022b). Organizations, destinations, and enterprises now have the capacity to display their services and goods to customers all over the world using a single device thanks to the use of newer technology. In contrast, as virtual reality technology has advanced to the next level and is being utilized to produce digital tourism, digitalization allows clients a wide range of choices, from choosing the appropriate location to making reservations for accommodations before their arrival (Yuce, 2022b). Researchers have lately started to analyze the effects of digital twins on the tourism business. It is critical to comprehend what digital twins technology is and how it may benefit the entire sector in order to boost the sustainability of tourist firms, destinations, places and unique natural resources.

What Is Digital Twins Technology? Historical Development of Digital Twins and Its Functionality

Over the past few years, technologies like big data, AI, and digital twins have become increasingly crucial for the industry. One of the newest among the others is the digital twin, which still needs time, progress in related technologies and commitment to maximize its potential but guarantees promising benefits across multiple sectors. The history of the digital twins concept began with Michael Grieves' introduction of it in 2003 while he was "in a course on Product Lifecycle Management (PLM)" (Grieves, 2015; Hartmann

& Van der Auweraer, 2021; Hribernik et al., 2021; Tao et al., 2019). However, the definition did not become well-known among academics and practitioners until recently. NASA made a public announcement about digital twins in 2012, according to Hartmann and Van der Auweraer (2021). According to some experts, the digital twin was first conceptualized in the year 2002 and was officially announced in 2010 (Chia et al., 2022). Because there is no common definition for digital twins, the academic discussion environment is complicated by the usage of a number of terminologies.

For example, some studies define a digital twin as a digital shadow or "digital representation of actual physical things," (Grieves, 2015) while others define it as a mirror image of a real-world object or location. In other words, a digital twins is a real-time virtual replication (like the blueprints) of objects, places, or any entity to detect the faults and enhance the product efficiency (Hribernik et al., 2021; Tzachor, Sabri, Richards, Rajabifard, & Acuto, 2022). According to Grieves (2015), The concept of digital twins consists of three main components. These are "a) physical products in Real Space; b) Virtual products in Virtual Space; c) the connections of data and information that ties virtual and real products together" (Grieves, 2015).

The primary characteristic of digital twins that sets it apart from competing technologies is its capacity to continuously and instantly gather data from physical locations utilizing sensors (Kurvinen et al., 2022; Qi et al., 2022). Although the purpose of the digital twins was to picture the product before it was actually built, as more qualities were included, it became possible to test the product prior to its production or manufacture (Grieves, 2015). The data collected during the "designing, manufacturing, distribution, maintenance, and recycling" phases of a product's lifecycle is analyzed using highly efficient algorithms by digital twins and other crucial technologies (Tao et al., 2019) in order to boost productivity and reduce failure risks. For instance, while GE and Chevron use digital twins to track the performance of wind turbines, NASA has been using them to track spacecraft. (Qi et al., 2022).

According to Tao et al. (2019) and (Kantaros et al., 2022), as mentioned above, digital twins, AI and big data are major cutting-edge technologies that are essential to smart manufacturing. However, sensors are the key elements of the digital twins technology in addition to the primary technologies. As a result of the data that is collected from the sensors and the virtual representation of the real thing created by the digital twins, the system enables developers or enterprises to decide on the best course of action for the manufacturing process (Qi et al., 2022). According to the authors Aheleroff et al., 2021; Cureton & Dunn, 2021; Grieves, 2015; Li et al., 2022, digital twin technology actively transfers a large amount of data from the physical representation to the virtual representation by using an advanced digital media in order to monitor and measure the replication of the actual space. As a result of analyzing the huge volume of data using advanced analytics, engineers or administrators begin monitoring the possible change in the virtual representation (Hribernik et al., 2021; Li et al., 2022). Furthermore, the system which is assumed to be controlled by AI technology, manages or intervenes in the ongoing process to achieve desired outcomes by predicting it on the virtual replication. Studies indicates that application of digital twin helped to optimize the product life cycle process and increased the total production in a real-world setting (Chia et al., 2022;Tao et al., 2019).

The digital twins technology has both advantages and disadvantages (Kantaros et al., 2022). The above-mentioned digital twins procedure is difficult since it requires cutting-edge algorithms and more modern computer gear such as CPUs and Hard drives (Li et al., 2022). The incorporation of these essential components will help in increasing the effectiveness of real-time detection and accuracy to handle all necessary operations without overheating or capacity difficulties while making predictions about virtual replication. On the other hand, in contrary to some research that suggest digital twins will have a number of advantages as previously described, there are also some disadvantages because there is a chance that the virtual depiction will be erroneous (Tzachor et al., 2022). This could lead to inaccurate data interpretation during data processing or insufficient data collection from sensors that were poorly chosen and deployed (Tzachor et al., 2022). Engineers or other decision-makers may make critical errors in this situation, leading to unavoidable repercussions that will terminate the real objects.

Sustainable Tourism Development and Digital Twins

The term "sustainability" has been misused throughout the past ten years in addition to being overused and exaggerated as a buzzword. In order to ensure responsible developments in the context of manufacturing and other businesses, sustainability is generally used to increase awareness about the need to cause less harm socially, culturally, and environmentally while producing and consuming products and services with "cleaner production concept" (Goffi, Cucculelli, & Masiero, 2019). In order to produce goods and services with less energy, water, and chemicals while consuming with awareness and natural sensitivity, without risking future generations ability to live in peace, sustainability development demands comprehensive accountability and decisiveness to engage with competitiveness indicators (Goffi et al., 2019; Tzachor et al., 2022). Many people think that technology has more beneficial effects than bad ones, despite the fact that some people attribute environmental issues like pollution and the loss of scarce natural resources on technology. Technology critics assert that people routinely replace their digital devices with the newest models as they hit the market. In addition to the significant increase in electronic trash in the environment, they criticize the fact that electronic devices use a lot of energy. On the other hand, there are people who think that technology improves the environment because they think that new and emerging technologies are more user- and environmentally-friendly goods that aid in lowering the consumption of both energy and natural resources.

How technology is influencing sustainable travel is one of the hottest debated issues among academics and industry professionals in the tourism and hospitality sectors (Huang et al., 2016; Xiang, 2018). The majority of research studies have emphasized how important technology is as a tool for increasing organizational effectiveness, enhancing consumer satisfaction, and lowering operating costs (Yuce, 2022c). Most research studies have stressed the significance of technology as a tool for boosting organizational effectiveness, improving customer happiness and cutting costs (Pirker et al., 2022; Yuce, 2022a). Some companies in the lodging industry have set aside a considerable portion of their budget to restructure their business operations in order to attain these aims. And they referred to this crucial investment in terms of strategy as 'sustainable tourism'. Another primary objective that drives their adoption of innovative technologies in business operations is to increase the number of visitors to their venues, attractions, destinations, or sites without taking into account the negative effects of tourism such as carrying capacity, ecological depletion and socioeconomic concerns. Advocates of tourism who simply focus on money thinks that 'the more tourists you have, the more money you make' without taking into account "at what cost". The biggest cost is one that we all bear because these special resources, whether historically, culturally, socially or environmentally, are vital for all living things. This cost is borne not only by the host community but by all of us. Numerous researches provide evidence that once these resources are ruined, it will be difficult to bring them back to the life again.

Contrary to popular belief, a database of tourism-related statistics may have offered precise data on incoming, domestic and exiting activities to evaluate the season's performance and forecast how and to what extent the future of tourism would be accomplished (Edwards, 1991; Volo, 2020). Tourism statistics can provide important information on the social sphere in addition to the economic indicators in the tourism industry (Antolini & Grassini, 2020). The negative social, cultural and environmental effects of tourism, such as resource abuse and waste management challenges, are rarely taken into account because the major emphasis has been on financial results. Furthermore, because the money is lost to the economies of other nations, the true impact of tourism-related economic advantage, which is frequently assessed by generated revenue and so-called foreign exchanges, is far away from the reality. According to studies, increased tourism does not always lead to the anticipated results, especially for the host communities, because there is a significant degree of leakage (Jönsson, 2015). Unless major tour operators and organizations are involved to bring the tourists, a local hotel or firm does not have much power over for directly marketing their establishment. Therefore, hotels, especially those of modest sizes, only receive a small portion of revenue that is produced abroad before the tourists arrive to the accommodation. Due to their reliance on imported commodities, services, and even labor, poor countries and islands experience leakage more frequently than developed countries (Jönsson, 2015). Fair economic distribution, equal employment opportunities, poor and unstable employment conditions, and an increase in the cost of living in the host community are some notable elements that are typically overlooked or excluded from those impressive figures. Therefore, sustainable tourism encompasses more than just the numbers, which do not include the exploitation of tourism workers or the loss of other particular resources. Digital twin technology might not be able to quickly reverse the negative effects described here. New digital products should enable local company owners to boost their own product's promotional power while also offering eco-friendly alternatives that will decrease the harmful consequences of tourism. The long-term efficiency and sustainability of organizations could greatly be enhanced by the convergence of cutting-edge technologies and digital twins that are in line with their goals.

With the Introduction of Digital Twins, a Newer Era Has Begun

Without changing its current vision and manner of thinking, tourism cannot continue in the present scenario. This new approach should aim to create and develop tourist programs while integrating the most recent technologies in order to make a fundamental change from a traditional notion of sustainable tourism to regenerative tourism. As previously said, one of the steps to establish this mindset among all the shareholders, including developers, investors, authorities and locals, is the integration of big data and AI with digital twins. Digital twins have the ability to offer the opportunity to virtually foresee the potential and current status of the things, places and dynamics as much as the immersive technology may physically deliver real-time and accurate information. Last but not least, even though the majority of the industry has adopted virtual reality and augmented reality as tools to advertise destinations and businesses to potential tourists (Yuce et al., 2020), virtual visitation can also be a vitally important innovative technology to monitor and measure the changes in attractions.

Researchers have highlighted the significant role that digital twins have played in developing alternative strategies for business growth across a variety of industries, including the tourism sector. Digital twins has shown that technology can increase organizations' effectiveness, provide inspiration and increase their productivity and profitability (James, 2021; Li et al., 2022; Pirker et al., 2022). Due to instant alerts and simultaneous physical issue detection, these two technologies give destinations and industry technology developers the ability to implement more customer-centric, goal-oriented, user-friendly and sophisticated applications that predict more accurate, straightforward and decisive experiences than conventional approaches and strategies (Aheleroff et al., 2021).

On the other hand, utilizing modern technology presents opportunities to change the perspectives of consumers and suppliers in order to raise or preserve the value of the tourism product. To the best of my knowledge, there is no credible empirical data in the existing literature on information and communication technology that demonstrates how to increase consumer and staff awareness of using environmentally friendly products and services. In addition to helping to lessen the negative socioeconomic and environmental repercussions of tourism, producing goods and services that are inexpensive, ecologically friendly and fuel-efficient will also enable businesses to maximize their integrity and reputation. Regardless of their position, highly engaged staff members with an eco-conscious outlook will provide enormous benefits, including aiding the business or organization in realizing its objectives and creating a positive customer experience. Utilizing contemporary technologies can also help to save natural resources before they are harmed or depleted. As was already mentioned, by actively monitoring the destination and integrating sensor technology, digital twins technology can help in the preservation of cultural heritage areas and the construction of more sustainable travel plans.

Drawbacks of Digital Twins

Since digital twins technology is still in its early stages of development, it is necessary for developers to make more advancements in order to reduce obstacles and constraints. Although recent technology developments are very exciting, it is still too early to say with certainty that using digital twins will soon be possible and will produce the greatest results. As Tzachor et al. (2022) claimed, "we must be prudent in considering the transformative potential of digital twins and pay close attention to socioeconomic and technological barriers". Some of these obstacles include a) digital divides, which highlight the unfairness of accessing or using digital tools as a result of unequal income distribution; b) a lack of real-time data in complex environments or systems, like cities, forests, or sites, which makes it challenging to present a virtual representation of the real-world objects. In other words, as the authors (Tzachor et al., 2022) indicate, to be used in a more sustainable environment and for green tourism, digital twins technology must go even further, along with other emerging technologies.; c) Due of insufficient input from the sensors, the present iteration of digital twins may not always receive precise information about the objects current status (Qi et al., 2022; Tzachor et al., 2022). This difficulty also results from the need for developing specialized algorithms for each target object or place.

CONCLUSION

In conclusion, today's technology comes with advanced reporting capability to help you improve the efficiency of your business. It enables you to gain insight into market trends, customer preferences, and business performance. With digital twins, technology makes it simpler to get hold of performance indicators and analytical insights that you may utilize to rethink your approaches. Representation of a real object with a digital equivalent has become possible for manufacturers and tourism shareholders with the development of AI, machine learning and digital twins. Despite the fact that digital twins are becoming more and more popular across a wide range of academic fields, this article examined how promising developing technology can be a driving force for the tourism and hospitality sectors. Tourism is a service industry, but its segments can benefit from utilizing digital twins technology in numerous ways. Hence, this conceptualized paper aimed not only to investigate the essentiality of digital twins but also to highlight and present the possible usage areas in the tourism industry. Qi et al. (2022) proposed that digital twins have enormous capacity to optimize organizations effectiveness by monitoring, simulating, optimizing and predicting maintenance before the service and products are manufactured. Qi et al. (2022) also claimed that digitalization helps organizations produce services and products according to the needs and expectations of consumers. This chapter also argued that digital twins, metaverse, artificial intelligence (AI), machine learning, big data, and immersive technologies (VR and AR) have been profoundly crucial technologies to sustain organizations' productivity. These technologies also provide significant opportunities and advantages for the tourism industry to improve organizational effectiveness while external conditions affect their operational sustainability and ability to achieve their goals.

This paper aimed to establish a roadmap for this evolution. As noted above, among all the emerging technologies, AI and big data are serving as the core pillars of other technologies that stand on them. When these essential technologies are integrated with other technologies such as internet of things (IoT) and immersion technologies, firstly, tourism organizations get greater benefits in developing more innovative, applicable and adoptable approaches and strategies to stay competitive in the exceedingly challenging tourism industry. Furthermore, these newest technologies also allow organizations to customize their products and services based on the users' preferences the system gathers during their online experiences. Lastly, modern technologies have also made it possible to influence potential consumers' perceptions, satisfaction, and decision-making processes by persuading them even before purchasing a tourist product.

Convergence of digital twins with internet of things also offers numerous benefits for the accommodations to control their most energy consuming utilities that help both paying less electric and water bill while protecting the natural resources. Finally, as mentioned above, merging of digital twins with the other state-of-the-art technologies also allow developers and practitioners to have a control mechanism over not only to predict how the products will look like, but it also makes it possible to measure the performance of the objects or products during the virtual replication process.

REFERENCES

Adie, B. A., Falk, M., & Savioli, M. (2020). Overtourism as a perceived threat to cultural heritage in Europe. *Current Issues in Tourism*, 23(14), 1737–1741. doi:10.1080/13683500.2019.1687661

Aheleroff, S., Xu, X., Zhong, R. Y., & Lu, Y. (2021). Digital Twin as a Service (DTaaS) in Industry 4.0: An Architecture Reference Model. *Advanced Engineering Informatics*, 47, 101225. doi:10.1016/j.aei.2020.101225

Allam, Z., & Jones, D. S. (2021). Future (post-COVID) digital, smart and sustainable cities in the wake of 6G: Digital twins, immersive realities and new urban economies. *Land Use Policy*, 101, 105201. doi:10.1016/j.landusepol.2020.105201

Antolini, F., & Grassini, L. (2020). Issues in tourism statistics: A critical review. *Social Indicators Research*, 150(3), 1021–1042. doi:10.100711205-020-02361-4

Buhalis, D., & O'Connor, P. (2005). Information Communication Technology Revolutionizing Tourism. *Tourism Recreation Research*, 30(3), 7–16. doi:10.1080/02508281.2005.11081482

Chang, Y., & Jang, I. (2021). Technology Trends in Digital Twins for Smart Cities. *Electronics and telecommunications trends, 36*(1), 99-108.

Chia, B. C. L., Yuen, K. Y., & Woon, K. S. (2022). Digital Twin for Overall Equipment Effectiveness in Intelligent Production Planning. *Paper presented at the Proceedings of the 12th Conference on Learning Factories (CLF 2022).* SSRN. https://ssrn.com/abstract=4076633 doi:10.2139/ssrn.4076633

Cronjé, D. F., & du Plessis, E. (2020). A review on tourism destination competitiveness. *Journal of Hospitality and Tourism Management, 45*, 256–265. doi:10.1016/j.jhtm.2020.06.012

Cureton, P., & Dunn, N. (2021). Digital twins of cities and evasive futures. In A. Aurigi & N. Odendaal (Eds.), *Shaping Smart for Better Cities* (pp. 267–282). Academic Press. doi:10.1016/B978-0-12-818636-7.00017-2

Darwish, A., & Hassanien, A. E. (2022). IoHCT: Internet of Cultural Heritage Things Digital Twins for Conservation and Health Monitoring of Cultural in the Age of Digital Transformation. Digital Twins for Digital Transformation: Innovation in Industry. Springer.

Edwards, A. (1991). The reliability of tourism statistics. *Travel & Tourism Analyst*, (1), 62–75.

Goffi, G., Cucculelli, M., & Masiero, L. (2019). Fostering tourism destination competitiveness in developing countries: The role of sustainability. *Journal of Cleaner Production, 209*, 101–115. doi:10.1016/j.jclepro.2018.10.208

Grieves, M. (2015). *Digital Twin: Manufacturing Excellence through Virtual Factory Replication.* Research Gate.

Hartmann, D., & Van der Auweraer, H. (2021). Digital twins. Progress in Industrial Mathematics: Success Stories. Springer.

Hribernik, K., Cabri, G., Mandreoli, F., & Mentzas, G. (2021). Autonomous, context-aware, adaptive Digital Twins—State of the art and roadmap. *Computers in Industry, 133*, 103508. doi:10.1016/j.compind.2021.103508

Huang, Y. C., Backman, K. F., Backman, S. J., & Chang, L. L. (2016). Exploring the implications of virtual reality technology in tourism marketing: An integrated research framework. *International Journal of Tourism Research, 18*(2), 116–128. doi:10.1002/jtr.2038

Ibănescu, B.-C., Stoleriu, O. M., Munteanu, A., & Iațu, C. (2018). The impact of tourism on sustainable development of rural areas: Evidence from Romania. *Sustainability, 10*(10), 3529. doi:10.3390u10103529

James, L. (2021). Digital twins will revolutionise healthcare: Digital twin technology has the potential to transform healthcare in a variety of ways–improving the diagnosis and treatment of patients, streamlining preventative care and facilitating new approaches for hospital planning. *Engineering & Technology, 16*(2), 50–53. doi:10.1049/et.2021.0210

Jönsson, C. (2015). Leakage, economic tourism. Encyclopedia of tourism, 1-2. Springer.

Kantaros, A., Piromalis, D., Tsaramirsis, G., Papageorgas, P., & Tamimi, H. (2022). 3D Printing and Implementation of Digital Twins: Current Trends and Limitations. *Applied System Innovation*, *5*(1), 7. doi:10.3390/asi5010007

KhanN.HassanA. U.FahadS.NaushadM. (2020). Factors affecting tourism industry and its impacts on global economy of the world. SSRN. doi:10.2139/ssrn.3559353

Li, X., Liu, H., Wang, W., Zheng, Y., Lv, H., & Lv, Z. (2022). Big data analysis of the Internet of Things in the digital twins of smart city based on deep learning. *Future Generation Computer Systems*, *128*, 167–177. doi:10.1016/j.future.2021.10.006

Marai, O. E., Taleb, T., & Song, J. (2021). Roads Infrastructure Digital Twin: A Step Toward Smarter Cities Realization. *IEEE Network*, *35*(2), 136–143. doi:10.1109/MNET.011.2000398

Mkrttchian, V., & Voronin, V. (2021). Digitalization of Lifecycle Management of Domestic Russian Tour Products Based on Problem-oriented Digital Twins-Avatars, Supply Chain, 3D-Hybrid, Federated, and Coordinated Blockchain. [IJDSGBT]. *International Journal of Digital Strategy, Governance, and Business Transformation*, *11*(1), 1–13. doi:10.4018/IJDSGBT.20210101.oa2

Mylonas, G., Kalogeras, A., Kalogeras, G., Anagnostopoulos, C., Alexakos, C., & Muñoz, L. (2021). Digital Twins From Smart Manufacturing to Smart Cities: A Survey. *IEEE Access: Practical Innovations, Open Solutions*, *9*, 143222–143249. doi:10.1109/ACCESS.2021.3120843

Namberger, P., Jackisch, S., Schmude, J., & Karl, M. (2019). Overcrowding, Overtourism and Local Level Disturbance: How Much Can Munich Handle? *Tourism Planning & Development*, *16*(4), 452–472. doi:10.1080/21568316.2019.1595706

Nyanga, C., Pansiri, J., & Chatibura, D. (2020). Enhancing competitiveness in the tourism industry through the use of business intelligence: A literature review. *Journal of Tourism Futures*, *6*(2), 139–151. doi:10.1108/JTF-11-2018-0069

Opoku, D.-G. J., Perera, S., Osei-Kyei, R., & Rashidi, M. (2021). Digital twin application in the construction industry: A literature review. *Journal of Building Engineering*, *40*, 102726. doi:10.1016/j.jobe.2021.102726

Pillai, S. G., Haldorai, K., Seo, W. S., & Kim, W. G. (2021). COVID-19 and hospitality 5.0: Redefining hospitality operations. *International Journal of Hospitality Management*, *94*, 102869. doi:10.1016/j.ijhm.2021.102869 PMID:34785847

Pirker, J., Loria, E., Safikhani, S., Künz, A., & Rosmann, S. (2022). Immersive Virtual Reality for Virtual and Digital Twins: A Literature Review to Identify State Of The Art and Perspectives. Paper presented at the *2022 IEEE Conference on Virtual Reality and 3D User Interfaces Abstracts and Workshops (VRW)*. IEEE. 10.1109/VRW55335.2022.00035

Qi, Q., Tao, F., & Nee, A. (2022). *From service to digital twin service Digital Twin Driven Service*. Elsevier.

Shubenkova, K., Valiev, A., Shepelev, V., Tsiulin, S., & Reinau, K. H. (2018). Possibility of Digital Twins Technology for Improving Efficiency of the Branded Service System. *2018 Global Smart Industry Conference (GloSIC)*. IEEE. 10.1109/GloSIC.2018.8570075

Tao, F., Zhang, H., Liu, A., & Nee, A. Y. C. (2019). Digital Twin in Industry: State-of-the-Art. *IEEE Transactions on Industrial Informatics*, *15*(4), 2405–2415. doi:10.1109/TII.2018.2873186

Tzachor, A., Sabri, S., Richards, C. E., Rajabifard, A., & Acuto, M. (2022). Potential and limitations of digital twins to achieve the Sustainable Development Goals. *Nature Sustainability*, *5*(10), 822–829. doi:10.103841893-022-00923-7

Volo, S. (2020). Tourism statistics, indicators and big data: A perspective article. *Tourism Review*, *75*(1), 304–309. doi:10.1108/TR-06-2019-0262

Xiang, Z. (2018). From digitization to the age of acceleration: On information technology and tourism. *Tourism Management Perspectives*, *25*, 147–150. doi:10.1016/j.tmp.2017.11.023

Yuce, A. (2022a). Digital Transformation-Oriented Innovation in Museum Settings via Digital Engagement: Virtual Reality. Handbook of Research on Museum Management in the Digital Era. IGI Global. doi:10.4018/978-1-7998-9656-2.ch013

Yuce, A. (2022b). ICT Pandemic Time Adoption and Immersive Technologies: A Comprehensive Review. *Digitalization as a Driver for Smart Economy in the Post-COVID-19 Era*, 243-255.

Yuce, A. (2022c). Impact of Technology in Sustainable Tourism Development: Virtual Reality. Mobile Computing and Technology Applications in Tourism and Hospitality. IGI Global.

Yuce, A., Arasli, H., Ozturen, A., & Daskin, M. (2020). Feeling the Service Product Closer: Triggering Visit Intention via Virtual Reality. *Sustainability*, *12*(16), 6632. doi:10.3390u12166632

Compilation of References

Abdul Ahad, M., Paiva, S., Tripathi, G., & Feroz, N. (2020). Enabling Technologies and Sustainable Smart Cities. *Sustainable Cities and Society*, *61*(102301).

Abdulsalam, M., & Aouf, N. (2020). Deep weed detector/classifier network for precision agriculture. In *2020 28th Mediterranean Conference on Control and Automation (MED)*. IEEE. 10.1109/MED48518.2020.9183325

Abid, M., Ngaruiya, G., Scheffran, J., & Zulfiqar, F. (2017). The Role of Social Networks in Agricultural Adaptation to Climate Change: Implications for Sustainable Agriculture in Pakistan. *Climate (Basel)*, *2017*(5), 85. doi:10.3390/cli5040085

Adate & Tripathy. (2022). A Survey on Deep Learning Methodologies of Recent Applications. In Deep Learning in Data Analytics- Recent Techniques, Practices and Applications. Springer. doi:10.1007/978-3-030-75855-4_9

Adhikari. (2018). Machine Learning Based Data Driven Diagnostics & Prognostics Framework for Aircraft Predictive Maintenance. Academic Press.

Adie, B. A., Falk, M., & Savioli, M. (2020). Overtourism as a perceived threat to cultural heritage in Europe. *Current Issues in Tourism*, *23*(14), 1737–1741. doi:10.1080/13683500.2019.1687661

Advantages and Disadvantages of Artificial Intelligence. (n.d.). https://www.javatpoint.com>advantages-and-disadvantages

Afzal, H. M. R., Luo, S., Afzal, M. K., Chaudhary, G., Khari, M., & Kumar, S. A. P. (2020). 3D Face Reconstruction From Single 2D Image Using Distinctive Features. *IEEE Access: Practical Innovations, Open Solutions*, *8*, 180681–180689. doi:10.1109/ACCESS.2020.3028106

Agale, R. R. (2017). Automated Irrigation and Crop Security System in Agriculture Using Internet of Things. *International Conference on Computing, Communication, Control and Automation (ICCUBEA)*, (pp. 1–5). IEEE. 10.1109/ICCUBEA.2017.8463726

Aggarwal, C. C. (2018). Neural networks and deep learning. Springer. doi:10.1007/978-3-319-94463-0

Aghion, P., Jones, B., & Jones, C. (2017). *Artificial Intelligence and Economic Growth*. NBER Working Paper N° 23928. doi:10.6/w23928

Agouzoul, Tabaa, Chegari, Simeu, & Dandache. (2021). Towards a Digital Twin model for Building Energy Management: Case of Morocco. Procedia Computer Science, 184, 404-410. doi:10.1016/j.procs.2021.03

Agrahari, R. K., Kobayashi, Y., Sonam, T., & Tanaka, T. (2021). Soil Science and Plant Nutrition Smart fertilizer management : The progress of imaging technologies and possible implementation of plant biomarkers in agriculture. *Soil Science and Plant Nutrition*, *67*(3), 248–258. doi:10.1080/00380768.2021.1897479

Aharonov, D., Van Dam, W., Kempe, J., Landau, Z., Lloyd, S., & Regev, O. (2008). Adiabatic quantum computation is equivalent to standard quantum computation. *SIAM Review*, *50*(4), 755–787. doi:10.1137/080734479

Aheleroff, S., Xu, X., Zhong, R. Y., & Lu, Y. (2021). Digital Twin as a Service (DTaaS) in Industry 4.0: An Architecture Reference Model. *Advanced Engineering Informatics*, *47*, 101225. doi:10.1016/j.aei.2020.101225

Aher, S. B., & Lobo, L. M. R. J. (2013). Combination of machine learning algorithms for recommendation of courses in E-Learning System based on historical data. *Knowledge-Based Systems*, *51*, 1–14. doi:10.1016/j.knosys.2013.04.015

Aïmeur, E., Brassard, G., & Gambs, S. (2007, June). Quantum clustering algorithms. In *Proceedings of the 24th international conference on machine learning* (pp. 1-8). Academic Press.

Aïmeur, E., Brassard, G., & Gambs, S. (2006, June). Machine learning in a quantum world. In *Conference of the Canadian Society for Computational Studies of Intelligence* (pp. 431–442). Springer.

Al-Ali, A. R., Al Nabulsi, A., Mukhopadhyay, S., Awal, M. S., Fernandes, S., & Ailabouni, K. (2019). IoT-solar energy powered smart farm irrigation system. *Journal of Electronic Science and Technology*.

Al-Ali, A. (2016). Internet of Things Role in the Renewable Energy Resources. *Energy Procedia*, *100*, 34–38. doi:10.1016/j.egypro.2016.10.144

Al-Ali, A. R., & Aburukba, R. (2015). Role of Internet of things in the smart grid technology. *Journal of Computer and Communications*, *3*(5), 229–233. doi:10.4236/jcc.2015.35029

Albizua, A., Bennett, E. M., Larocque, G., Krause, R. W., & Pascual, U. (2021). Social networks influence farming practices and agrarian sustainability. *PLoS One*, *16*(1), e0244619. doi:10.1371/journal.pone.0244619 PMID:33411756

Alexopoulos, K., Nikolakis, N., & Chryssolouris, G. (2020). Digital twin-driven supervised machine learning for the development of artificial intelligence applications in manufacturing. *International Journal of Computer Integrated Manufacturing*, *33*(5), 1–11. doi:10.1080/0951192X.2020.1747642

Alhmoud, L., & Al-Zoubi, H. (2019). IoT applications in wind energy conversion systems. *Open Engineering*, *9*(1), 490–499. doi:10.1515/eng-2019-0061

Ali, M. I., Patel, P., & Breslin, J. G. (2019). Middleware for real-time event detection and predictive analytics in smart manufacturing. *2019 15th International Conference on Distributed Computing in Sensor Systems (DCOSS)*, 370–376.

Ali, M. I., Patel, P., Datta, S. K., & Gyrard, A. (2017). Multi-layer cross domain reasoning over distributed autonomous IoT applications. *Open Journal of Internet Of Things*, *3*(1), 75–90.

Ali, M., Rahim, A., & Ya'akub, S. R. (2021). Solar Energy System for Brunei Residence. *International Journal of Engineering Materials and Manufacture*, *6*(4), 312–318. doi:10.26776/ijemm.06.04.2021.07

Ali, S., Glass, T., Parr, B., Potgieter, J., & Alam, F. (2021). Low-Cost Sensor With IoT LoRaWAN Connectivity and Machine Learning-Based Calibration for Air Pollution Monitoring. *IEEE Transactions on Instrumentation and Measurement*, *70*, 1-11. Advance online publication. doi:10.1109/TIM.2020.3034109

Alkhalidi, A., & Dulaimi, N. H. (2018). *Design of an off-grid solar PV system for a rural shelter*. School of Natural Resources Engineering and Management, Department of Energy Engineering.

Alkhodair, S. A., Ding, S. H. H., Fung, B. C. M., & Liu, J. (2020). Detecting breaking news rumors of emerging topics in social media. *Information Processing & Management*, *57*(2), 102018. doi:10.1016/j.ipm.2019.02.016

Allam, Z., & Dhunny, Z. A. (2019). On big data, artificial intelligence and smart cities. *Cities (London, England)*, *89*, 80–91. doi:10.1016/j.cities.2019.01.032

Allam, Z., & Jones, D. S. (2021). Future (post-COVID) digital, smart and sustainable cities in the wake of 6G: Digital twins, immersive realities and new urban economies. *Land Use Policy*, *101*, 105201. doi:10.1016/j.landusepol.2020.105201

Allam, Z., & Newman, P. (2018). Redefining the smart city: Culture, metabolism and governance. *Smart Cities, 1*(1), 4–25. doi:10.3390martcities1010002

Allan, G., Eromenko, I., Gilmartin, M., Kockar, I., & McGregor, P. (2015). The economics of distributed energy generation: A literature review. *Renewable & Sustainable Energy Reviews, 42*, 543–556. doi:10.1016/j.rser.2014.07.064

Allen, R., Pereira, L., Raes, D., Smith, M., & Ab, W. (1998). Guidelines for computing crop water requirements-FAO Irrigation and drainage document 56. *Crop Evapotranspiration*, pp. 1–15

Allen, A., Siefkas, A., Pellegrini, E., Burdick, H., Barnes, G., Calvert, J., Mao, Q., & Das, R. (2021). A Digital Twins Machine Learning Model for Forecasting Disease Progression in Stroke Patients. *Applied Sciences (Basel, Switzerland), 11*(12), 5576. doi:10.3390/app11125576

AlmasanP.GalmésM.F.PaillisséJ.Suárez-VarelaJ.PerinoD.LópezD.R.PeralesA.A.HarveyP.CiavagliaL.WongL. RamV.R.XiaoS.ShiX.ChengX.Cabellos-AparicioA.Barlet-RosP. (2022).

Altulyan, M., Yao, L., Wang, X., Huang, C., Kanhere, S. S., & Sheng, Q. Z. (2021). A Survey on Recommender Systems for Internet of Things: Techniques, Applications and Future Directions. *The Computer Journal*. Advance online publication. doi:10.1093/comjnl/bxab049

Ananthaswamy, A. (2018). What Does Quantum Theory Actually Tell Us about Reality? Scientific American, Published online: 3 Sept 2018, URL: https://blogs.scientificamerican.com/observations/what-does-quantum-theory-actually-tell-us-about-reality/, Last Accessed on: 05 Feb 2023.

Ang, K. L.-M., & Jasmine, K. P. S. (2021). Big data and machine learning with hyperspectral information in agriculture. *IEEE Access: Practical Innovations, Open Solutions, 9*, 36699–36718. doi:10.1109/ACCESS.2021.3051196

Anguita, D., Ridella, S., Rivieccio, F., & Zunino, R. (2003). Quantum optimization for training support vector machines. *Neural Networks, Elsevier, Vol, 16*(5-6), 763–770. doi:10.1016/S0893-6080(03)00087-X PMID:12850032

An, L., He, G., Liang, Z., & Liu, J. (2006). Impacts of demographic and socioeconomic factors on Spatio-temporal dynamics of panda habitat. *Biodiversity and Conservation, 15*(8), 2343–2363. doi:10.100710531-004-1064-6

Ansari, F., Glawar, R., & Sihn, W. (2020). Prescriptive maintenance of cpps by integrating multimodal data with dynamic Bayesian networks. In *Machine learning for Cyber-Physical Systems* (pp. 1–8). Springer.

Anthopoulos, L. (2015). *Defining Smart City Architecture for Sustainability* [Paper presentation]. 4th IFIP Electronic Government (EGOV) and 7th Electronic Participation (ePart) Conference. 10.3233/978-1-61499-570-8-140

Antolini, F., & Grassini, L. (2020). Issues in tourism statistics: A critical review. *Social Indicators Research, 150*(3), 1021–1042. doi:10.100711205-020-02361-4

Aphiwongsophon, & Chongstitvatana. (2018). *Detecting Fake News with Machine Learning Method*. CP Journal.

Ardebili, Longo, & Ficarella. (2021). Digital Twin (DT) in Smart Energy Systems - Systematic Literature Review of DT as a growing solution for Energy Internet of the Things (EioT). *E3S Web of Conferences, 312*, 09002

ArduinoU. N. O. R3. (2022). https://docs.arduino.cc/hardware/uno-rev3

Armendia, Ghassempouri, Ozturk, & Peysson. (Eds.). (2019). Twin-Control: A Digital Twin Approach to Improve Machine Tools Lifecycle. Springer.

Armstrong, M. M. (2020). *Cheat sheet: What is Digital Twin? Here's your quick guide to digital twins, what they are and why they matter for your organization.* https://www.ibm.com/blogs/internet-of-things/iot-cheat-sheet-digital-twin/

Arnold, M. H. (2021). Teasing out Artificial Intelligence in Medicine: An Ethical Critique of Artificial Intelligence and Machine Learning in Medicine. *Bioethical Inquiry*, *18*(1), 121–139. doi:10.100711673-020-10080-1 PMID:33415596

Artificial Intelligence (AI) Ethics: Ethics of AI and Ethical AI. (2020.) *Journal of Database Management, 31*(2), 74-87. doi:10.4018/JDM.2020040105

Arvind, G., Athira, V. G., Haripriya, H., Rani, R. A., & Aravind, S. (2017). Automated irrigation with advanced seed germination and pest control. *IEEE Technological Innovations in ICT for Agriculture and Rural Development*, 64–67. Advance online publication. doi:10.1109/TIAR.2017.8273687

Arya, S., & Kumar, S. (2020). E-waste in India at a glance: Current trends, regulations, challenges and management strategies. *Journal of Cleaner Production*, *271*, 122707. doi:10.1016/j.jclepro.2020.122707

Ashfaq, & Usman, Jia, Khan, Niaz, & Raza. (2021). Autonomous Driving Test Method Based on Digital Twin. *Survey (London, England)*, 1–7. doi:10.1109/ICECube53880.2021.9628341

Athani, S. & Tejeshwar, C. (2017). *Proceedings of the International Conference on IoT in Social, Mobile, Analytics and Cloud, I-SMAC 2017*. IEEE.

Atzori, L. I., & Morabito, G. (2010). The internet of things: A survey. *Computer Networks*, *54*(15), 2787–2805. doi:10.1016/j.comnet.2010.05.010

Auernhammer, H. (2001). Precision farming—The environmental challenge. *Computers and Electronics in Agriculture*, *30*(3), 31–43. doi:10.1016/S0168-1699(00)00153-8

Awad, E., Dsouza, S., Kim, R., Schulz, J., Henrich, J., Shariff, A., Bonnefon, J. F., & Rahwan, I. (2018, November). The Moral Machine experiment. *Nature*, *563*(7729), 59–64. doi:10.103841586-018-0637-6 PMID:30356211

Aziz, K., Haque, M. M., Rahman, A., Shamseldin, A. Y., & Shoaib, M. (2017). Flood estimation in ungauged catchments: Application of artificial intelligence based methods for Eastern Australia. *Stochastic Environmental Research and Risk Assessment*, *31*(6), 1499–1514. doi:10.100700477-016-1272-0

Azzouni, A., & Pujolle, G. (2017). *A long short-term memory recurrent neural network framework for network traffic matrix prediction*. arXiv preprint arXiv:1705.05690.

Bachinger Bachinger, F., Kronberger, G., & Affenzeller, M. (2021). Continuous improvement and adaptation of predictive models in smart manufacturing and model management. *IET Collab. Intell. Manuf, 3*(1), 48–63. doi:10.1049/cim2.12009

Bagdasaryan, E., Veit, A., Hua, Y., Estrin, D., & Shmatikov, V. (2018). *How To Backdoor Federated Learning*. https://arxiv.org/abs/1807.00459

Bajaj, G., Agarwal, R., Bouloukakis, G., Singh, P., Georgantas, N., & Issarny, V. (2016). Towards building real-time, convenient route recommendation system for public transit. *IEEE 2nd International Smart Cities Conference: Improving the Citizens Quality of Life, ISC2 2016 - Proceedings*. 10.1109/ISC2.2016.07580779

Balaji, S. RRadhakrishnan, MKarthikeyan, SSakthivel, R. (2020). Ultra Sound Imaging System of Kidney Stones Using Deep Neural Network. doi:10.1007/978-3-030-32150-5_117

Balasundaram & Tanveer. (2012). On proximal bilateral-weighted fuzzy support vector machine classifiers. *Int. J. Adv. Intell. Paradig.* . doi:10.1504/IJAIP.2012.052060

Baldauf, M., Dustdar, S., & Rosenberg, F. (2007). A survey on context-aware systems. *International Journal of Ad Hoc and Ubiquitous Computing*, *2*(4), 263–277. doi:10.1504/IJAHUC.2007.014070

Balogh, Z., Gatial, E., Barbosa, J., Leitão, P., & Matejka, T. (2018). Reference architecture for a collaborative predictive platform for smart maintenance in manufacturing. *2018 IEEE 22nd International Conference on Intelligent Engineering Systems (INES),* 299–304.

Bambura, R., Šolc, M., Dado, M., & Kotek, L. (2020). Implementation of Digital Twin for Engine Block Manufacturing Processes. *Applied Sciences (Basel, Switzerland), 10,* 6578. doi:10.3390/app10186578

Barbieri, A. F., & Soares-Filho, B. S. (2005). Population and land use effects on malaria prevalence in the southern Brazilian Amazon. *Human Ecology, 33*(6), 847–874. doi:10.100710745-005-8213-8

Baressi Šegota, S., Lorencin, I., Ohkura, K., & Car, Z. (2019). On the Traveling Salesman Problem in Nautical Environments: An Evolutionary Computing Approach to Optimization of Tourist Route Paths in Medulin, Croatia. *Journal of Maritime & Transportation Science, 57*(1), 71–87. doi:10.18048/2019.57.05.

Barocas, S., Hardt, M., & Narayanan, A. (2022, Nov. 20). *Fairness and machine learning: Limitations and opportunities.* https://fairmlbook.org/pdf/fairmlbook.pdf

Baskin, I. I., Winkler, D., & Tetko, I. V. (2016, August). A renaissance of neural networks in drug discovery. *Expert Opinion on Drug Discovery, 11*(8), 785–795. doi:10.1080/17460441.2016.1201262 PMID:27295548

Bedi, G., Venayagamoorthy, G. K., & Singh, R. (2016). Navigating the Challenges of Internet of Things (IoT) for Power and Energy Systems. In *Clemson University Power Systems Conference* (pp. 1-5). IEEE. 10.1109/PSC.2016.7462853

Beeharry, Y., & Bassoo, V. (2020). Performance of ANN and AlexNet for weed detection using UAV-based images. In *2020 3rd International Conference on Emerging Trends in Electrical, Electronic and Communications Engineering (ELECOM).* IEEE. 10.1109/ELECOM49001.2020.9296994

Behera, R. K., Reddy, K., & Roy, D. S. (2020). A novel context migration model for fog-enabled cross-vertical IoT applications. In *International Conference on Innovative Computing and Communications* (pp. 287-295). Springer. 10.1007/978-981-15-0324-5_25

Bell, J. S., & Bell, J. S. (2004). *Speakable and unspeakable in quantum mechanics: Collected papers on quantum philosophy.* Cambridge University Press. doi:10.1017/CBO9780511815676

Bendre, M. R., Thool, R. C., & Thool, V. R. (2015). Paper. *2015 1st International Conference on Next Generation Computing Technologies (NGCT),* 744-750. 10.1109/NGCT.2015.7375220

Benson, Reid, & Zhang. (2001). *Machine Vision Based Steering System for Agricultural Combines.* doi:10.13031/2013.3446

Benson, T., Akella, A., & Maltz, D. A. (2010). Network traffic characteristics of data centers in the wild. *Proc. of the ACM SIGCOMM Conf. on Internet Measure., ser. IMC '10.* 10.1145/1879141.1879175

Berghoff, C., Bielik, P., Neu, M., Tsankov, P., & von Twickel, A. (2021). Robustness Testing of AI Systems: A Case Study for Traffic Sign Recognition. *IFIP Advances in Information and Communication Technology, 627,* 256–267. doi:10.1007/978-3-030-79150-6_21

Berntzen, L., Johannessen, M. R., & El-Gazzar, R. (2018). Smart Cities, Big Data and Smart Decision-making-Understanding" Big Data" in Smart City Applications. *ICDS 2018, The Twelfth International Conference on Digital Society and eGovernments.*

Bestelmeye, B. (n.d.). Scaling Up Agricultural Research With Artificial Intelligence. *IT Professional, 22*(3), 33-38. . doi:10.1109/MITP.2020.2986062

Bhagat, M., Kumar, D., & Kumar, D. (2019). Role of Internet of Things (IoT) in Smart Farming: A Brief Survey. *Proceedings of 3rd International Conference on 2019 Devices for Integrated Circuit, DevIC 2019*, 141–145. 10.1109/DEVIC.2019.8783800

Bhatia, M., Sood, S. K., & Kumari, R. (2020). Fuzzy-inspired decision making for dependability recommendation in e-commerce industry. *Intelligent Decision Technologies*, *14*(2), 181–197. doi:10.3233/IDT-190143

Bhau, G. V., Deshmukh, R. G., Chowdhury, S., Sesharao, Y., & Abilmazhinov, Y. (2021). IoT based solar energy monitoring system. *Materials Today: Proceedings*. Advance online publication. doi:10.1016/j.matpr.2021.07.364

Bibri, S. E., & Krogstie, J. (2020). The emerging data–driven Smart City and its innovative applied solutions for sustainability: The cases of London and Barcelona. *Energy Informatics*, *3*(1), 1–42. doi:10.118642162-020-00108-6

Bilsborrow, R. E., & Okoth Ogendo, H. W. O. (1992). *Population-driven changes in land use in developing countries.* Ambio.

Bisen, S. V. (2020). *HowAI Can be Used in Smart Cities: Applications Role & Challenge.* Retrieved May 14, 2020, https://medium.com/vsinghbisen/how-ai-can-be-used-in-smart-cities-applications-role-challenge-8641fb52a1dd

Bisen, R. G., Rajurkar, A. M., & Manthalkar, R. R. (2020). Segmentation, Detection, and Classification of Liver Tumors for Designing a CAD System. In B. Iyer, P. Deshpande, S. Sharma, & U. Shiurkar (Eds.), *Computing in Engineering and Technology. Advances in Intelligent Systems and Computing* (Vol. 1025). Springer. doi:10.1007/978-981-32-9515-5_10

Blackmore, S. (1994). Precision Farming: An Introduction. *Outlook on Agriculture*, *23*(4), 275–280. doi:10.1177/003072709402300407

Blicq. (2021). *Digital Twins: The Next Human Revolution That Will Disrupt the Financial Services Industry.* Innovations Accelerated.

Bobadilla, J., Ortega, F., Hernando, A., & Gutiérrez, A. (2013). Knowledge-Based Systems Recommender systems survey. *Knowledge-Based Systems*, *46*, 109–132. doi:10.1016/j.knosys.2013.03.012

Boetticher, Menzies, & Ostrand. (2007). *Promise repository of empirical software engineering data.* Available: http://promisedata.org/repository

Bohr, A., & Memarzadeh, K. (2020). The rise of artificial intelligence in healthcare applications. *Artificial Intelligence in Healthcare*, 25–60. doi:10.1016/B978-0-12-818438-7.00002-2

Bokhari, S. A. A., & Myeong, S. (2022). Use of artificial intelligence in smart cities for smart decision-making: A social innovation perspective. *Sustainability*, *14*(2), 620. doi:10.3390u14020620

Bongaarts, J., O'Neill, B. C., & Gaffin, S. R. (1997). Global warming policy: Population left out in the cold. *Environment*, *39*(9), 40–48. doi:10.1080/00139159709604769

Boreale, Michele & Corradi, Fabio & Viscardi, Cecilia. (2019). Relative Privacy Threats and Learning From Anonymized Data. *IEEE Transactions on Information Forensics and Security*. IEEE. . doi:10.1109/TIFS.2019.2937640

Botta, A., De Donato, W., Persico, V., & Pescapé, A. (2016). Integration of cloud computing and internet of things: A survey. *Future Generation Computer Systems*, *56*, 684700. doi:10.1016/j.future.2015.09.021

Bottani, Assunta, Murino, & Vespoli. (2017). *From the Cyber-Physical System to the Digital Twin: the process development for behaviour modelling of a Cyber Guided Vehicle in M2M logic.* Academic Press.

Bourgonje, P., Schneider, J. M., & Rehm, G. (2017). From clickbait to fake news detection: an approach based on detecting the stance of headlines to articles. *Proceedings of the 2017 EMNLP workshop: natural language processing meets journalism*, 84–89. 10.18653/v1/W17-4215

Bousdekis, A., Mentzas, G., Hribernik, K., Lewandowski, M., von Stietencron, M., & Thoben, K.-D. (2019). A unified architecture for proactive maintenance in manufacturing enterprises. In *Enterprise Interoperability VIII* (pp. 307–317). Springer.

Boyes, H., Hallaq, B., Cunningham, J., & Watson, T. (2018). The industrial internet of things (iiot): An analysis framework. *Computers in Industry*, *101*, 1–12.

Boyle, G. (2004). *Renewable Energy: Power for a Sustainable Future*. Academic Press.

Bradley, P. (1997). The use of the area under the ROC curve in the evaluation of machine learning algorithms. *Pattern Recognition*, *30*(7), 1145–1159.

Brandtzaeg, P. B., & Følstad, A. (2018). Chatbots: Changing user needs and motivations. *Interactions*, *25*(5), 38-43.

Braunhofer, M., & Ricci, F. (2017). Selective contextual information acquisition in travel recommender systems. *Information Technology & Tourism*, *17*(1), 5–29. doi:10.100740558-017-0075-6

Brendan McMahan, H., Moore, E., Ramage, D., Hampson, S., & Agüera y Arcas, B. (2017). Communication-efficient learning of deep networks from decentralized data. *Proceedings of the 20th International Conference on Artificial Intelligence and Statistics, AISTATS 2017*, 54.

Brilli, F., Fares, S., Ghirardo, A., de Visser, P., Calatayud, V., Muñoz, A., Annesi-Maesano, I., Sebastiani, F., Alivernini, A., Varriale, V., & Menghini, F. (2018). Plants for sustainable improvement of indoor air quality. *Trends in Plant Science*, *23*(6), 507–512. doi:10.1016/j.tplants.2018.03.004 PMID:29681504

Bruce, A., Jackson, C., & Lamprinopoulou, C. (2021). Social networks and farming resilience. *Outlook on Agriculture*, *50*(2), 196–205. Advance online publication. doi:10.1177/0030727020984812

Bruschi, D., Diomede. (2022). N. A framework for assessing AI ethics with applications to cybersecurity. *AI Ethics*. doi:10.1007/s43681-022-00162-8

Bryson, J., & Winfield, A. (2017). Standardizing Ethical Design for Artificial Intelligence and Autonomous Systems. *Computer*, *50*(5), 116–119. doi:10.1109/MC.2017.154

Buddha, K. (2019). Weed Detection and Classification in High Altitude Aerial Images for Robot-Based Precision Agriculture. In *2019 27th Mediterranean Conference on Control and Automation (MED)*. IEEE. 10.1109/MED.2019.8798582

Bu, F., & Wang, X. (2019). A smart agriculture IoT system based on deep reinforcement learning. *Future Generation Computer Systems*, *99*, 500–507. doi:10.1016/j.future.2019.04.041

Bughin, J., Seong, J., Manyika, J., Chui, M., & Joshi, R. (2018). *Notes from the AI frontier: Modeling the global economic impact of AI*. McKinsey Global Institute.

Buhalis, D., & O'Connor, P. (2005). Information Communication Technology Revolutionizing Tourism. *Tourism Recreation Research*, *30*(3), 7–16. doi:10.1080/02508281.2005.11081482

Bühlmann, P., & Van De Geer, S. (2011). *Statistics for high-dimensional data: methods, theory and applications*. Springer Science & Business Media. doi:10.1007/978-3-642-20192-9

Buntain, C., & Golbeck, J. (2017). Automatically Identifying Fake News in Popular Twitter Threads. *IEEE International Conference on Smart Cloud (SmartCloud)*. 10.1109/SmartCloud.2017.40

Butt, Letchmunan, Ali, Hassan, Baqir, & Sherazi. (2021). Machine Learning Based Diabetes Classification and Prediction for Healthcare Applications. *Journal of Healthcare Engineering*. doi:10.1155/2021/9930985

Córdova-Cruzatty, Barreno Barreno, & Jacome. (2017). Precise weed and maize classification through convolutional neuronal networks. In *2017 IEEE Second Ecuador Technical Chapters Meeting (ETCM)*. IEEE.

Cai, J., Wang, Y., Liu, Y., Luo, J. Z., Wei, W., & Xu, X. (2018). Enhancing network capacity by weakening community structure in scale-free network. *Future Generation Computer Systems*, *87*, 765–771. doi:10.1016/j.future.2017.08.014

Campbell-Lendrum, D., & Woodruff, R. (2006). Comparative risk assessment of the burden of disease from climate change. *Environmental Health Perspectives*, *114*(12), 1935–1941. doi:10.1289/ehp.8432 PMID:17185288

Candrian, C., & Scherer, A. (2022). Rise of the machines: Delegating decisions to autonomous AI. *Computers in Human Behavior*, *134*, 107308. doi:10.1016/j.chb.2022.107308

Canny, J. (1986). A computational approach to edge detection. *IEEE Transactions on Pattern Analysis and Machine Intelligence*, (6), 679–698.

Cardullo, P., & Kitchin, R. (2019). Smart urbanism and smart citizenship: The neoliberal logic of 'citizen-focused' smart cities in Europe. *Environment and Planning C: Politics and Space, 37*(5), 813-830.

Carlini, & Wagner. (2017). Adversarial examples are not easily detected: Bypassing ten detection methods. In *Proceedings of the 10th ACM Workshop on Artificial Intelligence and Security*. ACM.

Carr, D. L., & Bilsborrow, R. E. (2001). Population and land use/cover change: A regional comparison between Central America and South America. *Journal of Geography Education*, *43*(8), 7–16.

Cassen, R. (Ed.). (1994). *Population and Development: Old debates, new conclusions* (Vol. 19). Transaction Publishers.

Castelli. (2019). Urban Intelligence: a Modular, Fully Integrated, and Evolving Model for Cities Digital Twinning. *IEEE 16th Int. conf. on Smart Cities: Improving Quality of Life Using ICT & IoT and AI (HONET-ICT)*, 33-37. 10.1109/HONET.2019.8907962

Cath, C., Wachter, S., Mittelstadt, B., Taddeo, M., & Floridi, L. (2018). Artificial Intelligence and the 'Good Society': The US, EU, and UK approach. *Science and Engineering Ethics*, *24*. doi:10.100711948-017-9901-7 PMID:28353045

Ch'ng, E. (2019). Art by computing machinery: Is machine art acceptable in the artworld. *ACM Transactions on Multimedia Computing Communications and Applications*, *15*(2s), 1–17. doi:10.1145/3326338

Chaitanya, S. M. K., & Rajesh Kumar, P. (2020). Oppositional Gravitational Search Algorithm and Artificial Neural Network-based Classification of Kidney Images. *Journal of Intelligent Systems*, *29*(1), 485–496. doi:10.1515/jisys-2017-0458

Chakraborty, S., & Adhikari, S. (2021). Machine learning-based digital twin for dynamical systems with multiple time scales. *Computers & Structures, 243*, 106410.

Chakraborty, A., Alam, M., Dey, V., Chattopadhyay, A., & Mukhopadhyay, D. (2018). Adversarial Attacks and Defences. *Survey*. https://arxiv.org/abs/1810.00069

Chamara, R. M. S. R., Senevirathne, S. M. P., Samarasinghe, S. A. I. L. N., Premasiri, M. W. R. C., Sandaruwani, K. H. C., Dissanayake, D. M. N. N., De Silva, S. H. N. P., Ariyaratne, W. M. T. P., & Marambe, B. (2020). Role of artificial intelligence in achieving global food security: A promising technology for future. *Sri Lanka Journal of Food and Agriculture*, *6*(2), 43–70. doi:10.4038ljfa.v6i2.88

Chan, A. K. W., & Case, K. (1994). Process planning by recognizing and learning machining features. *International Journal of Computer Integrated Manufacturing*, *7*(2), 77–99.

Chang, Y., & Jang, I. (2021). Technology Trends in Digital Twins for Smart Cities. *Electronics and telecommunications trends, 36*(1), 99-108.

Chang, P., Grinband, J., Weinberg, B. D., Bardis, M., Khy, M., Cadena, G., Su, M. Y., Cha, S., Filippi, C. G., Bota, D., Baldi, P., Poisson, L. M., Jain, R., & Chow, D. (2018, July). Deep-Learning Convolutional Neural Networks Accurately Classify Genetic Mutations in Gliomas. *AJNR. American Journal of Neuroradiology, 39*(7), 1201–1207. doi:10.3174/ajnr.A5667 PMID:29748206

Chan, H. C. S., Shan, H., Dahoun, T., Vogel, H., & Yuan, S. (2019, August). Advancing Drug Discovery via Artificial Intelligence. *Trends in Pharmacological Sciences, 40*(8), 592–604. doi:10.1016/j.tips.2019.06.004 PMID:31320117

Charles, A., Names, A., & Rodrigues, P. (2017). Comparison of data mining methods applied to a surface meteorological station. *Rbrh, 22.*

Chaudhuri, S., Roy, M., McDonald, L. M., & Emendack, Y. (2021). Reflections on farmers' social networks: A means for sustainable agricultural development? *Environment, Development and Sustainability, 23*(3), 2973–3008. doi:10.100710668-020-00762-6

Chauhan, R. M. (2015). Advantages And Challenging in E Agriculture. *Oriental Journal of Computer Science & Technology, 8*(3), 228–233. www.computerscijournal.org

Chavan, T. R., & Nandedkar, A. V. (2018). AgroAVNET for crops and weeds classification: A step forward in automatic farming. *Computers and Electronics in Agriculture, 154*, 361–372. doi:10.1016/j.compag.2018.09.021

Chavhan, S., Gupta, D., Nagaraju, C., Rammohan, A., Khanna, A., & Rodrigues, J. J. (2021). An efficient context-Aware vehicle incidents route service management for intelligent transport system. *IEEE Systems Journal, 16*(1), 487–498.

Cheatham, B. (2019). Confronting the risks of artificial intelligence. *The McKinsey Quarterly*, 1–9. https://www.health-industryhub.com.au/wp-content/uploads/2019/05/Confronting-the-risks-of-AI-2019.pdf

Chelladurai, J. (2020). The Role of New Media towards sustainable agricultural development among farmer's of Kancheepuram District, Tamilnadu. *International Journal of Social Research Methodology, 4*, 29-34.. doi:10.18231/2454-9150.2019.0227

Chen, F., Deng, P., Wan, J., Zhang, D., Vasilakos, A. V., & Rong, X. (2015). Data mining for the internet of things: Literature review and challenges. *International Journal of Distributed Sensor Networks, 2015*(i). doi:10.1155/2015/431047

Chen, D., & Lv, Z. (2022). Artificial intelligence-enabled Digital Twins for training autonomous cars. *Internet of Things and Cyber-Physical Systems, 2*, 31–41. doi:10.1016/j.iotcps.2022.05.001

Chen, G., Ding, C., Li, Y., Hu, X., Li, X., Ren, L., Ding, X., Tian, P., & Xue, W. (2020). Prediction of Chronic Kidney Disease Using Adaptive Hybridized Deep Convolutional Neural Network on the Internet of Medical Things Platform. *IEEE Access: Practical Innovations, Open Solutions, 8*, 100497–100508. doi:10.1109/ACCESS.2020.2995310

Chen, G., Li, X., Liu, X., Chen, Y., Liang, X., Leng, J., Xu, X., Liao, W., Qiu, Y., Wu, Q., & Huang, K. (2020). Global projections of future urban land expansion under shared socioeconomic pathways. *Nature Communications, 11*(1), 1–12. doi:10.103841467-020-14386-x PMID:31988288

Chen, H., Engkvist, O., Wang, Y., Olivecrona, M., & Blaschke, T. (2018, June). The rise of deep learning in drug discovery. *Drug Discovery Today, 23*(6), 1241–1250. doi:10.1016/j.drudis.2018.01.039 PMID:29366762

Chen, J. (n.d.). *Identification of plant disease images via a squeeze-and excitation MobileNet model and twice transfer learning*. doi:10.1049/ipr2.12090

Chen, Y. A., Hsieh, W. H., Ko, Y. S., & Huang, N. F. (2021). An Ensemble Learning Model for Agricultural Irrigation Prediction. *International Conference on Information Networking,* 311–316. 10.1109/ICOIN50884.2021.9333852

Chia, B. C. L., Yuen, K. Y., & Woon, K. S. (2022). Digital Twin for Overall Equipment Effectiveness in Intelligent Production Planning. *Paper presented at the Proceedings of the 12th Conference on Learning Factories (CLF 2022).* SSRN. https://ssrn.com/abstract=4076633 doi:10.2139/ssrn.4076633

Chollet, F. (2016). *Xception: Deep learning with depthwise separable convolutions.* https://arxiv.org/abs/1610.02357

Choudhury, T. T., Paul, S. K., Rahman, H. F., Jia, Z., & Shukla, N. (2020). A systematic literature review on the service supply chain: Research agenda and future research directions. *Production Planning and Control, 31*(16), 1363–1384. doi:10.1080/09537287.2019.1709132

Chu, E. K. (2016). The governance of climate change adaptation through urban policy experiments. *Environmental Policy and Governance, 26*(6), 439–451. doi:10.1002/eet.1727

Chukwuekwe, Glesnes, & Schjølberg. (n.d.). *Condition monitoring for predictive maintenance-towards systems prognosis within the industrial internet of things.* Academic Press.

Chung, P. R., Tzeng, C. T., Ke, M. T., & Lee, C. Y. (2013). Formaldehyde gas sensors: A review. *Sensors (Basel), 13*(4), 4468–4484. doi:10.3390130404468 PMID:23549368

Cicirelli, F., Guerrieri, A., Spezzano, G., & Vinci, A. (2017). An edge-based platform for dynamic smart city applications. *Future Generation Computer Systems, 76,* 106–118. doi:10.1016/j.future.2017.05.034

Cioara, T., Anghel, I., Antal, M., Salomie, I., Antal, C.D., & Ioan, A.G. (2021). *An Overview of Digital Twins Application Domains in Smart Energy Grid.* ArXiv, doi: abs/2104.07904.

CMU. (n.d.). https://wiki.sei.cmu.edu/confluence/display/seccode

Cohen, M. L. (2008). Essay: Fifty Years of Condensed Matter Physics. *Physical Review Letters, 101*(25). doi:10.1103/PhysRevLett.101.250001

Coley, C. W., Barzilay, R., Jaakkola, T. S., Green, W. H., & Jensen, K. F. (2017, May 24). Prediction of Organic Reaction Outcomes Using Machine Learning. *ACS Central Science, 3*(5), 434–443. doi:10.1021/acscentsci.7b00064 PMID:28573205

Comiter, M. (2019). *Attacking artificial intelligence: AI's security vulnerability and what policymakers can do about it.* Belfer Center for Science and International Affairs, Harvard Kennedy School.

Computer hardware. (n.d.). In *Wikipedia.* https://en.wikipedia.org/wiki/Computer_hardware

Constantin, S., Moldoveanu, F., Campeanu, R., Baciu, I., Grigorescu, S. M., & Carstea, B. (2006). GPRS based system for atmospheric pollution monitoring and warning. In *International conference on automation, quality and testing, robotics* (vol. 2, pp. 193-198). IEEE. 10.1109/AQTR.2006.254630

Cordero, P., Enciso, M., López, D., & Mora, A. (2020). A conversational recommender system for diagnosis using fuzzy rules. *Expert Systems with Applications, 154,* 113449. Advance online publication. doi:10.1016/j.eswa.2020.113449

Craglia, M., & Granell, C. (2014). *Citizen Science and Smart Cities.* Number EUR 26652 EN; Publications Office of the European Union.

Crawford, M. (2021). *7 Digital Twin Applications for Manufacturing.* https://www.asme.org/topics-resources/content/7-digital-twin-applications-for-manufacturing

Croatti, A., Gabellini, M., Montagna, S., & Ricci, A. (2020). On the integration of agents and digital twins in healthcare. *Journal of Medical Systems*, *44*(9), 1–8. doi:10.100710916-020-01623-5 PMID:32748066

Cronjé, D. F., & du Plessis, E. (2020). A review on tourism destination competitiveness. *Journal of Hospitality and Tourism Management*, *45*, 256–265. doi:10.1016/j.jhtm.2020.06.012

Cugurullo, F. (2016). Urban eco-modernisation and the policy context of new eco-city projects: Where Masdar City fails and why. *Urban Studies (Edinburgh, Scotland)*, *53*(11), 2417–2433. doi:10.1177/0042098015588727

Cugurullo, F. (2020). Urban artificial intelligence: From automation to autonomy in the smart city. *Frontiers in Sustainable Cities*, *2*, 38. doi:10.3389/frsc.2020.00038

Cugurullo, F., Acheampong, R. A., Gueriau, M., & Dusparic, I. (2021). The transition to autonomous cars, the redesign of cities and the future of urban sustainability. *Urban Geography*, *42*(6), 833–859. doi:10.1080/02723638.2020.1746096

Cupek, Drewniak, Ziębiński, & Fojcik. (2019). *"Digital Twins" for Highly Customized Electronic Devices – Case Study on a Rework Operation*. IEEE Access. . doi:10.1109/ACCESS.2019.2950955

Cureton, P., & Dunn, N. (2021). Digital twins of cities and evasive futures. In A. Aurigi & N. Odendaal (Eds.), *Shaping Smart for Better Cities* (pp. 267–282). Academic Press. doi:10.1016/B978-0-12-818636-7.00017-2

D'Aniello, G., Gaeta, M., Orciuoli, F., Sansonetti, G., & Sorgente, F. (2020). Knowledge-based smart city service system. *Electronics (Basel)*, *9*(6), 965.

Dagar, R., Som, S., & Khatri, S. K. (2018). Smart farming–IoT in agriculture. In *International Conference on Inventive Research in Computing Applications* (pp. 1052-1056). IEEE.

Dalton, M., O'Neill, B., Prskawetz, A., Jiang, L., & Pitkin, J. (2008). Population ageing and future carbon emissions in the United States. *Energy Economics*, *30*(2), 642–675. doi:10.1016/j.eneco.2006.07.002

Dameri, R. P. (2013). Searching for smart city definition: A comprehensive proposal. *International Journal of Computers and Technology*, *11*(5), 2544–2551. doi:10.24297/ijct.v11i5.1142

Damioli, G., Van Roy, V., & Vertesy, D. (2021). The impact of artificial intelligence on labor productivity. *Eurasian Bus Rev*, *11*(1), 1–25. doi:10.100740821-020-00172-8

Dang, H. V., Tatipamula, M., & Nguyen, H. X. (2021). Cloud-based digital twinning for structural health monitoring using deep learning. *IEEE Transactions on Industrial Informatics*, *18*(6), 3820–3830. doi:10.1109/TII.2021.3115119

Daptardar, V., & Gore, M. (2019). Smart Cities for Sustainable Development in India: Opportunities and Challenges. *European Journal of Sustainable Development*, *8*(3), 133. doi:10.14207/ejsd.2019.v8n3p133

Dargan, S., Kumar, M., Ayyagari, M. R., & Kumar, G. (2020). A survey of deep learning and its applications: A new paradigm to machine learning. *Archives of Computational Methods in Engineering*, *27*(4), 1071–1092. doi:10.100711831-019-09344-w

Darwish, A., & Hassanien, A. E. (2022). IoHCT: Internet of Cultural Heritage Things Digital Twins for Conservation and Health Monitoring of Cultural in the Age of Digital Transformation. Digital Twins for Digital Transformation: Innovation in Industry. Springer.

Das, S. D., Basak, A., & Dutta, S. (2021). *A Heuristic-driven Ensemble Framework for COVID-19 Fake News Detection*. doi:10.1007/978-3-030-73696-5_16

Dasgupta, Rahman, Lidbe, Lu, & Jones. (2021). *A Transportation Digital-Twin Approach for Adaptive Traffic Control Systems*. Cornell University.

Dasgupta, P. (2000). Population and resources: An exploration of reproductive and environmental externalities. *Population and Development Review*, *26*(4), 643–689. doi:10.1111/j.1728-4457.2000.00643.x

Daudon, M., Traxer, O., Conort, P., Lacour, B., & Jungers, P. (2006). Type 2 diabetes increases the risk for uric acid stones. *Journal of the American Society of Nephrology*, *17*(7), 2026–2033. doi:10.1681/ASN.2006030262 PMID:16775030

Davenport, T., Guha, A., Grewal, D., & Bressgott, T. (2020). How artificial intelligence will change the future of marketing. *Journal of the Academy of Marketing Science*, *48*(1), 24–42. doi:10.100711747-019-00696-0

De Laat, P. (2021). Companies Committed to Responsible AI: From Principles towards Implementation and Regulation? *Philosophy & Technology*, *34*(4), 1135–1193. doi:10.100713347-021-00474-3 PMID:34631392

Deac, C., Popa, C. L., & Ghinea, M. (2017). Machine Vision in Manufacturing Processes and the Digital Twin of Manufacturing Architectures. doi:10.2507/28th.daaam.proceedings.103

Dear, K. (2021). Artificial intelligence, security, and society. *The World Information War: Western Resilience, Campaigning, and Cognitive Effects*, *55*(1), 231–256. doi:10.4324/9781003046905-17

Della Vedova, M. L., Tacchini, E., Moret, S., Ballarin, G., DiPierro, M., & de Alfaro, L. (2018). Automatic Online Fake News Detect ion Combining Content and Social Signals. *2018 22nd Conference of Open Innovations Association (FRUCT)*, 272–279. (Das et al., 2021)10.23919/FRUCT.2018.8468301

Dembski, F., Wössner, U., Letzgus, M., Ruddat, M., & Yamu, C. (2020). Urban Digital Twins for Smart Cities and Citizens: The Case Study of Herrenberg. Journal of Sustainability, 12(6).

Deranty, J. P., & Corbin, T. (2022). Artificial intelligence and work: A critical review of recent research from the social sciences. *AI & Society*. doi:10.100700146-022-01496-x

Desai, J. (2020, June 16). *Rooftop solar pv system: basic guide.* Retrieved June 27, 2022, from GharPedia: https://gharpedia.com/blog/rooftop-solar-pv-system-basic-guide/

Dhiman, J. (2021, August 22). *Is Machine Learning the future of Data Quality?* Academic Press.

Diab. (2004). Automatic Tagging of Arabic Text: From Raw Text to Base Phrase Chunks. In *Proceedings of HLT-NAACL 2004: Short Papers* (pp. 149–152). Association for Computational Linguistics.(Das et al., 2021)

Dian Bah, M. (2018). Deep learning with unsupervised data labeling for weed detection in line crops in UAV images. *Remote Sensing*, *10*(11), 1690. doi:10.3390/rs10111690

Dietmar, P. (2021). Intelligent Manufacturing with Digital Twin. doi:10.1109/EIT51626.2021.9491874

Diharja, R., Rivai, M., Mujiono, T., & Pirngadi, H. (2019). Carbon Monoxide Sensor Based on Non-Dispersive Infrared Principle. *Journal of Physics: Conference Series*, 1201. 10.1088/1742-6596/1201/1/012012

Dominiković, I., Ćukušić, M., & Jadrić, M. (2021). The role of artificial intelligence in smart cities: systematic literature review. In *International conference on data and information in Online* (pp. 64-80). Springer. 10.1007/978-3-030-77417-2_5

Doorenbos, J. & Pruitt, W. (1977). Guidelines for forecasting crop water requirements. FAO Irrigation and Drainage Paper, *24*, 144.

dos Santos, F., Fernandes, P., Rockett, F., & de Oliveira, A. (2017). *The State of Food and Agriculture: Leveraging Food Systems for Inclusive Rural Transformation,* (*vol. 2*, no. 7929). Food and Agriculture Organization of the United Nations. http://www.fao.org/3/a- I7658e.pdfpercentApercent5Cn https://www.ncbi.nlm.nih.gov/pubmed/24897208

Douay, N., & Henriot, C. (2016). La Chine à l'heure des villes intelligentes. *L'Information Geographique*, *80*(3), 89–104. doi:10.3917/lig.803.0089

Dua & Du. (2016). *Data Mining and Machine Learning in Cybersecurity*. Auerbach Publications.

Dubey, Manisha, Deep, & Singh. (2016). Robotics and Image Processing for Plucking of Fruits. In *Proceedings of Fifth International Conference on Soft Computing for Problem Solving. Advances in Intelligent Systems and Computing* (vol. 437). Springer. 10.1007/978-981-10-0451-3_69

Duggar, D. (2022). Sarang Bang, B. K. Tripathy: Applications of Big Data Analytics in E-governance and other Aspects of Society. In *Encyclopedia of Data Science and Machine Learning*. IGI Publications.

Economic and Social Research Council. (n.d.). *Using Social Media*. Available at: https://esrc.ukri.org/research/impact-toolkit/social-media/using-social-media

Edwards, A. (1991). The reliability of tourism statistics. *Travel & Tourism Analyst*, (1), 62–75.

Einstein, A., Podolsky, B., & Rosen, N. (1935). Can quantum-mechanical description of physical reality be considered complete? *Physical Review*, *47*(10), 777–780. doi:10.1103/PhysRev.47.777

El Morr, C., & Ali-Hassan, H. (2019). Descriptive, predictive, and prescriptive analytics. In *Analytics in Healthcare* (pp. 31–55). Springer. doi:10.1007/978-3-030-04506-7_3

El Saddik, A. (2022). *Digital Twin for Healthcare: Design, Challenges, and Solutions*. Elsevier.

Electrical, E. (2014, August 15). *Created internally by a member of the Energy Education team. Adapted from: Ecogreen Electrical. Solar PV Systems*. Retrieved June 27, 2022, from ECOGREENELECTRICAL: http://ww1.ecogreenelectrical.com/

El-houari, H., Allouhi, A., Rehman, S., Buker, M., Kousksou, T., Jamil, A., & El Amrani, B. (2019). Design, simulation, and economic optimization of an off-grid photovoltaic system for rural electrification. *Energies*, *12*(24), 4735. doi:10.3390/en12244735

Erkoyuncu, J. A., Fernández del Amo, I., Ariansyah, D., Bulka, D., Vrabič, R., & Roy, R. (2020). A design framework for adaptive digital twins. *CIRP Annals*, *69*(1), 145–148. doi:10.1016/j.cirp.2020.04.086

Errandonea, I., Beltrán, S., & Arrizabalaga, S. (2020). Digital Twin for maintenance: A literature review. *Computers in Industry*, *123*, 103316. doi:10.1016/j.compind.2020.103316

Eswaran, H., Lal, R., & Reich, P. F. (2019). Land degradation: An overview. *Response to land degradation*, 20-35.

European Commission. (n.d.). *Smart cities: Cities using technological solutions to improve the management and efficiency of the urban environment*. Retrieved from: https://ec.europa.eu/info/eu-regional-and-urban-development/topics/cities-and-urban-development/city-initiatives/smart-cities_en

Evangeline, P. (Ed.). (2021). The Digital Twin Paradigm for Smarter Systems and Environments: The Industry Use Cases. Elsevier.

Evans, K., de Moura, N., Chauvier, S., Chatila, R., & Dogan, E. (2020). Ethical Decision Making in Autonomous Vehicles: The AV Ethics Project. *Science and Engineering Ethics*, *26*(6), 3285–3312. doi:10.100711948-020-00272-8 PMID:33048325

Eversheim, W., & Schneewind, J. (1993). Computer-aided process planning - state of the art and future development. *Robotics and Computer-integrated Manufacturing*, *10*(1/2), 65–70.

Falk, A., & Granqvist, D. (2017). *Combining Deep Learning with traditional algorithms in autonomous cars*. Academic Press.

FAO. (2016). *Aquastat*. FAO. https://www.fao.org/nr/water/aquastat/waterusage

Farahani, H., Wagiran, R., & Hamidon, M. N. (2014). Humidity sensors principle, mechanism, and fabrication technologies: A comprehensive review. *Sensors (Basel)*, *14*(5), 7881–7939. doi:10.3390140507881 PMID:24784036

Farsagli, S. (2019, August 20). *What are the developments, challenges, and opportunities for businesses provided by Digital Twin?* Ingenium.

Fauvel, S., & Yu, H. (2016). *A Survey on Artificial Intelligence and Data Mining for MOOCs*. https://images-insite.sgp1.digitaloceanspaces.com/dunia_buku/koleksi-buku-lainnya/a-survey-on-artificial-intelligence-and-data-mining-for-moocs-pdfdrivecom-10781581695980.pdf

FB. (2019). https://about.fb.com/news/2019/01/designingsecurity- for-billions/

Ferdousi, & Laamarti, Hossain, Yang, & El Saddik. (2021). Digital twins for well-being: An overview. *Digital Twin.*, *1*, 7. doi:10.12688/digitaltwin.17475.1

Fernando, L., Dur, C. S., Haag, S., Anderl, R., Sch, K., & Zancul, E. (2018). Digital Twin Requirements in the Context of Industry 4.0. In *Product Lifecycle Management to Support Industry 4.0*. doi:10.1007/978-3-030-01614-2

First, F. (2019). *Sustainable Agriculture*. Retrieved February 2019, from Farmers First- A Global coalition for sustainable agricultural development: https://farmingfirst.org

Floridi, L., Cowls, J., Beltrametti, M., Chatila, R., Chazerand, P., Dignum, V., Luetge, C., Madelin, R., Pagallo, U., Rossi, F., Schafer, B., Valcke, P., & Vayena, E. (2018). AI4People—An Ethical Framework for a Good AI Society: Opportunities, Risks, Principles, and Recommendations. *Minds and Machines*, *28*(4), 689–707. doi:10.100711023-018-9482-5 PMID:30930541

Forti, V., Baldé, C. P., Kuehr, R., & Bel, G. (2020). The global e-waste monitor 2020. *Quantities, flows, and the circular economy potential*, 1-119.

Freeman, L. (2004). *The Development of Social Network Analysis: A Study in the Sociology of Science*. Empirical Press.

Frey, C., & Osborne, M. (2017). The future of employment: How susceptible are jobs to computerization? *Technological Forecasting and Social Change*, *114*, 254–280. doi:10.1016/j.techfore.2016.08.019

Friedericha, Francisb, Lazarova-Molnara, & Mohamedc. (2022). A framework for data-driven digital twins of smart manufacturing systems. *Computers in Industry, 136*. doi:10.1016/j.compind.2021.103586

Friha, O., Ferrag, M. A., Shu, L., Maglaras, L., & Wang, X. (2021). Internet of Things for the Future of Smart Agriculture: A Comprehensive Survey of Emerging Technologies. *IEEE/CAA Journal of Automatica Sinica, 8*(4), 718–752. doi:10.1109/JAS.2021.1003925

Fuller, A., Fan, Z., Day, C., & Barlow, C. (2020). Digital Twin: Enabling Technologies, Challenges, and Open Research. *IEEE Access: Practical Innovations, Open Solutions*, *8*, 108952–108971. doi:10.1109/ACCESS.2020.2998358

Galang, M., Wicaksono, S., Suryani, E., & Hendrawan, R. A. (2022). Increasing productivity of rice plants based on IoT (Internet Of Things) to realize Smart Agriculture using System Thinking approach. *Procedia Computer Science*, *197*, 607–616. doi:10.1016/j.procs.2021.12.179

Ganguli, R., & Adhikari, S. (2020). The digital twin of discrete dynamic systems: Initial approaches and future challenges. *Applied Mathematical Modelling, 77*(2), 1110-1128. https://doi.org/ doi:10.1016/j.apm.2019.09.036

Garengo, P., Biazzo, S., & Bititci, U. S. (2005). Performance measurement systems in SMEs: A review for a research agenda. *International Journal of Management Reviews*, 7(1), 25–47.

Gaur, A., Scotney, B., Parr, G., & McClean, S. (2015). Smart city architecture and its applications based on IoT. *Procedia Computer Science*, 52, 1089–1094. doi:10.1016/j.procs.2015.05.122

Gelfert, A. (2018). Fake news: A definition. *Informal Logic*, 38(1), 84–117. doi:10.22329/il.v38i1.5068

Georgescu, M., & Popescul, D. (2016). The Importance of Internet of Things Security for Smart Cities. In Smart Cities Technologies (pp. 3-18). InTech. doi:10.5772/65206

Geothermal. (2021, January 1). *Using the Earth to save the Earth*. Retrieved June 27, 2022, from Geothermal: https://geothermal.org/

Gerald, Spindler. (2019). *Copyright Law and Artificial Intelligence*. IIC - International Review of Intellectual Property and Competition Law. . doi:10.1007/s40319-019-00879-w

Ghafoor, A., & Munir, A. (2015). Design and economics analysis of an off-grid PV system for household electrification. *Renewable & Sustainable Energy Reviews*, 42, 496–502. doi:10.1016/j.rser.2014.10.012

Ghasemi, F., Mehridehnavi, A., Pérez-Garrido, A., & Pérez-Sánchez, H. (2018, October). Neural network and deep-learning algorithms used in QSAR studies: Merits and drawbacks. *Drug Discovery Today*, 23(10), 1784–1790. doi:10.1016/j.drudis.2018.06.016 PMID:29936244

Gholamalinezhad, H., & Khosravi, H. (2020). *Pooling methods in deep neural networks, a review*. arXiv preprint arXiv:2009.07485.

Ghosh, A. K., Ullah, A. S., & Kubo, A. (2019). Hidden Markov model-based digital twin construction for futuristic manufacturing systems. *Artificial Intelligence for Engineering Design, Analysis and Manufacturing*, 33(3), 317–331. doi:10.1017/S089006041900012X

Ghosh, A. K., Ullah, A. S., Teti, R., & Kubo, A. (2021). Developing sensor signal-based digital twins for intelligent machine tools. *Journal of Industrial Information Integration*, 24, 100242. doi:10.1016/j.jii.2021.100242

Giffinger, R., Fertner, C., Kramar, H., Meijers, E., & Pichler-Milanović, N. (2007). *Ranking of European medium-sized cities*. Final Report. www.researchgate.net/publication/261367640_Smart_cities_-_Ranking_of_European_medium-sized_cities

Giffinger, R., Haindlmaier, G., & Strohmayer, F. (2014). *Typology of cities, Planning for Energy Efficient Cities*. https://publik.tuwien.ac.at/files/PubDat_240139.pdf

Giffinger, R., & Kramar, H. (2021). Benchmarking, profiling, and ranking of cities: The "European smart cities" approach. In *Performance Metrics for Sustainable Cities* (pp. 35–52). Routledge. doi:10.4324/9781003096566-4

Gilda, S. (2017). Evaluating Machine Learning Algorithms for Fake News Detection. *IEEE 15th Student Conference on Research and Development (SCOReD)*.

Gil-Garcia, J. R., Pardo, T. A., & Nam, T. (2015). What makes a city smart? Identifying core components and proposing an integrative and comprehensive conceptualization. *Information Polity*, 20(1), 61–87. doi:10.3233/IP-150354

Gilmer, Adams, Goodfellow, Andersen, & Dahl. (2018). *Motivating the rules of the game for adversarial example research*. arXiv preprint arXiv:1807.06732.

GilP. (2019). Available at: https://www.lifewire.com/what-exactly-is-twitter-2483331

Girletti, L., Groshev, M., Guimarães, C., Bernardos, C. J., & de la Oliva, A. (2020, December). An intelligent edge-based digital twin for robotics. In *2020 IEEE Globecom Workshops (GC Wkshps)* (pp. 1-6). IEEE. doi:10.1109/GC-Wkshps50303.2020.9367549

Girshick, R. (2014). Rich feature hierarchies for accurate object detection and semantic segmentation. *Proceedings of the IEEE conference on computer vision and pattern recognition*, 580–587. 10.1109/CVPR.2014.81

Girshick, R. (2015). Fast r-cnn. *Proceedings of the IEEE international conference on computer vision*, 1440–1448.

Github. (n.d.a). https://github.com/tensorflow/tensorflow/blob/master/SECURITY.md

Github. (n.d.b). Available: https://github.com/python-security/pyt

Glaessgen, E. H., & Stargel, D. S. (2013, August 25). *The Digital Twin Paradigm for Future NASA and U.S. Air Force Vehicles - NASA Technical Reports Server (NTRS)*. Retrieved September 21, 2022, from https://ntrs.nasa.gov/citations/20120008178

Godoy, A. J. C. (2019). Design and Implementation of Smart Micro-Grid and Its Digital Replica: First Steps. *16th Int. Conf. on Informatics in Control, Automation and Robotics*, 715-721. 10.5220/0007923707150721

Goel, R., & Jain, A. (2020). Improved Detection of Kidney Stone in Ultrasound Images Using Segmentation Techniques. In M. Kolhe, S. Tiwari, M. Trivedi, & K. Mishra (Eds.), *Advances in Data and Information Sciences. Lecture Notes in Networks and Systems* (Vol. 94). Springer. doi:10.1007/978-981-15-0694-9_58

Goffi, G., Cucculelli, M., & Masiero, L. (2019). Fostering tourism destination competitiveness in developing countries: The role of sustainability. *Journal of Cleaner Production*, *209*, 101–115. doi:10.1016/j.jclepro.2018.10.208

Gonzalez Perea, R., Camacho Poyato, E., Montesinos, P., & Rodriguez D'az, J. A. (2019). Optimization of water demand forecasting by artificial intelligence with short data sets. *Biosystems Engineering*, *177*, 59–66. doi:10.1016/j.biosystemseng.2018.03.011

Goodfellow, I., Bengio, Y., & Courville, A. (2016). *Deep learning*. MIT Press.

Gopalakrishnan, K., Chitturi, M. V., & Prentkovskis, O. (2015). Smart and sustainable transport: Short review of the special issue. *Transport*, *30*(3), 243–246. doi:10.3846/16484142.2015.1099407

Gope, J., & Jain, S. K. (2017). A survey on solving cold start problem in recommender systems. *Proceeding - IEEE International Conference on Computing, Communication and Automation, ICCCA 2017*, 133–138. 10.1109/CCAA.2017.8229786

Gordon, J. S., & Pasvenskiene, A. (2021). Pasvenskiene, A. Human rights for robots? A literature review. *AI Ethics*, *1*(4), 579–591. doi:10.100743681-021-00050-7

Gosavi, J. V. (2017). Electrical conductivity and pH of the substrate solution in gerbera cultivars under fertigation. *Horticultura Brasileira*, *31*(3), 356–360. https://www.ijraset.com/fileserve.php?FID=8625

Gothai, E. (2020). Weed Identification using Convolutional Neural Network and Convolutional Neural Network Architectures. In *2020 Fourth International Conference on Computing Methodologies and Communication (ICCMC)*. IEEE. 10.1109/ICCMC48092.2020.ICCMC-000178

Granacher, J., Nguyen, T.-V., Castro-Amoedo, R., & Maréchal, F. (2022). Overcoming decision paralysis—A digital twin for decision making in energy system design. *Applied Energy*, *306*, 117954. doi:10.1016/j.apenergy.2021.117954

Grand View Research. (n.d.). https://www.grandviewresearch.com/industry-analysis/digital-twin-market

Granik & Mesyura. (2017). Fake News Detection Using Naive Bayes Classifier. *IEEE First Ukraine Conference on Electrical and Computer Engineering (UKRCON).*(Das et al., 2021)

Gretzel, U. (2011). Intelligent systems in tourism: A Social Science Perspective. *Annals of Tourism Research, 38*(3), 757–779. doi:10.1016/j.annals.2011.04.014

Gries, T., & Naudé, W. (2022). Modelling artificial intelligence in economics. *Journal for Labour Market Research, 56*(1), 12. doi:10.118612651-022-00319-2

Grieves, M. (2015). *Digital Twin: Manufacturing Excellence through Virtual Factory Replication.* Research Gate.

Griffiths, D. J., & Schroeter, D. F. (2018). *Introduction to quantum mechanics.* Cambridge University Press. doi:10.1017/9781316995433

Grover, L. K. (1996). A fast quantum mechanical algorithm for database search. *Proc. STOC*, 212–219. 10.1145/237814.237866

Gubbi, J., Buyya, R., Marusic, S., & Palaniswami, M. (2013). Internet of Things (IoT): A vision, architectural elements, and future directions. *Future Generation Computer Systems, 29*(7), 1645–1660. doi:10.1016/j.future.2013.01.010

Gugler, J. (2020). *How social media influences sustainable food production.* https://www.austriajuice.com/news-blog/how-social-media-influences-sustainability

Guney, M. (2016). Solar power and application methods. *Renewable & Sustainable Energy Reviews, 57*, 776–785. doi:10.1016/j.rser.2015.12.055

Guo, H., Zhu, Y., Zhang, Y., Ren, Y., Chen, M., & Zhang, R. (2021). A digital twin-based layout optimization method for discrete manufacturing workshop. *International Journal of Advanced Manufacturing Technology, 112*, 1–12. doi:10.100700170-020-06568-0

Guo, J., & Lv, Z. (2022). *Application of Digital Twins in multiple fields.* Multimed Tools Appl. doi:10.100711042-022-12536-5

Guo, J., Zhao, N., Sun, L., & Saipeng, Z. (2019). Modular based flexible digital twin for factory design. *Journal of Ambient Intelligence and Humanized Computing, 10*. Advance online publication. doi:10.100712652-018-0953-6

Guo, Y., Liu, Y., Oerlemans, A., Lao, S., Wu, S., & Lew, M. S. (2016). Deep learning for visual understanding: A review. *Neurocomputing, 187*, 27–48. doi:10.1016/j.neucom.2015.09.116

Gupta, S., & Degbelo, A. (2022). *An Empirical Analysis of AI Contributions to Sustainable Cities (SDG11).* arXiv preprint arXiv:2202.02879.

Gupta, B., Madan, G., & Md, A. (2022). A smart agriculture framework for IoT-based plant decay detection using a smart croft algorithm. *Materials Today: Proceedings, 62*, 4758–4763. doi:10.1016/j.matpr.2022.03.314

Gupta, & Kaushal. (2015). Improving Spam Detection in Online Social Networks. *International Conference on Cognitive Computing and Information Processing(CCIP).*

Gupta, S., Langhans, S. D., Domisch, S., Fuso-Nerini, F., Felländer, A., Battaglini, M., Tegmark, M., & Vinuesa, R. (2021). Assessing whether artificial intelligence is an enabler or an inhibitor of sustainability at indicator level. *Transportation Engineering, 4*, 100064. doi:10.1016/j.treng.2021.100064

Gu, T., Pung, H. K., & Zhang, D. Q. (2005). A service-oriented middleware for building context-aware services. *Journal of Network and Computer Applications, 28*(1), 1–18. doi:10.1016/j.jnca.2004.06.002

Hagendorff, T. (2020). The Ethics of AI Ethics: An Evaluation of Guidelines. *Minds and Machines, 30*(1), 99–120. doi:10.100711023-020-09517-8

Hal. (1967, January). The WEKA data mining software: An update. *IEEE Transactions on Information Theory, IT-13*(1), 21–27.

Hamilton, I., Kennard, H. A., Höglund-Isaksso, L., Kiesewetter, G., Lott, M., & Watts, N. (2021). The public health implications of the Paris Agreement: A modelling study. *The Lancet. Planetary Health, 5*(2), e74–e83. doi:10.1016/S2542-5196(20)30249-7 PMID:33581069

Hansson, S. O., Belin, M. Å., & Lundgren, B. (2021). Self-Driving Vehicles—An Ethical Overview. *Philosophy & Technology, 34*(4), 1383–1408. doi:10.100713347-021-00464-5

Han, T. S., Sasaki, S., Yano, K., Ikebukuro, K., Kitayama, A., Nagamune, T., & Karube, I. (2002). Flow injection microbial trichloroethylene sensor. *Talanta, 57*(2), 271–276. doi:10.1016/S0039-9140(02)00027-9 PMID:18968627

Haponik, A. (2020, October 16). *Addepto*. Retrieved July 20, 2022, from https://addepto.com/blog/digital-twin-computer-vision-use-case/

Hardcastle, T. L. (2019). *Field Agent-the iPhone app that pays you: Unlocking the door behind attracting, retaining, and bringing back past agents*. Academic Press.

Hardy, S., Henecka, W., Ivey-Law, H., Nock, R., Patrini, G., Smith, G., & Thorne, B. (2017). *Private federated learning on vertically partitioned data via entity resolution and additively homomorphic encryption*. https://arxiv.org/abs/1711.10677

Harikrishnan, V. K., Vijarania, M., & Gambhir, A. (2020). Diabetic retinopathy identification using autoML. *Computational Intelligence and Its Applications in Healthcare*, 175.

Harrison, C., & Donnelly, I. A. (2011). A Theory of Smart Cities. *Proceedings of the 55th Annual Meeting of the ISSS, 55*(1). Retrieved from https://journals.isss.org/index.php/proceedings55th/article/view/1703

Harrow, A. W., Hassidim, A., & Lloyd, S. (2009). Quantum algorithm for linear systems of equations. *Physical Review Letters, 103*(15), 150502. doi:10.1103/PhysRevLett.103.150502 PMID:19905613

Hartatik, P., Purbayu, A., & Triyono, L. (2018). Dijkstra methode for optimalize recommendation system of garbage transportation time in Surakarta city. *IOP Conference Series. Materials Science and Engineering, 333*(1), 012106. Advance online publication. doi:10.1088/1757-899X/333/1/012106

Hartmann, D., & Van der Auweraer, H. (2021). Digital twins. Progress in Industrial Mathematics: Success Stories. Springer.

Hashimoto, Y., Murase, H., Morimoto, T., & Torii, T. (2001). Intelligent systems for agriculture in Japan. (2001). *IEEE Control Systems, 21*(5), 71–85. doi:10.1109/37.954520

Hassan, R., Scholes, R., & Ash, N. (2005). Ecosystems and human well-being: current state and trends. Academic Press.

Hassanalian, M., & Abdelkefi, A. (2017). Classifications, applications, and design challenges of drones: A review. *Progress in Aerospace Sciences, 91*, 99–131. doi:10.1016/j.paerosci.2017.04.003

Haupt, S. E., Cowie, J., Linden, S., McCandless, T., Kosovic, B., & Alessandrini, S. (2018). Machine Learning for Applied Weather Prediction. *2018 IEEE 14th International Conference on e-Science (e-Science)*, 276-277. 10.1109/eScience.2018.00047

Hawi, R. O., Alkhodary, D., & Hashem, T. (2015). Managerial Competencies and Organizations Performance. *Research Academy of Social Sciences, 5*(11), 723–735.

Hazem. (2022, Jan. 6). *What Is A Digital Twin? How Is It Useful In The Retail Industry?* https://thinkpalm.com/blogs/what-is-a-digital-twin-how-is-it-useful-in-the-retail-industry/

He, K., Zhang, X., Ren, S., & Sun, J. (2015). *Deep residual learning for image recognition.* https://arxiv.org/abs/1512.03385

Hecht, S. B. (2005). Soybeans, development and conservation on the Amazon frontier. *Development and Change, 36*(2), 375–404. doi:10.1111/j.0012-155X.2005.00415.x

He, K. (2016). Deep residual learning for image recognition. *Proceedings of the IEEE conference on computer vision and pattern recognition,* 770–778.

He, K. (2017). Mask r-cnn. *Proceedings of the IEEE international conference on computer vision,* 2961–2969.

Heleba, D. (2013). *Making Social Media Work in Sustainable Agriculture: 7 Lessons Learned.* Women's Agricultural Network Blog. Available at: https://blog.uvm.edu/wagn/2013/12/11/making-social-media-work-in-sustainable-agriculture-7-lessons-learned/

Helmstetter, & Paulheim. (2018). Weakly Supervised Learning for Fake News Detection on Twitter. *IEEE/ACM International Conference on Advances in Social Networks Analysis and Mining (ASONAM).*

Herwig, Pörtner, & Möller. (2021). *Digital Twins: Applications to the Design and Optimization of Bioprocesses.* Springer Nature.

Herzog, D., Massoud, H., & Wörndl, W. (2017). Routeme: A mobile recommender system for personalized, multi-modal route planning. *UMAP 2017 - Proceedings of the 25th Conference on User Modeling, Adaptation and Personalization,* 67–75. 10.1145/3079628.3079680

Hidary, J. D. (2019). *Quantum Computing: An Applied Approach.* Springer. doi:10.1007/978-3-030-23922-0

Hinton, G., Deng, L., Yu, D., Dahl, G., Mohamed, A., Jaitly, N., Senior, A., Vanhoucke, V., Nguyen, P., Sainath, T., & Kingsbury, B. (2012). Deep neural networks for acoustic modeling in speech recognition: The shared views of four research groups. *IEEE Signal Processing Magazine, 29*(6), 82–97. doi:10.1109/MSP.2012.2205597

Hiskens, I. (2011). Dynamics of type-3 wind turbine generator models. *IEEE Transactions on Power Systems, 27*(1), 465–474. doi:10.1109/TPWRS.2011.2161347

Hoang, D. A., Tung, T. T., Nguyen, C. M., & Nguyen, K. P. (2019). Rotating Sensor for Multi-Direction Light Intensity Measurement. *International Conference on System Science and Engineering (ICSSE),* 462-467. 10.1109/ICSSE.2019.8823447

Hofmann, W., & Branding, F. (2019). Implementation of an IoT-and cloud-based digital twin for real-time decision support in port operations. *IFAC-PapersOnLine, 52*(13), 2104–2109. doi:10.1016/j.ifacol.2019.11.516

Hossain, M. S., Al-Hamadani, S. M., & Rahman, M. T. (2015). E-waste: A challenge for sustainable development. *Journal of Health & Pollution, 5*(9), 3–11. doi:10.5696/2156-9614-5-9.3 PMID:30524771

Hosseini, S., & Barker, K. (2016). A Bayesian network model for resilience-based supplier selection. *International Journal of Production Economics, 180,* 68–87.

Hosseinzadeh Aghdam, M. (2019). Context-aware recommender systems using hierarchical hidden Markov model. *Physica A, 518,* 89–98. doi:10.1016/j.physa.2018.11.037

Houck, A. A., Türeci, H. E., & Koch, J. (2012). On-chip quantum simulation with superconducting circuits. *Nature Physics, 8*(4), 292–299. doi:10.1038/nphys2251

Howard, A. G., Zhu, M., Chen, B., Kalenichenko, D., Wang, W., Weyand, T., Andreetto, M., & Adam, H. (2017). *MobileNets: Efficient Convolutional Neural Networks for Mobile Vision Applications.* https://arxiv.org/abs/1704.04861

Howard. (2022, January 21). *5 Advantages of Integrating Neural Networks into Your Digital Twins.* Academic Press.

Hribernik, K., Cabri, G., Mandreoli, F., & Mentzas, G. (2021). Autonomous, context-aware, adaptive Digital Twins—State of the art and roadmap. *Computers in Industry, 133,* 103508. doi:10.1016/j.compind.2021.103508

Huang, G. (2017). Densely connected convolutional networks. Proceedings of the IEEE conference on computer vision and pattern recognition, 4700–4708. doi:10.1109/CVPR.2017.243

Huang, G., Liu, Z., van der Maaten, L., & Weinberger, K. Q. (2016). *Densely connected convolutional networks.* https://arxiv.org/abs/1608.06993

Huang, A., Chao, Y., de la Mora Velasco, E., Bilgihan, A., & Wei, W. (2021). *When artificial intelligence meets the hospitality and tourism industry: An assessment framework to inform theory and management.* J Hosp Tour Insights.

Huang, W., Song, G., Hong, H., & Xie, K. (2014). Deep architecture for traffic flow prediction: Deep belief networks with multitask learning. *IEEE Transactions on Intelligent Transportation Systems, 15*(5), 2191–2201. doi:10.1109/TITS.2014.2311123

Huang, Y. C., Backman, K. F., Backman, S. J., & Chang, L. L. (2016). Exploring the implications of virtual reality technology in tourism marketing: An integrated research framework. *International Journal of Tourism Research, 18*(2), 116–128. doi:10.1002/jtr.2038

Huang, Z., Shan, G., Cheng, J., & Sun, J. (2019). TRec: An efficient recommendation system for hunting passengers with deep neural networks. *Neural Computing & Applications, 31*(S1), 209–222. doi:10.100700521-018-3728-2

Hubel, D. H., & Wiesel, T. N. (1968). Receptive fields and functional architecture of monkey striate cortex. *The Journal of Physiology, 195*(1), 215–243. doi:10.1113/jphysiol.1968.sp008455 PMID:4966457

Huddlestone-Holmes, C., & Hayward, J. (2011). *The potential of geothermal energy.* CSIRO.

Huesemann, M. H. (2006). Can advances in science and technology prevent global warming? *Mitigation and Adaptation Strategies for Global Change, 11*(3), 539–577. doi:10.100711027-006-2166-0

Huitzil, I., Alegre, F., & Bobillo, F. (2020). GimmeHop: A recommender system for mobile devices using ontology reasoners and fuzzy logic. *Fuzzy Sets and Systems, 401,* 55–77. doi:10.1016/j.fss.2019.12.001

Hu, J., Shen, L., & Sun, G. (2018). Squeeze-and-excitation networks. *Proceedings of the IEEE conference on computer vision and pattern recognition,* 7132–7141.

Hussain, M. W., Reddy, K. H. K., Rodrigues, J. J., & Roy, D. S. (2020). An indirect controller-legacy switch forwarding scheme for link discovery in hybrid SDN. *IEEE Systems Journal, 15*(2), 3142–3149. doi:10.1109/JSYST.2020.3011902

Hussain, M. W., Reddy, K. H. K., & Roy, D. S. (2019). Resource aware execution of speculated tasks in Hadoop with SDN. *Int J Adv Sci Technol, 28*(13), 72–84.

Huval, B., Wang, T., Tandon, S., Kiske, J., Song, W., Pazhayampallil, J., . . . Ng, A. Y. (2015). *An empirical evaluation of deep learning on highway driving.* arXiv preprint arXiv:1504.01716.

Hwangbo, H., Kim, Y. S., & Cha, K. J. (2018). Recommendation system development for fashion retail e-commerce. *Electronic Commerce Research and Applications, 28,* 94–101. doi:10.1016/j.elerap.2018.01.012

Ibănescu, B.-C., Stoleriu, O. M., Munteanu, A., & Iațu, C. (2018). The impact of tourism on sustainable development of rural areas: Evidence from Romania. *Sustainability, 10*(10), 3529. doi:10.3390u10103529

Ibrahim, M. S., Fan, J., Yung, W. K. C., Prisacaru, A., Driel, W., Fan, X., & Zhang, G. (2020). Machine Learning and Digital Twin Driven Diagnostics and Prognostics of Light-Emitting Diodes. *Laser & Photonics Reviews, 14*(12), 2000254. doi:10.1002/lpor.202000254

IEC. (2006). *IEC61400-25-1: Communications for monitoring and control of wind power plants – Overall description of principles and models.* International Electrotechnical Commission.

Ilankoon, I. M. S. K., Ghorbani, Y., Chong, M. N., Herath, G., Moyo, T., & Petersen, J. (2018). E-waste in the international context–A review of trade flows, regulations, hazards, waste management strategies and technologies for value recovery. *Waste Management (New York, N.Y.), 82*, 258–275. doi:10.1016/j.wasman.2018.10.018 PMID:30509588

India Berry. (2021). *10 ways AI can be used in Smart Cities.* Retrieved November 14, 2021, https://aimagazine.com/top10/10-ways-ai-can-be-used-smart-cities

Iqbal, N. (2019). Investigation of alternate herbicides for effective weed management in glyphosate-tolerant cotton. Archives of Agronomy and Soil Science. doi:10.1080/03650340.2019.1579904

Islam, M. T., Dias, P., & Huda, N. (2021). Young consumers' e-waste awareness, consumption, disposal, and recycling behavior: A case study of university students in Sydney, Australia. *Journal of Cleaner Production, 282*, 124490. doi:10.1016/j.jclepro.2020.124490

Israilidis, J., Odusanya, K., & Mazhar, M. U. (2021). Exploring knowledge management perspectives in smart city research: A review and future research agenda. *International Journal of Information Management, 56*, 101989. doi:10.1016/j.ijinfomgt.2019.07.015

Iwanaga, J., Nishimura, N., Sukegawa, N., & Takano, Y. (2019). Improving collaborative filtering recommendations by estimating user preferences from clickstream data. *Electronic Commerce Research and Applications, 37*, 100877. doi:10.1016/j.elerap.2019.100877

Iyer, A. (2017). *Digital Twin: Possibilities of the new Digital twin technology.* Independently Published.

Jabir, B., & Falih, N. (2022). Deep learning-based decision support system for weeds detection in wheat fields. *Iranian Journal of Electrical and Computer Engineering, 12*(1), 816. doi:10.11591/ijece.v12i1.pp816-825

Jacobs, & Wallach. (2021). Measurement and fairness. *Conference on Fairness, Accountability, and Transparency*, 375–385.

Jagielski, M., Oprea, A., Biggio, B., Liu, C., Nita-rotaru, C., & Li, B. (2018). Manipulating Machine Learning. *Poisoning Attacks and Countermeasures for Regression Learning., 3*, 19–35. Advance online publication. doi:10.1109/SP.2018.00057

Jaihar, J., Lingayat, N., Vijaybhai, P. S., Venkatesh, G., & Upla, K. P. (2020). Smart home automation using machine learning algorithms. In *2020 International Conference for Emerging Technology (INCET)* (pp. 1-4). IEEE. 10.1109/INCET49848.2020.9154007

Jain & Kasbe. (2018). Fake News Detection. *IEEE International Students' Conference on Electrical, Electronics and Computer Sciences.*

James, L. (2021). Digital twins will revolutionise healthcare: Digital twin technology has the potential to transform healthcare in a variety of ways–improving the diagnosis and treatment of patients, streamlining preventative care and facilitating new approaches for hospital planning. *Engineering & Technology, 16*(2), 50–53. doi:10.1049/et.2021.0210

Jayaraman, PYavari, AGeorgakopoulous, DMorshed, AZaslavsky, A. (2016). Internet of Things Platform for Smart Farming: Experiences and Lessons Learned. *Sensors (Basel)*, *16*(11), 1–17.

Jeong, H. Y., Park, K. M., Lee, M. J., Yang, D. H., Kim, S. H., & Lee, S. Y. (2017). Vitamin D and hypertension. *Electrolyte & Blood Pressure*, *15*(1), 1–11. doi:10.5049/EBP.2017.15.1.1 PMID:29042901

Jiang, L., Cheng, Y., Yang, L., Li, J., Yan, H., & Wang, X. (2019). A trust-based collaborative filtering algorithm for E-commerce recommendation system. *Journal of Ambient Intelligence and Humanized Computing*, *10*(8), 3023–3034. doi:10.100712652-018-0928-7

Jiang, L., & O'Neill, B. C. (2004). The energy transition in rural China. *International Journal of Global Energy Issues*, *21*(1-2), 2–26. doi:10.1504/IJGEI.2004.004691

Ji, Z., Pi, H., Wei, W., Xiong, B., Wozniak, M., & Damasevicius, R. (2019). Recommendation Based on Review Texts and Social Communities: A Hybrid Model. *IEEE Access: Practical Innovations, Open Solutions*, *7*, 40416–40427. doi:10.1109/ACCESS.2019.2897586

Jo, Jo, Kim, Kim, & Han. (2020). Development of an IoT-Based Indoor Air Quality Monitoring Platform. *Journal of Sensors*. . doi:10.1155/2020/8749764

Jo, J. H., Jo, B., Kim, J. H., & Choi, I. (2020). Implementation of IoT-Based Air Quality Monitoring System for Investigating Particulate Matter (PM10) in Subway Tunnels. *International Journal of Environmental Research and Public Health*, *17*(15), 5429. doi:10.3390/ijerph17155429 PMID:32731501

Jönsson, C. (2015). Leakage, economic tourism. Encyclopedia of tourism, 1-2. Springer.

Joshi, N. (2020). *Exploring the limits of transfer learning.* https://www.bbntimes.com/technology/exploring-the-limits-of-transfer-learning

Kabeel, A., Abdelgaied, M., & Mahgoub, M. (2016). The performance of a modified solar still using hot air injection and PCM. *Desalination*, *379*, 102–107. doi:10.1016/j.desal.2015.11.007

Kahhat, R., Kim, J., Xu, M., Allenby, B., Williams, E., & Zhang, P. (2008). Exploring e-waste management systems in the United States. *Resources, Conservation and Recycling*, *52*(7), 955–964. doi:10.1016/j.resconrec.2008.03.002

Kalyanraj, D., Prakash, S. L., & Sabareswar, S. (2016). *Wind turbine monitoring and control systems using Internet of Things. In 21st Century Energy Needs Materials.* Systems and Applications.

Kamienski, J., Soininen, M., Taumberger, S., Fernandes, A., Toscano, T. S., Cinotti, R., Maia, F., & Neto, A. (2018). Swamp: an iot-based smart water management platform for precision irrigation in agriculture. In *2018 Global Internet of Things Summit (GIoTS),* (pp. 1-6). MDPI.

Kanamori, Y., Yoo, S. M., Pan, W. D., & Sheldon, F. T. (2006). A short survey on quantum computers. *International Journal of Computers and Applications*, *28*(3), 227–233. doi:10.1080/1206212X.2006.11441807

Kang, Y., Kim, K., Cho, B., Kwak, Y., & Kim, J. (2020). Highly Sensitive Detection of Benzene, Toluene, and Xylene Based on CoPP-Functionalized TiO2 Nanoparticles with Low Power Consumption. *ACS Sensors*, *5*(3), 754–763. doi:10.1021/acssensors.9b02310 PMID:32048833

Kannegiesser, M., & Günther, H. O. (2014). Sustainable development of global supply chains-part 1: Sustainability optimization framework. *Flexible Services and Manufacturing Journal*, *26*(1), 24–47. doi:10.100710696-013-9176-5

Kanschat, R., Gupta, S., & Degbelo, A. (2022). Wireless-Signal-Based Vehicle Counting and Classification in Different Road Environments. *IEEE Open Journal of Intelligent Transportation Systems*, *3*, 236–250. doi:10.1109/OJITS.2022.3160934

Kantaros, A., Piromalis, D., Tsaramirsis, G., Papageorgas, P., & Tamimi, H. (2022). 3D Printing and Implementation of Digital Twins: Current Trends and Limitations. *Applied System Innovation, 5*(1), 7. doi:10.3390/asi5010007

Kaplan, A., & Haenlein, M. (2019). Siri, Siri, in my hand: Who's the fairest in the land? On the interpretations, illustrations, and implications of artificial intelligence. *Business Horizons, 62*(1), 15–25. doi:10.1016/j.bushor.2018.08.004

Karimi, H., Roy, P., Saba-Sadiya, S., & Tang, J. (2018). Multi-source multi-class fake news detection. *Proceedings of the 27th International Conference on Computational Linguistics*, 1546-1557.

Karpathy, A. (2014). Large-scale video classification with convolutional neural networks. *Proceedings of the IEEE conference on Computer Vision and Pattern Recognition*, 1725–1732. 10.1109/CVPR.2014.223

Karvonen, A., Cugurullo, F., & Caprotti, F. (2018). Introduction: Situating smart cities. In Inside smart cities (pp. 1-12). Routledge.

Katarya, R., & Verma, O. P. (2017). An effective web page recommender system with fuzzy c-mean clustering. *Multimedia Tools and Applications, 76*(20), 21481–21496. doi:10.100711042-016-4078-7

Kaul, D., Raju, H., & Tripathy, B. K. (2022). Deep Learning in Healthcare. In Deep Learning in Data Analytics. Springer. doi:10.1007/978-3-030-75855-4_6

Kaur, R., & Juneja, M. (2018). *Comparison of Different Renal Imaging Modalities: An Overview.* doi:10.1007/978-981-10-3373-5_4

KBV Research. (2021). https://www.kbvresearch.com/digital-twin-market/

Keras Team. (n.d.). *Conv2D layer.* Keras.Io. Retrieved April 19, 2022, from https://keras.io/api/layers/convolution_layers/convolution2d/

Kermany, D. S., Goldbaum, M., Cai, W., Valentim, C. C., Liang, H., Baxter, S. L., McKeown, A., Yang, G., Wu, X., Yan, F., Dong, J., Prasadha, M. K., Pei, J., Ting, M. Y. L., Zhu, J., Li, C., Hewett, S., Dong, J., Ziyar, I., ... Zhang, K. (2018). Identifying medical diagnoses and treatable diseases by image-based deep learning. *Cell, 172*(5), 1122–1131. doi:10.1016/j.cell.2018.02.010 PMID:29474911

Kerremans, M., & Srivastava, T. (2021, July 13). *Market Guide for Technologies Supporting a Digital Twin of an Organization.* Gartner. Retrieved July 21, 2022, from https://www.gartner.com/en/documents/4003512

Kevan. (2020, January 31). *AI Rewrites the Possibilities of Digital Twin.* DE247 Digital Engineering.

Keyfitz, N. (1989). The growing human population. *Scientific American, 261*(3), 118–127. doi:10.1038cientificameric an0989-118 PMID:2772607

Khajavi, S. H., Motlagh, N. H., Jaribion, A., Werner, L. C., & Holmström, J. (2019). Digital twin: Vision, benefits, boundaries, and creation for buildings. *IEEE Access : Practical Innovations, Open Solutions, 7*, 147406–147419.

Khajenasiri, I., Estebsari, A., Verhelst, M., & Gielen, G. (2017). A review on Internet of Things solutions for intelligent energy control in buildings for smart city applications. *Energy Procedia, 111*, 770–779. doi:10.1016/j.egypro.2017.03.239

Khan, K. (2006). How IT governance is changing. *Journal of Corporate Finance, 17*(5), 21–25.

Khan, M. A. H., Rao, M. V., & Li, Q. (2019). Recent Advances in Electrochemical Sensors for Detecting Toxic Gases: NO_2, SO_2 and H_2S. *Sensors (Basel), 19*(4), 905. doi:10.339019040905 PMID:30795591

KhanN.HassanA. U.FahadS.NaushadM. (2020). Factors affecting tourism industry and its impacts on global economy of the world. SSRN. doi:10.2139/ssrn.3559353

Khan, S., Tufail, M., Khan, M. T., Khan, Z. A., & Anwar, S. (2021). Deep learning-based identification system of weeds and crops in strawberry and pea fields for a precision agriculture sprayer. *Precision Agriculture*, *22*(6), 1711–1727. doi:10.100711119-021-09808-9

Khayati, Y., Kang, J. E., Karwan, M., & Murray, C. (2021). Household use of autonomous vehicles with ride sourcing. *Transportation Research Part C: Emerging Technologies, 125*(May), 102998. doi:10.1016/j.trc.2021.102998

Kientopf, K., Raza, S., Lansing, S., & Güneş, M. (2017, October). Service management platform to support service migrations for IoT smart city applications. In *2017 IEEE 28th Annual International Symposium on Personal, Indoor, and Mobile Radio Communications (PIMRC)* (pp. 1-5). IEEE.

Kim, S. H., & Lee, C. M. (n.d.). *Advanced manufacturing systems through explicit and implicit learning.* Working Paper, KAIST Graduate School of Business, Seoul, South Korea.

Kitchin, R., & Dodge, M. (2017). The (in) security of smart cities: Vulnerabilities, risks, mitigation and prevention. *Journal of Urban Technology*, *26*(2), 47–65. doi:10.1080/10630732.2017.1408002

Kodali, R. K., Swamy, G., & Lakshmi, B. (2015). *An implementation of IoT for healthcare. In IEEE Recent Advances in Intelligent Computational Systems.* IEEE.

Kopardekar, P., & Anand, S. (1995). Tolerance allocation using neural networks. *Int. J. of Advanced Manufacturing Techn., 10.*

Korotkov, A., Tkachenko, V., Russo, D. P., & Ekins, S. (2017, December 4). Comparison of Deep Learning With Multiple Machine Learning Methods and Metrics Using Diverse Drug Discovery Data Sets. *Molecular Pharmaceutics*, *14*(12), 4462–4475. doi:10.1021/acs.molpharmaceut.7b00578 PMID:29096442

Kosmatos, E., Tselikas, N., & Boucouvalas, A. (2011). Integrating RFIDs and Smart Ob-jects into a Unified Internet of Things Architecture. *Advances in Internet of Things: Scientific Research*, *1*(01), 5–12. doi:10.4236/ait.2011.11002

Kosta, E. (2022). Algorithmic state surveillance: Challenging the notion of agency in human rights. *Regulation & Governance*, *16*(1), 212–224. doi:10.1111/rego.12331

Krishna, K., Silver, O., Malende, W., Anuradha, K. (2017). Internet of Things application for implementation of smart agriculture system. *Proceedings of the International Conference on IoT in Social, Mobile, Analytics and Cloud, I-SMAC* (pp. 54–59). Semantic Scholar.

Kritzinger, W., Karner, M., Traar, G., Henjes, J., & Sihn, W. (2018). Digital Twin in Manufacturing: A Categorical Literature Review and Classification. IFAC-Papers OnLine, *51*(11), 1016–1022. . doi:10.1016/j.ifacol.2018.08.474

Kritzinger, W., Karner, M., Traar, G., Henjes, J., & Sihn, W. (2018). Digital Twin in manufacturing: A categorical literature review and classification. *IFAC-Papers Online, 51*(11), 1016-1022. https://doi.org/10.1016/j.ifacol.2018.08.474

Krizhevsky, Sutskever, & Hinton. (2012). Imagenet classification with deep convolutional neural networks. *Advances in Neural Information Processing Systems, 25.*

Kruse, T., Pandey, A. K., Alami, R., & Kirsch, A. (2013). Humanaware robot navigation: A survey. *Robotics and Autonomous Systems*, *61*(12), 1726–1743. doi:10.1016/j.robot.2013.05.007

Kumar, K. A. (2020). An Internet of Thing-based Agribot (IOT- Agribot) for Precision Agriculture and Farm Monitoring. *International Journal of Education and Management Engineering*, *10*(4), 33–39. doi:10.5815/ijeme.2020.04.04

Kumar, P., Kumar, V., & Thakur, R. S. (2019). A new approach for rating prediction system using collaborative filtering. *Iran Journal of Computer Science*, *2*(2), 81–87. doi:10.100742044-018-00028-5

Kumar, P., & Thakur, R. S. (2018). Recommendation system techniques and related issues: A survey. *International Journal of Information Technology (Singapore)*, *10*(4), 495–501. doi:10.100741870-018-0138-8

Kumar, R., Yadav, S., Kumar, M., Kumar, J., & Kumar, M. (2020). Artificial Intelligence: New Technology to Improve Indian Agriculture. *International Journal of Chemical Studies*, *8*(2), 2999–3005. doi:10.22271/chemi.2020.v8.i2at.9208

Kumar, S., Bongale, A., Patil, S., Bongale, A. M., Kamat, P., & Kotecha, K. (2020). Demystifying Artificial Intelligence based Digital Twins in Manufacturing-A Bibliometric Analysis of Trends and Techniques. *Libr. Philos. Pract*, *2020*, 1–21.

Kumar, V., Rajan, B., Venkatesan, R., & Lecinski, J. (2019). Understanding the role of artificial intelligence in personalized engagement marketing. *California Management Review*, *61*(4), 135–155. doi:10.1177/0008125619859317

Kunst, R., Avila, L., Binotto, A., Pignaton, E., Bampi, S., & Rochol, J. (2019). Improving devices communication in industry 4.0 wireless networks. *Engineering Applications of Artificial Intelligence*, *83*, 1–12.

Kuo, Y. W., Wen, W. L., Hu, X. F., Shen, Y. T., & Miao, S. Y. (2021). A lora-based multisensor IoT platform for agriculture monitoring and submersible pump control in a water bamboo field. *Processes (Basel, Switzerland)*, *9*(5), 1–17. doi:10.3390/pr9050813

Laamarti, F., Badawi, H., Ding, Y., Arafsha, F., & Hafidh, B. (2020). *An ISO / IEEE 11073 Standardized Digital Twin Framework for Health and Well-being in Smart Cities*. doi:10.1109/ACCESS.2020.2999871

Lai, O. (2022). *Top 7 Smart Cities in the World*. Retrieved August 14, 2022, https://earth.org/top-7-smart-cities-in-the-world/

Lai, X., Yang, T., Wang, Z., & Chen, P. (2019). IoT Implementation of Kalman Filter to Improve Accuracy of Air Quality Monitoring and Prediction. *Applied Sciences (Basel, Switzerland)*, *9*(9), 1831. doi:10.3390/app9091831

Lakshmi, V., & Bahli, B. (2020). Understanding the robotization landscape transformation: A centering resonance analysis. *Journal of Innovation & Knowledge*, *5*(1), 59–67. doi:10.1016/j.jik.2019.01.005

Lavanya, G., Rani, C., & Ganeshkumar, P. (2020). An automated low-cost IoT-based Fertilizer Intimation System for smart agriculture. *Sustainable Computing : Informatics and Systems*, *28*, 1–12.

LeCun, Y., Bottou, L., Bengio, Y., & Haffner, P. (1998). Gradient-based learning applied to document recognition. *Proceedings of the IEEE*, *86*(11), 2278–2324. doi:10.1109/5.726791

Lee, J., Kao, H.-A., & Yang, S. (2014). Service innovation and smart analytics for industry 4.0 and big data environment. *Journal of Theoretical and Applied Information Technology, 95*(1).

Lepers, E., Lambin, E. F., Janetos, A. C., DeFries, R., Achard, F., Ramankutty, N., & Scholes, R. J. (2005). A synthesis of information on rapid land-cover change for the period 1981–2000. *Bioscience*, *55*(2), 115–124. doi:10.1641/0006-3568(2005)055[0115:ASOIOR]2.0.CO;2

Li, L., Aslam, S., Wileman, A., & Perinpanayagam, S. (2022). Digital Twin in Aerospace Industry: A Gentle Introduction. *IEEE Access: Practical Innovations, Open Solutions*, *10*, 9543–9562. doi:10.1109/ACCESS.2021.3136458

Lila, P. C., & Anjaneyulu, M. V. L. R. (2016). Modeling the Impact of ICT on the Activity and Travel Behaviour of Urban Dwellers in Indian Context. *Transportation Research Procedia*, *17*, 418–427. doi:10.1016/j.trpro.2016.11.083

Lim, H. S. M., & Taeihagh, A. (2018). Autonomous vehicles for smart and sustainable cities: An in-depth exploration of privacy and cybersecurity implications. *Energies*, *11*(5), 1062. doi:10.3390/en11051062

Lin, C. H., & Lee, C. S. G. (1991). Neural-network-based fuzzy logic control and decision system. *IEEE Transactions on Computers*, *40*(Dec), 1320–1336.

Lindemann, M. D. (2019). 169 awardee talk-nutrition from a risk management perspective. *Journal of Animal Science, 97*(Supplement_3), 174–175.

Lin, P. (2016). Why Ethics Matters for Autonomous Cars. In M. Maurer, J. Gerdes, B. Lenz, & H. Winner (Eds.), *Autonomous Driving*. Springer. doi:10.1007/978-3-662-48847-8_4

Liu, D., Yang, X., & Jiang, M. (2013, August). A novel classifier based on quantum computation. In *Proceedings of the 51st Annual Meeting of the Association for Computational Linguistics (*Volume 2*: Short Papers) (*pp. 484-488). Academic Press.

Liu, Y., Lyu, C., Liu, Z., & Cao, J. (2021). Exploring a large-scale multi-modal transportation recommendation system. *Transportation Research Part C: Emerging Technologies, 126*(September), 103070. doi:10.1016/j.trc.2021.103070

Liu, G.-C., & Chih-Hsiang, K. (2022). Exploring Multiple Application Scenarios of Visual Communication Course Using Deep Learning Under the Digital Twins. *Computational Intelligence and Neuroscience, 2022*, 5844290. doi:10.1155/2022/5844290 PMID:35211166

Liu, H., Tong, Y., Zhang, P., Lu, X., Duan, J., & Xiong, H. (2019). Hydra: A personalized and context-aware multi-modal transportation recommendation system. *Proceedings of the ACM SIGKDD International Conference on Knowledge Discovery and Data Mining*, 2314–2324. 10.1145/3292500.3330660

Liu, H.-Y., & Zawieska, K. (2020). From responsible robotics towards a human rights regime oriented to the challenges of robotics and artificial intelligence. *Ethics and Information Technology, 22*(4), 321–333. doi:10.100710676-017-9443-3

Liu, J., Abbas, I., & Noor, R. S. (2021). Development of Deep Learning-Based Variable Rate Agrochemical Spraying System for Targeted Weeds Control in Strawberry Crop. *Agronomy (Basel), 11*(8), 1480. doi:10.3390/agronomy11081480

Liu, N., Shapira, P., & Yue, X. (2021). Tracking developments in artificial intelligence research: Constructing and applying a new search strategy. *Scientometrics, 126*(4), 3153–3192. doi:10.100711192-021-03868-4 PMID:34720254

Liu, Y., Yang, C., Jiang, L., Xie, S., & Zhang, Y. (2019). Intelligent edge computing for IoT-based energy management in smart cities. *IEEE Network, 33*(2), 111–117. doi:10.1109/MNET.2019.1800254

Liu, Z., Jiang, A., Zhang, A., Xing, Z., & Du, X. (2021). Intelligent Prediction Method for Operation and Maintenance Safety of Prestressed Steel Structure Based on Digital Twin Technology. *Advances in Civil Engineering, 2021*. Advance online publication. doi:10.1155/2021/6640198

Li, X., Liu, H., Wang, W., Zheng, Y., Lv, H., & Lv, Z. (2022). Big data analysis of the Internet of Things in the digital twins of smart city based on deep learning. *Future Generation Computer Systems, 128*, 167–177. doi:10.1016/j.future.2021.10.006

Li, X., & She, J. (2017). Collaborative variational autoencoder for recommender systems. *Proceedings of the ACM SIGKDD International Conference on Knowledge Discovery and Data Mining, Part F1296*, 305–314. 10.1145/3097983.3098077

Li, Y., Qian, M., Liu, P., Cai, Q., Li, X., Guo, J., Yan, H., Yu, F., Yuan, K., Yu, J., Qin, L., Liu, H., Wu, W., Xiao, P., & Zhou, Z. (2019). The recognition of rice images by UAV based on capsule network. *Cluster Computing, 22*(4), 9515–9524. doi:10.100710586-018-2482-7

Ljubojevic, M., Simic, M., Babic, Z., & Zoric, M. (2016). Quality of life context influence factors improvement using houseplants and Internet of Things. *IEEE International Black Sea Conference on Communications and Networking (BlackSeaCom)*, 1-5. 10.1109/BlackSeaCom.2016.7901574

Lloyd, S., Mohseni, M., & Rebentrost, P. (2013). *Quantum algorithms for supervised and unsupervised machine learning*. arXiv preprint arXiv:1307.0411.

Lloyd, S. (1996). Universal quantum simulators. *Science, 273*(5278), 1073–1078. doi:10.1126cience.273.5278.1073 PMID:8688088

Logesh, R., Subramaniyaswamy, V., Vijayakumar, V., Gao, X. Z., & Indragandhi, V. (2018). A hybrid quantum-induced swarm intelligence clustering for the urban trip recommendation in smart city. *Future Generation Computer Systems, 83*, 653–673. doi:10.1016/j.future.2017.08.060

Lotfi, H., & Khodaei, A. (2016). *Levelized cost of energy calculations for microgrids. In IEEE power and energy society general meeting.* IEEE.

Lu, S., & Braunstein, S. L. (2014). Quantum decision tree classifier. In Quantum Inf Process. Springer. doi:10.100711128-013-0687-5

Lu, C., Zhang, L., Zhong, Y., Ren, W., Tobias, M., Mu, Z., & Xue, B. (2015). An overview of e-waste management in China. *Journal of Material Cycles and Waste Management, 17*(1), 1–12. doi:10.100710163-014-0256-8

Lucero, E., Barends, R., Chen, Y., Kelly, J., Mariantoni, M., Megrant, A., O'Malley, P., Sank, D., Vainsencher, A., Wenner, J., White, T., Yin, Y., Cleland, A. N., & Martinis, J. M. (2012). Computing prime factors with a Josephson phase qubit quantum processor. *Nature Physics, 8*(10), 719–723. doi:10.1038/nphys2385

Lu, J., Tan, L., & Jiang, H. (2021). Review on convolutional neural network (CNN) applied to plant leaf disease classification. *Agriculture, 11*(8), 707. doi:10.3390/agriculture11080707

Lu, S. C-VTcheng, D. KYerramareddy, S. (1991). Integration of simulation. learning and optimization to support engineering design. *CIRP Annals, 40*(1), 143–146.

Lu, S. Y. (1990). Machine learning approaches to knowledge synthesis and integration tasks for advanced engineering automation. *Computers in Industry, 15*, 105–120.

Lutz, W., Sanderson, W. C., & Scherbov, S. (2001). The end of world population growth. *Nature, 412*(6846), 543–545. doi:10.1038/35087589 PMID:11484054

Lv & Xie. (2021). *Artificial intelligence in the digital twins: State of the art, challenges, and future research topics.* https://digitaltwin1.org/articles/1-12

Lv, J., Song, B., Guo, J., Du, X., & Guizani, M. (2019). Interest-Related Item Similarity Model Based on Multimodal Data for Top-N Recommendation. *IEEE Access: Practical Innovations, Open Solutions, 7*(c), 12809–12821. doi:10.1109/ACCESS.2019.2893355

Lv, Y., Duan, Y., Kang, W., Li, Z., & Wang, F. Y. (2014). Traffic flow prediction with big data: A deep learning approach. *IEEE Transactions on Intelligent Transportation Systems, 16*(2), 865–873. doi:10.1109/TITS.2014.2345663

Madakam, S., & Lake, V. (2015). Internet of Things (IoT): A literature review. *Journal of Computer and Communications, 3*(5), 164–173. doi:10.4236/jcc.2015.35021

Mahmudul Hasan, A. S. M. (2021). A survey of deep learning techniques for weed detection from images. *Computers and Electronics in Agriculture, 184*, 106067. doi:10.1016/j.compag.2021.106067

Maia, R. & Tran, A. (2017). Precision agriculture employing remote monitoring systems in Brazil. *IEEE Global Humanitarian Technology Conference, Proceedings,* (pp. 1-6). IEEE.

Makanapura, N. (2022). Classification of plant seedlings using deep convolutional neural network architectures. Journal of Physics: Conference Series, 2161. doi:10.1088/1742-6596/2161/1/012006

Manallack, D., & Livingstone, D. (1999). Neural networks in drug discovery: Have they lived up to their promise? *European Journal of Medicinal Chemistry*, *34*(3), 195–208. doi:10.1016/S0223-5234(99)80052-X

Mangayarkarasi, T., & Jamal, D. N. (2017). PNN-based analysis system to classify renal pathologies in Kidney Ultrasound Images. *2017 2nd International Conference on Computing and Communications Technologies (ICCCT)*, 123-126. 10.1109/ICCCT2.2017.7972258

Marai, O. E., Taleb, T., & Song, J. (2021). Roads Infrastructure Digital Twin: A Step Toward Smarter Cities Realization. *IEEE Network*, *35*(2), 136–143. doi:10.1109/MNET.011.2000398

Marcoux, A. (1999). *Population and environmental change: from linkages to policy issues*. Academic Press.

Marghny, M. H., ElAziz, R. M. A., & Taloba, A. I. (2015). *Differential search algorithm-based parametric optimization of fuzzy generalized eigenvalue proximal support vector machine*. arXiv preprint arXiv:1501.00728.

Marr, B. (2017). What is digital twin technology-and why is it so important? *Forbes*, *6*(March), 2017.

Martin, C. J., Evans, J., & Karvonen, A. (2018). Smart and sustainable? Five tensions in the visions and practices of the smart-sustainable city in Europe and North America. *Technological Forecasting and Social Change*, *133*, 269–278. doi:10.1016/j.techfore.2018.01.005

Martinez, W. L., Martinez, A. R., & Solka, J. L. (2017). *Exploratory data analysis with MATLAB*. Chapman and Hall/CRC.

Maschler, Braun, Jazdi, & Weyrich. (2021). Transfer learning as an enabler of the intelligent digital twin. *Procedia CIRP, 100*, 127-132.

Maschler, B., Braun, D., Jazdi, N., & Weyrich, M. (2021). Transfer learning as an enabler of the intelligent digital twin. *Procedia CIRP*, *100*, 127–132. doi:10.1016/j.procir.2021.05.020

MathWorks. (2022, January 1). *ThingSpeak for IoT Projects*. Retrieved June 27, 2022, from ThingSpeak: https://thingspeak.com/

Matson, J. (2012, August 13). Quantum teleportation achieved over record distances. *Nature*. https://www.nature.com/articles/nature.2012.11163

Matsubara, T. (2020). *Incorporating AI & IoT into Power-Generating Facilities: Status of Development and Challenges*. Academic Press.

Mavridis, N. (2015). A review of verbal and non-verbal human–robot interactive communication. *Robotics and Autonomous Systems*, *63*, 22–35. doi:10.1016/j.robot.2014.09.031

McAfee, R. P. (2011). The design of advertising exchanges. *Review of Industrial Organization*, *39*(3), 169–185. doi:10.100711151-011-9300-1

McCallum, & Nigam. (1998). A comparison of event models for naive Bayes text classification. *AAAI-98 Workshop on Learning for Text Categorization*.

McCarthy, J. (2006). A Proposal for the Dartmouth Summer Research Project on Artificial Intelligence. *AI Magazine*, *27*(4), 12–14. doi:10.1609/aimag.v27i4.1904

Mehra, M., Saxena, S., Sankaranarayanan, S., Tom, R. J., & Veeramanikandan, M. (2018). IoT based hydroponics system using Deep Neural Networks. *Computers and Electronics in Agriculture, 155*, 473–486. . doi:10.1016/j.compag.2018.10.015

Meijer, A., & Thaens, M. (2018). Quantified street: Smart governance of urban safety. *Information Polity*, *23*(1), 29–41. doi:10.3233/IP-170422

Meyerson, F. A. (1998). Population, carbon emissions, and global warming: The forgotten relationship at Kyoto. *Population and Development Review*, *24*(1), 115–130. doi:10.2307/2808124

Miller, L. F. (2015). Granting automata human rights: Challenge to a basis of full-rights privilege. *Human Rights Review (Piscataway, N.J.)*, *16*(4), 369–391. doi:10.100712142-015-0387-x

Miranda, L., Viterbo, J., & Miranda, L. (2020). Association for Information Systems AIS Electronic Library (AISeL) Towards the Use of Clustering Algorithms in Recommender Systems Towards the Use of Clustering Algorithms in Recommender Systems. *Association for Information Systems AIS*, 0–10.

Misra, S., Goswami, R., Khawas, T., & Basu, D. (2015). Application of Social Network Analysis for Studying Agricultural Knowledge and Information System: A Case Study in Kalimpong-I Block of West Bengal. Sustainable Agriculture for Food Security and Better Environment At: BCKV, Nadia, West Bengal, India.

Mkrttchian, V., & Voronin, V. (2021). Digitalization of Lifecycle Management of Domestic Russian Tour Products Based on Problem-oriented Digital Twins-Avatars, Supply Chain, 3D-Hybrid, Federated, and Coordinated Blockchain. [IJDS-GBT]. *International Journal of Digital Strategy, Governance, and Business Transformation*, *11*(1), 1–13. doi:10.4018/IJDSGBT.20210101.oa2

Mks, S. (2005). Simplified algorithm to determine break point realys & relay coordination based on network topology. *2005 IEEE International Symposium on Circuits and Systems (ISCAS)*, 772-775. 10.1109/ISCAS.2005.1464702

Mohapatra, H., & Rath, A. K. (2022). IoE-based framework for smart agriculture. *Journal of Ambient Intelligence and Humanized Computing*, *13*(1), 407–424. doi:10.100712652-021-02908-4

Mohri, M., Rostamizadeh, A., & Talwalkar, A. (2018). *Foundations of machine learning*. MIT Press.

Molnár, M., & Vokony, I. (2019). The Cyber-Physical Security of the Power Grid. *2015 International Conference on Computational Intelligence and Communication Networks (CICN)*, 832-838. 10.1109/CICN.2015.169

Mona, Y., Do, T., Sekine, C., Suttakul, P., & Chaichana, C. (2022). Geothermal electricity generator using thermoelectric module for IoT monitoring. *Energy Reports*, *8*, 347–352. doi:10.1016/j.egyr.2022.02.114

Monti, F., Frasca, F., Eynard, D., Mannion, D., & Bronstein, M. M. (2019). *Fake news detection on social media using geometric deep learning*. arXiv preprint arXiv:1902.06673.

Moon, Y. K., Jeong, S.-Y., Jo, Y.-M., Jo, Y. K., Kang, Y. C., & Lee, J.-H. (2021). Highly Selective Detection of Benzene and Discrimination of Volatile Aromatic Compounds Using Oxide Chemiresistors with Tunable $Rh-TiO_2$ Catalytic Overlayers. *Advancement of Science*, *8*(6), 2004078. doi:10.1002/advs.202004078 PMID:33747750

Motlagh, N. H., Mohammadrezaei, M., Hunt, J., & Zakeri, B. (2020). Internet of Things (IoT) and the energy sector. *Energies*, *13*(2).

Moya, T. A., van den Dobbelsteen, A., Ottelé, M., & Bluyssen, P. M. (2019). A review of green systems within the indoor environment. *Indoor and Built Environment*, *28*(3), 298–309. doi:10.1177/1420326X18783042

Mujumdar & Vaidehi. (2019). Diabetes Prediction using Machine Learning Algorithms. *Procedia Computer Science*, *165*, 292-299. doi:10.1016/j.procs.2020.01.047

Musti, K. S. S. (2020). Quantification of Demand Response in Smart Grids. *IEEE Int. Conf. INDISCON*, 278-282. 10.1109/INDISCON50162.2020.00063

Musti, K. S., & Kapali, D. (2021). Digital Transformation of SMEs in the Energy Sector to Survive in a Post-COVID-19 Era. In N. Baporikar (Ed.), *Handbook of Research on Strategies and Interventions to Mitigate COVID-19 Impact on SMEs* (pp. 186–207). IGI Global. doi:10.4018/978-1-7998-7436-2.ch009

Myers, N. (1999). Environmental scientists: Advocates as well. *Environmental Conservation, 26*(3), 163–165. doi:10.1017/S0376892999000235

Mylonas, G., Kalogeras, A., Kalogeras, G., Anagnostopoulos, C., Alexakos, C., & Muñoz, L. (2021). Digital Twins From Smart Manufacturing to Smart Cities: A Survey. *IEEE Access: Practical Innovations, Open Solutions, 9*, 143222–143249. doi:10.1109/ACCESS.2021.3120843

MySQL. (2022). https://www.mysql.com

Nagaraja, G. S., A.B., S., Soumya, T., & Abhinith, A. (2019). IOT-based smart agriculture management system. *4th International Conference on Computational Systems and Information Technology for Sustainable Solution (CSITSS)*, 1–5.

Nahiduzzaman, K. M., Holland, M. E., Sikder, S., Shaw, P., Hewage, K., & Sadiq, R. (2021). Urban Transformation Toward a Smart City: An E-Commerce–Induced Path-Dependent Analysis. *Journal of Urban Planning and Development, 147*(1), 04020060. doi:10.1061/(ASCE)UP.1943-5444.0000648

Nakamura, H., Gao, Y., Gao, H., Zhang, H., Kiyohiro, A., & Mine, T. (2014). Toward personalized public transportation recommendation system with adaptive user interface. *Proceedings - 2014 IIAI 3rd International Conference on Advanced Applied Informatics, IIAI-AAI 2014*, 103–108. 10.1109/IIAI-AAI.2014.31

Nakicenovic, N., Alcamo, J., Davis, G., Vries, B. D., Fenhann, J., Gaffin, S., ... Zhou, D. (2000). *Special report on emissions scenarios*. Academic Press.

Namberger, P., Jackisch, S., Schmude, J., & Karl, M. (2019). Overcrowding, Overtourism and Local Level Disturbance: How Much Can Munich Handle? *Tourism Planning & Development, 16*(4), 452–472. doi:10.1080/21568316.2019.1595706

Nassar, N., Jafar, A., & Rahhal, Y. (2020). A novel deep multi-criteria collaborative filtering model for recommendation system. *Knowledge-Based Systems, 187*, 104811. Advance online publication. doi:10.1016/j.knosys.2019.06.019

Nassereddine, M. (2020). Machine learning roles in advancing the power network stability due to deployments of renewable energies and electric vehicles. *International Journal of Emerging Electric Power Systems*.

Natarajan, S., Vairavasundaram, S., Natarajan, S., & Gandomi, A. H. (2020). Resolving data sparsity and cold start problem in collaborative filtering recommender system using Linked Open Data. *Expert Systems with Applications, 149*, 113248. doi:10.1016/j.eswa.2020.113248

Nawara, D., & Kashef, R. (2020). IoT-based recommendation systems - An overview. *IEMTRONICS 2020 - International IOT, Electronics and Mechatronics Conference, Proceedings*. 10.1109/IEMTRONICS51293.2020.9216391

Nayak, S. K., & Panda, S. K. (2018). A user-oriented collaborative filtering algorithm for recommender systems. *PDGC 2018 - 2018 5th International Conference on Parallel, Distributed and Grid Computing*, 374–380. 10.1109/PDGC.2018.8745892

Necula, S.-C. (2017). Deep Learning for Distribution Channels' Management. *Informações Econômicas, 21*(4), 73–84. doi:10.12948/issn14531305/21.4.2017.06

Nee, A. Y. C., & Ong, S. K. (Eds.). (2021). Digital Twins in Industry. Applied Sciences, 11(14), 6437.

Nehrir, M., Wang, C., Strunz, K., Aki, H., Ramakumar, R., Bing, J., Miao, Z., & Salameh, Z. (2011). A review of hybrid renewable/alternative energy systems for electric power generation. *IEEE Transactions on Sustainable Energy*, *2*(4), 392–403. doi:10.1109/TSTE.2011.2157540

Neil Harker, K., & John, T. (2013). Recent weed control, weed management, and integrated weed management. *Weed Technology*, *27*(1), 1–11. doi:10.1614/WT-D-12-00109.1

Neloy, A. A., Alam, S., Bindu, R. A., & Moni, N. J. (2019). Machine Learning based Health Prediction System using IBM Cloud as PaaS. *2019 3rd International Conference on Trends in Electronics and Informatics (ICOEI)*, 444-450. 10.1109/ICOEI.2019.8862754

Neumayer, E. (2002). Can natural factors explain any cross-country differences in carbon dioxide emissions? *Energy Policy*, *30*(1), 7–12. doi:10.1016/S0301-4215(01)00045-3

Neumayer, E. (2004). National carbon dioxide emissions: Geography matters. *Area*, *36*(1), 33–40. doi:10.1111/j.0004-0894.2004.00317.x

NICResearch. (2019, February 26). *Is there a connection between diabetes & kidney stones - NICResearch*. National Institute of Clinical Research. https://www.nicresearch.com/connection-diabetes-kidney-stones/

Nielsen, M. A., & Chuang, I. L. (2010). *Computation and Quantum Information*. Academic Press.

Nikolaev, A. G., & Jacobson, S. H. (2010). Simulated annealing. In *Handbook of metaheuristics* (pp. 1–39). Springer. doi:10.1007/978-1-4419-1665-5_1

Nilashi, M., Ibrahim, O., & Bagherifard, K. (2018). A recommender system based on collaborative filtering using ontology and dimensionality reduction techniques. *Expert Systems with Applications*, *92*, 507–520. doi:10.1016/j.eswa.2017.09.058

Nivarthi, C. P. (2022). Transfer Learning as an Essential Tool for Digital Twins in Renewable Energy Systems. In S. Tomforde & C. Krupitzer (Ed.), *Organic Computing -- Doctoral Dissertation Colloquium 2021* (pp. 47-59). Kassel University Press.

Nnorom, I. C., & Osibanjo, O. (2008). Electronic waste (e-waste): Material flows and management practices in Nigeria. *Waste Management*, *28*(8), 1472-1479.

Noble Desktop. (2022). How is Quantum Computing Used in Data Analytics? Classes Near Me. published online: Jan 7, 2022, URL: https://www.nobledesktop.com/classes-near-me/blog/quantum-computing-in-data-analytics, Last Accessed on 05 Feb 2023.

NodeMcu. (n.d.). *Connect Things EASY (2014-2018)*. https://www.nodemcu.com/index_en

Noor-A-Rahim, M., Khyam, M. O., Li, X., & Pesch, D. (2019). Sensor fusion and state estimation of IoT enabled wind energy conversion system. *Sensors (Basel)*, *19*(7), 1566. doi:10.339019071566 PMID:30939747

Ntoutsi, E, Fafalios, P, & Gadiraju, U. (2020). Bias in data-driven artificial intelligence systems—An introductory survey. *WIREs Data Mining Knowl Discov*, *10*, e1356. doi:. doi:10.1002/widm.1356ry

Nyanga, C., Pansiri, J., & Chatibura, D. (2020). Enhancing competitiveness in the tourism industry through the use of business intelligence: A literature review. *Journal of Tourism Futures*, *6*(2), 139–151. doi:10.1108/JTF-11-2018-0069

O'Donovan, PGallagher, CLeahy, KO'Sullivan, D.T. (2019). A comparison of fog and cloud computing cyber-physical interfaces for industry 4.0 real-time embedded machine learning engineering applications. *Computers in Industry*, *110*, 12–35.

Obaidat, M. S., & Nicopolitidis, P. (2016). *Smart cities and homes: Key enabling technologies* (1st ed.). Kindle Edition.

OECD. (2018). *Mieux tirer parti de la transition numérique pour les villes intelligentes du futur.* https://www.oecd.org/cfe/cities/MIEUX-TIRER-PARTI-DE-LA-TRANSITION-NUM%C3%89RIQUE-POUR-LES-VILLES%20INTEL-LIGENTES%20DU%20FUTUR.pdf?fbclid=IwAR0CY4mup9H9JBq5a54R2-t_AhQTnwUr7mUOoRG4ChhX1kEv-5HQJ_Ib8Txk

Ofori & El-Gayar. (2020). *Towards deep learning for weed detection: Deep convolutional neural network architectures for plant seedling classification.* Academic Press.

Ojha, T., Bera, S., Misra, S., & Raghuwanshi, N. S. (2015). Dynamic duty scheduling for green sensor-cloud applications. *Proceedings of the International Conference on Cloud Computing Technology and Science, CloudCom,* 841–846. 10.1109/CloudCom.2014.169

Olsen, A., Konovalov, D. A., Philippa, B., Ridd, P., Wood, J. C., Johns, J., Banks, W., Girgenti, B., Kenny, O., Whinney, J., Calvert, B., Azghadi, M. R., & White, R. D. (2019). DeepWeeds: A multiclass weed species image dataset for deep learning. *Scientific Reports, 9*(1), 1–12. doi:10.103841598-018-38343-3 PMID:30765729

Oluwagbemi, O., Oluwagbemi, F., & Abimbola, O. (2016). Ebinformatics: Ebola fuzzy informatics systems on the diagnosis, prediction and recommendation of appropriate treatments for Ebola virus disease (EVD). *Informatics in Medicine Unlocked, 2,* 12–37. doi:10.1016/j.imu.2015.12.001

Onile, A., Machlev, R., Petlenkov, E., Levron, Y., & Belikov, J. (2021). Uses of the digital twins concept for energy services, intelligent recommendation systems, and demand side management: A review. *Energy Reports, 7,* 997–1015. doi:10.1016/j.egyr.2021.01.090

OpenLearn. (2019). *Smart Cities.* Retrieved September 4, 2019, https://www.open.edu/openlearn/science-maths-technology/smart-cities/content-section-overview?active-tab=description-tab

Opoku, D.-G. J., Perera, S., Osei-Kyei, R., & Rashidi, M. (2021). Digital twin application in the construction industry: A literature review. *Journal of Building Engineering, 40,* 102726. doi:10.1016/j.jobe.2021.102726

Oracle. (n.d.). *Developing Applications with Oracle Internet of Things Cloud Service.* https://docs.oracle.com/en/cloud/paas/iot-cloud/iotgs/iot-digital-twin-framework.html

Orumwense, E. F., Abo-al-ez, K., Orumwense, E. F., & Abo-al-ez, K. (2019). A systematic review to aligning research paths: Energy cyber-physical systems. *Cogent Engineering, 6*(1), 1700738. Advance online publication. doi:10.1080/23311916.2019.1700738

Osakada, K., Yang, G. B., Nakamura, T., & Mori, K. (1990). Expert system for cold-forging process based on FEM simulation. *CIRP Annals, 39*(1), 249–252.

Osibanjo, O., & Nnorom, I. C. (2007). The challenge of electronic waste (e-waste) management in developing countries. *Waste Management & Research, 25*(6), 489–501. doi:10.1177/0734242X07082028 PMID:18229743

Osisanwo, Akinsola, Awodele, Hinmikaiye, Olakanmi, & Akinjobi. (2017). Supervised Machine Learning Algorithms: Classification and Comparison. *Int. J. Comput. Trends Technol., 48*(3), 128–138. doi:10.14445/22312803/IJCTT-V48P126

Oskin, M., Chong, F. T., & Chuang, I. (2002). A practical architecture for reliable quantum computers. *IEEE Computer, 35*(January), 79–87. doi:10.1109/2.976922

Ouafiq, E. M., Saadane, R., & Chehri, A. (2022). Data Management and Integration of Low Power Consumption Embedded Devices IoT for Transforming Smart Agriculture into Actionable Knowledge. *Agriculture (Switzerland), 12*(3), 329. Advance online publication. doi:10.3390/agriculture12030329

Ousmane, D., Joel, J. P. C. R., Mbaye, S., & Jaime, L. (2013). Distributed Database Management Techniques for Wireless Sensor Networks. *Proceedings - 2013 International Conference on Computer, Electrical and Electronics Engineering: "Research Makes a Difference"*, 548–553. 10.1109/ICCEEE.2013.6633999

Paletta, Q., Arbod, G., & Lasenby, J. (2021). Benchmarking of deep learning irradiance forecasting models from sky images - an in-depth analysis. *Solar Energy, 224*, 855–867. doi:10.1016/j.solener.2021.05.056

Panchard, J., Rao, S., Prabhakar, T., Hubaux, J., & Jamadagni, H. (2007). Common Sense Net: A Wireless Sensor Network for Resource-Poor Agriculture in the Semi-Arid Areas of Developing Countries. *Information Technologies and International Development, 4*, 51–67.

Panch, T., Mattie, H., & Atun, R. (2019). Artificial intelligence and algorithmic bias: Implications for health systems. *Journal of Global Health, 9*(2), 010318. doi:10.7189/jogh.09.020318 PMID:31788229

Panda, S. K., Bhoi, S. K., & Singh, M. (2020). A collaborative filtering recommendation algorithm based on normalization approach. *Journal of Ambient Intelligence and Humanized Computing, 11*(11), 4643–4665. doi:10.100712652-020-01711-x

Pandey, A., & Ramesh, V. (2015). Quantum computing for big data analysis. *Indian Journal of Science, 14*(43), 98–104.

Pangbourne, K., Stead, D., Mladenović, M., & Milakis, D. (2018). The case of mobility as a service: A critical reflection on challenges for urban transport and mobility governance. In *Governance of the smart mobility transition*. Emerald Publishing Limited. doi:10.1108/978-1-78754-317-120181003

Panwar, N., Kaushik, S., & Kothari, S. (2011). Role of renewable energy sources in environmental protection: A review. *Renewable & Sustainable Energy Reviews, 15*(3), 1513–1524. doi:10.1016/j.rser.2010.11.037

Papernot. (2018). *A marauder's map of security and privacy in machine learning*. arXiv preprint arXiv: 1811.01134.

Parikh, S. B., & Atrey, P. K. (2018). Media-Rich Fake News Detection: A Survey. *IEEE Conference on Multimedia Information Processing and Retrieval*.

Park, C. H., & Ohan Shim, B. (2018). *Open Source IoT monitoring system of shallow geothermal energy integrated with OpenGeoSys*. EGU General Assembly Conference Abstracts.

Park, C., Shim, B., & Park, J. (2022). Open-source IoT monitoring system of a shallow geothermal system for heating and cooling year-round in Korea. *Energy, 250*, 123782. doi:10.1016/j.energy.2022.123782

Parkin, J., Clark, B., Clayton, W., Ricci, M., & Parkhurst, G. (2018). Autonomous vehicle interactions in the urban street environment: A research agenda. *Proceedings of the Institution of Civil Engineers. Municipal Engineer, 171*(1), 15–25. doi:10.1680/jmuen.16.00062

Park, J., & Yang, B. (2020). GIS-Enabled Digital Twin System for Sustainable Evaluation of Carbon Emissions: A Case Study of Jeonju City, South Korea. *Sustainability, 12*, 9186. doi:10.3390u12219186

Park, Y. J., Choe, Y. J., Park, O., Park, S. Y., Kim, Y. M., Kim, J., Kweon, S., Woo, Y., Gwack, J., Kim, S. S., Lee, J., Hyun, J., Ryu, B., Jang, Y. S., Kim, H., Shin, S. H., Yi, S., Lee, S., Kim, H. K., ... Jeong, E. K. (2020). Contact tracing during coronavirus disease outbreak, South Korea, 2020. *Emerging Infectious Diseases, 26*(10), 2465–2468. doi:10.3201/eid2610.201315 PMID:32673193

Parvatikar, S., & Parasar, D. (2021). Recommendation system using machine learning. *International Journal of Artificial Intelligence and Machine Learning, 1*(1), 24. doi:10.51483/IJAIML.1.1.2021.24-30

Patel, L., Shukla, T., Huang, X., Ussery, D. W., & Wang, S. (2020, November 12). Machine Learning Methods in Drug Discovery. *Molecules (Basel, Switzerland), 25*(22), 5277. doi:10.3390/molecules25225277 PMID:33198233

Patidar, S., Singh, U., & Sharma, S. K. (2020). Weed seedling detection using mask regional convolutional neural network. In *2020 International Conference on Electronics and Sustainable Communication Systems (ICESC)*. IEEE. 10.1109/ICESC48915.2020.9155701

Patil, R. A., & Ramakrishna, S. (2020). A comprehensive analysis of e-waste legislation worldwide. *Environmental Science and Pollution Research International*, 27(13), 14412–14431. doi:10.100711356-020-07992-1 PMID:32162230

Patil, S. M., Vijayalashmi, M., & Tapaskar, R. (2017). IoT based solar energy monitoring system. In *International Conference on Energy, Communication, Data Analytics and Soft Computing* (pp. 1574-1579). IEEE.

Patro, S. G. K., Mishra, B. K., Panda, S. K., Kumar, R., Long, H. V., Taniar, D., & Priyadarshini, I. (2020). A Hybrid Action-Related K-Nearest Neighbour (HAR-KNN) Approach for Recommendation Systems. *IEEE Access: Practical Innovations, Open Solutions*, 8, 90978–90991. doi:10.1109/ACCESS.2020.2994056

Peng, T., Liu, Q., Meng, D., & Wang, G. (2017). Collaborative trajectory privacy preserving scheme in location-based services. *Information Sciences*, 387, 165–179. doi:10.1016/j.ins.2016.08.010

Pereira, D. D. (2020, March 13). *Using the "internet of things" to improve geothermal energy production in Africa.* Retrieved June 27, 2022, from Unido: https://www.unido.org/stories/using-internet-things-improve-geothermal-energy-production-africa

Pereira, F. M. V., Milori, D. M. B. P., Pereira-Filho, E. R., Venâncio, A. L., Russo, M., Cardinali, M. C. B., Martins, P. K., & Freitas-Astúa, J. (2011). Laser-induced fluorescence imaging method to monitor citrus greening disease. *Computers and Electronics in Agriculture*, 79(1), 90–93. doi:10.1016/j.compag.2011.08.002

Pérez, L., Espeche, J., Loureiro, T., & Kavgić, A. (2020). DRIvE Project Unlocks Demand Response Potential with Digital Twins. Proceedings, 65, 1-14. doi:10.3390/proceedings2020065014

Perez-Rosas. (2018). Automatic Detection of Fake News. Academic Press.

Peteinatos, G. G., Reichel, P., Karouta, J., Andújar, D., & Gerhards, R. (2020). Weed identification in maize, sunflower, and potatoes with the aid of Convolutional Neural Networks. *Remote Sensing*, 12(24), 4185. doi:10.3390/rs12244185

Petit, J., & Shladover, S. E. (2014). Potential cyberattacks on automated vehicles. *IEEE Transactions on Intelligent Transportation Systems*, 16(2), 546–556.

Petropoulos, G. (2018). The impact of artificial intelligence on employment. *Praise for Work in the Digital Age*, 119.

Pettener, A. L. (2011). SCADA and communication networks for large scale offshore wind power systems. In *IET Conference on Renewable Power Generation* (p. 11). 10.1049/cp.2011.0101

Pham, X., & Stack, M. (2018). How data analytics is transforming agriculture. *Business Horizons*, 61(1), 125–133. doi:10.1016/j.bushor.2017.09.011

Philibert, C. (2005). The present and future use of solar thermal energy as a primary source of energy. International Energy Agency, 1-16.

Phung, M., Villefromoy, M. D., & Ha, Q. (2017). Management of solar energy in microgrids using IoT-based dependable control. *IEEE 20th international conference on electrical machines and systems (ICEMS)*, 1-6.

Pillai, S. G., Haldorai, K., Seo, W. S., & Kim, W. G. (2021). COVID-19 and hospitality 5.0: Redefining hospitality operations. *International Journal of Hospitality Management*, 94, 102869. doi:10.1016/j.ijhm.2021.102869 PMID:34785847

Pirker, J., Loria, E., Safikhani, S., Künz, A., & Rosmann, S. (2022). Immersive Virtual Reality for Virtual and Digital Twins: A Literature Review to Identify State Of The Art and Perspectives. Paper presented at the *2022 IEEE Conference on Virtual Reality and 3D User Interfaces Abstracts and Workshops (VRW)*. IEEE. 10.1109/VRW55335.2022.00035

Pitra, G. M., & Musti, K. S. S. (2021). Duck Curve with Renewable Energies and Storage Technologies. *13th International Conference on Computational Intelligence and Communication Networks (CICN)*, 66-71. 10.1109/CICN51697.2021.9574671

Pivoto, D., Waquil, D., Talamini, E., Finocchio, C., Corte, V., & Mores, G. (2018). Scientific development of smart agricultural technologies and their implementation in Brazil. Information Processing in Agriculture, 5(1), 21–32. https://linkinghub.elsevier.com/retrieve/pii/S2214317316301184

Plambeck, E., & Wang, Q. (2009). Effects of e-waste regulation on new product introduction. *Management Science, 55*(3), 333–347. doi:10.1287/mnsc.1080.0970

Platenius-Mohr, M., Malakuti, S., Grüner, S., Schmitt, J., & Goldschmidt, T. (2020). File- and API-based interoperability of digital twins by model transformation: An IIoT case study using asset administration shell. *Future Generation Computer Systems, 113*, 94–105. Advance online publication. doi:10.1016/j.future.2020.07.004

Popa, C. (2011). Adoption of Artificial Intelligence in Agriculture. *Bulletin of Agricultural Sciences and Veterinary Medicine, 68*(1), 284–293. doi:10.15835/buasvmcn-agr:6454

Popenici, S. A. D., & Kerr, S. (2017). Exploring the impact of artificial intelligence on teaching and learning in higher education. *Research and Practice in Technology Enhanced Learning, 12*(22), 1–13. doi:10.118641039-017-0062-8 PMID:30595727

Praharaj, S., Han, J. H., & Hawken, S. (2018). Urban innovation through policy integration: Critical perspectives from 100 smart cities mission in India. *City, Culture and Society, 12*, 35-43.

Pratama, M. T. (2020). Deep Learning-based Object Detection for Crop Monitoring in Soybean Fields. In *2020 International Joint Conference on Neural Networks (IJCNN)*. IEEE. 10.1109/IJCNN48605.2020.9207400

Premalatha, M., Abbasi, T., & Abbasi, S. A. (2014). The generation, impact, and management of e-waste: State of the art. *Critical Reviews in Environmental Science and Technology, 44*(14), 1577–1678. doi:10.1080/10643389.2013.782171

Preneel, B. (Ed.). (2000). Lecture Notes in Computer Science: Vol. 1807. *Factorization of a 512-bit RSA modules*. Springer Verlag.

Priyanka, E. B., Thangavel, S., Gao, X. Z., & Sivakumar, N. S. (2022). Digital twin for oil pipeline risk estimation using prognostic and machine learning techniques. *Journal of Industrial Information Integration, 26*, 100272. doi:10.1016/j.jii.2021.100272

Pujari, R. M., & Hajare, V. D. (2014). Analysis of ultrasound images for identification of Chronic Kidney Disease stages. *2014 First International Conference on Networks & Soft Computing (ICNSC2014)*, 380-383. 10.1109/CNSC.2014.6906704

Pulido-Velazquez, M., & Ward, F. A. (2020). Water conservation in irrigation can improve water use. *Proceedings of the National Academy of Sciences of the United States of America*, (vol. 105, no. 47, pp. 18 215–18 220).

Pundru, C. S. R. (2019). *An Adaptive Model for Forecasting Seasonal Rainfall Using Predictive Analytics*. doi:10.22266/ijies2019.1031.03

Puri, V., Nayyar, A., & Raja, L. (2017). Agriculture drones: A modern breakthrough in precision agriculture. *Journal of Statistics and Management Systems, 20*(4), 507–518. doi:10.1080/09720510.2017.1395171

Qiao, S., Qu, Y., Ma, Y., He, Y., Wang, Y., Hu, Y., Yu, X., Zhang, Z., & Tittel, F. K. (2019). A Sensitive Carbon Dioxide Sensor Based On Photoacoustic Spectroscopy With A Fixed Wavelength Quantum Cascade Laser. *Sensors (Basel)*, *19*(19), 4187. doi:10.339019194187 PMID:31561611

Qi, Q., Tao, F., & Nee, A. (2022). *From service to digital twin service Digital Twin Driven Service*. Elsevier.

Qi, Q., Tao, F., Zuo, Y., & Zhao, D. (2018). Digital twin service towards smart manufacturing. *Procedia CIRP*, *72*, 237242. doi:10.1016/j.procir.2018.03.103

Quan, L., Feng, H., Lv, Y., Wang, Q., Zhang, C., Liu, J., & Yuan, Z. (2019). Maize seedling detection under different growth stages and complex field environments based on an improved Faster R–CNN. *Biosystems Engineering*, *184*, 1–23. doi:10.1016/j.biosystemseng.2019.05.002

Quinn, P. (2021). Research under the GDPR – a level playing field for public and private sector research? *Life Sciences, Society and Policy*, *17*(1), 4. doi:10.118640504-021-00111-z PMID:33648586

Radianti, J. (2016). An Overview of Public Concerns During the Recovery Period after a Major Earthquake: Nepal Twitter Analysis. In *HICSS '16 Proceedings of the 2016 49th Hawaii International Conference on System Sciences (HICSS)* (pp. 136-145). IEEE. 10.1109/HICSS.2016.25

Raghunathan & Barma. (2019). *Digital Twin: A Complete Guide For The Complete Beginner*. Independently Published.

Rahman, N. R., Md, A. M. H., & Shin, J. (2020). Performance Comparison of Different Convolutional Neural Network Architectures for Plant Seedling Classification. In *2020 2nd International Conference on Advanced Information and Communication Technology (ICAICT)*. IEEE. 10.1109/ICAICT51780.2020.9333468

Raisch, S., & Krakowski, S. (2021). Artificial intelligence and management: The automation–augmentation paradox. *Academy of Management Review*, *46*(1), 192–210. doi:10.5465/amr.2018.0072

Ramamritham, K. (2006). *Innovative ICT tools for information provisioning via agricultural extensions*. 1st IEEE/ACM International Conference on ICT4D, Berkeley, CA.

Ramirez, A. (2013). The Influence of Social Networks on Agricultural Technology Adoption. *Procedia - Social and Behavioral Sciences*, *79*, 101-116. doi:10.1016/j.sbspro.2013.05.059

Ramkhelawan, R., & Sastry, M. (2019). Power System Load Flow Analysis using Microsoft Excel – Version 2. *Spreadsheets in Education, 12*(1).

Ranjan. (2003). Part of speech tagging and local word grouping techniques for natural language parsing in Hindi. In *Proceedings of the 1st International Conference on Natural Language Processing (ICON 2003)*. Semantic Scholar.

Ranjbar Kermany, N., & Alizadeh, S. H. (2017). A hybrid multi-criteria recommender system using ontology and neuro-fuzzy techniques. *Electronic Commerce Research and Applications*, *21*, 50–64. doi:10.1016/j.elerap.2016.12.005

Raspberry pi. (n.d.). https://www.raspberrypi.com/

Rath, S. K., Sahu, M., & Das, S. P. (n.d.). Software Reliability Prediction: A Review. *International Journal of Engineering Research & Technology*.

Rath, Madhusmita, Sahu, Das, & Mohapatra. (2022). Hybrid Software Reliability Prediction Model Using Feature Selection and Support Vector Classifier. *2022 International Conference on Emerging Smart Computing and Informatics (ESCI)*, 1-4. doi: 10.1109/ESCI53509.2022.9758339

Rath, S. K., Sahu, M., Das, S. P., & Bisoy, S. K. (2022). A Comparative Analysis of SVM and ELM Classification on Software Reliability Prediction Model. *Electronics (Basel)*, *11*(17), 2707.

Rath, S. K., Sahu, M., Das, S. P., & Pradhan, J. (2022a). Survey on Machine Learning Techniques for Software Reliability Accuracy Prediction. In *International Conference on Metaheuristics in Software Engineering and its Application* (pp. 43-55). Springer.

Rath, S. K., Sahu, M., Das, S. P., & Pradhan, J. (2022b). An Improved Software Reliability Prediction Model by Using Feature Selection and Extreme Learning Machine. In *International Conference on Metaheuristics in Software Engineering and its Application* (pp. 219-231). Springer.

Ratnaparkhi, S., Khan, S., Arya, C., Khapre, S., Singh, P., Diwakar, M., & Shankar, A. (2020). Smart agriculture sensors in IOT: A review. *Materials Today: Proceedings*. Advance online publication. doi:10.1016/j.matpr.2020.11.138

Rautela, R., Arya, S., Vishwakarma, S., Lee, J., Kim, K. H., & Kumar, S. (2021). E-waste management and its effects on the environment and human health. *The Science of the Total Environment*, *773*, 145623. doi:10.1016/j.scitotenv.2021.145623 PMID:33592459

Ray, S. (2017). https://www.analyticsvidhya.com/blog/2017/09/common-machine-learning-algorithms/(Das et al., 2021)

Ray, P. P. (2014). Home Health Hub Internet of Things (H3IoT): An architectural framework for monitoring the health of elderly people. *2014 International Conference on Science Engineering and Management Research, ICSEMR 2014*, 31–33. 10.1109/ICSEMR.2014.7043542

Razia Sulthana, A., & Ramasamy, S. (2019). Ontology and context based recommendation system using Neuro-Fuzzy Classification. *Computers & Electrical Engineering*, *74*, 498–510. doi:10.1016/j.compeleceng.2018.01.034

Rebentrost, P., Mohseni, M., & Lloyd, S. (2014). Quantum support vector machine for big data classification. *Physical Review Letters*, *113*(13), 130503. doi:10.1103/PhysRevLett.113.130503 PMID:25302877

Reddy, K. H. K., Behera, R. K., Chakrabarty, A., & Roy, D. S. (2020). A service delay minimization scheme for qos-constrained, context-aware unified iot applications. *IEEE Internet of Things Journal*, *7*(10), 10527–10534.

Redmon, J. (2016). You only look once: Unified, real-time object detection. *Proceedings of the IEEE conference on computer vision and pattern recognition*, 779–788. 10.1109/CVPR.2016.91

Reinecke, M., & Prinsloo, T. (2017). The influence of drone monitoring on crop health and harvest size. *2017 1st International Conference on Next Generation Computing Applications (NextComp)*, 5-10. 10.1109/NEXTCOMP.2017.8016168

Reis, Correia, Murai, Veloso, & Benevenuto. (2019). Supervised learning for fake news detection. *IEEE Intelligent Systems*, *34*(2), 76–81.

Ren, S. (2015). Advances in neural information processing systems: Vol. 28. Faster r-cnn: Towards real-time object detection with region proposal networks. Academic Press.

Renuka, K., Das, S. N., & Reddy, K. H. (2018). An Efficient Context Management Approach for IoT. *IUP Journal of Information Technology, 14*(2).

Renuka, K., Roy, D. S., & Reddy, K. H. K. (2021). An SDN empowered location aware routing for energy efficient next generation vehicular networks. *IET Intelligent Transport Systems*, *15*(2), 308–319. doi:10.1049/itr2.12026

Rezamand, M., Kordestani, M., Carriveau, R., Ting, D. S., Orchard, M. E., & Saif, M. (2020). Critical wind turbine components prognostics: A comprehensive review. *IEEE Transactions on Instrumentation and Measurement*, *69*(12), 9306–9328. doi:10.1109/TIM.2020.3030165

Richter, A. (2022, January 10). *ThinkGeoEnergy*. Retrieved June 27, 2022, from Top 10 Geothermal Countries 2021 – installed power generation capacity (MWe): https://www.thinkgeoenergy.com/thinkgeoenergys-top-10-geothermal-countries-2021-installed-power-generation-capacity-mwe/

Ritwik, M. G., Krishna, D., Shreyas, T. R., & Phamila, Y. A. V. (2018, September). Road Congestion based Traffic Management System with Dynamic Time Quantum. In *2018 International Conference on Recent Trends in Advance Computing (ICRTAC)* (pp. 1-6). IEEE.

Robinson, B. H. (2009). E-waste: An assessment of global production and environmental impacts. *The Science of the Total Environment, 408*(2), 183–191. doi:10.1016/j.scitotenv.2009.09.044 PMID:19846207

Robinson, D. A., Campbell, C. S., Hopmans, J. W., Hornbuckle, B. K., Jones, S. B., Knight, R., Ogden, F., Selker, J., & Wendroth, O. (2008). Soil moisture measurement for ecological and hydrological watershed-scale observatories: A review *Vadose Zone Journal, 7*(1), 358–389. doi:10.2136/vzj2007.0143

Röling, N., & Engel, P. G. H. (1990). Worldwide institutional evolution and forces for change. In W. Rivera & D. J. Gustafson (Eds.), *The Development of the Concept of Agricultural Knowledge Information Systems (AKIS): Implications for Extension*. Elsevier.

Romeo, L., Loncarski, J., Paolanti, M., Bocchini, G., Mancini, A., & Frontoni, E. (2020). Machine learning-based design support system for the prediction of heterogeneous machine parameters in industry 4.0. *Expert Systems with Applications, 140*, 112869.

Roselli, D., Matthews, J., & Talagala, N. (2019). Managing Bias in AI. WWW '19: *Companion Proceedings of the 2019 World Wide Web Conference,* (pp. 539-544). ACM. 10.1145/3308560.3317590

Rossi, G. P. (2003, Spring). Dual ACE and NEP inhibitors: A review of the pharmacological properties of MDL 100240. *Cardiovascular Drug Reviews, 21*(1), 51–66. doi:10.1111/j.1527-3466.2003.tb00105.x PMID:12595917

RouseM. (2018). https://searchenterpriseai.techtarget.com/definition/machine-learning

Roy, D. S., Behera, R. K., Reddy, K. H. K., & Buyya, R. (2018). A context-aware fog enabled scheme for real-time cross-vertical IoT applications. *IEEE Internet of Things Journal, 6*(2), 2400–2412.

Roy, D., Mazumder, O., Khandelwal, S., & Sinha, A. (2021, June). Wearable sensor-driven Cardiac model to derive hemodynamic insights during exercise. In *Proceedings of the Workshop on Body-Centric Computing Systems* (pp. 30-35). 10.1145/3469260.3469670

Rubin, V., Conroy, N., Chen, Y., & Cornwell, S. (2016). *Fake News or Truth?* Using Satirical Cues to Detect Potentially Misleading News. doi:10.18653/v1/W16-0802

Ruchansky, N., Seo, S., & Liu, Y. (2017). Csi: A hybrid deep model for fake news detection. *Proceedings of the 2017 ACM on Conference on Information and Knowledge Management,* 797-806. 10.1145/3132847.3132877

Rudisill, B. (2013, January 1). *The solar Ressource*. Retrieved June 27, 2022, from mcensustainableenergy: http://mcensustainableenergy.pbworks.com/w/page/20638192/The%20Solar%20Resource

Rudner, T. G. J., & Toner, H. (2021, Mar.). Key Concepts in AI Safety: An Overview. *CSET*.

Russakovsky, O., Deng, J., Su, H., Krause, J., Satheesh, S., Ma, S., Huang, Z., Karpathy, A., Khosla, A., Bernstein, M., Berg, A. C., & Fei-Fei, L. (2015). Imagenet large scale visual recognition challenge. *International Journal of Computer Vision, 115*(3), 211–252. doi:10.100711263-015-0816-y

Ryan, M. (2020). The future of transportation: Ethical, legal, social and economic impacts of self-driving vehicles in the year 2025. *Science and Engineering Ethics*, *26*(3), 1185–1208. doi:10.100711948-019-00130-2 PMID:31482471

Rzevski, G., Kozhevnikov, S., & Svitek, M. (2020, June). Smart city as an urban ecosystem. In *2020 Smart City Symposium Prague (SCSP)* (pp. 1-7). IEEE.

Saha, H. N., Roy, R., Chakraborty, M., & Sarkar, C. (2021). Development of IoT-based smart security and monitoring devices for agriculture. *Agricultural Informatics: Automation Using the IoT and Machine Learning*, 147–169.

Saheb, T. (202). Ethically contentious aspects of artificial intelligence surveillance: a social science perspective. *AI Ethics*. doi:10.1007/s43681-022-00196-y

Sa, I., Chen, Z., Popovic, M., Khanna, R., Liebisch, F., Nieto, J., & Siegwart, R. (2017). weednet: Dense semantic weed classification using multispectral images and mav for smart farming. *IEEE Robotics and Automation Letters*, *3*(1), 588–595. doi:10.1109/LRA.2017.2774979

Saifutdinov, Jackson, Zmanovska, & Tolujew. (2020). *Digital Twin as a Decision Support Tool for Airport Traffic Control*. . doi:10.1109/ITMS51158.2020.9259294

Sakellaropoulos, T., Vougas, K., Narang, S., Koinis, F., Kotsinas, A., Polyzos, A., Moss, T. J., Piha-Paul, S., Zhou, H., Kardala, E., Damianidou, E., Alexopoulos, L. G., Aifantis, I., Townsend, P. A., Panayiotidis, M. I., Sfikakis, P., Bartek, J., Fitzgerald, R. C., Thanos, D., ... Gorgoulis, V. G. (2019, December 10). A Deep Learning Framework for Predicting Response to Therapy in Cancer. *Cell Reports*, *29*(11), 3367–3373.e4. doi:10.1016/j.celrep.2019.11.017 PMID:31825821

Sani, A. S., Yuan, D., Jin, J., Gao, L., Yu, S., & Dong, Z. Y. (2019). Cyber security framework for Internet of Things-based Energy Internet. *Future Generation Computer Systems*, *93*, 849–859. doi:10.1016/j.future.2018.01.029

Sanjay, A., Vijarania, M., & Jaglan, V. (2021). Security Surveillance and Home Automation System using IoT. *EAI Endorsed Transactions on Smart Cities*, *5*(15), e1–e1.

Sarker, I. H. (2021). Machine learning: Algorithms, real-world applications and research directions. *SN Computer Science*, *2*(3), 1–21. doi:10.100742979-021-00592-x PMID:33778771

Sarker, S., Jamal, L., Ahmed, S. F., & Irtisam, N. (2021). Robotics and artificial intelligence in healthcare during COVID-19 pandemic: A systematic review. *Robotics and Autonomous Systems*, *146*, 103902. doi:10.1016/j.robot.2021.103902 PMID:34629751

Sarmah, S. (2019). *Concept of Artificial Intelligence, its Impact and Emerging Trends*. Retrieved from https://www.researchgate.net/publication/337704931

Sastry Musti, K. S. (2020). *Circular Economy in Energizing Smart Cities*. In Handbook of Research on Entrepreneurship Development and Opportunities in Circular Economy. doi:10.4018/978-1-7998-5116-5.ch013

Sastry Musti, K. S. (2020). *Industry 4.0-Based Enterprise Information System for Demand-Side Management and Energy Efficiency*. In Novel Approaches to Information Systems Design. doi:10.4018/978-1-7998-2975-1.ch007

Sastry Musti, K. S., Paulus, G. N. T., & Katende, J. (2021). *A Novel Framework for Energy Audit Based on Crowdsourcing Principles*. Springer. doi:10.1007/978-3-030-77841-5_11

Sastry, M. K., Bridge, J., Brown, A., & Williams, R. (2013, February). *Biomass Briquettes: A Sustainable and Environment Friendly Energy Option for the Caribbean*. In Fifth International Symposium on Energy, Laccei, Puerto Rico.

Sastry, M. K. S. (2007). Integrated Outage Management System: An effective solution for power utilities to address customer grievances. *International Journal of Electronic Customer Relationship Management, 1*(1), 30–40. doi:10.1504/IJECRM.2007.014424

Saxena, A., Brault, N., & Rashid, S. (2021). *Big Data and Artificial Intelligence for Healthcare Applications* (1st ed.). CRC Press. doi:10.1201/9781003093770

Schellin, H., Oberley, T., Patterson, K., Kim, B., Haring, K. S., Tossell, C. C., ... de Visser, E. J. (2020). Man's new best friend? Strengthening human-robot dog bonding by enhancing the doglikeness of Sony's Aibo. In *2020 Systems and Information Engineering Design Symposium (SIEDS)* (pp. 1-6). IEEE. 10.1109/SIEDS49339.2020.9106587

Schmidt, B., & Wang, L. (2018). Predictive maintenance of machine tool linear axes: A case from the manufacturing industry. *Proc. Manuf., 17*, 118–125.

Scholl, H. J., & AlAwadhi, S. (2016). Creating Smart Governance: The key to radical ICT overhaul at the City of Munich. *Information Polity, 21*(1), 21–42. doi:10.3233/IP-150369

Schröder, W. M. (2021). Robots and Rights: Reviewing Recent Positions in Legal Philosophy and Ethics. In: von Braun, J., S. Archer, M., Reichberg, G.M., Sánchez Sorondo, M. (eds) Robotics, AI, and Humanity. Springer. doi:10.1007/978-3-030-54173-6_16

Schrödinger, E. (1935, October). Discussion of probability relations between separated systems. *Mathematical Proceedings of the Cambridge Philosophical Society, 31*(4), 555–563. doi:10.1017/S0305004100013554

Schuld, M., Sinayskiy, I., & Petruccione, F. (2016). *Pattern classification with linear regression on a quantum computer.* arXiv preprint arXiv:1601.07823.

Schuld, M., Sinayskiy, I., & Petruccione, F. (2014, December). Quantum computing for pattern classification. In *Pacific Rim International Conference on Artificial Intelligence* (pp. 208-220). Springer.

Searcy, S. W. (1997). *Precision Farming: A New Approach to Crop Management.* The Texas Agricultural Extension Service. Retrieved from http://agrilife.org/lubbock/files/2011/10/PrecisionFarmNew.pdf

Segler, M. H. S., Kogej, T., Tyrchan, C., & Waller, M. P. (2018, January 24). Generating Focused Molecule Libraries for Drug Discovery with Recurrent Neural Networks. *ACS Central Science, 4*(1), 120–131. doi:10.1021/acscentsci.7b00512 PMID:29392184

Selukar, M., Jain, P., & Kumar, T. (2022). A device for effective weed removal for smart agriculture using convolutional neural network. International Journal of System Assurance Engineering and Management, 13(1), 397–404. doi:10.100713198-021-01441-z

Selvi, C., & Sivasankar, E. (2019). A novel Adaptive Genetic Neural Network (AGNN) model for recommender systems using modified k-means clustering approach. *Multimedia Tools and Applications, 78*(11), 14303–14330. doi:10.100711042-018-6790-y

Shahid, J., Ahmad, R., Kiani, A. K., Ahmad, T., Saeed, S., & Almuhaideb, A. M. (2022). Data Protection and Privacy of the Internet of Healthcare Things (IoHTs). *Applied Sciences (Switzerland), 12*(4), 1927. Advance online publication. doi:10.3390/app12041927

Shahinzadeh, H., Gharehpetian, G. B., Moazzami, M., Moradi, J., & Hosseinian, S. H. (2017). Unit commitment in smart grids with wind farms using virus colony search algorithm and considering adopted bidding strategy. In *Smart Grid Conference* (pp. 1-9). IEEE. 10.1109/SGC.2017.8308892

Shahinzadeh, H., Moradi, J., Gharehpetian, G. B., Nafisi, H., & Abedi, M. (2019). IoT architecture for smart grids. In *International Conference on Protection and Automation of Power System* (pp. 22-30). IEEE.

Shah, S. A., Shukla, D., Bentafat, E., & Bakiras, S. (2021). The Role of AI, Machine Learning, and Big Data in Digital Twinning: A Systematic Literature Review, Challenges, and Opportunities. *IEEE Access: Practical Innovations, Open Solutions*, 9, 32030–32052. doi:10.1109/ACCESS.2021.3060863

Shaikh, T. A., & Ali, R. (2016, December). Quantum computing in big data analytics: A survey. In *2016 IEEE international conference on computer and information technology (CIT)* (pp. 112-115). IEEE.

Shamma, Z., Rumman, I., Saikot, A., Reza, S. M. S., Islam, M. M., Mahmud, M., & Kaiser, M. S. (2021). *Kidney Care: Artificial Intelligence-Based Mobile Application for Diagnosing Kidney Disease.* doi:10.1007/978-981-15-7561-7_7

Shanmuganathan, Kadry, Vijayalakshmi, Pasupathi, & River. (2022). *Deep Learning for Video Analytics Using Digital Twin.* River Publishers.

Shao, C., Ciampaglia, G. L, Varol, O., Flammini. A., & Menczer, K. (2017). *The spread of fake news by socialbots.* arXiv preprint arAiv: 1707.07592.

Sharif, Bhagavatula, Bauer, & Reiter. (2017). *Adversarial generative nets: Neural network attacks on state-of-the-art face recognition.* arXiv preprint arXiv: 1801.00349.

Sharma, P. (2019). Crops and weeds classification using Convolutional Neural Networks via optimization of transfer learning parameters. International Journal of Engineering and Advanced Technology.

Sharma, S., Sharma, S., & Athaiya, A. (2017). Activation functions in neural networks. Towards Data Science, 6(12), 310–316.

Sharmila Banu, K., & Tripathy, B. K. (2016). Data analytics in spatial epidemiology: A survey. Jurnal Technology, 78(10), 159-165.

Sharp, M., Ak, R., & Hedberg, T. (2018). A survey of the advancing use and development of machine learning in smart manufacturing. *Journal of Manufacturing Systems*, 48, 170–179.

Sheng, Z., Yang, S., Yu, Y., Vasilakos, A. V., Mccann, J. A., & Leung, K. K. (2013). A Survey on the IETF Protocol Suite for the Internet of Things: Standards, Challenges, And Opportunities. Academic Press.

Shini, S., Shini, A., & Bryden, W. L. (2020). Unravelling fatty liver haemorrhagic syndrome: 1. Oestrogen and inflammation. *Avian Pathology*, 49(1), 87–98. doi:10.1080/03079457.2019.1674444 PMID:31565961

Shi, W., Cao, J., Zhang, Q., Li, Y., & Xu, L. (2016). Edge computing: Vision and challenges. *IEEE Internet of Things Journal*, 3(5), 637646. doi:10.1109/JIOT.2016.2579198

Shi, Y., Wang, Z., Wang, X., & Zhang, S. (2015). Internet of Things Application to Monitoring Plant Disease and Insect Pests. *Proceedings of the 2015 International Conference on Applied Science and Engineering Innovation, 12.* 10.2991/asei-15.2015.7

Shor, P. W. (1994). Algorithm for quantum computation: Discrete logarithm and factoring. *Proc. 35th IEEE Annual Symp. on Foundations of Computer Science*, 24–34. 10.1109/SFCS.1994.365700

Shor, P. W. (1997). *Polynomial-Time Algorithms for Prime Factorization and Discrete Logarithms on a Quantum Computer (SIAM). In Quantum Physics.* Springer.

Shu, Wang, & Liu. (2019). Beyond news contents: The role of social context for fake news detection. *Proceedings of the Twelfth ACM International Conference on Web Search and Data Mining*, 312-320. 10.1145/3289600.3290994

Shubenkova, K., Valiev, A., Shepelev, V., Tsiulin, S., & Reinau, K. H. (2018). Possibility of Digital Twins Technology for Improving Efficiency of the Branded Service System. *2018 Global Smart Industry Conference (GloSIC)*. IEEE. 10.1109/GloSIC.2018.8570075

Shu, K., Sliva, A., Wang, S., Tang, J., & Liu, H. (2017). Fake news detection on social media: A data mining perspective. *SIGKDD Explorations*, *19*(1), 22–36. doi:10.1145/3137597.3137600

Sigrist, L., May, K., Morch, A., Verboven, P., Vingerhoets, P., & Rouco, L. (2018). *On Scalability and Replicability of Smart Grid Projects — A Case Study*. doi:10.3390/en9030195

Sikder, A. K., Petracca, G., Aksu, H., Jaeger, T., & Uluagac, A. S. (2021). A survey on sensor-based threats and attacks to smart devices and applications. *IEEE Communications Surveys and Tutorials*, *23*(2), 1125–1159. doi:10.1109/COMST.2021.3064507

Silva, B. N., Khan, M., & Han, K. (2018). Towards sustainable smart cities: A review of trends, architectures, components, and open challenges in smart cities. *Sustainable Cities and Society*, *38*, 697–713. doi:10.1016/j.scs.2018.01.053

Simonyan, K., & Zisserman, A. (2014). *Very deep convolutional networks for large-scale image recognition*. arXiv preprint arXiv:1409.1556.

Simonyan, K., & Zisserman, A. (2014). *Very deep convolutional networks for large-scale image recognition*. https://arxiv.org/abs/1409.1556

Singh, M., Fuenmayor, E., Hinchy, E., Qiao, Y., Murray, N., & Devine, D. (2021). Digital Twin: Origin to Future. *Applied System Innovation.*, *4*, 36. doi:10.3390/asi4020036

Singh, N., Li, J., & Zeng, X. (2016). Global responses for recycling waste CRTs in e-waste. *Waste Management (New York, N.Y.)*, *57*, 187–197. doi:10.1016/j.wasman.2016.03.013 PMID:27072617

Singh, R. R., Banerjee, S., Manikandan, R., Kotecha, K., Indragandhi, V., & Vairavasundaram, S. (2022). Intelligent IoT Wind Emulation System Based on Real-Time Data Fetching Approach. *IEEE Access: Practical Innovations, Open Solutions*, *10*, 78253–78267. doi:10.1109/ACCESS.2022.3193774

Sistler, F. (1987). Robotics and intelligent machines in agriculture. *IEEE Journal on Robotics and Automation*, *3*(1), 3–6. doi:10.1109/JRA.1987.1087074

Sivaraj, P., & Philip, H. (2017). Social Networking for Agricultural and Rural Development -An Overview. In *5th Annual Agricultural Students Graduate Conference- Transforming Agriculture for Future*. Tamil Nadu Agricultural University.

Son, Chen, C.-F., Chen, C.-R., Thanh, B.-X., & Vuong, T.-H. (2017). Assessment of urbanization and urban heat islands in Ho Chi Minh City, Vietnam using Landsat data. *Sustainable Cities and Society*, *30*, 150–161. doi:10.1016/j.scs.2017.01.009

Song, Lichtenberg, & Xiao. (2015). Sun rgb-d: A rgb-d scene understanding benchmark suite. *Proceedings of the IEEE conference on computer vision and pattern recognition*, 567–576.

Son, J., & Kim, S. B. (2017). Content-based filtering for recommendation systems using multiattribute networks. *Expert Systems with Applications*, *89*, 404–412. doi:10.1016/j.eswa.2017.08.008

Soumyalatha, S. G. (2016). Study of IoT: understanding IoT architecture, applications, issues and challenges. *1st International Conference on Innovations in Computing & Net-working (ICICN16)*.

Soursos, S., Žarko, I. P., Zwickl, P., Gojmerac, I., Bianchi, G., & Carrozzo, G. (2016, June). Towards the cross-domain interoperability of IoT platforms. In *2016 European conference on networks and communications (EuCNC)* (pp. 398-402). IEEE. 10.1109/EuCNC.2016.7561070

Spanias, A. S. (2017). Solar energy management as an Internet of Things (IoT) application. In *8th International Conference on Information, Intelligence, Systems & Applications* (pp. 1-4). IEEE. 10.1109/IISA.2017.8316460

Srbinovski, B., Conte, G., Morrison, A. P., Leahy, P., & Popovici, E. (2017). ECO: An IoT platform for wireless data collection, energy control and optimization of a miniaturized wind turbine cluster: Power analysis and battery life estimation of IoT platform. In *International conference on industrial technology* (pp. 412-417). IEEE. 10.1109/ICIT.2017.7913266

Srinivasan, M., & Moon, Y. B. (1996). *A framework for a goal-driven approach to group technology applications using conceptual clustering*. Production Research.

Stafford, J. V., & Benlloch, J. V. (1997). Machine-assisted detection of weeds and weed patches. In *Precision agriculture'97: papers presented at the first European Conference on Precision Agriculture, Warwick University Conference Centre, UK, 7-10 September 1997*. BIOS Scientific Pub.

Stahl, B. C. (2021). Addressing Ethical Issues in AI. In *Artificial Intelligence for a Better Future. Briefs in Research and Innovation Governance*. Springer., doi:10.1007/978-3-030-69978-9_5

Steed, R., & Caliskan, A. (2021). Image representations learned with unsupervised pre-training contain human-like biases. *Conference on Fairness, Accountability, and Transparency*, 701–713. 10.1145/3442188.3445932

Sthiannopkao, S., & Wong, M. H. (2013). Handling e-waste in developed and developing countries: Initiatives, practices, and consequences. *The Science of the Total Environment*, *463*, 1147–1153. doi:10.1016/j.scitotenv.2012.06.088 PMID:22858354

Suakanto, S., Engel, V., Hutagalung, M., & Angela, D. (2016). *Sensor networks data gathering and job management for decision support of smart farming. International Conference on Information Technology*. Information Processing in Agriculture. https://linkinghub.elsevier.com/retrieve/pii/S2214317316301184

Subasi, A., Alickovic, E., & Kevric, J. (2017). Diagnosis of Chronic Kidney Disease by Using Random Forest. *CMBEBIH 2017. IFMBE Proceedings, 62*. 10.1007/978-981-10-4166-2_89

Subeesh, A. (2022). Deep convolutional neural network models for weed detection in polyhouse grown bell peppers. Artificial Intelligence in Agriculture, 6, 47–54. doi:10.1016/j.aiia.2022.01.002

Subrahmanyan, S., & Wozny, M. (1995). An overview of automatic feature recognition techniques for computer-aided process planning. *Computers in Industry*, *26*, 1–21.

Sudharson, S., & Kokil, P. (2019). Abnormality classification in the kidney ultrasound images using singular value decomposition features. *2019 IEEE Conference on Information and Communication Technology*, 1-5. 10.1109/CICT48419.2019.9066200

Suwa, S., Tsujimura, M., Kodate, N., Donnelly, S., Kitinoja, H., Hallila, J., Toivonen, M., Ide, H., Bergman-Kärpijoki, C., Takahashi, E., Ishimaru, M., Shimamura, A., & Yu, W. (2020). Exploring perceptions toward home-care robots for older people in Finland, Ireland, and Japan: A comparative questionnaire study. *Archives of Gerontology and Geriatrics*, *91*, 104178. doi:10.1016/j.archger.2020.104178 PMID:32717586

Sweet, M. (2014). Traffic congestion's economic impacts: Evidence from US metropolitan regions. *Urban Studies (Edinburgh, Scotland)*, *51*(10), 2088–2110.

Szegedy, C., Vanhoucke, V., Ioffe, S., Shlens, J., & Wojna, Z. (2015). *Rethinking the inception architecture for computer vision.* https://arxiv.org/abs/1512.00567

Szegedy, C. (2015). Going deeper with convolutions. *Proceedings of the IEEE conference on computer vision and pattern recognition*, 1–9.

Tacchini, Ballarin, Della Vedova, Moret, & de Alfaro. (2017). *Some like it Hoax: Automated fake news detect ion in social networks.* Academic Press.

Tahmasebi, F., Meghdadi, M., Ahmadian, S., & Valiallahi, K. (2021). A hybrid recommendation system based on profile expansion technique to alleviate cold start problem. *Multimedia Tools and Applications*, *80*(2), 2339–2354. doi:10.100711042-020-09768-8

Tahmid, T., & Hossain, E. (2017, December). Density based smart traffic control system using canny edge detection algorithm for congregating traffic information. In *2017 3rd International Conference on Electrical Information and Communication Technology (EICT)* (pp. 1-5). IEEE.

Takyar, A. (n.d.). *A Complete Knowledge Guide On Digital Twins.* LeewayHertz. https://www.leewayhertz.com/digital-twin/

Talaviya, T., Shah, D., Patel, N., Yagnik, H., & Shah, M. (2020). Implementation of artificial intelligence in agriculture for optimisation of irrigation and application of pesticides and herbicides. *Artificial Intelligence in Agriculture*, *4*, 58–73. doi:10.1016/j.aiia.2020.04.002

Tamilkodi, R., & Nesakumari, G. R. (2021). Image retrieval system based on multi feature extraction and its performance assessment. *International Journal of Information Technology*, *14*(2), 1161–1173.

Tan, M., & Le, Q. V. (2019). *EfficientNet: Rethinking model scaling for convolutional Neural Networks.* https://arxiv.org/abs/1905.11946

Tandoc, E.C., Lim, Z.W., & Ling, R. (2018). Defining "fake news" a typology of scholarly definitions. *Digital Journalism, 6*, 137–153.

Tandoc. (2017). Defining fake news a typology of scholarly definitions. *Digital Journalism*, 1–17.

Tang, W., Chen, X., Tong, Q., Gang, L., Li, M., & Li, L. (2020). Technologies and Applications of Digital Twin for Developing Smart Energy Systems. *Strategic Study of Chinese Academy of Engineering*, *2*(4), 74. Advance online publication. doi:10.15302/J-SSCAE-2020.04.010

Tao, F., Cheng, J., & Qi, Q. (2018). Digital twin-driven product design, manufacturing and service with big data. *International Journal of Advanced Manufacturing Technology*, *94*, 3563–3576. doi:10.100700170-017-0233-1

Tao, F., Qi, Q., Wang, L., & Nee, A. (2019). Digital Twins and Cyber-Physical Systems toward Smart Manufacturing and Industry 4.0: Correlation and Comparison. *Engineering.*, *5*, 653–661. doi:10.1016/j.eng.2019.01.014

Tao, F., Zhang, H., Liu, A., & Nee, A. Y. C. (2019). Digital Twin in Industry: State-of-the-Art. *IEEE Transactions on Industrial Informatics*, *15*(4), 2405–2415. doi:10.1109/TII.2018.2873186

Tao, F., Zhang, M., & Nee, A. (2019). *Digital Twin and Cloud.* Fog, Edge Computing., doi:10.1016/B978-0-12-817630-6.00008-4

Tapaswi. (2012). Treebank based deep grammar acquisition and Part-Of-Speech Tagging for Sanskrit m sentences. In Software Engineering (CONSEG), on Software Engineering (CONSEG) (pp. 1-4). IEEE. doi:10.1109/CONSEG.2012.6349476

Taylor, K. (n.d.). *Blockchain and Digital Twins: Amalgamating the Technologies.* HiTechNectar. https://www.hitechnectar.com/blogs/blockchain-and-digital-twins-amalgamating-the-two-technologies/

Tensorflow. (n.d.). https://bit.ly/2RDl3cm

Terazono, A., Murakami, S., Abe, N., Inanc, B., Moriguchi, Y., Sakai, S. I., & Williams, E. (2006). Current status and research on E-waste issues in Asia. *Journal of Material Cycles and Waste Management*, *8*(1), 1–12. doi:10.100710163-005-0147-0

Terciyanlı, E., Demirci, T., Küçük, D., Sarac, M., Çadırcı, I., & Ermiş, M. (2013). Enhanced nationwide wind-electric power monitoring and forecast system. *IEEE Transactions on Industrial Informatics*, *10*(2), 1171–1184. doi:10.1109/TII.2013.2294157

Thakur, P., & Kumar, S. (2021). Evaluation of e-waste status, management strategies, and legislations. *International Journal of Environmental Science and Technology*, 1–10.

The World Bank. (n.d.). *What a Waste*. https://datatopics.worldbank.org/what-a-waste/

ThinkTank European Parliament. (2021). *Artificial Intelligence in smart cities and urban mobility*. Retrieved July 23, 2021, https://www.europarl.europa.eu/thinktank/en/document/IPOL_BRI(2021)662937

Tian, Pei, Jana, & Ray. (2018). DeepTest: Automated testing of deep-neural-network-driven autonomous cars. *The 40th International Conference on Software Engineering (ICSE 2018)*, 303–314.

Torky, M., & Hassanien, A. E. (2020). Integrating Blockchain and the Internet of Things in Precision Agriculture : Analysis, Opportunities, and Challenges. *Computers and Electronics in Agriculture*, *178*(May), 105476. Advance online publication. doi:10.1016/j.compag.2020.105476

Torresen, J. (2018). A Review of Future and Ethical Perspectives of Robotics and AI. *Frontiers in Robotics and AI*, *4*, 75. Advance online publication. doi:10.3389/frobt.2017.00075

Tóth, Z., Caruana, R., Gruber, T., & Loebbecke, C. (2022). The Dawn of the AI Robots: Towards a New Framework of AI Robot Accountability. *Journal of Business Ethics*, *178*(4), 895–916. doi:10.100710551-022-05050-z

Tranfield, D., Denyer, D., & Smart, P. (2003). Towards a methodology for developing evidence-informed management knowledge utilizing systematic review. *British Journal of Management*, *14*, 207–222.

Tran, V. V., Park, D., & Lee, Y. C. (2020). Indoor Air Pollution, Related Human Diseases, and Recent Trends in the Control and Improvement of Indoor Air Quality. *International Journal of Environmental Research and Public Health*, *17*(8), 2927. doi:10.3390/ijerph17082927 PMID:32340311

Tripathy & Banu. (2018). Neighborhood Rough Sets Based Spatial Data Analytics. In *Encyclopedia for Science and technology*. IGI Publications.

Tripathy, B. K. (2017). Rough set and neighbourhood systems in Big Data Analysis. In Computational Intelligence Applications in Business Intelligence and Big Data Analytics. CRC Press.

Tripathy, B. K., & Deboleena, D. (2018). Trustworthiness in the Social internet of Things (SIoT). In Big Data Analytics: A social network approach. Taylor and Francis.

Tripathy, B. K., & Deepthi, P. H. (2017a). An Investigation of Fuzzy Techniques in clustering of Big Data. In Computational Intelligence Applications in Business Intelligence and Big Data Analytics. CRC Press.

Tripathy, B. K., & Deepthi, P. H. (2017b). Quantum Inspired Computational Intelligent Techniques in Image Segmentation. In S. Bhattacharya, U. Maulik, & P. Dutta (Eds.), Quantum Inspired Computational Intelligence: Research and Applications (pp. 233–258). Elsevier.

Tripathy, B. K., Raju, H., & Kaul, D. (2018). Quantum Computing inspired algorithms in machine learning. In Quantum inspired intelligent systems for multimedia data analysis. IGI Publications.

Tripathy, B. K., Sooraj, T. R., & Mohanty, R. K. (2018). Data Mining Techniques in Big Data for Social Network. In Big Data Analytics: A social network approach. Taylor and Francis.

Tripathy, B. K., Parimala, B., & Thippa Reddy, G. (2021). Prediction of Diseases using Innovative Classification and Regression Models. In *Data Analytics in Biomedical Engineering and Healthcare* (pp. 179–203). Academic Press. doi:10.1016/B978-0-12-819314-3.00012-4

True, J. (2022). Weed detection in soybean crops using custom lightweight deep learning models. Journal of Agriculture and Food Research, 100308.

Tsamados, A., Aggarwal, N., Cowls, J., Morley, J., Roberts, H., Taddeo, M., & Floridi, L. (2022). The ethics of algorithms: Key problems and solutions. *AI & Society*, *37*(1), 215–230. doi:10.100700146-021-01154-8

Tsang, S. W., & Jim, C. Y. (2016). Applying artificial intelligence modeling to optimize green roof irrigation. *Energy and Building*, *127*, 360–369. doi:10.1016/j.enbuild.2016.06.005

Tseng, C.-H. (2015). Type 2 diabetes mellitus and kidney cancer risk: A retrospective cohort analysis of the National Health Insurance. *PLoS One*, *10*(11), e0142480. doi:10.1371/journal.pone.0142480 PMID:26559055

Tu, C., He, X., Shuai, Z., & Jiang, F. (2017). Big data issues in smart grid–A review. *Renewable & Sustainable Energy Reviews*, *79*, 1099–1107. doi:10.1016/j.rser.2017.05.134

Turner, B. L. II, Matson, P. A., McCarthy, J. J., Corell, R. W., Christensen, L., Eckley, N., Hovelsrud-Broda, G. K., Kasperson, J. X., Kasperson, R. E., Luers, A., Martello, M. L., Mathiesen, S., Naylor, R., Polsky, C., Pulsipher, A., Schiller, A., Selin, H., & Tyler, N. (2003). Illustrating the coupled human-environment system for vulnerability analysis: Three case studies. *Proceedings of the National Academy of Sciences of the United States of America*, *100*(14), 8080–8085. doi:10.1073/pnas.1231334100 PMID:12815106

Tutorials Point. (n.d.). http://www.tutorialspoint.com/computer_fundamentals/computer_quick_guide.htm

Twycross, Aickelin, & Whitbrook. (2010). *Detecting anomalous process behavior using second generation artificial immune systems*. arXiv preprint arXiv: 1006.3654.

Tzachor, A., Sabri, S., Richards, C. E., Rajabifard, A., & Acuto, M. (2022). Potential and limitations of digital twins to achieve the Sustainable Development Goals. *Nature Sustainability*, *5*(10), 822–829. doi:10.103841893-022-00923-7

Udhbav, M., Kumar, R., Kumar, N., Kumar, R., Vijarania, D., & Gupta, S. (2022, May 27). Prediction of Home Loan Status Eligibility using Machine Learning. Swati, Prediction of Home Loan Status Eligibility using. *Machine Learning*.

Undzyte, G., Patasius, A., Linkeviciute-Ulinskiene, D., Zabuliene, L., Stukas, R., Dulskas, A., & Smailyte, G. (2020). Increased kidney cancer risk in diabetes mellitus patients: A population-based cohort study in Lithuania. The Aging Male. *The Official Journal of the International Society for the Study of the Aging Male*, *23*(5), 1241–1245. doi:10.1080/13685538.2020.1755249 PMID:32342709

United Nations. (n.d.). *Goal 2: Zero Hunger*. United Nations. https://www.un.org/sustainabledevelopment/hunger/

Vaish, P., Bharath, R., Rajalakshmi, P., & Desai, U. B. (2016). Smartphone based automatic abnormality detection of kidney in ultrasound images. *2016 IEEE 18th International Conference on e-Health Networking, Applications and Services (Healthcom)*, 1-6. 10.1109/HealthCom.2016.7749492

Van der Aalst, M., & de Medeiros, A. K. A. (2005). Process mining and security: Detecting anomalous process executions and checking process conformance. *Electronic Notes in Theoretical Computer Science, 121*, 3–21.

van der Merwe, D., Burchfield, D. R., Witt, T. D., Price, K. P., & Sharda, A. (2020). Drones in agriculture. *Advances in Agronomy, 162*, 1–30. doi:10.1016/bs.agron.2020.03.001

Vasanthselvakumar, R. (2020). Automatic Detection and Classification of Chronic Kidney Diseases Using CNN Architecture. doi:10.1007/978-981-15-1097-7_62

Vatcheva, I., De Jong, H., & Mars, N. J. (2000, August). Selection of perturbation experiments for model discrimination. In ECAI (pp. 191-198). Academic Press.

Vats, M. C., & Singh, S. K. (2014). E-Waste characteristic and its disposal. *International Journal of Ecological Science and Environmental Engineering, 1*(2), 49-61.

Veeragandham, S., & Santhi, H. (2021). A Detailed Review on Challenges and Imperatives of Various CNN Algorithms in Weed Detection. In *2021 International Conference on Artificial Intelligence and Smart Systems (ICAIS)*. IEEE. 10.1109/ICAIS50930.2021.9395986

Veloso, M. (1995). Integrating planning and learning: The Prodigy architecture, 1. *Experimental and Theoretical AI, 7*, 81–120.

Verdicchio, M., & Perin, A. (2022). When Doctors and AI Interact: On Human Responsibility for Artificial Risks. *Philosophy & Technology, 35*(1), 11. doi:10.100713347-022-00506-6 PMID:35223383

Verdouw, C. (2016). Internet of Things in agriculture. *CAB Reviews: Perspectives in Agriculture, Veterinary Science, Nutrition, and Natural Resources, 11*(35). http://www.cabi.org/cabreviews/review/20163379897

Vergara, S. E., & Tchobanoglous, G. (2012). Municipal solid waste and the environment: A global perspective. *Annual Review of Environment and Resources, 37*(1), 277–309. doi:10.1146/annurev-environ-050511-122532

Verma, S., Sharma, R., Deb, S., & Maitra, D. (2021). Artificial intelligence in marketing: Systematic review and future research direction. *International Journal of Information Management Data Insights, 1*(1), 100002. doi:10.1016/j.jjimei.2020.100002

Vieira, A. (2015). *Predicting online user behaviour using deep learning algorithms.* Academic Press.

Vieira, G. (2020, February 1). *Diabetes & kidney stones.* Diabetes Strong. https://diabetesstrong.com/diabetes-kidney-stones/

Vieto, I., & Sun, J. (2015). Small-signal impedance modelling of type-III wind turbine. *2015 IEEE Power & Energy Society General Meeting.*

Vijay, D., Goetze, P., Wulf, R., & Gross, U. (2018). Homogenized and pore-scale analyses of forced convection through open cell foams. *International Journal of Heat and Mass Transfer, 123*, 787–804. doi:10.1016/j.ijheatmasstransfer.2018.03.008

Villani, C. (2018). *Pour une intelligence artificielle significative. Vers une stratégie française et européenne.* Une mission parlementaire du 8 septembre 2017 au 8 mars 2018. https://www.aiforhumanity.fr/pdfs/MissionVillani_Report_ENG-VF.pdf

Vi, N. T. L., Ahderom, S., & Alameh, K. (2020). Performances of the lbp based algorithm over cnn models for detecting crops and weeds with similar morphologies. *Sensors (Basel), 20*(8), 2193. doi:10.339020082193 PMID:32295097

Viscarra Rossel, R. A., Minasny, B., Roudier, P., & McBratney, A. B. (2006). Colour space models for soil science. *Geoderma, 133*(3-4), 320–337. doi:10.1016/j.geoderma.2005.07.017

Visvizi, A., Lytras, M. D., & Mudri, G. (2018). Smart Villages in the EU and Beyond. Emerald Publishing Limited.

Vitali, G., Francia, M., Golfarelli, M., & Canavari, M. (2021). Crop Management with the IoT : An Interdisciplinary Survey. *Agronomy (Basel)*, *11*(1), 1–18. doi:10.3390/agronomy11010181

Volo, S. (2020). Tourism statistics, indicators and big data: A perspective article. *Tourism Review*, *75*(1), 304–309. doi:10.1108/TR-06-2019-0262

Wadekar, S., Vakare, V., Prajapati, R., Yadav, S., & Yadav, V. (2016). Smart water management using IoT. In *5th International Conference on Wireless Networks and Embedded Systems (WECON)* (pp. 1-4). IEEE.

Walsh, S. J., Crawford, T. W., Welsh, W. F., & Crews-Meyer, K. A. (2001). A multiscale analysis of LULC and NDVI variation in Nang Rong district, northeast Thailand. *Agriculture, Ecosystems & Environment*, *85*(1-3), 47–64. doi:10.1016/S0167-8809(01)00202-X

Walter, A., Finger, R., Huber, R., & Buchmann, N. (2017). Smart farming is key to developing sustainable agriculture. *Proceedings of the National Academy of Sciences of the United States of America*, *114*(24), 6148–6150. doi:10.1073/pnas.1707462114 PMID:28611194

Wang, J., Qiao, L., Lv, H., & Lv, Z. (2022). Deep Transfer Learning-based Multi-modal Digital Twins for Enhancement and Diagnostic Analysis of Brain MRI Image. IEEE/ACM Transactions on Computational Biology and Bioinformatics. doi:10.1109/TCBB.2022.3168189

Wang, P., Aalipur, B., & Wang, D. (2021). Microprocessors and Microsystems An improved multilayer perceptron approach for detecting sugarcane yield production in IoT-based smart agriculture. *Microprocessors and Microsystems*, *82*(November), 103822. doi:10.1016/j.micpro.2021.103822

Wang, Q., Jiao, W., & Zhang, Y. M. (2020). Deep learning-empowered digital twin for visualized weld joint growth monitoring and penetration control. *Journal of Manufacturing Systems, 57*, 429-439.

Wang, Z., Song, M., Zhang, Z., Song, Y., Wang, Q., & Qi, H. (2019). Beyond Inferring Class Representatives: User-Level Privacy Leakage from Federated Learning. *Proceedings - IEEE INFOCOM*, 2512–2520. doi:10.1109/INFOCOM.2019.8737416

Wang, A., Zhang, W., & Wei, X. (2019). A review on weed detection using ground-based machine vision and image processing techniques. *Computers and Electronics in Agriculture*, *158*, 226–240. doi:10.1016/j.compag.2019.02.005

Wang, B., Kong, W., Guan, H., & Xiong, N. N. (2019). Air Quality Forecasting Based on Gated Recurrent Long Short-Term Memory Model in Internet of Things. *IEEE Access: Practical Innovations, Open Solutions*, *7*, 69524–69534. doi:10.1109/ACCESS.2019.2917277

Wang, C. D., Deng, Z. H., Lai, J. H., & Yu, P. S. (2019). Serendipitous recommendation in e-commerce using innovator-based collaborative filtering. *IEEE Transactions on Cybernetics*, *49*(7), 2678–2692. doi:10.1109/TCYB.2018.2841924 PMID:29994495

Wang, C., & Jiang, P. (2018). Manifold learning-based rescheduling decision mechanism for recessive disturbances in RFIDdriven job shops. *Journal of Intelligent Manufacturing*, *29*(7), 1485–1500.

Wang, C., Liu, B., Liu, L., Zhu, Y., Hou, J., Liu, P., & Li, X. (2021). A review of deep learning used in the hyperspectral image analysis for agriculture. *Artificial Intelligence Review*, *54*(7), 5205–5253. doi:10.100710462-021-10018-y

Wang, H., Wu, Y., Min, G., & Miao, W. (2022, February). A Graph Neural Network-Based Digital Twin for Network Slicing Management. *IEEE Transactions on Industrial Informatics*, *18*(2), 1367–1376. doi:10.1109/TII.2020.3047843

Wang, J., Lu, Y., Wang, X., Dong, J., & Hu, X. (2018). SAR: A social-aware route recommendation system for intelligent transportation. *The Computer Journal*, *61*(7), 987–997. doi:10.1093/comjnl/bxy042

Wang, J., Zhu, H., Wang, S. H., & Zhang, Y.-D. (2021). A Review of Deep Learning on Medical Image Analysis. *Mobile Networks and Applications, 26*(1), 351–380. doi:10.100711036-020-01672-7

Wang, K., & Wang, Y. (2017). How AI affects the future predictive maintenance: a primer of deep learning. In *International Workshop of Advanced Manufacturing and Automation.* Springer.

Wang, K., Zhang, T., Xue, T., Lu, Y., & Na, S. G. (2020). E-commerce personalized recommendation analysis by deeply-learned clustering. *Journal of Visual Communication and Image Representation, 71,* 102735. Advance online publication. doi:10.1016/j.jvcir.2019.102735

Wang, T., Li, J., Deng, Y., Wang, C., Snoussi, H., & Tao, F. (2021). Digital twin for human-machine interaction with a convolutional neural network.Issue7-8: Digital Twin-enabled Smart Industrial Systems. *Recent Developments and Future Perspectives, 34,* 888–897.

Wang, Y. (2012). Quantum computation and quantum information. *Statistical Science, 27*(3), 373–394. doi:10.1214/11-STS378

Wang, Y. (2022). When Quantum Computation Meets Data Science: Making Data Science Quantum. *Harvard Data Science Review, 4*(1). Advance online publication. doi:10.1162/99608f92.ef5d8928

Wang, Y., & Song, X. (2020). Quantum science and quantum technology. *Statistical Science, 35*(1), 51–74. doi:10.1214/19-STS745

Wasserman, S., & Faust, K. (1994). *Social Network Analysis.* Cambridge University Press. doi:10.1017/CBO9780511815478

Webster, J., & Watson, R. T. (2002). Analyzing The Past to Prepare for the future: Writing A Literature Review. *Management Information Systems Quarterly, 26*(2), 13–23.

Welfare, G. o. (2016). *State of Indian Agriculture 2015-16. Krishi Bhavan.* Government of India Ministry of Agriculture & Farmers Welfare.

Whitmore, A., Agarwal, A., & Da Xu, L. (2015). The Internet of Things—A survey of topics and trends. *Information Systems Frontiers, 17*(2), 261–274. doi:10.100710796-014-9489-2

Widmer, R., Oswald-Krapf, H., Sinha-Khetriwal, D., Schnellmann, M., & Böni, H. (2005). Global perspectives on e-waste. *Environmental Impact Assessment Review, 25*(5), 436–458. doi:10.1016/j.eiar.2005.04.001

Wilde, M. M. (2019). *Quantum information theory* (2nd ed.). Cambridge University Press.

Williams, C. P., & Clearwater, S. H. (1997). *Exploration in quantum computing.* Springer-Verlag.

Williams, C. P., & Clearwater, S. H. (1998). *Explorations in quantum computing.* Springer.

Wolfert, S., Ge, L., Verdouw, C., & Bogaardt, M.-J. (2017). Big Data in Smart Farming - A review *Agricultural Systems, 153,* 69–80. doi:10.1016/j.agsy.2017.01.023

Wolfram, J. S., Timothy, J. K., Norman, A.-G., Lucia, H., & Jeroen, C. J. G. (2021) Putting social networks to practical use: Improving last-mile dissemination systems for climate and market information services in developing countries. *Climate Services, 23.* doi:10.1016/j.cliser.2021.100248

Wood, J. (2022, March 29). *These are the countries bidding to become wind power superpowers.* Retrieved June 27, 2022, from Weforum: https://www.weforum.org/agenda/2022/03/offshore-onshore-wind-power-auction-capacity/

Woodbury, R. (1960). The Legend of Eli Whitney and Interchangeable Parts. *Technology and Culture, 1*(3), 235–253. doi:10.2307/3101392

Woyte, A., Richter, M., Moser, D., Mau, S., Reich, N., & Jahn, U. (2013). Monitoring Of Photovoltaic Systems: Good Practices And Systematic Analysis. *Proc. 28th European Photovoltaic Solar Energy Conference*, 3686-3694.

Wulf, A. J., & Seizov, O. (2022). Please understand we cannot provide further information": Evaluating content and transparency of GDPR-mandated AI disclosures. *AI & Society*. doi:10.100700146-022-01424-z

Xiang, Z. (2018). From digitization to the age of acceleration: On information technology and tourism. *Tourism Management Perspectives*, 25, 147–150. doi:10.1016/j.tmp.2017.11.023

Xiao, Q., Li, K., Zhang, D., & Xu, W. (2018). Security risks in deep learning implementations. *Proceedings - 2018 IEEE Symposium on Security and Privacy Workshops*, 123–128. 10.1109/SPW.2018.00027

Xiao, H., Zeng, H., Jiang, W., Zhou, Y., & Tu, X. (2022, December). HMM-TCN-based health assessment and state prediction for robot mechanical axis. *International Journal of Intelligent Systems*, 37(12), 10476–10494. Advance online publication. doi:10.1002/int.22621

Xiaojun, C., Xianpeng, L., & Peng, X. (2015). *IOT-based air pollution monitoring and forecasting system. In 2015 international conference on computer and computational sciences*. IEEE.

Xu, Y., Yao, H., & Lin, K. (2018, December). An overview of neural networks for drug discovery and the inputs used. *Expert Opinion on Drug Discovery*, 13(12), 1091–1102. doi:10.1080/17460441.2018.1547278 PMID:30449189

Yaïci, W., Krishnamurthy, K., Entchev, E., & Longo, M. (2020). Internet of things for power and energy systems applications in buildings: An overview. *2020 IEEE International Conference on Environment and Electrical Engineering*, 1-6. 10.1109/EEEIC/ICPSEurope49358.2020.9160522

Yamashita, R., Nishio, M., Do, R. K. G., & Togashi, K. (2018). Convolutional neural networks: An overview and application in radiology. *Insights Into Imaging*, 9(4), 611–629. doi:10.100713244-018-0639-9 PMID:29934920

Yampolskiy, R. V., & Spellchecker, M. S. (2016). *Artificial Intelligence Safety and Cybersecurity: a Timeline of AI Failures*. https://arxiv.org/abs/1610.07997

Yang, C., Li, Y., Yang, Y., Liu, Z., & Liao, M. (2022). Transfer Learning-enabled Modelling Framework for Digital Twin. *IEEE 25th International Conference on Computer Supported Cooperative Work in Design (CSCWD)*, 113-118. 10.1109/CSCWD54268.2022.9776083

Yang, Z., Sun, Q., & Zhang, B. (2018). Evaluating prediction error for anomaly detection by exploiting matrix factorization in rating systems. *IEEE Access: Practical Innovations, Open Solutions*, 6, 50014–50029. doi:10.1109/ACCESS.2018.2869271

Yaqub, U., Al-Nasser, A., & Sheltami, T. (2019). Implementation of a hybrid wind-solar desalination plant from an Internet of Things (IoT) perspective on a network simulation tool. *Applied Computing and Informatics*, 7-11.

Yeh, Nee, Tao, & Zhang. (2019). *Digital Twin Driven Smart Manufacturing*. Academic Press.

Yi. (2003). Sentiment analyzer: Extracting sentiments about a given topic using natural language processing techniques. In *Data Mining, ICDM 2003. Third IEEE International Conference* (pp. 427-434). http://citeseerx.ist.psu.edu

Yigitcanlar, T., & Cugurullo, F. (2020). The sustainability of artificial intelligence: An urbanistic viewpoint from the lens of smart and sustainable cities. *Sustainability*, 12(20), 8548. doi:10.3390u12208548

Yigitcanlar, T., Han, H., Kamruzzaman, M., Ioppolo, G., & Sabatini-Marques, J. (2019). The making of smart cities: Are Songdo, Masdar, Amsterdam, San Francisco and Brisbane the best we could build? *Land Use Policy*, 88, 104187. doi:10.1016/j.landusepol.2019.104187

Yigitcanlar, T., & Inkinen, T. (2019). *Geographies of disruption.* Springer International Publishing. doi:10.1007/978-3-030-03207-4

Yin, J., Cao, Y., Yong, H. L., Ren, J. G., Liang, H., Liao, S. K., . . . Pan, J. W. (2013). *Bounding the speed of spooky action at a distance.* arXiv preprint arXiv:1303.0614.

Young, M. M., Bullock, J. B., & Lecy, J. D. (2019). Artificial discretion as a tool of governance: A framework for understanding the impact of artificial intelligence on public administration. *Perspectives on Public Management and Governance, 2*(4), 301–313. doi:10.1093/ppmgov/gvz014

You, Y., Chen, C., Hu, F., Liu, Y., & Ji, Z. (2022). Advances of Digital Twins for Predictive Maintenance. *Procedia Computer Science, 200,* 1471–1480. doi:10.1016/j.procs.2022.01.348

Yuce, A. (2022a). Digital Transformation-Oriented Innovation in Museum Settings via Digital Engagement: Virtual Reality. Handbook of Research on Museum Management in the Digital Era. IGI Global. doi:10.4018/978-1-7998-9656-2.ch013

Yuce, A. (2022b). ICT Pandemic Time Adoption and Immersive Technologies: A Comprehensive Review. *Digitalization as a Driver for Smart Economy in the Post-COVID-19 Era,* 243-255.

Yuce, A. (2022c). Impact of Technology in Sustainable Tourism Development: Virtual Reality. Mobile Computing and Technology Applications in Tourism and Hospitality. IGI Global.

Yuce, A., Arasli, H., Ozturen, A., & Daskin, M. (2020). Feeling the Service Product Closer: Triggering Visit Intention via Virtual Reality. *Sustainability, 12*(16), 6632. doi:10.3390u12166632

Yumeng, Q. (2018). Predicting Future Rumours. *Chinese Journal of Electronics.*

Yun, H., & Park, D. (2021). Simulation of Self-driving System by implementing Digital Twin with GTA5. *2021 International Conference on Electronics, Information, and Communication (ICEIC),* 1-2. doi: 10.1109/ICEIC51217.2021.9369807

Yun, Y., Hooshyar, D., Jo, J., & Lim, H. (2018). Developing a hybrid collaborative filtering recommendation system with opinion mining on purchase review. *Journal of Information Science, 44*(3), 331–344. doi:10.1177/0165551517692955

Yu, X., & Xue, Y. (2016). Smart Grids: A Cyber – Physical Systems Perspective. *Proceedings of the IEEE, 104*(5), 1058–1070. doi:10.1109/JPROC.2015.2503119

Yu, Y., & Zou, Y. L. (2014). Application of technology of the Internet of Things on the monitoring of geothermal field. *Advanced Materials Research, 860,* 563–567.

Zaveri, E., Grogan, D., Fisher-Vanden, K., Frolking, S., Lammers, R., Wrenn, D., Proussevitch, A., & Nicholas, R. (2016). Invisible water, visible impact: Groundwater use and Indian agriculture under climate change. *Environmental Research Letters, 11*(8), 084005. doi:10.1088/1748-9326/11/8/084005

Zeiler & Fergus. (2014). Visualizing and understanding convolutional networks. In *European conference on computer vision.* Springer.

Zeng, T., Semiari, O., Saad, W., & Bennis, M. (2019). Joint communication and control for wireless autonomous vehicular platoon systems. *IEEE Transactions on Communications, 67*(11), 7907–7922.

Zhang, J., Dong, B., & Yu Philip, S. (2020). Fakedetector: Effective fake news detection with deep diffusive neural network. In *2020 IEEE 36th International Conference on Data Engineering (ICDE)* (pp. 1826-1829). IEEE. 10.1109/ICDE48307.2020.00180

Zhang, Y., Huang, T., & Bompard, E. F. (2018). Big data analytics in smart grids: A review. *Energy Informatics,* 1-24.

Zhang, & Chen, Zhu, Yu, Yin & Zhou. (2021). Digital Twin Based on 3D Visualization and Computer Image Recognition Technology in Coal Preparation Plant. *Journal of Physics: Conference Series, 2083*, 042068. doi:10.1088/1742-6596/2083/4/042068

Zhang, J., Li, C., Ye, J., & Qu, G. (2020). Privacy threats and protection in machine learning. *Proceedings of the ACM Great Lakes Symposium on VLSI, GLSVLSI, September*, 531–536. 10.1145/3386263.3407599

Zhang, K., Schnoor, J. L., & Zeng, E. Y. (2012). E-waste recycling: Where does it go from here? *Environmental Science & Technology, 46*(20), 10861–10867. doi:10.1021/es303166s PMID:22998401

Zhang, Rui, & Alexander Shapiro, Y. X., & H. (2019). Stastical Rank Selection for Incomplete Low-rank Matrices. *IEEE Access: Practical Innovations, Open Solutions, 3*, 2912–2916.

Zhao, L., Hu, Q., & Wang, W. (2015). Heterogeneous feature selection with multi-modal deep neural networks and sparse group lasso. *IEEE Transactions on Multimedia, 17*(11), 1936–1948.

Zheng, C., Yuan, J., Zhu, L., Zhang, Y., & Shao, Q. (2020). From digital to sustainable: A scientometric review of smart city literature between 1990 and 2019. *Journal of Cleaner Production, 258*, 120689. doi:10.1016/j.jclepro.2020.120689

Zhong, H. X., Jiang, S. L., Liu, M., & Lin, J. H. (2016). A prediction-based online soft scheduling algorithm for real-world steelmaking-continuous casting production. *Knowledge-Based Systems, 111*, 159–172.

Zhou, C., & Tham, C.-K. (2018). Graphel: A graph-based ensemble learning method for distributed diagnostics and prognostics in the industrial internet of things. In *2018 IEEE 24th International Conference on Parallel and Distributed Systems (ICPADS)*. IEEE.

Zhou, N., Zhang, Z., Nair, V. N., Singhal, H., Chen, J., & Sudjianto, A. (2022). Bias, Fairness and Accountability with Artificial Intelligence and Machine Learning Algorithms. *International Statistical Review, 90*(3), 468–480. doi:10.1111/insr.12492

Zhou, Z., Li, X., & Zare, R. (2017). Optimizing Chemical Reactions with Deep Reinforcement Learning. *ACS Central Science, 3*(12), 1337–1344. Advance online publication. doi:10.1021/acscentsci.7b00492 PMID:29296675

About the Contributors

Brojo Kishore Mishra awarded Ph.D. in Computer Science from Berhampur University in the year 2012 for his excellent work in the field of Web Mining. He worked in several reputed private Engineering Colleges and state University at a different level for more than last 15 years. Presently, he is a Professor with the Department of Computer Science & Engineering and Associate Dean - International Affairs at GIET University, Gunupur, India and also working as Joint Secretary of IEEE Bhubaneswar subsection. He has published more than 80 publications in reputed international conferences, journals and online book chapter contributions (Indexed By: SCI, SCIE, SSCI, Scopus, DBLP) and 13 edited books, 02 authored books, 02 patents, 01 copyright and 03 book series. He has successfully guided 01 Ph.D. research scholar and currently 06 research scholars are continuing. He served in the capacity of keynote speaker, program chair, proceeding chair, publicity chair, and as advisory board members of many International conferences also. He is also a life member of ISTE, CSI, and senior member of IEEE.

***

Gaurav Agarwal has earned the degrees of Ph.D (CSE), M.Tech (IT), B.Tech (CSE); his expertise areas are Cryptography and Network Security, Cloud Computing. During his teaching career, he has published more then 45 national and International Research Publications, he is having 16 years of teaching experience in computer science and engineering department. Recently published a paper in Springer with topic A novel generalized fuzzy intelligence-based ant lion optimization for internet of things based disease prediction and diagnosis. Also filed a patent in his field. In the deep neural network, he is having contribution of A Deep Neural Network-Based Approach for Extracting Textual Images from Deteriorate Images paper in EAI Endorsed Transactions on Industrial Networks and Intelligent Systems.

Manisha Agarwal is an associate professor in the Computer Science Department of Banasthali Vidyapith, where she has been a faculty member since 2004. During 2003 to 2004 she was serving as a guest faculty in MNIT,Jaipur. She received her Ph.D. in Computer Science from the Banasthali Vidyapith in 2017. Her research interests lie in the area of AI,ML, Data Analytics and HPC, ranging from theory to design to implementation. She has also collaborated actively with researchers in several other disciplines of computer science. Dr. Agarwal has served on many conference and workshop program committees and editorial boards of national and International journals. She has many publications in conferences and journals and have contributed book chapters in books, apart from all others at present she is having approximately 30 Scopus publications.

Akshat Agrawal completed B.Tech in Computer Science & Engineering from UPTU & M.Tech from USICT, GGSIPU. He is currently pursuing PhD. from GGSIPU, Delhi. He works as an Assistant Professor in Amity School of Engineering & Technology, Amity University Haryana. he has a total of 10 years of teaching & research experience. His major research interest is Artificial Intelligence, Deep Learning & Machine Learning, Artificial Neural Network, Speech processing, and Image processing. He has published a total of 29 research papers in Scopus indexed and reputed refereed international journals. He has guided 20 M.Tech thesis and 42 B.Tech projects. He has been visiting faculty at Technical University Kosice, Slovakia in June 2019. He actively participated in the reviewing process of research papers and book chapters and was a Program Committee member of various Conferences. He has edited (under process) one Special Issue on Sustainable technological solutions for next generation intelligent buildings in smart cities for EAI Endorsed Transactions on Smart Cities– EUDL (ISSN: 2518-3893).

Basavaraj S. Anami has pursued his Ph.D. from University of Mysore, Mysore in the year 2003. He has obtained his M.Tech., (Computer Science), from IIT Madras in the year 1986. He has obtained his Engineering degree from Karnataka University Dharawad in the year 1981. He has 35 years of professional experience and 14 years of research experience. He is presently working as Principal, KLE Institute of Tchnology, Hubli-30 since July-2008. He is the chairman of Board of studies in computer science and engineering of Visvesvarayya Technological University, Belagavi.

Hanène Babay B'Chir holds a PhD and a master's degree in marketing from the Faculty of Economics and Management of Tunis. She is currently professor of marketing at the Fashion Institute of Monastir, Tunisia. She is also the author / co-author of several marketing research works, particularly around social network marketing, consumer-brand relationship, e-learning, etc. Her areas of research interest are in relationship marketing, brand management, digital marketing, consumer behavior, e-commerce, e-learning, etc. She is also a trainer and marketing consultant for Tunisian companies. She has provided numerous training and team building activities on behalf of several organizations and companies in Tunisia.

Maringanti Hima Bindu has a B.Tech from Osmania University, Hyderabad in Electronics & Communication Engg & M.Tech from Indian School of Mines (now IIT) Dhanbad in Computer Science & Applications, Ph.D from IIIT, Allahabad in the field of Emotional Intelligence and Semiotics; A total of 29 years of teaching experience in various institutes of repute, including OEC, ITER, CVREC, MGR University, IIITA, JAYPEE University and presently Professor in MSCBD University, Odisha, India. Bindu was a research associate with BARC, Bombay at ISM, Dhanbad. Selected and Nominated as Senior Scientist by NCST, Mumbai, India. She is a life member of ISTE, CSI and executive member of IEEE, ACM, LSI and ACS. Executive board member of International Institute of Information Science, Florida, USA. Editorial board member of JoC, Global Science and Technology Forum, Singapore. TPC (technical programme committee) member of a no. of National / International conferences, Member of Association of Cognitive Science and Linguistics Society of India. Bindu has around 103 research publications in various journals, ISBN serial numbers and conference proceedings, book chapters with highest IF of 6.3 and 7.97 and H-index 47; CI 300. Areas of interest and research include Heuristic algorithms, Natural Language Processing, Cognitive Science, Psycho. and Neuro-linguistics, Emotion Modeling and Affective Computing.

Neeraj Chugh has a Ph.D. from Uttarakhand Technical University in Computer Science and Engineering, and received his M.Tech. degree from Kurukshetra University, Haryana in year 2001. Presently, he is working as Assistant Professor (Selection Grade), School of Computer Science, at the University of Petroleum and Energy Studies, Dehradun, Uttarakhand. He has research publications in various international journals and conferences with SCI/SCOPUS/UGC indexing. His research interests include data mining, intrusion detection, Ad Hoc Network, and Machine Learning, Knowledge Management, Technical Debt etc. He has been associated with many conferences throughout India as TPC member and session chair and reviewer for number of journals. He is a lifetime member of CSI.

Shom Das is an associate professor at the Dept of CSE, Birla Global University, Bhubaneswar, Odisha.

Kunal Dhibar is an energetic and passionate college student working towards a B.Tech in CSE at the Bengal College of Engineering and Technology, Durgapur, West Bengal, India. Aiming to use knowledge of coding, machine learning, software development, and data science strategies to satisfy the book chapter.

Iris Efthymiou is an author, speaker, and CEO of Noimosini. Her multifaceted background has earned her a reputation as a visionary. With publications (more than 35) spanning a wide range of topics (Environment, Politics, AI, Wellbeing, Healthcare), she firmly believes in the power of combining different disciplines to reach a balanced view. She is a Board Member of HAPSc, of CATS London, Womanitee, Trustee of Sadie Bristow Foundation, and Associate Researcher of LabHEM of the University of Piraeus. https://www.linkedin.com/in/iris-efthymiou-egleton-9a95a06b/.cdc8022d-bae2-4cd8-8c42-68f1e3a52c63

Harry Efthymiou Egleton is a student at the London School of Economics, in the UK, and Vice President of HAPSc Abroad. He has a passion for new technologies, politics, and philosophy. He has worked in and with the Hellenic Association of Political Scientists (HAPSc*) to help widen access to education for students of all backgrounds as well as having helped organise events that attempt to broaden the political debate with leaders and academics from around Europe. https://www.linkedin.com/in/harry-efthymiou-egleton-38a3041b3/.17d04f75-50d5-4e54-b153-898dbd6ab42c

Amal El Arid is a lab engineer and instructor in the electrical and computer engineering department at Rafik Hariri University in Lebanon. She is currently doing a lot of research on information technology in education. She did her Master's Degree in Electrical and Computer Engineering at the American University of Beirut in Lebanon.

Rajat Subhra Goswami received his Doctor of Philosophy in Computer Science & Engineering in 2015 from National Institute of Technology, Arunachal Pradesh, Master of Technology in Multimedia Development 2009 from Jadavpur University, West Bengal, and Bachelor of Technology in Information Technology in 2005 from West Bengal University of Technology, West Bengal. His area of interest lies Information Security, Cryptography, Image Processing, Big Data, Network Traffic Classification.

Megha Gupta is a PhD holder in Computer Engg. from University of Delhi. Her areas of expertise include networks based on radio, cognitive, sensor, opportunistic etc. During her studies of Bachelor and M.Tech, she was rank holder in the respective Universities. Holding more than 14 years of experience from academic and corporate journey. She has presented papers in various reputed International conferences and also, published research works in various SCIE, Scopus indexed International journals. Presently she is working in the field of ML and IoT.

Swati Gupta is currently working as Associate Professor in Department of Computer Science in KR Mangalam University, Gurugram. Her areas of research are database, data mining, machine learning and artificial intelligence. Prior to her appointment at KRMU, she was working in Amity University, Gurugram. Dr. Swati has received her undergraduate as well as her postgraduate degree in the field of computer science and her PhD is in field of Database and Data Mining. She has published a large number of papers in reputed Journals, conferences and books chapter.

Vighhnesh Hegde is an electronics undergrad interested in software development and design.

Amrutashree Hota is a research scholar at GIET University, Gunupur.

Fredrick Ishengoma is a lecturer at the Department of Information Systems and Technology (IST), College of Informatics and Virtual Education (CIVE), the University of Dodoma (UDOM), Tanzania. He received his PhD in information systems from the University of Dodoma in 2021. He holds a Master's degree in computer and information engineering from Daegu University, South Korea, and a Bachelor's degree in Information and Communication Technology Management (ICTM) from Mzumbe University, Tanzania. His current research interests are focused on e/m-Government, innovative teaching and learning processes, and Information and Communication Technologies for Development (ICT4D).

Manisha Jailia is an associate professor in the Department of Computer Science.

Swatantra Kumar Jaiswal is a fulltime Ph.D. researcher in Department of Mechanical Engineering, National Institute of Technology, Raipur, India. His topic of the research is E-Waste Management. He has been published more than 3 articles in reputed journal with high indexing and impact factors. His area of interest is not limited to E-Waste Management only, but he also published some paper related to forecasting of short lifecycle product. He has participated and presented more than 5 articles in international conference. He is life time member of Indian Institution of Industrial Engineering (IIIE).

Nida Khan has completed her bachelor's in computer science (B.Sc Honours) from University of Delhi. Presently, she is pursuing her master's in computer application. Her several research papers have been published in various prestigious international conferences. Presently she is working in the field of ML and IoT.

Robin Kumar is a B.Tech CSE student of K R Mangalam University Gurugram. He has good experience in Machine learning, Deep Learning projects. He has published few papers in International Conferences and Book chapters.

Sanjay Kumar has earned the degrees of MBBS, MD, DNB in Nephrology, and is currently serving as assistant professor at Nephrologist at Department of Nephropathy, Shri Ram Murti Smarak Institute of Medical Sciences, Bareilly since 2009. He is having past experience in Rajendra Institute of Medical Sciences, Ranchi, as junior resident doctor. He aware people about the nephrology issues and kidney transplant functions, he is also an expert in renal process.

Kshvamasagar Mahanta has a B.tech from Biju Patnaik University of technology, Odisha in Computer Science & Engg., M.Tech from North Orissa University(now MSCBD University), Odisha in Computer Science & Engg. Now doing Ph.D at MSCBD University, Odisha, India. Total 4 years of teaching experience in various institutions. 2 years of experience as Software Developer. Currently working as Asst. Prof. at C.V.Raman Global University, Bhubaneswar. Areas of interest include Cyber Security, Cryptography, Machine Learning, Artificial Intelligence, Software Engineering, Operating systems.

Prasenjit Maji is a professor at Bengal College of Engineering and Technology, Durgapur; has keen knowledge on Image Processing, Data Structures in C, C++.

Akshay Mendon is an electronics undergrad interested in AI and ML hoping to contribute significantly to the world of science.

Anirban Mitra is currently working as an Associate Professor in the Department of Computer Science Engineering, Amity School of Engineering and Technology at Amity University Kolkata. He is a senior member of IEEE and ACM. His research area includes Knowledge Management, Social Network Analysis, Knowledge Discovery, and Computational Intelligence. He had around 80 publications at national and international levels, both in journals and conferences. He is reviewer of many international journals and conferences. He had an experience of nearly 17 years of teaching and research.

Suraj Kumar Mukti is working as an assistant professor at the Department of Mechanical Engineering, National Institute of Technology Raipur. He has completed his Ph.D. research work at his own institute i.e., NIT Raipur under the supervision of Dr. A. M. Rawani, Director and Professor NIT Raipur. His fields of interest are Industrial Engineering & Management, Enterprise Resource Planning, Management Information System, Knowledge Management, Change Management, Customer Relationship Management and Production Engineering & Technology. In institutional level Dr. Suraj Kumar Mukti is Taking care of CPDA review Committee, Institutional Start-up Cell, Anti-Ragging Committee, In-Charge Mechanical Engineering Departmental Library and Training Cell (Internal) under Career Development Centre at NIT Raipur presently. He has teaching and research experience of more than 21 years and also served as an Engineer at Chhattisgarh Electricity Board, in State Government. He has published, more than 40 papers in reputed journals and attended & presented research papers in many important International Conference within the country and abroad as well. He is handling the sponsored project by Science and Engineering Research board (SERB), Govt. of India and has organized many short-term training programs, Expert Talks, Technical Sessions and other important events at his institute. Dr. Suraj Kumar Mukti has authored many books viz. Customer Relationship Management: A Management Perspective, Execution of ERP system: A Case Study Approach, Knowledge Management: Implementation Methods and Strategies and Industry 4.0: Advances and Applications. He is lifetime member of Institute of Engineers (India), Indian Society for Technical Education (ISTE), Indian

Institution of Industrial Engineering (IIIE), South Asia Institute of Science and Engineering (SAISE) and many more technical and educational bodies. He is the recipient of many prestigious awards like Mahatma Jyotiba Phule Fellowship Award, Shikshak Ratna Samman etc. He is Editorial Board Member International Journal of Core Engg. and Mgt. (iJCEM) and may other reputed journals.

S. Sastry Musti is presently with Namibia University of Science and Technology, Windhoek, Namibia. He has than 30 years of professional experience. He obtained his BTech in Electrical Engineering from JNTU, Kakinada (A.P.) in 1990, MTech and PhD from NIT, Warangal in the years 1996 and 2002 respectively. Some of his earlier employments include University of the West Indies, St Augustine, Trinidad, ESIGELEC, Rouen, France and Sophia University, Tokyo, Japan. His research interests include Power and Energy Systems, Information Systems and Engineering Education.

I **Leela Rajani Myla** is a student earning a B.Tech, at the Department of CSE, 2019-23 batch, Koneru Lakshmaiah Education Foundation, Vaddeswaram, Andhra Pradesh, India. Working in the field of Recommendation system, and machine learning under the supervision of S Gopal Krishna Patro with the specialization of Java.

Mauparna Nandan is presently engaged as an Associate Professor in the Dept. Of Computer Applications, Haldia Institute of Technology, Haldia, India. She is a doctorate from National Institute of Technology (NIT), Durgapur in the year 2019. Her dissertation title was "A study on some collective phenomena in coupled nonlinear dynamical systems". Her research interests include Machine Learning, Deep Learning, Image Processing, Optimization Techniques, Chaos Synchronization, Collective phenomena in complex dynamical systems, Time-Series Analysis etc. She has won the Best Paper Award in the 3rd International Conference on Communication, Devices and Computing (ICCDC 2021). She is the first author of the book entitled "Introduction to Computer Applications" from Bluerose Publisher. She also holds 11 patents (both International-Australian and Indian) and Copyrights. At present, she is engaged in research collaborative work with renowned Professors from premier Institutes of the country.

Ghalia Nassreddine is an associate professor at the Jinan University, Lebanon. She is a Ph.D holder in information technology and systems from University of Technology of Compiegne, France since 2009. Currently, she is serving as a chairperson in Business Computing School in Jinan University of Lebanon. She is currently doing a lot of research in Machine Learning, education and Dempster Shafer theory.

Mohamed Nassereddine received a Ph.D. degree in the field of High Voltage Power Systems from Western Sydney University where he also received his MEng (Hons) in Research in the field of Electric Machine and Renewable Energy. Dr. Mohamad has over 17 years of experience in industry and academia. He delivered a large number of engineering courses across universities in Australia, the Gulf, and the Middle East.

Moumita Pal is working as associate professor in the dept of ECE at JIS college of engineering. She got her PhD degree in the year of 2022. She has several numbers of papers and articles in reputed journals.

Gopal Patro is working as an asst. professor (Department of CSE) at Koneru Lakshmaiah Education Foundation, India.

Subrata Paul is currently working as Assistant Professor of Department of CSE, School of Engineering at Brainware University and is also a PhD scholar under MAKAUT. He had completed his B.E(CSE) from VTU – Belgaum, Karnataka in 2010 and M.Tech (CS) from Berhampur University in the year 2013. His research area includes Social Network Analysis, Computational Intelligence and Cloud Computing. He has 30 publications at national and international levels, both in journals and conferences. He is also a reviewer of few referred Journals. He is a member of several Professional Associations like ACM, ICSES, SDIWC etc. He had an experience of nearly 9 years in teaching undergraduate courses and 4 year in handling post graduate classes.

Shin Prasad is working as assistant professor in Computer Science & Engineering department of Bengal College of Engineering & Technology from last 9 Years. Research Area: Image Processing, Cloud Computing.

Divya R. was born on 24th March 2000 in Tamil Nadu. She did her high schooling in Vivekananda Kendra Vidyalaya, Portblair, and senior secondary in Government Model Senior Secondary school. Her passion to serve plants and animals lead her to select biotechnology as her career. She had completed her undergraduation in B.Tech Biotechnology at B.S. Abdur Rahman Crescent Institute of Science and Technology. Currently she is pursuing post-graduation in food and nutritional biotechnology. Her research interests include agrotechnology, agronomy, food sustainability, food technology, and new product development.

Karthikeyan Ramalingam is Dean of student affairs and professor, BSA Crescent Institute of Science and Technology with over 20 years of laboratory knowledge, including academic, government, and industrial projects, handling experience with excellent supervisory skills and a strong record of scientific accomplishments and publications. In nanoemulsion sciences experienced from the University of Texas Health Science Center at San Antonio, Texas, USA, US Naval Medical Research Unit, San Antonio, Texas, USA, New York University, USA, Nottingham University, UK and received funds for nanoemulsions research from Department of Defense, Navy, USA ($105,900), DST-SERB (Rs. 23 lakhs) and ICMR (15 lakhs) and USA-NSF-SBIR ($475,766) as principle investigator.

Kali Charan Rath is presently working as Associate Professor, Department of Mechanical Engineering, GIET University, Gunupur, Odisha, India. He has more than 17yrs of experience in academic and research. He awarded with Ph.D. degree by National Institute of Technology, Jamshedpur, India, year 2013, in the area of CAD/CAM. He guided more than 20 M.Tech students as project supervisor and scholars received their degree. Recently he is supervising 3 Ph.D scholar work. He attended more than 300 webinars during pandemic time. He presented his research work in various national and International conferences. His work is not only published in various reputed journals but also published as book chapters by reputed publishers. He attended a bunch of FDP and STTP programme conducted by reputed organizations. He published a bunch of research papers in various National and International journals as well as conferences. He is the Ambassador of "Bentham Science Publication", and also Ambassadorship of SPSC- support to Sustainable Development Goals. He has one Australian patent (Granted) and one more patent applied to India patent house. He is the member of IEI, CSI, ISTE, IAENG, ISRD, IFERP, Member of "All India Council for Technical Skill Development" and also the member of "National Institute For Technical Training & Skill Development". He is also acting as Mendeley Advisor community (Elsevier) . Received 40 certificates with knowledge from research academy- Elsevier, after completion of various research modules. Two Certificate of Excellence received for successfully completed every module within Going through peer review, from research academy- Elsevier. He delivered his research talk in various FDP, STTP, and Conferences as a keynote speaker. Accredited professional certificate on (a) ISO 9001 Quality Management System Associate, (b) Foundation of Business and Entrepreneurship, (c) Lean Foundations Professional certification (LFPC), (d) "Focus on peer Review", Nature Master classes (Springer Nature), (e) "The Fundamental of Digital Marketing", Google Digital Garage . His research field: Robotics and Automation; Smart Manufacturing System; IOT applications, Product design, Modeling and Simulation; CAD/CAM/CIM ; Finite Element Analysis, etc.

Suneel Rath is a research scholar of C.V.Raman Global University, Bhubaneswar, Odisha

K. Hemant Reddy received the Ph.D. degree from Berhampur University, Berhampur, India, in 2014. He is currently an Associate Professor with the Department of Computer Science and Engineering, VIT AP University, Andhra Pradesh. His current research interests include Internet of Things, fog computing, big data, and cloud computing.

Diptendu Sinha Roy (Senior Member, IEEE) received the Ph.D. degree in engineering from the Birla Institute of Technology, Mesra, India, in 2010. He is currently an Associate Professor with the Department of Computer Science and Engineering, National Institute of Technology Meghalaya, Shillong, India. His current research interests include Internet of Things, big data, machine learning, and soft and evolutionary computing.

Madhusmita Sahu is an assistant professor, C.V. Raman Global University, Bhubaneswar, Odisha.

Naga Venkata Sai Deekshitha Sandaka is a student studying for the B.Tech, Department of CSE, 2019-23 batch, Koneru Lakshmaiah Education Foundation, Vaddeswaram, Andhra Pradesh, India. Working in the field of Recommendation system, and machine learning under the supervision of S. Gopal Krishna Patro with the specialization of Java.

Sakya Sarkar is presently engaged as a Lecturer in the Dept. of Computer Science and Technology, Asansol Institute of Engineering and Management-Polytechnic, Asansol, India. His research interests include Machine Learning, Deep Learning, NLP and Image Processing. He is an aspiring researcher in this field.

Sachin Kumar Saxena is pursuing Ph.D. in study and analysis of diabetic patients in India, written an International paper on nephrology issues such as Comparison based Prediction of Diabetic Nephropathy using Deep Learning Algorithm, has more than 12 years of teaching experience in computer science and engineering. He knows Machine Learning, Data Science, Statistics using Python, tensorflow and PyCharm. As far as other languages are concerned, he knows Java, BootStrap, C,C++. He is also Assistant Professor at Shri Ram Murti Smarak College of Engineering and Technology, Bareilly since

2019. For various research work he has collected huge radiology images dataset of patients suffering from cyst, stone, lesion, early stages of cancer, normal etc., aiming to classify these four classes patients or prediction of chronic kidney disease (CKD), having good experience in Computer Vision, Artificial Intelligence, Deep Learning and ML.

Jitendra Shrivastava is a Professor in the Department of Computer Science & Engineering. He has been the Vice-Chancellor, Officer on Special Duty (OSD), and Advisor to the proctorial Board in the past. He is having more than 26 years of experience in teaching, research & administration. He has more than 26 research papers in international & national journals of repute to his credit. He has also delivered many expert lectures in various reputed academic institutions. His research area of expertise involves data mining, artificial intelligence, and database management system. He always attempts to provide a student-friendly environment in the campus.

Abhishek Sinha works at the department of BCA, GIET University, Gunupur, Odisha India.

K. Sunitha has a B.E. in Computer Science and Engineering, an M tech. in Computer Science and Engineering, and has experience in IT industry for 3 years in Software Testing domain and experience in Teaching in Engineering college of 15 years. Pursuing PhD in Software Engineering. Currently working as assistant professor in the department of CSE AI & ML.

Geetam Tomar has more than 30 years of working experience and has published good number of patents, papers, and books; currently working as Head of the Institute at Uttarakhand Government Institute.

B. K. Tripathy is now working as a Professor (Higher Academic Grade) in School of Information Technology and Engineering (S ITE), VIT, Vellore, India. He has received research/academic fellowships from UGC, DST, SERC and DOE of Govt. of India. Dr. Tripathy has published more than 700 technical papers in international journals, proceedings of international conferences and edited research volumes. He has produced 30 PhDs, 13 MPhils and 5 M.S (By research) under his supervision. Dr. Tripathy has published two text books on Soft Computing and Computer Graphics. Also. he has two monographs on Social networks with IGI and Dimensionality reduction with CRC Press. Dr. Tripathy has served as the member of Advisory board or Technical Programme Committee member of over 130 International conferences inside India and abroad. Also, he has edited 5 research volumes for different publications including IGI, Springer and CRC. He is a Fellow of IETE; life/senior member of IEEE, ACM, IRSS, CSI, ACEEE, OMS and IMS. Dr.Tripathy is an editorial board member/reviewer of more than 100 international journals of repute.

Milind Udbhav is a B.Tech CSE student of K R Mangalam University Gurugram. He has good experience in Machine learning, Deep Learning projects. He has published few papers in International Conferences and Book chapters.

Sneha Unnikrishnan completed her B.tech. Biotechnology from Jeppiaar Engineering College, Chennai, in 2011 and received the Anna University rank. She did her M.tech. Biotechnology at Jeppiaar Engineering College, Chennai, (affiliated to Anna University, Chennai) in 2013 and was the Anna University Gold medalist. From 2013-2014, she worked as a lecturer at Shri Devi Institute of Science and Technology, Tumkur. From 2014-2016, she worked as Assistant Professor at Jeppiaar Engineering College, Chennai. She joined Ph.D. in Biotechnology, School of Life Sciences, B.S. Abdur Rahman Crescent Institute of Science and Technology, Chennai, under the guidance of Dr. Karthikeyan R., in July 2016. From 2017-2020 she has worked in the AYUSH-EMR project as Junior Research Fellow and Senior Research Fellow. She has been selected as ICMR-SRF and has been awarded Swachtha Saarthi Fellowship in 2021. Dr. Sneha Unnikrishnan is currently working as DST Woman Scientist in B.S. Abdur Rahman Crescent Institute of Science and Technology.

Meenu Vijarania received her Ph.D degree from Amity University Haryana in 2019 and M.Tech (I.T) degree from GGSIPU, New Delhi in 2007 and B.Tech degree in Information Technology from MDU university Haryana in 2005. She has 14 years of experience in teaching. Currently she is working at K R Mangalam University Gurugram Haryana as Associate Professor in Department of Computer Science, Centre of Excellence, School of Engineering and Technology. She has published more than 30 research papers in International Journals/ conferences and book chapters of high repute. Her research area includes topics of wireless networks and genetic algorithm, machine learning, internet of things.

Ankit Vijayvargiya (Student Member, IEEE) received the B.Tech. (Hons.) degree in electrical engineering from Rajasthan Technical University, Kota, India, in 2010, the M.Tech. degree in instrumentation from Devi Ahilya University, Indore, India, in 2014. He is currently pursuing the Ph.D. degree in electrical engineering from the Malaviya National Institute of Technology, Jaipur, India. He is also an Associate Professor with the Department of Electrical Engineering, Swami Keshvanand Institute of Technology, Management & Gramothan, Jaipur. His research interests include biomedical signal processing, pattern recognition, and machine learning.

Prabhakar Yadlapalli is a student pursing a B.Tech, Department of CSE, 2019-23 batch, Koneru Lakshmaiah Education Foundation, Vaddeswaram, Andhra Pradesh, India. Working in the field of Recommendation system, and machine learning under the supervision of S Gopal Krishna Patro with the specialization of Java.

Ali Yuce was born and grew up in Turkey. He altered his life dramatically and profoundly to pursue his passion for academia after working independently for his business. After receiving his bachelor's degree from DePaul University, he obtained his Master's and Doctoral degrees from Eastern Mediterranean University. Before graduating from the Ph.D. program, he worked as an independent researcher concerning tourism and digital technologies and was a part-time instructor at Cappadocia University. Following his graduation, he became a full-time teaching faculty member at the Tourist Guidance Department of Cappadocia University. Ali Yuce has been teaching at Cappadocia University since 2019, at the undergraduate and graduate levels. Since 2016, he has concentrated his academic work and research on sustainable tourism development strategies, tourism development paradoxes, and the effects of climate change on travel destinations. Moreover, he has also provided scholarly discussion in the tourism literature by investigating the role of emerging technologies and education in sustainability-related topics like protecting natural resources and improving livelihoods while highlighting the most prevalent tourism-oriented problems like overpopulation, traffic congestion, and a poor perception of local people towards tourism. He is the author of several articles and book chapters in peer-reviewed international journals and books, along with several congress papers about the impact of technology on the landscape of sustainable tourism, education, and marketing. His research areas include but are not limited to innovation in tourism, innovation networks, smart tourism, technology competencies, research philosophy, and sustainable destination planning and development. On the other hand, he is a lifelong learner who loves conveying every bit of knowledge that he learns. Last but not least, he enjoys swimming, cooking, jogging, and reading about history, technology, and more; and lastly, he loves animals and nature.

Index

A

Actuator 94, 185, 324
Affinity 332-333, 335, 409
Agricultural Social Network 124, 137
Agricultural System 124, 126
Agrotechnology 139
Amalgamate 332-333, 336
Artificial Intelligence 1-2, 4-12, 17, 31, 41, 43-44, 61-62, 66, 87-88, 90-91, 93-94, 99-100, 102-103, 108-112, 122, 139-142, 146-147, 149, 152-158, 247, 253, 286, 291-294, 296, 302-308, 311-313, 319, 328-330, 333, 337-338, 341-342, 344-347, 354-356, 358, 379, 403-404, 407, 417-418, 422-425, 433, 437-438, 445, 447-448, 451, 456-459, 461-463
Artificial Intelligent 12
AtomNet 404-406, 408, 411-416, 418
Automation 4, 7, 9, 11, 31, 44, 46, 90, 109-110, 112, 117, 139, 153-155, 157, 160, 181, 183, 199, 269, 284, 294, 310, 319, 337, 342, 347, 378, 399, 402, 423-424, 436, 445, 450-451
Autonomous Vehicle 11, 17, 350, 460

B

Back-End Subsystem 255, 259, 263-264
Big Data 8, 13, 16, 28, 37, 40, 44, 50, 175, 184-185, 187, 191, 236, 247, 249, 252-254, 267, 286, 293, 307, 312, 319, 325, 328, 331, 344-345, 348, 357-358, 360, 383, 399, 427, 438-439, 446, 459, 461, 463-465, 467, 469, 471-472

C

Case Studies 186, 188, 194, 196, 310, 436
Circular Economy 220, 267-269, 285
Cloud Computing 38, 45, 187, 191, 194, 198, 259, 293, 306-307, 310-311, 323-325, 329, 332-333,

337-338, 341, 344, 358, 464
Cloud Database 255, 259, 263
Cold Start Problem 361-364, 367, 369, 373-379
Collaborative Filtering 223-224, 227, 233-234, 362, 366-367, 375-379
Computer Vision 14, 30, 53, 60, 94, 103, 108-109, 193, 344-345, 354, 384, 400-403, 407
Confidentiality 87, 92, 94, 99, 289
Convolutional Neural Networks 59-60, 316, 318, 381, 383-384, 399, 401-403, 405-407, 417
COVID-19 4, 6, 64-65, 84, 115, 284, 286, 300, 333, 341, 459, 471
Crop Management 157, 186, 189-190, 199
Cutting-Edge Technology 108, 111, 257, 332-333, 358, 463
Cyber Physical System 267, 276, 279-280, 282, 285

D

Data Privacy 42, 92, 450, 460
Data Security 94, 101, 289, 460
Deep Fakes 453, 459
Deep Learning 10, 14, 17, 27-28, 38, 41, 46-47, 49, 51, 55-56, 59-60, 65-66, 68, 82, 84, 88, 99, 102, 107, 110, 251-252, 286, 291, 293, 303-305, 310, 316, 318-319, 328-330, 343, 348, 381-383, 388-389, 399-401, 403-405, 407, 417-418, 426, 428, 453-454, 471
Deep Neural Network 14, 51, 58, 88-89, 320
Design Prototyping 344
Digital Transformation 267, 269, 277-279, 283-286, 423, 470
Digital Twin 267-270, 275, 277, 280-285, 306-312, 314-360, 437-439, 444-445, 461, 463-465, 467, 469-472
Digital Twins Application Domains 283, 334, 339
DRONE- Dynamic Remotely Operated Navigation Equipment 158
Drug Discovery 404, 407-408, 411, 417-418

Ensure Quality Research is Introduced to the Academic Community

Become an Evaluator for IGI Global Authored Book Projects

Premier Reference Source

Stabilizing Currency and Preserving Economic Sovereignty Using the Grondona System

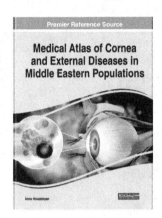

Premier Reference Source

Medical Atlas of Cornea and External Diseases in Middle Eastern Populations

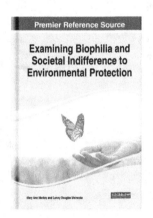

Premier Reference Source

Examining Biophilia and Societal Indifference to Environmental Protection

Premier Reference Source

Using Narratives and Storytelling to Promote Cultural Diversity on College Campuses

The overall success of an authored book project is dependent on quality and timely manuscript evaluations.

Applications and Inquiries may be sent to:
development@igi-global.com

Applicants must have a doctorate (or equivalent degree) as well as publishing, research, and reviewing experience. Authored Book Evaluators are appointed for one-year terms and are expected to complete at least three evaluations per term. Upon successful completion of this term, evaluators can be considered for an additional term.

If you have a colleague that may be interested in this opportunity, we encourage you to share this information with them.

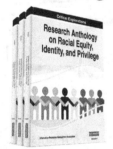

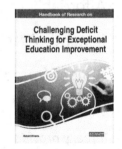

Printed in the United States
by Baker & Taylor Publisher Services